EDUCATION POLICY
IN
TWENTIETH CENTURY IRELAND

TOPICS IN MODERN IRISH HISTORY
General Editor: R. V. Comerford

Published

Priest, politics and society in post-famine Ireland
A study of County Tipperary, 1850-1891
James O'Shea

Towards a National University: William Delaney S.J.
(1835-1924) and an era of initiative in Irish education
Thomas Morrisey S.J.

The Fenians in context: Irish politics and society, 1848-1882
R. V. Comerford

Education policy in twentieth century Ireland
Séamas Ó Buachalla

EDUCATION POLICY
IN
TWENTIETH CENTURY
IRELAND

Séamas Ó Buachalla

WOLFHOUND PRESS

First published 1988

WOLFHOUND PRESS
68 Mountjoy Square, Dublin 1.

© Séamas Ó Buachalla 1988

British Library Cataloguing in Publication Data
  Ó Buachalla, Séamas
  Education policy in twentieth century Ireland
  ——— (Topics in modern Irish history,
  ISSN 0790-0783).
  1. Education and state ——— Ireland
  I. Title   II. Series
  379.417   LC93.I73

  ISBN 0-86327-146-4

Cover design by Jan de Fouw
Printed by Billings & Sons, Worcestershire, UK.
Typesetting and layout by Redsetter Ltd., Dublin.

Table of Contents

LIST OF TABLES

6

LIST OF FIGURES

LIST OF APPENDICES

PREFACE

This is an outstanding contribution to scholarly research on official Irish education policy. It is well-written, comprehensive, detached and fair in its judgements; there is a total absence of polemics, although the author must often have been tempted. Scarcity of available primary sources made his work unusually difficult. From personal experience I can understand his formidable task in seeking factual material on policy making from the files of the Department of Education; fortunately he fared better in the Department of Finance. His survey, however, is in no sense an attack on the Department of Education; it merely states the regrettable truth about the lack of detailed documentation which, I feel sure, any official there today deplores no less. An impressive feature of this splendid book, therefore, is its success in reaching convincing conclusions from evidence that is often sparse.

Séamas Ó Buachalla begins by demonstrating conclusively the dominating influence of Cardinal Cullen down to the end of the nineteenth century, the political commitment to education reform of the Chief Secretary, Augustine Birrell and the vision and energy of the Resident Commissioner, Dr W. J. M. Starkie in the early decades of the present century. He goes on to consider the pusillanimity of native governments towards education from the outset. What had happened to the passionate aspirations of Pearse and the eloquence of Michael Tierney in *Education in a Free Ireland*, published in 1919?

The answers are clearly and unequivocally presented here. There is no longer need for astonishment that the First Dáil in November 1919 should have shirked the issue of education and appointed a Minister for Irish instead of a Minister for Education despite the glowing rhetoric of The Democratic Programme of that same Dáil. Mr de Valera, it appears had 'some good reasons' for the decision. The words are not Dr Ó Buachalla's but those of Cathal Brugha. The surviving documentation is thin but even with it, one may surmise that the First Dáil was influenced in its timidity towards education by the fierce hostility of the Catholic bishops to the bill introduced by the British Chief Secretary McPherson. This mild measure proposed to substitute one form of the British education system for another. It

9

had been immoderately denounced by the Catholic bishops as replacing a satisfactory Irish system by a foreign one at a time when, to quote them, 'Mr de Valera and his associates are labouring for Irish freedom'. The bishops' enthusiasm for de Valera's labours in this direction was later to diminish.

All this was an ominous beginning to education in a free Ireland and the spectre of the McPherson Bill was to haunt policy-making in the Department of Education for years after its creation in 1924. Dr Ó Buachalla gives a vivid account of the feebleness of policy-making in the early decades of the Department and of the unrelenting opposition to positive state action in education of Eoin Mac Neill and John Marcus O'Sullivan as Ministers. Neither of them understood the political, social and economic implications of education or if they did understand it, left not a scintilla of evidence to support that understanding. They had no sympathy with the conviction of many that their Department should be responsible for systematic modes of education in the formation of which parents and the public should have a legitimate democratic part as well as the churches, professional educationists and teachers. Variants of this negative ministerial view surprisingly continued to survive for decades.

As late as 1949, the then Minister for Education General Richard Mulcahy declared: 'It is the function of the Minister to watch out for causes of irritation and having found them, to go around with the oil can'. Mulcahy perceived his own role as minister as a modest one, 'a kind of dungarees man' who 'will take the knock out of the pipes and will link up everything'. This was a far cry from the brave words of the same man thirty-four years earlier when he moved the acceptance of the Democratic Programme of the First Dáil.

The Catholic Church had never liked the Vocational Education system and Dr Ó Buachalla states that it was tacitly accepted because of the ministerial assurance given to the bishops that the vocational schools 'would not be allowed to develop so as to impinge upon the field covered by the denominationally-run secondary schools'.

The nadir of the Department's education inactivity must surely have been reached in 1944 (ironically the year of Mr R. A. Butler's education revolution in the United Kingdom) when the Taoiseach, Mr de Valera, wrote to his Minister for Education, Mr Deirg, suggesting to him that he should consult the postwar plans and White Papers published in Britain and Northern Ireland 'to ascertain if we could derive any benefit from them'. Our thinking had undergone a sea-change since the First Dáil took fright at the mere thought of the McPherson bill.

Yet despite Mr de Valera's quest for a positive education policy we still had a long wait for a minister who appreciated the social and technological significance of education and its broad political implications. This was to be the thoughtful and questioning Dr Hillery. He was succeeded by Mr George Colley and he, in turn, by Mr Donagh

O'Malley, described by the author, as introducing in 1967 'the single most significant advance in Irish education in the century' with his 'free' education and school transport scheme. (Half a century earlier, the despised and derided English Minister McPherson had proposed to provide school transport, school books and compulsory school attendance.) O'Malley's decision, Ó Buachalla writes, derived 'from some very deep convictions on the social role of education, the innate injustice of educational inequality and the long-term national benefit to be derived from expanding educational opportunity'. This is a tribute that Mr O'Malley richly deserves.

This exhaustive study is full of sad and dismal revelations of the handling of our education affairs since 1922 and few major institutions emerge unscarred. The Catholic Church rightly insisted on the primacy of parental rights and on the dangers – unlikely though they were – of statism being imposed through ill-conceived policies in the Department. But Dr Ó Buachalla points to inconsistencies. In spite of official church teaching, there was in 1934, he states, an episcopal prohibition on parent involvement. Over long periods the spinelessness of the Department was matched by what he describes as 'the non-involvement of the lay public and politicians, a low level of professional autonomy within the education system and an overall complacency which was oblivious of the social and geographical inequalities characterising it'. As a result, the promise of Augustine Birrell and the energies of Starkie at the beginning of the century were not met by comparable effort until the late 1960s.

This book deserves to be read, not merely by professional educationists, teachers and politicians. School managers, in particular, will find much to think about in the records of the attitudes and actions of many of their predecessors.

Patrick Lynch

Dublin, March 1988

Publisher's Acknowledgement

The publisher wishes to acknowledge with thanks the following for responding to his request for financial contribution towards the typesetting costs: The Educational Building Society; The Irish National Teachers' Organisation; The Association of Secondary Teachers of Ireland; The Teachers' Union of Ireland.

INTRODUCTION

In the preparation and writing of this volume I have been assisted by many individuals, organisations, government departments, libraries and archives. To all those who have supplied information or materials, offered opinions, granted interviews or facilitated access to public or private archival materials I am deeply indebted. I am equally grateful to those who, having assisted my quest in various ways, requested that their cooperation remain unrecorded. I wish to express my special indebtedness to Professor Basil Chubb whose generous assistance and deep interest constituted a sustaining force throughout the exercise. The major portion of the archival materials consulted was made available to me in the Department of Finance and in the former Department of the Public Service; access to this material was made possible by the enlightened attitude adopted to my request by the senior officers of these Departments. I wish particularly to thank R. J. Curran, Second Secretary, P. H. Mullarkey, Assistant Secretary and J. J. McCaffrey, Principal Officer of the Department of Finance, and Séamas Ó Cíosáin, Assistant Secretary of the Department of the Public Service. I am indebted to them both for the manner in which my request to consult official files was acceded to and for the facilities provided for me in doing so. I am also indebted to Richard Stokes, Assistant Secretary of the Department of the Taoiseach for valuable assistance in locating archival materials.

Research on the education policy of the Gaelic League and of the early decades of the state was significantly helped by gaining access to the MacNeill and Mulcahy papers; I am especially grateful to Mrs Michael Tierney and to Professor Risteard Mulcahy for permitting and facilitating such access. Ar an mbealach céanna táim go mór faoi chomaoin ag Isolde Ní Dheirg as ucht na cabhrach a thug sí go fial dom. I wish to thank the directors, librarians and staffs of the following libraries for their unfailing assistance and courtesy: Trinity College Library, UCD Archives Department, the State Paper Office, the Public Record Office, the National Library of Ireland and the Church of Ireland Library, Braemor Park. The annual officers and the permanent headquarter staffs of the teacher and managerial organisations were most helpful in locating and providing relevant records

13

and papers to supplement the published records of their organisations. I wish to record my deep gratitude to the individuals and the organisations whose cooperation proved so valuable and especially to those who requested that such assistance would not be personally attributed. I am similarly indebted to a large number of former and present Chief Executive Officers of Vocational Education Committees for their help in gaining a deeper understanding of the system; I wish to thank particularly Michael Cryan, D. Mac Suibhne, Olibhéar Ó hEidhin, Liam Ó Maolchatha, E. Gibson and the late Fred Cronin of Co. Leitrim. I am especially indebted to my wife, Eilís, for her invaluable help in the preparation of the manuscript and the editing of the computerised version of the text. I wish to record my gratitude to Ms Vivienne Jenkins, Ms Olive Murtagh and Ms Margaret Lawlor of the Arts Faculty Offices of Trinity College for their assistance in the computerisation process. I am indebted to Rev Professor F. X. Martin and Professor John Kelly, TD, of UCD, to Rev Professors Enda McDonagh and the late T. P. Cunningham of St Patrick's College, Maynooth, and to my colleagues in Trinity College, Professors Martin O'Donoghue, Tom Mitchell and Seán Freyne, for providing information on specific topics or facilitating access to relevant archival materials. I also wish to express my indebtedness to the late Provost of Trinity College, Professor F. S. L. Lyons, to Professor T. P. O'Neill, University College, Galway, to Dr Michael Ryan, NIHE, Dublin and to Dr Vincent Comerford, St Patrick's College, Maynooth.

Táim faoi chomaoin ar bhealaí éagsúla ag Riobard Mac Góráin agus ag an Dr Seán Mac Donagh. Imeasc iad siud a chuir comaoin ar leith orm agus atá ar shlí na fírinne, tá an tiar-Aire Seoirse Ó Colla, an Dr Toirdhealach Ó Raifeartaigh agus Mícheál Ó Siochfradha. I owe a special debt of gratitude to Liam Ó Laidhin, Chairman of the HEA and former Secretary of the Department of Education, who granted me permission to examine Department files and papers under the 'thirty year rule'. However it did not prove possible to examine more than a fraction of the Department files, mainly, though not totally, due to the unorganised state of the materials. Happily the department of Finance archives contained most, if not all, of the significant policy documentation originating in the Department of Education as well as its own records relative to policy formation in education. In the fullness of time, when the records of the Department of Education are made completely available to researchers, some further points of detail may be revealed; I am confident, however, that the larger picture presented here will not require substantial alteration. I am very indebted to those who have read the work either in full or in part; in this context I am indebted to Professors Basil Chubb, Guy Neave, Maurice Kogan and Patrick Lynch. I am doubly indebted to Professor Patrick Lynch for contributing the preface and I am honoured by having associated with the volume one whose contributions to public and academic life have been so singularly distinguished; his major contribution in education, the report *Investment in Education* was undoubtedly the main catalyst, if not the *fons et origo*, of the expansion and reforms which have occurred since 1965.

I wish to record my appreciation of and gratitude for the assistance received in support of this research project from the Arts and Economic and Social Science Benefaction Fund of Trinity College, Dublin.

The policy process in Irish and other European systems has been of interest to me since my years in the Secondary Inspectorate and the Development Branch of the Department of Education. In this study I sought to analyse and evaluate the various contributions to policy in this century and to examine the policy process in its formulation and implementation stages. In conducting the study I was fortunate to gain access to government and department papers, and to other archival records, which had not been previously available for research purposes. The availability of this type of primary material is especially significant in studying the early stages of the policy process and in gaining an understanding of those policy determinants which are not usually identified in official publications. The study is presented in three sections. Section I examines the historical residue within the system, the influence of the last century and the main lines of policy development in this century. The policy contributors and their contributions are presented in Section II which examines in turn the roles of teachers, managers, churches, political parties, ministers and government departments in the process. Section III addresses the question of policy mechanism and models in the context of current policy theory; in this section two case studies are presented and an analysis of the historical evolution of the policy process. The work concludes with some observations on the quality of the policy process and with some proposals on measures to improve it. I trust that this volume may help to promote and stimulate the systematic study of the policy process, not only in education but also in other public policy sectors.

Séamas Ó Buachalla,
Trinity College.

September 1988.

SECTION I
THE HISTORICAL RESIDUE

CHAPTER ONE

Educational Developments
in the Nineteenth Century

While educational developments in the nineteenth century were the focus for frequent, prolonged and deep controversy, they constitute nevertheless a remarkable achievement in a society characterised by political unrest and widespread social and economic deprivation. This educational achievement was due ultimately and equally to church initiatives and to positive state intervention; the controversy and the conflict arose inevitably from the divergent perspectives of the churches and the state on education and on its structure and on their respective roles in its provision and management.[1] The growth of the system especially the geographical spread of the national schools after 1831 is clearly reflected in the reduction in the rates of reported illiteracy evident in the decennial censuses for the period from 1841 to 1901.[2] Coincidental with a significant decline in illiteracy there occurred a crucial phase of the language shift from Irish to English, a shift to which the education system contributed significantly by the exclusion from the schools in many areas of the country of the only language spoken by local majorities.[3]

While the century witnessed an expansion of educational provision at all three levels and while various controversies attached to secondary, technical and university education, it was undoubtedly the issues involved in the elementary 'national' schools which dominated the educational scene throughout the century. The political idealism which inspired the national school system, introduced by Stanley on behalf of the Whig government in 1831, was a brave, though ultimately unsuccessful, excursion into promoting community harmony and local cohesion by means of interdenominational education.[4] Such a school system, providing universal elementary education was available in very few European countries at the time; Prussia, and France (after the Guizot Law of 1833) were among the few countries possessing similar elaborate systems. Whereas the French scheme was modelled on a report by Cousin on the Prussian system, the plan proposed by Stanley was derived mainly from the recommendations of a parliamentary select committee and from the detailed proposals made by Thomas Wyse M.P. in 1830.[5]

19

Prior to the introduction of the National School system in 1831, there was no systematic educational provision except the schools of the Kildare Place Society and the emerging system of the Catholic teaching orders. There had been numerous church-related agencies providing schools, with or without some government aid, which were associated mainly with the established church many of which were suspected by Catholics of proselytism.[6] Consequently equality of educational provision had become a priority among Catholic leaders in the struggle for emancipation culminating in the passing of the Act of 1829. Significant steps towards that equality of educational provision for Catholics had been taken by the establishment of the teaching orders of nuns and brothers at and before the dawn of the nineteenth century.[7] The Presentation Sisters founded by Nano Nagle in Cork in 1791, the Mercy Sisters founded by Catherine Mc Auley in 1828 and the Irish Christian Brothers founded by Edmund Rice in Waterford in 1802, provided the first systematic network of schools catering extensively for Catholics.[8] These teaching orders spread rapidly in Ireland and abroad; the geographical distribution of their school systems in Ireland is closely correlated with educational opportunity during the last century and for most of this.[9]

The provision of elementary education by the state under the scheme of 1831 can be viewed as the fruitful outcome of the public concern and controversy concerning education which had characterised the previous decades; it can also be regarded as the logical political endpoint of the objections which the Roman Catholic authorities had increasingly lodged against the educational activities of the government-aided voluntary education societies.[10]

The Board of seven commissioners established under the 1831 scheme, was characterised in its membership by a delicate balance of denominational interests; presided over by the Duke of Leinster, it included clerical and lay representatives of the different denominations. The Board was obliged under the Stanley instructions to allocate the funds for the erection of schools, the organisation of inspection, subsidising the provision of school texts, paying gratuities to teachers and for the purpose of erecting a teacher training establishment. The objective of the National Board, as indeed of the 1828 select committee which greatly influenced the Stanley scheme, was to provide 'combined literary and separate religious education' in schools which under multidenominational management, would enrol all the children of an area, irrespective of denomination. The emphasis in the 1831 national education system, upon integrated schools and community commitment, is clear from the provision in the Stanley scheme whereby priority was to be given by the Board to applications for school funds proceeding from:

1. the Protestant and Roman Catholic clergy of the parish *or*

2. one of the clergy and a certain number of parishioners professing the opposite creed, *or*

3. parishoners of both denominations.[11]

However, such admirable intentions, as to the management and enrolment, were not translated into firm administrative practice in the distribution of the board's funds, nor indeed in the local management of the schools. Within twenty years the system had become a denominational system, in which the term 'manager' had become synonymous with local clergyman. Despite the many controversies which beset the early years, controversies which derived mainly from inter-church suspicion and from ecclesiastical mistrust of a state-initiated education scheme, the national school system enjoyed a period of rapid growth and quickly established its credibility. The period 1833-1849 witnessed the erection or attachment to the Board of 3,500 schools providing 370,000 student places and a four-fold increase in the parliamentary public finance voted for these schools. This rapid growth and geographical spread of the national system in the period to the mid-century, was accompanied by a definite dilution of the multidenominational principle espoused and envisaged by Stanley in 1831.

It would have been unrealistic, given the varied reactions of the main denominations to the scheme and given the intolerant relationships between them at the more senior levels, to expect the Anglican, Catholic and Presbyterian churches to cooperate in the 'combined' management of mixed national schools. Moreover in very few areas of the system were the denominations so represented in the population as to justify a widespread rather than token cooperation. Presbyterian reactions to the national schools prompted a policy, especially in Ulster during the period 1831-1840, of independent denominational schools. Eventually the Ulster Synod had gained sufficient concessions by 1840 to allow their schools to join the national scheme, secure in the knowledge that they were being guaranteed effective denominational instruction. Among the prelates of the Anglican church, Dr Whately, Archbishop of Dublin, was the exception in his total espousal of the national system. Since he did not share the fear of state initiative in education, so common among Anglican clergy of the period, Whately devoted his talents and energies both as commissioner and as prelate to gaining support for the system. Anglican opposition to the national schools produced in 1832 a parliamentary petition signed by seventeen of the bishops which protested that the system deprived the Anglican clergy of their legal trust of superintending national education. Such opposition drew widespread support in Britain especially from prominent clerics and politicians, among them, W. E. Gladstone. As an alternative to the national school system the Anglican church founded the Church Education Society in 1839. This efficiently organised society, distributed funds to diocesan societies to manage schools open to children of all faiths. According to its annual reports, the C.E.S. in its prime was managing 1,861 schools which included over 46,000 Catholics and 15,000 Presbyterians in their total enrolment of 120,000.[12]

Roman Catholic support for the national schools was immediate, if not unanimous, among the higher clergy. The new system was regarded as providing a workable alternative to the schools of the education societies, especially to those of the Kildare Place Society; it was envisaged as an interim stage in the desired development of a state-financed but Church-controlled denominational system. The disunity among the Catholic bishops on the issue, especially the public dispute in the press between Archbishop Murray of Dublin, a Commissioner, and Archbishop MacHale of Tuam, produced a prolonged controversy which split the hierarchy and was eventually referred for arbitration to Rome. Whereas the Irish Catholic bishops in 1838 formally approved of the national system and of the Commissioners, the Vatican authorities, in the same year, declared that the participation of Catholics in the national system could not be tolerated. This impasse was finally resolved in 1841 by a document from Pope Gregory XVI, which, recognising that the operation of the system for ten years had not injured the Catholic religion, effectively withdrew the 1838 declaration. It stipulated that henceforth all such questions should be resolved at the prudent discretion of each bishop and further directed that bishops and clergy would refrain from public controversy on this matter.

The strategies adopted in the three churches to secure implementation of the national system according to their own terms ensured that by 1850 the national school system was effectively a denominational system in all but name, 'undenominational in theory but denominational in practice'. Thus in 1852 a mere 175 out of a total of 4,795 schools were managed on a joint basis and by 1867 approximately 10% of all national schools showed any degree of interdenominational staffing.[13] While the bishops of both the Anglican and Roman Catholic churches increasingly benefited from the national system in the extension of their educational domain, the Catholic teaching orders established early in the century found it extremely difficult to accommodate the religious aims and educational principles of their founders within the rules and demands of the commissioners relating to combined literary and moral but separate religious education. This was especially so of the Irish Christian Brothers who, by 1831 had established about thirty schools in Ireland and England and refused to connect their school system to the Board. They agreed, under episcopal persuasion, to attach six of their schools in 1834 as an experiment; by 1836 they had withdrawn four of these and henceforth operated their schools independent of the national system until 1925. The various teaching orders of sisters, however, especially the Sisters

of Mercy and Presentation Sisters, in their attitude to the National
Board showed a keen adherence to episcopal policy on education; by
1858 there were 44,161 girls enrolled in 112 convent schools which
were affiliated to the Board as national schools; towards the end of the
century, less than forty schools conducted by teaching brothers were
operated under the National Board.

A major source of controversy from the founding of the national
school system concerned teacher training and the control of training
colleges. The original plan of Stanley included the provision of a
central training or model school in Dublin which was opened in 1834
and continued in operation until 1922. In 1835 the Commissioners
produced a plan whereby each one of thirty two school districts was
to have a model school providing initial training and two years of
apprentice teaching for those proceeding to the Central Model School
in Dublin. The first district model school was opened at Newry in
1849 and over twenty more were provided during the following two
decades. These district model schools were vested in, financed fully
and managed by the Commissioners and provided a higher level of
education than the normal national school. Each one contained an
infant, a male and female division, with a total enrolment of 300 and
provided boarding accommodation for the candidate teachers and
teacher residences at the board's expense. Some of these model
schools are still in operation as national schools with the management
now shared between the churches and the Department of Education.
The model schools and the principles under which they were established were consistently opposed by the Roman Catholic bishops and
clergy on the grounds that they provided interdenominational education under public management and as such were unacceptable to
Catholics. At the synod of Thurles in 1850, the principle of denominationally mixed education was condemned and specific regulations
were issued in relation to model schools and the Queen's Colleges.[14]
In 1863 the Bishops instructed the clergy to withdraw all Catholic
children attending the model schools and directed that henceforth
teachers trained in the model schools were not to be employed in
national schools under their management, a directive which
remained in force until 1924. The government, in reaction to the
sustained Catholic opposition to the model schools, succeeded in
retaining the existing institutions, while promising in 1861 that
no further model schools would be erected without reference to
parliament, and in 1863 permitted the larger national schools to
train their own teachers.[15] This interim provision succeeded in
mitigating Catholic opposition to the model schools but did not solve
the serious quantitative problem of teacher supply.[16] The Powis
Commission of 1870 recommended that the model schools be gradually abolished and that denominational training colleges be
sanctioned. The long controversy concerning the model schools and
the implementation of the decrees of the Synod of Thurles produced

the inevitable result; by the mid-seventies no more than approximately 38% of the total teachers in national schools were trained. The ban on the employment of model school-trained teachers in national schools under Catholic management is reflected in the higher percentage of untrained teachers in these schools, 66% as against 48% in the other national schools.[17] An adequate supply of teachers was ensured and the controversy was resolved to the satisfaction of all when denominational training colleges were established in Dublin in 1883 and in Waterford, Limerick and Belfast at the turn of the century.[18]

The Powis Commission of Inquiry of 1870 reflected in its recommendations many of the educational concepts and practices then emerging in Britain.[19] The implementation of these recommendations excerised a major influence on the evolution of the national schools in the remaining decades of the century and in some respects shaped the development of some aspects of Irish education to this day. As D. A. Akenson has written, the Powis recommendations embodied measures which would transform completely the national system in a manner which reflected 'the increasing weakness of the National Commissioners and the increasing aggressiveness of the Roman Catholic prelates' in the period prior to 1870.[20] In designing this transformation, the Commission was significantly aided by its denominational composition; the seven Roman Catholic and the five Anglican commissioners were of one voice in seeking an extension of the power of denominational groups at the expense of the National Board.[21] The two Presbyterian members alone of the Powis Commission consistently resisted such moves.[22] The fact that the Government had sought by circular in 1868 to learn from all the Irish bishops how they would wish to reform the national school system must have encouraged the Powis Commissioners in their enthusiasm for radical change.[23]

The Powis report contained the following concrete proposals:

i)   that a 'payment-by-results' system be introduced to aid teacher renumeration,

ii) that in a locality where there were two existing schools with mixed enrolments, they be recognised as two schools catering for single denominations,

iii) that attendance at school be made compulsory for children of school age not at work,

iv) that where voluntary local support was not forthcoming the local contribution be raised by local tax or rates,

v)   that the district model schools be abolished.[24]

Proposals i) and ii) were implemented without delay, proposals iii) and iv) generated some long-term controversy in the various attempted implementations during the ensuing sixty years and proposal v) was implemented indirectly by the establishment of denominational training colleges in the last decades of the century.

The 'payment-by-results' system was introduced as an element in computing teacher salary in 1871. It meant that a payment additional to the basic salary of each teacher was payable in respect of each pupil who performed satisfactorily in the annual inspection and who achieved a minimum annual attendance. The skewed distribution of pupils over the various standards and the high concentration in the lower standards was assumed by the Powis Commissioners to indicate inadequate progress and inefficient instruction.[25] A contributory factor to this possible low efficiency of instruction, was undoubtedly the level of pedagogic training among the teachers in the national schools, a situation which was directly linked to the episcopal ban on Catholics attending the model schools and the Central Training College in Dublin.[26]

The introduction of 'payment-by-results' into the Irish national schools and its incorporation in the intermediate education scheme of 1878 was a further indication of the convergence of educational thinking in Britain and Ireland. The parliamentary resistance to the growing costs of an expanding education system and the counter demand that the quality of the system be raised produced the compromise enunciated by the Newcastle commission when it sought 'sound and cheap elementary education'.[27] Sir Robert Lowe, the vice-president of the new Education Department established in Britain in 1856, introduced 'payment-by-results' in 1862 with the rather frank statement 'If it is not cheap it will be efficient, if it is not efficient it will be cheap'. The operation of the 'payment-by-results' system in both the national schools (until 1900) and in the secondary schools (until 1924) of Ireland, left an indelible character on the quality of the instruction and allowed the external examinations to exert a dominant influence on Irish schools, an influence which still persists to some extent.

The Powis proposal that overt recognition be accorded to separate denominational schools in the same locality was implemented without delay; this policy change clearly indicated that 'the days of lip-service to Lord Stanley's ideas were over and that a new era was about to begin'.[28] By 1870, the Stanley ideas had been effectively abandoned; the national schools had become *de facto* denominational parish schools with extensive 'mixed' enrolment but with very little of the interdenominational management and staffing so central to those ideals. The Powis Commission, in its espousal of complete denominationalism, promoted an increase in the number of small rural schools and thus contributed significantly to the creation of one of the system's continuing problems. Despite a population drop of a million in the period from 1870 to 1900, the number of national schools increased by over 2,000 to a total of 8,692.[29] In the same period the percentage of schools having denominationally homogeneous enrolment rose from 50% to 70%. Undoubtedly the multiplication of small rural schools was not due totally to the increasing denominationalism of the system; demographic, economic and social factors and the limited availability and range of transport made the small local school a characteristic feature of most of rural Ireland. The accelerated demographic decline of the present century has tended to exacerbate the problem; by the nineteen sixties over one third of all national schools had less than 50 pupils. These schools while they contained 11.5% of all pupils were staffed by 21% of all teachers.[30]

The two Powis proposals which generated prolonged controversy concerned compulsory school attendance and the provision of support from local rates for schools. These two issues, while seemingly unrelated, provoked reactions in Ireland, similar in some respects to those provoked in Britain at the same time by the educational reform sponsored by the Nonconformist and radical lobbies.[31] The questions of local financial support for the Irish schools and compulsory attendance though advocated widely were merely of academic interest in the absence of a statutory local government system providing a complete national network of competent authorities. The development of such a network had to await the passing of the Local Government Act of 1898.

The low average daily attendance at the national schools had been a cause for concern to the Commissioners prior to 1870. The introduction of the 'payment-by-results' system would seem to have promoted improved attendance in the period after Powis, perhaps due to the enhanced enthusiasm of both teachers and pupils. The Irish Education Act of 1892, introduced a number of measures which sought to make education free and compulsory and to adjust teachers' income to compensate for loss of pupil fees.[32] Under the act, fees were abolished in schools where they had been six shillings per annum or less and in other schools only the fee in excess of that amount was chargeable. Teachers were compensated by means of increased salaries or capitation rates. By the end of the century, only 6% of the 8,684 national schools were charging fees.[33] The 1892 act introduced compulsory attendance for those between six and fourteen, the implementation of which was to be the administrative responsibility of school attendance committees established by local authorities. The act, in relation to attendance, applied only to towns and cities which already had local authorities; it provided for the extension of the provisions by county councils, if and when such were established.[34] The Roman Catholic bishops in 1892 formally opposed compulsory education on principle, declaring it to be an infringement of parental right.[35] In opposing the compulsory education measures, the Catholic bishops, were reiterating the principles set forth previously by them to the effect that 'education is not a function of the state but an inalienable office of the parents', and that 'the church can claim on two distinct grounds, a right to exercise control over the education of the Catholic child'.[36] The bishops, supported by a number of local town councils which refused to operate the act, were also effectively protesting at the exclusion from the financial terms of the act of those religious order schools, mainly those of the Christian Brothers, which had not been affiliated to the Board of National Education and for which the bishops had been agitating.[37] When it was proposed to amend the 1892 Act in 1896, the bishops successfully opposed the amending measure.[38] The Local Government Act of 1898 created country and rural district councils which acquired responsibility for school attendance. By 1899 the national average attendance figure was 64.5% whereas in the urban areas in which the 1892 Act had been implemented, the average daily attendance exceeded 71%.[39] The problem of school attendance continued to be an issue of concern to the National Board and the teachers and was again the subject of state legislation and associated controversy in 1926; in 1942 the constitutionality of a School Attendance Act was successfully challenged in the courts.[40]

In the context of the specified aim of 'sound and cheap education', it is not surprising that the financing of the national schools should have been an issue of concern to the British Treasury. In the period in question, the Treasury engaged the Commissioners of National Education in a number of controversies on expenditure, the outcome of which yielded an enhanced role to the Lords of the Treasury as 'the final arbiters on educational policy and priorities'.[41] In the process, while the total amounts voted for education trebled in the period 1870-1900, reaching £1.1 million in the latter year, the internal allocations and the acceptance or rejection of specific policy items were decided on non-educational grounds and mainly on fiscal grounds promoted by the Treasury.[42] Questions such as recruitment to the inspectorate, the improvement of teacher's conditions, fees in model schools, the building and improvement of national schools, results fees and extra subject fees were decided by a Treasury dictat which proved more effective than the advocacy of the commissioners.[43] In 1875 the Treasury sought to alleviate the burden on the central government arising from the total education bill for Ireland being a charge on its funds by initiating a local rate for education to be struck by the boards of Poor Law Guardians - the only elected local authorities covering the entire country. The National School Teachers Act of 1875 specified that one third of the amount of the results-fees be collected locally by rate as a condition of the other two thirds being provided by the imperial exchequer.[44] This scheme which lacked the support of an adequate local authority structure and whose sanctions penalised only the teachers was not the most suitable legislative basis on which to introduce the concept of education as a local responsibility. By 1892, when local contributions were abolished various modifications had been introduced which ensured that very few schools failed to receive the total amount of earned fees.[45] The concept of local contribution and the associated local lay involvement in school management were not likely to gain acceptance in an education system which had become firmly established on a clerical denominational basis; the association of additional taxation with this policy, merely guaranteed its rejection in an Ireland where popular awareness of over-taxation was confirmed in the Childers report of 1896.[46] The implementation of the various Powis recommendations over the three decades to 1900 was a major factor in shaping the national schools system and in emphasising certain features which characterise it to this day. By the end of the century, education for the majority of children was received in schools which were parochially organised, denominationally segregated and clerically managed. The state's role was defined as responding to the needs and demands of educational providers by means of building and teacher grants amounting to the major portion of such costs. The development of the national school system and its evolution throughout the century was also accompanied by the emergence of teacher and managerial organisations.

What can now be discerned as the predecessors of the Irish National Teachers Organisation were active in local groups in the forties and fifties on a scale which drew censorious comment from the Commissioners of National Education.[47] The organisation was formally established in August 1868 at its first congress which was followed by a second more formal congress in December chaired by its first president, Vere Foster, the Belfast philanthropist[48]

For the teachers the achievement of employment security and improved salary and pension conditions were the main immediate objects of the organisation. In the activities designed to achieve these ends the INTO met determined opposition from the managers who interpreted any modification of the existing scheme as a direct diminution of their own power under the managerial system.[49] Various cases of dismissal of teachers gained national publicity and some of these reached the courts.[50] The teacher-manager relationship was further threatened in 1899 when the Catholic managers of the ecclesiastical provinces of Tuam and Armagh placed a ban on the INTO.[51] Under this ban, the Catholic managers refused to employ any teacher who had not supplied satisfactory proof that he/she was not a member of the organisation and given a written guarantee to have no connection with the organisation in the future.[52] Among the indirect consequences were the formation in Portadown in 1899 of the Irish Protestant National Teachers Union and a call from the Armagh clergy to form a Catholic managers' association. This call was answered in October 1903 when the Catholic hierarchy formally established the Catholic Clerical Managers' Association.[53]

When one examines the growth of secondary and higher education during the nineteenth century, those same points of tension and controversy can be identified which marked the development of national education. The respective roles of state and churches, the local or central control of education, the management and trusteeship of school buildings, interdenominational schools and colleges – these were the major issues. The experiences of the British government and its representative institutions in Ireland in the education controversies associated with national education based on Stanley's scheme, had diminished the earlier appetite for educational initiative and may have conditioned it by the seventies towards a policy of minimal involvement as regards secondary education. Various developments in national and university education and in English political thinking and sustained Catholic and Presbyterian pressure for equality of treatment in educational endowment, ensured that any government initiative in secondary education would follow a formula which would avoid the essential features of the 1831 National education scheme.

Irish secondary or superior education has been described as 'a record of poverty, of abused endowments and of numerous inquiries preceding tardy reform'.[54] In the early nineteenth century some attempts were made to rectify the abuses and to accelerate reform. Sir Thomas Wyse, M.P. for Waterford, chaired a select committee established by the house of commons in 1835, which examined the state of existing endowed schools and proposed the establishment of new schools according to a nation-wide plan.[55] Elementary education would be provided for all in parochial schools. Each county would have a government-founded and locally maintained county academy which would be interdenominational and whose curriculum would include scientific as well as classical subjects. In each of the four provinces a Provincial College and an Agricultural College would offer opportunity for higher education to all denominations equally. This comprehensive scheme was to be supervised by a centralised council or committee of secondary education of the National Board. The final report of this Commmittee drew attention to the value of the supplementary education provided by museums, libraries, botanical gardens, art galleries and observatories which 'enlarge and perpetuate the advantages of other branches of education', a concept which has gained a permanent place in educational thinking within this century. Despite the intrinsic quality of Wyse's scheme and the integrity of the parliamentary legislative programme which he proposed to give effect to his scheme, nothing came of the report of the select committee.

A royal commission, under the chairmanship of the Earl of Kildare, was established in 1854 to examine the position of the endowed schools and its report published in 1858 proposed structural and curricular changes.[56] It recommended that the curriculum be widened to include commercial, literary and scientific subjects, sentiments which were to be repeated in the reports of the Clarendon (1861) and the Taunton (1864) commissions in Britain.[57] The Kildare commission also proposed the establishment of an interdenominational secondary education system which would enjoy state aid to supplement the funds of local committees which would manage the schools. Such proposals, embodying the principle of mixed denominational enrolment, local management and united literary education which the Catholic hierarchy especially after 1850 had rejected totally in the national and model schools were certain to experience a similar fate in a period in which Catholic influence in public affairs was asserting itself effectively under the leadership of Cardinal Cullen. At a special public meeting in Cork in March 1859, the official Catholic position was stated in the following terms:

No form of intermediate education is suited to a Catholic people, unless it be granted to them in separate schools and on terms always strictly in accordance with the teaching and discipline of the Catholic church.[58]

Catholic reaction to the report of the Kildare commission stimulated a rapid growth and expansion in the number of Catholic secondary schools, strengthened the resolve of the hierarchy in defence of the denominational principle and ultimately influenced the nature of the Intermediate Education Act of 1878. In 1867 Cardinal Cullen affirmed the need 'to preserve our intermediate educational establishments free from all government control'.[59] 'Government aid, without government control, to denominational schools', was to be the acceptable formula for Catholic secondary education, a formula which would prove acceptable also to the other religious denominations.

The schools which provided secondary or superior education for the 24,710 pupils receiving it in 1871, showed a wide variability as to size, facilities, curriculum, teacher qualification and the nature and quality of the instruction imparted.[60] Some owed their existence to private and royal endowments in the seventeenth century; others were church foundations of diocesan origin, while the most rapidly growing category were the schools established by the Catholic teaching orders of men and women. The wide variability as to size and status is reflected in the census returns for 1871 which show 587 schools as offering intermediate education.[61] Those schools were mainly dependent on private endowments and on the slender fees which the pupils could afford; many of the schools conducted by the teaching orders charged no fees. Consequently the quality of staff, facilities and the level of teaching aids available were inadequate and the absence of systematic criteria weakened the general standard of work. The performance objectives for these schools were often set by the entrance examinations of universities and of various government agencies especially branches of the home and colonial Civil Service in which Irish students were very successful.[62] The Intermediate Education Bill which was introduced in parliament in June 1878 and became law in August, established a Board of Commissioners of Intermediate Education for Ireland composed of seven members. The Board would institute a system of public examinations, on the basis of which prizes, exhibitions and certificates would be awarded to students; it would also make payments of fees to school managers relative to the examination results of their students who had complied with certain rules. There would be no public expenditure in respect of religious instruction. A detailed schedule of rules was included in the act, which specified the structure of the examination and awards scheme and identified the seven subject divisions which were examinable in three grades. Exhibitions would be awarded of £20, £30 and £50 in each grade as well as medals and book prizes. The school fees payable to managers in respect of pupils who had made 100 attendances per annum ranged from £5 per capita for passes in two divisons to £10 per capita for passes in six divisions.[63]

The swift passage of the Intermediate Bill in parliament was due in some measure to the fact that its funding would not fall as a charge on the exchequer; the Commissioners of Church Temporalities in Ireland would, out of property deriving from the Irish Church Act of 1869, which disestablished the Anglican Church, make the income from one million pounds available to the Commissioners of Intermediate Education. This main but variable source of finance was supplemented in 1890 by monies from customs and excise revenues. The scheme of secondary education introduced under the Intermediate Education Act of 1878, did little to improve the quality or extend the geographical provision of secondary education in Ireland; it merely aided financially the existing institutions and, in the process, reinforced their defects. The act made no provision for the inspection of schools, established no entry standards and demanded no minimum professional qualifications nor any specified minimum criteria as regards staff or facilities to secure entry to the scheme. Once the examination rules were complied with, schools could operate as they wished. Examinations and results became the central concern of all, both teachers and students, for on both depended the school income under the 'payment-by-results' principle.

As already indicated, the 1878 scheme studiously avoided those aspects of educational provision which, in the Irish context, would have potential for controversy. Thus, no provision was made for the establishment, building, equipping or maintenance of secondary schools. The consensus of English political thought at the time would have made any such direct state aid to schools conditional on the acceptance of the principle of interdenominational intake or at least on that of local civil control. Both of these principles were anathema to the Irish Catholic bishops, whose acceptance of the 1878 scheme was a prime political consideration for the administration.[64]

Under the aegis of the Board of Intermediate Education the secondary schools in the remaining two decades of the century gradually acquired a distinctive character. While the undue emphasis on examination success and the associated teaching methods may have offended against the canons of sound modern pedagogy, nevertheless the majority of those institutions offered educational opportunity to a growing number of able scholars from that section of the population which previously seldom continued their education beyond the elementary stage.[65] Thus while in its initial operation the secondary system may have suffered from serious faults, in the larger socio-economic perspective it offered enhanced life chances and access to higher education to many thousands of children, mainly urban and middle class, at a critical stage in the political and economic development of the society.

By the end of the century the education system had acquired permanent structures which differed fundamentally for the different school types both centrally and institutionally. Thus for primary and secondary education there were two distinct central boards of commissioners, representative of political, ecclesiastical and educational interests. In each parish elementary education was provided in national schools affiliated to the National Board and managed predominantly by parochial clergy *ex officio*. Intermediate or secondary schools were organised, owned and managed by church bodies, by teaching orders or by private individuals. The absence of any specifications in the 1878 act as to school recognition or teacher qualifications promoted a rapid increase in the number of small academies which specialised in the 'grinding' procedures which the 'payment-by- results' system encouraged.[66] The availability of secondary education in a particular locality was determined mainly by a number of factors concerned with size of town, ecclesiastical geography, the interest, presence or availability of a teaching order and the quality of the relationship between that order and the bishop of the diocese. In the absence of any state or local public responsibility for the establishment of schools, the operation of these arbitrary factors determined the location and distribution of secondary schools. While the counties of Munster were, relatively speaking, generously provided for, some counties in Connacht were practically lacking in secondary schools. Of the 264 secondary schools operating in 1904, Leinster, Munster and Ulster contained 248, while of the 16 secondary schools in Connacht, Galway and Sligo had 11 between them and Leitrim had none.[67]

The reliance upon examination success as a basis for the award of school grants encouraged a keen, but educationally unhealthy competitive spirit between the schools. Examination results became the final criterion of educational performance and consequently schools tended to select for presentation only those pupils on whose examination prowess they could depend. Examinations unduly influenced the whole educational experience in secondary schools; in 1901 of the 38,000 students in secondary schools only 8,000 were presented for examination at any of the four levels of the system.[68]

The rapid growth of technical education, which manifested itself in Britain and in Germany during the closing decades of the century, was not so readily apparent in Ireland. This was mainly due to the absence of the catalytic effect of heavy industry and the dominance of agriculture in the economy. Nevertheless provision was made for technical and vocational education in a variety of formats and under various agencies especially in urban areas. The Commissioners of National education also in a variety of institutions provided on an ambitious scale for agricultural education during the century until the establishment in 1900 of the Department of Agriculture and Technical Instruction. In addition to the Albert College in Glasnevin (1838) and the Munster Model Farm in Cork (1853) the Board also operated model agricultural schools and ordinary agricultural schools in which the students gained practical experience in the farms attached to the schools; during the seventies there were over 200 of these agricultural schools operating. The Powis Commission recommended that the model agricultural schools be discontinued but that the local agricultural national schools be encouraged. When the Department of Agriculture and Technical Instruction assumed responsibility for agricultural education in 1900 there were still over 150 national schools to which farms or gardens were attached.

One of the most serious consequences of the 1878 act was the delay in introducing any specifications of minimum qualifications for teachers in secondary schools. The absence of an inspection system and the total emphasis upon examination success in the 'payment-by-results' system, delayed further the emergence of a professional corps of secondary teachers. The ecclesiastical ban on Catholics attending Trinity College, and the disarray attending the establishment of a university acceptable to the Roman Catholic bishops, resulted in very few Catholics attaining to higher education. Consequently it is not surprising that in 1905 only 11.5% of the male teachers and 8% of the female teachers in Catholic secondary schools possessed a degree.[69] The lay assistant teacher in secondary schools had no contract, no fixity of tenure, no stipulated salary scale and was operating in a results system which did not benefit him financially for his examination 'successes' but might punish him drastically for his failures by reducing his assurance of continuity of employment. The professionalisation of the secondary teacher and the establishment of satisfactory employment conditions were to demand the united energies of the teachers over a long period. In this they were aided by the efforts of Birrell in 1914 and the work of the Association of Secondary Teachers, Ireland, founded in 1909. An earlier association, the

Intermediate Teachers' Association, was active in the closing decades of the century and presented evidence to the Royal Commission of 1899.[70]

By the end of the century, there was a general awareness of the need for reform in Irish education; this awareness was fanned by the movements for educational innovation and change which characterised the 1890s in Britain and in Europe. The New Education movement in Europe influenced education developments in Ireland at the end of the century mainly through the work of the two commissions which examined the national and intermediate systems in 1897 and 1898 respectively and through the Slojd movement in Europe which promoted practical subjects on the curricula, and through generating a growing public discussion of the quality of the educational provision. The spread of liberal political thought, which traditionally had afforded such a central role to educational reform, contributed also to the public debate on education in numerous journals, both academic and popular. Professional societies such as The Statistical and Social Inquiry Society of Ireland contributed actively to the promotion of informed educational debate.[71] The Irish Ecclesiastical Record and The Irish Monthly published a variety of articles on educational topics usually though not always expressing the official Catholic demands and policies.[72] Popular journals such as Hibernia and The New Ireland Review offered frequent comment and critical reviews of educational issues, while the more academic publications catered for those with a professional interest in educational matters.[73]

Educational policy and provision throughout the nineteenth century were never far from fundamental controversy, which divided not only the churches one from the other, but frequently occasioned a rift between them and the state and for a period even precipitated a sharp division within the ranks of the Catholic hierarchy. Such controversy however, should not occlude the very substantial advances made in the elaboration of a national school system providing elementary education for close on a million children by the century's end and a secondary system which offered further education to a growing minority. The Queen's Colleges at Cork, Belfast and Galway, though unsupported generally by Catholics, and the older Dublin University had established the nucleus of a higher education system whose continuation and wider acceptance would be guaranteed by the creation of the National University in 1908. By the last decade of the century teacher education was provided in well-endowed training colleges and the proportion of trained qualified teachers was rising rapidly. Technical education was available in the larger urban areas in institutions funded and managed by local authorities.

These various advances constitute in aggregate a significant achievement and denoted a growing rapprochement between the churches and state which effectively removed education from the arena of state/church conflict. The churches had, especially after 1870, assumed a dominant role in education policy and provision; the Catholic church especially had enhanced its public and national status considerably by means of the education policies it pursued from 1850 onwards. The structures for the provision and management of education which had evolved in the course of the century had been consolidated by 1900 in a manner which explicitly recognised the dominant role of the churches; these structures would emerge as an early controversial issue but would prove resistant to substantial modification for most of the new century.

CHAPTER TWO

Power and Patronage in Irish Education in the Nineteenth Century

In examining educational developments in nineteenth century Ireland the interaction between the churches and the state is of central importance. The outcome of the various controversies surrounding that interaction had by the century's end significantly influenced the status and power of the churches. Furthermore the mechanisms and strategies by which that power had been achieved would in turn directly shape education policy and provision throughout most of the following century. The Roman Catholic church in the early decades of the nineteenth century enjoyed none of the overt power and patronage attaching to the Church of Ireland. As an established state church, the Church of Ireland exercised a major influence in the cultural, political and educational spheres, an influence which was resented and envied by the leaders and members of the majority church. By the end of the century those positions of power and disadvantage had virtually been reversed. While the Catholic Emancipation Act of 1829 and the Irish Church Act of 1869 made far-reaching legal changes, it was mainly in and by the education system that the Roman Catholic Church extended its sphere of power and influence during the century.[1] That church's position of weakness in the early decades, a residual legacy of the penal laws, was transformed by the seventies into a position of considerable strength and influence in Irish life. The process of transformation was promoted and catalysed mainly by a prolonged campaign involving a series of resounding victories on education issues carried by the church against various govenments. This strategy of church enlargement and power brokerage in the education system was presided over by a succession of able prelates notably by Murray, Crolly, Cullen and Walsh, all of whom placed the education question high on their list of priorities.[2] In the early decades of the century the Catholic church leaders successfully countered the alleged proselytism of the education societies with the growing power of the recently founded teaching orders. Stanley's national school scheme of 1831 introduced a new phase, in which state financial aid allied to interdenominational education proved to be a source of temporary disunity and controversy among the Irish

Catholic bishops.[3] Archbishop Murray of Dublin, an enthusiastic supporter of Stanley's scheme, served as one of the first Commissioners of National Education; Dr Doyle, Bishop of Kildare and Leighlin, was another active supporter, who canvassed support for the national schools in a circular to his priests in 1831.[4] The Archbishop of Armagh, Dr William Crolly also gave enthusiastic support to the national schools system until 1849, when he was succeeded by Dr Cullen. Two years later when Cullen transferred to Dublin to succeed Murray, his refusal to accept the proffered position of Commissioner of National Education signalled a significant reorientation in the Church's education policy and a rising hostility among the hierarchy towards the national school system. Cullen's specific mandate from Rome was to unify the Catholic Church in Ireland and to bring it into alignment with Roman discipline and policy. His objective was to defeat Gallicanism in the Irish church and to replace it by those features which are collectively recognised as the hallmarks of Ultramontanism.[5] Chief among these was ecclesiastical liberty from the state, which Cullen saw to be especially critical in the field of education. He was particularly opposed to 'mixed' or 'interdenominational' education which he suspected would promote proselytism and indifferentism, an attitude difficult to reconcile with his own early happy experiences at the Quaker School at Ballitore, Co. Kildare.

Within a short time, Cullen had demonstrated his ascendancy over the Irish Church by summoning the first national synod held in Ireland since the twelfth century; it met at Thurles in 1850 and dealt predominantly with issues in education.[6] Nationalist political opinion and some clerical opinion were not at all favourable to Cullen. To the Maynooth students in 1866 he was not 'so patriotic as he ought to be'.[7] Those clerics who supported McHale regarded Cullen, after his long sojourn in Rome, as failing to understand or sympathise with Irish conditions.[8] To O'Neill-Daunt he was a 'most virtuous man, but narrow-minded and not at all an Irish nationalist'.[9] His attitude to Fenianism sprang from his Roman experiences and his basic political viewpoint; the attempt by him to link the separatist secret organisation with the schools under the National Board, especially the Model Schools, was misplaced and opportunist, as were similar claims which he made before the Powis Commission.[10] The Fenians made no secret of their criticism of Cullen who had, in their view, 'no feeling about his country other than that it was a good Catholic machine fashioned mainly to spread the faith over the world'.[11] Another Fenian comment to the effect that with Cullen's arrival in Ireland in 1849, 'the Cullenisation of Ireland began' contains an accurate observation, for he quickly stamped his own mark on much of the public life of the country and especially on those sectors such as education that involved the interaction of church and state. In this regard the newspaper comment of 1865 that 'Dr Cullen *is* the hierarchy' accurately conveys the dominant role he exercised for thirty years.[12] In establishing that dominance and in exercising it so effectively in moulding church and education policy, Cullen was aided by some significant factors. His outstanding success in creating a cohesive national church structure, over which he exercised positive legatine powers of direction, afforded him a position of great power vis-a-vis the state. In education questions this structure yielded a ready and coherent supportive set of policies, representative of majority lay and clerical opinion, which undoubtedly enhanced the political weight of his educational demands.

His perception of the interaction of the moral law and political activity is neatly summarised in his assertion that: 'Political and moral virtue can never be rightly dissociated from each other'[13] This perspective gave him a decided advantage in deciding the particular domain into which various public issues fell, a tactical advantage which was specially evident in the education issues which arose during the thirty years of his leadership. A recent biography illustrates the manner in which Cullen, during his long Roman term, maintained an extensive correspondence with clerical friends in Ireland, providing him with a valuable information network and a band of allies when appointed to Armagh in 1849.[14]

Finally his close high level Roman contacts were especially useful as an internal instrument of government in the Irish church and in raising the level of his political leverage and intelligence in Dublin and Westminster. The friendships he had formed while rector of the Irish College and as Roman agent for many of the Irish bishops enabled him to deal effectively with any opposition within the hierarchy, especially with McHale, whose Gallicanism and nationalism were anathema alike to Cullen and to the Vatican bureaucracy. At the Vatican Council of 1868-70 the Pope had commented favourably on the unity and discipline of the Irish bishops under Cullen. However, such unity was more apparent than real; in the Council debate on Papal infallibility four of the Irish bishops opposed Cullen in his advocacy of the dogma and two, McHale and Moriarty, sustained their opposition to the end though they did not vote against.[15] In many of his public utterances and political stances, Cullen seemed to put immediate church gain in relation to educational issues before wider considerations. Thus in the seventies, in order to retain the collaboration of the Liberals in the hope of securing an acceptable settlement of the university question, he informed Cardinal Manning that he 'had determined to have nothing to do with the Home Rule movement for the present'.[16] His ultramontanism suffered a severe setback in the famous O'Keeffe case, which arose initially in Callan, Co. Kilkenny, over the managership of a national school but which before its conclusion in 1875 had been through many courts and parliamentary committees and had raised a question of much deeper significance, the supremacy of civil over ecclesiastical authority.[17]

By the end of his illustrious career (he died in 1878) Cardinal Cullen had left a permanent stamp on Irish education; he had set the scene, if not the terms, for the scheme of secondary education and had established the battle lines on which the university question would finally be settled thirty years after his death. He had contributed largely to transforming the national schools into *de facto* denominational parish schools, had secured a pattern of denominational representation on the National Board which gave the Catholics an effective majority, had strangled the model schools in their infancy and had established in their place the principle of denominational training colleges. The vehemence with which he had defended denominational education had decided the minimal degree of state involvement contained in the Intermediate Act of 1878. At Thurles in 1850 he had roundly condemned the Queen's Colleges and identified the long-term Catholic demand as equality of treatment in higher education in a denominational institution. His major achievement was to confer a new status on the education question as a public issue; he achieved this by organising and modulating the expression of lay opinion, by lobbying politicians, by collective resolutions of the hierarchy and by numerous public meetings, statements, pastoral letters and pamphlets.[18] His statements on the Catholic demands in education were so formulated theologically that they formed an ideological base camp from which only further advances could come. It remained for his successors to consolidate and to expand, to extend the structural organisation which he had established and to make it seem plausible and even natural that, in Ireland, education policy was strictly a matter between the churches and the state. Thus in the post-Cullen period of the century, the main Catholic demands related to university education and to securing equitable funding and conditions for secondary schools; the major campaigns had been won convincingly by Cullen.[19] His successor, Cardinal McCabe, was a man of mediocre ability, who, in his short six years of office, succeeded in alienating a significant section of lay and clerical opinion mainly by his alignment with Dublin Castle on some issues; he also displeased many of his fellow bishops by what his successor described as 'deplorable weakness', consequences of the prolonged dominance of Cullen.[20] In 1885 when William Walsh was appointed to succeed McCabe a new era began, which mainly due to Walsh's progressive educational ideals, to his political skill and his established academic standing, produced in 1908 an acceptable solution to the higher education question in the National University of Ireland Act.[21]

The final decades of the century witnessed also the growth of managerial and teacher associations. Their origins and development illustrate some of the tensions which had become dominant elements of the education system, especially its confirmed denominationalism and the reaction of the teachers to their depressed state. Upon the passage of the Intermediate Education Act of 1878, three prominent

Catholic educationalists, among them Dr William Walsh, were invited by the existing Schoolmasters' Association, mainly representative of Protestant schools, to join with them in a managerial body.[22] The offer was rejected and the Catholic headmasters formed an *ad hoc* committee, out of which evolved the Catholic Headmasters' Association.This initiative by Dr Walsh and his associates, Fr Delaney, S.J. and Fr Reffé, C.S.Sp., attracted criticism and reprimand from some of the Catholic bishops whose model of the policy making process in education made no provision for inputs other than episcopal. Dr Gillooley, Bishop of Elphin regarded it as 'presumptious' of Dr Walsh, while Cardinal Cullen's nephew, Dr Moran, Bishop of Ossory, regarded it as a mistake for such priests to hold meetings 'on a matter they know very little about'.[23] If some of the bishops did not readily concede the right of Catholic college principals to form a professional association, chaired by the Vice-President of Maynooth, it is hardly surprising that they resented the emergence of a strong national teachers' organisation, the more so since that organisation, from its foundation in 1868 was the only remaining feature of the national school system which was interdenominational in its membership, a factor which, apart from others, was unlikely to win approval from the church authorities.

Prior to the foundation of the INTO, the commissioners had established a court of appeal in 1849 to which teachers could submit for investigation any cause of complaint against a manager; this concession however was accompanied by restrictions on the freedom of teachers to make public comment on matters educational.[24] This did not deter some teachers from forming the Teachers' Redress Committee which was described in a second circular in 1850 by the Commissioners as 'wholly unnecessary'.[25] Despite the very low level of remuneration, the majority of teachers earning less than ten shillings per week, security of tenure was a priority with the INTO, even from its first congress in August 1868. Within twenty years of its foundation, the INTO had secured improved salary and pension arrangements; its campaign to secure protection against summary dismissal and a right to due process in disputes with managers, encountered a much longer period of agitation, litigation, episcopal admonitions and pastorals and an ecclesiastical ban on the INTO in two of the ecclesiastical provinces of the country.[26] This campaign produced some celebrated dismissal cases, which revealed the determination of the teachers to secure common justice in an issue in respect of which there was frequently a discontinuity between central episcopal policy and the implementation of that policy by managers at parish level.[27]

The enlightened attitude of Dr Croke of Cashel, was hopefully indicative of a changing episcopal policy; writing to the aggrieved teachers of Limerick in 1885, he assured them that the bishops 'would soon put it out of the power of the school managers to unjustly dismiss a teacher'.[28] However Dr Power, Bishop of Waterford, was unable in 1887 to restore Mr and Mrs Healy of Clonmel whose dismissal by their manager he disapproved of; emigration for the family and a new diocesan law forbidding summary dismissal by a priest were the outcome.[29] In 1892, the case of the Careys of Leighlinbridge demonstrated the need for urgent measures to delimit the arbitrary abuse of managerial power within some reasonable diocesan structure. Mrs Carey, an efficient teacher of twenty years experience, was pressurised by her manager, Fr Connolly, to appoint as monitoress a girl who had failed the qualifying examination. On the day on which the monitoress was appointed, Fr Connolly, gave Mrs Carey three months notice of dismissal; a request from the teacher for an explanation was described by the manager as 'an offensive and impertinent letter'. Before the three months notice had expired, Fr Connolly requested her to leave the school on payment of three months salary; when she refused to accept the salary, he threatened to dismiss her husband, principal of the male school. To avoid the greater calamity, she accepted and placed her case before the bishop who promptly reinstated her in October and reprimanded Fr Connolly for attacking Mrs Carey from the pulpit. Undaunted by episcopal sanctions, the manager, organised a boycott of his parish school and opened a private school in opposition, to which parishioners were exhorted by anonymous notes to send their children. His campaign broke the health of Mrs Carey who was committed to Carlow Hospital in 1893. The Commissioners and the INTO investigated the case and both fully exonerated Mrs Carey.[30] By 1894 when she was finally restored to health and position, she and her husband were cleared of all charges and their case had offered the INTO one of its most decisive victories in the campaign for protection against summary dismissal. The teachers through the INTO secured some redress when, after another dismissal case in Foxford and a sustained campaign in the press, the 'Maynooth Resolution', was introduced which, while it gave teachers some protection, did not prove effective against summary dismissal nor allow the teacher to offer evidence in his own defence.[31] In an effort to contain teacher anger and to separate the body of the teachers from the central executive of the INTO, the bishops issued a solemn admonition to Catholic national school teachers in 1896 which, while praising the body of the teachers for their dedication, drew attention to the 'wiles and sophisms of men who have no claim whatever to act either as their guides or spokesmen'.[32] By implication, those in the leadership of the INTO who advocated securing fixity of tenure were to be regarded as 'advocates of a purely secular and godless system of education' and as such 'dangerous guides for our Catholic teachers'. The validity of the teachers' criticism of the 1894 Maynooth Resolution was clearly demonstrated in the O'Sullivan dismissal in Leixlip in the Dublin archdiocese which occurred in 1897.[33] This case, in which a young curate summarily dismissed an experienced lady principal teacher, in which parents petitioned for action from

Archbishop Walsh who pleaded inability to intervene and in which the manager lost a court case which found for Mrs O'Sullivan, showed conclusively the need for an adequate formula to regulate teacher/manager relations. It was abundantly clear that the anonymous school manager who stated that 'teachers themselves are only educational servants hired by the quarter', did not represent the majority viewpoint among managers no more than the description of the INTO executive by Bishop Clancy of Elphin, as 'Protestants, Presbyterians and anticlerical Catholics' accurately represented the disposition or the denominational allegiance of the executive.[34] The question was of such concern to the bishops that it merited an official pastoral, *The management of Catholic schools*, issued in June 1898.[35] This pastoral offered a defence of the clerical managerial system, describing those who would weaken it as 'enemies of the Catholic church'; it also included a modified form of the Maynooth Resolution of 1894 which offered a teacher the right to be heard in his own defence and protection against summary dismissal.

The executive of the INTO sent a memorial to the Commissioners of National Education in June 1898 which appealed, in the light of recent dismissal cases, for effective action to protect them from 'irresponsible managers', having the power of 'dismissing state-paid servants at their own whim without assigning any cause'.[36] A request in the memorial that the commissioners receive a deputation was not acceded to. This memorial proved to be detrimental to the INTO cause; it provoked an angry response among the Catholic hierarchy and less than full support among some INTO members who repudiated it and hastened to assure the bishops of their allegiance. Dr Walsh of Dublin, in a letter to an INTO branch, made it quite clear that the amended 1898 Maynooth Resolution was the final settlement of the managerial question and indicated unspecified consequences should the teachers not abide by its terms.[37] In response to this, the executive of the INTO, in August 1898, thanked the bishops for their recent decision and accepted it as a satisfactory settlement of the managerial question.[38] However, this conciliatory response did not terminate the controversy, nor did it pacify those in the INTO who objected to the executive's pluralist composition. At the Limerick congress of the INTO in April 1899, those responsible for the 1898 memorial as well as the president and vice-president were voted out of office and the denominational composition of the executive was radically changed to three Protestants and ten Catholics. The ban by the archdioceses of Armagh and Tuam, which was introduced in April 1899, excluded from employment any teacher who would not sign the following declaration:

> I hereby declare I am not a member of the National Teachers' Organisation and I furthermore undertake not to become a member of the aforesaid association, as at present constituted,

without first tendering my resignation.[39]

This ban which was formally revoked in the Tuam province in 1904 and in Armagh in 1905, was unevenly applied; nevertheless it served as a painful reminder to the INTO of their ecclesiastical disfavour.[40] In 1899 a separate union for Protestant teachers was formed and at the 1900 INTO congress, the organisation elected an executive containing only one Protestant member.[41] It apologised once again by resolution to the Catholic bishops for the 1898 memorial and swore unswerving loyalty to the system of clerical management.

The humble depressed status of the individual teacher may have been improved by the turn of the century, yet the organisation by which he achieved that improved status, was made to endure harsh treatment. In 1900, to consolidate their unquestionable victory and to defuse the widespread growing demands for educational reform, the Catholic bishops issued a further pastoral, in which the efforts of the teachers to achieve protection from dismissal and fixity of tenure are described as 'this anticlerical and almost secularist movement', with which 'the great majority of national school teachers are not in sympathy'.[42] Referring to the 'machinations of a few designing persons' on the executive, the pastoral demanded that these persons 'put themselves right as Catholics' and requested that unless the association 'takes up and maintains unequivocally a correct and becoming attitude towards the bishops and priests of the church', the members should sever their connection with the organisation 'as no longer in harmony with the principles of faith or with their duties as members of the Catholic church'. Such sharp ecclesiastical demands, seeking total submission, drew a comprehensive response from the teachers; the INTO issued a circular from the executive in October 1900, in which they stated that 'any other position than that of correct and becoming attitude towards the Bishops and Priests of Ireland shall never find sympathy, favour or toleration with us'.[43] Obviously the bishops had viewed the movement by the teachers for modification of the manager/teacher relationship as being part of a much larger threat to the clerical school management system. While they were ultimately sympathetic to the just demands of dismissed teachers, the bishops were not prepared to tolerate any diminution of the power and patronage in education which the church's efforts had secured in the preceding century. As a sure guarantee against such an outcome, clerical control in denominational schools was presented as a necessary condition for satisfactory religious and moral education. In essence, the bishops by their victory over the national teachers, had signalled their preeminence within the educational field; more significantly they indicated their intention to conserve and defend that position against all interests. This subjugation of the teachers was a major step towards reducing the number of effective participants in policy making and in guaranteeing a near monopoly to the churches in this field.

The nineteenth century witnessed a distinct redefinition and clarification of the agencies concerned with policy making in education. In the early decades a multiplicity of agencies, denominational leaders, associated church bodies, education societies and political groups sought to participate in the formation of education policy. By mid-century, the churches had begun to exercise a dominant role, to the partial exclusion of almost all other groups; certainly after 1869 and possibly as early as 1850, the church of the majority had sensed the possibility of attracting to itself significant power in the domain of education. At the end of the century, the system had been completely polarised on denominational lines and within that polarisation, 'clerical' and 'denominational' had become synonymous; church managed schools meant clerically managed schools, especially in the Roman Catholic church. The only issue which contained a serious threat to church monopoly was the question of local popular control and rate aid for schools. The local control and local rate which had been proposed in the sixties and the seventies had been promptly swept aside by the energetic opposition of Cardinal Cullen. At the same time that the church asserted that 'education is not a function of the state, but an inalienable office of the parents', it emphasised that in education matters the clergy acted 'in loco parentis' and hence could claim on two distinct grounds, a right to exercise control.[44] Any measures which involved a local democratic body participating in educational administration was construed as not representing the parents and being a threat to clerical control and was accordingly opposed. The 1892 Education Act establishing attendance committees was opposed by the Catholic bishops as an infringement of parental rights and an amending act was withdrawn in 1896 due to similar opposition.[45] This official church ambivalence towards parental rights and democratic control in education is manifest in the declaration of the bishops of May 1899 against denominationally 'mixed' agricultural colleges:

> While we are prepared to support an agitation for the reform of the National Board that will give adequate representation to the educational interests of our people, we wish to warn our priests and people against any movement that may result in a change calculated to interfere with or endanger the authority or control of our Catholic managers, which is our chief security for the safety of religion in our schools.[46]

The questions of local popular control, rate aid for schools and attendant issues were to promote sharp controversy in the opening decades of the new century; they were also the issues which the Catholic church would find most difficult to resolve within the tenets of its own declared doctrines on parental rights. The pastoral letter issued by Cardinal Logue and the bishops in 1900 contained the following:

> . . . the system of National Education has itself undergone a radical change and in a great part of Ireland is now, in fact, whatever it is in name, as denominational almost as we could desire.[47]

This enthusiastic though qualified acceptance of the National School system bears testimony to the modifications wrought over the century in Stanley's original scheme of 1831, mainly by the effort of the churches. The 1900 pastoral of the bishops marked the first major watershed in the evolution of power in Irish education. It sealed with ecclesiastical approval the herculean work of Catholic prelates such as Murray, Cullen and Walsh; it also indicated the defeat of those who advocated any reform of the structure which had evolved in the course of the century. That structure was centred especially on the managerial system of the national school and its essential significance rested on the *ex officio* roles of the bishop as patron and the parish priest/rector as manager of the schools, whose buildings and site were normally vested in diocesan trustees. This system which was installed firmly on a large scale by the last decades of the century delivered a significant degree of patronage and power to the churches. The bishop nominated and exercised ecclesiastical control over the parochial managers whose decisions on all major issues and specifically on the employment and dismissal of teachers were subject to his sanction; furthermore all parochial school property was controlled by diocesan trustees nominated by the bishop while all school funds were under the manager's control. Collectively, the bishops were represented on the national board which administered the system and they formed a body of opinion without whose implicit support no education policy had much prospect of acceptance or political viability.

In secondary and higher education the churches exercised a similar degree of indirect influence and power through agencies which had close church connections and were generally subject to ecclesiastical discipline; the degree of connection, control and discipline however differed as between the two main churches. Many secondary schools which were nominally under Protestant management had no direct organic links with the official church. A similar phenomenon is observable on the Catholic side, especially where male teaching orders which were not subject to diocesan control were involved; throughout the century cases arose where the desire of such orders to provide secondary education in specific locations or invitations to them by local parents were opposed by the local bishop. In higher education, while Trinity College was closely identified with the Church of Ireland, the various campaigns to secure equality of treatment for Catholics in higher education revealed some strange conflicts and tensions not only among the bishops but also among the two principal orders of priests involved.[48] These points of conflict however referred to the apex of the Irish education cone which catered for a small minority; the base of the system covering the national schools catering for almost a million pupils, was securely settled within a managerial structure which was firmly controlled by the churches.

Most of the various attempts to modify that structure, or mould it in an alternative pattern were doomed to failure in the course of the century: their political genesis or motivation could frequently be construed as external in origin and alien in philosophy or could usually be presented as such and thus rendered politically unacceptable.

Few Irish political groups or leaders in the nineteenth century offered any policies bearing upon alternative educational structures; the exceptions were the Young Irelanders and Michael Davitt. The policies advocated by Thomas Davis and the Young Irelanders centred mainly on the principle of interdenominational or mixed education. They supported the essentials of Stanley's scheme, urged Catholic and Protestant to attend the same schools and favoured the Queen's Colleges and the model schools in opposition to O'Connell. Their policy is neatly summarised in the words of Davis which, strangely, are in strong alignment with the sentiments of some Catholic bishops in the period prior to Cullen's ascendancy:

> The reasons for separate education are reasons for separate life, for mutual animosity, for penal laws, for religious wars . . . let those who insist on unqualified separate education follow out their principles . . . let them prohibit Catholic and Protestant boys from playing or talking or walking together . . . let them rail off each set into a separate quarter.[49]

However the idealism of Davis and the Young Irelanders stood little chance against the demographic reality and the inter- church bitterness of post-famine Ireland; the widespread social deprivation and the growing network of Catholic teaching orders ensured that the outcome would be an education system which was decidedly denominational. In the reversal of the relative roles of the two main churches, the development of a strong denominational education system was to prove both an effective weapon and a symbol of victory for the Catholic church. By the 1870s that weapon had been effectively and strategically used and the campaigns for intermediate and higher education were waged under the banner of the successes achieved in the national schools. By the end of the century the national and intermediate systems had settled into mature, stable, organisational models, which reflected the reality of education provision as a bilateral undertaking of churches and state.

By century's end the island had the benefit of an education network which was geographically extensive and offered the benefits of its national schools to all its children, few of whom however could remain on its rolls to the theoretical limit of eighteen or avail of the secondary education which was becoming increasingly available. In the school year beginning September 1899 there were 8,670 national schools in operation catering for 796,163 enrolled pupils of whom 50.8% were girls; these schools were managed by 2,936 managers of whom 617 were lay, 1,316 were Roman Catholic and 960 were Protestant. A closer analysis of the denominational composition of the student body however will reveal that, despite the evolution of a strongly denominational system, there was a residual significant degree of mixed education in evidence in the system, seventy years after Stanley's experiment, though it was rapidly declining and unevenly distributed over the four provinces.[50] As shown in Table 2.1, over the last decade of the century the percentage of national schools which had Roman Catholic and Protestant pupils in attendance fell from 46.7% to 37.5% and as late as 1899 almost half of the schools in Ulster had a mixed attendance. The degree of mixing however is of some significance for it seldom exceeded 10% in schools under either Catholic or Protestant management and staffed exclusively by teachers of the same denomination, whereas in the small number of schools, 43 in 1899, staffed conjointly by Catholic and Protestant teachers the pupil ratios were almost equal. Of the 3,235 schools which had a mixed attendance, 2,238 were under Catholic management and 954 were under Protestant management. Surprisingly, the same pattern is observable in the intake to the Central Training College in Marlborough Street despite forty years of a vigorous Catholic campaign against the state-managed training institu-

TABLE 2.1

The percentage of national schools which had Roman Catholic and Protestant pupils in attendance for selected years 1890-1899 in each province and throughout the system.

PROVINCE	1890	1895	1897	1899
Ulster	68.2	57.4	50.4	49.2
Munster	32.9	33.3	29.7	28.6
Leinster	43.2	42.3	34.4	35.0
Connacht	36.4	35.4	29.5	27.0
TOTAL	46.7	44.4	38.4	37.5

Source: Sixty-Sixth Report of the Commissioners 1899/1900, 12.

tion following 1850. In 1899, of the 307 students who enrolled in Marlborough Street, Presbyterians formed over 50%, while Catholics and the Church of Ireland supplied 59 and 54 students respectively.

These patterns of mixed attendance should be seen as a residual feature which by 1920 would have declined even further. Their presence however does not diminish the reality that by the century's end the education system had acquired a denominational structure at all levels. Futhermore the controversies and educationally-linked political contests of the century had reduced the power structure in Irish education to a binary model involving the state and its education boards interacting with the churches and their managerial bodies. The extension and elaboration of that power structure, to include teachers, political parties and indeed parents would constitute a central aspect of the development of Irish education in the twentieth century.

CHAPTER THREE

Policy and Provision 1900-86

While the nineteenth century was characterised by sustained educational controversy, the first eight decades of the twentieth century in contrast present a different pattern. The opening and closing periods were marked by lively debate and expansion policies whereas the middle decades were characterised by a distinct inertia in policy; in this period from the twenties to the early sixties, access to and participation in the education system beyond the compulsory age were governed by conservative social values which also accorded a low political priority to education policy and provision.

The internal structures and the related power patterns which emerged from the controversies of the last century proved remarkably resilient and their preservation and defence became central factors in the determination of policy in this century. The dominant role of the churches and their relationship to the state in the organisation and management of the education system remained as major influences on policy throughout this century. Nevertheless some modifications and evolution can be observed in the power structure, perhaps as early as the forties and certainly from the mid-sixties. The simple binary power structure which operated at the turn of the century excluded all but the state and the churches from the policy process. In the course of this century that simple model was extended to encompass in turn the political parties from 1922, the local authorities from 1930, the national teachers from 1946 and other teachers later; the quantitative and qualitative expansion of the system in the last two decades has been accompanied by the gradual inclusion in the power structure of industrial and socio-economic interests and eventually of parents and students. However these inclusions do not represent a serious or significant departure from the reality of the old binary model; the major portion of the system at first and second levels still lies within the direct sphere of influence and managerial direction of the churches and is funded mainly by the state, a situation which yields dominant roles to the state and the churches.

In examining education policy and its implementation, it is possible to identify three dimensions; these are the dimensions of policy relat-

49

ing to *access, process and structure*. Policies in the *access* dimension relate to strategies and measures which influence, promote or facilitate access to and participation in education; the *process* dimension covers the central question of what goes on in the heart of any education system, in the individual school and classroom and includes the quality of instruction and the curriculum, the physical and instructional environment of the school and other determinants of quality. The *structure* dimension covers the issues relating to the national and local organisation of the system, the details of management and funding and the articulation mechanism governing the links between different sectors of the system.

The major developments in education in this century will be outlined in this chapter to provide an historical framework within which to examine the policy formation process; in doing so the relative emphasis on the different policy dimensions of access, process and structure will be illustrated and referred to as occasion arises. This historical framework is most conveniently presented in three phases or periods, formed by taking the years 1922 and 1957 as demarcation points. The early period, 1900-22 forms a natural unit not only in the politico-historical sense but more especially in that it was characterised by a very high level of educational initiative and debate and by the presence of a number of prominent figures for whom educational reform and policy were of high priority. This period is especially significant for the emphasis placed upon structural change, an emphasis which despite various attempts yielded no significant modifications in the structure. The middle period, 1922-57, manifests not only the initiation of the education policies of the new state but the consolidation of these policies within a political orientation which approached educational issues with a deep caution and sensitivity. In those thirty five years, the emphasis placed by various governments on education was directed mainly, if not exclusively towards the *process* dimension, whereas issues of *access* and participation were generally avoided. When such questions were raised at government or department level, as they were in 1934, 1937 and 1945, they were seldom acted upon because they inevitably raised associated questions of structure and the possibility of precipitating church-state conflict. The dividing line between the middle and third periods is not easily identified with any finality because the associated changes which accompanied the transition occurred over half a decade, from the mid-fifties to the early sixties. The year 1957, however, represents a defensible choice as marking a new phase in education, not least because the economic planning then begun was so crucial in the generation of the resources so vital to the educational expansion of the sixties. This last period is characterised above all by a significant change of attitude among people and politicians towards education and an emerging political commitment to seeking equality of educational opportunity. These fundamental changes are reflected in increased public funding, in a rapid increase in post-compulsory participation rates and in some structural modifications at second and third levels. The early impetus has not been maintained however; economic recession has exercised a restraining influence since the early seventies and the state has found it increasingly difficult to provide for the educational demands of a growing youth population. These recessionary pressures have not however deflected fully the reformist thrust of this period and some changes at present under consideration hold considerable potential.

Phase 1: 1900-22.
The nineteenth century closed with high hopes and great expectations in education; two commissions, the Belmore Commission (1898) on the primary school and the Commission on Intermediate Education (1899) examined both foreign and domestic evidence and proposed significant changes in the national and intermediate schools.[1] New programmes and regulations were introduced in 1900 which governed the development of these schools until the change of administration in 1922 and the formation of the Department of Education in 1924.

With the introduction of a new programme in 1900, a new era in primary education was ushered in.[2] However the teachers were never happy with the new programme, in the preparation of which they had not been consulted; the progressive ideas underlying the new emphasis on 'child-centred' education and practical subjects were ultimately obstructed by the absence of the necessary levels of funding, teacher training and school facilities.[3]

The Commission on Intermediate Education recommended the establishment of an inspectorate, the diversification of courses to reflect student differences, the vesting of additional powers in the Intermediate Board in relation to school staffing and premises and the retention of the external examinations as the basis of state aid to schools. The Education Act of 1900, and the revised regulations of the commissioners for 1902, gave legal effect to some of these innovations.[4] Inspectors were to participate in the evaluation of school performance and a degree of specialisation was introduced into the curriculum by means of separate grammar and modern courses. The effect in the schools of these alternative courses and of the further specialisation introduced in 1903, was diminished considerably for the same reasons that obstructed the new measures in the national schools i.e. teacher qualification and lack of resources. These inherent weaknesses of primary and intermediate education in the first decade were trenchantly exposed in the commissioned reports of the two English inspectors, Dale and Stephens.[5] They criticised the dominance of the external examinations, the associated and resultant features of schoolwork, the absence of a permanent inspectorate and the depressed role of assistant teachers within the system. Their proposals included a central authority to coordinate all educational provision, the abolition of school grants related to examination success and the recasting of the examination system to reduce the number of examinations to two.

The educational work of the Gaelic League, founded in 1893, encompassed much more than the question of Irish in the education system.[6] Its deep involvement in the major education issues of the day attracted a wide readership to its weekly bilingual paper wherein educational questions ranging from infant school to university were given extensive coverage.[7] In the first two decades of the century the issue which generated the deepest controversy and which contained the most fundamental implications for the system concerned the establishment of a central coordinating education authority in conjunction with local democratic education bodies. Proposals to introduce such structures emerged in the Wyndham Bill of 1904, the Irish Council Bill of 1907, and in McPherson's Irish Education Bill of 1919.[8] Wyndham's bill proposed a gradual move towards local control and rate support, beginning with technical and secondary education and later including primary education. The Irish Council Bill of 1907, involving the principle of devolution, proposed the establishement of a Council with autonomous responsibility for eight of the forty five departments or boards in Ireland, including Local Government, Education and Agriculture. The Bill proposed the abolition of the various boards controlling education and the establishment for the first time of a department of education, a proposal to which Birrell personally attached 'most enormous importance'. While opposition to the bill in general was widespread among the Nationalist party, who opposed it as falling short of Home Rule, and while those of the Catholic clergy who opposed it did so mainly because of its education measures, unqualified support for the Bill came from P. H. Pearse in his role as an educationalist and as editor of *An Claidheamh Soluis*. To Pearse, the bill, which would give effect to the Gaelic League demand for 'educational Home Rule', would also 'give the people of Ireland virtual control of their own education' and thereby place us 'on the eve of the greatest and most beneficial revolution in the modern history of Ireland'.[9] Others, like Terence MacSwiney and D. P. Moran of *The Leader*, supported Pearse in counselling acceptance on political as well as educational grounds; however, the active lobbying and caucus activity of the Ancient Order of Hibernians ensured the rejection of the bill and its withdrawal in parliament.

The Killanin and Molony commissions examined primary and secondary education and collectively they constitute a clear indictment of the existing structures and their functioning during the opening decades of the century. The report on primary education drew attention to the many inadequacies of the national schools and proposed various remedial measures, among them, the levying of a local education rate in support of local education committees which would exercise managerial functions. The Molony report in which some of the educational ideas of Pearse found an echo, recognised 'that the whole system should be reconstructed', and realised the impossibility of effectively coordinating Irish education in the absence of a single central authority.[10] It proposed a Department of Education, a statutory Council of Education, a national education rate and other reforms relating to examinations, teacher tenure and salary and the abolition of 'payment-by results'.[11]

These two reports influenced and contributed substantially to the contents and the spirit of the Irish Education Bill which was introduced by McPherson on 14 November 1919.[12] This bill, introduced amidst the tensions and expectations of the War of Independence, offered a veritable *magna carta* for Irish education which would have given a similar coherent educational structure to all parts of the island. A central Department of Education would replace the old boards, an advisory council would be established and each county would have an education committee with managerial functions and rate income. Among other reform measures the bill proposed the provision of school transport and school books and the enforcement of compulsory school attendance. Public reaction to this significant bill divided mainly on denominational lines; the Catholic clergy, the Catholic educational bodies and the Catholic press vehemently opposed it while the Protestant churches, the Protestant managerial bodies and the Protestant press generally supported the bill with equal vehemence.

It is necessary to assess the reaction to the McPherson bill in the light of the unfolding political situation and especially to consider it in the context of the political solution, which, under the 1920 Government of Ireland Act, would partition the island and establish two parliaments. Some of those who opposed the bill did so in the expectation that a self-governing 'southern' state would offer a more satisfactory educational formula. The bill was condemned by the Catholic hierarchy in a statement which opposed 'the abolition of the semi-independent boards, to be replaced by a British Department, at the instigation of an intolerant minority in one angle of the country'.[13] The episcopal statement called on ratepayers and public bodies to 'weigh the overwhelming burden of foreign origin which the bill would impose on them' and the General Council of County Councils obliged by roundly condemning the measure.[14] When the Nationalist Party were reluctant to commit themselves to the measure in advance of a clear consensus and obstructed its passage in parliament, they drew severe criticism from Carson who saw in their reaction to the bill some indications of the nature of a possible future Irish parliament which 'would be dominated by the influences which killed the Education Bill'.[15] On the other hand, the measure was seen by some opponents as 'a proselytising bill' and 'at once anti-Catholic and anti-Irish' while the *Irish Independent*, in opposing the bill, described it as 'reactionary and non-democratic'.[16]

The bill, on its re-introduction early in 1920 generated a considerable public controversy, which reached a climax in March when Cardinal Logue issued a pastoral letter describing the 'pernicious education bill' as threatening the eternal and temporal interests of generations of Irish children; having restated the rights of parents he claimed that this bill 'trenches upon their parental rights'.[17] Describing the bill as tending 'in the direction of extreme Socialism', the cardinal called for a national solemn novena in honour of St Patrick 'to avert from us the threatened calamity' and as a measure of public protest, the fathers of families were to be invited on Passion Sunday to assemble in church to register their votes.[18]

Dáil Éireann, which had been established in January 1919 was functioning in certain sectors and was asserting its authority widely, often in competition with the corresponding statutory bodies.[19] Already in 1920 questions of education policy were coming before the meetings of the Dáil aireacht or cabinet and in addition other questions with wider implications relating to state-church interaction were under discussion.[20] During the controversy of March 1920, the McPherson bill was discussed at a meeting of the Dáil Aireacht under 'other business'. The following terse and vague minute probably covers a lengthy discussion of which there is no more complete record available:

> Other business:
> (b) *Educational Bill*: Dáil will support the
> bishops in setting up and maintaining a national
> system of education.[21]

Although Sinn Féin did not make any public statement on the bill, it could be implied from this minute that they supported the stand taken by the bishops on the issue. If so, the 'support' in question may explain the strength and self-assurance with which the bishops and clergy mounted the March 1920 offensive against the educational reforms of McPherson's bill. It also explains their appeals to cultural and political nationalism and the related terms in which they couched their opposition to the bill. Bishop Foley of Kildare and Leighlin saw the bill as 'binding in foreign fetters the mind and soul of the Irish nation'.[22] The Bishop of Ossory saw the object of the bill as 'aiming a deadly blow at Irish nationalism and perhaps later on to secularise the schools'.[23] Despite the fact that the bill was merely substituting one form of British education system for another, it was presented widely by its opponents as replacing a satisfactory Irish system by a foreign one at a time when 'Mr deValera and his associates are labouring for Irish freedom'.[24]

The infant Dáil Éireann, in its first foray into education controversy, seemed to learn an early lesson as to the political sensitivity attaching to such questions. The Dáil during 1919 and 1920 adopted a very tentative approach to matters impinging on education as is evidenced in the surviving documentation. De Valera did not appoint a Minister for Education when constituting his Ministry, for which, according to one colleague, 'he had some good reason'.[25] Pending the return home from America of the President, it was decided that, instead of a Minister for Education, a Minister for Irish be appointed and this was done at a cabinet meeting in November 1919.[26]

The prolonged controversy surrounding the McPherson bill reflects not only the tensions attaching to the emerging political situation but also illustrates the fundamental place occupied by the education question in the realm of church-state relations. The outcome of the controversy has influenced education policy ever since in both Irish states and has imbued educational questions with a degree of political sensitivity which has remained to this day. However, many of the McPherson measures were implemented by the government of Northern Ireland in the early twenties. Whereas some of its peripheral reforms were introduced in later years under the various governments in the South, that concerned with popular elected control of education, a central feature of the bill, has never been implemented.

Two other major issues dominated the first two decades of the century, the long-standing university question and the status and employment conditions of secondary teachers. Birrell, having tasted bitter defeat on the Devolution Bill of 1907, increased his efforts to seek a solution of these pressing education issues. He succeeded admirably in solving the sixty year old univeristy question with his Irish Universities Act of 1908; in relation to the many grievances of secondary teachers his strenuous efforts aroused deep and protracted controversy though he did eventually achieve a partial success.

The university question had been a source of controversy and of Catholic grievance since the 1840s and while various reform schemes had been proposed, all had been rejected by one or more of the parties involved. The university institutions, Trinity College, the Queen's Colleges at Cork, Belfast and Galway and the residue of Newman's University catered for a very small minority of students, collectively around a thousand in 1908, while the Royal University was merely an examining body having no teaching function. Two Royal Commissions, the Robertson Commission of 1901 and the Fry Commission of 1906 proposed different solutions, each one embodying a new multi-collegiate university, one excluding Trinity College, the other including it and both providing a new college for Catholics.[27] When in 1903, Trinity College, in an effort to meet the objections to Catholics attending, offered to provide additional safeguards for faith and morals, the offer was rejected.[28] A compromise proposal was offered by Lord Dunraven in 1904 in which a new University of Dublin would embrace Trinity College Dublin, Queen's College Belfast, and a new King's College Dublin, each of which would mainly serve the interests of a different denomination.[29] The Fry Commission concentrated its solution mainly on extending the University of Dublin to include all existing colleges and a new college in Dublin to meet the needs of Roman Catholic students.

In a statement on university reform in 1906, the Roman Catholic hierarchy indicated that they would be prepared to accept any of three solutions, 'a university for Catholics' being accorded priority, the others being a new college in either the University of Dublin or the Royal University.[30] One further scheme was proposed in 1907, that of James Bryce, the chief secretary; this would have located a new college for Catholics inside an enlarged University of Dublin, a move which was acceptable to and possibly encouraged by the Catholic bishops.[31] This scheme which provoked instant adverse reaction in Trinity College and rallied some British universities in support, was quickly abandoned. The principal political achievement of Birrell in 1908 was to design a formula which created two new universities, and in doing so to meet the long-standing Catholic demands while not diminishing the status of Trinity College. The Irish Universities Bill introduced in March 1908, provided for the dissolution of the Royal University, the establishment of Queen's University, Belfast and a new National University of Ireland, having three constituent colleges at Cork, Galway and Dublin.[32]

While The NUI would be legally undenominational and while no religious test might be applied and no ecclesiastical authorities were to have de jure representation on its governing bodies, yet it received unqualified support and acceptance from the Catholic hierarchy, one of whose members, Archbishop W. J. Walsh of Dublin, became its first Chancellor. The particular solution contained in the 1908 Act, while confirming the denominational divide in Irish education, extended for another sixty years the social and cultural isolation of Trinity College.

Birrell's remarkable success with the university question was not to be repeated when he tackled the other problems of Irish education. Speaking in Parliament in 1911, he described as 'miserably inadequate' the salary and conditions of teachers in secondary schools and he set himself 'to try to raise the standard of the secondary teacher in Ireland'.[33] Commenting in Parliament on the low status of secondary teachers, John Dillon said that those who drifted into secondary teaching 'came afterwards to have one desire in life and that was to escape from the servitude in which they found themselves'.[34]

It required three years of patient negotiations and political determination on Birrell's part to transform his parliamentary intentions of 1911 into legislative reality. In this project while he received active support from the newly-founded Association of Secondary Teachers he found the Catholic Headmasters Association reluctant to agree to the measures by which he hoped to improve the status and employment conditions of the lay teachers. While both the ASTI and the CHA were agreed on the need to provide Treasury grants for secondary schools, they differed as to the priorities on those grants.[35] When in 1912 Birrell secured an Exchequer grant of £40,000 specifically for raising the status of the lay teachers in Ireland, he outlined a scheme which included a fixed ratio of lay teachers and did not include religious teachers.[36] The CHA and the Catholic bishops opposed the proposals which would 'admit the right of the Government to regulate their staffs and alter the very foundations of their constitution as Catholic religious schools'.[37]

The Bill which Birrell introduced in 1914 provided for the allocation of the £40,000 grant and for the establishment of a Teachers' Registration Council, which met for the first time in 1915 and the regulations of which came into force in July 1918.[38] While Birrell's 1914 measure provided for direct payment to registered secondary teachers, it was not universally adhered to in all its provisions by the schools; the final satisfactory resolution of the teachers' grievances required almost fifty years of agitation and negotiation in search of adequate remuneration and security of tenure. Secondary teachers generally were not satisfied with the majority findings of the 1918 Vice-Regal Committee on Conditions of Service. The two ASTI representatives produced a minority report founded on the principle of public accountability by which they claimed, that those paid out of state funds had a right to due process in cases of dismissal. The case fought by the primary teachers of the INTO in the nineties was being fought all over again within the same context of dismissals, appeal boards and counter appeals to church laws. The intensity of the teachers' campaign can be judged from the fact that both primary and secondary teachers organised school strikes in 1918 and 1920.

The issues and developments in the period 1900-1922, were of major significance in shaping the future education system. The reform measures attempted, especially those of 1904, 1907 and 1919 which involved fundamental structural changes possessed considerable potential. Had they succeeded the result would have been a radical modification of the structures moulded by the controversies of the nineteenth century. Their implementation, especially that of McPherson's bill would also have, in time, extended the power structures beyond the binary model of churches and state at national level, to include local elected representatives, teachers and parents at local level. The defeat of these various measures meant the conservation of the power structure in Irish education as it operated in 1900; it also meant that in the Irish Free State education policy and structural control would be monopolised by the churches and the state.

The *process* dimension of policy received considerable attention in this critical period; at primary and secondary levels, curricula and syllabuses were devised according to current progressive thinking. Scientific, practical and commercial subjects were promoted and initially some efforts were made to provide professional training for teachers in these areas. The influence of the training colleges was beginning to show in the rapidly rising professional calibre of the teaching force. Under the energetic direction of Commissioner Starkie from 1899 to 1920, the physical environment of the national schools was improved and a programme of amalgamation and rebuilding was begun. These *process* reforms however, while accelerated by the political support of Augustine Birrell as Chief Secretary from 1907, were frustrated frequently by the alienation of teachers from the inspectorate and the central authority and were considerably diluted in their impact by the economic disruption occasioned by the first World War.

Questions relating to educational opportunity and access to secondary education were seldom raised in the opening decades of the century. Completion of the primary school course represented the limit of educational experience for the majority, while one third of students left school long before completing the primary programme. Access to secondary education was severely limited and entrants seldom exceeded 10% of the cohort; a scholarship scheme from primary to secondary, devised in 1912, was designed to offer 25 day and 50 boarding scholarships per annum.[39] The geographical availability of secondary schools constituted a greater restriction on educational opportunity than the cost factor attaching to fees, which in many cases were negligible. In 1920, out of a total of 356 secondary schools, Connacht had 33; while Galway had 13 and Mayo 11, Leitrim had 1. While the peripheral areas of the Atlantic region were inadequately provided for in general, the Gaeltacht areas in particular endured even greater educational disability. During the early decades of the century there was only one secondary school in the Gaeltacht areas and that school in Dingle, Co. Kerry, used English as a medium of instruction.[40]

In general while this phase witnessed considerable education activity and debate, with the exception of higher education it resolved few if any of the major problems in Irish education. It bequeathed to the new Irish state a legacy of poor school attendance, a school network requiring considerable funding and maintenance and a body of teachers who were dissatisfied with conditions and status, issues which would constitute the agenda for the education policy process for half a century. On curricular and *process* issues the new regime would share no continuity with the previous order; the ideals and ideology of independence demanded a new *process* and consequently curricular issues would dominate policy for many decades. Only on structural aspects of policy was there to be direct continuity between the old and the new; the educational structures of 1900 would form the keystone of the education system in the Irish Free State.

Phase II 1922-57

Many of the political and cultural organisations which formed the independence movement shared a deep commitment to reform in education; a native government would, it was expected, accord a high place to education in its policy priorities. The Gaelic League from its foundation in 1893 engaged in a campaign of national regeneration of which education was regarded as a major element; in its papers, and by means of a host of pamphlets, it illustrated the importance of education reform in the overall programme of national resurgence.[41] In the editorial columns of *An Claidheamh Soluis*, especially under the editorship of P. H. Pearse, the educational expectations for the new Ireland were articulated in detail.[42]

In 1919 the Gaelic League had published an educational plan which while concentrating on the inclusion of the Irish language, history and music in the curriculum, showed, in proposing a differential linguistic policy for different areas, a solid grasp of educational and linguistic realities. When Seán Ó Ceallaigh ('Sceilg'), who was appointed Minister for Irish in November 1919 in the first Dáil, was later appointed Minister for Education in August 1921, the existing link with the Gaelic League was formally strengthened.[43] As president of the Gaelic League, he was in a position to channel the educational proposals of the League into the Dáil and aireacht programmes. Despite the Dáil's lack of effective power over or formal contact with the educational system until 1922, it would appear that some useful work was undertaken in the period from 1919 to the treaty of December 1921. The reports of Aireacht na Gaeilge to the Dáil of June 1920 and August 1921 reveal a rational and systematic policy operating in collaboration with the League; they also indicate a network of emergent contacts with Catholic bishops and managers, with teachers, local bodies and parents.[44] The 1921 report reveals that the Dáil department had taken counsel with most of the bishops of the Irish-speaking areas, all but two of whom promised their active cooperation and that the minister had addressed large meetings in ten different counties. Moreover, by means of eight district organisers, the department had established direct contact with primary and secondary schools and with local committees of parents; it also offered prizes, scholarships and incentive schemes to teachers. For the year 1920/21 the voted estimate of Aireacht na Gaeilge amounted to £10,000 which included grants to schools, parish commitees, to cooperatives and subsidies to promote creative literature. The 1921 Report confirms what is clear from the Dáil Éireann papers, that all matters concerning education in general were referred to Aireacht na Gaeilge, among which were many requests from County Councils and local authorities asking the department to prepare a national scheme of education. The Dáil Éireann cabinet instructed the minister in February 1920 'to get a committee together to formulate a general scheme of national education', a reference to the First

Programme Conference which was convened in January 1921 and reported a year later.[45] The 1921 report of Aireacht na Gaeilge refers also to the other conference on intermediate education, which 'it had summoned at the beginning of August'. Having expressed deep dissatisfaction with the status of the Irish language in the National University, particularly in Dublin, the report sees the solution to lie with the Senate, which body unless it reacts favourably, 'must receive attention'.[46] Such attention would involve President de Valera becoming chancellor of the National University and a commission on university education which would be established, the report proposed, as soon as the committees on primary and secondary education had concluded.[47]

The main administrative changes which accompanied the transfer of power to the Provisional Government in February 1922 concerned the amalgamation of the various branches under a single department, the structure and curriculum of the secondary examination system and the manner of payment of public grants to secondary schools. Eoin MacNeill who became Minister for Education in September 1922 held strong views on the role of the state in education which made it highly unlikely that he would introduce any fundamental structural changes in the system.[48] The political echoes of the defeat of the 1919 McPherson Bill especially as to the role of the state in education, were reinforced by statements such as that issued by the Catholic Clerical Managers' Association in 1921, in which they expressed their confidence that the new state 'would recognise and respect the principles which must regulate and govern Catholic education'.[49] The structural provisions involved in the establishment of the Department of Education in June 1924, under the Ministers and Secretaries Act (1924), introduced no fundamental change; it offered an administrative device which centralised under one minister the parliamentary responsibility for three school systems which continued their independent uncoordinated existence. The structural reforms which various bodies and writers had campaigned for were not part of the policy pursued by the Free State government despite MacNeill's commitment to the creation of a 'broad highway' in Irish education from infant school to university. At its annual congresses from 1920 to 1928 the INTO called for radical examination of the system and for legislation based on progressive lines. The Labour Party, which formed the main opposition party, had repeatedly stressed the importance of education and had published in 1925 a major policy document advocating comprehensive reforms in all sectors of the system.[50]

A number of significant factors prevented the emergence of radical changes in education under the Cosgrave governments from 1922 to 1932. The government's socio-economic policies throughout the twenties were mainly policies of deflation and general retrenchment designed to counter the economic setback of the early years.[51] Furthermore a government whose Minister for Finance, Ernest Blythe, found it necessary in 1923 to reduce the salary of national teachers by 10% was unlikely to accept enthusiastically any proposals for educational reform which carried budgetary implications.[52] Quite apart from any economic constraints, the Free State government envisaged its role in education as one of minimal interference, an approach revealed by Eoin MacNeill, and his cabinet colleagues, Blythe and O'Higgins, as early as the debate on the Free State Constitution in 1922 and which MacNeill had subsequently reinforced.[53] This administration's caution in education policy is clearly reflected in its timid approach to the Intermediate Education Act of 1924 and in the paucity of legislation on education in the early years despite a veritable avalanche of government measures during the life of the Fourth Dáil from 1923 to 1927.[54]

The third constraining factor inhibiting educational reform in the twenties, derives from the close symbiotic relationship between the government party and the Roman Catholic church. The personal political alignments of many of the clergy would have automatically attracted them to the conservatism of Cosgrave rather than the republicanism of de Valera or the feared radicalism of the Labour Party. Mr Cosgrave in power was in a position to give effect to his own set of political beliefs on church-state relations. As a member of the ministry of the first Dáil, he had proposed in February 1921 the establishment of a 'Theological board or upper house to the Dáil which would decide whether any enactments of Dáil Éireann were contrary to faith or morals or not'.[55] He had also proposed that a guarantee be given to the pope that 'the Dáil will not make laws contrary to the teachings of the Church'. Such a church-orientated stance in a member of a republican government was bound to attract support later from church leaders who were as yet uncertain of their relationship with the emerging new state. In the 1923 election campaign Cardinal Logue issued a statement which supported the Cosgrave government and warned the electorate against voting for independent candidates.[56] Thus the economic situation, the political stance of the government and its relationship with the majority church, combined to determine the nature of the education policy of the twenties. Such a policy of minimal interference was probably a valid reflection of majority opinion in the Irish Free State of 1923, in which, it has been observed, 'there was little use for idealism and less scope for utopianism'.[57]

The main emphasis of education policy in the twenties was curricular rather than structural; this emphasis however should not obscure the scale or the significance of the administrative initiatives undertaken under Eoin MacNeill and John Marcus O'Sullivan as ministers from 1922 to 1932. The department was created and its procedures established, systematic investigations were launched into various issues, a new secondary examination and curricular structure was devised, a primary certificate was introduced, a network of preparatory colleges was established and legislation was successfully promoted in the late twenties on school attendance, the universities and vocational education.[58]

Following the formulation of a new curricular policy for national schools by the first programme conference , the government promulgated a new programme in April 1922 which reduced the number of subjects and introduced the Irish language as an element of the curriculum; according to a regulation issued in that year, Irish was 'to be taught or used as a medium of instruction for at least one hour each day where there is a teacher competent to teach it'.[59] This programme was modified, in detail if not in its general objective, by the revised programme issued in 1926 following a second conference; it was modified again in September 1934 by ministerial decision without the benefit of a representative conference.[60]

In 1921 a conference on secondary education under the auspices of Dáil Éireann met in Dublin and prepared a new curriculum for secondary education for which it proposed only two external examinations.[61] The Intermediate Act of 1924 introduced this new programme of 'open' courses with no prescribed texts; it also substituted capitation payments to secondary schools for the 'payment-by-results' system. From 1924 to 1927, candidates for the public examinations had a choice between Irish and English as an essential required subject; it was decided in 1927 that Irish would henceforth be an essential subject in the Intermediate examination.[62]

Despite the expressions of social concern which accompanied many political statements in the period, and the commitment to equality of opportunity in education which was proclaimed and advocated, access to education beyond the primary stage outside urban areas, was available only to about 8% of the age group[63]. The School Attendance Act which became law in October 1926 made compulsory attendance mandatory for those between 6-14 years of age and raised the average rate of attendance; it also empowered the minister to raise the school leaving age to 16 eventually. Had the latter been implemented a heavy immediate demand for school places and teachers would have resulted.[64]

Under John M. O'Sullivan as minister, from 1926-32, the Cumann na nGael government introduced a number of significant changes which had long-term effects. The most important undoubtedly was the Vocational Education Act of 1930. Furthermore, in an effort to rationalise the distribution of school accommodation and raise the rate of return on capital expenditure, a policy of amalgamation of small national schools was initiated in 1928 and pursued systematically up to 1932 when the Fianna Fáil government reversed the policy.[65]

In an effort to improve the quality and stabilise the supply of trained national teachers and to extend educational opportunity seven preparatory colleges were established by the State to provide secondary education for teacher candidates; these colleges were built, owned and maintained by the state, managed by church bodies on a denominational basis and were located mainly in the peripheral Irish-speaking areas where they provided the only second level education available.[66]

As a result of teacher pressure, an investigation of the primary inspectorial system was carried out in 1927 by an independent committee; its findings when implemented helped somewhat to diminish the strain between primary teachers and the department.[67] Arising from this inquiry, it was proposed that a terminal written examination be introduced in the national schools and such an examination, the primary certificate, was introduced on a voluntary basis in 1929 despite very strong opposition from the teachers.

The question of teachers' salaries was a constant issue during the twenties and thirties. Complaint centred on the reduction on the 1920 scales effected by successive governments; this continuous teacher dissatisfaction was one of the main factors which fuelled national teacher antagonism and eventually precipitated the teachers' strike of 1946. Further reductions in fees for extra subjects in 1928 was responsible for the abolition of night schools for adults in national schools, a provision which had been running for almost forty years. Pension arrangements for secondary teachers were introduced in 1929 and an improved scheme for national teachers was agreed to in 1931.[68]

In the sphere of higher education the government, following its earlier promise, established a committee on university education in November 1925 which considered in particular the role of University College Galway and the question of Irish in the universities. Under the University Education Act of 1926 some new faculties were etablished within the National University and the Royal College of Science was incorporated in University College Dublin, where a new faculty of General Agriculture was established, while a faculty of Dairy Science was established at University College, Cork. By legislation of 1929 University College Galway was appointed to do 'special work with and through the Irish language'.[69]

During the twenties, arising from some early steps in industrialisation and the growing criticism of existing facilities, demands arose for a coherent provision in technical education. Following an internal departmental survey, the Commission on Technical Education was established in 1926. This was representative of public departments, teachers, organised labour and employers and included also Swiss and Swedish experts.[70] The report of this commission not only offered a detailed analysis of existing technical education but made trenchant criticism of aspects of primary, secondary and general education policy. The acceptance of the report by the minister was followed by the introduction of the Vocational Education Bill in May 1930, which established statutory local education authorities supported by local rates and providing continuation, apprentice and technical education.[71] An Apprenticeship Act of 1931, also based on the 1927 report, gave considerable support to the development of the vocational system. Despite some negative reactions to the 1930 Act, on the grounds of state interference, there was no official objection by the Catholic church to a statutory education scheme which contained provisions to which the church had so vehemently objected in 1919. It has been observed that the tacit acceptance by the church of the vocational education scheme was due to the assurance given to the bishops by the minister that the vocational schools 'would not be allowed to develop so as to impinge upon the field covered by the denominationally run secondary schools'.[72] This assurance, contained in a letter of October 1930 to Bishop Keane of Limerick, meant that vocational schools would not be allowed to teach those subjects nor prepare for those examinations which gave access to university and white collar employment. In practice this meant that the Intermediate and Leaving Certificate examinations were not available to students of vocational schools from 1930 until the middle sixties when the restriction was removed.

The policies pursued by Cumann na nGael in the twenties are singularly important in that they established a model which the education system followed with minor modifications for almost forty years. The relative roles of government, churches, teachers, managerial bodies, politicians and parents were established during this period with a degree of permanence which normal socio-political forces were powerless to disturb. If in independent Ireland education has only rarely been an issue between church and state, the political orientation conducive to that situation was securely laid by the governments led by W. T. Cosgrave.[73]

In the general election campaign of 1932 which brought Éamon de Valera to power, Fianna Fáil found it necessary to include in its manifesto a disavowal to the effect that they had 'no leaning towards Communism and no belief in Communist doctrines'.[74] Such a disavowal was thought necessary to consolidate the image of orthodoxy to which the party had laid claim during the period from its entry to the Dáil in 1927. On various public issues, it claimed that it was as qualified, if not more qualified, 'to act as spokesman for Catholic interests as were its political opponents'.[75] Consequently when it came to education policy and the appointment of a minister in his first cabinet, de Valera could naturally be expected to exercise a prudent care lest any disturbance of the equilibrium established by the previous administration should rebound to his political disadvantage; his choice of Tomás Deirg as minister illustrates very clearly this political prudence. His choice came as a surprise to many, especially as Frank Fahy, who was experienced professionally and politically in education was available and had proved a very capable shadow minister. It has been suggested that from an education point of view Fianna Fáil made a great mistake in not appointing Fahy, who might have been a very successful minister.[76] Obviously de Valera's criteria encompassed much more than education considerations; in selecting Fahy as Ceann Chomhairle (Speaker) and nominating Deirg to education he derived a double advantage for he was thereby in a better position to personally influence policy in a department where there was ample scope for church-state conflict. Deirg remained Minister for Education during the sixteen continuous years of Fianna Fáil government, except for a short spell from September 1939 to June 1940 during most of which period de Valera took direct charge of the department.

In a period which witnessed a demographic decline, a related falling school population and an internal economic climate which was seldom far from crisis, education policies tended to be conservative rather than expansionist and to focus mainly on curricular issues. Throughout the sixteen years of Deirg's ministry the disenchantment of the teachers grew steadily, reaching a climax in the protracted Dublin strike of national teachers in 1946, a strike which may have marginally contributed to the defeat of the government in the general election of 1948. Many factors contributed to the teacher dissatisfaction, salary reductions, the ban on married women teachers, the refusal to establish a council of education, the implementation of the language policy in the schools, the curtailment of training opportunity and the establishment of the primary certificate as compulsory. In all these issues Deirg tended to act with a rigidity which the teachers interpreted as authoritarian and unyielding, attitudes which they later perceived to be once again dominant in the government's reaction to the 1946 strike.

Prior to the 1932 election the Cumann na nGael government proposed a 6% reduction in teacher salaries which de Valera promised Fianna Fáil would not implement,if elected.[77]When elected to office however, they failed to honour the promise and in an Economies Bill of 1933 introduced salary cuts for teachers and other public servants, a measure that led to a one day strike.[78] In its Irish language policy also the Fianna Fáil administration generated some teacher opposition. The basic aim of this policy was to extend the use of Irish as a medium of instruction at both primary and secondary levels and to raise the required competency level among teachers. This policy was furthered by means of the revised programme introduced in 1934 in national schools, by incentive schemes in secondary schools, by special university scholarships for Gaeltacht areas and by promoting the acquisition of the language in teacher training.[79] The policy reached its high point of implementation and success in the early forties when 12% of the national schools and 28% of the secondary schools in English-speaking areas used Irish as the medium of instruction.[80]

DeValera's tenure of the education portfolio in 1939-40, though short, is of special significance for it involved both progressive and reactionary measures and revealed his philosophy of education to be socially conservative. Under pressure from the schools he restored the earlier practice of detailed specification of syllabus content and prescribed texts in classical and modern languages and was strongly in favour of increasing the number of external examinations. In higher education he showed considerable enterprise and imagination in the foundation of the Dublin Institute for Advanced Studies in 1940 to which he attracted some eminent emigré academics; he further advanced higher education by making substantial annual grants available to Trinity College Dublin.[81] In his social philosophy, however, de Valera showed no great political concern for the inherent inequality of opportunity obtaining in the system. He viewed the socially stratified participation in the system as answering to the future role structure of society; while he expressed satisfaction with the secondary system which trained the future leaders of the society, he was not sure if the vocational system which extended opportunity to rural areas was worthy of the public money expended on it.[82]

Though constrained by de Valera's close supervision of education policy and by his own political caution, Deirg launched a number of policy initiatives of some significance, mainly in the early years of the Fianna Fáil administration. An inter-departmental committee which reported in 1935 against a general raising of the school leaving age suggested that local experiments be conducted to combat unemployment in cities. Deirg implemented this by applying Part V of the 1930 Vocational Act to raise the age to 16 for the cities of Cork in 1938 and for Limerick and Waterford in 1942.[83] When his 1934 plan to extend educational opportunity in the Gaeltacht was not supported by the Catholic bishops, he established instead a number of vocational schools in the Gaeltacht areas in 1938.[84] While his campaigns to accelerate the rate of building and replacement of rural national schools were less than successful, he was eminently successful in planning and providing schools in the various new Dublin suburbs in the postwar period. In his approach to school funding and teachers' salaries he was the protesting victim of Department of Finance policy and was forced to cut grants and reduce salaries. In the process dimensions of his policy he adhered faithfully to the government's strong line on language policy and under his aegis the policy achieved its maximum impact within the schools and training colleges. He reformed the approach to physical education, promoted radio broadcasts for schools in 1936, and sanctioned a scheme in 1939 for the production of gramophone discs as teaching aids.

While adventurous in some respects, the Fianna Fáil governments in general tended to concentrate their education policy in the *process* domain, devoting much attention to curriculum and to examinations; their efforts in the policy realm of *access* were tentative and were finally confined to the vocational sector, thereby avoiding any structural implications with political consequences. In the postwar planning process, an education plan was devised by a department group in 1947 which involved raising the school leaving age to 16 and the creation of new senior schools, catering for the less able pupils aged 12-15.[85] A decision was taken by the cabinet in October 1947 to introduce legislation to raise the school leaving age to 15 as a first step to raising it ultimately to 16. The general character of Fianna Fáil policy in education was due as much to the close supervision by de Valera as to the party's reluctance to depart in any significant way from the policy pattern and the *status quo* established by their predecessors in government.[86]

During the two periods of Inter-Party government, 1948-51 and 1954-57, Richard Mulcahy was Minister for Education; as leader of the majority coalition party, Fine Gael, he was possibly in a position to seek the education portfolio and thus continue his earlier deep involvement in education and in the language movement.[87] Besides, his deep political conservatism would have offered the party the necessary assurance of avoiding any church-state confrontation in a cabinet in which there was deep polarisation and little unanimity on some basic issues. Mulcahy showed promise in the early years of generating a new spirit in the education system by honouring his pre-election promises and implementing those reforms which he had consistently advocated while in opposition. In his election addresses in 1948, he emphasised that Fine Gael would pursue different policies in education and he pledged that Ireland should be a leader in the new approach to education that was emerging in all progessive countries in the postwar period.[88]

In his first period of office, Mulcahy was concerned almost exclusively with solving the pressing problems of primary education and with the establishment of the Council of Education. He introduced some early marginal measures which placated the teachers. However the militancy of the national teachers following the 1946 strike was still alive and was clearly expressed in their demand for a new salary scheme at their 1948 congress.[89] Mulcahy's rejection of the Roe Committee's report on teacher salaries and his minimal changes in language policy caused his standing with the teachers to suffer.

The Mulcahy reform which possessed the greatest potential for fundamental change was undoubtedly the establishment of the Council of Education in 1950. Such a council had been advocated for over forty years by various bodies and individuals, was in line with the 1944 report of the Commission on Vocational Organisation and had also been proposed in 1945.[90] Mulcahy's advocacy of such a council reveals a rather limited understanding of its function which was at variance with the concept as contained in the election manifesto of his cabinet colleagues in the new Clann na Poblachta party who envisaged the council as democratically representative and comprehensive in its role.[91] When finally established in April 1950, the Council of Education was presented by the Minister with narrow defensive terms of reference which excluded any consideration of structural questions. Its membership of 29, nominated by the minister, consisted of 26 professional educators (including 11 clerics of various denominations) and 3 members who represented rural interests.[92] Some aspects of the council were severely criticised, its urban bias, the exclusion of the trade unions and of parents as parents.[93] This latter exclusion is difficult to reconcile with the minister's statement that 'one of the foremost functions which the council would perform would be to emphasise the rights and responsibilities of parents in the matter of education'.[94]

The council examined at the request of the minister, in turn, the curricula of the primary and the secondary schools, topics which it was difficult to examine meaningfully without reference to the administrative and structural aspects of the education system. The two reports from the council reveal a conservative and reactionary value system which on the one hand did not see any compelling need for change in the primary school curriculum and on the other rejected a rising demand for wider access to free secondary education. This latter demand it described as being untenable, utopian, socially and pedagogically undesirable and economically impossible.[95] The Council of Education in its reports revealed a sterility and an irrelevance which may have reflected accurately the views of the educational establishment of the fifties and answered to the innate conservatism of most politicians. As educational blueprints its reports were totally alien to the rising hopes and expectations of a younger generation which saw clearly the immense potential of the education system for economic and social development, a generation which was slowly realising that historically in education, all the childern of the nation had not been equally cherished.

Education policy during the two inter-party periods revealed an attitude to the role of government very similar to that obtaining in the twenties. In his first ministerial Dáil speech, Richard Mulcahy wished to have it understood that 'the function of the Minister for Education is a very, very narrow one'.[96] At the INTO congress in 1949, elaborating further, he declared: 'It is the function of the minister to watch out for causes of irritation and having found them, to go round with the oil can'.[97] It would seem that both minister and government were satisfied with the size of the oil can; neither envisaged an enlarged education system, the lubrication of which would require a much larger supply of oil.

In between the two inter-party governments, Fianna Fáil returned to power in 1951-54 with Seán Moylan as Minister for Education. In his choice of Moylan to replace Deirg as minister, de Valera was recognising the need to conciliate the teachers and also to suggest that his earlier language policy was to be modified. Moylan, an efficient military leader, who in the twenties was credited with holding radical and socialist views, has been described by a colleague, Peadar

O'Donnell, as 'that self-educated most cultured carpenter'.[98] His term as Minister coincided with a period which was dogged by economic stagnation, high inflation and persistent and deep-rooted emigration. Teacher remuneration was a major issue, yet surprisingly he chose instead to concentrate the scarce resources on school building, especially of vocational schools. In order to cope with an acute shortage of primary teachers it was proposed that the department's ban on married women teachers be rescinded; he refused to do so, preferring to sanction instead the employment of untrained assistant teachers.[99] The question of equality of opportunity and of wider access to education was one which, coming into prominence at the time, might have been expected to attract the spontaneous political attention of Moylan. Speaking at the opening of a rural school in 1953 he referred to the non-availability of second-level education for 'eighty per cent of our children who leave school at the age of fourteen'; yet speaking in the Dáil, he declared that he did not agree with 'this idea of equal opportunities for all'.[100] In his ministerial preference for vocational education he sought, perhaps to combine his rural commitment, his egalitarianism, his obvious disenchantment with secondary education and his allegiance as a former vocational teacher. During his term of office 160 new vocational schools were provided and the numbers attending full-time vocational courses rose from 18,000 to 20,000 between 1951 and 1954.[101]

On language policy, Moylan reflected very much the optimism of de Valera; he advocated a policy of bilingualism while maintaining that the compulsion which was widely complained of, did not exist in the schools. In 1953 he introduced an imaginative change in the national school; the free enterprise half-day in which the teacher was free to teach as and what he wished, was a precursor of the fundamental reforms to come in primary education. This reform may indicate that Moylan possessed the policy vision and the educational perspective which with more adequate public resources might have flourished and blossomed.

Speaking at the INTO congress in 1952, Moylan advocated stablility and continuity in education policy, irrespective of political change and in observing the decades following independence there is evidence of a remarkable stability irrespecitve of political party. Continuity was indeed the most striking characteristic of policy over the thirty five years from independence, continuity in the emphasis placed on process aspects and continuity in the avoidance of structural changes. Measures to actively promote wider access to post-compulsory education were seldom considered and the various steps taken to raise the school leaving age were limited and inconclusive or were abandoned in the face of economic or political obstacles. Nevertheless participation in the system increased at a slow but steady pace during this phase; the numbers transferring to secondary

and vocational schools rose steadily, the overall number of postprimary schools increased and the completion rates at Intermediate and
Leaving Certificate levels rose also. Table 3.1 illustrates this gradual
extension of educational opportunity in the secondary schools in the
thirty years to the mid-fifties. However this extension of opportunity
was marginal, involving only a small percentage of the relevant age
groups; there were areas and social groups for whom the national
school constituted the entire educational experience. This is clearly
illustrated in the education fate of the 14-16 age group in the period
from the late twenties to the early sixties. The data in Table 3.2
indicate that very little significant change had taken place by the mid-
forties; two out of every three had left school altogether and more of
the 14-16 age group stayed on in the national school than transferred
to secondary. This pattern had changed by the early sixties when
those who transferred to secondary or vocational school almost equalled the 49% who had left the system and the proportion remaining on
in the national school had dropped considerably. In the development
of Irish education in the period 1922-57, one is observing the interaction of a feeble economy subject to heavy constraints, a political
culture in which education policy was not accorded high priority and
a range of political leaders most of whom did not perceive the central
role of education within any coherent socio-economic policy of
national development. Such a policy had to await the arrival on the
political scene of a younger generation who viewed the education
system and its operation within the wider context of a planned
economy and a more equitable social system.

Phase III: 1957-86

The quarter century since 1957 has been marked by developments in
education which render this period totally different from what went
before. Political, economic and social factors combined from the late
fifties onwards to generate an era of expansion and initiative in
education, the momentum of which has only recently slackened
somewhat in the economic recessions of the late seventies and the
eighties.[102]

The Fianna Fáil government which was returned to power in 1957
for what was to be a second continuous period of sixteen years,
though facing major problems, was fortified by political support for
its electoral promise of initiative and leadership. This government,
unlike earlier administrations, included a number of younger
members who brought to government a new dynamism and political
dedication which seemed to respond to and reflect the popular mood
demanding urgent solutions for the country's social and economic
problems. This dynamism found expression in the introduction of
coherent economic and social planning which eventually encompassed education policy. With the departure of de Valera in 1959 and the
accession of Lemass, the image of drive and energetic government

was further emphasised.

This change in the general political situation was accompanied by a marked change in the political status of education. From the thirties to the fifties the portfolio of education occupied a low rank in the cabinet hierarchy. The sensitivity surrounding the portfolio usually attracted a political supervision which diminished the status of the minister; the absence of a coherent policy seldom offered the stimulus of cabinet discussion. In the sixties however the Department of Education was increasingly regarded as an important cabinet post, which secured enhanced resources and brought some energetic young ministers to the position. This is evidenced by the succession from 1957 to 1973 of Lynch, Hillery, Colley, O'Malley, Lenihan and Faulkner, ministers for whom the Department of Education was a significant step in their progress to political prominence. The increasing willingness of the government to invest in education reflected a growing public awareness of the importance of education and a growing political commitment to extend educational opportunity and to link the education system more directly with economic and social development.

The economic expansion of the sixties made available the resources which permitted a more generous education provision; in turn the same economic expansion demanded of the education system a higher output of skills and attitudes conducive to industrialisation and economic expansion. The vastly increased public financial commitment to education attracted and generated a wider political public debate on education which in turn occasioned intense competition among the political parties. The parties, especially those in opposition, devoted time and energy to the fomulation of policies, realising that the electorate favoured major changes in education. Fine Gael took steps, while in opposition, to prepare a set of coordinated policies under the general heading of *The just society*. In 1966 it published a detailed policy document on education in the introduction to which the party leader, Liam Cosgrave , complained that we had been for half a century content to tinker with the system but had nevert really attempted to reform it. He further committed Fine Gael to a 'concern for educational reform and a willingness to grasp the many nettles involved'.[103] This comprehensive opposition document may have played some part in shaping detailed aspects of the government's policy as it evolved during the sixties. The Labour Party also gave close attention to the elaboration of policy which continued the traditional commitment of that party to educational reform. In 1963, its policy document, *Challenge and change in education*, urged greater public investment in education and advocated 'free' secondary education for all, while its document of 1969 advocated community control of the education system.[104] Fianna Fáil on the contrary continued its traditional strategy of not publishing formal policy statements and of utilising government commissioned research studies, formal Dáil statements and occasional ministerial speeches as contributory elements in the formulation of policy.

The documents however which most closely influenced policy throughout this period were not the policy documents of the opposition parties nor the dire emanations from the Council of Education, but some basic quantitative studies and planning documents, among which *Investment in education* (1965) and the *Report on regional technical colleges* (1967), were the most significant.[105] Following an OECD Conference at Washington in 1961 on 'Ecomonic growth and investment in education', Ireland became one of the participants in the Education Investment Programme for developed European countries.[106] This EIP project promoted a series of comprehensive studies of education in Ireland, Sweden, Britain, Holland, Norway, Austria and other European countries; the project was twinned with the Mediterranean Regional Project for the southern underdeveloped European countries. Under the EIP project, a national survey team was established here in 1962 under Professor Patrick Lynch as director, which conducted a major pioneering, quantitative analysis of the system. Its report, *Investment in education*, offered a systematic examination of the performance of the education system, of the demands which would emerge within the immediate future and of the structural and organisational weaknesses within the system. It identified as major faults, the social and geographical inequalities of opportunity, the inefficient use of resources and the imbalance of the system's output; it also drew attention to the inadequacy of the statistical data available on the system, the absence of any forward planning mechanism and proposed as its only recommendation the establishment within the Department of Education of a planning and development branch.[107] *Investment in education* offered the quantitative basis for a coherent rational policy which might well tax the political energies and economic resources of an enthusiastic government for a few decades. It illustrated convincingly the nature and the extent of inequality; it drew attention to the low rate of participation in post-compulsory education by children of the lower social groups and to the high rates of early leaving from vocational schools and the small proportion of students from these schools entering higher education, and it highlighted the problems arising from size of school.[108] While social groups A,B,C formed 45% of the population, their children formed 64% of the entrants to secondary school, 68% of those sitting the Leaving Certificate and 85% of university entrants in 1963.[109] Participation in full-time education in the age range 13-17 showed pronounced geographical variation; while all the Munster counties exceeded the national average participation rate of 43.82%, Donegal, Cavan, Monaghan, Laois, Meath and Kildare were below it and occupied the lowest places.[110] In relation to the utilisation of resources in national schools, the *Investment* study showed that 38% of the schools had less than 50 pupils and 76% had less than 100 pupils; the schools with less than 50 pupils, employed 21% of the teachers to cater for 11.5% of the pupils while the larger schools of over 200 pupils catered for 45% of the pupils with 34% of the teachers.[111]

These and similar findings offered the empirical evidence which helped to shape the general objectives of policy in the sixties namely to promote equality of educational opportunity, to increase the efficiency of the system and to broaden the curricular content. Such a policy however, did not emerge with any great clarity until the mid-sixties and there is ample evidence of confusion and uncertainty in some policy statements in the early sixties. This confusion and uncertainty may reflect some hidden political tensions or may express the caution and pragmatism characteristic of Fianna Fáil in government in relation to education; alternatively such speeches as that of Hillery in May 1963 may be construed as holding statements while discussions and negotiations were in progress with the churches.

The general policy of the Lemass government on educational opportunity was outlined in 1959 during a Dáil debate on a motion tabled by Dr Noel Browne TD, proposing that the minimum school leaving age be raised to 15 and that postprimary education be provided for all childern irrespective of economic status.[112] It is obvious from this debate that education policy was beginning to occupy a more central place in government discussion; Lemass, as taoiseach, intervened in the debate and outlined his government's approach to educational opportunity. While they agreed with the objective of the motion of extending educational opportunity, they disagreed with the proposed method of achieving it:

> The aim of government policy was to bring about a situation in which all children will continue their schooling until they are at least fifteen years of age.[113]

They hoped to achieve this not by statutory compulsion but by 'increasing the facilities for postprimary education'. This cautious and gradual approach illustrates the growing pragmatism which sought wider popular support before espousing more adventurous policies. It was Hillery's task, as minister, to formulate policies which would lay claim to all the new political ground and to outline the way forward with maximum flexibility. This he did by means of innovative measures in secondary and university education which facilitated the building and extension of school facilities, promoted the sciences and modern languages and provided more scholarships to second level and higher education.[114]

By 1963 the central issues had been identified and quantified and were expressed in a major policy statement by the minister on 20 May.[115] This speech contains promise of many of the reforms of the following decade, the extension of educational opportunity, the establishment of regional technical colleges, access by students of vocational schools to all public examinations, the creation by the state of comprehensive schools in remote areas, and the promotion of higher technological education. The minister however was unable to say where the new schools would be located, he thought the local Vocational Education Committees would bear some of the costs, he expected the new schools to operate only to 15 years of age, after which the more able students would proceed to a secondary school; he envisaged reasonable fees being charged and a flat transport cost being charged to parents. In relation to the management of these schools, since he expected that all or the vast majority of pupils would be Catholic and 'having regard to the rights of parents, who in relation to the fundamental principles of education are represented by the church and in view of the church's teaching authority', the minister had consulted the Catholic hierarchy on the management of these schools, and was satisfied that it would be possible to constitute a management structure acceptable to all the interested parties.[116] Since no decision had been made as to the location of these new schools, he had not been in a position to consult with any Vocational Education Committee. While this speech contained many reform measures to be introduced later, its general tentative tone indicates that department policy had not yet been formulated with any measure of finality.

However the sharper definition of these policies was hastened by the publication of *Investment in Education* and the establishemnt of the planning and development branch within the Department of Education in 1965 following the appointment of George Colley as minister. The detailed county reports prepared in 1965 and 1966 revealed the extent of educational inequality and provided the statistical basis for the O'Malley 'free' postprimary and transport scheme introduced in 1967. This single measure in its immediate impact and its long-term influence transformed the Irish education system. Enrolment in secondary and vocational schools which had been increasing steadily from the mid-fifties was accelerated dramatically following the O'Malley measures and continued to increase throughout the seventies as Table 3.3. illustrates.

The establishment of comprehensive and community schools in the late sixties and early seventies has extended the capacity of the postprimary system significantly and has enhanced educational opportunity in many areas; of the 300,000 enrolled in full-time postprimary courses in 1980, over 25,000 were enrolled in comprehensive and community schools.[117]

The impact of the changes wrought in the educational system from the mid-sixties is clearly evident in the participation rates by age group as shown in Table 3.4. This expansion of educational opportunity at second level has in turn generated a related increased demand for higher education, the sector which towards the end of the sixties became the main focus of government policy.[118] Policy in higher education has sought to expand the physical provision, to extend participation socially and geographically and to broaden the technical and technological elements in the curriculum. Within this broad policy a national network, of nine Regional Technical Colleges and two National Institutes of Higher Education (NIHE), was established having a pronounced emphasis in their remit on technology, industry and commerce. By the late seventies, these new institutions formed in conjunction with the Dublin Institute of Technology and other colleges, a coherent technological sector, which offered extended opportunity in higher education, a sector likely to attract preferential funding from government throughout the eighties. The scale of the recent expansion in higher education and its current sectoral composition may be seen from Table 3.5.

The quantitative expansion of the education system in the past two decades has been accompanied by some structural change mainly at third level. At first and second levels the structural changes have been marginal; non-executive management boards have been established for primary schools and at second level three additional school types, comprehensive, community schools and community colleges have been established in a period when policy was attempting to coordinate, if not unify, the existing competing secondary and vocational schools. These changes have not altered in any significant way the existing power structure except to introduce parents in a formal fashion into the system. At third level, where few super-institutional structures existed, new administrative and policy bodies have been created at national level; the Higher Education Authority (1968) has a coordinating and planning role in higher education generally while exercising a funding role in relation to designated institutions. The National Council for Educational Awards (1972) was established to promote, coordinate and develop higher education in the non-university sector. These structural changes in third level reflect the rapid expansion and binary nature of the system and the marked shift in the sectoral distribution of students as presented in Table 3.5. Whereas twenty years ago the universities catered for 80% of all students in higher education, in 1980 one half of all new entrants enrolled in the technological sector; in the years from 1965 to 1982 full-time enrolments in the technological sector have grown by a factor of six.

The quantitative and qualitative changes since the sixties in all three levels have constituted a heavy financial burden on the state; in the decade following 1963 while total enrolment in the formal system rose from 642,000 to 831,000, total public expenditure on education rose from £25 million to £144 million, representing an increase from 3.4% to 6.29% of Gross National Product.[119] From the mid-seventies to date educational expansion has been hampered by a growing demand encountering the effects of recessionary pressures on resources and a demographic pattern characterised by a high dependency rate. Despite these factors, however, expenditure on education continues to grow and the public expenditure for 1985 exceeded £1 billion.[120]

In the period from 1957 to 1985 significant advances were made in extending provision at second and third levels yet little progress was made in diminishing inequalities especially those arising from social class. Social class, type of second-level school attended and domiciliary location still operate as differential factors in determining access to higher education. In 1979 while the four higher socio-economic groups constituted only 21% of the population of County Dublin, their children constituted 72% of the entrants to higher education.[121] A study of the entrants to higher education in 1980 shows marked social and regional disparities in access and participation rates and a marked advantage in transfer rates to higher education enjoyed by students of the private fee-paying secondary schools. Among the 1980 entrants, the children of the four upper social groups, representing 16% of the total population, constituted 46% of the entrants; skilled and semi-skilled workers represented 27% of the population, yet their children formed only 13.6% of the entrants.[122]

Curricular issues were not neglected in a period dominated by an expansion of educational opportunity; at first and second levels various reforms were introduced designed to improve the instructional process and enrich the curricular experience of the student. A new curriculum inspired by a child-centred pedagogy was introduced into the national schools in 1971 and the professional training of national teachers was extended to three years and linked to the universities for the award of a degree. In postprimary schools common syllabuses were introduced and a new emphasis was accorded to modern languages, the sciences and various practical subjects. These curricular reforms have had one deleterious effect however in that traditional subjects, such as Latin and Greek, have all but disappeared from the curriculum of the average postprimary school. This general movement of reform and development has promoted in the mid-eighties a general examination of the postprimary curriculum under a Curriculum and Examinations Board established in 1984.[123]

In reviewing the major developments in Irish education in this century one is aware of a pronounced continuity which can be observed over eight decades. This continuity is provided partly by the intractability attaching to some of the structural features of the system but mainly by the constancy of the power structure. In terms of the basic management arrangements in the system little has changed since 1900 with the exception of the creation of the vocational system. Continuity is also provided in the rather hesitant and cautious approach adopted to the education system and policy by the political parties; in fact this particular continuity would logically link the Irish Parliamentary Party with Cumann na nGael, Fine Gael and Fianna Fáil and assign a certain consistency to the Irish Labour Party in its earlier and post-Treaty manifestations. There is one other continuity which is more marked in the middle phase than in the other two, the emphasis upon process elements of policy and the exclusion of major structural reforms. However in relation to access and educational opportunity the system shows no continuity over the century. In the last phase we find an emphasis on increasing access and a commitment to basic equality of opportunity; earlier attempts to introduce similar measures were abandoned at early moments in the political debate. Even the policy of equality of opportunity which was espoused in the sixties was seldom, if ever, defined in operational terms which would allow of effective implementation. In general the system in its availability has reflected many aspects of the socio-economic reality characterising Irish society in this century. While it would be unreasonable to expect the education system to undo the social inequalities of a society, yet the expansion of opportunity of the past two decades has contributed somewhat to promoting social mobility.[124]

In both the early and later decades of this century education was a central issue and enjoyed a high political status; prior to independence structural questions were foremost in the educational debate. In independent Ireland educational structure has seldom been an issue of open political debate though it has certainly been the subject of critical church-state discussions. When in the last quarter century education policy raised isues of equality of opportunity and access, these were resolved without disturbing the existing structures. Throughout this century the inherited educational structures of the nineteenth century have been conserved and indeed consolidated; we may count them among those institutional features which, according to Chubb, have been preserved as if in amber amidst the changes of 1922.[125]

Despite this structural conservatism, there have been major

TABLE 3.1

The number of secondary schools, their enrolments and numbers entered for Intermediate and Leaving Certificate Examinations in selected years from 1925-1954.

Year	Secondary Schools	Pupils	Intermediate Certificate	Leaving Certificate
1925	278	22,897	2,903	995
1935	319	33,499	5,803	2,165
1944	379	41,178	8,561	3,702
1954	458	56,411	12,311	6,098

Source: Tuarascáil na Roinne.

TABLE 3.2

The distribution of the 14-16 age group in various school types and not in full-time education for the years 1929, 1944 and 1962.

Year		Age Group 14-16	In Primary School	In Secondary School	In Vocational School	Not in School
1929	N	118,900	32,200	12,750	—	74,012
	%	100%	27%	10.7%	—	62%
1944	N	107,000	20,800	16,400	7,400	62,400
	%	100%	19%	15%	7%	58%
1962	N	169,000	7,035	55,750	22,500	83,700
	%	100%	4.16%	33%	13.3%	49%

Source: Compiled from D.F., S 84/13/29; S.P.O., S12891; *Investment in Education*, Vol. 1.

TABLE 3.3

Enrolment in full-time second-level education at Secondary and Vocational schools and separately at each for selected school years 1957-81.

Year	Secondary Schools	Vocational Schools	Secondary & Vocational Schools
1957/58	60×10^3	25×10^3	83×10^3
1960/61	77	27	104
1963/4	89	32	121
1966/67	104	40	144
1967/68	114	45	159
1968/69	119	50	169
1969/70	144	52	196
1975/76	183	68*	251
1980/81	201	70*	271

*These totals contain enrolments at Regional Technical Colleges.
Source: Tuarascáil na Roinne Oideachais.

changes in the system throughout the century, not all of which occur-red in the last few decades. Access and participation have been considerably extended; whereas the minimum school leaving age was raised to 15 as late as 1972, by the late seventies 50% of all 17 year olds were in full-time education. While implementing a new curriculum in the seventies the primary sector managed successfully to cater for an enrolment which increased from 473,000 in 1964/65 to 541,000 in 1980/81.[126] These patterns of expansion have been repeated in higher education which in 1983 enrolled a total of 44,500 students, equal approximately to the total enrolment in second level in 1939. The gradual expansion of the system since the foundation of the state and the rapid increase in participation of the recent past may be clearly seen if we compare total enrolments in the twenties and the eighties; at the establishment of the Department of Education (1924) there were 572,000 students enrolled of whom 522,000 were in national schools, sixty years later total enrolment stood at 911,000 of whom 568,000 were in the national schools.[127]

This quantitative expansion has been accompanied by a number of significant changes; these relate mainly to the relative participation by girls in the non-compulsory levels and the expansion and elabora-tion of the consultative policy processes and of the power structure. Prior to 1922 girls formed from 25% to 30% of those sitting for the various examinations of the Intermediate Board. At the Intermediate and Leaving Certificate examinations in 1925, they formed 36% and 25% respectively of the entrants. Participation by girls improved throughout the forties and by the early fifties they achieved parity with boys at Intermediate level, rising to 55% of Intermediate entrants by 1962 when they had also achieved parity at Leaving Certificate level.[128] At present while more girls than boys complete senior cycle by taking the Leaving Certificate, they form only 46% of the entrants to higher education. A recent extensive study of sex differences in provision and subject choice has made some funda-mental policy proposals.[129]

At the close of the last century the consultative process and the power structure were effectively confined to the state agencies and the churches or church bodies. That situation persisted until the middle years of this century when the prolonged primary teachers strike of 1946 changed teacher attitudes considerably; similar confrontation situations dramatically changed the secondary teachers in the early sixties and re-affiliation as a trade union immersed them with their professional colleagues in a movement which was adopting a more militant stance and taking a greater interest in policy.[130] Since the mid-1960s under the umbrella of the Irish Congress of Trade Unions, teachers have acquired a greater voice in policy formation, have improved considerably their condi-tions of employment and are a more significant element in a slightly modified power structure. In a similar fashion, the managerial bodies have, in the past twenty years and mainly in response to state initiative, elaborated their network of organisations and have created a number of umbrella bodies which channel their views and their influence into the central process of negotiation and consultation. The policy process and its consultative machinery of 1900 was simple, if not primitive, compared to the labyrinthine structures and networks operating in 1986. Teachers and parents were excluded then whereas they are now included as well as other interest groups representing agriculture and industry. The growing complexity of the system and the growing mass of its central administrative machinery may very soon necessitate some fundamental structural adjustments and decentralisation.

TABLE 3.4

Percentage participation rates in full-time education
by stated age groups in 1964 and 1974

Age	14	15	16	17	18	18	20-24
1964	66	51	36	24	14	9	6
1974	95	86	68	46	27	15	8

Source: Tuarascáil na Roinne.

TABLE 3.5

Full-time student enrolment in higher education by sector
for selected years 1965-1982.

Sector		1965/66	1975/76	1980/81	1981/82
University	N	15,049	21,936	23,949	24,662
	%	85.9	66.5	57.7	55.9
College of Education	N	1,435	2,584	3,278	3,269
	%	8.2	7.8	7.9	7.4
Technological	N	1,031	8,483	14,289	16,164
	%	5.9	25.7	34.4	36.7
Total	N	17,515	33,003	41,516	44,095
	%	100	100	100	100

Source: Commission on Higher Education, 1967;
HEA Accounts and Student Statistics 1975, 1980, 1981.

SECTION II

CONTRIBUTORS AND CONTRIBUTIONS
TO
EDUCATION POLICY
1900-86

INTRODUCTION

The policy making process in Irish education has undergone a significant change in the course of this century in so far as the number of participating groups has been increased considerably. If we accept Lindblom's dictum that 'policy is made through the complex processes by which people exert power or influence over each other' and if we also accept that the 'proximate policy-makers' and those other groups who influence them are all participants, then in the Irish context we are confronted with a large number of groups who are involved in one role or another of Lindblom's typology.[1] Leaving aside the task of identifying the proximate policy-makers to a later chapter, it is necessary at this stage to identify all the main contributors to education policy and to examine their contributions in this century.

Primary, secondary, vocational and other postprimary teachers number about forty thousand and are represented by three trade unions or organisations. The owners and managers of schools are organised in managerial bodies according to level and denomination and some also by sex. These various bodies are linked in networks of cooperating umbrella groups which in turn coalesce, through senior church bodies to form a Joint Mangerial Body at national level. On the government side there are the Cabinet, the Minister for Education and his/her Department with its professional and administrative officials. There are also other government departments involved, principally the Department of Finance in its fiscal role and the Office of Public Works in relation to the building and maintenance of school buildings at primary level. Historically and logistically the churches form a significant part of the education system for the main denominations in Ireland exercise managerial and proprietorial control over a major portion of the system. The political parties in their contests to gain and exercise power place policies including those on education before the electorate and when in government usually seek to have the Department of Education implement these policies.

Parents possess the fundamental legal rights in education as stipulated in the Constitution. According to the doctrinal teaching of the major churches they have inalienable rights, yet until quite recently they have not exercised these rights nor have they organised corporately within the system; since 1976 they are involved in the management of primary and in some postprimary schools. There are also small interest groups, who have campaigned on various aspects of education policy such as corporal punishment, interdenominational education and Irish language policy.

Throughout the century research findings and empirical studies have exercised influence on policy by providing evidence or exploring new approaches. There are also individual educationalists who have by their writings, their political actions or their research influenced education policy or thinking and whose contributions may be regarded as significant.

At the turn of the century, the policy making process had been reduced in scale to include only the churches and the state or their related respective agencies. As a result of the various controversies of the last century, additional power within the education system was acquired by the churches and their managerial bodies; the various boards which administered the system were also manned by nominees of the state and the churches.[2] In the early decades of the century other groups, especially some Liberal politicians, teachers and the emergent nationalist political and cultural groups attempted to influence policy. In the twenties, the political parties of the Free State were formally admitted to the policy process where in addition to the normal party policy mechanism they also excerise, in Chubb's terms, the 'appraisal, amendment and approval' roles of the Oireachtas.[3] Throughout most of the period from the twenties to the sixties, there is an interesting contrast between the involvement of the management bodies and the teachers; both are directly involved in conducting the schools, yet in a sense the managerial bodies play a much more central, if not a double role in policy making because of their organic connections with the churches. They engage in direct negotiations with the Department at institutional and organisational levels and through their bishops and church leaders they also contribute to policy making at a higher political level.

It is proposed in this section to examine systematically the contributions of the various groups and agencies already identified by examining their policy documents, official pronouncements and their reactions to specific issues. Chapters 4 and 5 examine the primary and postprimary teachers, while Chapter 6 presents the contributions of the various managerial bodies. The main political parties are discussed in Chapter 7 while the churches form the subject of Chapter 8. The Ministers for Education and the Department of Education are examined in Chapter 9 while the Department of Finance and its role form the subject matter of Chapter 10.

The evaluation of the relative efficacy of the various contributions, the analysis of the policy making process and the identity of the 'proximate' policy-makers will form the subject matter of Section III.

Chapter 4

The Irish National Teachers' Organisation

The Irish National Teachers' Organisation which represents the vast majority of teachers in the national or elementary schools was founded in Dublin in August 1868.[4] Prior to the formal establishment of a national representative organisation, various local and regional associations had been active, some as early as the 1840's. Such groups, known as Redress Committees or Teacher Improvement Societies were mainly concerned with securing improved salaries and employment conditions for teachers; their activities frequently attracted the censure of the Commissioners who disapproved of teachers making public comment on education policy.[5]

The rapid growth of the organisation and its development as an efficient national organ of educational opinion were due mainly to the involvement of some talented, energetic individuals, the availability of a journal and the coincidence of the birth of the organisation with the Powis Commission which was then examining all aspects of the national school system. Vere Foster (1819-1900), who devoted his fortune and his talents to many philanthropic works, became the first president of the organisation, provided leadership and inspiration and was instrumental in launching the organisation's professional monthly, *The Irish Teachers' Journal*. In the preparation for the first congress a major part was played by a Dublin-based association representing teachers in Counties Kildare, Wicklow, Meath and Dublin. Perhaps the most active of those involved in the Dublin group was Jeremiah Henly who in 1863 from his school in Callary, Co. Wicklow, revitalised the moribund Dublin association and became the principal contributor to the teachers' journal on its foundation.[6]

From its early years the organisation was active on behalf of its members and immersed itself in the various controversies arising from the report of the Powis Commission. As early as January 1871 a deputation from the INTO presented a coherent set of policy proposals to Gladstone, which showed that, while they sought primarily to improve the material position of their members, the organisation was equally conscious of the need to legislate for regular school attendance, to provide for the education needs of sparsely populated areas and to assess the long-term consequences of measures such as the 'payment-by-results' scheme which, though administratively attractive and politically plausible, was not acceptable to the teachers.

During its early decades the INTO was seldom far removed from the issues and controversies surrounding the titanic struggle waged by the state and the churches over the control and management of the education system. In many of those issues the teachers were the victims of a system in which a battle was still being waged; in others on the contrary they were sometimes rendered helpless by the politically expedient alliance of churches and state. Nevertheless by the end of the century the national teachers had established their own position in Irish education and had acquired a high degree of skill in negotiating the maze of educational politics. This skill deserted them temporarily however in their conflict with the Catholic bishops on unfair dismissals; the ecclesiastical ban on the Organisation from 1899 to 1905 though not universally applied, split the membership denominationally and caused internal discord. Their experience of the complex and sensitive balance of control which existed between local clerical managers, religious orders, bishops, inspectors and the commissioners had made the national teachers acutely aware of the need to develop a strategy by which their corporate body could play a role in policy making. By the end of the century the Irish National Teachers' Organisation had evolved such a strategy in its organised strength at national and local level. Its efficacy was further enhanced by the regular meetings of its elected bodies and by its annual congress at Easter which by 1900 had become a major occasion in the calendar of education. By the turn of the century the political parties regarded the INTO Easter congress as a public occasion not to be missed and the National Board regarded the president's address at that congress as a policy statement which could not be ignored. However the teachers and their organisation were still outside the power structure, which was dominated by the state and the churches. It would require the sustained efforts of their organisation over much of the next century to achieve an effective place in that structure.

Policy Formulation and Expression

By the early years of the century the affairs of the INTO had acquired a regularity and a ritual which indicated the existence of an efficient and vibrant association. The annual congress, at Easter, which had become the supreme governing body of the organisation, was attended by representatives from each district committee on a national basis and from the central executive in Dublin. At each congress the outgoing president delivered an address which encompassed the education issues which had concerned the Organisation during the year. The resolutions debated at congress reflect the variety of questions which were of importance to branches and to the members; the presidential addresses, on the other hand, present a more coherent picture of the INTO policy as expressed by its elected officers.

On issues of particular importance, the organisation has occasionally published lengthy documents or research reports such as the *Report on Irish* (1941), the *Plan of education* (1947) and the report on the organisation, *Eighty years of progress* (1948). These provide a collection of specific policy documents which together with some individual presidential addresses offer insights into the organisation's policies at critical points in its history.[7] However, it is the annual presidential addresses which provide the most reliable source for the education policies pursued by the organisation in the period under survey. Inevitably, the presidential address includes aspects of the personal educational vision of the paticular president; the dominant elements of the address, however, normally reflect the consensus of opinion established in regular meetings of the Central Executive Committee, significantly coloured by the major issues raised in the resolutions submitted to the annual congress. Thus these addresses delivered to the Easter Congress outline comprehensively the policy of the organisation and its viewpoint on the various problems in Irish education during the past eight decades[8].

Throughout this century there have been issues or controversies which have been of special significance to national teachers, on which they have taken a strong stand and on which their organisation adopted a specific policy. Such issues are of particular significance in observing the development and continuity in INTO policy. Among the more significant of these issues one would count inspection and the Dill Inquiry 1913, the perennial question of salary, promotion prospects and an issue which figures frequently on the agenda, the physical condition of school buildings. The first two of these issues involved the organisation in prolonged negotiation or conflict with the state and the Department of Education; the latter two involved in addition, the managers and the churches. These various controversies, even those which drew strong responses from the organisation, were dwarfed in significance however by the 1946 strike of Dublin teachers, a strike which, lasting for six months, generated very deep feelings and may have exerted a fundamental influence on the oganisation.

The presidential addresses, the reaction of the organisation to some critical issues, and the occasional policy documents collectively constitute a broad body of policy statements and stances which provide a reliable guide to the organisation's contribution to policy in education; it is proposed to examine each of these component elements in turn.

Presidential Addresses.
If one disregards the peripheral issues it is possible to categorise the addresses according to their main themes which fall into a number of

predictable groups. The topics covered in the presidential addresses delivered from 1900-1980 may be grouped under five major headings:

I General Education Policy
II School Organisation
III Employment Conditions
IV Curricular Policy
V Other Sectors of the System

The presidential addresses are content analysed by decade in Table 4.1; from an examination of this data it will be apparent that in the period 1900-80 the INTO was concerned with many issues which ranged beyond those questions of salary and conditions which are the primary function of a trade union. Undoubtedly questions relating to salary, pensions, promotion prospects and other factors affecting working conditions were prominent as themes in presidential addresses at annual congress. These however have never, except in crisis periods, dominated policy to the exclusion of issues relating to general policy and particularly to those factors determining the administrative and educational efficiency of the system especially in the national schools. This inherent balance within the organisation's policies between the immediate material and professional interests of members and the wider interests of the education system, is clearly evident in the frequency with which issues relating to fundamental educational considerations figure in the presidential addresses. These include issues such as school conditions, school attendance, educational opportunity and slow learners, all of which have a direct bearing on the quality of the education available to the individual child. This balance however, does not imply that the INTO had been equally radical in its policies throughout the period under review. There are patterns evident in the data presented in Table 4.1. which would suggest that the INTO reflected at various periods in its education policy both the political stance of its leaders and the general current socio-political climate. It would appear that in the substance and formulation of its policies during the first half of our period (1900-40) the organisation was more radical in its orientation than in most of the later four decades. Questions such as the civil rights of teachers, equality of opportunity, the structure, funding and central administration of the system figure largely in INTO policy statements in the first three decades of the century while such issues recede in the later years. Undoubtedly the political radicalism of the INTO in the period 1900-40 was related directly to its close links with the Irish Labour Party, mainly in the person of its general secretary, T. J. O'Connell, and also to the fact that, prior to 1920, its membership contained a significant number of teachers from the North whose socio-political horizons were less circumscribed than those of their southern colleagues. The leaders of the organisation in later decades were more overtly identifiable with the larger political parties; while many teachers were elected to the Dáil on behalf of Fianna Fáil and Fine Gael, only one teacher was elected on behalf of the Labour Party after 1932.

Controversial Issues.
Some policy issues have arisen which, because of the strong stand adopted, have assumed a dramatic significance for the organisation. Among such questions, one must include the Dill Inquiry of 1913 into inspection and the prolonged struggle for adequate salary. In addition there were the controversies in relation to the transfer of lay schools to religious orders and the refusal of teachers to teach in schools which were inadequately maintained; these two issues culminated respectively in the 'Ballina case' of 1956 and the 'Kerry campaign' of 1968.

Inspection.
From the early decades of the century to recent years, inspection has regularly been an issue. At the 1914 congress, the INTO unanimously called by resolution for the resignation of Dr Starkie and for the replacement of the National Board by a body composed of elected representatives of the various interests involved in primary education. Such a radical policy was prompted by the level of frustration and alienation generated by the authoritarianism of the National Board and its officials in the period from 1900. The climax of the teachers' agitation was associated with the Mansfield dismissal of October 1912 and the Vice-Regal Committee of Inquiry into Inspection (the Dill Inquiry) of 1913; however these were merely the tip of the iceberg as many more aspects of the education system were involved. According to the teachers, the administration of education under the board during the period was characterised by 'injustice, mismanagement and abuse of authority'.[9] Reviewing the period from the beginning of the century, Miss Catherine Mahon, in her presidential address of 1913 claimed that 'the state of unrest, indignation and panic which had culminated in the Mansfield dismissal had been rife, with short occasional lulls, for the previous thirteen years; during which the organisation, had been spending most of its energies practising the arts of war'.[10] According to Miss Mahon, relations between the teachers and the inspectors had worsened and Starkie had assumed an autocratic and dominant role in which he became 'the sole arbiter of the destinies of twelve thousand teachers'; furthermore, lack of consultation with teachers and managers had dampened enthusiasm for the curricular reforms introduced in 1900, a policy of amalgamation of small schools threatened the income of teachers and in many aspects teachers were denied civil rights available to their British colleagues.

However, it was the new system of teacher classification introduced in 1900 and the amended rules for promotion which created the principal issues on which the friction between inspectors and teachers developed. With the new programme of 1900, annual examinations by inspectors were abolished and an impressionist general verdict by an inspector during an unnotified visit became the sole determining factor on which the teacher's salary depended. Teachers objected to the lack of objectivity involved and the absence of a measurable recordable standard. Furthermore the classification and promotion scheme was treated as an official secret so that teachers were not aware of the criteria on which they were officially classified; as late as 1910 Starkie refused to say officially in public what the precise rules were regulating promotion and increments. Appeals by teachers in Tipperary and Clare against lowering of their annual marks drew no response, except an inspectorial visit by Starkie in the course of which he further aggravated an already inflamed situation. The president of the INTO, Edward Mansfield, in his address of 1911 gave vent to the widespread anger among teachers when he requested that offending inspectors be transferred and specifically that the inspector be changed, whose advent to a district meant 'the worry of the teachers and the ruin of education'.[11] Following the dismissal of their president from his school in Co. Tipperary, the organisation rallied to his support and sought political support for their demand for a public inquiry into the operation of the National Board. In November 1912 a limited inquiry was instituted which was chaired by Sir Samuel Dill of Queen's University Belfast and submitted its report early in 1914.[12] The INTO initially refused to submit evidence to the inquiry but later relented and appeared before the committee with telling effect. The Dill Report provided unassailable evidence that the national teachers had a just grievance and that Starkie had ruled the primary system with an iron hand. Nevertheless the report according to the INTO was weak in two respects: its findings were constrained by a narrow interpretation of its terms of reference and the language in which it was written was mild and inoffensive. It had little effect on subsequent administrative policy; it did little to diminish the spirit of suspicion and hostility which existed between the teachers and the National Board, a spirit which continued even after the demise of Starkie in 1920 and the change of administration in 1922. There are indications however that the Dill Inquiry did lead to some changes of attitude on the part of the National Board's education office; only two teachers out of five thousand were promoted in the thirteen years prior to the inquiry, while in the twelve months following the publication of its report, sixty teachers were promoted under the same rule.[13] The residual tension between teachers and inspectors was re-awakened in the twenties in the context of the system of merit marks used by inspectors. The INTO congress of 1926 demanded an inquiry into inspection and the report of the representative committee of 1927 chaired by

Fr L. McKenna, S.J., resulted in the establishment of an appeals board on which the teachers were represented.[14]

The Mansfield crisis and the Dill Inquiry led the INTO to seek structural reforms which were more radical than the general body of their policies. At its annual congress in 1913, the organisation called for an education system wherein teachers would enjoy 'reasonable peace, security and encouragement'; they further demanded an end to the system characterised by 'distrust of teachers, disregard for their vested rights, incredulity to their appeals and hostility to their organisation'.[15] To effect this required reform the teachers demanded that 'a popular and elective board' should replace the National Board consisting of commissioners whose guaranteed life tenure and secret procedures were responsible for the indifference, the reaction and despotism which characterised its administration. The new board advocated by the INTO would work via sub-committees, would conduct its meetings in public and have its proceedings fully reported in the public press; furthermore its members would serve for a limited period and its decisions could be appealed to Westminster. The constitution of the Board would reflect equal representation, of five members each, for 'the parts of the nation directly interested and experienced in primary education i.e. the people, managers and the teachers'.[16] These elements would be represented by the General Council of County Councils, the managerial bodies of the churches, and by the INTO; the government would nominate five further members to bring the total to twenty. According to the teachers in 1913 such a reformed Board administering the national schools would realise popular control in the truest sense.

Salary

Throughout the eight decades covered in this study there was seldom a period during which questions relating to salary, pensions and related service issues have not been prominent items of INTO policy. There were two main aims in this policy: to secure improved salary structures and absolute salary levels and to achieve parity of salary with secondary and vocational teachers. In addition, the related questions of pensions and promotion prospects frequently engaged the attention of the organisation. The sensitivity of teachers' salaries and employment conditions to socio-economic conditions and the constant temptation for governments in times of economic crisis to reduce annual expenditure on education of which teachers' salaries usually form over 80%, are both clearly evident in the struggle of the national teachers on the question of salaries. Salary cuts were imposed by the government on three occasions, 1923, 1933 and 1934 and the teachers organised strike action in support of their salary claims in 1918, 1933 and 1946. During the first two decades of the century, the INTO had campaigned repeatedly for improved salary scales and for a reform of the mechanism by which salary was determined and paid; they also sought an end to the practice by which salary was transmitted quarterly to the teacher's manager and above all they requested that their conditions of remuneration be decided on criteria similar to those employed in the public service. In 1906 and 1907 they organised national campaigns to secure public support for their policy of having the level of education expenditure in Ireland raised to that attained in England and Scotland, thanks to the 1902 education act. The financial stranglehold exercised by the Treasury was condemned in the Belfast speech of Dr Starkie in 1911, in which he claimed that the Treasury accepted the new programmes of 1900 '. . . with the proviso that they should cost nothing in addition to the existing grants'. Referring to the role of the English inspector, Dale, Starkie further asserted: 'Dale was sent not to help the reformers of Irish education but to effect reductions or obviate increases in an already insufficient grant.'[17] However the Liberal government of Campbell-Bannerman brought a distinct change in policy and when the Chief Secretary, Augustine Birrell, spoke to the 1907 congress, he secured the immediate support of the teachers by declaring them to be 'the victims of a bad system' and affirmed that their salary scales were meagre and insufficient. Birrell matched his words with political action when he secured a special grant in 1908 to provide a salary increase for national teachers. This increase, though small, was the only salary improvement granted between 1900 and the war bonus of 1916. 'Those lean and frustrating years for teachers', according to T. J. O'Connell, generated a new determination in the organisation to campaign effectively for their salary demands; by 1920 they had achieved major results.

These gains were not achieved however without militant action by the teachers; a special delegate congress was convened in September 1917 to discuss the Duke award (a supplementary estimate), which was deemed inadequate even on the basis of the Goschen ratio.[18] An alternative agreed policy emerged from this congress which sought a common basic salary of £80 to £180 per annum. The rejection of their claim and their exclusion by the government from the scope of the Burnham Committee inevitably led the INTO to strike action. Their strike of 1918 achieved a major victory.

Between 1918 and 1920 the teachers secured three bonus awards from the Civil Service Arbitration Board and in November 1920 secured what they had sought for so long, a permanent salary structure.[19] This major advance embodied not only substantial improvements on the Killanin proposals but significant gains in administrative details as well. In effect it won for Irish national teachers conditions of service approximately equivalent to those secured for their British counterparts under the Burnham Committee. This 1920 agreement, which figured so largely in later controversy, included the following:

(i)   a common scale, with annual increments, reaching a maximum of £370 for men and £300 for women;

(ii)   a 'supernormal' scale for those rated 'highly efficient' with maxima of £460 and £360 respectively;

(iii)   lay teachers in convent and monastery schools were for the first time to receive salaries equivalent to teachers of similar standing in lay national schools;

(iv)   in schools of over 160 enrolment, a post of vice-principal was to be created.

In addition to these substantive national gains, the teachers derived significant psychological advantage from the new arrangements whereby salaries were no longer paid to the manager quarterly but dispatched to each teacher directly monthly.[20]

However these gains were short-lived; the new salary scales fell victim to the 10% cut on public service pay introduced in 1923.[21] The lack of prior consultation with the teachers and the rejection by the minister of their objections created growing dissatisfaction among them. Teachers were further aggrieved by the Economies Act of 1933 which reduced their salaries despite deValera's pre-election promise to the contrary.[22] They claimed that they were being asked to shoulder an undue share of the reductions; while their salaries represented 23½% of state expenditure on salaries, they were being required to contribute 60% of the total economy sought under the bill.[23] Despite a protest march by Dublin teachers in April and a one-day strike on 26 April the response from political or public opinion was minimal. The 1934 cut of 9% was imposed by the government to fund the pension scheme.[24]

INTO policy on salary in the years to 1940 centred on seeking restoration of the 1920 salary scales and the abolition of the various economy cuts. From 1940 onwards this policy changed to one of seeking a cost-of-living salary increase; this however was not acceded to by the government, following its wage freeze of 1941. Teachers again registered a sense of discrimination in view of the disparity between their treatment and that of other public employees; while the normal maximum for male teachers in 1942 was £318, the corresponding salary for civil servants with equivalent entry requirements i.e. junior executive officers, was £514. Of the 10,000 national teachers only 7% had salaries in excess of £400 p.a., while over 50% received less than £200.[25] A growing sense of frustration and militancy is evident in the INTO from about 1942, accompanied by a growing alienation from the Fianna Fáil government.

This growing militancy produced a coherent salary claim by the INTO which was presented to the government in 1944. The claim embodied a maximum of £600 p.a. for all trained teachers and a pension scheme on Civil Service lines.[26] The rising tide of anger among teachers caused by repeated government rejection of their demands was indicated by the demonstration organised by teachers in the public gallery of the Dáil during the 1945 estimate debate. After the Easter congress of 1945 had authorised industrial action by the teachers, preparations were begun for a strike by Dublin teachers; a monster meeting of Dublin teachers held in the Mansion House in October declared their willingness to take action. In November the Minister for Education, Tomás Deirg, produced a new salary structure which was unacceptable to the teachers and was doubly so because the minister could give no assurance as to when his scheme would commence. Following repeated negotiations, the strike by Dublin teachers was begun on 20 March 1946, sanctioned by an INTO referendum which rejected the Minister's final offer.

The strike in lay national schools which lasted from March to October, was funded by the contributions of teachers outside Dublin; convent and monastery schools remained open though without lay staff. The strike affected about 45% of the school children of Dublin some of whose parents became vocal in support of the teachers' cause by means of Parents' Associations which called on the government to seek a settlement.[27] The teachers attracted widespread support from the press and from some elements of the trade union movement and from the Catholic Archbishop of Dublin, Dr John Charles McQuaid, who offered his services as mediator and urged both sides towards a settlement. Politicians of all parties supported the teachers and opposition spokesmen, Richard Mulcahy and Patrick McGilligan, pleaded with the government to realise the justice inherent in the INTO stance and to accept offers of mediation or conciliation.

The government position was one of firm resistance; its spokesmen, including Seán Lemass and Deirg, laid repeated charges against the teachers of seeking to challenge the authority of the government and refused all offers of mediation or negotiation while the strike continued. Support from parents was further expressed in a mass demonstration of Dublin Parents Associations in September; at Croke Park in October, the 70,000 people at the All-Ireland final embarrassed the Government ministers present when they loudly applauded a demonstration by teachers.

An offer by Dublin Corporation to arbitrate was rejected and a Dáil motion of 23 October by Richard Mulcahy, proposing an independent conciliation tribunal, was rejected by the votes of the 72 Fianna Fáil deputies. On 28 October, Dr McQuaid wrote to the INTO inviting the teachers to return to work and the executive of the organisation decided to direct the teachers to return to work without prejudice to their natural rights or their just and equitable claims. While the decision of the executive was accepted there was however a large body of teachers in Dublin who disagreed with the decision.

Nevertheless the schools closed by the strike reopened 31 October.

The 1946 strike, which concluded on a note of abject defeat for the teachers, had a profound effect on the organisation; it may also have exercised some influence on Irish political life and would seem also to have given a higher political and public profile to policy issues in education. The internal cohesion generated by the strike and the depth of public support which it attracted gave a new strength to the INTO. The leaders of the Dublin teachers gained rapid recognition in the organisation; two of then, Seán Brosnahan and Matt Griffin, were elected to office shortly afterwards and were appointed as General Secretary and Treasurer in which offices they played significant roles for three decades. The spirit of the 1946 strike seems to have remained alive within the organisation and has been invoked since on many occasions.[28] The shift in political allegiance by many teachers following the strike, while not a crucial factor in the electoral defeat of Fianna Fáil in 1948, was however a contributory factor in so far as many of the dissatisfied teachers joined a new radical party and contributed to the considerable though short-lived impact which Clann na Poblachta had on Irish politics.

It would appear that Fianna Fáil in retrospect realised that the 1946 policy had been a mistake, a lesson that seems to have been remembered when they were in government in the 1960s. During crucial salary negotiations in 1963, when INTO claims were being resisted, one of the delegation addressed Lemass directly and said 'We tore the Fianna Fáil government out of power before and we will do so again'.[29] Within a few days the INTO claim was acceded to. It would appear that the 1946 strike had sharpened the politicians' perception of teacher power and had thereby sensitised them to education as an issue of growing political importance.

Following the introduction of abitration and conciliation procedures in 1951 which stabilised teachers' salaries viv-a-vis cost of living increases, INTO policy in the years from 1951 to 1968 was largely concerned with restoring or establishing relativities with other public servants and with securing parity with the other teacher groups, which the organisation saw as a major step to achieving a unified profession. In pursuit of such policies the INTO submitted a 'status' claim in 1962 which, under arbitration, yielded a salary structure preserving the 1955 relativity as between secondary and national teachers, in favour of the former.[30] Reaction among national teachers was such that preparations were completed for a strike in September 1963 and the organisation threatened to withdraw from the Conciliation and Arbitration scheme. However such drastic action did not take place for the government yielded and a fresh claim produced acceptable findings and a government fiscal policy which became progressively more favourable to teachers.

Parity of salary with other teachers had been a major policy of the INTO from the late forties and resolutions and presidential speeches reiterated its importance at various congresses. National teachers resented deeply the differential status and the public esteem which was implied in the salary differentials which existed between themselves, vocational and secondary teachers. Two unsuccessful 'parity' claims were submitted in the fifties and when a joint Teachers' Salary Committee of 1958 recommended that salary differentials be retained, the INTO intensified its campaign against the system. Various increases granted to secondary teachers in the sixties depressed the relative position of national teachers further; in 1964 the maximum salary of a male national teacher stood at 84% of that of his secondary counterpart.[31] The Ryan Tribunal established in 1967 was requested to determine a common basic salary scale for all teachers and to recommend suitable additional remuneration for service, qualifications and function. The findings of this tribunal embodying the principles of common scale and common Conciliation and Arbitration machinery for all teachers were acepted by the INTO and by the Vocational Teachers' Association; the opposition of the secondary teachers and of the ASTI continued until 1973 when they joined their colleagues.[32] Since then the common scale has operated satisfactorily and has been accompanied by growing cooperation and joint action by the teachers' unions.

The two major issues already discussed, i.e. inspection and salaries, concerned questions which involved only the teachers and the government directly. Other issues arose however which widened considerably the network of participants, since they concerned the clerical managers and church authorities and thereby touched upon the sensitive issues of the control and the management of schools. Two principal issues in this category conern us here, promotion and the physical conditions of schools.

Promotion
In the course of the century the INTO policies on questions of promotion for lay national teachers show a gradual but pronounced shift. In the early decades, as indeed almost from its foundation the organisation was actively involved in securing basic contractual rights for its members, in resisting summary dismissals and in establishing due process governing termination of employment. In the period following the 1946 strike the emphasis shifted to widening the range and quality of promotional outlets available to lay teachers; in the latter part of the seventies the national teachers were deeply involved in securing acceptable participation with clergy and parents in the amended managerial structure of national schools.

Reference has already been made in Chapter 2, to some cases of dismissal towards the end of the last century which the INTO had contested, as a result of which fixity of tenure was a major item of policy for many decades. The 'Maynooth Resolution' of 1894 was intended by the Catholic bishops to provide a measure of protection;

under it teachers could not be served with notice of dismissal by a manager unless he had previously sought and secured the assent of his bishop. An amendment of 1898 extended the teachers' right of appeal and episcopal sanction to cases of summary dismissal.[33]

In the early decades of the century the relations between the INTO and the Catholic managerial bodies were characterised by hostility and mutual mistrust which arose mainly over the issue of fixity of tenure. The teachers questioned the inherent justice of having the bishop as final court of appeal in cases of dismissal; they had experience as well of cases where the bishops, who had unilaterally drawn up the 'Maynooth Resolution', had refused to abide by its terms, and of one bishop who preached from his pulpit in support of his dismissal of a teacher whose personal character and professional competence, he admitted were beyond reproach.[34]

The O'Shea case at Fanore, Co Clare (1914) convinced the teachers of the weakness of the 'Maynooth Resolution' as a guarantor of their contractual rights in the face of authoritarian priests or prelates.[35] In this case, the Bishop of Galway, Dr O'Dea, claimed that he had never heard of the resolution and that it had 'no force in law'. The parents strongly supported the teacher and founded an opposition school; their children were refused confirmation by Dr O'Dea and the parents were threatened with deprivation of the sacraments should they continue to disobey their priest and bishop in the exercise of their parental rights. The outcome was that O'Shea lost his position and was later employed as a teacher by the Gaelic League. The Fanore case and other incidents gravely disturbed the teachers and they sought to have an agreed uniform procedure adopted governing dismissal and the operation of the 'Maynooth Resolution'. A further modification of the Resolution was proposed by the bishops in 1916 whereby neither service of notice nor dismissal could be carried out before notifying the bishop so that the teacher could be heard in his own defence. In this format the resolution was incorporated as a church law in the Maynooth statutes in 1927.[36]

This formal church legislation would seem to have introduced an era of calm and some mutual trust between Catholic managers and the INTO; according to the general secretary of the teachers' organisation, most of the dismissal cases which came to his notice were settled satisfactorily within the terms of the 1927 Statute.[37] The one significant exception was the dismissal of Mrs Keenan of Killeen near Newry in 1938, a case which involved Cardinal McRory as Archbishop of Armagh, failed to find a resolution within or without the agreed procedures after a decade of negotiation and created serious doubt among teachers as to the contractual protection afforded teachers and as to the possibility of appeal, either secular or ecclesiastical, from the decision of the bishop. The INTO congress of 1939, held in Belfast, declared by resolution that the Keenan dismissal was 'a harsh, unwarranted and arbitrary exercise of managerial authority'; the

INTO regarded this particular case as constituting 'one of the most unhappy chapters in their relations with the clerical authorities'.[38]

There were other cases of dismissal however which did not attract the support of the INTO. Where, as in a few instances, radical socialist or republican opinions held by teachers led to official censure and dismissal the INTO were not inclined to support the teachers.[39]

After the 1946 strike there were few cases of dismissal, and INTO policy was increasingly more concerned with the positive issue of securing and extending avenues of promotion for its members. The lay teachers had two main grievances against the existing system;

(i)   that, due to the size distribution of schools and the capitation principle on which promotional posts were created, lay teachers enjoyed lower promotional prospects than members of religious orders in whose management most of the larger schools were;

(ii)   that schools formerly staffed by lay teachers had been handed over to religious orders, whose members held the principalship as a reserved post.

It will be seen from Table 4.2 that between 1929 and 1981 while the total number of national schools decreased by almost 40%, the percentage of convent and monastery schools doubled to 16.6%. This arose mainly from the establishment and expansion of schools in newly-built urban areas, especially in Dublin, whose management in most cases was allocated to religious orders. The vast majority of convent and monastery schools managed by religious orders were usually funded totally on a capitation basis; a small minority of them and all other schools were funded by means of personal salaries paid to individual qualified teachers. Convent and monastery schools tended to have larger enrolments; while they constituted 8.4% of all national schools in 1929 they catered for 26% of all pupils and in 1968 the corresponding figures were 14% and 42% as shown in Table 4.2. By the seventies it seems that more large urban schools were being staffed by lay teachers.

There were a number of reasons which led to the majority of larger schools being managed by religious; the location of convents and monasteries in larger towns and cities, the preference of the religious orders for the capitation system of funding which produces its optimum return in larger schools staffed by religious and the desire for pastoral and logistical reasons to reach as large a school apostolate as possible with the given manpower. Furthermore diocesan authorities welcomed religious orders for financial reasons as their capital contribution relieved the new urban parishes of a heavy burden; the Department of Education concurred as it extracted a higher local contribution from the orders than from the diocesan authorities.[40]

As a result of this situation the promotional prospects of lay teachers were diminished; they could either remain as assistant teachers in the larger schools where only religious occupied principalships and vice-principalships or they could seek principalships in much smaller schools. In this century, the percentage of national schools with less than 50 enrolment has never fallen below 25% of the total; the percentage with less than 100 enrolment has never been less than 50% while the percentage of schools with more than 300 has reached 16% in 1980.[41] Given that the allowances payable to principals and vice-principals are directly related to school enrolment and the number of such posts is a function of school size, it seems obvious that the religious enjoyed an advantage over lay teachers in terms of promotional prospects. These restricted promotional possibilities strengthened the resolve of the INTO to protect their existing situation and especially to resist any efforts by bishops to transfer schools which were staffed by lay teachers to the management of religious.

In the period from 1922 to the mid-forties, the INTO was actively concerned with the number of large schools passing into the control of religious and especially with cases where existing lay schools had been transferred to teaching orders.[42] In a reply in 1943 to a letter from the organisation on this question, the bishops stated that they did not favour, as a rule, such transfers, and that very few such transfers had taken place in recent years except where strong parental demand prompted such changes. In spite of such claims however, the general secretary of the INTO has asserted that in the period 1923-48 over a dozen large schools in the provinces had been transferred to religious communities and he also claimed that any parental activity in these questions had been usually stimulated by the managers.[43]

The issue which marked a turning point in this question was the 'Ballina' case which began in 1956 and was terminated formally in 1962. It concerned one of the two seven-teacher schools outside the cities, the boy's national school in Ballina, whose lay principal was about to retire. The bishop introduced a religious order of brothers, the Marists, one of whom was appointed principal without any prior consultation with the teachers. The INTO, convinced that this was a significant test case, sought first to negotiate with the manager and the bishop and with individual members of the hierarchy who dissuaded them from calling a strike, finally appealed to the Vatican and called the Ballina teachers out on strike in 1962. The response from Rome, transmitted in 1959, declined to offer judgement, adding that it was 'always sympathetic to the point of view of the bishops' and urging that these matters be settled at home.[44] Through the mediation of Archbishop McQuaid of Dublin a settlement formula was drawn up which was acceptable to the INTO but this was rejected out of hand by the bishop of Killala; under it the school would be divided into two units, junior and senior, one staffed by the lay teachers and the other by the religious. This particular controversy was finally resolved by the acceptance of proposals put forward by the Minister, Dr P. J. Hillery in February 1962, which stipulated that as long as the school was conducted by the Marist order, an annual allowance, equivalent to that of a principal, would be paid to a lay teacher selected by the manager. Since all salaries and allowances to national teachers are paid by the department, it is significant in relation to the justice of the teachers' case that this annual allowance is paid by the manager of the school and not by the department. The willingness of the INTO to accept such a solution was strongly conditioned by the assurances, explicit and implied, given by the hierarchy and by the minister, that there would be no further cases of take-over of lay schools by religious orders.[45] The data in Table 4.3 would suggest that the practice has ceased in recent years.

The stand taken by the INTO on the Ballina case and the manner of its resolution had immediate and significant effects on policy in two respects (i) additional posts of responsibility and wider promotional prospects were created in national schools for lay teachers, and (ii) convent and monastery national schools switched from a capitation basis of funding to one based on personal salaries. Even while the Ballina controversy was still in progress, the INTO sought to have more new large schools staffed by lay teachers exclusively, a demand that was conceded and implemented in the late sixties and through-out the seventies. In 1962 special posts of lay assistant were created in convent and monastery capitation schools which were of monetary advantage only and carried no duties or responsibilities.

Throughout the sixties INTO congresses emphasised the need to provide greater promotional avenues for lay teachers and this policy was formalised in a memorandum sent to the Department of Education. The Ryan Tribunal, reporting in 1968, advocated the estab-lishemnt of new posts of responsibility in all schools and that their distribution be based on the staffing ratio as between lay and religi-ous teachers; it also proposed that all schools have posts of principal and vice-principal.[46] In 1970 the Minister introduced a scheme under which every school over one hundred enrolment was to have a vice-principal and new posts of responsibility were created and distri-buted according to the proposals of the Ryan Report. Finally when the value of principals' and vice-principals' allowances were revised significantly in 1973, it would appear that the long policy campaign of the INTO on promotion had been successful.

The data in Table 4.4 indicate that a significant shift in the pattern of funding of convent and monastery schools occurred during the same period in which the INTO was campaigning on the question of promotion. This change occurred initially only in the convent schools and to such an extent that it suggests a fundamental policy change. At the turn of the century, the principle of capitation was introduced as a partial funding mechanism in national schools; when in 1920 a scheme was introduced which gave a common salary structure to all trained national teachers, most of the convent and monastery schools opted to base their funding on the capitation principle. Such has been their practice up to the late fifties or early sixties as the data in Table 4.4 show. Between 1960 and 1976 the convent national schools switched to personal salaries; the monastery schools followed and by 1980 only one convent national school remained on the capitation scheme. As the availability of professional training for all nuns entitled more of them to personal salary, it made more economic sense in a situation where religious orders could not staff schools because of depleted manpower to switch to personal salaries. Furthermore the personal salary scheme entailed a pension which is not available under the capitation scheme.

The Physical Condition of Schools

Questions concerning the physical conditions and maintenance of national schools have constituted a major element in INTO policy throughout the period under review; the topic has figured prominently and continuously in presidential addresses at annual congresses during every decade of this century.[47] The various solutions and measures put forward by the organisation to guarantee the proper upkeep of school buildings inevitably provoked a strong reaction from the bishops and school managers who feared that any modification of the existing procedures and responsibilities contained a significant threat to the clerical management of national schools. This complex problem arose from the dual capital funding mechanism in the provision of schools and from the large number of small schools in rural areas with decreasing populations, populations which sometimes found it difficult to provide the local contributions to building and maintenance costs which church and state authorities regarded as the cornerstone of the managerial system.

The system under which the national schools were built required a capital contribution of one third and the provision of the site from the local agency providing the school, usually the local parish whose parish priest or rector was *ex officio* manager. In schools organised and managed by teaching orders these capital contributions were made from the general funds of the order. Where the locality could not provide the one-third contribution, this was frequently reduced or sometimes waived, without any consequent diminution of the rights of the manager; this occurred both under the Board of National Education and after 1924, under the Department of Eduction. In the various new suburban housing schemes erected in Dublin from 1937 to 1957 schools were provided on the basis of a 'reasonable' local contribution, which was usually about 10%.[48] In the case of the 386 schools erected between 1957 and 1962, the average local contribution was 13.7%.[49]

The maintenance of a school, is the responsibility of the manager for which no state aid was available until 1962. A state grant for the cleaning and heating of schools was provided in 1911 on a basis of the grant equalling the local vouched expenditure. The state grant was related to school enrolment which imposed a severe disadvantage on small rural schools.

From the beginning of the century, the INTO drew attention to the neglected state of many school buildings. In the presidential addresses to congress in 1904, 1906, 1907 and 1908, there is a sustained emphasis on the need for an urgent programme to replace unsuitable and unhealthy schools and to institute regular cleaning, heating and sanitary procedures. Judging by the descriptions provided by the INTO presidential addresses, the speaker was not guilty of undue exaggeration who claimed in 1908 that 'the ducks in St. Stephen's Green are better housed, better cared for and better looked after than the majority of children attending our national schools'.[50] A confidential report prepared by the inspectors for the Commissioners of National Education in 1907, offers precise information; according to this report 12% of the 8,684 national schools needed to be replaced by new schools and 38% required improvements and extensions.[51] According to the INTO, Starkie's attempts in the early years of the century and Birrell's accelerated school building programme made little impact on the problem.[52] The decline in education expenditure during World War I and the political unrest in the period 1916-24 carried the crisis forward to the Free State government and its newly created Department of Education. In 1928 John Marcus O'Sullivan, quoting a departmental survey, stated that of the 5,500 schools in the Free State, 350 required to be replaced and 550 needed extensions.[53] In the years 1932-47 despite the material shortages caused by the second World War, over 570 new schools were built, some of which were designed to cater for urban expansion.[54] In 1940 Éamon de Valera, as Minister for Education, reported that 300 schools were in need of replacement and 600 needed attention.[55] At the same time, it was reported to the Public Accounts Committee of the Dáil, that the total money allocated for the heating and cleaning of national schools had not been spent because approximately 10% of the school managers in western areas had not applied for the grant.[56] In the two decades following the war, a vigorous building campaign was initiated and an average of 73 new schools were erected annually with the local contribution falling to an average of 15%.[57] In the early sixties, official policy was to erect 100 new schools and to complete major improvements on 50 schools each year.[58] On this basis it was estimated that by 1980 a significant shift in the age structure of the buildings would have occurred with the virtual elimination of all nineteenth century buildings. Following the report of an inter-departmental committee on school buildings, a state grant was introduced in 1962 towards the cost of school maintenance.

At its congress in 1926, the INTO passed a resolution calling on the government to establish in each county borough 'an education authority whose main function shall be to make provision for adequate and suitable school accommodation and the heating, cleaning and general upkeep and maintenance of school buildings'.[59] This demand was the cornerstone of policy on school buildings for thirty years; it derived mainly from the Report of the Killanin Commission of 1918 and it owes something also to the Irish Labour Party's *Policy on Education* of 1925. This demand sought merely to change the procedure whereby schools were built and maintained; it did not seek to alter directly or indirectly the rights or privileges of the clerical managers. The policy was restated by spokesmen and in various congress resolutions during the succeeding decades. In 1927 an ingenious proposal was made by T. J. O'Connell, that the special local authority rate (6p in the £) which had been levied to fund reconstruction after the War of Independence (under the Damage to Property Act 1923) should, after 1928 be applied to the problem of school maintenance.[60] The proposal was welcomed by some clerical authorities but when it was rejected by the Catholic Clerical Managers' Association, it was not presented to the government or to the opposition parties.[61]

At the 1932 congress in Athlone, the president called for 'a new system of building schools as the financial burden is altogether too great for a voluntary agency'. He was answered promptly by Monsignor Waters, chairman of the CCMA, who claimed that 'the church could not allow the managers to be ousted, because if they were, the security would be gone as to religious teaching in the schools'.[62] The policy of the INTO was effectively supported by the reports of local authority Medical Officers of Health, many of whom reserved their harshest comments for the insanitary and unhealthy conditions of national schools.[63] In their 1947 document *A Plan for Education*, the INTO devoted significant attention to school buildings and the health of the pupils. They suggested that the state should bear the entire cost of building and equipping schools and that the local authority should be responsible for maintenance and decoration; the plan also contained proposals for a proper medical and dental school service and for the provision of school meals.[64] While the response of politicians to such proposals was generally cautious, circumspect and ambivalent, that of clerical leaders was generally dismissive.[5] There was one government politician however, Patrick Smith, Parliamentary Secretary to the Minister for Finance, who, when the issue was under discussion in government in 1945, urged that the unsatisfactory situation be no longer tolerated. When it was suggested that the blame lay with the Department of Education and/or the Office of Public Works, Smith wrote to the Taoiseach enclosing a detailed memorandum containing a digest of twenty specific cases from the files of the Board of Works. His conclusion was that the principal cause was the neglect by the managers and he urged that unless a new method were found the problem would continue for many years.[66]

In June 1952 an INTO letter to Cardinal D'Alton on the issue received a reply that not only rejected the INTO proposals on funding school buildings but requested that the organisation desist from advocating such policies 'now that they had been made fully aware of their (the bishops) views of the managerial system'; the reply continued: 'the bishops would hope that the organisation's energies would be directed in future mainly towards securing a better allocation of state funds'. The INTO executive acceded to the request contained in the cardinal's letter and abondoned its previous policy.[67]

The problem arose again in dramatic form fifteen years later when the general secretary of the INTO, Senator Seán Brosnahan, issued an ultimatum to the clerical managers, the Department of Education and the Board of Works stating that after 1 November 1967, on receipt of a serious complaint on sub-standard conditions in any national school, the executive would after investigation, withdraw the staff. This strategy prompted immediate action at department and diocesan levels and a scheme was initiated to hasten overdue repairs. A withdrawal of teachers, as threatened, was implemented in five schools in the Ardfert area of Co Kerry in January 1968.[68] The immediate renovation of the schools and the appointment of an acting manager were the direct outcome of the strike which lasted a month. The Ardfert strike had much more than a parochial effect; it signalled the intention of the INTO to deal effectively with a long-standing problem and grievance and it had a marked demonstration effect on tardy managers throughout the system.

In each of the issues discussed the INTO pursued its policy objectives with determination and energy; in each case it achieved ultimate success though in most cases the struggle lasted for many decades and in the case of salary and the physical condition of schools required strike action. Such successful prosecution of its objectives can be attributed to the national strength, cohesion and professionalism of the organisation and to its impressive political sense especially after the major strike of 1946.

Occasional Documents

While the controversial issues in the main concerned questions bearing on the working conditions of teachers, they did refer indirectly to some elements of general education policy as in the question of the physical conditions of schools. However it is in the occasional documents that we find the education philosophy and broad policy of the organisation stated in detail. There are three such documents from the forties, *Report of committee of inquiry into the use of Irish as a teaching medium (1941)*, *A plan for education (1947)* and *Eighty years of progress (1948)*. The report on Irish will be discussed in a later chapter on language policy (Chapter 12) and the 1948 document is concerned solely with the history of the organisation. *A plan for education* however, represents the organisation's articulation of its general policy at a critical time in the postwar period. It may not be totally coincidental that during the time when the plan was being written a high level team in the Department of Education was examining the education system in response to the government's request to conduct a systematic analysis as part of its postwar planning exercise. The result of the department's analysis was never published but was presented to the Minister as an internal department memorandum.[69]

In its range and cohesion, the Plan indicated that the organisation, although immersed in a long struggle on salaries and promotion, had been aware of the contemporary movements in postwar European education and that it had its finger on the pulse of Irish education at all levels. The report dealt in detail with each level in turn, advocated a planned integrated system and identified the defects in the existing system; it advocated equality of opportunity and specified measures towards achieving such equality. It criticised the absence of provision for the individual student and the tyranny of the examinations, identified the obsession with academic subjects and the neglect of practical elements in the curriculum and in many ways it presaged some of the fundamental reforms introduced in the sixties and seventies. In some aspects it echoes the early reform measures contained in the Killanin Commission and in the 1925 document of the Labour Party; in its forward vision however and in the comprehensive political perspective which inspired its chapters, it belongs rightfully to the era of *Investment in Education*.

Throughout most of its existence the Irish National Teachers' Organisation has of necessity been deeply involved as a trade union in securing and protecting its members' rights and in improving their working conditions as professional educators. This however has not prevented it as an organisation from making a significant contribution to public debate and to the formulation of education policy. As the oldest teacher union it has been a major force in Irish education during all of this century; its close ties with the Irish Labour Party in the early decades enhanced its political impact and sharpened its ideological commitment. Its strike in 1946, while not successful, generated a new spirit in the organisation which secured a greater commitment to education reform. The success of its struggle for parity with other teachers has conferred a new vigour on the organisation which during the past two decades has enabled it to contribute significantly to general policy developments while successfully continuing its long tradition of furthering the professional interests of its members. During those recent decades it has also extended its international contacts, played a major role in national trade union activities, promoted closer links between the teacher unions and contributed in a major way to education debate by means of its various published reports.[70] In the closing decades of the twentieth century the INTO is as deeply involved in the various aspects of general policy as it was a century earlier when it presented Gladstone with a comprehensive and critical memorandum on Irish education.

TABLE 4.1

Content Analysis of the Presidential Addresses at I.N.T.O. Congresses 1900-80 showing the frequency of various topics by decade.

TOPICS	1900/10	1911/20	1921/30	1931/40	1941/50	1951/60	1961/70	1971/80	TOTAL
Educational Planning	—	—	1	—	2	—	—	—	3
School Buildings	6	3	1	4	5	5	3	1	28
Slow Learners	—	—	—	—	—	3	5	3	11
Council of Education	—	—	1	5	2	—	—	—	8
Integrated System	—	—	—	—	2	5	2	5	14
Equality of Educational Opportunity	5	3	3	—	—	—	—	3	13
School Attendance	5	2	4	1	1	—	—	—	14
School Leaving Age	—	—	—	2	2	—	—	1	5
Financing of Education	8	3	—	—	—	—	—	2	13
Class Size	—	—	—	—	3	8	3	7	21
Administrative Structure	3	4	—	—	—	—	—	3	10
Salaries	4	3	1	5	8	6	2	2	31
Pensions	2	1	4	2	1	—	—	—	10
Civil Rights	3	4	—	4	1	—	—	1	13
Promotions	3	3	—	4	1	—	—	1	12
United Profession	—	—	—	—	—	—	—	1	1
Teacher Training	2	1	6	1	3	7	7	8	35
Inspection	3	6	2	4	2	—	—	—	17
Irish Language	2	1	3	4	5	5	5	5	30
Curriculum	6	6	2	3	8	6	7	6	44
Post Primary Education	—	—	1	—	—	—	1	—	2
University Education	—	3	1	—	—	—	1	—	5

Source: Complied by author.

TABLE 4.2

The total number of national schools in operation in the years 1929, 1958, 1968 and 1981, the number of these which were 'Convent and Monastery Schools' and the number of these schools on a salary and a capitation basis.

Year	Total Number of National Schools	Number of Convent & Monastery Schools		Manner of Funding Salary from Capitation	
		N	%		
1929	5,447	460	8.4	77	383
1958	4,869	567	11.6	127	440
1968	4,294	617	14.4	271	346
1981	3,403	565	16.6	564	1

Source: *Tuarascáil na Roinne Oideachais* and *Tuarascáil Staitistiuil.*

TABLE 4.3

Convent and Monastery Schools as a percentage of all National Schools and their enrolments as a percentage of all pupils for 1929,1958, 1960, 1976 and 1981.

Year	1929	1958	1962	1976	1981
% Total Schools	8.4	11.7	14.1	15.2	16.6
% All Pupils	26	38	42	38	33.6

Source: *Tuarascáil na Roinne Oideachais.*

TABLE 4.4

The number of Convent and Monastery Schools opting for Capitation and Personal Salary as a Funding Mechanism for selected years 1929-80.

	1929	1958	1968	1971	1974	1976	1980
Convent Schools							
Capitation	311	350	257	117	53	7	1
Personal Salary	31	67	201	326	395	426	416
Total	342	417	458	443	448	433	417
Monastery Schools							
Capitation	72	90	89	87	87	84	—
Personal Salary	46	60	70	67	68	69	148
Total	118	150	159	154	155	153	148

Source: *Tuarascáil na Roinne Oideachais* and *Tuarascáil Statistiúil na Roinne.*

Chapter 5

Postprimary Teachers

In the postprimary sector there were until the sixties two school types, secondary and vocational; the reforms of the sixties have created three more, comprehensive schools, community schools and community colleges. Comprehensive and community schools are managed by boards composed of church, local authority, department, parental and teacher representatives. Teachers in secondary schools are employed by the management of their schools and paid mainly by the Department of Education and partly by their school; those in vocational schools are employed and paid by their Vocational Education Committee. Teachers in comprehensive and community schools are employed by their management boards and remunerated by the Department of Education.

Entry requirements to the profession are controlled by the Registration Council for secondary teachers and by the Department of Education for vocational and other teachers. The Association of Secondary Teachers, Ireland (ASTI) represents lay teachers in secondary schools and the Teachers' Union of Ireland (TUI), formerly the Vocational Teachers' Association, represents the teachers in vocational schools; both organisations represent teachers in comprehensive and community schools. There are approximately 20,000 full-time teachers in postprimary schools of whom almost 12,000 are in secondary schools.

The Association of Secondary Teachers, Ireland
The Association of Secondary Teachers, Ireland, represents the interests of the majority of lay teachers in Irish secondary schools and some teachers in comprehensive and community schools.[1] It was founded in 1909 following the initiative taken by six lay teachers in St Colman's College, Fermoy, who organised an exploratory meeting in Cork in March of that year.[2] The Cork meeting was concerned mainly with organisational details and with generating a common awareness among lay teachers of the need to combat collectively those conditions of 'ignoble slavery' and 'lonely subordination', under which they worked.[3] Teachers from the Dublin region met at Easter 1909 and, encouraged by the efforts of their Munster colleagues, resolved

to amalgamate their memberships to form a national organisation. A joint meeting was held in the Mansion House, Dublin in July 1909 at which the Association of Secondary Teachers, Ireland was inaugurated and a Central Executive Committee established. The association, in the process of its formation, absorbed another organisation, The Association of Intermediate and University Teachers in Ireland, which, founded in 1897, had by this time lost most of its early initiative and membership. The earlier association had, however, in its short existence, achieved some positive results; its short pamphlet of 1904, *Secondary education in Ireland, a plea for reform*, outlined succinctly the main grievances of teachers and related them to general education policy. In the concluding section of this pamphlet the issues and policies which exercised the ASTI on its foundation are already identified:

> Registration, adequate salary, security of tenure and good service pensions, these are the legitimate claims of teachers, nor will they cease to agitate until they get them.[4]

By early 1910 the ASTI had developed an embryonic national structure, had elected annual officers and had adopted a constitution under which membership was open to all lay secondary teachers in Ireland.[5] Its aims were specified as follows:

(i)   to secure a system of registration of secondary teachers;

(ii)   to secure an adequate minimum salary with regular increments;

(iii) to obtain reasonable security of tenure and pension rights.[6]

During its first year, the Association showed unusual initiative and organisational energy; it founded its own education journal, organised a major public meeting and sent a deputation to the Commissioners of Intermediate Education. In January 1910, *The Irish Journal of Education* was launched by which it was hoped to generate among members a collective awareness and a commitment to reform. The *Journal* during seven years and its fifty-one issues acted as the Association's mouthpiece in furthering its aims and also acted as a counterfoil to the journal of the Catholic Headmasters' Association, *The Irish Educational Review* (1907-1914). The *Review* while supporting in general terms the case for more financial aid for the secondary system, was more directly concerned with advancing the interests of school authorities and managers.[7] Early in the 1910 academic year the CHA sought a meeting with the ASTI to discuss its aims; subsequently the managerial association issued a guarded statement supporting the ASTI demands for salary and pension reforms but significantly omitting any reference to security of tenure and registration.[8]

In November 1910 however, teachers and managers shared both a common platform and a common cause at the public meeting in the Mansion House, organised by the ASTI.[9] The meeting, by formal resolutions, expressed itself in favour of improving the status of teachers and of increasing the investment from government sources in Irish secondary education; the fluctuating annual amounts available and the inequalities suffered by Ireland under the existing arrangements were the sources of managerial, political and teacher dissatisfaction.[10]

It is evident from the activities of the association in its early years that it had a keen awareness of the efficacy of political action and lobbying in advancing its cause. During 1911, local deputations from the association waited on various local authorities, county councils and corporations and secured their support; resolutions embodying the elements of the teachers' demands were passed by the County Councils of Limerick, Clare and Kerry, the Corporations of Dublin, Derry, Cork, Limerick, Waterford and Clonmel and by other smaller authorities.[11] Furthermore by the end of its first year in existence, the association had branches operating in the main centres, had established provincial councils and had launched a vigorous membership campaign.[12] By late 1911, women's branches had been established in Dublin and Belfast which attracted membership among teachers from both Catholic and Protestant schools in both cities. It is of interest also that at a time when the term 'trade union' was not highly regarded in Ireland the association was happy to proclaim itself as such. Reacting to a speech by Dr O'Dwyer, Catholic Bishop of Limerick, who deplored the fact that teachers had been driven to agitate and had 'been turned into a kind of trade union', the *Journal* editorial notes that progress had been made in that 'the poor dumb driven cattle of Irish Intermediate schools had at length found a voice', a voice which had met with sympathy in powerful quarters.[13]

By the early twenties the association had acquired a coherent structure, involving an annual convention as the supreme authority, a central executive committee meeting twice yearly, having representatives from all branches and a smaller body, the standing committee, meeting more regularly. Its first formal convention was held in 1923 and has been held annually since then, traditionally at Easter. Policy is determined by convention and occasionally by special conferences; the address delivered by the president is a major feature of the convention as it is usually concerned with those issues of policy which are under current discussion or are of most urgent priority to the association.

Presidential Addresses and Congress Resolutions
For the first thirty years of its activity, the Association was concerned almost exclusively with the immediate trade union aspects of its objectives, i.e. security, salary and registration. From the mid-

thirties onwards one can discern in the presidential addresses a broadening of the range of policy issues discussed so that items of general policy and matters arising from professional practice gradually come to dominate the annual presidential occasion.[14]

Over the forty years covered by the presidential addresses which survive, curricular issues predominate, followed closely by questions deriving from conditions of service; other issues such as school facilities, educational philosophy, the dominance of examinations, teacher education, and the need for a representative consultative Council of Education figure prominently from time to time. Only from the early sixties onwards do issues of national education policy emerge as central themes, catalysed no doubt, by the emerging public debate on education which characterised the period.

The role of specific subjects in the curriculum has been a constant theme; the case for more modern languages has been made frequently, (1936, 1938, 1958, 1959, 1961, 1962) while appeals for more scientific and mathematical studies (1936, 1960, 1961, 1962), have been counterbalanced by pleas for a balance between the humanities and the sciences. Support for the inclusion of practical and aesthetic subjects in the academically biassed curriculum appear spasmodically (1936, 1954, 1956, 1959) and are effectively countered by strong condemnations of specialisation (1950, 1956) and the assertion that the programme should not be vocationally oriented (1960). Condemnation of the dominance of written examinations has been frequent (1936, 1950, 1947, 1975), sometimes accompanied by a plea for the clarification of the aims, philosophy or guiding purpose of the system (1947, 1954, 1956, 1959). On the conduct of the examinations there were periodic references to standards of marking in particular subjects, condemnation of the practice of 'cramming' (1957, 1958), complaints against prescribed texts, (1938) and a rather strange appeal for a third public examination (1939, 1940). One brave president struck an unusual note in a profession noted for its complacency by declaring secondary education to be irrelevant for the majority of students as early as 1936.

The place of the Irish language in the curriculum and various aspects of teaching methods and syllabuses figure consistently in the addresses, especially in the forties and fifties when it was customary to deliver some portion of the address in Irish. The emphasis on written skills and the absence of an oral test in Irish were frequently condemned (1938, 1951, 1954, 1955, 1957, 1958, 1959) while following the introduction of an oral test, the methods employed were criticised (1960, 1962, 1963). The decline of Irish as a medium of instruction was noted in 1957.

On questions of tenure, conditions of employment, salary and pensions, there is as marked a contrast between the issues which dominated the early decades and those of the last decade as there is between the teacher attitudes which characterised these periods.

Prior to 1950 many issues concerning tenure and continuity of employment were contested by the ASTI against a background of employer dominance and erratic dismissals; in the last two decades matters concerning salary, contract and service conditions have been handled within the normal procedures of the Irish Congress of Trade Unions to which the ASTI reaffiliated in 1966 or within the ambit of the Employer-Labour Conference.

Insecurity of tenure and lack of promotional prospects are frequently referred to (1938, 1940, 1942, 1956, 1957, 1958), while the references to dismissals and appeal procedures reflect current negotiation or incidents (1936, 1940, 1942). The question of lay teacher status, promotion, and lay posts of authority became a major issue within the past two decades (1964, 1974, 1975, 1976); also in the recent past the associaton has sought to have employment contracts specify such conditions as maximum class size and maximum number of class hours per week (1974). On questions of salary and pensions, presidential addresses have inevitably sung the same constant tune though not always at the same pitch; 'teacher salaries have never been adequate and pensions have not kept pace with rising costs of living'. The enactment of the recommendations of the Ryan tribunal on teacher salaries of 1968 whose basic principle of parity of salary for all teachers, primary, secondary, and vocational, had long been opposed by the ASTI, precipitated a three week strike by secondary teachers in February 1969. This secured an improved salary agreement for the ASTI and some *ad hoc* allowances which directly caused a long feud between the department and the secondary teachers. The gradual acceptance by the ASTI of the principle of parity and of a common conciliation and arbitration scheme for all teachers removed a major source of friction between the different teacher groups. This released the energies of the ASTI for other issues of policy and many of these issues dominated the seventies. The more effective political power of the ASTI in the seventies is reflected in the more radical aspects of its policy and in the manner in which it has canvassed and publicly espoused its policies. It has been facilitated in these developments by its greatly increased membership and by the institutional and ideological strength which it derived from its membership of the Irish Congress of Trade Unions.

While issues relating to salary and service conditions continue to appear in the presidential addresses of the seventies, there is a marked shift apparent towards issues involving a wider perspective on general policy and reform measures. This dramatic shift was considerably helped by the 1974 address which issued a call to the association to be innovative and to abandon its traditional role as a reactive organisation. Later addresses express concern for the educational fate of slow learners (1975) and the adverse effects of high pupil/teacher ratios are highlighted (1975, 1976). By the mid-seventies a new radical spirit is clearly discernible within the ASTI which is reflected both in the annual addresses and in its relationship with school authorities. The management of schools (1976), arbitary decision-making on school closures (1975), principalships for lay teachers (1976) and demands for consultation on a regionalisation proposal (1974) are issues which clearly indicate a radical change of climate.

The general pattern of ASTI policy as enunciated in conference presidential addresses is also reflected in the annual reports of the Central Executive Committee and in the resolutions proposed for discussion at the annual conferences. The resolutions passed at the conferences in the periods 1953-64 and 1968-78 are tabulated in Table 5.1 under a number of category headings.[15] Throughout this period employment conditions and association business figure consistently as major areas of concern as expressed by these resolutions; this emphasis reflects the centrality of the long struggle waged by the association in securing basic contractual employment rights and of the associated issues which this struggle raised. Half a century after its foundation the ASTI was still engaged in consolidating its initial gains in relation to contracts of employment, arbitrary dismissals and salary issues which in the first three decades of its history were central to its activities. To understand the contribution of the ASTI to education policy it is essential to outline the manner in which it achieved its basic objectives in the period from 1909-1959. If one compares the professional status and economic plight of secondary teachers in 1909 and in the late sixties it becomes apparent that their association in the space of fifty years achieved a remarkable advance. In the first half century of its existence the Association of Secondary Teachers not only attained its founding objectives, and thereby enhanced the material and professional interests of its members; in doing so it made a significant contribution to policy on teacher status and employment conditions and altered many central features of the system.

Teachers and Managers
As indicated previously, the Intermediate Education Act of 1878 which established a Board of Commissioners to allocate grants to secondary schools on the basis of examinations, was an educational measure of very limited efficacy. It required no recognition criteria of schools, specified no minimal qualifications for teachers and made no provision in relation to their employment conditions. By the opening years of this century these same conditions still governed the operation of the 400 secondary schools and the employment of their 1,300 teachers. The Commissioners of Intermediate Education were well aware of this major problem and referred frequently in their reports to the reluctance or inability of school managers to employ adequately qualified teachers.[16] Whether due to reluctance or inability on the part of the schools, graduates were not plentiful among

those employed as teachers in the secondary schools at the turn of the century; 11.5% of the male teachers and 8% of the female teachers in Catholic secondary schools were university graduates whereas the corresponding figures for Protestant schools were 55% and 30% respectively.[17] The disparity between the denominations was due as much to the inadequate provision for higher education for Catholics and the ecclesiastical ban on their attendance at Trinity College as it was due to the depressed and unattractive status of the lay teacher in Catholic secondary schools[18]. The Dale and Stephens Report observed in 1905 that few Irish graduates were inclined to adopt teaching as a profession due to the low status and insecurity of tenure and the inadequate salaries; it reported an average salary of £82 for men and £48 for women for 1904. In relation to salary, professional standing and security of tenure the secondary teachers were in a far inferior position to their counterparts in the national schools. This differential, of which the secondary teachers were well aware, deepened their commitment to securing a betterment of their conditions.

In addition to the inspiration of their colleagues in the INTO, the secondary teachers received solid support from some public figures especially from Dr Starkie, and from Chief Secretary Augustine Birrell; they were also encouraged by the qualified support of the Catholic bishops and the Catholic school authorities. The ASTI however could not rely upon the unqualified support of the Catholic Headmasters Association (CHA) whose attitude to the teachers' demands was coloured by the genuine scarcity of funds afflicting secondary education and by an equally genuine resistance by the headmasters to recognising the rights of lay teachers to security of tenure in secondary schools, owned and managed by the clergy or by religious orders. On the general issue of securing adequate salary and pensions for teachers by means of increased government funding for secondary education, the church authorities, the managers of secondary schools and their employees, the lay teachers, were in total accord, but on the more basic issue of the contractual rights of employees there was little, if any, agreement between them. This fundamental difference persisted for over forty years and surfaced many times and in different contexts. When the Commissioners of Intermediate Education appointed permanent secondary inspectors in 1909, the gravity of the plight of the lay secondary teachers prompted the Commissioners to investigate the staff conditions obtaining in the schools. When however the inspectors attempted to secure detailed information from the schools as to the qualifications, conditions of employment and length of service of the lay teachers they encountered an official silence and resistance on the part of the Catholic school authorities; such an inquiry according to a spokesman for the CHA would interfere with the private nature of the schools and the freedom of the managers.[19] In September 1909 the CHA had resolved not to supply the Commissioners, through the inspectors, with any details as to the salaries of the lay teachers; this action was a major cause of discord between the managers and the lay teachers.[20]

The teachers gave frequent expression to their feelings and grievances through their association and in the columns of *The Irish Journal of Education*. The *Journal* publicised the teachers' case, generated some corporate spirit and commitment among ASTI members and, by means of trenchant editorial comment and rousing articles, broadcast the association's message. One such article, typical of the *Journal's* ebullient style, quoted an eminent British statesman, as expressing sentiments of shame and horror upon hearing of the plight of Irish secondary teachers:

> ... their salary was a pittance, their tenure was uncertainty itself and their qualifications might range from anything to nothing: so that a teacher is, in Ireland on a level with the unskilled artisan, a nobody, a hireling, a nondescript, a harmless necessary person, whose function anyone, who has failed at all else, may in the last resort fall back upon.[21]

The author of these words had identified correctly the kernel of the ASTI case and expressed in forceful language the policy objective which the association introduced successfully into the wider political arena in 1910 and 1911, thereby securing the political support of the Irish Party at Westminster, the active backing of Starkie and the commitment to reform measures of Augustine Birrell. The joint managerial associations and the Catholic bishops also gave support but confined that support to the 'reasonable demands of lay teachers in the secondary schools of Ireland'.[22] Such reasonable demands included, according to the chairman of the CHA, 'status , salaries and pensions' but not, significantly, security of tenure.[23] The monster public meeting in Dublin organised by the ASTI in December 1910, in association with the two managerial bodies and attended by prominent political and educational figures, signalled that after years of agitation, the teachers were about to elicit a positive response from the government.

Augustine Birrell and the Initial Struggles

Augustine Birrell came to the position of Chief Secretary in 1907 with deep experience of the politics of education at Westminster and with a personal commitment to securing education reform in Ireland. Having successfully negotiated an acceptable solution to the thorny problem of university education in the Irish Universities Act of 1908, Birrell turned his attention enthusiastically to alleviating the plight of secondary teachers. Speaking in parliament in 1911, he announced the allocation of funds 'to raise the status of secondary schools which can only be done by raising the present status of the teachers in these schools'.[24] His proposals became an issue of sharp controversy between Birrell, the CHA, the ASTI and the Catholic bishops, especially in relation to the conditions governing the award of the grant. The draft scheme as announced by Birrell in 1912, would form part of an education act providing for the establishment of a professional register of teachers and securing for them adequate salaries and contractual security of employment. Birrell had clearly indicated in 1911 that his sympathies were totally with the lay teachers; in his Westminster speech he stated 'The life of an assistant master in Ireland is detestable, the remuneration is miserably inadequate and he has no tenure of office at all'.[25] By the end of his chief secretaryship, Birrell had secured a register and an improved salary scale for the secondary teachers but had failed to secure security of tenure; thirty years later it was still a major aim of ASTI policy.

Under the Birrell scheme published in September 1912 a special grant of £40,000 was allocated to improve the status of the lay secondary teacher in Ireland; the allocation of the grant would be governed by the following conditions:

(i)   each secondary school to employ one lay registered teacher for each 40 pupils enrolled, such teachers to be in receipt of a minimum salary of £120 p.a. (men) and £80 p.a. (women);

(ii) these lay assistant teachers to be entitled to six months notice or six months salary in the case of dismissal except on grounds of misconduct;

(iii) a teachers' register would be established.

These proposals, satisfying some, if not all, of the ASTI demands received instant support from the association; however, the Catholic secondary school managers and the CHA viewed the Birrell scheme as constituting an attack on the autonomy of their schools as private institutions and they opposed the proposals vigorously on various grounds. Fundamentally, the CHA were not concerned unduly with the detailed mechanism of the proposals which were negotiable, but they rejected the right of the public authorities to decide how the schools should be staffed. When Birrell emphasised that his concern was with improving the status of the lay teacher, the CHA claimed that he was guilty of 'gross discrimination against priests and religious'; his proposals were viewed as the first step in a policy leading to the complete laicisation of the schools.[26] It was further claimed that, since most if not all staff in Protestant schools were lay, this scheme would favour them and thereby constitute a discriminatory endowment of Protestant education. A joint statement from the CHA and the convent secondary schools in October 1912, while reasserting support for the lay teachers, claimed that the amount of the allocated grant at £40,000 was totally inadequate and that any such grant should be applied to the system generally not to the lay teachers only. This was supported by a statement from the Catholic bishops in which they expressed a wish to see the position of the lay teachers improved but by a mechanism other than that proposed by Birrell.[27] When a deputation from the CHA was received by Birrell in London on 18 December 1912 to request him to amend his scheme, he invited the school authorities to submit their amendments in writing. There followed a lengthy correspondence between Birrell and Canon Andrew Murphy of Limerick (hon. secretary of the CHA) which terminated in June 1913 with little agreement of substance emerging except a resolve on both sides to publish the correspondence in full.[28]

The ASTI policy throughout this controversy was consistently and trenchantly expressed, mainly in the pages of their *Journal*. The teachers saw the issue essentially as one of achieving security and fair terms of employment in a publicly regulated profession. When the headmasters described Birrell's scheme as creating 'preserves' for laymen, the ASTI counterclaimed that the scheme, on the contrary: 'would remove a little of the barbed wire fence and some of the trespass notices that already mark out preserves that are not for laymen'. They also claimed that the Birrell correspondence revealed a total unwillingness on the part of the Catholic headmasters to grant some security or recognition to the lay teachers. In addition, both before and during the controversy, the number of arbitrary dismissals of lay teachers rose dramatically, leading the *Journal* to claim that 'lay teachers are being ruthlessly driven out of a certain section of the schools'.[29] In 1911 the Munster Council of the ASTI condemned by resolution what they described as an established annual feature of certain schools, 'the wholesale dismissal without notice or cause assigned, of capable and well conducted secondary teachers'[30] When the headmasters described the statements made by Birrell in parliament as 'extravagant', the ASTI answered by providing details of dismissal cases and offering evidence from dismissed teachers. In one such case, a teacher dismissed from a religious college, reported his headmaster as communicating his dismissal to him in the following words:

> I have learned that I shall probably be able to get one of our members (of the order) to do your work. I regret therefore that I shall not have a vacancy for you next year. I am sorry for this, because your example both in and out of the college was calculated to produce the best possible effect.[31]

In an effort to persuade the ASTI to abandon their campaign before the act was introduced, the CHA at a joint conference in 1913 requested the teachers to accept an alternative solution based upon 'trusting the honour of the headmasters'. In reply, the ASTI rejected the suggestion which they termed 'childish', and stated

> We ask that our position be put on a business basis; we do work
> of public utility and we are entitled to some of that protection
> and recompense which the public grants to the humblest of its
> civil servants.[32]

Such a statement of the ASTI claim to security of tenure, drawing
upon the argument of public utility, would never be acceptable to the
school authorities, who regarded the secondary teachers as being
employed in private institutions. The controversy between the CHA
and Birrell and the ASTI campaign to gain their basic objectives,
demonstrated again the resilient power of the Catholic authorities in
education. It also became apparent by 1914 that, even with a catalyst
of the calibre of Augustine Birrell, the structural problems of Irish
secondary education were not amenble to easy and ready solutions.

Eventually the Birrell proposals in modified form were incorporated in the Intermediate Education Act of August 1914. The Act
created a Teacher Registration Council, provided £40,000 for a
teachers' salary grant and empowered the Lord Lieutenant to draft
rules for the administration of the grant. The Registration Council
was constituted in 1915 having representatives of the teaching
profession, the Intermediate Board, the Department of Agriculture
and Technical Instruction, the Universities and of other bodies
interested in education. At its first meeting in December 1915,
chaired by Starkie and attended by fifteen representatives of the
designated bodies, the ASTI was represented by W. J. Williams and
by Miss F. Steele. The rules governing the registration process were
published in July 1918; in order to allow for those seeking registration
on the basis of age and experience, a transition period to 1925 was
granted, after which a degree, a postgraduate diploma and three
years' teaching experience were required.

Under the 1914 Act, the teachers' salary grant was specified as
being 'for the purpose of promoting the employment upon reasonable terms of an adequate number of duly qualified lay teachers in
intermediate schools'.[33] Under the rules governing the grant, schools
under Catholic and Protestant management were to be treated as
separate groups, within each of which the total number of duly
qualified lay teachers should not be less than 1:40 of the total pupils
attending the schools in the group. Only those teachers could be
included who taught at least ten hours per week, received, under
contract, specified minimum salary and whose contract of employment involved provision for three months' dismissal notice in
writing.[34] It was stipulated in the act that the grant was to be distributed to the managers of schools in proportion to the amount of
examination results fees received in the preceding year. Power was
vested in the Lord Lieutenant to alter the manner of distibution of the

grant if the conditions as to the employment conditions of lay teachers were not adhered to. To facilitate this review process, the manager of each school was required to furnish any information required to the Intermediate Education Commissioners who were to report annually to the Lord Lieutenant on the scheme.

While welcoming the benefits of the 1914 Act, the ASTI were under no illusion as to the compromise nature of its provisions, especially as to the obligations on groups of schools to maintain global lay teacher employment levels. It soon became clear to the teachers that many schools were not abiding by the rules and that the Lord Lieutenant was reluctant to take corrective action in relation to such violations of the 1914 measure. During the ten years in which the Birrell scheme operated (from 1914/15 to 1923/24) the teachers expressed sustained criticism of many aspects of its operation. They claimed that many secondary school managers accepted the increased funding without extending its benefits to the lay teachers and they asserted that many of the Catholic schools did not discharge their obligations under the 1914 act. In this latter charge the claim by the teachers is substantiated by the data presented in the annual reports on the scheme prepared by the Intermediate Commissioners and reproduced in Table 5.2.

By 1917 less than 35% of the 1,142 lay teachers in secondary schools had salaries and the related security of tenure which satisfied the modest requirements of the 1914 act and many teachers had salaries less than £100 p.a.[35] In the remaining years to 1922, the ASTI availed of every opportunity to press for government and school initiatives with a view to improving the employment conditions of lay teachers. While the special Duke grant in 1918 of £50,000 improved matters for the schools, the teachers were so deeply dissatisfied with the system that they sought legal advice as to the failure of the Catholic group of schools to observe the 1914 rules. The vice-regal committee of inquiry of 1918, chaired by Chief Justice Molony, which was established to inquire into conditions of service and remuneration of secondary teachers and into the funding of secondary schools can be construed as an implied acknowledgement of the validity of the ASTI claim as to the failure of the 1914 scheme. The ASTI representatives on the committee disagreed with the majority report in relation to security of tenure although they welcomed the proposals on a uniform minimum salary and a superannuation scale. They and Professor R. M. Henry of Queen's University Belfast signed a minority report which made the case for a guaranteed security of tenure and an impartial forum of appeal in cases of dismissal; they proposed an independent referee nominated or approved by the public education authority. Such a measure seemed highly unlikely to be acceptable to the CHA; in 1917 a Board of Appeal consisting of equal representatives and a neutral chairman, as proposed by the ASTI, had been rejected out of hand by the bishops and by the Catholic headmasters.[36] The minority report also disagreed with the majority proposal to merge all school grants then in operation lest the removal of the Birrell Grant rules would further endanger the security of lay teachers. The official Catholic view on security of tenure was expounded by Canon Marshall and Professor T. J. Corcoran S.J., members of the Molony committee; it was obvious that the deep divergence of views would not permit of a ready solution of the question of tenure.

The draft of the McPherson Bill incorporating the findings of the Molony Committee and the inactivity of the government in relation to the proposed measures to improve the conditions of teachers, prompted the ASTI early in 1920 to initiate a campaign for a living wage and improved conditions. They publicised their case, sought the support of local trade councils and of the Irish Trades Union Congress, to which the ASTI had affiliated in 1919, and referred effectively to the social encyclical of Leo XIII, *Rerum Novarum* , the principles of justice of which, they claimed, had been violated singly and collectively by the Catholic schools.[37]

The degree of disenchantment and militancy with which the ASTI was imbued at this period is clearly indicated in the national strike which they organised in May 1920. Upon the refusal of the CHA to grant a satisfactory salary scale, similar to that introduced in Britain under the Fisher Act of 1918, the association sanctioned a strike in the Cork secondary schools. It began on 6 May and was later declared a general strike to begin on 10 May 1920.[38] While the school authorities had gained from the Duke award of £50,000 in 1918 and the interim grant of 1920, the teachers, according to the ASTI had received no improvement on their miserable salaries despite a rise of 135% in the cost of living. The widespread support for the ASTI from primary and vocational teachers and collectively from the trade union movement forced an early settlement along lines agreeable to the secondary teachers. While the national strike was terminated within a few days, it continued in Limerick schools for three weeks because local school authorities denounced the settlement and the CHA decision to concede the ASTI claim. It also continued in the schools of the Christian Brothers who claimed that their meagre financial resources did not allow them to meet the increases, with the granting of which they agreed in principle. The active and generous support of the INTO was probably a major factor in procuring the resolution of the issue by 29 May.

The conduct of the strike and its outcomes had important effects. It generated a new spirit within the association and inspired teachers to further collective action in pursuit of their objectives; from some of the school authorities it produced a new and harsh reaction towards lay teachers. Lay teachers suffered arbitrary dismissal following the strike; some schools which subsequently refused to employ any lay teachers persevered in that policy for over a generation and many teachers opted to emigrate to England and Scotland where secure employment was available at very attractive salaries. Before the change of administration in 1922 the ASTI organised a conference on secondary education in collaboration with the managers and the Intermediate Board in January 1921 which presented a report to the Chief Secretary outlining the urgency of providing adequate funds for secondary education and the application of the English salary scales in Irish schools.[39]

Within the short space of twelve or thirteen years from its foundation, the ASTI had achieved significant advances for its members in relation to professional registration and improved salary conditions. If security of tenure had not been achieved yet, the case had been effectively made and wide public and political support had been garnered, especially in the years after 1916. In the period following independence, security of tenure would form the central element of ASTI policy; its eventual achievement would require over two decades of patient negotiation and eventually compromise on some points.

Security of Tenure after 1922

Following the change of administration in 1922, the ASTI concentrated its energies mainly on the issues of security of tenure, pensions and a uniform contract. Encouraged by the outcome of the 1920 strike and perhaps by the remembrance of the solid support of Birrell, Starkie and the Commissioners of Intermediate Education, the ASTI entertained a high expectation that the Minister for Education in the governemnt of a free Ireland would be found convincingly on their side in any question of basic rights as to tenure of employment. They held the view that, since the state was providing most of the funding for secondary schools, any tribunal established to arbitrate between school authorities and secondary teachers should be assisted by the state in an impartial role. In numerous submissions to the Department of Education and to three ministers between 1922 and 1934, they sought the impartial intervention of the minister in an issue which they described as of crucial importance to the functioning of the education system. The association received the same reaction from Eoin MacNeill, John Marcus O'Sullivan and Tomás Deirg, each of whom refused to get involved in the issue while professing to accept the case made by the teachers. In a Dáil debate in December 1922, for which the ASTI had prepared a detailed memorandum, the minister, Eoin MacNeill, while acknowledging that the tenure of secondary teachers was unsatisfactory, was of the opinion that an initiative towards a solution should not come from him.[40] Upon being pressed by the ASTI in 1923 as to his obligations on the matter of an independent appeal board, MacNeill offered to consult the Catholic hierarchy but his efforts were fruitless.

When the government introduced the Intermediate Education Act of 1924, involving a new system of funding for secondary schools based upon capitation grants, the ASTI feared that the abolition of the 1914 Birrell grant would endanger the degree of contractual security already achieved by lay teachers under the rules governing the Birrell scheme. When, in 1925, the Department rules were redrafted in accordance with the 1924 Act, the rule deriving from the 1914 scheme requiring the employment of a stated proportion of registerd lay teachers was rescinded. According to the attorney general, such a rule constituted a discrimination in favour of lay teachers and as such was in contravention of Article 8 of the 1922 constitution which guaranteed protection from disability on account of religious status.[41] This official initiative effectively diminished the security of the lay teachers at a crucial moment and confirmed the Catholic school authorities, the CHA and the bishops in their sustained opposition to the Birrell rules. It may also have been linked to the simultaneous decision by the bishops in October 1925 to extend the protection of the 'Maynooth Resolution' to secondary teachers.[42]

Since the departmental regulations of 1925 required a contract of employment for the minimum registered staff, the ASTI approached the department and the minister seeking an agreed standard form of contract in 1925; the official response was an equivocal assertion that the rule merely required the contract to be satisfactory.[43] When, following conferences between the ASTI and the CHA in 1925, the school authorities rejected the right of the association to act on behalf of a dismissed member, the ASTI appealed to the minister, Eoin MacNeill, to propose a satisfactory solution. Mac Neill responded that while he desired a settlement, he did not propose to take any action since the matter could be resolved by the CHA and the ASTI.[44]

When, in 1931, the ASTI urged the minister, John Marcus O'Sullivan, to assist in securing an appeal board to deal with dismissals, he replied that such an issue was outside his province and refused to be involved. When the teachers were campaigning against the practice, especially prevalent in convent schools, of replacing teachers due for registration (and hence entitled to higher specified salaries) by non-registered teachers, they requested the minister to introduce a regulation to prevent the practice. The department's response was to the effect that such a regulation would not be possible or equitable.[45] When in May 1932 the teachers, in deputation to Mr Deirg, pleaded the case of female secondary teachers, whose position was particularly vulnerable under the existing tenure conditions, the minister's response was one of helplessness and a suggestion that the obvious solution was a reduction in the number of lady graduates produced by the universities.[46] Undismayed by such negative reactions, the 1933 annual convention of the ASTI sought to secure the right of appeal to the minister in dismissal cases, quoting the practice in Northern Ireland; the ministerial response was a consistent refusal.[47] In the period to 1935 it became very clear that the ministers were not willing to assume the role of arbitrator as between the lay secondary teachers and the clerical school authorities.

In the same period the ASTI approached the bishops and the school authorities on a number of occasions. The official church policy on appeal procedures and tenure had been enunciated earlier in regard to the Birrell scheme, in the report of the Molony committee of 1919, and in the rejection of various proposals by the ASTI on having a neutral chairman for a board of appeal with equal representation. When the ASTI sought in 1923 to obtain from the CHA a list of the schools represented by the association, the information was refused by the officers of the managerial association; such a basic negotiating document was later made available to the ASTI in 1931 by eighteen of the twenty four dioceses.[48] The official ecclesiastical approach to security of tenure for lay teachers was outlined in an article entitled 'Catholic Secondary Teachers' Security of Tenure' published in *The Irish Monthly* in 1924, the authorship of which was attributed to 'S.J.'.[49] It claimed that the secondary teacher in the Catholic secondary school was not to be viewed as operating in a standard professional milieu where certain norms operate. Hence, suitability for employment on moral, religious or professional grounds could not be adjudicated upon by any independent or state-appointed board of appeal. The only acceptable arbitration mechanism in Catholic schools was that based upon appeal to the bishop of the diocese or the authorities of a religious order; any other arrangement was described as 'a grave lesion on the liberty of the school'. Following negotiations between the CHA and the ASTI in 1925, an agreed document incorporating proposals from both sides was prepared with a view to wider discussion within each organisation. Later in the same year the CHA offered a scheme to the ASTI based upon acceptance of their own and rejection of the ASTI proposals including that which demanded members be representd by the ASTI in appeal procedures.[50]

The ASTI, in frustration, suspended all negotiation with the school authorities and appealed to the bishops on the basis that the CHA in refusing the ASTI's claim to represent members in proceedings, were rejecting the principle of collective bargaining; the teachers claimed that such a stance denied them a right which was operative in both civil and ecclesiastical life. The bishops responded that the CHA offer was adequate to meet all known grievances and emphasised that the 'bishops have given to secondary school teachers in all schools under their control the same safeguards as those given by the 'Maynooth resolution' to primary teachers'.[51] The 'Maynooth resolution' as introduced in 1894 and amended in 1898, secured for national teachers protection against summary dismissal, appeal to the bishop and the right to be heard in defence. Mention by the bishops of the resolution in the context of 1925 is significant. They had formally adopted two similar resolutions in relation to secondary teachers, one at the meeting of the standing committee of 15 January 1924 and the other at a general meeting, 6 October 1925. The resolutions are as follows:

(i)   When a teacher in a secondary school considers himself aggrieved by the action or threatened action of any headmaster of any college or school under our control, the teacher will be heard in his own defence by the Ordinary of the place before any notice of dismissal is issued. (Standing committee, 15 January 1924).

(ii) That lay secondary teachers employed in convent schools (diocesan) have the right of appeal to the Ordinary, as in the case of primary teachers. (General meeting, 6 October 1925).

These resolutions were incorporated in the statutes adopted at the national synod of Maynooth in 1927 and were published in 1929.[52] It was on the basis of these resolutions that negotiations with the ASTI had been conducted; however the association was not aware of the resolutions until after the publication of the synod statutes when they came to the notice of the teachers by accident in 1930. It was reported to the central executive of the ASTI in November 1926 that Dr O'Doherty, Bishop of Galway, had indicated to the general secretary that the bishops were not prepared to go any further on the question of appeal and that they were not likely to agree to having teachers represented by the ASTI at appeal hearings.[53]

However, some dismissal cases were heard following the Maynooth synod in which the association was represented. A significant case in 1935 in the archdiocese of Tuam, in which the general secretary acted, involved a major breakthrough for the teachers and a case in Wexford some time later confirmed the ASTI position that the question should be negotiated further. A special convention convened in December 1934 to examine the question of tenure published a special report and a survey of the dismissal cases of the previous decade.[54] This convention mandated the executive to reopen discussions with the CHA and nominated a special working group to do so. In the negotiations which opened in March 1935 the ASTI reintroduced some of its earlier demands, namely a board of appeal with an independent chairman, a guaranteed quota of lay teachers in Catholic secondary schools according to group and an assurance of alternative employment for redundant teachers.[55] These demands were rejected by the CHA, whose chairman, Dr J. C. McQuaid, of Blackrock College, was requested by the ASTI to draft alternative proposals. Finally, after prolonged negotiations, agreement was achieved in June 1936 and within a few months all the religious orders and managerial authorities associated with the CHA had signed agreements with the ASTI on appeal procedures. This agreement while conceding the right to be represented to the association, was framed along the lines of the 'Maynooth resolution' and was clearly modelled on the earlier provision for national teachers. By 1940 the teaching orders not affiliated to the CHA had negotiated and signed similar agreements with the teachers. However the agreement of 1936 caused division within the ASTI and led eventually to the resignation of the general secretary.[56]

Despite these agreements, issues regarding tenure, dimissals and contracts continued to arise, especially where lay teachers were employed on a temporary basis; the association was involved in the period from 1935 to 1950 in over sixty such appeals, in one of which it considered appealing to a Roman ecclesiastical court. Even after the lengthy negotiations and the formal agreements, cases arose where local bishops refused to abide by the agreed procedures or where interpretations of the rubrics differed from place to place.[57] The remaining outstanding issue pertaining to tenure was that of a uniform written contract which the association was anxious to see introduced. Following discussions with the CHA an agreed form was achieved and this was introduced on a national basis in 1940; by 1942 it was reported that 60% of secondary schools employing ASTI members were using the new contract.[58] When in 1950 separate forms of contract were provided by agreement for probationary, temporary and continuous teaching service, the remaining issues of contention were resolved.

Security of tenure was a major issue for the ASTI; the campaign which it waged in search of that measure of security which was achieved by 1940, was synonymous with its history from its foundation. The major part of that thirty years represented an herculean struggle by a small, inexperienced association to gain the rudiments of professional recognition in a school system where they represented a small minority of those employed. Some of the lay secondary teachers who had frequently heard it asserted that 'No layman has the right to teach in Ireland', survived to witness lay teachers forming 40% of the incremental staffs of secondary schools and enjoying contractual tenure by 1942; their successors in the ASTI in the eighties constitute 82% of a profession which is four times larger than it was in 1942. Secondary teachers of recent decades enjoy salary levels, working condition and a pension scheme which would have been regarded as utopian by the founding fathers of the ASTI.

Pension and Salaries

Securing the associations's aims in relation to pensions and salaries did not involve the ASTI in such a prolonged or complicated campaign as that required in the struggle for security of tenure; moreover these issue were matters touching upon the availability of public resources rather than of questions touching upon the respective roles of church and state in education. Essentially the campaign for an adequate salary and pension rights was waged mainly in the political arena with a view to influencing the politicians and the Departments of Finance and Education. In the early phase, while the secondary teachers struggled to secure an adequate salary and pension scheme, they enjoyed the wholehearted support of the Minister for Education and his department against the resistance of the Department of Finance. This support however did not persist during the period from 1948 to 1968 when the ASTI opposed the claim by the INTO for parity of salary for all teachers, a claim which found ready support in the Departments of Education and Finance.

Following its formal convention in 1923 the ASTI mounted a sustained programme of political action in support of its salary claims. They were supported surprisingly in their claims by the Commissioners of Intermediate Education who in their annual reports of 1921 and 1922 expressed the hope that these reforms which they had 'unavailingly advocated in the past' would be introduced by the new government. When the teachers approached the new government, however, even with the explicit support of the school authorities, the response was neither immediate nor generous. The ASTI in its campaign enjoyed the vigorous leadership of T. J. Burke as general secretary who exercised considerable influence in political circles and who was tellingly effective as a propagandist. Under the provisional government of 1922 and during the civil war, the ASTI succeeded in having their case raised, debated and supported in the Dáil.[59] They also secured the support of Dublin Corporation in April 1922 for a formal resolution which, on circulation to other local authorities, was adopted by most county councils and corporations.[60] The address of the governor general, T. M. Healy, to the Oireachtas in October 1923, outlining the government's policy programme, contained hopeful reference to 'the reorganisation of secondary education'; the omission of any mention of improving conditions for secondary teachers sharpened considerably the frustration of the ASTI.[61] They intensified their campaign, circularised deputies, met senior officials of the department and eventually had an interview with the ministers, Eoin MacNeill and Ernest Blythe.[62] The scheme, embodying most of the ASTI demands, which was submitted by the Department of Education to the Department of Finance in October 1923 was undoubtedly considerably influenced by the vigorous campaign of the association. In conducting that campaign its leadership was assisted by the INTO, whose general secretary, T. J. O'Connell T.D., as Labour spokesman on Education, exercised extensive political influence.

The whole question of the funding of secondary schools and salaries for teachers was examined in an internal departmental memorandum prepared for the Minister for Education in 1924.[63] It would appear that the minister and his department were fully in support of the teachers and of the schools in their quest for a higher level of funding and adequate salaries. This departmental memorandum outlined the inadequacy of the funding system in operation in 1923. Funds consisted mainly of interim grants; if schools used these interim grant only to pay the recommended minimum salaries to registered teachers the schools would suffer a collective heavy loss, whereas if the teachers received no more than these salaries they were in danger of drifting close to the poverty line. The Department of Education in attacking the injustice of the system used critical and uncommonly strong language in relation to the Department of Finance:

> The only thing that remains certain under this vicious system is that even in a 'lucky' year the secondary teachers can never receive a living wage, while in an 'unlucky' year when the Department of Finance has hardened its heart, they may find themselves on the brink of starvation.[64]

In October 1923 the Minister for Education forwarded an alternative scheme to the Department of Finance, under which schools would receive capitation grants from the state enabling them to pay basic salaries to teachers which, together with the incremental salaries from the state, would guarantee gross salaries comparable to those in Northern Ireland.[65] The response of the Department of Finance was sharply negative, even if predictable in a period when salary cuts in the public services were the order of the day.[66] The Department of Finance, in refusing sanction for the scheme, suggested that schools should charge higher fees and where they could not or would not do so, the necessary funds might be secured by savings in the salaries of the religious community.[67] Furthermore 'the Minister for Finance would require strong evidence to convince him of the unworkability of the exisiting system of funding for secondary education'.

The school authorities and the secondary teachers responded to the refusal with an orchestrated campaign, the intensity of which suggests that they may have been made aware of the details of the official response. In May 1924, a deputation representative of the Catholic and Protestant secondary authorities, the Irish Christian Brothers and the ASTI, met the Minister for Education, Eoin MacNeill and presented him with a joint statement demanding adequate salaries and pensions for teachers and capitation grants for schools. They quoted various official bodies and individuals in support of their demands and asserted that the extensive curricular reforms, planned by the minister, would be severely handicapped unless accompanied by adequate financial provision.[68] Within a week of this joint deputation, the ASTI issued a memorandum on the position of the lay secondary teacher in which the language is more militant and the argument more direct than the measured tones of the deputation's document. Ideologically, the memorandum distanced the association from the policy of the Catholic authorities when it stated:

> The interests of the nation imperatively demand that education should be a state service and the conditions of employment of

teachers a matter of state concern and state control.[69]

The trenchant style of the document is also conveyed in its comment on the absence of a pension scheme:

> Cases of acute distress are on record in which lay secondary teachers who had spent their lives in the public service ended them in public institutions.[70]

The ASTI attributed the rejection of the proposed scheme to the Department of Finance and to its fears of the future costs involved, costs which the association estimated would not reach their maximum of £250,000 until the school year 1931/32.

The campaign by the ASTI and the school authorities achieved its political objective by July 1924 when the Minister for Education announced in the Dáil that Department of Finance approval for his scheme had been obtained. It would appear that government approval for the scheme had been secured in principle only and that no details had been agreed. When Eoin MacNeill made the announcement in the Dáil he refrained from giving any salary details, confining himself to the general terms: a fixed minimum basic salary to be paid to the teachers by the schools and a system of yearly increments to be paid to the teachers by the state.[71] The scheme was to come into effect for the school year 1924/25 and would involve new regulations for staffing and recognition of schools. Discussions on the details of the scheme continued until early in 1925 when the complete scheme was announced. Schools were required to employ a specified minimum of recognised teachers; each such teacher would receive a basic salary from the school of £200 (men) and £180 (women) and an incremental salary from the state of maximum value £210 and £120 respectively after sixteen and twelve years service.[72]

These salary levels, with some minor modifications remained in force until 1946 when the incremental scales were increased significantly to compensate for the standstill caused by the war.[73] Following the establishment of a system of conciliation and arbitration for the public service, the ASTI demanded that secondary teachers be included. This was acceded to in March 1951.[74] Between then and 1969 all salary claims by the ASTI were submitted to a Conciliation Council representative of government interests, school managerial bodies and teacher organisations; failing agreement in this forum the claims were presented to an Arbitration Board composed of equal numbers from each side and chaired by an independent chairman, a nominee of the governemnt. From the inception of the conciliation and arbitration procedure until 1964, the organised bodies representing the management of Catholic secondary schools refused to participate until the Conciliation Council was revised in 1964.[75]

A major feature of the conciliation and arbitration scheme was the pattern of claims and counterclaims submitted by the ASTI and the INTO respectively in an effort to retain or abolish the differential established and upheld in all previous salary structures. In addition to retaining the differential within the profession, the ASTI sought as a policy priority to re-establish comparability with civil service salary scales in the postwar years. When the government responded to pressure from the INTO in 1958 and established a teachers' salaries committee, it was widely expected that the INTO objective of parity of salary would be the recommended outcome. The ASTI in its submissions to the committee, held that differentials in salary between teachers in different levels were a common feature of education systems and that the existing differentials as between secondary, vocational and national teachers were conservatively based.[76] They based their case on arguments derived from differential qualifications and professional preparation, the nature of the work and the structural absence of promotional opportunities in the secondary system. The committee found in favour of retaining the differentials, a recommendation which prompted the INTO representatives to sign a minority report in which they described the majority decision as being based upon 'a materialistic conception of the function of the education system'.[77]

Salary claims which the ASTI initiated in 1961 and 1963 in attempts to redress comparability lapses, generated a running battle with the Department of Education and marked a new level of militancy within the organisation. Following an unfavourable arbitration hearing on the 1963 claim, the ASTI organised a national boycott of the department examinations of 1964 by their members. No ASTI member was available to the department to superintend or examine; it was believed by the teachers that this measure would obstruct the examination process and force the government to yield. However the examinations were held, supervised by civil servants and by other recruited personnel; there was an air of emergency about the operation and in a few places confrontation occurred between teachers and the personnel conducting the examinations. The bitterness generated by the 1964 boycott influenced negatively the relations between the teachers and the government throughout the sixties and diminished the acceptability of various reforms. The long-standing controversy concerning parity of salary was resolved by the establishment in December 1967 of a tribunal on teachers' salaries, chaired by Professor W. J. L. Ryan. The ASTI in its submission repeated its 1958 claim that teacher salaries should be related to training, academic level of work and the nature of qualifications; they seemed to alter their previous stance by asserting that they had no rooted objection to a common basic scale for all teachers provided that additional allowances rendered secondary teachers' salaries comparable to those obtaining in Northern Ireland.[78] Their submission also contained a strong argument in favour of posts of responsibility for lay teachers in secondary schools.

Despite its specific and narrow terms of reference, the Ryan tribunal produced a report with the following wide-ranging proposals: a common basic scale salary and conciliation scheme for all teachers, a coherent system of allowances for qualifications, a system of posts of responsibility for all schools, and a proposal that the total salary of secondary teachers be paid by the Department of Education.[79]

The ASTI formally rejected all the major recommendations of the report and were especially critical of the proposed scales, of the allowances and of the mechanism for the allocation of posts. Two special conventions of the association held in the summer and autumn of 1968 reflected a deep dissatisfaction among secondary teachers and a spirit which resembled the earlier militancy of 1920. A new salary claim submitted to the Conciliation Council in September by the ASTI and an improved offer to all teachers by the minister in October, based upon the Ryan principles, failed to modify the anger of the ASTI who decided on strike action if an acceptable offer had not been negotiated by January 1969. Following the rejection of such an offer, a total stike by ASTI members resulted in February which closed all secondary schools for three weeks.[80] The fragile peace in the education system was threatened once again in September 1969 when the Minister for Education introduced a new salary structure for all teachers, which the ASTI regarded as negativing their strike settlement. The main issue was the apparent conflict between the posts of responsiblity provided for in the minister's scheme and the 'definable special functions' of the ASTI negotiated scheme; the former entailed no extra duties, whereas the latter did. The long-term outcome was that by 1971 all three teacher unions were functioning happily under the umbrella of the Ryan tribunal scheme. If in the process the ASTI had to submit to government policy and accept the dreaded policy of parity, it salvaged its own institutional pride by an effective strike action and by an increased militancy in the growing ranks of its younger members.[81]

A Broader Perspective after 1971

In evaluating the contribution of secondary teachers and of their association to education policy in this century, it is necessary to bear in mind the relevance of their depressed conditions to the policies which they pursued. It is also of some significance that their confreres in the INTO had enjoyed a settled institutional and unionised existence, with many of the associated material benefits, long before the foundation of the ASTI in 1909. The impact of the ASTI on the contemporary education scene was moderated in the early decades by their small membership and by their depressed status within a school system in which they occupied the role of 'hired help', a well-defined role in a mainly agricultural society. Arising from their depressed employment conditions relating to security of tenure, salary and pensions, the members of the association had to endure a prolonged, frustrating and painful purgatory before emerging into full professional security in the late fifties. That purgatorial period, lasting three decades, by necessity sharpened the focus of the ASTI on the necessities of professional existence. The threatening insecurity of tenure, the reluctance of the Department of Education to intervene and the hostility encountered from some school authorities meant that very little professional energy remained for loftier questions of idealism and education policy, beyond the routine annual details of curricular policy. These adverse conditions may also have engendered a spirit of complacency, if not of docile conservatism, in a social group among whom the experience of higher education might have been expected to generate a more daring spirit of innovation.

Perhaps the damping effect of the decades of frustration and professional depression may have generated a very tangible, if indirect, result. The defiant militant spirit of the sixties owes as much to the decades of professional suppression as it does to the changing socio-cultural climate of the society and the growing numerical majority of lay teachers in religious schools. Once the turbulence of the sixties had released the head of steam generated by the frustration of the previous decades, the ASTI and its membership contributed to education policy with a maturity and a professionalism which previously had received little scope for expression.

The sixties and their developments transformed the association. The expansion of postprimary education brought into the teaching profession in large numbers younger members whose perspectives and career expectations were not circumscribed by the more traditional and passive stances of the association. The government policies pursued in the sixties raised questions which were new to the agenda of debate in Irish education and which demanded some fresh thinking and new responses from both teacher and managerial associations. The secondary system had developed throughout this century as an elitist system in which whatever expansion occurred up to the mid-sixties was based on the gradualism characteristic of the 'non-interventionist' approach outlined by Lemass in 1959. When confronted with the prospect of free education for all and mass access to secondary schools by the O'Malley proposals of 1966, the authorities and teachers in secondary schools found it difficult to respond in terms of the rhetoric which had dominated their policies for half a century. The idealism which had fired the early members of the ASTI and had influenced the Labour Party's *Policy on Education* of 1925, had been diminished and diluted by the crushing experience of its members serving in a school system where for many decades they enjoyed little security of tenure, where their consultative role was grudgingly acknowledged and where their salary structure and promotion prospects were dismal.

However once the association had overcome the major difficulties of the sixties and in particular, once the implications of the Ryan salary tibunal had been institutionally assimilated, the early seventies proved to be a watershed in the history of the ASTI. The secondary teachers derived the same collective psychological benefit from the 1969 strike and the associated controversies as their colleagues in the INTO derived from the unsuccessful strike of 1946. Since the early seventies the ASTI has grown in numerical strength, has been active in the Congress of Trade Unions, has cooperated closely with the other teacher organisations and has made substantial contributions to general education policy. It represents teachers in secondary, comprehensive and community schools, whereas formerly its remit was confined to secondary schools; the association in 1984 had over ten thousand members whereas fifty years earlier it had under three hundred and in the early sixties it still had as few as 1,200.

Its enlarged membership has both necessitated and facilitated a more sophisticated structure and professional staff; such a structure has provided a highly efficient negotiation service and has also enhanced the association's contribution to policy debates. On issues relating to working conditions and contractual rights, the ASTI has been active in negotiating redundancy schemes, revised contracts, and contracts for teachers in community schools; it has sought representation for teachers on boards of management of secondary schools where it sought equal representation for school authorities, parents and teachers. Arising from the growing radicalism of the association, issues and proposals arose in the seventies which would have seemed unthinkable to the typical ASTI members of the fifties; parent-teacher contact was one such question, in which the teachers sought a professional fee for their attendance at parent-teacher meetings. The association has secured substantial salary increases and fee increases for examination work in recent years and has rectified various anomalies in pension schemes which discriminated against female secondary teachers.

On general policy issues secondary teachers have contributed to the policy discussion on curricular reform, the modification of the examination system, the alignment of the primary and postprimary sectors and corporal punishment. It has been formally involved in a number of government committees and working groups including those on educational broadcasting, in-service education for teachers, adult education and transition from primary education. It has responded critically to the 1980 *White paper on educational development*, sought by negotiation to ameliorate the school effects of 1983 expenditure cuts, and has expressed lack of confidence in the Curriculum and Examination Board announced in 1984 because its membership included so few practising teachers.

When in December 1984, the association celebrated the seventy-fifth anniversary of its foundation with the publication of its history, it had ample reason to rejoice in its achievements. The education system in which it now plays such a prominent and effective role is far removed from the poorly endowed network of intermediate schools of 1909, in which its early members, enjoyed low status and were helpless to improve their conditions. The herculean efforts of the Association by which the professional status of its members was secured have contributed equally to modifying and modernising the system in which they serve.

The Teachers' Union of Ireland

Since 1955 most teachers in vocational schools, colleges of technology, regional technical colleges and the non-university sector generally are organised and represented by the Vocational Teachers' Association (VTA) which in 1973 changed its name to the Teachers Union of Ireland (TUI). Prior to the establishment of the VTA there had been two earlier organisations, the Association of Technical and Agricultural Officers, founded in the early years of the century and the Vocational Education Officers' Association which, following the Vocational Education Act of 1930, represented both officers and teachers of the vocational system. The succession and evolution of these various organisations were hastened by the growing awareness of the specific identity and educational role of the vocational system. The transitions were generally conducted without serious tension though in the mid-fifties sharp criticism by Dublin teachers of the negotiating capacity of the VEOA led to the formation of the VTA.[82] The continuity of these organisations is reflected in the general practice of dating the VTA and the present union to the original association founded for the staff of Horace Plunkett's Department of Agriculture and Technical Instruction.

The objects of the union embrace both conventional union activities and the prosecution of educational aims; these include the organisation of teachers, the improvement of their working conditions, the regulation of relationship of members to colleagues and to employers and the expression of the collective opinion of members on education issues.[83]

While the TUI and the VTA did not have to face a prolonged struggle similar to that endured by the ASTI in pursuit of basic contractual rights, issues bearing on working conditions have always enjoyed a priority with them. In the early fifties, salary levels, superannuation, arbitration and conciliation machinery and the specification of working conditions as contained in Memorandum V of the Department were of concern to the union in seeking to promote and protect the interests of their members.[84]

In defending the rights and employment conditions of teachers the Union has engaged in a few major controversies. The use of political patronage in teacher appointments was strongly condemned and in 1967 they succeeded in having the selection and appointment process

TABLE 5.1
The frequency of resolutions tabled at ASTI conventions on various topics
in the periods 1953-1964 and 1968-1978.

YEAR	Association Business	Employment Conditions	Curriculum & Examinations	Academic Issues	Irish Language	General Policy	Funding	Other Sectors
1953	13	13	5	1	1	3	1	—
1954	9	13	4	2	1	1	—	—
1956	6	14	4	4	—	—	—	—
1957	5	12	2	—	1	—	—	—
1958	3	6	5	—	—	1	—	1
1959	3	11	5	2	3	1	—	—
1961	13	18	8	1	1	—	—	1
1962	1	6	—	—	—	1	—	—
1963	1	5	—	2	1	—	—	—
1964	7	4	1	—	1	3	1	—
1953-64	61	102	34	12	9	10	2	1
YEAR	Association Business	Employment Conditions	Curriculum & Examinations	Academic Issues	Irish Language	General policy	Funding	Other Sectors
1968	6	6	—	—	—	3	—	—
1969	5	7	—	—	—	—	—	—
1970	3	6	1	1	—	—	2	—
1971	6	2	—	—	—	2	—	—
1972	4	7	—	—	—	3	—	1
1973	6	6	1	2	—	3	—	—
1974	9	5	4	1	2	2	—	—
1975	6	8	3	3	—	2	1	—
1976	9	5	4	5	1	1	—	—
1977	7	5	—	3	1	3	3	—
1978	4	9	4	2	—	5	—	—
1968-78	65	66	17	17	4	24	6	1

Source: Compiled by author.

regularised and modified accordingly.[85] When in 1967 the negotiating rights of the Union were questioned by the Co. Galway VEC, the association (VTA) initiated proceedings in the high court; the issue was resolved however out of court by the mediation of the Department of Education[86] A lengthy dispute in Co. Wexford, which lasted from 1956 to 1974 and provoked strikes in 1972 and 1974 and a special congress, was resolved by proposals entailing boards of management in each school.[87]

Over a number of years the Union has been concerned with the reform of teacher training for vocational teachers and urged the extension of training to three years, the raising of entry standards and the provision of a permanent training institution for the courses provided by the Department of Education.[88] The department accepted the proposals in principle and these were implemented with the establishment of Thomond College in Limerick in 1972. The Union was strongly in favour of the creation of a Council with responsibility for the teaching profession which would keep training requirements under review.[89] An earlier major proposal from the VTA involved the creation of an Institute of Education which would control, design and implement all training programmes for teachers both initial and inservice. This concept was again formally submitted to the Higher Education Authority in 1969 and was incorporated in its report on teacher education.[90]

With the expansion of the sixties and the growing convergence of secondary and vocational schools, the vocational teachers were deeply concerned with some aspects of the reforms. Equality of opportunity had been a frequent theme of policy especially in view of the absence of equality for the pupils in vocational schools who could not gain access to the universities. In 1959 a congress resolution directed the association to approach the universities with a view to securing admission for vocational pupils.[91] The following year the association's president advocated the establishment of regional technical schools which would enable vocational pupils to prepare for academic and technological higher education; scholarships and family grants should be provided and the association also recommended that vocational education be extended to 17 or 18 years of age.[92]

While concerned with the inequality of opportunity obtaining in vocational schools, the association was also worried about the dangers inherent in the vocational schools becoming weaker versions of the secondary schools; the president in 1961 warned that vocational schools should not become pale imitations of the secondary route to higher education. The traditional character of vocational education had to be conserved and in this spirit the Common Intemediate Certificate advocated by Dr Hillery in 1963 was opposed in favour of an extended Group Certificate which would become a Technical Intermediate.[93] It would appear that the general reforms of the sixties have diluted the character of vocational education somewhat, according to a former General Secretary of the VTA.[94]

The development of the community schools in 1970 and 1971 and especially the nature of the management board proposed by the Department of Education posed serious problems for the association. While the VTA welcomed and supported the central concept of the community schools, they rejected the management structure and resented the absence of consultation with all interested parties.[95] The teachers contended that the Minister's proposed structure would mean that the community schools would be owned and managed by the diocesan authorities. They proposed that vocational school interests and secondary school interests should have equal representation in management, that parent representatives should be elected not selected and that other interests from industry, commerce, farming and trade unions should also be represented.[96] The contribution by postprimary teachers to the policy process has been diminished somewhat by their relative numbers and their depressed status in the early decades; their influence was also constrained by the extent to which the system was dominated by the state and the churches. The expansion of the system over the past three decades and the associated modifications in the power structure have opened up the policy process so that it has begun to utilises the enhanced professionalism of a larger lay teaching profession.

TABLE 5.2

The numbers of lay secondary teachers (a) specified under the Birrell scheme 1914 for Catholic and Protestant schools separately and (b) the actual number of teachers employed in these schools for the years 1914-1924 during which the Birrell scheme operated.

YEAR	CATHOLIC SCHOOLS		PROTESTANT SCHOOLS	
	Pupils/40 (a)	Lay teachers employed (b)	Pupils/40 (a)	Teachers employed (b)
1914-15	300	46	137	237
1915-16	319	125	144	273
1916-17	330	164	149	295
1917-18	368	264	164	370
1918-19	369	318	161	407
1919-20	434	299	181	356
1920-21	415	240	183	381
1921-22	388	215	81	162
1922-23	394	230	79	172

Note: (i) The number given under (i) is one-fortieth of the total number of pupils in the group of schools.

(ii) The decrease in the figures from 1921-22 in relation to Protestant schools was caused by the large number of such schools which, under the Government Act of 1920, were henceforth subject to the Ministry of Eduaction in Northern Ireland.

Source: *Annual Reports*, Commissioners of Intermediate Education.

Chapter 6

The Managerial Bodies

A Complex Network

The managerial bodies are the representatives of those agencies, mostly church or church-related groups, which own and/or manage educational institutions at first and second levels; they constitute an organisational structure representing the interests of the providers of education. Due to the variety of school types, the gradations within religious groups, and the division by sex and denomination found in the school system, the number of managerial bodies is very large. In relation to secondary schools alone, there were in 1985 fourteen managerial bodies functioning and four umbrella groups. Parallel structures exist for the schools of both the Catholic and Protestant denominations at first and second levels and a third set exists for the vocational education system.

While the oldest of the managerial bodies were founded in the last century and derived their specific roles from the education structures of the period, many of the current bodies especially the significant umbrella groups concerned with secondary education, have come into existence in the period since the mid-fifties. Table 6.1 lists in chronological order the various managerial bodies for first and second level and summarises the interests represented by each body.

The early sixties constituted a major watershed in the history and evolution of the managerial bodies which is directly associated with the development of government policy and the extension of educational provision characterising that period. Prior to that period the managerial bodies which existed were denominationally specific, homogeneous in membership and operated mainly in an isolated fashion; while the bodies attached to the various major churches cooperated in a formal fashion on denominational lines, the degree of cohesion and alignment on policy issues was minimal. At the beginning of this century there were only three managerial bodies in existence, the Irish Schoolmasters' Association (1869), The Catholic Headmasters' Association (1879) and the Association of Irish Headmistresses (1882), all three concerned directly with Intermediate (or Secondary) education.[1] The uneasy relationship between the INTO and the Catholic hierarchy which characterised the turn of the century and the fears among national school managers which Starkie's amalgamation policy generated, led to the formation of the Catholic Primary Managers' Association in 1903. Surprisingly, the corresponding national body for Church of Ireland national schools, was not formally constituted until 1973, although some diocesan managerial structures operated prior to that date. The establishment in 1929 of the Conference of Convent Secondary Schools and the creation, on its initiative, of a similar body for primary schools, the Conference of Convent Primary Schools, in 1950, constituted significant additions to the growing managerial network.

The only lay managerial body in the secondary sector, The Federation of Lay Catholic Secondary Schools, was established in 1952 to represent the growing number of secondary schools conducted by lay Catholics. Finally the last of the homogeneous managerial groups, The Teaching Brothers' Association, emerged in 1965, with a mandate covering both primary and secondary education and representing those orders of religious brothers which conduct national or secondary schools.[2] Of the bodies listed so far two or three figured more prominently than the others in the period from 1900 to the early sixties; those were The Irish Schoolmasters' Association, The Catholic Headmasters' Association and The Conference of Convent Secondary Schools. Their history and their contribution to education policy merit closer examination.

The Irish Schoolmasters' Association

The Irish Schoolmasters' Association or the Schoolmasters' Association as it was initially known, owes its origins to a prominent educationalist, Maurice C. Hime, who in 1869, when Headmaster of the Diocesan School, Monaghan, invited some thirteen of his colleagues in endowed and private schools to meet in Dublin on 29 June 1869 with a view to planning an association.[3] The inaugural meeting took place in December 1869 when the following objectives were agreed:

(i)   to advance the interests of upper-class schools in Ireland;

(ii) to afford its members the advantage of mutual counsel and support.[4]

The second of its two objects was modified in 1916 to read: 'To advance the interests of secondary education in Ireland'.

Membership of the Association was initially confined to the headmasters of the (Protestant) diocesan schools and of the endowed grammar schools and to such headmasters of other schools who were university graduates and whose schools had been in existence for two years; from 1872 to 1905 assistant masters were eligible for membership provided they served in schools presided over by members of the association. A parallel organisation, the Association of Irish Headmistresses, founded in 1882, catered for the heads of similar girls' schools; the two organisations cooperated closely and members of the latter attended meetings of the Schoolmasters' Association as associates in the period from 1904 to 1941. In 1968 headmistresses were admitted to full membership of the ISA and while the principals of all girls' Protestant secondary schools are automatically offered membership of the Schoolmasters' Association, the Association of Irish Headmistresses still exists and is represented in the managerial network.

Since its foundation, the Irish Schoolmasters' Association has been actively involved in most of the developments in secondary or intermediate education and its voice has been heard on many of the educational issues surrounding such developments and on general policy. Being in existence prior to the Intermediate Education Act of 1878, it is not surprising that it was active in canvassing for such a measure and in attempting to influence its terms. The submissions by the association to the Chief Secretary in 1876 urging government action on intermediate education undoubtedly contributed to the preparation of the 1878 scheme but the claim by the association that the provisions in the Intermediate Act proceeded from suggestions by them, can hardly be upheld in view of the earlier work of Sir Patick Keenan and Sir Michael Hicks-Beach, the Chief Secretary.[5]

Following the passing of the Intermediate Act, the Schoolmasters' Association sought to unite all who were involved in secondary education by inviting the principals and heads of Catholic secondary schools and colleges to join their association; rejection of this invitation led in turn to the foundation in 1879 of the Catholic Headmasters' Association by Dr William J. Walsh of Maynooth.[6] Despite the reluctance to cross denominational boundaries, the two associations sometimes cooperated and by means of joint deputations to the Chief Secretary, exercised a significant influence on the administrative and curricular details of the Intermediate Act.

In the early years of this century the Schoolmasters' Association played an active part especially in seeking extra funding and structural reforms in the system. Following the foundation of the ASTI in 1909 the association, by resolution, affirmed its support for the claims of the lay secondary teachers and assured a deputation of the teachers of their support for the aims of the ASTI.[7] When Birrell proposed a scheme for primary to secondary school scholarships in 1911, the Schoolmasters' Association responded by arguing that measures to improve the status of secondary teachers by means of salary and pension schemes should have priority over scholarship schemes. When in 1912 Birrell proposed his scheme providing for a Teacher Registration Council and a salary grant on condition that schools would employ a certain ratio of registered lay teachers, the association strongly supported the scheme and the teachers, throughout the prolonged controversy which led eventually to the 1914 Intermediate Education Act.[8]

Perhaps the most outstanding policy proposal which emanated from the Schoolmasters' Association was contained in the document presented to the Chief Secretary in May 1917, a move very likely inspired by the Fisher reform measures introduced in Britain in the same year. This policy document advocated:

(i)   an improved funding from imperial funds for Irish education yielding amounts equivalent to those available to England and Scotland;

(ii)   the creation of a new structure for the system involving a minister and a department with responsibility for all branches coherently organised;

(iii) a new examination system;

(iv)   a school funding system based on a capitation principle;

(v)   a planning mechanism which could oversee and decide on the location of schools, establish the number required in a district, and foster and encourage different school types.[9]

It is not surprising that the Schoolmasters' Association strongly supported the Vice-Regal Committee (Molony) and its findings and gave equally staunch support to the McPherson bill based upon the same findings.

In the sharp controversy surrounding the 1919 Bill, the association was to the forefront in defence of the reform measure; in its campaign it secured the support of the Irish Headmistresses' Association, convened special meetings, passed trenchant resolutions which it forwarded to the Chief Secretary and sought the support of a special delegation of the British Labour Party which visited Dublin in January 1920[10] The defeat of McPherson's bill created a significant residue of disillusion and alienation among the association and in the Protestant schools generally. With the change of administration in 1922, the ranks of the association were depleted by partition and the enthusiasm of its members for the education policies of the new state was diminished.

Though the period from 1922 to the mid-fifties witnessed a decline in the level of activity of the Schoolmasters' Association, nevertheless its voice was never silent for any lengthy period especially on curricular policy. While it fully supported the claims of the ASTI on employment conditions, the issues of tenure and contract, which dominated teacher/manager relations in the Catholic schools in the decades following independence, were of no direct relevance to the schools of the Association in which satisfactory employment terms had been already established.

The association advocated with a sustained voice the curricular importance of modern languages; it bemoaned the fact that as few as 13% of candidates in boys' schools offered a modern language in the Intermediate Certificate of 1930.[11] During the same period the association made a plea for reform of the examination system, involving abolition of the Intermediate Certificate and the development of the Leaving Certificate along the lines of the French Baccalaureate.[12] Undoubtedly the curricular question which most stirred the association was the role of the Irish language; its officials and spokesmen maintained that the policy of compulsory Irish militated against other subjects especially other modern European languages.[13] When in 1926 the department announced its intention to require that Irish be taken as an essential subject in the Intermediate certificate in and after 1928 the association protested by resolution and repeated similar protests annually to 1929.[14]

When a deputation went to meet the new Fianna Fáil minister in 1932, its members were assured by Tomás Deirg that his policy had the support of both the political parties and the will of the people; he could not promise any general concession but individual schools could make appropriate representations which would be considered by the department. Deirg further asserted that if the headmasters and headmistresses had been genuinely supportive of government policy there should be more progress to show as a result; his department was in the position of financing schools which did not take Irish seriously. Nevertheless, the minister did grant a concession whereby one or more pupils could be exempted from the requirement of taking Irish as an essential subject, in schools where suitable provision was already made for the teaching of the language. This question lingered on as an issue and surfaced spasmodically up to the fifties; it would appear that while the association and its related school authorities were assuring the department that they were favourable to the language and would make every reasonable effort to meet department requirements, the department and its senior officials were not at all convinced on the matter.[15]

By the middle of the fifties curricular matters had ceased to be an issue of major concern for the association; the future pattern of Protestant secondary education was emerging as a crucial question. The officers of the association had already sensed the need to formulate a rational and coherent education policy for the scattered Protestant population in an era when the future of some of their secondary schools seemed doubtful. In his presidential address in October 1956, P. J. Southgate issued an inspiring challenge to his colleagues urging them to galvanise themselves into coherent action on behalf of secondary education for the minority denominations. He rejected forcefully the appeal to minority privilege and appealed to the members in the following terms:

> The welfare of the schools is not the concern of a few individuals but a duty laid upon our community as a whole. Our hope of survival depends on our ability to combine. It seems to me that we are a proper body to take the lead in such a campaign.

These dynamic words proved prophetic of the manner in which Protestant education policy has moved in the last two decades; it sought rationalisation and cohesion in structure and provision and did so within the context of emerging government policy. In a later section of this chapter these developments will be described and the relevant role of the Schoolmasters' Association outlined.

The Catholic Headmasters' Association

For most of the period since its foundation the Catholic Headmasters' Association has been the most prominent and influential of the bodies repesenting the interests of secondary schools; from 1922 to the early sixties, it was seen as the major voice representing the educational views of Catholic secondary schools. The association secured that prominent position by virtue of its origins in the passing of the Intermediate Act of 1878, by means of the many eminent clerical leaders who guided its destiny and by the absence before 1929 of any organised body representing convent secondary schools. Thus for the first half century of its existence the CHA represented and negotiated on behalf of all the Catholic secondary schools except those conducted by the Irish Christian Brothers; even after the formation of the Conference of Convent Secondary Schools the male association continued as the dominant body at least until the early sixties.

When the Intermediate Act of 1878 was introduced, relations between the major churches, especially in the education field, were coloured by mutual mistrust and sharp competition. The basic competitive nature of the principle underlying the Intermediate grants scheme i.e. 'payment-by-results' did nothing to diminish that distrust. With a view to maximising the benefit to Catholic colleges under the act, Dr William J. Walsh of Maynooth wrote in September 1878 to the bishops, suggesting that a conference should be held of 'the heads or representatives of all those Catholic schools or colleges which are under ecclesiastical management'.[16] In doing so he envisaged the objects of such a conference as follows:

(i) the mutual exchange of ideas as to teaching methods, textbooks and special training to meet the requirements of the new examination;

(ii)   the alignment of the content of the entrance examination to Maynooth with that of the new system;

(iii) careful consideration of the new Act;

(iv)   the formation of a standing committee;

(v)   establising liaision with leading book publishers.

It is of interest to note that Dr Walsh in his letter to the bishops was at pains to indicate that such a conference would not alter the existing balance of power in Irish Catholic education; he did not contemplate 'any arrangement which would have the effect of placing any control-ling power in the hands either of the conference itself or of the stand-ing committee'.[17] This feature of the foundation of the association was an early indicator of the sensitive nature of the relationship which would exist between the CHA and the hierarchy.[18]

The early concern of the association with the mechanics of the examination system, introduced by the 1878 act is central to its activities in the early decades. As early as 1881 we find Dr Walsh writing to the press as chairman of the CHA, outlining in great detail 'the marvellous success of our Catholic Intermediate schools and colleges in the examinations of this year'.[19] The number of exhibi-tions, of gold medals and the aggregate marks, as well as the very crucial total money prizes, are quoted to show 'that the victory of the Catholic schools must be accepted as an established fact in any discussion which may take place in parliament or elsewhere on the removal of the religious inequality which at present exists in matters of even secular education in Ireland'. So committed were the Catholic schools to the Intermediate competitive examination system that when in 1883 they introduced a national programme for religious instruction for the secondary schools they modelled its examination system on the Intermediate plan. Amidst a rising tide of criticism of the worst excesses of competitive examinations, the association in the same year expressed its total satisfaction with the system which had a 'beneficial influence on education' and which far from encouraging 'cramming', 'could not fail to be a splendid training for life'.[20]

In the first two decades of this century while the curricular issues arising from the examination system continued to be of concern to the CHA, more sensitive policy questions arose concerning the employ-ment conditions of lay teachers and measures to restructure the system upon which the association took a coherent, firm and active stance. This cohesion was forged mainly though the association's journal, *The Irish Educational Review*, which flourished from 1907 to 1914 under the editorship of Fr Andrew Murphy of Limerick, the secretary of the association; the association's policies received consistent support also from the Bishop of Limerick, Dr O'Dwyer.

From the establishment of the ASTI in 1909, the CHA while wholeheartedly espousing the salary and pensions claims of the teachers, was decidedly opposed to recognising the claim of lay teachers to security of tenure in secondary schools, owned and managed by clergy and religious orders; the association was equally negative in regard to the teachers' demand for a professional register.[21] These latter issues were central to the measures proposed by Birrell in 1912 'to raise the status of the lay teacher'; this scheme proposed to make contractual provision, at a stipulated salary, for a number of lay teachers linked to the number of pupils in each school. The Catholic Headmasters' Association saw Birrell's scheme as 'an attack on the autonomy of the schools'; the association's *Review* described the measures as tantamount to the forcible confiscation of church schools 'as practised by the anticlerical governments of France and Portugal'.[22]

The eventual outcome of the Birrell controversy, the Irish Education Act of 1914, constituted a major victory for the CHA, a victory however which merely extended the stuggle between the ASTI and the association into the decades following independence, especially in relation to the crucial issue of tenured contractual employment.

In each of the education controversies surrounding the reform measures of 1904, 1907 and 1919, the Catholic managerial bodies were ranged in total opposition to the Protestant managerial bodies who supported the structural changes. In the controversy surrounding the McPherson Bill of 1919, the interdenominational antagonism was deepened further and the hostility sharpened to the point of animosity. The Catholic Headmasters' Association was confirmed in its dominant position within the education structure by the retention of the *status quo* and by the continuing depressed status of teachers following the strike of 1920.

In the decades following independence the CHA was almost totally occupied in seeking an acceptable solution to the major question of the contractual employment conditions for lay teachers. While some issues relating to this question were still unresolved in the sixties and seventies the question was settled for the most part by the agreement on appeal procedures of 1936 and the agreement on contracts of 1940. Throughout the period of negotiation leading to the 1940 solution relations between the association and the secondary teachers were frequently strained and were sometimes at breaking point. On those rarer occasions of joint action, as in the conference of 1921 and the joint deputation of managerial bodies and teachers of May 1924, making a plea for higher levels of state funding for schools and salaries for teachers, the apparent harmony cannot have been extensive. Whereas the teachers claimed that education was a state service and the conditions of employment a matter of public policy and control, the CHA rejected such a claim and contended that no independent or state-appointed arbitrator could be tolerated in cases of dismissal. Furthermore, according to the CHA, secondary teachers, as employees of private institutions, could not expect the state or other public authority to interfere by arbitration or enforced contract; this question had been settled at least for the Commissioners of Intermediate Education in 1921 by the legal advice which they received, a development which was known alike to the CHA and the ASTI.[23] The only acceptable appeal mechanism was that based upon ecclesiastical practice, involving appeal to a bishop or to a religious major superior. When the CHA refused to concede to the teachers the right to be represented by their association at such appeal procedures, it was claimed that they were departing from a practice and denying a right which are central to all ecclesiastical procedures.

There is one strange aspect to the CHA/ASTI negotiations on security of tenure in the delay in bringing the matter to a conclusion following the 1927 synod. While the issue as far as the bishops and the managers were concerned had been settled in the statutes of the National Synod of 1927, negotiations with the teachers were carried on until 1936 before yielding a settlement based upon those very same statutes. It is difficult to establish to what extent if any, the officers of the CHA were free agents in this question; it seems certain that the bishops played a very active, if vicarious, role. It is possible also that there was disunity within the CHA, based upon the diocesan and religious order priests. This question of tenure for lay secondary teachers was of no great importance to the diocesan colleges which seldom employed them; it was however of immediate concern to both the bishops from a national ecclesiastical perspective and to the religious orders of priests on an institutional basis. While the religious order members of the CHA sought an early resolution, the diocesan members were more likely to sanction only a settlement which was in total conformity with the 1927 ecclesiastical statutes. In this context it may be of some significance that it was a member of a religious order, Dr J. C. McQuaid C.S.Sp., of Blackrock College, who, as chairman of the CHA, conducted the negotiations leading to the 1936 agreement.

In the negotiations on security of tenure the absence from the table of the Department of Education is of basic significance. Given his deeply-held and frequently expressed views on the role of the state in education, it is not surprising that as minister, Eoin MacNeill, should eschew all responsibility for involvement and participation in the CHA/ASTI negotiations on security of tenure. The various appeals by the teachers to the minister were rejected on the grounds that no initiative should come from him; the request by the teachers for him to act as mediator was similarly refused.[24] When pressed in 1923 by the teachers as to his obligations as minister concerning an independent appeal board, MacNeill's reaction was to consult the Catholic hierarchy who were on record as being opposed in principle to any appeal board other than an ecclesiastical one. His successors as minister, John Marcus O'Sullivan and Tomás Deirg followed identical lines of policy. The outcome of such policies was to weaken further the already weak position of the lay teachers and to strengthen the position of the CHA as the dominant, if not the sole, authority in this sector of education policy. When MacNeill asserted in the Dáil:

> The mere fact that the religious bodies state an objection is all sufficient, since it is not for the minister or anybody else to question whether it is well-based or not,

he was articulating a principle in tune with his own published opinions, by which supremacy was guaranteed to the education policies advocated by the Catholic Headmasters' Association and the other church bodies.[25] The other basic issue arising from such a statement concerning the minister's political responsibility in the democratic political process is examined later in the context of the role of the Minister for Education.[26]

The dominance of the CHA in the formulation of policy continued undisturbed until the early sixties when its role was modified by the creation of a more elaborate managerial network in which other bodies especially the Convent Conference and the TBA emerged. In the intervening decades no great policy issues arose in the secondary sector other than routine questions of a curricular nature and the unfinished business relating to contracts, dismissals and the basic salary of lay teachers; the fragmentation within the managerial bodies frequently caused difficulties in negotiation and a diminished cohesion in policy in the fifties.[27] The *modus operandi* employed by the association involved a small number of general meetings per year held in Dublin, between which a standing committee conducted the business of the association and was consulted by the Department of Education. The Dublin-based members of this standing committee were in close contact with the department and with teacher and other organisations and so were in a position to function effectively on behalf of their members. However, the efficacy and influence of a body with such an informal functional mechanism was greatly enhanced by the prestige and status of its various chairmen and secretaries.[28] At various stages in its recent history the association was presided over by such prominent and experienced presidents as Dr Fergal McGrath S. J., Dr J. C. McQuaid, C.S.Sp., Dr D. Cregan, C.M. and Fr John Hughes, S. J. Despite the agreements on security of tenure and contracts negotiated by 1940, many issues impinging on the contractual employment conditions continued to occupy the centre of the stage. In the mid-forties the convent schools sought to extend the probation period of young teachers to three years, the ASTI sought to retain the *status quo* of one year while the CHA favoured a two year probation.[29] When the issue was finally decided in 1947 the decision to support a two-year probation was taken by the CHA at the behest of the bishops. On the question of issuing contracts to lay teachers, it would seem that the CHA adhered more rigidly to the agreed procedures than their colleagues in the convent schools as is evident from the frequent complaints by the ASTI.[30] Whereas a general agreement concerning a common contract was negotiated in 1956 by all the Catholic managerial bodies there is evidence to indicate that some convent schools throughout the fifties and sixties did not issue any contracts of employment.[31]

The basic salary paid by the school to recognised secondary teachers may not appear to be a significant issue in education policy; indeed to the recipients and to most managers it always did seem insignificant in amount! However it retained a residual significance in the managerial viewpoint as symbolising the employment link between teacher and school even when the state paid the bulk of the salary. Various attempts were made to have the total teacher salary paid by the state, a development which, though favoured by the bishops, was totally rejected by the CHA[32]. A related move by the Association, seeking to have the amount of the basic salary paid by the schools determined by Department regulation, was just as firmly resisted by the Department.

It may appear that the CHA involvement in policy was mainly concerned with managerial questions of salary, contractual arrangements and issues arising from teacher dismissals. However, these issues were the squalls and perturbations upon a sea which was more regularly traversed by the routine merchant shipping of annual examinations and curricular content. The most constant interactions with the Department concerned the standard of the examinations, the results, the content of courses and the regulations governing subject choice, the weighting of subjects, teacher quotas and the school timetable. Perhaps the most significant curricular change introduced in secondary education was the reversion to specified texts in language courses in 1940. The 'open' courses, with no prescribed texts, were introduced in 1924 as a direct reaction to the grinding text-ridden 'murder machine'.[33] By the mid-thirties the schools were finding it very difficult to cope with the demanding courses and frequent requests were made by the managerial bodies for a return to 'the prescribed texts approach'. The change was introduced by Mr de Valera during his term as Minister for Education in 1940.[34]

Surprisingly the significant influence exercised by the CHA in the area of policy is disproportionate to the number of the secondary schools represented by the association; in 1980 it represented 12% or 61 out of a total of over 500 Catholic secondary schools and only a third of boy's schools. Of the 61 schools represented in the CHA, 32 are conducted by priests of religious orders, 28 are diocesan colleges and one is conducted by Opus Dei. The distribution of schools by religious group and managerial organisation is outlined in Table 6.2.

However, the size of its constituency in the secondary sector is overshadowed by the central role which the CHA has played and still plays as a leading element among the Catholic managerial bodies. For many decades it and the Irish Christian Brothers were the only Catholic managerial bodies consulted by the educational authorities. It was through the initiative of the CHA that the convent secondary schools achieved corporate representation in the Conference of Convent Secondary Schools and for many decades after 1929 the conference's orientation was closely influenced by the CHA. Though there have been sixteen different orders in memberhip of the CHA over the decades, its dominant leadership has been drawn from three or four orders, especially the Jesuits, the Vincentians and the Holy Ghost Fathers. Some eminent members of those orders by their personal stature and their involvement in the association have enabled it to influence educational thinking and to contribute to national policy. Such influence and contributions have been augmented significantly by the close personal friendship between the CHA leaders and prominent politicians.[35]

In the exercise of its functions the CHA would seem to have been hindered if not frustrated at times by the knowledge that on the central issues of policy, a superior body, the hierarchy, was operating in the same field, a situation rendered all the more sensitive by the existence within the CHA of religious orders whose authority structure was independent of episcopal rule.[36] It would seem that this phenomenon contributed somewhat to the confusion surrounding the Catholic managerial reaction to the innovative policies of the sixties; it may also have catalysed the complex structural changes which emerged in the managerial bodies. Those changes which constitute a veritable metamorphosis among the Protestant as well as the Catholic bodies will be studied later in this chapter after an examination of the origins and contributions of the Conference of Convent Secondary Schools.

The Conference of Convent Secondary Schools

Representing the biggest category of secondary schools, those conducted by nuns, the Conference of Convent Secondary Schools was formally established in 1929 following an invitation to schools from the Department of Education to participate in a review of examination standards. Prior to that date however, the convent secondary schools had acted collectively on a number of occasions, usually in collaboration with the Catholic Headmasters' Association. The earliest such occasion would appear to have been in 1904 when the Irish Schoolmasters' Association and the Catholic Headmasters' Association urged the Commissioners of Intermediate Education to establish a schools' consultative committee to enable the heads of schools to communicate their views on the programme and subject syllabus.[37] In the Birrell controversy of 1912 the CHA and the convent secondary schools issued a joint statement opposing the scheme as outlined by the Chief Secretary. When in 1929 the Department of Education wished to establish a mechanism whereby the annual examinations could be monitored by committees representative of the secondary schools, there was no corporate body in existence representing the convent secondary schools.[38] With a view to solving this problem a senior official of the department, Dr W. F. Butler approached the Prioress of the Dominicans and sought her good offices in persuading the heads of a few of the more important convent schools, the Ursulines, the St. Louis and Loreto orders, to participate in the meeting which would establish the various subject committees.[39] Representatives of the Dominican, Ursuline and St. Louis orders met and on the advice of the Archbishop of Dublin, proceeded to organise the inaugural meeting of the conference to which the heads of all convent secondary schools were invited. This meeting took place on 25 May when representatives of fourteen religious orders from eighty four secondary schools met under the chairmanship of Dr Cullen C.M., representing the Archbishop of Dublin. The Rules of the Conference as adopted in 1929 were based directly upon those of the Catholic Headmasters' Association and included the following objectives:

(i)   to watch over Catholic interests in all matters concerning our schools and to take such steps as may be considered advisable to ensure the due consideration of such interests;

(ii) to facilitate the interchange of ideas and information in all school matters e.g. teaching, examinations, internal management and organisation generally.[40]

In its formation and in its early years the conference was closely linked to the CHA; indeed throughout the half century of its existence both organisations were, with few exceptions, at one on most policy issues. This close collaboration has at times appeared almost as a form of domination, which in the decades before Vatican II was considered to be the normal ecclesiastical lot of female religious. In the early decades the conference would not respond to any departmental initiative or undertake any negotiations independent of the CHA. In 1946 two members of the CHA were commissioned by the bishops to investigate the salaries paid to lay teachers in convent secondary schools subsequent to a memorandum on the subject being sent to the bishops by the conference. As late as 1962 the conference declined an invitation to make a submission to the Commission on Higher Education but indicated that they supported the submission already made by the CHA. Up to recent years the annual meeting of the conference was presided over by a senior clerical nominee of the Archbishop of Dublin and the conference was usually represented at foreign conferences by members of the CHA. The link between the

Conference and the hierarchy was further strengthened by the effective support of Archbishop McQuaid and of Dr Lyons, Bishop of Kilmore, whose sister, Mother Reginald, was a founding member and president of the conference for sixteen years.

Such dependence however did not seem to inhibit the conference in its deep involvement in every aspect of Irish education; of the Catholic management bodies it has displayed the highest level of corporate and organisational energy and has published the most detailed reports of its activities. The Conference now represents a membership of two hundred and eighty five secondary schools conducted by thirty seven different orders. Initially the president and standing committee of the conference were elected on an institutional or order basis, with each elected order subsequently nominating a member to the committee. In 1961 provincial branches of the conference were founded and this led in turn to the establishment in 1966 of a central executive committee composed of delegates of the various branches. In 1976 the earlier standing committee was restored, based upon individual not institutional representation.[41] If the conference was heavily dependent on male clerical direction it certainly was not reluctant to offer its own members a very decisive brand of leadership. From the beginning it was enshrined in its charter that members were to have no interaction with the Department of Education or with other bodies except through the conference. A departure from that practice in 1949 drew a rather sharp admonition from the president.[42]

The conference during much of its early decades of activity was concerned with those same issues which had locked the CHA and the ASTI in frequent combat, security of tenure and conditions of employment; as soon as these were resolved by the CHA the solution was made available to the conference and the convent schools on similar if not identical terms. It would appear that at times some convent schools departed from the agreements as to contracts and procedures which had been formally entered into; in 1950 the cases brought to the attention of the standing committee by the ASTI showed so much lack of clarity as to procedures that the president thought it necessary to circulate a document outlining the arrangements to be followed.[43]

Among the issues which concerned the conference over the decades many belong to the realm of routine educational adminstration and school organisation such as staffing, courses, examinations, and finance. Other issues while seeming at the time to be of major importance to the conference members would seem at this distance, to have been of minor significance; the mild unsuitability of a prescribed French text in 1949 or the support for a proposal by the department in 1946 that science should merit higher marks represent this type of issue. The latter proposal was opposed by the CHA on grounds that it posed a threat to the classics in boys' schools.[44]

There are a number of issues in the proceedings of the conference which, though not of direct relevance to the central questions in educational policy, do throw valuable light on the period. In the thirties Catholic convents were discouraged from participating in the annual Dublin Feis Cheoil because some of its competitions were held in the Metropolitan Hall, a Protestant premises decorated with scriptural extracts and regarded as 'an environment so distasteful to their feelings'.[45] In 1946 the Conference protested very strongly against those sections of the Public Health Bill, then before the Dáil, under which a school medical service was proposed for secondary school pupils; its letter of protest, addressed directly to Éamon deVal-era, claimed that the sections referred to represented a 'serious infringement of the natural rights of parents and of the liberty both of the family and of the school' and that 'compulsory medical inspection of girls especially those of adolescent age is altogether undesirable'.[46] In 1961 the conference supported a campaign initiated at the request of Archbishop McQuaid 'to check the growing lack of reticence' and especially the use of life-size models in the shop windows of Dublin.[47] Questions of personal liability for the payment of income tax were raised frequently in the conference; when demands were received from the Revenue Commissioners for school accounts to be furnished in 1952, the move was interpreted as a counter to the claim by the secondary schools for increased capitation grants.[48]

The major educational issues of policy which exercised the conference arose mainly during the forties and can be construed as revolving round the role of the state in education, the suitability of the secondary curriculum, and the growth of the vocational system. In 1943 the conference members established an internal commission charged with critically examining the existing educational system as to aims, curricular provision and examination demands; this commission consisted of three members, one each from the Dominican, Sacred Heart and St. Louis orders.[49] Reporting back in 1945, in a series of papers presented to the annual meeting, the commission found that the education imparted in girls' secondary schools was dominated by the economic factor, was conditioned as to content and method by the requirements of the examination system and was evaluated mainly in terms of examination success. Specifically the commission found that the secondary curriculum was 'designed for boys in preparation for university work, was over-intellectual and bookish'.[50] It also found that such a programme prevented the schools from serving the needs and best interests of their pupils by training them for the 'real work of life' as woman, wife and mother.

A growing percentage of the girls in secondary schools were seen as 'definitely not satisfactory'; they were 'light, irresponsible, pleasure-loving, ready to follow the latest fashion and lacking in womanly dignity and reserve'.[51] As a solution the conference proposed that an alternative course be available for girls throughout the secondary system in which special emphasis would be laid on home-making subjects which would foster 'those qualities of head and heart that will fit a girl to fulfil her function as wife and mother'.[52] The conference further proposed that there should be two Leaving Certificate courses, one to cater for the intellectual 20% and the other designed for the needs of the majority. The examination process for the latter course would include as an essential element a certificate of personal reliability and efficiency awarded by the school authorities, based on records kept by the school.[53]

This concern among the members of the conference with a fundamental restructuring of the postprimary system may have been partly occasioned by the postwar reforms in the United Kingdom and in Northern Ireland. When at the 1945 annual meeting, representatives of the Northern Conference of Convent Schools lectured on postwar educational planning in Northern Ireland, the members expressed great interest in the concepts of 'equal opportunity for all' and the extension of secondary education to all.[54] The new northern postprimary structure of Junior and Senior Secondary Schools would seem to have appealed to those among the conference who had earlier advocated a restructured Leaving Certificate. The president however was more cautious; she advised her members to study the various new schemes being advocated 'so that they may be in a position to offer sound criticism if the department proposes any changes in our present system'.[55]

In 1947 the standing committee of the conference reported on three issues which it regarded as of major importance:

(i)   the growing tendency of the government to assume control of education;

(ii)   the growth of lay schools;

(iii) the growing dissatisfaction with the present scheme of education.[56]

The tendency of the government to assume control was associated, in the eyes of the conference, with a department requirement as to the necessary qualifications of secondary teachers, the inspection of junior primary schools by department inspectors and especially with the growth of vocational education.

When in 1946 the ASTI urged the conference to appoint only 'qualified' secondary teachers in their schools (i.e. those holding a degree and a postgraduate diploma) and sent a memorandum to the bishops on the question, the conference rejected the claim that in a Catholic school a degree is the most important qualification for a teacher. According to the conference, religious, moral and social convictions, were of much greater import, for the possession of which a degree gives no assurance.[57] The CHA and the Conference declared jointly in 1947 that they would hold to the practice of placing on their staffs teachers whom they considered qualified, whether they possessed a degree or not.

The controversy over the inspection of private junior schools arose following the 1942 School Attendance Act under which schools were required to get from the Department a certificate of suitability. Throughout 1946 and 1947 complaints were received from convents that private junior schools, hitherto not subject to inspection of any kind, were visited by department inspectors. While the department disclaimed all responsibility for the development, the conference consulted the bishops, legal opinion was sought on the 1942 Act, and the state was reminded that it had only a delegated authority in education from the family and the church; the policy of the conference was to refuse to allow the state to inspect private primary schools.[58]

Perhaps the issue which most clearly reveals the mood of concern among conference members in the forties was the question of vocational education. The Education estimate for 1947/48 contained provision, under the vocational vote, for the building of one hundred new schools. This prompted an immediate alarm among the CCSS, the CHA and the ASTI; all three bodies were of the opinion that similar provision should be made for secondary schools.[59] At the 1947 annual meeting the conference devoted a special session to the issue of the vocational school 'which has become a cause of grave anxiety to those interested in the future of religion in this country'.[60] The members saw these schools as filling a real need and the education they provided as suited to the majority of boys and girls; the vocational school corresponded to the junior secondary in Northern Ireland and 'must form part of any new educational scheme'. The defects which the members perceived in the vocational schools were as follows:

(i) they were strictly lay schools, staffed completely by lay men and women, giving education to boys and girls in the same classroom;

(ii) they were conducted on a principle of free discipline;

(iii) they were staffed by teachers who were, for all practical purposes civil servants and whose positions were dependent neither on pupil numbers nor examination results.

A scheme such as the vocational system was thought to be admirably suited to adults whose minds and characters are formed but for children in the impressionable years of early adolescence, it could not but have disastrous results. In addition the scant knowledge of religion possessed by the pupils was a cause of alarm to the clergy.[61]

When examining the government's intention to build one hundred new vocational schools and to raise the school leaving age to 15, the conference foresaw as immediate consequences that the pupil numbers in primary and secondary schools would decrease and 'that the secularisation of education will progress still further'.[62] It agreed that secondary education of the intellectual type was not suited to the majority of pupils who attended their own schools. But this solution of building more vocational schools did nothing 'to solve the grave problem of how the pupils in vocational schools were to be made good Catholics, strong in the faith, ready and able not only to live but to die, if need be'.

'The only satisfactory answer', as the conference saw it, 'was to scrap the vocational system as at present administered, turn the existing schools into schools for adult education . . . and then start the vocational system over again on new and thoroughly Catholic lines'. The conference regarded it as amazing that since Ireland was a Catholic country and with 95% of the population Catholic, 'we could not have a Catholic system of education'. As a practical outcome of this debate the conference suggested that secondary schools should build 'vocational blocks' as additions to their premises and that vocational sections be added to national schools as 'vocational tops'. One of the immediate outcomes of this unusual discussion was that the question of seeking state aid for the building of secondary schools was raised again. While the Irish Christian Brothers agreed with the ASTI proposal of seeking state building loans, the CCSS and the CHA were slow to seek any aid which might give the state too much control over education. Among the long-term outcomes from these issues of concern to the conference was the growth of collaboration and consultation between the Catholic secondary managerial bodies, the CCSS, the CHA and the Irish Christian Brothers, a development which foreshadowed the alliances and reorganisation attempted in 1958 but not achieved until the sixties.

One other issue from the late forties was the establishment in 1949 by Richard Mulcahy of the long-promised Council of Education. The announcement by the Minister of his intention at Easter 1948 caused the CCSS and the CHA to devote their April meetings to the question. While agreeing with the concept of a body of expert advice being available to the Minister, the CCSS thought that 'one of the dangers of such a Council would be the inclusion amongst its members of persons of different religions'. The President of the CHA, Dr Kennedy C.S.Sp., arranged to consult theologians on the issue and also to see the Minister so that he could make a mature statement on the question.[63] When in June the Minister for Education addressed the annual meeting of the CCSS, he devoted much of his address to the Council of Education and to its role as he envisaged it. 'What is wanted', he stated 'is a council which will recognise and proclaim the Catholic philosophy upon which our Irish system is based, the rights of parents, the church, the State'.[64] When he had assured the conference that the Catholic hierarchy had already sanctioned the council and had particularly approved of its being advisory, non-representative and having no function in relation to finance, one would expect that total acceptance of his proposal by the assembled CCSS members was guaranteed. However, in the discussion which followed, 'several members expressed doubts as to the utility or advisability of a Council of Education in which members of different denominations participated'.[65]

In conclusion, it is worth recalling a statement by the president of the English Association of Convent Schools, when addressing the 1949 meeting of the CCSS. She described, with a detectable note of envy, the role of the conference in Irish education in the following words:

> It is wonderful to see the power that you have in education. In fact, the nuns have all power to guide and control educational policy. You have the Education Department in the hollow of your hands. [66]

The validity of such an assessment of the influence of the Convent Conference especially in the early decades of the state, is open to question; the dominance of the CHA and the absence of structures which would guarantee the nuns a voice in proportion to their numbers, were inhibiting factors. The educational expansion of the sixties however and the growing spirit of sexual equality enabled them to participate more fully in the new managerial structures which they helped to create; in the past decade or two these new structures have enabled them to play a major innovative role in postprimary education.

Complex Developments in the Sixties

The elaboration of policy in the sixties and the various measures promoted by the state under its general policy of extending educational opportunity involved a major change in the environment in which the managerial bodies operated. The manner in which the various organisations reacted and responded to these government measures reflected, especially among the Catholic bodies, not only the fundamental educational ethos characterising each organisation, but the emerging liberating influences abroad in Irish Catholicism in the sixties and the relationship of each managerial body to the guiding influence of the hierarchy. Before examining the specific issues which arose, there are some general tendencies to be observed in the managerial bodies which began early in the sixties and continued throughout the seventies.

The most pronounced tendency involved the growth of umbrella groups of various kinds, both among Catholic and Protestant bodies, a tendency which while conferring cohesion and efficiency on previously incoherent structures, nevertheless signified a strong centralisation of power in national high-level ecclesiastical bodies. Such a process of centralisation was already partially in existence in the major Protestant church; its establishment among the Catholic bodies was not achieved without deep and sometimes sharp controversy and a prolonged power struggle mainly between the managerial bodies and the bishops.

In an era when for the first time a major increase in public educational resources was proposed the managerial bodies sought to strengthen and improve their capacity to engage in effective negotiations with the state. Whereas formerly their interactions with the minister and department involved relatively minor issues, the policies of the sixties raised questions of central importance such as equal access to education, the relationship of the minister to the private secondary schools, the acceptability of vocational education and the implications of building grants being available to secondary schools. The search among the bodies for increased leverage and mutual strength impelled them to a greater cooperation even across denominational lines, catalysed the formation of central secretariats and the creation in 1964 of a Joint Managerial Body to represent all the managerial associations responsible for secondary schools.

Perhaps the most significant, if least obvious, change concerned the major shifts in power which occurred in some of the associations. The Conference of Convent Secondary Schools appeared to be less dependent upon the Catholic Headmasters' Association for guidance and direction in policy matters and functioned more as an equal than as a dependent relative. The emergence of a strong internal leadership in the CCSS significantly strengthened its contribution to policy, a contribution which on occasions was resented and regarded as assertive by some members of the CHA. This change of leadership style within the convent conference was accompanied by a definite shift in the balance of power; traditionally the conference was dominated by those orders whose schools, while few in number, enjoyed a high social prestige. Of the 285 secondary schools run by the 37 different orders or congregations, 230 schools are conducted by 8 of the orders of which group, the Mercy and Presentation Sisters are the most numerous with 160 schools. The shift in power within the conference represented a greater voice for the provinces and for those orders whose schools had traditionally provided education for the masses; the growing influence of the Presentation Sisters and Sisters of Mercy may also reflect the growth of the influence of other members of the hierarchy as the power of Archbishop McQuaid declined. Within the CHA while no major structural change occurred, the established rift between the diocesan colleges and the religious orders would seem to have been confirmed, if not intensified, by the formation of a separate informal body within the CHA, the Association of Diocesan Colleges.

The general realignment of power and influence within the managerial bodies was emphasised by the emergence of one new body, The Teaching Brothers' Association in 1965, and the growing influence of the existing Federation of Lay Catholic Secondary Schools. These two bodies require some comment and description at this point.

The Teaching Brothers' Association

Of the 120 secondary schools conducted by religious orders of brothers, 85 are conducted by the Irish Christian Brothers, 17 by the de La Salle Brothers and 8 by the Patrician Brothers; the other 10 schools are conducted by Presentation (5), Marist (2), Marianist (2) and Franciscan (1) Brothers. Most of these orders had been members of the CHA with the exception of the Irish Christian Brothers; the latter through their own Education Committee had been one of the managerial bodies consulted by central government and educational authorities throughout the century and had figured in most of the commissions and education conferences.[67] In the thorny issues surrounding the ASTI campaign for security of tenure and forms of contract, the Christian Brothers tended to adopt a line of policy independent of that followed by the CHA; they favoured and followed a one year probation period for secondary teachers whereas the CHA and the CCSS favoured two or three years. In the sixties when the question of basic salary became an issue, their formula linking the basic salary by ratio to total salary was accepted in 1964 and imposed by episcopal direction on the other managerial bodies. Their representatives were directly involved with those of the CHA and the CCSS in establishing the Joint Managerial Body in 1964, an effort to provide one coherent negotiating body representing all secondary schools, Catholic and Protestant.[68]

In September 1965 the Teaching Brothers' Association was established to represent all the schools conducted by orders of brothers; since however, some of the smaller orders continued their membership of the CHA, recognition of the TBA was deferred by the Department of Education until 1967 when its membership represented all such orders. The aim of the TBA was stated as follows:

> To discuss every aspect of educational policy, to ascertain the thinking of the different orders in matters educational and to advise the Executive of the TBA on all such matters.

This objective marks a significant development in that it envisages the association as having an active interest in all aspects of education policy, unlike the other managerial bodies whose main concern had traditionally centred on routine or sectoral aspects of curriculum and management. In accordance with their main aim, the TBA played a very central role in the structural developments among the Catholic bodies in the sixties and in their response to the policies of the period.

The Federation of Lay Catholic Secondary Schools

The Federation of Lay Catholic Secondary Schools, (1952), represents the interests of those secondary schools which are owned or managed by lay Catholics; in the early sixties the federation had a membership of about fifty. This managerial association differed in some fundamental respects from the other associations already described; it had a most comprehensive set of aims, it perceived its role vis-a-vis policy as active rather than reactive and had a vision of education policy which found it at times well ahead of ministerial thinking. Besides its representative function, it sought also, according to its stated aims, 'to foster the growth and improve the quality of secondary education in Ireland', to promote discussion on education issues with interested parties both at home and abroad, to conduct research into education problems and issues in Ireland and to publish and disseminate in an impartial manner the findings of such research and also information on other education systems.[69] In its contributions to education policy in the fifties and sixties, it was conscious of the importance of systematic comparative data, it relied upon realistic examination of the issues and showed scant regard for those in the education establishments who did not seem to agree with Macauley's dictum 'that men are never so likely to settle a question rightly as when they discuss it freely'.[70] In 1960 it presented a comprehensive policy memorandum to the Minister for Education, Dr P. J. Hillery, emphasising i) the need to improve the quality of teaching and examining especially in science, mathematics and modern languages, ii) the comparative unit costs in secondary and vocational education, iii) the need for the state to invest more in secondary education by means of higher capitation grants, iv) the recognition of teaching service abroad, and v) the introduction of special allowances for headmasters and teachers holding posts of responsibility.[71] Perhaps its most significant and ambitious effort was the detailed research study, conducted by P. J. Cannon, *Investment in Education in the Republic of Ireland* (1962), which foreshadowed and identified some of the findings of its major namesake, *Investment in Education* (1965) in relation to participation patterns and obstacles to equality of opportunity in postprimary education.[72] For its quality, detail and methodology this study received wide acclaim, but not from the Minister for Education, who claimed in the Dáil 'that the whole aim of the booklet was to show up this country in a bad light'.[73]

It would appear that in 1958 the federation sought to unite in one organisation all the managerial bodies in secondary education; with this end in view it changed its own title to the Federation of Irish Secondary Schools. The move towards unification foundered on the refusal of the other bodies, but the change of title drew upon the federation the fury of the minister who refused to supply it with statistical information, withdrew official recognition and removed it from membership of the Teacher Registration Council.[74] When the issue was raised in the Dáil, the minister asserted that there could be no question of recognising the association 'which represents about one tenth of our secondary schools and had abrogated to itself the new title Federation of Irish Secondary Schools', a title which he regarded as misleading.[75] Deputy Declan Costello, who championed the cause of the federation, indicated to the minister that two other managerial bodies, The Irish Schoolmasters' Association and The Catholic Headmasters' Association, bore titles which were equally 'misleading'; he contended that the question of title was not the real reason for refusal of recognition by the minister:

> It is quite clear that the real reason lies in the strong objection which it has been thought fit to have towards this association. I believe that the attacks made on the Association- and I think 'attack' is the proper word- are completely unjustified and that the real reason why this association has been refused recognition is the objection that has been taken to the fact that the federation has been concerning itself actively with secondary education matters in this country; that its actions in this field were regarded as interference in the field of secondary education and that there was suspicion of the efforts made by this federation to get reform in secondary education, reform which we all know to be urgently necessary.[76]

The former title, the status and role of the federation as a recognised body were restored following the intervention of George Colley as Minister in 1966. The federation continued to play an active part in the developments of the sixties and participates to date in the umbrella groups, the Joint Managerial Body and the Council of Managers of Catholic Secondary Schools.[77]

Church Responses in the 1960s

Looking at the major issues of policy in the sixties, the Hillery scheme of 1963 and the O'Malley 'free' education plan of 1966, we find a distinct difference in the manner in which the Catholic and Protestant managerial bodies reacted to these efforts by the state to expand and reform the education system. For both groups there was a need for discussion, analysis and perhaps re-definition of education policies and values; new managerial structures were also required on both sides. The Protestant bodies and their church agencies would seem to have conducted the transition with more discipline and efficacy; on the Catholic side, the lines of authority and communication seemed confused and at times there were clear signs of conflict, power struggles and questioning of authority with the result that the response to the official policies was indecisive and even when positive, seemed reluctant.

The General Synod of the Church of Ireland since 1875 had as part of its structure a Board of Education which was concerned mainly with religious education until 1917 when its remit was extended to cover all aspects of primary and secondary education.[78] Towards the end of the fifties the Board of Education was deeply concerned with various aspects of primary and secondary education and in particular with the educational problems posed by the size of their schools.[79] In 1962 the board established an Advisory Committee to examine the existing network of secondary schools, their resources, facilities and staffing, to assess the impact of geographical distribution on the economics of provision and to consider the possibility of collaborating with other Protestant denominations in matters affecting secondary schools.[80] This Advisory Committee reported to the General Synod in 1965 and in its *Report on secondary education* outlined a blueprint for Protestant secondary education which called for 'radical steps' without which the existing schools would not be able to maintain standards. Its strategy was clear and unambiguous:

> We are strongly of the opinion that improved standards can be provided only through fewer and larger schools with more specialised staff, with suitable buildings, adequate equipment and with better facilities for both teachers and pupils. We therefore consider that there must be substantial planned reduction in the number of schools.[81]

The report strongly advocated the appointment of a joint committee with the Presbyterian and Methodist Churches and the Religious Society of Friends 'to formulate a common policy for Protestant secondary education and to enter into discussion with the Minister for Education and the governing bodies of Protestant secondary schools for the purpose of implementing such policy'.[82] The General Synod of 1965 regarded this report as critically important for the future welfare of the Church of Ireland and acted accordingly. A Secondary Education Committee (SEC) spearheaded the implementation of the policy under the chairmanship of the Bishop of Cork, Dr G. Perdue, with a commitment which reflected the final words of the report: 'Time is short and the sands are running out'.[83]

It is of some significance that the Advisory Committee on secondary education coincided in time with the *Investment in Education* inquiry established by the Department; there was close liaison between the two projects and this liaison is reflected in the degree to which the Protestant policy and strategy was in close alignment with the general policy strategy of the department in the mid-sixties. The SEC applied itself to its appointed task with obvious energy, meeting monthly throughout 1966/67 and some of its sub-committees meeting weekly. When the O'Malley scheme was launched in 1966, the SEC pointed out to the minister and the department that for various reasons a scheme for free education which met the needs of the majority would not necessarily meet theirs.[84] The minister responded by announcing an alternative scheme which would guarantee an equitable and corresponding benefit to Protestant pupils as that received by pupils in the Catholic schools; the state block grant for this scheme would be administered by the SEC.

In the context of the countrywide analysis of educational provision and demand contained in its county reports, the Department of Education prepared a report on *Postprimary provision for the Protestant community*, which was discussed at public meetings in Dublin, Cork, Sligo and Limerick between representatives of church, schools, parents and department officials. The discussions at these meetings helped to catalyse a movement, already underway, designed to amalgamate and relocate many of the Dublin schools; within a short time five large centre-city schools had moved to new spacious suburban locations and the state had also proposed to build a number of Protestant comprehensive schools, two in Dublin, one in Cork and one in Raphoe. The SEC had also achieved a modification of the school transport scheme which enabled Protestant pupils living within the catchment area of a vocational school to secure free transport to the nearest Protestant school.

Prior to the teachers' salary strike of 1969, the SEC was instrumental in arranging a conference of school governors at which representatives of the minister, the ASTI and the school heads attended to discuss the issues involved. The strike, when it occurred, showed clearly the need for a consultative council of governing bodies to act as a medium for the exchange of advice and information between schools. Such a body had existed but had been moribund for years; through the good offices of the SEC a new body was created, the Council of School Governors.[85]

Ten years after its establishment the Secondary Education Committee had significant achievements to its credit. It had created a new structure in Protestant secondary education (Fig. 6.1) involving the establishment of many new schools, it had negotiated a variant of the O'Malley 'free' education scheme which met the specific requirements of the Protestant community; morever, it had achieved these results more by informed discussion and gentle diplomacy than by centralised directive. By 1975 the SEC was administratively responsible for the government grant of £260,000 by which boarding grants were provided for 946 students out of 2,353 boarding students and tutorial grants were made available to 1,195 of the 3,112 day students in the Protestant secondary schools; in addition 1,600 pupils were receiving free postprimary education in the four Protestant comprehensive schools. The SEC was also the main catalyst in the structural changes which occurred, the creation of the Council of

School Governors and especially in stimulating the various Protestant churches to adopt and implement a very advantageous education policy. As a result of the developments of the sixties the Protestant managerial and school bodies had evolved a coherent policy and had adopted a negotiating structure as illustrated in Figure 6.1. The SEC provides a forum for direct common systematic negotiation on behalf of the various churches and the various churches through their own central structures can also interact with government at department or political levels.

It is difficult to examine the reaction of the Catholic managerial bodies to the education developments of the sixties in isolation from the structural changes introduced and the new bodies established; these bodies were created mainly as a result of the different approaches adopted to the new policies by different elements and at different levels within the complex array of Catholic managerial and education interests. Various moves were made throughout the sixties to seek more coherent structures among the various bodies especially by the CHA, the CCSS, and the TBA. In 1959 these three bodies met to consider the possibility and need for an umbrella organisation, a move however which was regarded by the bishops as undesirable unless the emerging body were subject to episcopal control.[86] The Catholic and Protestant bodies came together in 1964 to form the Joint Managerial Body, a venture which owed much to the efforts of the president of the CHA; however the Catholic bishops refused to recognise the JMB as the sole negotiating body for secondary education. In February 1966 a new organisation was formed, the Catholic Managerial Consultative Committee and within the same month the bishops established the Episcopal Commission on Postprimary Education; the formation of both of these bodies would seem to have been occasioned by the policy letter sent to the secondary and vocational schools by Mr George Colley on 1 January 1966.[87] The former organisation had a short life however for in June 1967, arising from a memorandum which it sent to the hierarchy on the problems facing private secondary schools and their relationship with the state, the bishops established and nominated a special committee to draw up concrete proposals to be submitted to the Episcopal Commission on Postprimary Education.[88] This special committee proposed the establishment of a permanent council or commission of managers, which would have direct negotiating rights with the department, would act as the executive of the combined managerial associations and have a professional staff. The bishops accepted the proposal to establish a Council of Catholic Managers but indicated that the remit of the council would need to draw a clear distinction between matters of policy which should be reserved to the bishops and other matters. This clear distinction was formalised in the constitution of the Council under which it is required that all agreements reached by the Council shall be submitted via the Episcopal Commission to the hierarchy and to the Conference of Major Religious Superiors.[89] In addition it is stipulated that it is the duty of the Council to keep the Episcopal Commission and the Conference of Major Religious Superiors informed of all proposals as also of policies proposed to be followed. This injunction is more specific in some instances:

> Before adopting any policy or concluding any agreement with the Department of Education, the Minister for Education or other parties which may affect: (1) Religion (2) Catholic educational policy; (3) Change in the management of the schools; (4) Contracts with lay staff, the council shall obtain the specific approval of the hierarchy through the said Episcopal Commission for Postprimary Education and of the Conference of Major Religious Superiors through the said Education Commission of the Conference of Major Religious Superiors.[90]

It was also stipulated that the Council of Managers would be kept informed whenever any direct negotiations are in progress between the hierarchy and the Department or the Minister; the Department of Education was to be requested to consult the council on all questions concerning secondary education.[91] The council was established in May 1968. As a result of these developments, by the early seventies a very clear structure had been created with its apex located firmly within the episcopal domain. This was quite evident when the creation of community schools was first raised in 1970; the initial plans were discussed with Cardinal Conway in Armagh before being released for discussion with other parties. The absence of such a recognised line of command throughout the early sixties produced much confusion and dissatisfaction among the managerial bodies in their response to the various government policy measures.

The report of the Council of Education on the secondary curriculum (1962) is generally regarded as being a document of little significance; it does however show most of the managerial bodies, both Catholic and Protestant, to have been opposed to a policy of 'secondary education for all'. This particular stance was extended by the CHA in its general reaction to the major policy statement made by Dr P. J. Hillery in May 1963. This policy statement announced the establishment of comprehensive schools, regional technical colleges, the extension to vocational schools of the right to enter pupils for the state examinations at Intermediate and Leaving Certificate levels, the initiation of a school transport service, a Technical Leaving Certificate and a Common Intermediate Certificate examination which would give parity of standard to both types of postprimary schools.[92] In addition Dr Hillery defined his policy of equality of educational opportunity as entailing 'the opportunity of some postprimary education for all' and announced the introduction of 'a new principle into Irish education namely direct state provision of a postprimary school building'.[93] The CHA in response to this policy initiative were rather fearful of the threat posed to the secondary schools by the extension of the state's role in education. The introduction of building grants for secondary schools in 1964 prompted some members of the managerial bodies to interpret the scheme as undermining the 'private status' of the secondary schools, this status being defined in terms of school management and the selection and admission of pupils. The relations between the minister and the managerial bodies throughout 1964 and 1965 were generally uneasy and this situation was aggravated by a department circular which proposed giving effect to some of the measures in Hillery's 1963 policy statement on 'the extension of the Intermedidate Certificate to cater for pupils from secondary, vocational and comprehensive schools'.[94]

The CHA and the other Catholic managerial bodies were highly critical of the proposal and saw the extension of the Intermediate Cerfificate to vocational schools as bringing into being a state system of secondary education. They were gravely concerned as to the impact of such a strengthened vocational system on the smaller secondary schools in rural areas. They recognised that such a measure might be intended to provide equality of opportunity, an objective which they welcomed; they disagreed however, with the means proposed by the department. The Minister, they argued, should have first sought the assistance of the private secondary schools in seeking a solution before setting up state schools which would inevitably be operated in opposition to voluntary schools. This particular policy development proved to be a major revelation to the managerial bodies. When they approached the hierarchy on the issue they were informed that the bishops had been in active consultation with the department on all questions over the previous two years; furthermore it was the hierarchy's intention that all such questions would receive their continued attention. When the Catholic managerial bodies sought a written detailed statement of the department policies and plans, the request was refused and the managerial bodies were left in no doubt by the department that all these questions had been discussed with the hierarchy.

Upon the appointment of George Colley as minister in June 1965 relations would seem to have improved between the Catholic managerial bodies and the department, a development which, it was hoped would be furthered by the establishment of an Advisory Council on Education as proposed by the Minister. The managerial bodies responded enthusiastically to this proposal but it seems to have disappeared from discussion as quickly as it first appeared. The major initiative from Colley was his letter to schools in January 1966 advocating that local secondary and vocational schools should cooperate to provide a comprehensive curriculum in each centre and urging the school authorities of each area to meet to discuss the local educational needs. While the CHA reacted to this proposal by pointing out the various problems regarding staffing, funding and the constitutional rights of parents, they were in entire agreement in principle with the policy of cooperation which they regarded as highly desirable. Equally, the TBA expressed themselves as being entirely in favour of the minister's proposal and assured him of their willingness to assist him; they pointed out some practical problems in the proposal and suggested that the policy be implemented on a limited pilot basis. Problems associated with planning educational provision in the greater Dublin area were assigned by the minister in June 1966 to a special council which he established and on which all the managerial bodies were represented.

The O'Malley 'free' education scheme announced in September 1966 posed some basic problems for the managerial bodies and raised again the question of their relationship to the consultative process taking place between the bishops and the minister. While the managerial associations were anxious to meet the minister to discuss his scheme such an interview did not take place until the Minister had already consulted the authorities of both churches and had announced his plans in the Dáil on 30 November.[95] The Catholic managerial bodies considered the scheme, as presented, less than satisfactory especially in relation to the differentiated grant and the exclusion of high-fee schools. As an alternative interim solution it was proposed to the minister that if he increased the capitation grant to all schools by a fixed amount, the fees of each school would be reduced by that same amount, thus producing free places in some schools.[96] A permanent solution could come, according to the managerial bodies, only when an act of the Oireachtas specified the future relationship 'between the state and the voluntary church-linked parental schools'. They were of the opinion that any scheme for free education, whereby a school's total income is derived from public funds, was objectionable; under the O'Malley scheme, in the absence of legal guarantees, the situation of the schools could be intolerable. However, once again the role of the bishops proved decisive; by February 1967 the issue was settled by an episcopal directive that the Committee of Catholic Managers would recommend acceptance of the scheme to those schools which found it financially feasible to do so. It would appear that, while there were strong opinions within the managerial bodies both in favour and in opposition to the scheme, among the bishops the possibility of rejection of a politically popular scheme by the Catholic managerial bodies would not be entertained.

By the time in 1970 when the next major issue arose, the community school plan, the new managerial umbrella structures were well established; however the decline in the number of religious posed major manpower problems for many teaching orders. This very factor, which has sometimes been identified as a justification for the emergence of a stronger public presence in postprimary educational management, was effectively the reason why the bishops sought and secured a firmer and more formal place for central ecclesiastical control not only in the policy-making bodies but in the various school management structures. The hierarchy and its corporate bodies, it was believed, were far more permanent than some of the religious orders, some of which were already suffering a decline in numbers and influence. The community schools, as introduced and developed in the seventies offer a clear example of the implementation of this strategy.

In reviewing the influence of the managerial bodies on education policy, one cannot conclude without considering the question within the larger context of state-church relations on education policy, a topic which will be examined in a later chapter. However each group of managerial bodies, Catholic and Protestant, is subject to a superior group of church leaders or bishops, with whom issues of policy are discussed by the minister or senior department officials before these issues reach the managerial bodies. Such a procedural formula has been followed on most if not all educational issues since the foundation of the state. The result is that the field of education policy effectively open to the managerial bodies is reduced by the prior consultative process at the higher level. In effect the managerial bodies have the diminished satisfaction of engaging in direct negotiations with the Department while both sides are aware that the real limits to the discussions have already been set. This mechanism has frequently produced, especially among the Catholic bodies, a high level of frustration and irritation directed mainly against the department but sometimes against the bishops; occasionally this frustration has found expression in the publication of hysterical attacks on department policy by groups who are aware that the same policies had already been negotiated in direct consultation with the bishops.[97]

Prior to the early sixties, very few educational issues of major importance surfaced or were the subject of sustained public debate.

TABLE 6.1

The managerial bodies at first and second levels, their foundation dates and the educational interests each represents.

— FIRST LEVEL —		
Title	Founded	Interests Represented
1. Catholic Primary Managers Association (C.P.M.A.)	1903	Clerical Managers of Catholic National Schools
2. Church of Ireland National School Managers' Association	1973	Clerical Managers of Church of Ireland National Schools
3. Conference of Convent Primary Schools (C.C.P.S.)	1950	The Principals and Managers of National Schools under the management of orders of sisters
4. Teaching Brothers Association (T.B.A.)	1965	Teaching members of the orders of religious brothers which conduct National Schools

Table continued next page

	— SECOND LEVEL —		
5.	The Irish Schoolmasters' Association[1] (I.S.A.)	1869	Principals and Headmasters of Protestant Boys' Secondary Schools
6.	The Catholic Headmasters' Association (C.H.A.)	1879	Headmasters of Catholic Boys' Secondary Schools managed by priests
7.	Association of Irish Headmistresses[2] (A.I.H.)	1882	Principals and Headmistresses of Protestant Girls' Secondary Schools
8.	Conference of Convent Secondary Schools (C.C.S.S.)	1929	Principals and Managers of Secondary Schools conducted by orders of of religious sisters
9.	Federation of Lay Catholic Secondary Schools (F.L.C.S.S.)[3]	1952	The Principals/Managers of Lay Catholic Secondary Schools
10.	The Teaching Brothers' Association (T.B.A.)	1965	The members of the religious brotherhoods which conduct secondary schools
11.	The Council of School (C.S.G.) Governors	1969	The Governing Bodies of all Protestant Secondary Schools
12.	The Secondary Education Committee (S.E.C.)	1965	The four main Protestant Churches and their central education policy-making bodies
13.	The Council of Managers of Catholic Secondary Schools[4] (C.M.C.S.S.)	1967	All the corporate managerial bodies of Catholic Secondary Schools and the educational bodies of the Hierarchy and the Religious Superiors
14.	The Episcopal Commission on Post-Primary Education (E.C.P.P.E.)	1966	The Catholic Hierarchy
15.	The Education Commission of the Conference of Major Religious Superiors (E.C.C.M.R.S.)	1966	The Catholic Religious Orders involved in education
16.	The Joint Education Commission (J.E.C.)	1967	Representatives of the Catholic Episcopal Commission on Post-Primary Education and of the Conference of Major Religious Superiors
17.	The Church of Ireland Board of Education[5] (C.I.B.E.)	1875	A stautory body reporting to the Annual Synod representing all aspects of the Church of Ireland educational activities
18.	The Joint Managerial Body (J.M.B.)	1964	All the corporate managerial bodies, Catholic, Protestant and Lay, involved in secondary education
	— SECOND LEVEL: VOCATIONAL SECTOR —		
19.	The Irish Vocational Education Association		The managerial interests in the vocational system i.e. the various Vocational Education Committees
20.	The Vocational School Principals' Association		The headmasters of vocational schools

Footnotes:
1. From its foundation to 1968 was known as *The Schoolmasters' Association*. 2. The Association of Irish Headmistresses merged in 1968 with The Irish Schoolmasters' Association. 3. The original title was *The Federation of Irish Secondary Schools*. 4. The Council should not be confused with the *Catholic Managerial Consultative Committee* of 1966 which proposed its establishment. 5. The central educational bodies of the other Protestant churches, contribute to the work of the S.E.C.

Consequently the managerial bodies had been mainly concerned with negotiating with the department on routine low-level questions relating to staffing, curriculum, examinations and school finance. It would appear also that the minister and the department seldom felt compelled to discuss any central issues of policy with the managerial bodies; they did however rely on the goodwill and cooperation of the various bodies to ensure the smooth running of the school system. Whenever in these consultations issues arose which proved highly contentious or which either side regarded as belonging to the realm of higher level consultation, such issues were referred upwards; this two-level process of consultation has existed practically from the foundation of the state but it has been formalised and structured by the developments of the last two decades. In these developments the individual managerial bodies would seem to have been diminished in their autonomy by the umbrella groups which have been inserted between them and the process of negotiation and consultation.[98] Their own attempt in 1964 to prevent such a loss of autonomy by the creation of the Joint Managerial Body would seem to have failed since it is now the main vehicle for the regular low-level consultation. However it may be of some significance that the Catholic managerial bodies are now anxious to seek arbitration by a non-ecclesiastical agency in disputes with teachers; in 1974 in a dispute between the Council of Managers of Catholic Secondary Schools and the Association of Secondary Teachers concerning the maximum number of teaching hours, it was the managerial side which initiated the move to have the issue adjudicated by the Adjudication Conference of the Employer-Labour Conference.[99]

Since the middle sixties it seems certain that the important and decisive consultative process in relation to major policy issues occurs at the senior levels i.e. between the bishops and church leaders and the minister and his department as is illustrated in Fig. 6.2. The symmetry of the mechanism is of some interest. Both the Catholic and Protestant managerial bodies have representation on the Joint Managerial Body (JMB) through a central umbrella body (CMCSS and SEC respectively); through this umbrella body contact is maintained with all the superior church structures which thus are in a controlling position vis-a-vis the negotiation and implementation of policy. There is however one significant difference between the Catholic and Protestant managerial stuctures; the involvement of elected lay membership of the senior governing church bodies in the Protestant structure provides a democratic element which is absent in the Catholic structures. The growing complexity of the managerial structures reflects the intensity of the political debate which has attached to education policy in the past two decades and the continuing sensitivity which characterises state-church relations in the field of education policy.

TABLE 6.2

Orders and other Church groups which conduct secondary schools, the number of schools in each category and the managerial bodies to which they belong (1980).

Managerial Body	C.C.S.S.	T.B.A.	C.H.A.	S.E.C.	F.L.C.C.S
No. Schools	285	120	61	26	28
Mercy & Presentation	160	Christian Brothers 85	Diocesan 28	Church of Ireland 22	
Loreto		de la Salle 17	Holy Ghost 6	Friends 1	
Charity		Patrician 8	Jesuits 4	Methodist 1	
Holy Faith	70	Presentation 5	Marists 3	Presbyterian 2	
Dominican		Marist 2	Carmelites 3		
Louis		Marianist 2	Vincentian 2		
Ursuline		Franciscan 1	Rosminians 2		
29 Others	55		Salesians 2		
			Augustinian 2		
			Oblates 1		
			Opus Dei 1		
			Dominicans 1		
			Missionary Sacred Heart 1		
			Capuchins 1		
			Benedictines 1		
			Redemptorists 1		
			Franciscans 1		
			Cistercians 1		

Notes:

(i) The Jewish community also conduct a secondary school.

(ii) There are also 5 schools conducted jointly by two 2 different church agencies i.e. by a diocese and a convent or by two different orders.

FIGURE 6.1
The various managerial bodies and umbrella groups.

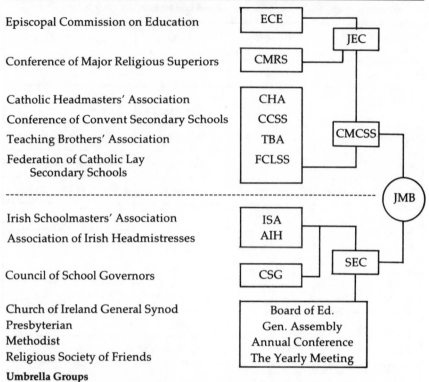

Episcopal Commission on Education	ECE	
Conference of Major Religious Superiors	CMRS	JEC
Catholic Headmasters' Association	CHA	
Conference of Convent Secondary Schools	CCSS	
Teaching Brothers' Association	TBA	CMCSS
Federation of Catholic Lay Secondary Schools	FCLSS	
Irish Schoolmasters' Association	ISA	JMB
Association of Irish Headmistresses	AIH	
Council of School Governors	CSG	SEC
Church of Ireland General Synod	Board of Ed.	
Presbyterian	Gen. Assembly	
Methodist	Annual Conference	
Religious Society of Friends	The Yearly Meeting	

Umbrella Groups
JEC: The Joint Education Committee.
CMCSS: The Conference of Managers of Catholic Secondary Schools.

SEC: The Secondary Education Committee.
JMB: The Joint Managerial Body.

Source: Devised by author.

FIGURE 6.2
The Catholic and Protestant organisational structure, their Managerial Bodies and their relationship in the policy process.

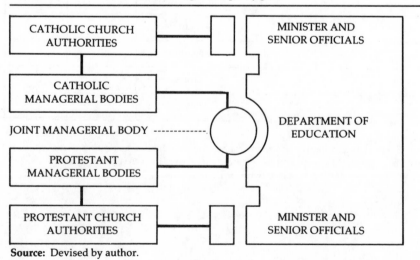

CATHOLIC CHURCH AUTHORITIES	MINISTER AND SENIOR OFFICIALS
CATHOLIC MANAGERIAL BODIES	
JOINT MANAGERIAL BODY	DEPARTMENT OF EDUCATION
PROTESTANT MANAGERIAL BODIES	
PROTESTANT CHURCH AUTHORITIES	MINISTER AND SENIOR OFFICIALS

Source: Devised by author.

Chapter 7

The Political Parties

Education systems, even when operating as 'aided' systems, depend on the public sector not only for much of their financial resources but also for part of their pedagogical and organisational direction. It has been argued that, since education systems utilise public resources to provide a service which directly or indirectly affects the lives of the whole population, education policy and political opinion cannot be separated.[1] The amount and allocation of these resources and the extent and the nature of the education service provided are basically and validly functions of government and ultimately the subject of political debate. In examining the nature of the political debate on education in this century, the role of the political parties is of central importance.

Of the major parties now functioning in the state, only one, the Irish Labour Party, existed prior to independence. Founded in 1912, it forms the main party strand linking the political process of the early decades of the century with that of post-independence Ireland.[2] This continuity is due to the fact that the Labour Party, though it committed itself unreservedly in the national opposition to conscription of 1918, stood aside as a party from the basic political struggle attendant upon the independence movement.[3] This experience sharply differentiated it from Fine Gael and Fianna Fáil, both of which, though originating in opposing reactions to the Treaty of 1921 and the resultant civil war had some organisational links with pre-independence political movements.[4] Sinn Féin, the political organisation which fostered the independence movement, having effectively eliminated the Irish Parliamentary Party in the 1918 election was itself displaced by the birth of Cumann na nGael in 1923 and by that of Fianna Fáil in 1926. The other main pre-independence grouping, the Irish Unionist Party, found its main support in Northern Ireland following the Government of Ireland Act 1920, although some of its members later entered Free State politics, mainly through Cumann na nGael.

Since the foundation of the state party politics have been dominated by Cumann na nGael, Fine Gael , Fianna Fáil and the Labour Party; the various governments have been constituted from these and with occasional support from smaller parties, principally

Clann na Talmhan, a farmers' party and Clann na Poblachta, a short-lived radical republican party. While both of the major parties originated in different responses to a constitutional question, they have in recent decades acquired a more diffuse 'catchall' character and they have also become very similar in the socio-economic character of their support and of those they elect to office.[5] In national politics, while farmers, professionals and the self-employed constitute almost 90% of the deputies of Fianna Fáil and Fine Gael (1965), these groups constitute only 40% of the Labour deputies, among whom trade union officials however form an equally large group.[6] Recent studies throw some interesting light on electors' perceptions of the main parties; only one third of the respondents in a 1969 survey believed that there were any important differences between the parties and a majority saw no difference between Fianna Fáil, Fine Gael and Labour.[7]

The various governments in the period since 1922, their terms of office, their constituent parties and the party identity of the Minister for Education are shown in Table 7.1; the Ministers for Education have come exclusively from the two larger parties, Fianna Fáil and Fine Gael. For forty of the sixty years since 1922, Fianna Fáil ministers have occupied the Department of Education and twice their occupation lasted for sixteen consecutive years.[8]

All the main parties, Labour, Fine Gael and Fianna Fáil, have utilised the same methods for mobilising the electorate. Thus, local branch activity, election manifestos, special policy documents, public speeches by leaders and the annual party gatherings provide the parties with a range of means by which their policies can be publicised and support for them evoked. The emphasis placed on each of these various means varies among the parties; the Labour Party has tended to produce and publish more policy documents than the other parties, while Fianna Fáil has relied significantly on the strength of its local and national organisational structure and Fine Gael has favoured the public statement and the structured document. A recent study, observing that the tradition of election manifestos is comparatively rather weak in Irish politics, identifies the present growing emphasis as deriving exclusively from the recent past when each party prepared at least one significant election document.[9] This same study argued that the manifesto is less important than the election leaflets which are distributed on a constituency basis to every voter; it also shows that the mechanism by which manifestos are prepared varies but does not usually involve a wide range of party members.[10]

It needs to be borne in mind however that political parties tend to be much more radical when in opposition; all if not most of the party documents published have come from the parties when in opposition. In Kogan's terms, parties in opposition attempt to appeal to the stongest interest groups whereas in office reality forces a wider range of interests on their attention.[11]

The Labour Party

Founded on a resolution at the 1912 Clonmel conference of the Trade Union Congress, the Irish Labour Party while never achieving a large volume of electoral support, has always been a persistent, if not always prominent, force in Irish political life.[12] Earlier attempts to develop a political wing in the Congress had foundered mainly due to fear of disunity on the national issue; however the imminence of Home Rule and the growing political activity in Congress of the Irish Transport and General Workers' Union (founded 1909) secured a majority in favour of the resolution proposed by Connolly in 1912. In the first decade of its activities the new party adopted a neutral stance on the issue of national independence despite the central involvement of James Connolly and the Irish Citizen Army in the rising of 1916; on the same basis it eschewed the general elections of 1918 and 1921 although it had unsuccessfully contested a Dublin by-election of 1915.[13]

Following the general election of 1922, Labour's seventeen deputies led by Thomas Johnson entered Dáil Éireann as the official opposition to the Cosgrave Cumann na nGael government. Since then its strength in the Dáil has varied from 8 (1933) to 22 (1965); its mean percentage share of votes has been 11.6% while its highest share of valid votes cast was 17% in 1969.[14] This support however was centred in the early decades among the rural working class and not in the industrial urban areas; prior to 1940 Labour's share of the Dublin poll never exceeded 10%.[15] In recent years it has been gaining ground significantly in the younger age cohorts; its urban support has grown considerably but in western regions its support is still weak.[16]

Since its participation in the first Inter-Party government of 1948-1951, Labour has on a number of occasions shared government with other parties; in none of these administrations has it occupied any office associated with education, either as Minister or as Junior Minister. Despite this however, education has been a consistent theme of its policies, has been the subject of special policy documents and has from the beginning been the focus for party political action. This was very much in line with the traditional emphasis placed by the unions and Labour on education as a powerful agent of social mobility. Thus a certain ideological and substantive continuity links the major party documents on education, *Labour's policy on education* (1925), *Labour's programme for a better Ireland* (1943), *Labour's constructive programme* (1952), *Challenge and change in education* (1963), *Labour Party outline policy (education)* (1969) and *Education at first level- a policy for our children's future* (1975).[17]

This historical continuity of interest in education stems largely from the party's formal commitment to social and economic reform and from the early close association of the INTO and the ASTI and other teachers with the party. The party's origins in a period when educational reforms were major public issues also helped to imprint on the party members the central importance of education policy.

Moreover the deep interest in education policy evinced by the Irish Trades Union Congress from its foundation in 1894 and the emphasis on education reforms expressed by various socialist leaders had created a body of political opinion which eventually took shape in the policy document of 1925. A brief review of such expressions will provide a suitable introduction to the party's formal policy statements on education.

The Irish Democratic Labour Federation, founded by Michael Davitt in 1890, which did not survive the Parnell split of 1891, included in its advanced social programme a call for free education.[18] The Irish Socialist Republican Party, founded by Connolly in Dublin in 1896, adopted the following demand in its initial party programme:

> Public control and management of national schools by boards elected by popular ballot for that purpose alone. Free education up to the highest university grades.[19]

The question of popular and local control of education was an issue of some political importance in the closing decades of the last century and the various structural proposals of Wyndham, Birrell and Starkie made it a topical issue in the first decades of this century. Connolly advocated greater public control of education in the following argument:

> Education seems to be the one ground from which the public guardianship and responsibility welcomed elsewhere are here most resolutely forbidden to enter. Public responsibility indeed, is admitted in a half-hearted form, but the right of control, of guardianship that goes, or should go with responsiblity is bluntly denied, and its assertion treated as a veritable attack on public morality.[20]

Connolly's analysis of the existing system as 'an attempt to perform by a mixture of bureaucracy and clericalism what can only be accomplished by a full and complete application of democratic trust in the people', found an echo and implicit support in the writings of Dr Walter McDonald of Maynooth.[21]

Following the establishment of the Labour Party, education was a frequent topic of discussion and of formal resolution especially at the annual conferences. At the Sligo conference in 1916, John Good of the Cork Trades Council condemned the education system as involving 'a policy of cramming the minds of the few and ignoring the fate of the many'.[22] The following year at Derry the president, T. McPartlin identified education reform as a subject of primary concern for the party.[23] At the same conference a cornerstone of Labour's education policy was outlined in a resolution moved by a Mr Stewart of the

Railway Clerk's Association in which he claimed:

> A free educational highway from the primary school to the
> university is the only educational system which can satisfy the
> needs of a democratic community.[24]

The sophistication and range of the argument advanced in support of
this particular resolution are impressive and of interest; Stewart
emphasised that in the absence of maintenance grants, free access to
secondary and higher education would not bring any advantage to
those who could not afford the opportunity cost. Significantly, a call
was made also for the establishment of technical colleges which
would enjoy equal status with universities.

At the 1918 conference, the first attended by the recently affiliated
INTO, the National Board of Education was condemned, the 1917
education proposals were reiterated and the executive was requested
to 'appoint a committee to deal with the question of educational
reform'.[25] Education policy also figured prominently in the manifesto,
Let Labour Lead, issued by the Dublin United Trades Council for May
Day 1918, in which specific proposals were made to meet the needs of
the Dublin area. This document advocated public control of schools
and free education:

> The citizens through the Corporation should obtain a direct
> interest and influence in the schools . . . All public schools,
> primary and intermediate, should be absolutely free and all
> books should be provided at the public expense.[26]

This manifesto also advocated free school meals for the necessitous, a
medical and dental service for the schools, special schools for
handicapped children and the inclusion of practical subjects in the
primary curriculum. It also emphasised the need to improve school
buildings, provide sporting facilities, conduct evening classes for
adults and allow apprentices to avail of full-time education on a day
release basis. This manifesto contained many of the policy elements
which were to figure repeatedly in the later policy documents.

The Killanin and Molony Commissions established in 1918 were
crucial instruments in the planned postwar reform of Irish education.
Aware of their significance and conscious of their own growing
commitment to reform in education, the National Executive of the
Labour Party sought unsuccessfully to be represented on both
commissions:

> Your executive have demanded as representatives of the parents
> of the children that on any such commission set up, they shall be
> fully represented.[27]

Though not participating in the First Dáil in 1919, the Labour Party through Thomas Johnson and William O'Brien, exercised considerable influence on the wording of the Democratic Programme adopted by the Dáil. According to Cathal O'Shannon, Séan T. Ó Ceallaigh contributed about one third of the document as adopted by the Dáil and Johnson about two thirds, which eventually represented only one half of the Labour draft.[28] It would appear that the following extract is from the Johnson/Labour contribution:

> It shall be the first duty of the Government of the Republic to make provision for the physical, mental and spiritual well-being of the children, to ensure that no child suffer hunger or cold from lack of food, clothing or shelter, that all shall be provided with the means and facilities requisite for their proper education and training as citizens of a free and Gaelic Ireland.[29]

Some excerpts in the Johnson draft relating to public good and private rights were excluded by Ó Ceallaigh from the final version and he also omitted the following sentence referring to education:

> A condition precedent to such education is to encourage by every reasonable means the most capable and sympathetic men and women to devote their talents to the education of the young.[30]

While the Democratic Programme could be regarded as 'a genuflection to the aspirations of the working class interest', even in such a token role it might not have secured assent from all the deputies of the First Dáil; nevertheless it represented a formal affirmation of the Dáil's social aspirations and also reflected the social policies of the Labour Party in which education figured prominently.

One further and highly significant issue arose before Labour entered on its parliamentary career; the McPherson Education Bill, introduced on 24 November 1919 proposed many of the reforms which had been advocated by Labour and also secured improved salary scales for teachers, yet surprisingly the executive of the party found some aspects of the bill 'obnoxious'. While recognising that the measure would bring valuable improvements, the party was opposed to the creation of a central department which would deprive 'the popularly elected local Councils' of their already restricted influence in education.[31] Significantly the party's outing in the local elections of 1920 had been an outstanding success in which its programme was vindicated by the election of 324 of its 505 candidates.[32]

More significantly, however, this election afforded Labour a golden opportunity to forge cooperative links with Sinn Féin and thus redeem its credentials with the majority political group. The paradox of its attitude to the McPherson Bill may be explained in terms of its new-found power on the local authorities; or perhaps it may have adopted an ambiguous neutral stance on the advice of Sinn Féin, whose own leadership, depite intense pressure on it to condemn the Bill, recorded in its cabinet minutes the following vague resolution:

Education Bill: Dáil will support the Bishops in setting up and maintaining a national system of education.[33]

The Labour Party further cemented its growing alignment with Sinn Féin at its 1920 conference when it resolved to seek a democratically controlled education system 'which reflected the national, social and economic aspirations of the Irish people'.[34] It also resolved to cooperate with the INTO, the ASTI and the Gaelic League in the education conference proposed by the Dáil Cabinet, expressing the hope that the conference would extend its agenda to include the wider subjects of control and administration of educational affairs.[35] Three members, T. Johnson, T. Farren and J. J. O'Farrell were nominated to represent the party on this First Programme Conference, which drew up a curricular programme for national education but did not address questions of control and administration.

When in 1922 the seventeen Labour deputies under the leadership of Thomas Johnson entered the Dáil they had long since abandoned the policy of standing aside, from which the party undoubtedly suffered. They had now established a credible niche in national and local politics and their broad range of radical policies lent authority and enthusiasm to their parliamentary role as official opposition. Their party cohesion more than compensated for their numerical weakness in the Dáil especially in view of the absence of such cohesion on the government benches prior to the formation of Cumann na nGael in April 1923.[36] Whereas the Labour deputies were committed to a wide programme of social and economic reform in which the restructuring of the education system figured prominently, neither the Provisional nor the Free State government gave high priority to social issues despite the fact that social distress had increased considerably since 1918 and that the number of unemployed had reached 130,000 by 1922.[37]

While its formal attitude was one of neutrality, the Labour Party was *de facto* a pro-Treaty party and while engaging in very radical rhetoric as in the 1922 conference, the acid test was its willingness to cooperate with the provisional government from September 1922. This cooperation, should cause no surprise; there was little if any revolutionary marxism remaining in the party and according to Johnson, the party felt it to be their duty to enter constitutional politics to promote the interests of trade unionists and rural workers.[38] However moderate its general policy, its educational programme as contained in *Labour's policy on education*, must be seen as very radical in the Irish context and especially so in the context of the policy pursued by Eoin MacNeill, as minister, from 1922-1925.

The National Executive at its conference in May 1924, appointed a special committee to advise the executive on a national system of education 'adapted to the needs and circumstances of the children of workers'.[39] They were asked to report on 'the aim of a national system of education', 'on the methods by which such an aim might be realised' and on the various congress resolutions on education adopted previously. This Education Committee under the chairmanship of Thomas Johnson and with representatives of all three teacher organisations, met on twenty occasions and by June 1925 had produced a concise systematic report which was adopted as policy by the annual conference at Newry in August 1925 and published as *Labour's policy on education*.[40] The report contains sections on aims, structure and finance, school buildings, staffing and inspection, the training, remuneration and status of teachers, pupil attendance and medical care, curriculum and educational provision for adults; each section contains a summary and critique of the existing position followed by the committee's recommendations. The report also contains a five page summary of the historical evolution of the education system which seldom sacrifices accuracy to brevity; the report concludes with a short minority report from the representatives of technical education.[41] In identifying an aim for a national system of education, the report commends the account of education in a free Ireland outlined by Pearse and quotes extensively from it.[42] In so far as Irish education had any aim it was the 'killing of nationality and the perpetuation of class distinction'. The aim proposed was one which combined a personal with a social dimension:

> The aim of any national system of education should be in our opinion, to produce men and women who are governors of themselves; whose object in life will be to become civilised Christian human beings, citizens of an Irish commonwealth; who will be sufficient wealth producers, not because, as the prevailing school of economists would have us believe, that the production of wealth is the essential object of all human endeavours but because the production of more wealth will increase the comfort of all people.[43]

In regard to the structure of the system and access to education it made some fundamental proposals:

(i)   that the Department of Education be in the charge of a minister who was not a member of the Executive Council;

(ii)   that the minister be assisted by a Council of Education of which he would be chairman, composed of elected members from all those engaged in education (two-thirds) and nominated members representing the Oireachtas (one-third);

(iii) that the council be consulted on all questions of education policy and legislative proposals and have the right to initiate proposals for submission to the minister;

(iv) that an Educational Authority be established in each county and county borough, composed equally of elected public representative and representatives of the educational interests;

(v) that each County Education Authority should have responsibility for school provision and maintenance, school transport, coordination of all educational services including school meals, medical care, special education and scholarship schemes. The committee which would be advised by local school committees or school groups, would not have any function in the appointment and dismissal of teachers;

(vi) where the cost of the proposed educational scheme exceeds the state estimate on education, the balance to be met by local rates;

(vii) education in all types of schools should be free and 'a broad highway' should be provided for all children having the desire and ability to pass right through to university without disability or hindrance. Maintenance allowances should be paid to working class parents to enable them to keep their children at school to beyond the compulsory age limit.[44]

The report recommended age limits for the different school types with compulsory school attendance from 6-15 years, that the powers in the school attendance act be invested in the Gárdaí, that all teachers have a common training linked to the universities, form one teaching body, have a common salary structure, superannuation scheme and employment security and that the pupil-teacher ratio be reduced to 32:1. It advocated a new role for the inspector as 'a Director of Education rather than as a Departmental Detective'.[45]

The report laid special emphasis on adult education, which it described as being regarded for generations as 'a luxury for the children of the rich' whereas they saw it as 'a permanent national necessity' upon which depended not only the economic recovery of the nation but the development of an informed intelligent public opinion. In a democracy the educational process failed if it did not fit the individual for his duties as a citizen as well as for his personal domestic and vocational duties. To do so, education should aim at developing an open habit of mind, 'proof against sophism, shibboleths, clap-trap phrases and cant', and should enable all to form a sound judgement on the many issues that arise.[46] The report in the context of adult education pays tribute to the education work of the Gaelic League but advocates an adult education movement wider in scope which 'would create a new social spirit and a higher social consciousness in the minds of our people'. The committee envisaged the universities and the county education authorities combining to provide various forms of adult education, including Danish-type Folk High Schools, and it urged that state assistance be given to voluntary agencies which organise adult education.[47]

Though the report deliberately avoided making any major proposals on the curriculum, since the executive had already contributed to the Programme Conference of 1920, it nevertheless decried the fact that education in rural areas had tended to promote migration from the land. The committee devoted considerable time to the curricular position of the Irish language, yet the document contains only six or seven lines on it; bilingualism should be the policy objective and Irish should be stressed in the school programme with the ultimate aim that Irish be the dominant language of the country. These proposals are formulated in a fashion which suggests an absence of unanimity among the committee on this topic.[48]

In the context of Ireland in the twenties, the 1925 policy document is a significant item. In replacing the major initiative on education which was promised but not provided by Cumann na nGael, it synthesised most of the radical education policies inherited by the party from its political forebears; it also introduced into the education debate some current European concepts and in its format and quality it set a headline for the future policy makers in the party. Nevertheless its impact was minimal in a society in which the politics of reaction were dominant and at a time when 'there was little use for idealism and less scope for utopianism'.[49]

The headline set by the 1925 document was not matched for almost forty years and then in an Ireland where there was widespread political support for educational expansion and reform. In the intervening decades the Labour Party, though marked by internal conflict, division and the rejection of progressive policies, nevertheless produced some documents. The party's weak condition in those decades is faithfully reflected in the muted tone of *Labour's programme for a better Ireland* (1943) and *Labour's constructive programme* (1952); nevertheless these two documents do echo some of the current concern in relation to the Irish language policy and the physical condition of schools. These documents also reveal a commitment to postwar planning in education, possibly prompted by deValera's early Cabinet exercise in this field in 1941 and 1942.[50]

The party's 1963 policy document, *Challenge and change in education*, represents a new beginning and contains many of the aspirations towards education innovation which characterised the early sixties; there are also signs that the committee which prepared the document were aware of the general implications of the OECD project *Investment in Education*, then under way. In the early sixties there was keen competition between the three parties to produce a policy on education which would reflect the expansive trend in public opinion and thus capture a growing constituency. Fine Gael and Labour established working parties while Fianna Fáil, though having no published policy document, was in a position to utilise the findings of the report, *Investment in Education* and thus to upstage its rivals. Because of this fluid political situation, *Challenge and change in education*, while maintaining a radical stance and articulating policies based upon traditional Labour egalitarian principles, was nevertheless tentative in its approach and somewhat diffuse in its focus. It advocated free postprimary education for all and access to and participation in higher education according to ability.[51] It contained frequent echoes of the rhetoric of the 1925 document and also some new concepts emanating from the international fora of the early sixties, 'education as an investment in human capital', 'education planning' and 'manpower requirements'. The document proposed the establishment of a national planning branch in the department of education which would consist of representatives of the department, local authorities, the churches, managerial and teacher bodies.

It reserved its most trenchant criticism for the secondary system, 'by which in the past the financial contributions of the state have tended to endow the rich and buttress privilege'.[52] It decried the class-conscious basis of secondary education, the absence of any coherent framework in the system, the uneven geographical distribution of schools whereby in some areas no secondary schools existed, in many towns a number of small schools competed whereas in Dublin there was widespread duplication. The document advocated the amalgamation of small secondary schools, the provision of school transport and proposed as a general principle 'that public money should only be spent on secondary schools open to all'. The mechanism advocated to ensure free education involved increasing the existing capitation grant to schools which abolished tuition fees for day pupils.[53] While in higher education Labour's aim was free education, it recognised in the 1963 document the existing limitations on public finances and proposed to introduce a gradual approach to 'free higher education'.

As regards vocational education, the 1963 document advocated an extension of the school network, the abolition of fees and the establishment in each region of a Regional College which would provide a bridge between the vocational schools and higher education and forge a close link with the economic and industrial life of the region.

On curricular issues, *Challenge and change in education* espoused the broadening of the existing over-academic curricula, schools broadcasting, a new approach to the teaching of history, and the utilisation in subjects such as geography and history of local and regional subject material. It rejected as unrealistic and dated the argument of the 'two cultures' and advocated a balanced core curriculum which would accommodate comfortably both the sciences and the humanities.[54] It urged a revolution in modern languages, castigated the quality of English teaching in schools and urged a comprehensive modern course in language and literature. On the curricular position of Irish it offered some candid comment, identifying the failure to teach the language as the central issue and advocating radical change in teaching methods and syllabus content. In teacher education, the policy proposed that all teachers, primary and postprimary, should attend both Colleges of Education and universities and complement their academic education with appropriate professional pedagogic elements.

In general the 1963 document touched upon most if not all of the major issues in the system, proposed solutions which were in tune with the reformist tradition of the party and in many instances were in advance of the cautious measures being canvassed by the government in the early sixties. However the document itself reveals a caution and a political prudence in some of its vaguer proposals, a prudence which may have been due in equal parts to the residual dominance of conservative party elements and to the fluid nature of political opinion on education at the time.

Growing support for the party and the emergence of a close liaison with the trade unions during the sixties prompted Labour to hope that it might shake off its third party status. Encouraged by the return of 21 members in 1965, it fielded 100 candidates in the general election of 1969; though it increased its total vote to 223,250 it returned only 18 members.[55] In preparation for this election it prepared and published a comprehensive policy document, *Labour party outline policy* , in which 'education' figured as a substantial chapter.[56] The document committed the party to equality of educational opportunity, identified the existing system as part of a structure of social and financial privilege and claimed that the government exercised an uneasy and uncertain control over most of the system, a system from which the parents were effectively excluded. Labour proposed to replace the existing structure by a three-tiered structure as follows:

A. *The General Level*: an integrated basic school covering ages 6-16 on comprehensive lines under local community control.

B. *The Emphatic Level*: covering ages 16-18 involving a core curriculum and four possible specialist lines, under local community control.

C. *The Specialist Level*: a third level system embracing all institutions on equal footing under the coordination of the Higher Education Authority.

This structural blueprint, which was presented as offering a contrast with the non-structural reform of the government, entailed public ownership and management of all schools forming the General and Emphatic levels. This would be secured by means of Education Committees (LEC) acting as the administrative basic elements and by Regional Education Authorities (REA) at county or borough level; both would be democratically elected bodies composed of representatives of local authorities, the churches, parent/teacher oganisations and economic organisations.[57]

The concept of permanent education was central to the policy of equality of opportunity and consequently re-entry for those who had dropped out was advocated. The document identified the following as specific objectives for the education system: education for work, education for leisure, education for mental health and education for tolerance. In higher education, Labour proposed reform of the structures at institutional level and a reformed admissions procedure; it also advocated separate university status for all the defederated colleges of the NUI and for the Technological University of Limerick. It proposed changing the compulsory status of Irish in the curriculum though retaining it initially as an essential school subject and also supported the improvement of teaching methods and the production of modern scientific teaching materials and aids.

This 1969 document was comprehensive, detailed and radical, as befits an education policy designed for the seventies, a decade which the party proclaimed would be socialist. Its most radical element however, involving the total restructuring of the existing system at first and second levels, lacks any indication of the mechanism whereby the existing church-linked schools would be brought into the public ownership and mangement advocated. The document furthermore did not contain any attempt at costing the reforms outlined, although the chapter on taxation policy contained provisions for a capital gains tax, a wealth tax, taxation of farmers and other measures designed to create an equitable taxation system, the returns from which, it was expected, would adequately fund increased expenditure on education.[58]

The policy documents examined in detail, those of 1925, 1963 and 1969, reveal a consistent concern with education policy in the Labour Party, a concern which only appears intermittently in the other parties. Labour, in the legacy of its ideological progenitors and in its early parliamentary years was nurtured in a political ethos which accorded a high priority to education policy. Except during the middle decades it would seem that the party remained faithful to that ethos; however its various terms in government as minority coalition partner offered it very limited opportunities to promote its cherished policy measures.

Cumann na nGael / Fine Gael

Before the Civil War ended in 1923 those Dáil deputies elected in the Pact election of 1922 who supported the Treaty had already taken formal steps to establish a regular political party. Deputies who took the government whip, known collectively and variously as the 'Treaty Party' and the 'Government Party' met in April 1923 and held the inaugural meeting of *Cumann na nGael* in the Dublin Mansion House.[59] The new party commanded the allegiance of only 56 deputies of the total of 153; nevertheless under the leadership of W. T. Cosgrave, aided by the abstention of the anti-Treaty deputies and the active support of the Labour Party and of independent deputies, it provided the Free State with its early governments in the decade following the Treaty. The apparent unity conferred on Cumann na nGael by the common support for the Treaty, concealed a range of views held within the party which made crisis and possible fragmentation highly probable. Such fragmentation occured in 1924 when nine deputies, including a cabinet minister, resigned on the issue of the army mutiny; in 1925, in protest over the Boundary Commission debacle, three further deputies resigned. Such departures however did not seriously impede the overall progress of the party; in the elections between 1922 and 1933 it reached a high point in the second election of 1927 with 62 seats after which the advance of Fianna Fáil implied a growing threat to its retention of power. The electoral fortunes of Cumann na nGael throughout the decade, as shown in Table 7.2 accurately reflected the unstable political situation and the inherent cautious conservatism of its policies which were in sharp contrast with the confident radicalism characterising the early policies of Fianna Fail.

The general character of Cumann na nGael has been decribed in the following terms:

> In the 1920's it looked and behaved like a conservative party and attracted to itself those who desired peace and stable government, those who thought that the Treaty and the Irish Free State and the close Commonwealth connection were the best guarantee of these, and those who could not abide de Valera.[60]

Having suffered defeat at the hands of deValera and Fianna Fáil in 1932 and 1933, the party engaged in some fundamental soul searching and in the resulting metamorphosis it changed its name to Fine Gael.[61] Essentially the new party at parliamentary level, was a union between the old Cumann na nGael and the small National Centre Party; this latter had evolved from Farmer and Independent groups and having won 11 seats in the 1933 election found itself on many issues in agreement with Cumann na nGael. The early years of Fine Gael were marked by confusion, disillusionment, internal conflict and electoral defeat. The period from 1933 to 1948 proved electorally disastrous for the party; its own share of the popular vote fell to 20.5% and its Dáil representation fell to its lowest ever at 30 seats in 1944, while in the same period Fianna Fáil for the first time exceeded the

50% mark in popular support.[62] It achieved government in 1948 as major partner despite returning only 31 deputies and registering its lowest share ever of popular support at 19.8%.

The formation of the Inter-Party government proved a turning point for Fine Gael for it restored the party's flagging morale and helped to create a new public image of a party which had the capacity and desire to govern.[63] Furthermore by its declaration of the Republic in 1949, Fine Gael had successfully distanced itself from its earlier Free State stance and had launched itself on the road to resume its *vocation majoritaire*.[64] The decision of Labour to follow an independent electoral strategy throughout the sixties, while diminishing the possibility of further inter-party administrations, offered Fine Gael a golden opportunity to recast its policies at a time when economic expansion called for fresh socio-economic strategies.

The major party development of the sixties centred on the efforts of the younger and more radical members, led by Declan Costello, to forge more progressive social and economic policies. Despite the adoption of a comprehensive range of policies under the attractive title of *The just society* before the 1965 general election, the persistent tension within the party prevented any major advances. The leadership change in Fine Gael whereby Garret FitzGerald replaced Liam Cosgrave in 1977 ushered in a new era of promise and renewal for the party; it also attracted some youthful vigorous support and created a new image.

Fine Gael's parliamentary strength over the half century since 1933 has varied from 30 to 70; its percentage first preference votes fell below 20% in 1948 and rose to 40% in 1982.[65] Its fortunes as a major party have improved considerably since the mid-seventies and for the first time it seems possible for the party to achieve an overall majority. Accompanying this electoral transformation the basis of its support and the nature of its policies have undergone significant changes since its formation in 1933. By the end of the thirties, the Treaty, which had provided the basic issue as between the two main parties, ceased to be a question of political substance. It became increasingly difficult, according to Rumpf, to distinguish between the policies of the two main parties; while both parties retain policies of national unity and language revival as major goals it seems clear that the bulk of opinion in each party regards both as unrealistic aims.[66] The recent convergence of the two main parties towards a 'catchall' status indicates relative movement on the part of both over the last four decades.

The absence of cleavage bases other than constitutional in the evolution of the major political parties from the Treaty split of 1922 has been widely commented upon.[67] It has been suggested by Garvin that the intensity of the constitutional cleavage effectively swamped not only a left/right bias but that 'it also absorbed liberalism and conservatism as coherent political doctrines'.[68] The party system which developed in the Free State showed little continuity either with the British model or with the system obtaining in Ireland prior to independence; according to Chubb, it was further insulated from European influences by the 'screening' effect of geographical proximity to Britain and by its brand of home-grown Catholicism.[69] Yet the simple bipolar or bimodal party division generated by the Treaty concealed policy differences between Cumann na nGael/Fine Gael and Fianna Fáil which extended beyond the Treaty and 'the desirable and practicable relationships between the new state and the British Empire'.[70] As the constitutional issues died the other underlying differences became more obvious and politically significant. Cumann na nGael and its successor, Fine Gael, were predominantly middle-class in character, supported by the business world and by medium and big farmers.[71] They attracted considerable support also from the Catholic clergy, especially the middle-aged and elderly, who regarded their political values 'as a bastion against the twin dangers to the faith of radical nationalism and socialism'.[72] Fine Gael and Cumann na nGael enjoyed the support of most Protestants in the early decades of the state's existence; the party's involvement in the 1949 declaration of the Republic may have alienated some of that support, though by that time constitutional issues had diminished in importance.[73]

The earliest scientific data available on the sources of party support, confirm the view of Fine Gael as being 'a predominantly middle-class and middle-aged party'; while over 40% of each of the occupational groups C1 (lower middle), C2 (skilled manual) and DE (unskilled manual) supported Fianna Fáil, 26%, 21% and 14% of these groups supported Fine Gael.[74] Furthermore Fianna Fáil's support among working class trade unionists was three times that of Fine Gael's; the latter's support among farmers was stronger than Fianna Fail's in Munster and slightly lower in Leinster. A similar survey conducted in 1977, at a point when Fine Gael's electoral position was low, showed that Fine Gael's support had held only in two groups, 'lower middle-class' and 'semi-skilled and unskilled'; while its support among small farmers had increased by 20%, in all other occupational groups it had suffered serious erosion in support. The party's revival in the past five years and especially its major advance manifest in the general election of November 1982, reveal an increase in support in all the major regions and in Dublin; within five years it has more than doubled its percentage support in Dublin and Munster while in Leinster and Connacht/Ulster it has increased its support by over 50% and 30% respectively.[75] With such a uniform support base, it seems that in the early eighties, Fine Gael had finally shed 'the somewhat tired air of resignation' and that it had re-established itself as a party capable of achieving a majority.[76]

Education as a policy issue did not figure prominently among the priorities of Cumann na nGael or Fine Gael in the early decades of the state despite the large number of leading party personalities who had a keen personal and professional interest in education. Eoin MacNeill, Fionán Lynch, Michael Hayes, Richard Mulcahy, Michael Tierney and John Marcus O'Sullivan had prior to 1922 and in government from 1922 to 1932, taken a keen interest in fundamental educational issues. Michael Tierney's *Education in a free Ireland* (1919) contained a comprehensive blueprint for reform, set within a wider cultural and socio-political context; one would have expected that such a document would have been readily available to the party in which he was so active. Yet it seems that the party in the twenties and thirties was not very enthusiastic about adopting such a comprehensive policy, a stance which may have stemmed from its own inherent conservatism, from a recognition of the political need to avoid church-state conflict or from the need to give attention to more pressing, social, political and economic questions. The party aim which W. T. Cosgrave articulated at the inaugural meeting of Cumann na nGael in 1923, towards the playing down of class, sectional and denominational differences was certainly not realised in the education policies of the party which proved to be reactionary and cautious.

The party's conservative approach to education and its reluctance to encourage any expansion of the role of the state was clearly outlined in the Dáil debate on the Free State Constitution in October 1922. This interesting debate arose on motions by T. J. O'Connell and Professor Magennis to amend the proposed Article 11 and to insert an additional article whereby private schools catering for children of school-going age be conducted on conditions determined by law. The proposed amendment of Article 11 read:

> Provision shall be made by Saorstat Éireann for the free education of the young and for their compulsory attendance at school up to such an age and to such a stage of instruction as shall be prescribed by law.[77]

The draft article stated 'all citizens of the Irish Free State have the right to free elementary education'. Those seeking to amend it deemed the proposed article to be weak, indefinite and leading to confusion. In reply, MacNeill as minister, rejected the amendment on the following grounds:

(i)   the right of education belongs fundamentally to the parents of the children and such a right was a higher right than any possessed by the state;

(ii) the state exists for the benefit of the citizens and not the citizens for the benefit of the state;

(iii) we must be extremely careful that we do not say or appear to say that the control of education belongs as by right to the state; it belongs to the state as by right of service,

(iv) responding to the charge that the proposed article 11 was indefinite, MacNeill claimed that it was essential that it be indefinite for 'none of us is wise enough to define what is sufficient education for children',[78]

(v) the right of a child to education, when the state undertakes the responsibility of providing it is akin to the right to equal liberty i.e. 'equal opportunity in proportion to capacity',

(vi) rejecting the compulsory school attendance, MacNeill stated that he would reject such a proposal in any form as it ran counter to the principle he had already laid down.[79]

When T. J. O'Connell and Tom Johnson claimed that the very arguments made by MacNeill could be validly adduced in favour of the proposed amendment and that their proposed article would cater for parental and church schools, the Minister for Home Affairs, Kevin O'Higgins came to the aid of his colleague, claiming that the proposed amendment was 'loose' for:

If you fix the age at 14/15, you will have some desperately precocious youngster 'sticking' the state for not merely his elementary education but for secondary education and possibly for a certain amount of university education.[80]

The possibility existed, according to O'Higgins, that under such an amended constitutional article, people might claim free secondary education, to which comment Johnson responded: 'succeeding parliaments will do that'. It is necessary to bear in mind that in 1922, the average daily attendance at primary school was under 70% of those enrolled, that the cohort retention rate at sixth standard was under 40% and that less than 10% of those finishing primary school gained access to secondary school.[81]

On the second education amendment moved by O'Connell and supported by Magennis and Johnson, it was proposed that a new article be added to the constitution as follows:

Private schools for the instruction of young persons within the limits of age which may be prescribed for compulsory attendance, shall not be established except on conditions to be determined by law and every person engaged as a teacher in any school attended by such young persons must possess educational qualifications to be prescribed by law.[82]

O'Connell, introducing the motion, claimed that its object was the protection of young persons against exploitation especially for greed, against which it was the duty of the state to protect them. There are strong echoes of the nineteenth century in his reference to 'an impression in many quarters that advocacy of state interference of any kind in education is an advocacy of what is sometimes termed 'godless' education'. Replying, MacNeill seems to have missed O'Connell's main point when he deplored the great folly of those boards and individuals who assume they have all the wisdom in matters such as this . . . 'when some private individual may by private enterprise do something far wiser than they ever conceived'. He then apealed to the memory of Pearse's school, St. Enda's, which bold experiment, he claimed, would have been prevented by a constitutional provision such as that proposed. Concluding, MacNeill asserted that 'it would be very wrong to lay down any principle in the constitution that would prevent initiative in the matter of education'.[83] The amendment was opposed by MacNeill aided by the Minister for Agriculture, Patrick Hogan, and was lost on a vote.

Though these early expressions of policy are mainly statements by a few prominent leaders in the party, they represent the essence of the de facto party line, since in this sector the minister responsible was given wide discretion. MacNeill made full use of such discretion, judging by the numerous occasions on which he expressed his own strong views with vigour. Perhaps such utterances are best typified and illustrated by his speech in March 1923 on the governor general's address to the Dáil. He observes with apparent jubilation that 'the soverign power over their own education was at last come to the people of Ireland' and he pleads with deputies to bring that reality home to the people and so convince them of their enormous responsibility.[84] He states categorically his own position on the role of the state in education:

To speak plainly I assure you, I have, what I could hardly describe with any other word, a horror of state-made education. I think the action of the state in a matter of this kind should be as far as possible a reponse to the feelings and demand of the people.

He further urged the deputies to rouse up the people as to 'that belief which they did not possess in the reality and importance of education'. Finally he raised a topic to which he frequently returned, the structure of the primary and secondary systems; he urged that a fusion be sought between primary and secondary education as he regarded the existing division as totally artificial.

The policies pursued by MacNeill as minister and subsequently followed by his successor, John Marcus O'Sullivan, contain a number of paradoxes which are not easily resolved; either his various statements of policy did not reliably reflect his views or his words and his political actions were fundamentally at variance. He had a horror of 'statism' in education yet he created by legislation in 1924 the first Department of Education which gave to the pubic authority a central role in the system. In his Dáil appeal to deputies to convince the people that 'the sovereign power over their own education' was at last in their hands he seems to contradict his other Dail statement that it is not the role of the minister or anybody else to question an objection raised by the religious bodies.[85] He was opposed to compulsion in education and especially in relation to school attendance and the learning of any specific subject, yet it was under his political leadership that a policy of compulsory Irish was introduced and preparations completed for the introduction of the School Attendance Act of 1926. His ideal structure for Irish education envisaged 'a clear educational highway' from the elementary school to the university, a concept borrowed from the Labour Party, yet in the absence of a recognised state function in policy direction it was not reasonable to expect such structural articulation to emerge.[86]

In their long sojourn in opposition after 1932, Fine Gael seldom gave serious thought to a coherent policy until the sixties yet they seldom missed a chance of responding opportunely to passing items or issues in education. Thus in the thirties the party supported the payment by the state of the total cost of building national schools when the INTO was raising the issue; their scepticism of the wisdom of the Irish language policy was already being expressed in the late thirties and forties. While the party proposed a commission of inquiry in 1943 into the education system they did not seem to have any progressive ideas to add to the process of postwar planning; they rejected the INTO suggestion of a local committee to deal with school maintenance and their education spokesman was of the opinion that the vocational schools should avoid commercial education and concentrate on manual skills and agriculture.[87]

The influence of the conservative policies and procedures laid down by Eoin MacNeill and the early Fine Gael leaders in the twenties persisted not only in the system but also in the party. Towards the end of the fifties, however, a new perspective emerged in which education policy was viewed within the wider context of socio-economic planning. In the early sixties a policy group was established to examine party policy in detail and to draw up a comprehensive party programme of reform. This group constituted an expert committee whose work was part of the wider 'Just Society' movement. The formal result of their work was a substantial policy document, *Fine Gael policy for a just society - education* (1966) in the introduction to which, the party leader committed his party to 'giving priority to education over other important policy matters' and to a White Paper based upon the document as a working blueprint for Fine Gael's Minister for Education when in government.

The document is systematic, detailed and professionally comprehensive; it deals in turn with the policy making process and the role of the department, primary, postprimary and higher education, teacher education and educational research. Among party policy documents it is singularly distinguished in that it quantified realistically the cost of its reform measures and estimated both their current and capital implications over a five year span.[88]

The document criticised the policy making process, which is described as dominated by the administrative officers of the department; policy making lacked the direct input of the professional officers of the department and also the statistical data and research activity essential to any planning process. It endorsed the analysis and recommendations of *Investment in Education*, stressed the need for planning and emphasised the role of the Development Unit in the transformation of the Department.[89] It advocated the usual reform measures designed to improve the education process, i.e. lowering of class size, increased grants, the extension and improvement of school facilities, the enlargement of curricular provision and facilities for in-service education.

Its most progressive proposals concerned access to education and aspects of the structure of the system, many of which though previously canvassed as desirable had not received formal commitment from the government. This policy document committed Fine Gael to a radical extension of opportunity by means of a stipulated minimum of three years postprimary education to 15 for all, a review of state capital assistance to private secondary schools, the provision by the state of comprehensive schools in sparsely populated areas, a review of apprentice and technician education and the provision of maintenance grants to cover opportunity costs in higher education. Perhaps its most significant proposal was that which sought to provide free postprimary education in 'a scheme under which almost all secondary schools will be enabled without financial loss to offer free education in most cases to all the children in the school'.[90] This scheme would offer increased capitation grants to schools in lieu of fees; where these grants equalled income from fees, schools would offer free places to all, in other schools a proportion of places would be free. The document claimed that such a scheme would promote social mixing and would avoid the danger of creating a barrier between fee-paying and free schools.

In relation to structural changes the document offers a wide range of reforms designed to decentralise the structure and raise the efficiency of what it termed 'an out-of-date, rigid and unimaginative educational system'.[91] Its twin aims were to improve the policy making machinery of the central Department and the delegation of specified functions to appropriate professional interests and subsidiary groups. Proposals were put forward for a reorganisation of the department as a progressive development-orientated organisation staffed at the highest level by qualified personnel and working in close collaboration with teachers and schools.[92] Two new bodies are proposed, an Educational Planning Committee responsible for physical and human resources and a Schools Committee responsible for curricular policy, evaluation and teaching methodology at primary and postprimary levels. In the politically sensitive area of primary school management, Fine Gael proposed to 'encourage the establishment of school committees to work with the school managers in the management of the national schools'.[93] With a view to solving the problems of school maintenance and funding, the document proposed 'to seek the collaboration of the religious authorities in establishing diocesan or regional school offices' with which would be associated regional school banks, somewhat akin to the Landeschulkasse of the German system. Among the other structural reforms advocated were a University Advisory Committee, the creation of posts of responsibility in primary and postprimary schools and the association of primary teacher training with the universities.

The *Just Society* document on Education owed a debt to the OECD report *Investment in Education* whose quantitative analysis and observations its authors found very acceptable; moreover, many of the reforms advocated in the party's proposals had gained common currency among professional educationalists and interested parties throughout the sixties. Like much more of the *Just Society* policy proposals, the education document did not find favour among all the party's members. Nevertheless, it bore some substantial fruit; among politicians it raised the level of political commitment to educational reform, not least in Fianna Fáil who were prompted in 1966 to propose 'free education to 18'. In addition, when in the more recent Fine Gael administrations of the early 1980s, the reformist authors of the 1966 document had achieved power, their checklist of education reforms was already drawn up.

The second major Fine Gael policy document, *Action programme for education in the 80's*, was published in 1980 following work over three years by an expert committee; it was sanctioned by the party front bench and approved by the parliamentary party as part of its preparation for the 1981 general election. In contrast with the era of economic expansion and political optimism in which the *Just Society* document of 1966 was conceived, the *Action programme* of 1980 reflects the recessionary pressures and the resultant constraints operating on the system in the late seventies and early eighties.[94] Unlike the earlier party document and the government white paper of 1980 it does not examine the various structural levels of the system seriatim but discusses various reform and expansion measures under three general dimensions of policy i.e. social, educational and organisational/administrative priorities. Long-term reform measures are identified from which a list of high priority reforms is constructed.

Some of these measures are of high significance in that they mark a sharp contrast between the policy of Fine Gael and that of Fianna Fáil especially in relation to higher education, the administration of the system and the postprimary curriculum and evaluation process. Fine Gael favours a comprehensive system of higher education rather than the binary structure advocated by Fianna Fáil; in the *Action programme* it proposed the creation of a Conference of Irish Universities and a parallel Conference of Technological Education, both participating in the Higher Education Authority, thus unifying the higher education sector.[95] The *Action programme* proposed the establishment of regional education authorities and of school management boards with a view to 'lessening the monolithic control by a centralised Department of Education and devolving administrative responsibility to local control centres'.[96] This proposal is rather tentative, indicative perhaps of the flexibility required in such potentially explosive areas of educational policy. The document's proposals on postprimary curricular policy however are far from tentative; they make a heavy commitment to an independent curriculum and examination board having full responsibility for curricular provision and evaluation at second level. This commitment is made without any critical analysis of the existing mechanisms involving inspectorial staff and teachers; neither is any attempt made to cost the proposal.

This *Action programme* recognises both the need to ensure 'that education be given a just and adequate share of the annual budget' and the 'obligation to ensure that the money invested in education is used to maximum effect and where the need is greatest'.[97] In the light of this recognition, however, the absence of any attempt to quantify the cost implications of the proposals is a major weakness. In this sense the *Just society* education policy document of 1966 was a political document of superior character.

Fine Gael at its foundation was heir to a legacy of conservatism and caution in education policy, a legacy which was enshrined in party tradition and thus safeguarded by the high standing of Eoin MacNeill in the party. That legacy was further fortified by the important role played by Cumann na nGael governments and Ministers for Education in laying down the precedents which would govern policy for four decades. This legacy was sustained, if not augmented, by the innate conservatism of Richard Mulachy as Minister in the forties and fifties. The political caution and reticence thus established did not diminish significantly until the late fifties and early sixties when educational reform had become a major issue in political and public debate. The two major policy documents recently published by Fine Gael reflect both the enhanced position of education as a political issue and the growing influence within the party of the younger liberal element.

Fianna Fáil

Fianna Fáil has been described and has traditionally seen itself as a national movement or organisation rather than a conventional political party. The justification for such a description lies in its origins and in the role which Éamon de Valera assigned to it in its early years. In an interview given by him to United Press in April 1926, de Valera said:

> The new Republican organisation, Fianna Fáil, has for its purpose the re-uniting of the Irish people and the bonding of them together for the tenacious pursuit of the following ultimate aims, using at every moment such means as are rightfully available.

Among the ultimate aims identified were, political independence and unity as a republic, restoration of the Irish language and the development of a mature Irish culture, a social system in which as far as possible equal opportunity will be afforded to every Irish citizen to live a noble and useful Christian life, land distribution to maximise the number of rural families and an economic self-sufficiency based on a balance between agriculture and other essential industries.[98]

Fianna Fáil was formally launched as a political party at a meeting in the La Scala Theatre, Dublin on 16 May 1926, at which deValera delivered an address outlining the political philosophy of the new party which was later published in pamphlet form as *A National Policy*.[99] In this inaugural speech deValera committed his new party not only to political independence and republican autonomy but also to 'taking an effective part in improving the social and material conditions of the people and in building up the strength and morale of the nation as a whole'. He envisaged such a social programme as involving an attack upon the problems of emigration and unemployment; he was realist enough to recognise that such a programme of social reconstruction could not be achieved overnight 'while the people were asleep'. In this address de Valera also committed Fianna Fáil to a reduction in the state bureaucracy and the constitutional structure of the state; he favoured the election of the Executive or cabinet directly by the people independent of the Dáil. He also proposed that the Dáil membership be reduced from 153 to 100 and that the Free State Senate or upper house be abolished and replaced by an Advisory Council of a vocational character.[100]

The period from 1927 to 1932, when the party was on the threshold of power, was a significant period in the development of Fianna Fáil; it began to recover the electoral support which Sinn Féin had lost in the years between 1923 and 1926 and 'quickly became the heir to the main body of popular republican sentiment'.[101] The years following entry to the Dáil exercised some fundamental influences on the party's structure and political philosophy; according to Garvin:

The experience of political and military humiliation and the collapse of its political ideas and postures had a hardening, sobering and maturing effect on the Republican Party, taught it the importance of popular organisation and sensitivity to popular opinion and also gave it an internal unity and cohesion which Cumann na nGael lacked.[102]

Fianna Fáil's rapid growth and its early electoral success are linked to the fine structure of the party organisation and to the ideological ancestry of its local units. Recent studies have shown that the party's organisation 'echoed the branch structures of older pan-nationalist parties dating back to the 1880's', while the third Sinn Féin (1924) showed little organisational links either with the pre-Treaty organisations or with the later Fianna Fáil patterns of the 1930's.[103] In establishing its local party structure, Fianna Fáil relied heavily on old IRA units and personnel but unlike Cumann na nGael, it did not utilise any of the ecclesiastical network. Presiding over this national organisation deValera provided the stability and centripetal cohesion which the new party needed; his central charismatic role has prompted one commentator to describe Fianna Fáil as a lay church and deValera as its political pope.[104]

In the half-century since it first achieved power in 1932, electoral support for the party has never fallen below 40%, its total of elected deputies has never been outside the range 65-84 and it has formed 14 of the 18 governments which have ruled during the period. During the sixteen years of Fianna Fáil's first period in office support for the party increased and diversified and its policies were accordingly modified. From its initial power base among 'the poorer and more radical element', it quickly extended its support among 'the growing Catholic commercial and industrial middle class, mainly composed of operators of small family businesses, who prospered in a modest way under the party's protection policies'.[105] According to Chubb, the longer Fianna Fáil remained in power the more acceptable deValera's image as a conservative and devout Catholic became and the more supportive links were established between the party and the business community.

The periods in opposition, 1948-51, and 1954-57, were widely interpreted within the party as temporary aberrational phenomena; long periods in office, its established political dominance of the local authority structure and the stability of its administrations had helped to establish Fianna Fáil in the popular mind as the normal government party and 'the only party capable of ensuring the stablility of single-party government'.[106]

Before discussing the educational policies pursued by Fianna Fáil it will be useful to review the broader social economic and cultural goals advocated by the party. In the period from its foundation to the outbreak of World War II the party's policies followed a pattern which could be broadly classified as radical; this early radicalism was identified with its espousal of 'an expansion of state initiative and a long-term social and economic policy clearly rooted in republicanism' and 'of a frugal Gaelic Ireland, as little despoiled as possible by the forces of civilisation especially English civilisation; a state wherein there would be no rich and no poor, but rather a countryside scattered with small farms and small industries'.[107] The effect of this radical posture on the electorate is evidenced in the extent to which Fianna Fáil made inroads on the natural support base of the Labour Party; in its *Annual Report* for 1932 the Labour Party reported that 'the workers expected Fianna Fáil to fulfil all their wishes'.[108] According to Rumpf it was frequently asserted, especially by its own supporters, that Fianna Fáil was 'Ireland's Labour Party'.[109] Despite such assertions however, de Valera and his party were cautiously conservative in their radicalism. This paradoxical situation was achieved mainly by the dexterity displayed by de Valera in his numerous policy statements and by his 'characteristic fondness for ambiguous political formulae and for the manipulation of political symbols rather than of political ideas'.[110] It has been claimed that:

(Fianna Fáil) by 1938 while still managing to give the impression of being the party for the underprivileged and so retaining a wide base of support, was at the same time becoming a party of irreproachably respectable dye and was beginning to attract the men of property and position.[111]

This early espousal by Fianna Fáil of radical social and economic policies is clearly reflected in the speeches of its leader. It is of some significance that in the years of its initial radicalism, de Valera repeatedly committed Fianna Fáil to the social and economic policies of the 1916 leaders and of the First Dáil. Speaking at Arbour Hill in April 1933, he urged his party to resolve in their hearts to complete the work of the men of Easter Week. They should bear in mind that 'to the leaders of Easter Week the Republic meant more than a form of government, that it meant more than an independent Ireland'. The leaders of 1916 were not men who used words lightly and when in the Proclamation they guaranteed 'equal rights and equal opportunities to all citizens' they meant it. According to de Valera, this meant that the circumstances which made it all but impossible for so many of our poorer citizens to live the life of rational beings should no longer be tolerated. In urging his party followers to follow the idealism of the Proclamation, de Valera asserted:

If we are truly followers of the men we commemorate today, Ireland must mean for us not merely a combination of chemical elements but the living people of our own country. We must be prepared in the words of the proclamation 'to cherish all the children of the nation equally'.[112]

This statement, delivered at the graves of the 1916 leaders, outlined a general principle of socio-economic policy to which de Valera committed his party, a principle which carries a direct implication for the party's policy on education. When, however, sixteen years later he came to evaluate the nation's progress since 1916, de Valera had reformulated his interpretation of the aims of the 1916 leaders. His exposition in 1949 differs fundamentally from that of 1933 in its avoidance of the basic egalitarianism and of the assertion of 'equal rights and equal opportunities' so central to the 1933 speech. According to the 1949 version if we wished to know how our society should be organised, we would find guidance in the sound principles of de Valera's 1937 constitution. Fianna Fáil, it would appear, was no longer committed to its early undiluted republicanism and it no longer attached priority status to 'cherishing all the children of the nation equally'. In 1949, after a year in opposition, deValera restated the aims of the 1916 leaders in the following terms:

> To make our nation once more a free nation and an Irish-speaking nation and thus to lay the foundation from which could be rebult a Gaelic national state, within which the traditional distinctive qualities of our people might find adequate and just expression; these were the foremost aims of the leaders who rose in arms in 1916.[113]

This fundamental change or moderation in his policies by deValera can be linked to a more general shift to the right observable in both Fine Gael and Fianna Fáil. According to Rumpf, as the left was captured by radical republicans so the mainstream of Irish national politics moved steadily to the right; on the pro-Treaty side this development took place between 1916 and the end of the Fine Gael administration in 1932. In Fianna Fáil a similar shift is apparent 'from the radical republicanism of the civil war period and the economic war, to the conservative period which began with the signing of the Anglo-Irish agreement of 1938'.[114] In areas of the world which have nationality problems, nationalist radical parties in general enjoy considerably more political flexibility than do Labour parties. This very flexibility, while enabling them to win power 'suggests that in the long run, like Fianna Fáil, they will not be very reliable vehicles for wide-ranging social reform'.[115] Such social reform would have been a natural concomitant of a republicanism which was properly understood; however on the anti-Treaty side, according to P. S. O'Hegarty 'the Republic was worshipped for its own sake, without reference to the meaning of the word or the conditions which would establish its meaning'.[116] Such worship was, in the view of the same contemporary observer, 'mystical, hysterical and remote' and as such promoted adherence more to the symbols rather than to the substance of political discussion.

While terms such as 'radical' and 'semi-revolutionary' have been applied to Fianna Fáil in its early phase, by 1938 such terms do not describe the more cautious policies emerging. If by the 1938 agreement deValera had effectively dismantled the Treaty, he had also begun to attract support from the Protestant population and from many who had previously derived no joy from his electoral success in 1932.[117] A significant part of Fianna Fáil's radicalism in the 1920s and 1930s centred upon its relationship with the Catholic church and its clergy. The favourable attitude towards the Treaty expressed by the Catholic hierarchy even before the Dáil had voted on it, determined largely the later relationships between the Church and the two parties emerging from the Civil War. The episcopal joint letter of October 1922, supporting the Provisional Government and declaring the republican stance to be without moral justification, caused antagonism towards the bishops and prompted deValera to appeal to Rome against the episcopal judgement. At a personal level the harsh pastoral treatment received by republicans from some clergy generated a deep resentment among many of those who later formed the nucleus of Fianna Fáil.[118] Ten years after the episcopal pastoral, when de Valera had come to power, he expressed to Cardinal Lauri, his belief that a decade of misunderstanding between the church and republicanism had come to an end. That outcome had been achieved mainly by de Valera's control over his party and especially by his success in smothering the latent anti-clericalism of some of his colleagues; it was also achieved by Fianna Fáil's pragmatic sensitivity to an electorate which frequently confused piety with political guidance. In a number of spheres, however, deValera especially in the thirties showed himself to be more independent of the Catholic church than Cumann na nGael had been; this independence is more than countered by the extent to which he was influened by Catholic theology and Catholic social thinking in drafting his constitution in 1937. The 1937 constitution, in its 'distinctly Catholic and Irish flavour' stands in marked contrast with the more secular constitution of 1922 introduced by a party which was regarded as clericalist and reactionary.[119]

It is obvious that de Valera and his party regarded the Catholic church as much more than another, though very significant, interest group which played a major role in Irish politics. In the Fianna Fáil view, it has been suggested, that Ireland and Irish society rested on three central pillars, the Catholic church, the Gaelic Athletic Association and the party; there were other important structural elements but they were peripheral and secondary. Some of the 'independent' stances deValera adopted could validly be classified as 'symbolic', designed more to secure wayward segments of his following than to thwart church interests. According to Garvin:

In the nationalist community, the Church could wield massive direct political power not only through its participation in party politics but also through its role in shaping and organising public opinion through the educational system, the pulpit and the popular press.[120]

Acceptance of this reality would induce in most political leaders a resolve to avoid major conflict with the church; so astute a politician as de Valera reacted by ensuring that no major policy advocated by his party could be construed as antagonistic to church teaching or interests, especially in those fields in which the church claimed a special interest, competence or commitment.[121] Education was high on the list of such fields and in this sensitive sector, as in many others, deValera was never short of close clerical friends who kept him in direct touch with ecclesiastical thinking and church intentions. It is of some significance that the only major education policy on which the state and the church seemed to differ, the reforms of the sixties, arose after deValera's retirement from active politics. It may be of greater general significance that in his periods of office reform proposals were abandoned once deValera detected signs of episcopal opposition.

In examining the education policies advocated by Fianna Fáil, one is constrained by the dearth of published policy documents; there are some documents available, one White Paper and some circulars which represent ministerial and departmental thinking but very little which originated within the party.[122] This contrasts sharply with the practice of the other main parties and reflects the consummate caution and pragmatism generated within Fianna Fáil by long periods of office. Furthermore deValera's personal interest in education and the dominance exercised by him in the elaboration of policy generally confined party discussion of education policy to those issues outlined by him. Thus his direct influence on his ministers, especially on Tomás Deirg, his own brief but crucial occupation of the Department of Education in 1939/40, and his frequent speeches on education and cultural issues justify us in regarding his utterances as a faithful résumé and determinant of party policy on education.

A fundamental plank in Fianna Fáil's policy on education, its language revival policy, stems directly from the second of the party's five basic aims enunciated in 1926, which seeks: 'The restoration of the Irish language and the development of a native Irish culture'.[123] Prior to 1932 however this party aim does not figure prominently in deValera's many speeches either in the Dáil or to the party. In the election manifesto of 1932 the language policy is stated more precisely and in a larger socio-economic context:

To endevour by systematic effort to preserve the Irish language and make it again the spoken language of the people; to save the native speaker from the emigration ship, to provide employment for him in the Gaeltacht, and make it possible for the language to spread out naturally from the Gaeltacht to the surrounding areas.[124]

By 1937 de Valera in an important speech to the party Ard-Fheis identified language revival and national unity as co-equal aims, a statement which, in theory at least, has survived as representing party policy for almost half a century. The role of language revival as an element of education policy will be examined in detail in a later chapter; the topic needs no further examination here except to establish its central significance in deValera's overall socio-cultural philosophy and also to note a significant shift in his language policy in regard to the role of the schools.

According to deValera, it was essential to revive the Irish language if we were to preserve our national identity:

> If we want to stand as a really distinctive nation we must preserve that one great attribute of nationhood that is our language. For that we have to depend on the schools, the grown-up people and we have to depend on other organisations in Irish life.[125]

In 1943 he devoted a large part of the famous and oft-quoted speech, 'The Ireland that we dreamed of' to the question of the langauge; drawing upon the philosophy of Thomas Davis he declared:

> It is for us what no other language can be. It is our very own. It is more than a symbol; it is an essential part of our nationhood. It has been moulded by the thought of a hundred generations of our forebears. As a vehicle of three thousand years of our history, the language for us is precious beyond measure.[126]

Though it was Cumann na nGael who introduced the policy of promoting the revival of Irish through the formal education system, from the accession to power of Fianna Fáil in 1932, this policy was implemented with greater vigour. However by June 1940 de Valera had changed his position especially in relation to the use of the language as the sole medium of instruction in the infant school. Reflecting perhaps the doubts about the policy expressed in the iterim report of the INTO survey, he indicated in his estimate speech, as Minister for Education, that he did not agree with the language policy as introduced in 1922; he had grave doubts about the wisdom of using the language as the medium of instruction in the early stages; had he been in charge of policy then he would have concentrated first on increasing mastery of the language itself.[127]

There was however much more to the education policy of Fianna Fáil and de Valera than a strong commitment to language revival; it embraced such topics as curricular content, accountability in the primary school and the relative educational efficiency of each school type. These and other issues were raised by deValera in his speech on the education estimate in June 1940. This Dáil speech is of special significance. It examined the relative performance of primary, secondary and vocational schools, it acknowledged the restricted access to postprimary education then obtaining, yet it condemns the vocational system out of hand. This issue will be examined later in greater detail when discussing the ministers and the Department of Education.

It would be unfair to regard the ministers who served in Education in de Valera's governments as feeble puppets of the master; Tomás Deirg and Seán Moylan were strong political characters, who were steadfast in their personal viewpoint and not short of educational ideas. In the thirties and forties Fianna Fáil attempted to extend educational opportunity in the Gaeltacht and under the vocational system in the urban areas, introduced a compulsory primary certificate examination, examined the raising of the school leaving age and attempted to provide a mechanism by which national school building and maintenance be organised and funded by a collective diocesan effort. In the process of postwar planning, educational issues were not deemed to merit a White Paper and the departmental committee examining the question of reform produced a disappointing document. Throughout much of this period Fianna Fáil seemed to be insensitive to the just demand of teachers and suffered a resultant loss of support following the teachers' strike of 1946.

The party, however, returned to the early professed egalitarianism of deValera when he had gone; in the sixties when it fell to Fianna Fáil's lot to make provision for extended educational opportunity, it garnished the political deed with profuse and appropriate references to 'equality of opportunity' and the party's commitment to 'cherishing all the children of the nation equally'. Ten years later in the election manifesto of 1977, Fianna Fáil committed itself once more to 'a guarantee of equality of opportunity', which it claimed was not being achieved, and to a re-appraisal of education priorities.[128]

In the half century since 1932 one can detect two phases in Fianna Fail's approach to education policy, between which deValera's departure from active politics in 1959 marks the transition point. The first phase is dominated by deValera and Deirg; the second is characterised by the efforts of a succession of young ministers who were anxious to respond to the demands of a changed electorate. In neither phase did the party compile and publish a policy document on education; for de Valera, in response to a higher dictat, the education system and its structure were as immutable as a mathematical constant. To his younger proteges, especially to Hillery, Colley, O'Malley and Lenihan in the sixties, education and its expanding budget offered the ideal platform for advancement. Though lacking the support of a party policy document, these young ministers were unerring in identifying the potential public support for specific policies and in adopting these policies without delay. Because of this supreme pragmatism, few would question the validity of the claim in its 1977 Manifesto,that Fianna Fáil was 'the party of Investment in Education and of free education'.[129]

In reviewing the contributions of the political parties to education policy one observes a very sharp distinction between the Labour Party and the larger parties. For Labour education policy has been a constant element of party concern almost from its foundation; its international contacts and especially its links with English trade unionism and socialist opinion kept it in touch with progressive thinking in education. Furthermore, Labour enjoyed a direct continuity with pre-Treaty politics which enabled it to carry over into the post-Treaty period those education issues which were central to the McPherson Bill of 1919.[130] For Fine Gael and Fianna Fáil innate conservatism and consummate pragmatism respectively dominated the political process and overcame whatever claims the proclamation of 1916 and the 'Democratic Programme' of the First Dáil exercised on their collective political consciences. Until the mid-fifties neither party engaged in any serious consideration of questions relating to *structure* or *access* in the education system; both parties limited policy discussion to politically safe curricular and other *process* issues. When in the sixties both major parties espoused policies of expansion in education, the impetus for such policies came less from the parties than from an electorate which was ideologically in advance of the politicians.

TABLE 7.1

The various governments in the period 1922-88, the constituent parties and the
party identity of the Minister for Education.

Government	Term of Office	Parties	Minister for Education	Minister's Party
First Dáil	Jan 1919-Aug 1921	Sinn Féin	None	—
Second Dáil	Aug 1921-Sept 1922	Sinn Féin	J. J. O'Kelly	Sinn Féin
			M. Hayes	
Provisional	Jan 1922-Aug 1922	Pro-Treaty	F. Lynch	Pro-Treaty
	Aug 1922-Sept 1922	Pro-Treaty	E. MacNeill	Pro-Treaty
Cum. na nGael	Sept 1922-Sept 1923	Cum. na nGael	E. MacNeill	Cum. na nGael
Cum. na nGael	Sept 1923-June 1927	Cum. na nGael	E. MacNeill	Cum. na nGael
			J. M. O'Sullivan	Cum. na nGael
			(from Jan 1926)	
Cum. na nGael	June 1927-Oct 1927	Cum. na nGael	J. M. O'Sullivan	Cum. na nGael
Cum. na nGael	Oct 1927-Mar 1932	Cum. na nGael	J. M. O'Sullivan	Cum. na nGael
Fianna Fáil	Mar 1932-Feb 1933	Fianna Fáil	T. Deirg	Fianna Fáil
Fianna Fáil	Feb 1933-July 1937	Fianna Fáil	T. Deirg	Fianna Fáil
Fianna Fáil	July 1937-June 1938	Fianna Fáil	T. Deirg	Fianna Fáil
Fianna Fáil	June 1938-July 1943	Fianna Fáil	T. Deirg	Fianna Fáil
			(to 8/9/39)	
Fianna Fáil			S. T. Ó Ceallaigh	Fianna Fáil
			(to 27/9/39)	
Fianna Fáil			E. de Valera	Fianna Fáil
			(to 18/6/40)	
Fianna Fáil			T. Deirg	Fianna Fáil
			(to July 1943)	
Fianna Fáil	July 1943-May 1944	Fianna Fáil	T. Deirg	Fianna Fáil
Fianna Fáil	May 1944-Feb 1948	Fianna Fáil	T. Deirg	Fianna Fáil
Inter-Party	Feb 1948-June 1951	Fine Gael/Lab.	R. Mulcahy	Fine Gael
		Clann na Pobl.		
		Clann na Talm.		
Fianna Fáil	June 1951-June 1954	Fianna Fáil	S. Moylan	Fianna Fáil
Inter-Party	June 1954-March 1957	Fine Gael/Lab.	R. Mulcahy	Fine Gael
		Clann na Pobl.		
		Clann na Talm.		
Fianna Fáil	March 1957-June 1959	Fianna Fáil	J. Lynch	Fianna Fáil
Fianna Fáil	June 1959-Oct 1961	Fianna Fáil	P. J. Hillery	Fianna Fáil
Fianna Fáil	Oct 1961-April 1965	Fianna Fáil	P. J. Hillery	Fianna Fáil
Fianna Fáil	April 1965-Nov 1966	Fianna Fáil	G. Colley	Fianna Fáil
Fianna Fáil			(to 13/7/66	Fianna Fáil
Fianna Fáil	July 1966-Nov 1966	Fianna Fáil	D. O'Malley	Fianna Fáil
Fianna Fáil	Nov 1966-Dec 1968	Fianna Fáil	D. O'Malley	Fianna Fáil
			(to 10/3/68)	Fianna Fáil
		Fianna Fáil	B. Lenihan	Fianna Fáil
Fianna Fáil	Dec 1968-June 1969	Fianna Fáil	B. Lenihan	Fianna Fáil
Fianna Fáil	June 1969-Feb 1973	Fianna Fáil	P. Faulkner	Fianna Fáil
Coalition	Feb 1973-June 1977	Fine Gael/Lab.	R. Burke	Fine Gael
			(to 31/2/1976)	
			P. Barry	Fine Gael
			(to June 1977)	
Fianna Fáil	June 1977-June 1981	Fianna Fáil	J. Wilson	Fianna Fáil
Coalition	June 1981-Feb 1982	Fine Gael/Lab.	J. Boland	Fine Gael
Fianna Fáil	Feb 1982-Nov 1982	Fianna Fáil	M. O'Donoghue	Fianna Fáil
			(to Oct 1982)	
			G. Brady	Fianna Fáil
			(to Nov 1982)	
Coalition	Dec 1982-Feb 1986	Fine Gael/Lab.	Gemma Hussey	Fine Gael
	Feb 1986-Mar 1987	Fine Gael/Lab.	P. Cooney	Fine Gael
Fianna Fáil	Mar 1987-to date	Fianna Fáil	Mary O'Rourke	Fianna Fáil

TABLE 7.2

The number of Dáil deputies returned by the two main political groups pro-Treaty/
Cumann na nGael and anti-Treaty/Fianna Fáil in the elections held 1922-33.

Election	6/1922	9/1923	6/1927	10/1927	1932	1933
Pro-Treaty C. na nG	56	63	47	62	57	49
Anti-Treaty Fianna Fáil	36	44	44	57	72	77

TABLE 7.3

The electoral support for each of the main parties in the general elections from 1923 to 1987
expressed in percentage of first preference votes and (seats) secured.

General Election	Fianna Fáil %	C. na nG./F.G. %	Labour %	Others	
1923 (153)	27.4(44)	39.0(63)	10.6(14)	12.1(15)	10.9(17)
1927(153)	26.1(44)	27.4(47)	12.6(22)	8.9(11)	25.0(29)
1927(153)193	35.2(57)	38.7(62)	9.1(13)	6.4 (6)	15.7(15)
1932(153)	44.5(72)	35.3(57)	7.7 (7)	2.1 (5)	10.5(12)
1933(153)	49.7(77)	30.5(48)	5.7 (8)	—	14.1(20)
1937(138)	45.2(69)	34.8(48)	10.3(13)	—	9.7 (8)
1938(138)	51.9(77)	33.3(45)	10.0 (9)	—	4.7 (7)
1943(138)	41.9(67)	23.1(32)	15.7(17)	10.3(13)	9.0 (9)
1944(138)	48.9(76)	20.5(30)	11.5(12)	10.8(11)	8.4 (9)
1948(147)	41.9(68)	19.8(31)	11.3(19)	5.3 (7)	21.7(22)
1951(147)	46.3(69)	25.7(40)	11.4(16)	2.9 (6)	13.7(16)
1954(147)	43.4(65)	32.0(50)	12.0(19)	3.1 (5)	9.5 (8)
1957(147)	48.3(78)	26.6(40)	9.1(12)	2.4 (3)	3.6(14)
1961(144)	43.8(70)	32.0(47)	11.6(16)	1.5 (2)	11.1 (9)
1965(144)	47.8(72)	33.9(47)	15.4(22)	—	2.8 (3)
1969(144)	45.7(75)	34.1(50)	17.0(18)	—	3.2 (1)
1973(144)	46.2(69)	35.1(54)	13.7(19)	—	5.0 (2)
1977(148)	50.6(84)	30.5(43)	11.6(17)	—	7.3 (4)
1981(166)	45.3(78)	36.5(65)	9.9(15)	—	8.3 (8)
1982(166)(Feb)	47.0(81)	37.0(63)	9.1(15)	—	(7)
1982(166)(Nov)	45.0(75)	39.0(70)	9.3(16)	—	(5)
1987(166)(Feb)	44.15(81)	27.07(51)	6.44(12)	—	(22)

Source: Compiled from Chubb, B. *The Government and Politics of Ireland*, (1974), Table B. 5,
p.334 and from other sources.

CHAPTER 8

The Churches

The Irish education system is most accurately characterised as an 'aided' system, in which the state assists other agencies, mainly by means of funding, to provide education services at all three levels. At both first and second levels, with the sole exception of the vocational system, the majority of the aided agencies are churches, church bodies or trusts, or corporate bodies in which the churches exercise a large influence. This applies equally to the churches of both main denominations, Catholic and Protestant; in the vocational system the aided agency is the local authority or its specialist sub- committee. At third level the state funds universities and colleges of technology either directly, through the Higher Education Authority or by means of the appropriate local authority.

Thus throughout the formal education system the churches or their agencies occupy a prominent structural position, both proprietorial and managerial. Practically all of the national schools are managed by boards which are chaired *ex officio* by clergymen and whose other membership is determined partly by church decision; in addition the legal trustees of the school property also come from the ranks of senior diocesan clergymen and church parochial officers. In the second level the vast majority of secondary schools are owned and managed by church bodies, religious orders or trusts; in the more recently consti- tuted comprehensive and community schools diocesan authorities and religious orders have been given a share in the management and trusteeship. Of the 548 secondary schools, 494 are owned and conducted by Catholic agencies and 26 by Protestant boards or governing bodies; the balance, 28 schools, are owned and managed by lay persons, the majority of whom are Catholic.[1] In the vocational system which conducts 246 schools, the churches have not played a dominant role yet they are involved, mainly through membership of the controlling Vocational Education Committees. Each of the 38 Committees contains 14 members of whom 8 are elected local council- lors and the remaining 6 are coopted from among local representa- tives of cultural, commerical, trade union and educational interests. Of the 38 committees operating in 1982/83, 6 committees had no clergyman among their members while of the other 32 committees,

10 were chaired by Catholic clergymen; 10 of the committees had 3 or more clergymen, 22 had 2 or less and there were twenty committees each of which had one Protestant clerical member.[2] In an earlier chapter, the interaction of the managerial bodies and the Department of Education has been described and its stuctural features outlined; the high and low processes involved in that interaction provide the main locus for the influence exercised by the churches on education policy.

In addition to the strong quantitative presence of the churches at all levels of the system, the controversies of the last century and the signal victories achieved have invested education with a special significance for both churches. According to D.A. Akenson, referring to the national system:

> The second important effect upon the Irish religious situation was that, in addition to saving the churches considerable money, the national system delivered a great deal of patronage into their hands.[3]

Compared to the education structures in other European states where the churches were losing ground to public initiative, the system obtaining in Ireland by the turn of the century gave economic relief, political power and ideological satisfaction to the churches. In other states where the churches rejected public education, the main price of rejection was the creation out of church funds of an alternative autonomous system; in Ireland the churches had secured a system which was acceptable to and controlled by them, but was funded mainly by the state. The acceptability of such a system to the Catholic church and its satisfaction with the outcome of the educational struggles of the nineteenth century were clearly indicated by Cardinal Logue in 1900. His pastoral letter issued following the national Synod, expressed satisfaction that the national school system was *de facto* as denominational as could be desired and that there was very little mixed education whatsoever.[4] This satisfaction with the structure of the system was on the whole shared by the Protestant churches; the denominationalisation of the system had produced at first and second level an effective partitioned structure in which each denomination exercised control over its own sector.

This position of stasis as between the churches did not mean that they were *ad idem* on all issues of education policy. They were certainly united on their shared intention to defend the denominational *status quo*, with the Protestant churches perhaps more sympathetic to lay involvement than the majority church. They differed fundamentally however on the various structural reforms attempted in the early decades of the century, Wyndham's 1904 measure, the 1907 Irish Council Bill and the Irish Educational Bill of 1919.[5] In these measures the common issue of local popular control and rate-aided funding, divided the churches; the Protestant churches and associated bodies generally supported the principle of localised popular control. The question of university education, a major issue from the middle of the nineteenth century also continued to divide the churches as the Catholic leadership sought a university which was as avowedly Catholic as they claimed Trinity College to be Protestant. When, after 1908, the National University and its constituent colleges satisfied the major Catholic demands, university education still remained as a basic difference; the ban by the Catholic bishops on Catholic students attending Trinity College was retained and implemented with vigour. For the Protestant churches the policies introduced in 1922 in primary and secondary schools provided problems especially as regards the place of Irish on the curriculum. As late as 1950 this issue and the general treatment of minority denominations within the education system was the subject of high-level negotiations. Towards the end of our period, however, there is a convergence observable in the policy stances of the churches; since 1964 both have gained from the enlarged education system and especially from the significant increase in capital and recurrent state expenditure on education. This convergence of interest is clearly reflected in their willingness to construct inter-denominational umbrella managerial bodies to conduct policy negotiations with the Department.[6]

Despite such recently developed convergence among the churches in their approach to education policy they differ in practice on the internal mechanisms by which such policy is generated and formulated. In the Protestant churches generally there are annual formal meetings in which all church matters including education are discussed by elected clerical and lay members. In the Catholic church no such participatory mechanisms exist and the formulation of education policy is predominantly a clerical function and more usually an episcopal function with appropriate assistance from subsidiary clerical bodies; within the recent past some limited lay consultation has been added to the mechanism. It is proposed to examine in turn the contributions of the main churches to policy by reference to the statements made by offical spokesmen and by their stances on specific issues.

THE CATHOLIC CHURCH

Pre-Independence Policy Statements and Issues
The hierarchy of the Catholic church conducted an almost continuous crusade on education from the introduction of Stanley's scheme of 1831 to the end of the century. Their victory in that crusade, in so far as primary and secondary education were concerned, constituted a remarkable feat; the partially acceptable educational structures of 1850 were adopted and by 1900 moulded and modified to the almost

total satisfaction of the church. From the later decades of the century their representatives on the Boards of National and Intermediate Education exercised a major central influence on a system in which their clergy occupied a dominant managerial role at local level. It is not surprising then that, in the opening decades of this century, the bishops opted to employ a strategy of defence and consolidation; this strategy generated a sensitivity to structural reforms especially those which would diminish clerical control within the education system.[7] Consequently most of the episcopal statements on education during the early decades of this century are almost exclusively concerned with structural aspects of the system or with issues which they regarded as threatening the structures they favoured.

The basic position of the Catholic church on existing structures had been expressed in the 1898 pastoral letter which emphasised the central importance of the managerial system in promoting the efficiency of the schools, safeguarding the faith and morals of pupils, supervising the conduct of teachers and controlling the choice of school books.[8] The pastoral of 1900 repeats the same episcopal message on the importance of education, the most important question, according to the bishops, on which progress had been made since the previous national synod of 1875.[9]

The establishment of the Department of Agriculture and Technical Instruction (DATI) in 1899 under which rate-aided technical education would be provided, caused the bishops some concern. This concern is evident in the specially convened meeting of May 1900 which issued a 'Declaration on agriculture and technical instruction', condemning any use of public funds by DATI to bolster the Queen's Colleges and urging that the model schools be used for agriculture or technical instruction and proposing that some 'bright capable well-conducted boys be sent to industrial centres in the Catholic districts of Germany'.[10]

The early years of the century were marked by an unusually high level of education debate in which questions of structural reform predominated; this debate was prompted by the Dale reports, by the various parliamentary measures of 1904, 1907 and 1919/20 and the related controversies which were significantly fuelled by the strong personality of Starkie and the political commitment of Augustine Birrell as Chief Secretary. Starkie's Belfast paper of 1902 on *Recent Reforms in Irish Education with a View to their Coordination*, in which he accused the school managers of neglect of their duties and called for more local involvement in the funding and management of schools, caused consternation and led directly to a decision of the Catholic bishops 'to have an association of clerical managers founded in each diocese forthwith'.[11] In response to Starkie's argument and Dale's report in support of local democratic control and rate-aid, the bishops issued a major statement on education in 1904, which was read in all churches and which can be seen as a rejection of Wyndham's reforms.[12] This defended the managerial system and the existing Boards of Education, claimed that any structural changes would be unacceptable to the Irish people and themselves on religious, political and educational grounds; they asserted further that any changes involving reduced clerical control would be so injurious to the religious interests of the people that it would be imperative for the bishops to resist them.[13]

The same defensive strategy employed successfully against Wyndham's measure was employed by the bishops with equal effect against Birrell's devolution bill of 1907 and McPherson's education bill of 1919-20. These three measures collectively constituted an assault on the structural *status quo*; by defeating each measure decisively, the bishops indicated to the people and the politicians that, in this century they were intent on consolidating the dominant position gained for the church by Cardinal Cullen in the nineteenth century. Opposing the devolution bill was significantly facilitated for the bishops by the widespread political disappointment surrounding what was seen as 'two-thirds Home-Rule'; under such an effective strategic umbrella they could easily dismiss the education reforms of Birrell's measure even though these sought to promote popular participation and democratic local involvement.[14] The climax to these structural controversies was generated by McPherson's bill of 1919 which, introduced on the eve of independence, evoked a national campaign by the church in which the rhetoric was more unmeasured than any previously employed. According to one authority, 'one of the church's most vital interests as churchmen perceived it, the prevention of popular control of education, was at stake'.[15] The gravity of the measure for the church is clearly evident in the assertion by Cardinal Logue, that if the bill were passed, the eighty years struggle to shape the education system as a sympathetic instrument for the preservation of the faith, would have to be fought again.[16] Individual statements by bishops were supported by two official collective statements; in these the bishops opposed the setting up of a Department of Education as proposed, defended the existing Boards and attributed the political motivation surrounding the bill to 'an intolerant minority in one angle of the country'.[17]

The significance of the defeat of the McPherson bill lies not in the total victory of the bishops but in the manner in which it was accomplished and in the residual influence which it exercised on education policy in the new Irish states. The First Dáil was in existence a month when Cardinal Logue issued a general warning on education:

An attempt was being made by their enemies to interfere in the matter of education and if that attempt succeeded, it would be disastrous to Catholic interests. Education required to be most carefully watched so that no assault should be made on it.[18]

This statement, delivered at a local occasion in Armagh and intended as a general statement, sufficiently vague to apply to the emerging situations north and south, marked the opening of a campaign on education which was to last two years. It was followed in April 1919 by a specific statement condemning the anticipated structural changes as being 'at variance no less with Irish feeling and Irish national rights than with Irish education interests'[19]

These statements on education, however, were part of a larger scenario in which the bishops had been attempting to exercise more direct influence on the evolving political scene. In connection with the 1918 general election their efforts to orchestrate the electoral strategies of the parliamentary party and Sinn Féin were only partially successful, despite best efforts of John Dillon and Eoin Mac Neill.[20] The episcopal statement of June 1919 on the political situation appealed for peace and a just settlement; they asked that their words be heeded in Ireland just as Mercier's were by the Belgians; When Belgium lay prostrate under the heel of oppression they listened to Cardinal Mercier. It shall be so with our people also.[21] The statement of the standing committee of the bishops issued on 9 December 1919 on the introduction of the Mc Pherson bill reveals a deep and growing sense of grievance against the government allied to a cautious but blossoming support for the political forces seeking independence. However, the main thrust of the statement is focussed on the creation of a public opinion among nationalists hostile to the bill, mainly by frequent references to a future native government and its predicted reaction to such a measure; it also revealed a general objection to the need for legislation in education. The bishops were of the opinion that 'such reforms as were needed could best be carried out under the auspices of native government' and that much of these reforms did not need 'any great legislative effort'[22]

This strong expression of episcopal expectations may have been aimed at Dáil Éireann. If so, it was highly successful for in March 1920 the Cabinet resolved that the Dáil 'would support the bishops in setting up and maintaining a national system of education'.[23] The other item in the bishops' statement which must have been of topical as well as of long-term interest to the members of the First Dáil was the reference to the suitability of party political hacks as Minister of Education. The bishops declared:

> Educationalists had fondly hoped that they had seen the last of the appointment of political party hacks to the important post of Minister of Education,

adding that the only department which the majority of the Irish people would tolerate was one established by its own parliament and which would have 'as Minister of Education a man who shall be acknowledged as the highest educational authority in the land'.[24] These episcopal assertions must have convinced de Valera of the correctness of his decision of April not to appoint a Minister of Education in the Cabinet, a decision for which, Cathal Brugha thought, 'President deValera had some definite reason'.[25]

The bishops' statement of January 1920 indicates that they were already confident of the satisfactory outcome of the education issue in any new administration controlled by Sinn Féin and Dáil Éireann. The response of the cabinet, in the March resolution, assured them that the education demands of the church were clearly understood by the nationalist politicians and accepted unquestioningly by the majority of them. The remaining episcopal statements of 1920 on the McPherson issue and the associated political exercises were mainly intended to convince the country at large and to attract popular support for the episcopal policy.

Catholic Policy Statements 1922-1984

By their defeat of the McPherson bill, the bishops had decided the question of structure in Irish education at least for that portion of the island which became the Irish Free State in 1922. In Northern Ireland, the sensitive questions raised by McPherson's measure were resurrected in 1922 by the work of the Lynn Committee. This body, on which the Catholic authorities refused representation, recommended a scheme for elementary schools involving local rate aid and local popular control, measures which were incorporated in the education act of 1923.[26] The northern bishops in various statements restated the Catholic position; while acknowledging the difficulties inherent in a pluralist society, they demanded equity for Catholic schools in funding and facilities, a central role for religious instruction in the formal school day and separate institutional provision for the professional training of Catholic teachers.[27] Dr McRory summarised the position in 1924 when de declared that 'it was the duty of the government to make such educational provision as Catholics could conscientiously accept'.[28]

When the Free State administration came to office in 1922 there could be no remaining doubt among its leaders as to official Catholic education policy. The position was presented succinctly in a statement issued by the central council of the Catholic Primary Managers' Association:

> We feel confident that an Irish government established by the people, while safeguarding the material interests of the new state, will always recognise and respect the principles which must regulate and govern Catholic education and in view of pending changes in Irish education we wish to assert the great fundamental principle that the only satisfactory system of education for Catholics is one wherein Catholic children are taught in Catholic schools by Catholic teachers under Catholic control.[29]

The educational structures and policies of the new state were seemingly very acceptable to the Catholic hierarchy, some members of which publicly expressed their satisfaction in quite specific terms.[30] However the pastoral letter of 1927, issued after the national synod, while welcoming the changed situation makes it quite clear that the system was still *de jure* unacceptable:

> The education for a Christian people is education permeated by religion. In Ireland, however we have had to make the most of systems that in theory fall short of that ideal. But for years past in practice, the character of our primary, as of our secondary schools from a religious point of view, depends mainly upon ourselves and there is no ground for complaint in the greater part of Ireland.[31]

In the decades following the establishment of the state, official episcopal statements of Catholic policy on education were less frequent. However, the Catholic position was constantly put forward energetically by specialist spokesmen foremost among whom were the Jesuits, Lambert McKenna, Edward Cahill, Richard Devane and Timothy J. Corcoran, Professors Martin Brenan and Cornelius Lucey of Maynooth and Dr Edward Leen C.S.Sp and Dr John C. McQuaid C.S.Sp. The latter as chairman of the Catholic Headmasters' Association in the thirties and as Archbishop of Dublin from 1941 to 1972 exercised a major influence on education policy. The writings of these important spokesmen appeared in a number of influential journals which played a critical role in the formation of Catholic public opinion. Among these spokesmen, Leen and Corcoran were mainly, though not solely concerned with process and curricular matters while the others were interested in the larger questions of educational structures and the role of the state; all of them drew heavily on the papal encyclical on education, *Divini Illius Magistri* (1929). Since this encyclical of Pope Pius XI was central to what was written by many of these spokesmen, it may prove useful to examine in summary the encyclical's teaching.

The function of education according to Pius XI belongs in due proportion to the family, the state, and the church, according to the proper end of each. The church's role in education is derived from 'a supernatural title conferred by God upon her alone, transcending in authority and validity any title of the natural order'; therefore education is supereminently the function of the church and her rights are independent of any earthly power, universal in their scope and include the supervision of any education given to her members.[32] The family's rights and responsibilities in education are God-given, prior to those of the state and inviolate; these family rights should not be eliminated or absorbed by the state and can in no way be attenuated or supplanted.

The encyclical defines the right and duty of the state in education as to protect the prior right of the parents to give their children a Christian education and therefore to respect the rights of the church over such Christian education; the chief duty of the state is to promote and assist the work of the church and the family, to supplement that work where it is deficient and to build its own schools and institutions.[33]

The encyclical criticises among contemporary education developments, 'an excessive cult of athletic prowess', 'naturalism in education', 'co-education' and 'modern theories which appeal to the child's so-called autonomy and unrestricted liberty and belittle or suppress entirely the authority and activity of the teacher'. The strongest strictures in the encyclical are reserved for 'neutral or secular schools' and 'mixed schools', attendance at which is forbidden to Catholics on any pretext whatsoever.[34] Finally the encyclical described the ideal Catholic school as one in which the whole training and teaching, the whole organisation must be so impregnated with the Christian spirit that religion comes to provide the foundation and the culminating perfection of the whole training.

This encyclical of 1929 was most influential in moulding Irish Catholic opinion; its promulgation mid-way between the establishment of the Free State and the adoption of the new Constitution of 1937 increased Catholic dissatisfaction with the former and influenced significantly the contents of the latter. The encyclical is furthermore important in that its contents suffused the main Catholic writings on education in the thirties and forties; this is especially so in relation to *The Framework of a Christian State* (1932) by Edward Cahill, S. J., Professor of Social Science in Milltown Park, Dublin, whose work was especially influential and whose contribution to the framing of the 1937 constitution was significant.[35]

Cahill's presentation of Catholic teaching on education is virtually a paraphrase of the papal encyclical, repeating very closely its contents and terminology while offering additional relevant background material.[36] In particular he outlines the provisions of canon law bearing on the inalienable rights of the church to supervise secular teaching, extending to all manner of schools, whether religious or otherwise, in which Catholics are educated.[37] Furthermore Cahill's work attempted to interpret the encyclical in relation to Irish conditions; the national schools were 'neutral' or 'mixed' in their conception and legal constitution although in their practical working they have in the course of time approximated more and more to the ideal. In 1932 they were only tolerated as being sufficiently safe for Catholics. Model schools, on the other hand, remained under the Church's ban, as 'neutral' or 'mixed' and therefore unsuitable for Catholics. Elaborating on the episcopal ban on Catholic students attending Trinity College, Dublin, Cahill explained that the colleges of the National University, although 'neutral' or 'mixed' are allowed owing to special circumstances as being 'sufficiently safe for Catholics as far as faith and morals are concerned'.

In a concluding section Cahill offered some comment on education issues of the day, some of which may seem irrelevant fifty years later. The principles implied in the shibboleth 'free education for all' are condemned totally as being under the influence of liberalism and socialism and as being 'full of danger to the interests of family life, especially where the free education is to be given at the public expense in State schools'. The provision of 'school-books, stationery, medical attention and even free meals' is also condemned as diminishing the role of parents. Under such systems, according to Cahill, parents take less interest in their children's education; 'hence it seems most desirable, in the best interests of both child and parent that the latter should in all cases pay directly at least a small portion and where possible even a considerable portion of the educational expenses'.[38]

Since in the selection of teachers, moral character and religious training are of such importance, priests, nuns and members of religious orders, according to Catholic tradition, are usually preferred to all others and 'it should be the policy of a Christian government to encourage and multiply efficient schools under religious control'. Teachers are not civil servants even when paid wholly or in part by the state; indeed the teacher, according to Cahill, is under the natural and divine law, 'the mandatory of the church and of the parents in his dealings with the child'. Consequently in the appointment, retention and dismissal of a teacher, the authority of the church and the parents must be supreme; for similar reasons, it is considered improper and incongruous that teachers' organisations should in any way be affiliated to the ordinary labour unions. Equally undesirable were 'neutral' or 'mixed' organisations of teachers; since the Catholic teacher is primarily and essentially the mandatory of the Catholic church, an office which cannot be reconciled with the principles and general outlook of the non- Catholic teacher. According to Cahill there was an urgent need for the establishment of Catholic Teachers' Guilds with a view to refashioning the social organisation. Cahill concludes by asserting that the Irish education system, though improved, was still far fom perfect and free from danger; neither the national school, nor the vocational, nor the university system, nor even the secondary system (owing to the state programme) realised the ideals of Catholic education; this hope was that 'they will now be gradually refashioned in accordance with the full Catholic ideal'.[39]

The encyclical of 1929 and Cahill's statement on Catholic social teaching of 1932 collectively exercised major influences both on thinking and practice in the decades following the establishment of the state; their contents are frequently echoed in the writings of those clerical leaders who were most influential in the shaping of state policy from 1920 to the fifties. Fr Lambert McKenna S.J.chaired both the Department Committee on Inspection of Primary Schools in 1927 and the Second Programme Conference of 1925. In an obvious reference to the emerging vocational system, he warned of the dangers of state control in education, defined the state role as an auxiliary one of providing financial assistance to the private providers of education, a provision which should be made without diminishing the autonomy of the schools.[40] He was not in favour of an official department inspectorate of schools and proposed that the inspectorate should be employed by and answerable to the school managers.[41] Professor T. J. Corcoran, S.J., Professor of Education in University College, Dublin 1909-42, was a member of the Molony Committee and of the Dáil Commission on Secondary Education and was a major influence on many aspects of policy in the Free State.[42] He wrote extensively on education and contributed editorially to a number of influential Catholic journals.[43] He outlined his views on the autonomy of the Catholic school thus:

> The most essential issue in the Catholic nature of Catholic schools is full Catholic control of the choice of teachers, retention of teachers and removal of teachers.[44]

He expressed the same sentiments later, using the language of the encyclical, when he summarised the Catholic policy on education as 'Catholic education in Catholic schools for all Catholic youth'.[45]

Fr R. Devane, S.J., author of *Challenge from Youth* (1942)[46] and of *The Failure of Individualism* (1948), was a keen admirer of Salazar's youth programmes, made a major contribution to youth policy here and may also have been instrumental in the establishment of An Comhairle le Leas Óige in 1942. Writing in 1930 he contrasted the Vocational Education scheme with the Bavarian scheme of continuation education in which religious education was included:

> There is one incidental, or shall we say, fundamental aspect which has attracted relatively little notice and to which immediate attention ought to be directed that is the devising of some plan, either within or without the Vocational system for the moral and religious formation of the nation's youth.[47]

Fr Martin Brenan, Professor of Education in Maynooth, writing in 1938 on the church-state aspects of the education system, described the national school system as composed of private or non-state schools and defined the teacher's *licentia docendi* as depending ultimately on the church:

> The situation really is that the Catholic people or parents of Ireland, for whom the bishops and parish priests are trustees, submit their schools to a system of national education, as a result

of which the state pays the teachers and gives other financial assistance.[48]

Brenan's opinion of the Irish system from a church perspective is one of complete satisfaction and while bemoaning the absence of legal denominationalism, he is happier to have the reality. This acceptable reality is evident to him in the section on religious instruction of the department's *Primary Programme* of 1926 and 1932 which he says 'might have been taken from the encyclical on the Christian Education of Youth'. His proximate objective or target in some of his writings was a proposed Council of Education, to which he was vehemently opposed, but to which his Maynooth colleague, Dr Lucey, was equally committed and concerning which they conducted a controversy on the pages of the *Irish Ecclesiastical Record*.[49] Lucey rejected Brenan's thesis as to the acceptability of the system; 'to be Catholic the system must realise the Catholic ideal and not just approximate very closely to it'. What the church wanted, according to the future bishop of Cork, was a 'system giving us both the legal form and the reality of Catholic education'. The church's ownership of the school buildings and her nomination of the staff was not tantamount to control of the system unless she also directed and supervised what was taught. Drawing an analogy from the medical profession, he stated: 'whoever controls the educational fare really controls education, since what is taught is so much more vital than where it is taught or who teaches it'.[50] The Council of Education, which Dr Lucey and those who advocated vocational organisation proposed, would be endowed with some of the prerogatives of the Department of Education but not with any of the powers of the school managers. It would largely eliminate the red-tape and formalism of our centralised system and would also seek improvement in curricular provision; such a vocationally-organised Council of Education would 'bring better results than any other form of educational organisation' and 'bring us nearer to the ideal educational system'.[51]

Despite such specific criticisms of the system as it operated in the decades following independence, the church leadership would seem to have been generally satisfied. The joint pastoral letter issued in 1927 expressed the bishops' judgement that they had 'no grounds for complaint' and various individual statements reflected this general satisfaction. As late as 1950, in his inaugural speech as chairman of the Council of Education, Rev. Canon D. O'Keeffe, Professor of Ethics and Politics at UCD, identified one fundamental point on which the Irish education system was superior to any other he knew of:

> There lies beneath all our educational efforts a sane and balanced philosophy – an exact appreciation of what is and what is not the legitimate function of the state. On this there is almost universal agreement.[52]

In addition to the major structural elements of the system, there were some other aspects of Irish education which conformed closely to Catholic thinking as already outlined. Coeducation was not encountered frequently throughout the system; as early as 1931, 10% of the secondary schools and one third of the national schools were coeducational. The practice was not encouraged except where demographic reality and departmental regulations left no alternative and this occurred mainly in the peripheral regions. From the twenties to the sixties the Association of Secondary Teachers was disaffiliated from the Irish Congress of Trade Unions and did not function as a normal trade union again until 1969. In regard to the establishment of lay secondary schools under Catholic lay management the Department of Education did not recognise these schools unless they were first sanctioned by the Catholic bishop in whose diocese they were situated. Throughout most of the system while field games of various kinds were enthusiastically promoted, regular physical education classes were not introduced until the late sixties, although the department had made an earlier attempt in 1936.[53] The model schools, of which there were 17 in 1930, were managed and owned by the state and in Catholic terminology were 'mixed' and 'neutral'; within ten years they were placed under joint church-state management. The modern approaches to early education associated with the names of Montessori, Froebel and Pestalozzi which were criticised in the 1929 encyclical, were not encouraged offically by the Department of Education until the late sixties.

In the matter of higher education, the church's policy was generally adhered to; most of the Catholics who had the opportunity of university education attended the colleges of the National University of Ireland. Trinity College, Dublin, which Catholics were forbidden to attend under the statutes of the Plenary Councils of the bishops, was described in 1961 by Archbishop J. C. McQuaid in the following terms: 'Trinity College, Dublin, as a non-Catholic University, has never been acceptable and is not now acceptable to Catholics'.[54] In June 1970 the hierarchy removed the ban on Catholics attending Trinity College when the following statement was issued:

For over a hundred years the Irish hierarchy has felt obliged to restrict by synodal decree the entry of Catholics into Trinity College, Dublin. That decree was last re-enacted by statute of the 1956 plenary synod. Some hope of a change that would make this institution acceptable to the Catholic conscience was provided by the announcement of a proposed merger - as it was called - of Trinity College and University College Dublin. This announcement enabled the bishops to reconsider the attitude that might be adopted towards a new Trinity College. In consequence, the aptness of the existing statute has been examined on more than one occasion recently by the bishops. In view of the substantial agreement that has been reached between the National University of Ireland and Trinity College, the hierarchy has decided to seek approval from the Holy See for the repeal of statute 287 of the plenary synod.[55]

Despite what is implied in this statement, it seems that the removal of the ban owed more to the increasing number of Catholics who ignored its terms rather than to any fundamental change in Trinity College as a university. During the sixties, as access to higher education grew, many urban Catholics were unwilling to forego the convenience of a centre-city campus. It was probably their rebellion rather than any actual or contemplated change in Trinity College which prompted the removal of the ban.

This one instance of policy reversal merely emphasised the continuity and consistency which marked Catholic policy over most of the century. Throughout five or six decades the central policy emanating from the 'supereminent' role of the church in education and the complementary but subsidiary role of the state, was presented, implemented and defended. The expansion of the system in the sixties evoked a change of tactic but no fundamental shift in policy; the church's response to the state's innovative policies involved not only the creation of defensive sectoral and umbrella bodies but a desire and decision to involve itself centrally in the emerging new educational structures at second level despite the decreasing manpower available to it.

These developments however, especially the creation of umbrella groups, far from diminishing the primacy of the hierarchy in the formulation and enunciation of policy, merely formalised and confirmed that primacy. The recognition of that primacy was illustrated in the community school controversy of 1970 and in the consultative process employed by the Department of Education. Cardinal Conway in his *Catholic Schools* (1971) restates many of the essential elements of Catholic policy especially in relation to the need for continuity between the home and the school:

> The fact is that the child's basic formation for life, whether social, moral or religious is likely to be gravely affected if the two great formative influences, home and school, do not corroborate and support each other. Probably the most important factor in preserving this religious atmosphere of the school is the attitude to religion of the teachers.[56]

The 1907 Lenten pastoral of Cardinal Conway's predecessor, Cardinal Logue, illustrates the continuity of policy and the confident consistency with which it has been promulgated; this early formulation will also serve as a useful summary of its main elements.

One of the chief duties of the Catholic pastor is that of watching over the education of the children of his flock especially in the primary school where their character is formed. It is a duty from which the pastors of the church cannot shirk, a right which they cannot abdicate. It is a mission given neither to elected boards nor to county councils, nor to local bodies, nor as far as Christian education is concerned, even to the democracy. It is the chief security which Catholics have for the faith and religious education of their little children. There is reason to fear from the tone of recent agitation and recent utterances of doctrinaire writers that the notion has arisen that this arrangement can be easily upset. I believe that whatever other changes may be made, he who tries to remove this safeguard, whether he be politician or writer, will find his work cut out for him, a work too, not easily accomplished.[57]

Before turning to the concrete issues of policy which arose since 1922, it is necessary to look briefly at the question of dissent from official policy within the church. The intense public controversies among the hierarchy and senior clergy over church education policy for much of the nineteenth century never arose again; church policy in this century was marked by almost total unanimity and adherence.[58] As one might expect the main examples of dissent occurred when educational debate was highest, in the first decade and in the sixties and seventies. Dr Walter McDonald, Professor of Dogmatic Theology in Maynooth, intervened publicly on the university question and on the management of national schools in terms which differed from the official church policy.[59] He favoured acceptance of a policy of 'making terms with Trinity' by which a Catholic college would be provided within Dublin University. His statements and published articles, which questioned the validity of the clerical right of direct control of state-endowed schools, sparked off a controversy in the pages of *The Irish Educational Review* in 1908. According to McDonald's reading of theology and canon law,

In schools endowed by the state, churchmen as such have no right to direct control, but only to indirect supervision to see that the laws of religion and morality are observed. Those who provide the funds, the people in all democratic states, have direct control involving the right of appointing teachers, inspectors and other officers as well as of prescribing courses and textbooks. The Church has a right to see that in all this religion and morality do not suffer loss, the appeal being ultimately of course, to the higher, the ecclesiastical tribunal.

His practical advice to the clergy was as follows:

If churchmen thought it better for the nation that the management should remain as it is, they would do well to base their claim, not on any inherent right that the church has to direct control of state-endowed schools, but on the presumed delegation of the children's parents who are also taxpayers and the electors. It is those only who, in my opinion have the right to direct control in this democratic country; and they are within their right in delegating this managerial authority either to a committee or council of themselves or to those in whom it is vested at present.[60]

In the late sixties Dr James Good, Professor of Catholic Philosophy and Theology in University College Cork, and later Professor of Education, questioned Church policy in education in relation to the role of the laity, the dominance of clerical personnel and the need to unify the postprimary system in the form of community schools. In the context of the community school controversy in 1970 he wrote:

One must question whether control of second-level education should necessarily rest in the hands of the Catholic hierarchy in order that it continues to be suitable for Catholics; above all one must question whether a take-over by the hierarchy of vocational education is desirable or even tolerable.[61]

During the controversy surrounding the department proposal to establish Community Schools in 1970/71, there was a body of opinion which claimed that the establishment of such schools on the basis sought by the bishops would weaken the vocational system and transform the proposed community schools into denominational institutions. In an effort to stop such a development, a number of prominent clergymen from all the churches and religious groups, presented a joint petition to the President, Éamon de Valera, seeking his support to have the policy altered as not being in the national interest. The petition was not successful as the president maintained that he had no role in political questions. The petition was signed by seven Catholic priests, among whom were three Jesuits, two Dominicans and two diocesan priests.[62] It can be seen then that clerical dissent from the Catholic church's official policy on education has been rare and that the church's policy was supported thoughout the century by a majority of the clergy. A major instance of official church policy yielding to clerical and lay dissent arose on the issue of the Irish language in the National University in 1909, in which Rev. Dr Mícheál Ó hIceadha was deprived of the Chair of Irish in Maynooth. The remaining question concerns how, in the light of its policy, the church reacted to the various policy issues which arose.

Policy Issues 1922-85

Defence and consolidation were frequently the objectives of policy in relation to the concrete issues which arose in the six decades since independence. The structural *status quo* and the dominant role of the church in the education system were to be defended; the position was to be consolidated by the removal of surviving structural features which were not favoured and the assimilation into the favoured structures of any new institutions established. Thus the surviving model schools and the schools of domestic economy run by the state were among the institutions not favoured and the preparatory colleges established in 1927 were accommodated within the church managerial system though funded entirely by the state. The fluctuating demand and supply of national teachers raised the associated question of the establishment of new training colleges. The physical condition of national schools and the inability of clerical managers to maintain the buildings adequately constituted a major threat to the managerial system; though persisting as a burning issue from the days of Starkie and Birrell to the seventies, it did not produce any significant structural change or effective church response. Two issues in particular raised directly the question of structure, the Vocational Education Act of 1930 and the various attempts from the early thirties onwards to extend educational opportunity and raise the school leaving age. In neither of these issues did the church have to accept a major policy upset; if in 1930 the Vocational Act introduced a new element in the postprimary sector, the church secured that the new vocational schools operated on its own terms. The attempts to extend educational opportunity by means of the Gaeltacht senior schools of 1934 and the proposals to raise the school leaving age in the thirties and forties were thwarted mainly because they could not be accommodated within an acceptable managerial system.

In all of these policy questions the bishops were consulted directly by the minister or his department; where the issue warranted it, the bishops of the Church of Ireland and the leaders of the other churches were also consulted. In one instance, the cabinet discussion on the proposal to establish senior schools in the Gaeltacht was adjourned without decision so that the minister might consult with members of the hierarchy. The postwar scheme for a major restructuring of the system proposed by a department committee in 1947 was not taken further than its submission by the minister to the hierarchy, though the change of government in early 1948 may have diminished the political support for such reforms. In most of these policy issues, the bishops discussed the issues at their formal meetings and sent a collective opinion to the minister, though on some issues, as on the question of the ban on married women teachers, they did not provide any agreed viewpoint.[63] The colleges of domestic economy at Kilmacud and Killarney, which had been established under and conducted by the Department of Agriculture and Technical Instruction, were the subject of negotiations in 1928 and alternative institutions were sanctioned in 1929.[64] The model schools were the object of a decree of the 1927 Synod of Maynooth:

> It will be the task of the diocesan Ordinary in particular cases to negotiate with the government to place a model school where it exists in a diocese under the control of at least one clerical manager so that Catholic children can lawfully attend that school.[65]

In 1929 there were 17 model schools in operation, most of which had a large majority of Catholic students; those at Monaghan, Clonmel, Waterford and Sligo, however were effectively Protestant schools although attended also by Catholics. By early 1930, the Catholic bishops had initiated discussions with the Department of Education, in which they stressed 'the undersirability of allowing the present state of affairs to continue, under which these schools are officially banned by the Catholic church and in consequence are not attended for religious and moral supervision by any of the Catholic clergy.'[66]

The Department of Education in a letter of June 1930 to Dr O'Doherty, secretary to the hierarchy, proposed a scheme whereby, subject to satisfactory arrangements regarding heating, cleaning and caretaking, the minister was prepared, in his capacity as patron to nominate as joint managers, 'a representative of the Department who would be a Catholic and a representative proposed by the Catholic bishop of the diocese'. The bishops at their 1931 meeting decided that in relation to the management of the model schools, each bishop would act as he thought fit.

Within a few years discussions were begun in relation to the model schools in Cork, Limerick, Clonmel, Enniscorthy, Trim and Galway with a view to their transfer; the latter school was transferred to University College Galway to house the Chemistry Department in 1932 on a long lease with all maintenance costs to be borne by the college.[67]

The preparatory colleges established in 1926, though they were the first new institutions established in the Free State, were not the subject of legislation; their managerial structure was decided upon after detailed consultation by the department with the Catholic bishops.[68] A memorandum of agreement was drawn up in 1925 with each bishop involved, stipulating that the bishop as manager should appoint the principal and vice-principal and that where the college was not conducted by diocesan clergy, the bishop should have the right to select the religious order in charge. In the negotiations it was also agreed that 'in one of the Roman Catholic colleges it is possible, that under certain conditions both principal and vice-principal as well as professors might be lay persons'.[69] The structure of the colleges was formally discussed by the bishops in June 1925; to the proposal of the department that the staff be appointed by the department after consultation with the manager, the bishops counter proposed that appointments be made by the manager subject to the sanction of the department.[70] The department's view prevailed however and in a further letter of 1926, the bishops were assured as to the method of selection and received the further guarantee that 'it is not intended to appoint any person not approved by the manager of the college'.[71]

The perceived similarity of the managerial system in the preparatory colleges and the well-established system of the national schools, is clearly illustrated in the proceedings of the two legal actions in the thirties, taken by dismissed teachers against their managers; in both cases the clerical managers sought to be regarded as agents of the department and to have their legal costs paid by the state.[72] Arising from the first of these cases, deValera issued an express direction that in no circumstances would a similar payment be made in future from state funds to cover legal costs of school managers.[73] This direction was departed from when the Archbishop of Tuam, as manager of a preparatory college, was sued in 1937 by a staff member who was dismissed from her post following her marriage.[74]

The introduction of the Vocational Education Act of 1930 seems on the surface to be totally at variance with what had been repeatedly stated to be acceptable to the Catholic church; it involved provision by the local authority of a form of postprimary education over which the church would exercise no formal control or supervision and as such would seem to have been in conflict with church policy. Surprisingly there was no public criticism from any of the bishops though they had been consulted beforehand by the minister, John Marcus O'Sullivan; furthermore they would have had lengthy advance notice since the act was based on the report of the Commission on Technical Education, published in 1927. Following the passing of the measure, three members of the hierarchy met the Minister and 'discussed certain aspects of the act in which the church was particularly interested'. In a subsequent letter to Dr Keane, Bishop of Limerick, the minister discussed and clarified the issues raised at the meeting and assured the bishops as to the exact nature of the schools and the education to be provided.[75] It would appear that the bishops were perturbed by the provision of continuation education in the vocational schools and were questioning the relationship of continuation education to primary and secondary education. In his letter, the minister was adamant that 'Vocational, not general education was the subject of the act' and that 'it is not and was never intended to be, in any degree, a general education act'.

While the vocational education proposed in the act was divided into continuation and technical education, both these branches remained essentially vocational. By their very nature, the minister continued, the vocational schools are not schools for general education; they will provide 'technical education of a general character'. The minister reassured the bishops that 'general education after the age of 14 years, as well as before the age of 14 years, will continue to be given in primary and secondary schools'. Neither did he envisage the vocational schools ever providing general education even in a system of universal postprimary provision. Asserting that there is no new principle of control in education involved and that he strove successfully to secure that the act should not run counter to established Catholic practice in this country or to the spirit of the Maynooth decrees governing these matters, the minister assured them that there is no need for them to be uneasy about the act.

It would appear that the bishops were also worried about the powers conferred on the minister to extend compulsory school attendance in particular districts under Part V of the act, lest that be interpreted in favour of any one school type. The question of coeducation and night schools in rural districts were also raised and the minister suggested that the committees should arrange their timetables so that boys and girls would not attend the same classes and that as far as possible night classes should be avoided.[76]

Finally the minister explains that since the act does not mention subjects of instruction, no mention is made of religious instruction; he is certain that no committee will fail in this respect and should any such case arise he would use his statutory powers to make provision for it. The provision of the actual teaching of religious instruction would be undertaken by the bishops; the minister concludes by assuring the bishops that the department would issue instructions to committees in which these matters would be brought to their notice.

The specific assurances contained in the minister's letter to Dr Keane would undoubtedly have diminished the bishops' fears about the vocational system. Furthermore, once they were assured that only vocational and technical skills and not general education would be provided in the new schools, the bishops could validly claim that the vocational system fell within the provision of the decree of the 1927 Synod which states:

> Since it seems to us that knowledge of technical skills and of agriculture is useful and necessary for our people we consider it permissible for Catholic young people to attend schools with non-Catholics where this knowledge, but not general instruction or education is given.[77]

Despite some possible ambiguity on the minister's part, it seems that both state and church accepted the letter of 1930 as defining the strict parameters within which vocational schools should operate. Thus vocational pupils could not enter for the Intermediate and Leaving Certificate examinations of the department and were thereby excluded from entry to the universities. Where subjects such as History or English were taught in the vocational schools they were frequently officially described as Commercial History or Commercial English. The church may also have been encouraged in its initial tolerance of the vocational schools by the informal intelligence that the scheme was not intended to be implemented on a general scale for about twenty years.[78] Perhaps the most surprising feature of this letter is the assurance that the vocational schools would not be used for general education in the future even 'when we can afford to make more universal a system of general education for postprimary pupils.' It is hardly surprising that when in the sixties, the department proposed to do exactly that, the church and the secondary school authorities protested.

Some policy questions relating to primary education and the supply of teachers were the subject of regular consultation between the Department of Education and the bishops over a number of decades; these included the physical condition of schools, the supply and training of national teachers (both questions which involved the managerial system in relation to schools and training colleges) and the mechanism for financing the building and maintenance of schools.

Demographic fluctuations and the resultant impact on pupil numbers caused problems in relation to training college accommmodation and teacher employment. These fluctuations evoked various policy measures ranging from the closure of, or restiction of entry to, training colleges or preparatory colleges (1939), to elaborate administrative measures to alleviate unemployment among teachers (1937), and also, at the other extreme, proposals to erect an extra training college at various times when teacher supply fell below demand.

The question of building a new training college was raised as early as 1926 when University College Galway proposed that a new college, located in the Galway Model School, be attached to the University Department of Education, which would train nuns from all over the country. This proposal, approved of by the bishops, assured of the cooperation of the Sisters of Mercy in Galway and personally supported by Ernest Blythe as Minister for Finance, came to nothing.[79] A second proposal, also strongly supported by the Minister for Finance, was made in 1928 to provide a large college in Galway for 160 women students including nuns. A site was purchased, contracts issued and construction work begun in 1931; the project was abondoned late in 1932 and the partially completed building allocated to the preparatory college for boys, Coláiste Éinde.[80] When the question of this training college was discussed at cabinet in November 1932 it was reported that 'the Department of Education cannot agree with the bishop of the diocese as to the management of the new college, on which point, there is no prospect apparently of giving way, on one side or the other'.[81] The question at issue was not the structure of the management but the choice of order to manage the college; the order which the bishop was insisting upon was regarded as inefficient by the Department and the order proposed by the department was unacceptable to the bishop. This episode illustrates quite clearly the sensitivity and disequilibrium which could surround church-state questions in education even when respective roles and rights had been the subject of earlier written agreement.

By the late thirties there was a serious over-supply of teachers despite the effects of the ban on married women national teachers which had come into effect in 1934. In 1939 the number of unemployed teachers and the total numbers in the preparatory and training colleges was equivalent to eight years supply of men and six years supply of women teachers.[82] This resulted in the permanent closure of one of the Preparatory Colleges for boys (Coláiste Chaoimhín) and the policy decision that one training college for men was adequate. By the early fifties the Department of Education was again seeking to have an extra training college established by adapting the premises of the preparatory College in Galway, Coláiste Éinde, which it proposed to close permanently. This move to open an extra college was repeatedly opposed by the Department of Finance; alternative measures based on the temporary relaxation of the 1934 ban on married women teachers and the admission of university graduates to posts in national schools were decided on by the cabinet. In June 1954 the Minister for Education submitted two proposals to the hierarchy with a view to overcoming the shortage of trained teachers. These were (i) that suitable university graduates be selected for acceptance for recognition as trained teachers, and (ii) that suitable candidates be accepted as extern students of the training colleges.[83] In reply, the bishops rejected the recruitment of graduates as 'altogether unacceptable' and urged the expansion of internal capacity in the colleges and the raising of retiral age; in the event of these measures failing, they were willing to accept the admission of extern students as a temporary measure for two years.[84]

The various questions surrounding the construction and maintenance of national schools, their physical condition and the size of the local contribution towards their erection and maintenance raised crucial issues which were continuously under discussion. The local contribution to the erection of national schools of one third of total cost proved difficult for many local managers to provide. In 1926 the department, seeing the need to provide additional accommodation and to improve the standard of school buildings, was only too well aware that except in a limited number of cases the managers had been unable to collect the normal quota of the cost and that in the western areas especially they had frequently not been able to provide any contribution from local sources.[85] In such circumstances the Department was empowered to allow more than the usual two thirds from the state but the grand total of such excess grants paid in any one year could not exceed one eighth of the total annual allocation. When the Minister proposed a significant increase in allocation over a number of years and also to abolish the restriction on excess contributions by the state, the Department of Finance promptly raised the question of the waste of public money due to neglect of maintenance by managers and also the relative roles of the state and the managers should the principle of local contribution be abandoned. However the issue was never taken further as the economy drive of 1927 did not allow of any additional funds being allocated to school building.

The problem however did not thereby disappear but disimproved steadily throughout the thirties. The INTO had been campaigning from 1926 for improved school buildings and had advocated that a county education authority be given the responsiblity for providing and maintaining primary school buildings.[86] When the INTO proposed that the special Civil War reconstruction rate be redirected to such a purpose the proposal was rejected by the Catholic Clerical Managers' Association. This policy of the INTO survived until 1954 when, having proposed to the bishops that schools be built by the state and maintained by local authorities, the reply from Cadinal D'Alton, outlining the threat which such measures involved for the managerial system, caused the teachers to abandon the policy. The essence of the bishops' attitude is revealed in the further letter to the INTO from Cardinal D'Alton in October 1954, which displays the hierarchy's resolve:

> to guard the foundation of the managerial system and the system of denominational education which it ensures, the moral basis of which was the right of parents and the legal basis of which was the ownership of the school, resting upon ownership of the site and the contribution of some portion of the erection costs. The state contribution was a grant in aid and did not involve any claim to ownership.[87]

To surrender the existing system would be to surrender the right to the managerial system, according to the Cardinal, and the right to denominational education which it guarded.

Arising from the renewed pressure by the teachers expressed in their 1932 Congress and the possibility that the new Fianna Fáil Government might be inclined to alter some aspects of the existing system, the bishops established a sub-committee in 1933 to consider in conjunction with the Central Council of the Catholic Clerical Managers' Association, the various questions concerning the costs of erection, extension, maintenance, heating and cleaning of national schools. Following the general meeting of the bishops in October 1934 the following decisions were conveyed to the Minister for Education by letter from Dr O'Doherty of Galway:

Decisions of the General Meeting of Bishops 9.10.1934

1. That the state be requested to pay to the Managers the full cost of

maintenance, heating and cleaning of all national schools.

2. Cost of Building and Extension of Schools

(i)   the state, as at present, should pay two thirds and the manager is to provide one third from local resources;

(ii) in necessitous areas, a manager may apply for more than two thirds of costs;

3. Recommendations of the Managers' Council adopted:

(i)   that the present rights of the managers be maintaind intact;

(ii) any additional monies to be given to managers should come from the central fund and not from local rates;

(iii) no lay committee of any kind is to be associated with the manager in school management;

(iv) the site of the school must remain in the names of trustees, one of whom is to be the bishop.[88]

The question of local contribution and cost of site arose again in 1937 in Dublin when the erection of schools for the slum clearance schemes was under discussion. When the Coadjutor Bishop of Dublin complained of the prohibitive price charged by the corporation for church and school sites and suggested that the local authority should contribute, the Minister for Finance, Seán MacEntee, agreed and wrote to the Minister for Education urging him to take the matter up with the archbishop, promising him his own support. This may have been a ploy to move the archbishop from his stated position that the parishes in question could not pay any local contribution to a position of agreement to pay £6,000 as local contribution to a total cost of £90,000 for three schools.[89] In the discussions, however, the archbishop made it perfectly clear to Deirg that he would not countenance any contribution towards the cost of erection of national schools being provided by Dublin Corporation.[90]

The Minister for Education in an effort to hasten progress in 1935 secured a government decision 'that money should be made available at once in all cases where only the normal grant of two-thirds is required'.[91] Despite this however the minister was disappointed at the rate of progress; the general recession of the war period did not permit very much building and by 1942 the condition of some schools was such that parents in Co Mayo organised a strike of pupils in protest during the winter term in 1942.[92]

In the postwar planning programme of the government, the Department of Education proposed to make primary school building and improvement a major priority. The minister proposed in 1943 to complete the task of replacing all defective buildings within ten years at a total state cost of five million pounds. To secure a coordinated response at local level, the minister proposed to the bishops that a committee be established in each diocese which would provide the local contribution, act as a supervisory agency, and liaise with the department in arranging an ordered programme of school building in each diocese and in securing that adequate attention be given to the maintenance, sanitation, heating and cleaning of school buildings.[93] The minister also initiated a national survey by diocese with a view to providing each bishop with particulars of the works necessary to enable a diocesan programme to be planned. In their reply in October 1943, the bishops while expressing total agreement with the minister's desire to improve school accommodation, could not accept his proposals regarding the roles of diocesan committees.[94] They unanimously agreed that a committee of managers be established in each diocese to promote the provision of suitable school accommodation and the adequate maintenance of school buildings and in general to further the minister's aims. However the bishops 'did not consider it wise that this committee should take away from the manager his prime and basic responsibility with regard to the school as any lessening of the final responsibility of the manager would defeat the end of the committee's formation'. It also decided to leave to each bishop to decide on the financial arrangements most suitable to his diocese. Several bishops had mentioned cases where delay was caused not by lack of local contributions but by delays in procuring the government grant.

In the forties the question continued to be an urgent priority of the government, involving the Ministers for Education and Finance as well as the parliamentary secretary with responsibility for the Board of Works. There was a growing political awareness of the inability of managers in many parts of the country to raise the required one third and the Department of Education was in favour of reducing it to one sixth; the average national contribution since 1922 had been between 20% and 25%. The survey conducted in 1944 had revealed the situation to be very serious; of the 4,966 national schools, 503 were so bad as to require replacement as a matter of urgency, 1,500 schools required reconstruction and 550 schools were generally unsuitable but could by repair work be rendered passable for a short period of years.[95]

In 1945 Deirg reopened correspondence with the bishops on the issue in which he outlined the extent to which local contributions had fallen below the theoretical one third; in all cases in the financial year to March 1944, in each of thirteen dioceses the average contribution had been below one sixth and in only one diocese was the normal one third provided, it being between one third and one sixth in all the others.[96]

The minister expressed concern at the increasing number of managers who 'are not prepared to guarantee the provision of the local contribution when officially assessed'. A survey in 1944 by the Office of Public Works revealed that there were over a hundred national schools without any sanitary arrangements of which 29 were in Co Kerry.[97] The serious state of some schools prompted the parliamentary secretary in charge of the Board of Works, Patrick Smith, to undertake a survey of the worst cases on the files of the Board of Works, which led him to conclude that 'the principal cause for the present condition of many of our schools is due entirely to neglect by the managers'.[98] He urged the Minister for Education to intimate to the hierarchy that 'the past and present lackadaisical methods can no longer be tolerated'. The Minister for Education, however, despite his serious concern, was unable to get agreement from the bishops on a mechanism which would secure the local contribution and supervise the work on a diocesan basis. Consequently the issue remained a serious problem which the restriction on capital expenditure of 1948 exacerbated; in 1953 the department prepared a plan whereby one hundred new schools would be built annually. Despite the emergence of diocesan liaison groups in some dioceses and the erection of many new schools, there were still some unsatisfactory cases into the sixties which led the INTO to organise official protests as late as 1968.[99]

The questions of school leaving age and the extension of educational opportunity, universally or for specific areas or groups, are obviously inter-related and both in turn are linked to possible resultant changes in educational structures. A number of initiatives were taken after the School Attendance Act of 1926 established fourteen years as the minimum school leaving age; yet despite numerous reports and committees, the age was not raised to fifteen until 1972.[100] Following the report of the Inter-Departmental Committee on the School Leaving Age of 1935, some schemes were introduced in the forties under part V of the Vocational Education Act, mainly to cater for the 14-16 age group in the cities of Cork, Limerick and Waterford. The Commission on the Gaeltacht which reported in 1926, had drawn attention to and expressed its concern at the fact that 'the only type of education available to the Irish-speaking child is primary education'.[101] The Commission recommended the establishment of day secondary schools in twenty five centres in the Gaeltacht. Nothing was done in this regard until 1933 when the Cabinet Committee on the Gaeltacht asked the Department of Education to prepare a plan for increasing secondary and vocational education in the Gaeltacht.[102] This plan proposed the establishment of twenty one central Senior or Higher Primary Schools with a practical curriculum, each of which would cater for children aged twelve and over from the surrounding national schools which, as junior schools, would cater for pupils in and below fifth standard. Since each senior school would cater for an area of 200 square miles it was proposed to provide free bicycle transport and waterproof clothing for students. These higher primary schools would supply 'the equivalent of a secondary school suited to a rural population and to the requirements of an agricultural community'.[103] The scheme was communicated to the bishops early in 1934 including the proposal that (i) the total costs of site, buildings, equipment and maintenance might be borne by the state and (ii) the management of the schools might be on a joint basis.[104] The hierarchy at their June meeting established an episcopal committee to consider the scheme; its report to the October meeting was adopted unanimously and forwarded to the Department:

Copy of Minutes of the General Meeting of the Hierarchy held on 9 October 1934

Section III.   Higher primary schools in Irish-speaking districts

Report received from the Episcopal Committee appointed last June to consider a communication from the Ministry of Education. The following is a copy of the Report:-

While welcoming increased facilities for education we have some doubts regarding the proposed scheme.

I.   Management. The scheme involves a further extension of State control.

II.   From the moral point of view there is danger from boys and girls from 12-16 years of age coming from long distances without any supervision.

III.   The need for such schools does not seem to be apparent in view of the existence of vocational schools.

IV.   In different districts of the Gaeltacht different conditions prevail. In some very congested areas the people are very poor and many of the children from 12 to 14 years of age have either to give assistance at home or go out earning in order to help to support the family. Such economic conditions should be kept in mind in any new educational arrangement which the Ministry may wish to make. Consequently we think that in any such scheme the schools should be part-time. The Report was adopted unanimously.

(Sd) Thomas O'Doherty,
Bishop of Galway.[105]

This scheme had been discussed at Cabinet in February 1934 and a decision had been deferred 'to allow the Minister for Education, following the approval of the Minister for Finance, to discuss certain aspects of the scheme with members of the Catholic hierarchy'.[106] To compensate for the rejection of this scheme, de Valera in 1938 proposed the establishment of vocational schools in the Gaeltacht at Dingle, Cnoc Spidéal and Cill Ronáin.

In June 1944 the chairman of the Commission on Youth Unemployment, Archbishop J. C. McQuaid, indicated to the Department of Education that the commission had unanimously decided to recommend:

(i)   that the school leaving age should ultimately be raised to sixteen;

(ii) that, as soon as conditions shall permit, education up to the age of sixteen should be full-time, and;

(iii) that immediate steps should be taken to provide the accommodation, equipment and teaching staff required to give effect to these recommendations.[107]

Following close on this encouraging policy contribution and urged on by de Valera, the Minister for Education appointed a department committee in 1945 'to examine the existing educational system and to make recommendations as to the changes and reforms necessary in order to raise the standard of education and to provide greater educational facilities for our people'.[108] This committee reporting in 1947 based its proposals on the assumption that the school-leaving age would be raised to fifteen years, an assumption which was strengthened by the decision of the government that legislation be promoted to raise the school leaving age to fifteen as a first step to raising it to sixteen. The 1947 report proposed the establishement of a new school type, a senior school, to cater for the 12-16 age group; continuation education under the vocational system would be abandoned although some vocational schools would be utilised as senior schools. Copies of the committee's report were presented to the bishops in April 1948 for their confidential information with a request that 'it be regarded solely as a document setting out the nature of the problem and making proposals which might be capable of offering a solution'.[109]

The issue of extending educational opportunity did not arise again until the sixties when extensive consultation with the hierarchy preceded the major policy measures of 1963, 1966 and 1970. Perhaps the major contribution of the Catholic bishops to policy in that decade lay not only in shaping the nature of the proposals coming forward but in securing acceptance of the government policies by the

Catholic managerial bodies, in the creation of effective consultative infrastructures and in influencing the character of the comprehensive and community schools so that they approximated as closely as possible to the Catholic ideal in management, ownership and staffing.[110]

In examining the interpenetration of Church and State in Ireland, John Whyte claims that it is most clearly seen in education, in which the church 'has carved out for itself a more extensive control in Ireland than in any other country in the world'.[111] The Church's role and influence in Irish politics, according to Whyte, is determined by the variables of topic, period and party. Yet when education was the topic neither period nor party have been discriminant factors. Throughout all of this century the church has built up and confirmed its dominant and major role in Irish education irrespective of party in power; it has been as successful with Augustine Birrell as Chief Secretary as it has been with Eoin MacNeill or Donagh O'Malley as Minister for Education. This long-term success is directly due to a number of important factors characterising the Catholic church's role in Irish education. From the end of the last century the church has constituted the greatest proprietorial and managerial presence in the system, a presence which surprisingly has been consolidated in recent decades despite increasing manpower problems. This presence makes of the church and its leadership much more than another major interest group in education; in effect due merely to the extent of its presence no policy measure can be realistically implemented in the system without the tacit consent of the Church. To this proprietorial significance must be added the readiness with which politicians have harkened to expressions of episcopal and church opinions and their reluctance to question or query church policy. In expressing church policy on education the hierarchy has been in this century remarkably coherent and unanimous, a feature which had enabled it to speak with assurance and has guaranteed a more receptive hearing especially among political leaders.[112]

If the enunciation of church policy has been consistent, the strategy employed has not; the response by the bishops to practical issues presents a sharp contrast between the line followed in the thirties and forties and the policy pursued in the sixties and seventies. Policies proposed by the government in the thirties to extend educational opportunity were rejected by the bishops when they involved structures which they did not favour. Those same policies, or more radical ones, were acceptable in the sixties and seventies when the associated structures were amenable to church control. Senior schools for the Gaeltacht, general education in vocational schools and parental involvement in the management of national schools were specifically rejected in the thirties while comprehensive and community schools, management committees, free education and school transport were welcomed in the sixties. In the midst of these changes however, the residual core of church policy, the clerical management of schools, has been conserved and perhaps extended. In removing its ban on Catholics attending Trinity College, the church was responding pragmatically to a changing situation in which one of its laws was being increasingly flouted.

It would seem that, despite its unchanging official policy statements, based on theological principles and papal teaching, the church's approach to educational issues in the last sixty years has been governed by a basic, flexible pragmatism. This pragmatic approach has enabled it to extend its involvement and participation in an evolving system without diminishing its control over the basic structures.

The cohesion in the expression of church policy in education has been reinforced by the church's laws on education as expressed in the decrees of national synods. The legal basis of its policy in education can be traced within the *Acta et Decreta* of the National Synods from 1850 onwards. The consistency found within these laws is reflected in the historical consistency of church policy and in the continuity of its response to policy issues involving questions of structure.

The continuity in the legal system underlying the policy is clearly evident in the decrees of the 1900, 1927 and 1956 Synods, especially in relation to the topics of denominational education and the managerial system which constitute the kernel of church policy. In relation to the former, the 1900 Synod decreed 'we consider it our duty to declare, with the Council of Thurles (1850) that the separate education of Catholic youth is to be altogether preferred'.[113] The synod of 1927 is more specific; decree 385 states: 'Catholic children should not attend non- Catholic, non-denominational or mixed schools, which presumably are open to non-Catholics', a provision which is repeated in the acts of the 1956 synod.[114]

The decrees governing the managerial system lay down procedural rules and legal requirements, in which there is, over the period a growing precision and detail accompanying a growing acceptance of the national system. The Synod of 1900 enacted some rules so 'that the dangers in the system of national education may be minimised'; the school site is required to be entrusted to curators or trustees consisting of the bishop, the parish priest and others nominated by the bishop, in whose names all titles or instruments are to be completed according to civil law.[115] It was also forbidden to priests to accept help towards the building of schools under any arrangement not approved of by the hierarchy.[116] The synod of 1927 decreed that 'the precautions prescribed by preceding synods for making national schools safe for Catholics must be maintained'.[117] It added decrees concerning managers being approved of by bishops and the appointment and dismissal of teachers. In view of the proposals made by the minister in 1943, Decree 389 is of special interest:

A Council of Managers should be retained in each diocese

whose function will be to supervise everything that pertains to primary schools.[118]

The 1927 decrees also dealt with model schools, to which 'in conformity with the statements of preceding synods, we give the lowest level of approval'; bishops are also urged to seek to modify the management structure of these schools. The growing specificity of the synodal decrees is evident in the decree which required the parish priest and his deputies to visit each school in the parish once a week; failure in this regard was to be regarded as a serious matter.

In the 1956 synod's decrees the national school system receives more favourable comment and the various elements of the managerial system are legally defined in a systematic fashion. It was decreed that 'the system under which primary schools are under the direction of managers approved of by the local bishop, as it especially suits our conditions, should be preserved by every means'.[119] There is also an obvious effort to legislate for internal uniformity of practice as between secular clergy and religious orders in their managerial functions- 'so that one mode of procedure may be observed by Catholics'.[120]

The central issue is covered in Decree 261 which states:

We prohibit entering into any agreement for the building of schools except under the following conditions:

1. that ownership of the site and school be in the hands of trustess approved by the local bishop;

2. that the manager of the school be approved by the bishop.

The duties and rights of a manager are also detailed as follows:

1. The manager should carefully learn his rights and duties and fulfill them in all that pertains to the buildings, pupils and teachers;

2. He should keep the school building repaired and roofed and see that all requirements relating to maintenance, cleaning and heating are supplied at the proper time;

3. He has the duty to insure the building, pupils and teachers against damage or danger;

4. He should be present himself when the school building is examined by the public medical officer.[121]

In the 1956 decrees the function of the diocesan council of school managers is modified considerably and generalised in its intent:

> The Diocesan Board of school managers should oversee all that
> pertains to the Christian education of children and the defence
> of the rights of managers. (Decree 266)

The item on schools providing technical education, present in the
decree of all three synods, is of special significance in the context of
vocational education and the act of 1930. In the 1900 and 1927 decrees,
Catholic young people were permitted to attend schools with others
of a different faith, where technical or agricultural training but not
general education is imparted.[122] This does not appear in the 1956
decrees, but instead, a decree specifically deals with vocational
schools:

> Decree 274: Care must be taken by every means that pupils in
> vocational schools are trained to the full in moral and religious
> teaching and are protected against dangers morally damaging to
> young people. Therefore, in these schools instruction should be
> given separately to boys and girls, indeed, in so far as possible
> in separate halls.

As regards higher education the acts of all the synods contained a
decree prohibiting Catholics from attending Trinity College, Dublin;
the synod of 1900 also expressed disapproval of the Queen's Colleges
and discouraged contact with them.[123]

Throughout this century the Catholic church has been systematic
and coherent in the enunciation of its education policy; in the
implementation of the policy however it has been pragmatic and at
times inconsistent. Its policy has been systematic in that it has been
the subject of regular episcopal discussion and statement and has
been founded closely on a definable body of papal teaching and
church legislation. Its coherence derives from the unanimity of its
spokesmen and the close alignment between the elements of the
policy and the large segment of the Irish system which operates
according to that policy. In some respects, the policy has lacked internal consistency. The church's teaching has always accorded parents a
primary role in education and described their rights as God-given
and inviolate; yet in practice up to very recent years, parents have
been effectively excluded from all church education structures and
this exclusion was formalised in an episcopal decision of 1934. The
church policy of 'Catholic education in Catholic schools for all
Catholic youth' would in logic require that the church espouse a
policy of equality of educational opportunity so that all Catholic
youth might benefit from such desirable education. It would also
seem logical that the vocational system be encouraged to function to
its full potential and not be regarded solely as a potential rival to the

church secondary schools. While educational opportunity was widely provided by the larger teaching orders, the church leadership did not formally advocate equality of opportunity nor accept the principle of 'secondary education for all' until state policy and popular opinion had rendered them politically imperative in the sixties.

The effectiveness of the church's policy and its impact have been significantly enhanced by the nature and the continuity of the response it has evoked from political parties and their leaders. Its success has been guaranteed and its dominant role assured by the virtual absence of alternative policies which were comparably coherent and as vigorously pursued and by the total absence of any alternative policies at critical formative points during the century.

The Church of Ireland and the other Protestant Churches

Though the Church of Ireland constitutes the major component among the Protestant denominations and has the most developed educational infrastructure, it would seem preferable to examine as a unit the contribution of the Protestant churches to education policy, since they have frequently acted in concert during this century. Furthermore, especially after 1922 they shared the same structural and organisational problems centred upon making educational provision for a scattered population in schools which were for the most part rural and small. Questions concerning church and state and their respective and appropriate roles have seldom been of major concern to the Protestant churches since, after 1922, the denominational structures and educational role provided by the state for the majority church were accorded by extension to the minority churches.

The Church of Ireland Board of Education which reports annually to the General Synod has played a central role in the formulation and implementation of education policy especially since 1917 when its remit was enlarged to encompass both religious and secular education. The board's annual report provides a detailed account of policy and developments in the national and secondary schools under Church of Ireland management. The board has also been the vehicle by which cooperation with the other Protestant churches is fostered; indeed the early and closing decades of our period were equally marked by very fruitful joint ventures by the Church of Ireland, the Presbyterians, Methodists and the Society of Friends.

In the period prior to 1922 the Board of Education in many of its policies reflects the major current issues and their impact upon the scattered educational network of the minority churches. The policy of small school amalgamation launched by Starkie posed serious problems for the Protestant churches out of which developed a Joint Education Committee of the Church of Ireland and the Presbyterians and in 1908 the establishment of a Committee for the Defence of

Small Schools.[124] In an effort to minimise the adverse effects of amalgamations, rules and conditions were agreed in 1906 by the various churches under which in each diocese they would accept closures and amalgamations. Where schools of different denominations were concerned, the principalship was to go to the majority denomination, religious education was to be provided for each denomination and any committees formed in connection with the resulting school should reflect the denominational composition of the pupils; where these arrangements could not be guaranteed, amalgamations were to be resisted.

Closely linked to the question of school closure and amalgamation was the question of school transport for those living in remote areas. While by 1914 the pace of amalgamations had slackened, cooperation between the Church of Ireland and the Presbyterians had continued; in 1917 there were nine cases of amalgamation reported and 'an increased willingness to cooperate'.[125] In 1913 the Board of Education gained a significant concession from the Commissioners whereby in areas where enrolment had fallen below ten but where closure would cause hardship, the school could be retained on condition that the parish would pay portion of the teacher's salary.[126]

Throughout the entire system questions relating to conditions of employment of teachers were prominent during the first two decades of the century and this feature is faithfully reflected in the Church of Ireland policy discussions. In 1906 the Diocesan Education Boards were urged to promote cordial relations and cooperation between managers and teachers and were asked to recognise the principle 'that no teacher be compelled to do service for the church in return for salary paid entirely by the state'.[127] It was decided in 1908 that where issues connected with dismissals arose teachers were to have a contractual right to a referee of their choice from an agreed list which would include a senior clergyman and commissioners of education or senior inspectors of a Protestant denomination. In 1918 this was modified so that the referee would be either a bishop or a commissioner of education, the choice resting with the teacher; in the previous year teachers from national and secondary schools in association with the Church of Ireland were given formal representation on the Board of Education.[128] By 1915 it was proving difficult to secure an adequate number of male teachers for the national schools under Church of Ireland management; commissioners of the National Board who were members of the church prepared a report on the question and proposed a solution based on the monitorial system. The problem continued however and in 1916 the rules were relaxed to allow newly-trained teachers of three years' standing to be appointed as principal teachers.[129]

Some curricular issues arose during the early decades which though few in number are significant in that they concern issues which were to become frequent policy questions among the Protestant churches after 1922; these involved the role of the Irish language and the suitability of officially sanctioned school textbooks. Stimulated perhaps by the National Board's bilingual programme of 1904, the Board of Education of the Church of Ireland passed the following resolution in 1907:

> That in the case of children in primary schools, in whose homes English is the spoken language and whose opportunity for mastering necessary subjects are so limited, it is inexpedient to compel them to learn a language which cannot be of any practical use in the struggle of everyday life and work.[130]

Commenting further the *Annual Report* states that while the objection does not refer to *bona fide* Irish-speaking districts, it does apply to any system of fees which might tempt teachers to introduce a subject which could not become part of a primary curriculum on its merits. In 1909 it was decided by the Commissioners that, as and from 1911, candidates for admission to the training colleges would be required to offer two languages, one of which must be English. The Church of Ireland Board of Education objected to this rule, which, it claimed, would inflict hardship on many candidates; as an alternative it proposed that additional marks be given to those offering two languages.[131]

The question of the suitability of school texts arose in 1914 and in 1918; the series entitled *Stories from Irish History* was severely criticised as unsuitable in 1914 and Macmillan's *History Reader* was recommended as an alternative for Protestant schools. In 1918 texts in Irish history were cited as containing bias and members of the Education Board were asked to forward to the Church's members on the Board of Commissioners any examples they might find of false statements of fact in Irish history.[132] The extension of educational opportunity at second and third levels was an object of church policy prior to 1922. Under resolution of the 1903 Synod a committee was established to examine secondary education as it affected the interests of the Church of Ireland. This committee reported that while there was a large number of ill-equipped schools in connection with the Church for pupils who can pay from £30 to £50 p.a. as boarders and from £6 to £12 as day pupils, there were also many districts in which schools were needed for secondary and technical education.[133] In 1912 when the provision of scholarships was under discussion, the Board of Education criticised those County Councils which required their Catholic scholarship holders to study at the Colleges of the National University. In a measure designed to increase opportunity, the Commissioners proposed the establishment of higher grade national schools and advanced departments in ordinary schools in 1912; these measures were discussed by the Protestant managers and teachers at meetings presided over by Commissioner Mahaffy. In 1918 the

Protestant churches were also interested in technical training and the promotion of domestic economy when it was proposed that a School of Domestic Economy and Housewifery should be established in connection with the Church of Ireland especially for County Council scholarship holders.[134]

The Church of Ireland and the other Protestant churches solidly supported the findings of the vice-regal committees of 1919 and the resulting McPherson bill; when the lattter did not receive a second reading the Board of Education passed the following resolution:

> That this board wishes to express its hearty approval of the main principles of the Irish Education bill and believes that if carried into law, would, with certain modifications, confer signal benefits on Irish education.[135]

The Board of Education also welcomed the liberal and democratic features of the bill as well as the manner in which it protected the managerial system, the provision for religious education and the representation of the various denominations in primary and secondary education. They wished, however, to see the control of the proposed Department of Education widened to more than three experts, so that all interests might be represented. The General Synod of 1920 urged the government to proceed with expedition to carry the bill into law while also improving the salaries of teachers.[136] However the political changes consequent upon the Treaty of December 1921 ushered in a new education era for Protestants north and south and new challenging education structures in Belfast and Dublin for churches which themselves retained their pre-Treaty national structures.

This all-Ireland organisational perspective among the Protestant churches is clearly reflected in an interesting, if doomed, initiative taken by the Church of Ireland Board of Education in 1922. Following discussions between Dr Miller, Bishop of Cashel and Mr. Lynn, Chairman of the Northern Education Committee, on the possibility of securing a common scheme of education for all Ireland, the following resolution was passed and forwarded to Ministers, north and south;

> That the Education Board of the General Synod earnestly request the Ministers of Education, of Northern and Southern Ireland to consider whether a scheme of education could be drafted which could be suitable for all Ireland.[137]

Despite the failure of this initiative, the Protestant churches adjusted quickly to the new education structures and within a few years were involved again in the consultative process. The major adjustments required concerned the drastic reduction in their own school network and the replacement of the old Boards of Education by a Department of Education in which there was no controlling denominational balance.

In effect the number of national schools under Protestant management in the twenty-six county area fell to approximately 50% of what it had been prior to 1922 and this reduction also produced a shift in the size pattern of the schools. The figures for the Church of Ireland schools alone reveal these changes quite clearly.

It will be seen that after 1922 the Church of Ireland school network had fewer large and more small schools; in 1927 whereas 13% of the schools had more than 50 pupils, 46% had less than 20 enrolled. This pattern of school size was to raise policy issues continually as to school transport, teacher numbers and school closure. (Table 8.1)

The establishment of a department and the departure of the denominationally balanced Boards of Commissioners meant in effect that those who had represented the Protestant churches on the National and Intermediate Boards were no longer at the centre in shaping education policy. Consequently, it was very natural that Protestant educational interests would feel estranged from the new administration in which there was no longer a Mahaffy or a Traill to plead their cause. This estrangement was likely to be exacerbated by some of the policies pursued by the new state especially those in relation to the Irish language. Despite those initial predictable reactions however, the Protestant churches, by 1925, were actively involved in the Second Programme Conference in which Dr Kingsmill Moore and Professor W. E. Thrift represented their interests.[138] By the end of the twenties official church publications were reflecting a growing accommodation and the leaders of Protestant education were becoming familiar with the new administrative machinery.[139]

In the decades from the twenties to the early sixties the major issues on which the Protestant churches formulated their policies were the problems of small schools and curricular issues; they were also interested in other questions but these two issues dominated their thinking. The questions deriving from size of school were crucial throughout most of this century and in one sense they are an extreme case of the problems of the mass of national schools; even after successive policy campaigns of amalgamation of small schools, one in four have now less than 50 pupils and over half have less than 100 pupils on roll.

From the twenties onwards the organisation of transport schemes for remote pupils was an important strategy in the retention of small marginal schools; the magnitude of this task and the development of the problem can be seen from Table 8.2. It will be noticed that, over three decades, while the total number of schools dropped by 20%, the number of 'large' schools (>50) dropped by over 22% and the proportion of small schools increased considerably.

Even though the question of government aid for a transport scheme was raised as early as 1924, nothing significant was achieved until 1929 when the education facilities in rural districts was discussed at the synod.[140] The problem had been described in dramatic terms at the previous synod when it was claimed that in many rural areas, Protestant children, due to the School Attendance Act of 1926, had to attend Catholic schools 'where they must naturally become acquainted with Roman Catholic doctrine and practices which are not in accordance with our reformed faith'.[141] In many cases there were children with no suitable school within twenty miles of their homes. The synod of 1929 urged dioceses to draw up rationalisation plans and having identified those schools which must be kept open at all costs, to approach the Department of Education which would most likely give a sympathetic hearing to proposals presented at diocesan level. In discussions with the Minister for Education in 1930 and 1931 evidence was presented that there were 1,500 Protestant children living outside reasonable walking distance (as defined in the School Attendance Act) from any school except one under Catholic management. It was also claimed that a modest government funded transport scheme, costing £7,000 would enable 1,000 of these to attend a Protestant school.[142] This long awaited scheme was sanctioned in 1934 by which time there were 32 diocesan transport schemes in operation in ten dioceses. By 1936 the schemes were credited with improving significantly the attendance patterns in rural schools; seventy schemes were funded by the government in 1937. As the policy of school amalgamation was intensified,numbers, distances, and costs escalated so that special grants were periodically necessary.[143] While the financial burden on the church was heavy it was convinced of the absolute necessity of the policy and frequently expressed its appreciation of the generosity of the state.[144] A request from the synod of 1953 to the Ministry of Education in Belfast for information as to the transport schemes provided for Roman Catholic children in Northern Ireland was refused on the grounds that 'records were not kept of the denomination of pupils'.[145] When in 1957 the church sought to have a transport grant paid for individual children irrespective of a stipulated minimum number, the department replied that 'providing a grant for one or two children might in fact result in subsidising a parent to send his children to school, which is not in accordance with normal state policy'.[146]

After thirty years of the transport schemes the need for them was as great as ever in 1962; while in that year 700 children were conveyed at a cost of £17,000 there were 400 others in need of transport.[147] Children in very remote areas were catered for in 1963 in a special scheme when the minimum was reduced to two. The whole issue took a new turn in 1965 when the Report of the Advisory Committee on Primary Education outlined the educational consequences and the great vulnerability of one- teacher schools and recommended a policy of centralisation aimed at a network of larger schools each with three or more teachers. This policy was adopted and implemented with vigour supported by a parallel state policy of school building and curricular initiative.

Despite the success of the centralisation policy, there are still many small schools in operation and it would appear that this pattern will persist. In its submission to the government in preparation for the 1980 white paper, the Board of Education of the Church of Ireland made a special plea that one and two- teacher schools be protected by special policy measures; the demographic reality would seem to indicate that such will continue to be a basic education policy for the Protestant churches within the system.

In the thirty years after 1922 the Irish language and the denominational suitability of school textbooks were the major and dominant curricular issues of concern to the Protestant churches. Very early in the life of the Free State the textbooks sanctioned by the department were regarded as unsuitable; in 1922 the Board of Education passed the followng resolution in relation to books in Irish used in primary schools and in training colleges:

> Since there are expressions in the Irish textbooks now in use in National schools which violate the principles hitherto recognised in national schools that there should be no interference with the religious beliefs of any child attending them, they desire to urge in the strongest terms that books containing such expressions should no longer be permitted in the national schools and they request the Minister for Education to receive a deputation on the matter.[148]

An expert committee comprising Dr Gregg, Archbishop of Dublin, Canon H. Kingsmill Moore, Principal of the Church of Ireland Training College and Professor E. P. Culverwell of Trinity College, acted in conjunction with the other Protestant churches and examined a large number of books. This committee reported that phrase and reading books used in national schools contained some and many contained much Roman Catholic doctrine and that books by P.H. Pearse used in the training colleges were open to grave objections. In December 1922 this committee met the Minister, Eoin MacNeill, who, in reply to their complaints, gave them assurances that inspectors would not be permitted to expect, much less to enforce, in Protestant schools anything not in accord with Protestant teaching.[149] Arising from this assurance the Board of Education issued a circular to all managers of Church of Ireland schools informing them of the state's policy and reminding them of their duty of 'carefully inquiring into the nature of the Irish books in their schools and of conveying to teachers the intentions of Mr MacNeill, that nothing was expected of pupils not in accord with their faith and that protection would be afforded to the clergymen of children compelled to attend schools not under Protestant management'. In drawing the attention of managers 'to the nakedly sectarian character of many of the Irish phrase books and readers used in schools under Catholic management', the circular seemed to exonerate the works of Fr Peadar Ó Laoghaire whose *An Easy Irish Phrase Book*, it recommends wholeheartedly.[150] This issue of the suitability of textbooks evolved quickly into the separate issues of Irish language policy and general textbooks in English.

The textbook question was partially resolved in 1926 when a special Protestant edition of the *Saorstát Readers* was published, which received strong recommendation from the Board of Education.[151] The issue arose again in 1934 when differences of opinion between school managers and inspectors generated some friction.[152] The department response was to issue a special list of sanctioned books which was extended or modified at regular intervals. Texts for the teaching of Irish history continued to present problems and in 1936 the Board of Education organised a competition from which a suitable textbook was published in 1941.[153] Throughout the late forties and fifties the basis for complaint shifted from specific subject matter to 'the general tendency' of the textbooks; a special committee reported in 1950 that 'generally speaking no series of readers in English or Irish as specified in the official list can be regarded as wholly acceptable to our school authorities'.[154] The problem was still present in the early sixties when the right of every school manager to select reading books of his own choice in addition to those on the official list, was affirmed, after which the question does not feature in the annual reports.[155] The question would seem to have been resolved by 1967 when a new textbook was presented as totally acceptable.[156]

While the question of the Irish language arose prior to 1922 and continued to be of concern to the Protestant churches up to the late fifties, there were a number of occasions when it constituted an issue of importance involving ministerial interviews and the submission of memoranda by the Board of Education. When the new regulations of 1924 required secondary schools to include Irish in their curriculum the Board of Education made representations and sought modifications or a guarantee that the regulations would be administered with flexibility.[157] The revisions made in the primary programme by the Programme Conference of 1925 were welcomed by the Board of Education; while they regretted the retention of compulsory Irish, they were satisfied with the recognition of English in the Infant classes and the conditions governing the teaching of other subjects through Irish. An interview with the minister in 1930 secured a considerable concession for teachers in one-teacher schools; the regulation requiring one hour's instruction in Irish could be interpreted so as to effectively reduce the amount of direct teaching.

When the primary programme of 1934 restored the earlier more demanding regulations regarding Irish in the Infant classes, the

Board of Education sought an interview with the Minister, Tomás Deirg, in 1935. The Church delegation emphasised the importance of allowing parents to decide the essential features of their childrens' education and pointed out 'the psychological, humanitarian and educational effects on infants of teaching exclusively through Irish'.[158] The minister replied that the policy adopted ten years earlier could, with general cooperation, be successful; he also undertook to give due consideration to their views and to consult the inspectors. The matter was considered again by the Board of Education in 1935 and 1936; its opinion which remained unaltered was conveyed to the minister and discussed with officials of the department; no agreement was reached except that in relation to schools where the 1934 programme was not carried out in full, no blame would be attached directly to the teachers.[159]

In 1939 a survey, conducted on the use of the language in Church of Ireland schools both national and secondary, claimed that department policy on Irish had the following results:

(i) the curriculum had been restricted by the exclusion of subjects of cultural and practical value;

(ii) except in schools where the teachers and pupils are of supernormal capacity the development of pupils had been retarded by the teaching of Irish and more particularly by teaching through Irish;

(iii) teacher salaries were seriously affected by lacking certain qualifications in Irish;

(iv) parents tended to remove pupils from schools where the department's policy was implemented and send them to other schools and to Northern Ireland.[160]

This inquiry which may have been prompted by a similar INTO survey, then in progress, was continued in 1940 and 1941. Replies received from 576 teachers in 483 schools claimed that the vast majority were highly qualified in Irish, that over 150 had less than the required qualifications, and that on average two hours were devoted to Irish per day, which they claimed reduced the efficiency of the work of the school. Ninety per cent of the managers regarded the pressure on the teaching of Irish as inadvisable. The survey also reported from Protestant secondary schools that over fifteen years lower standards had been observed in mathematics, general intelligence and knowledge, in association with an increased interest in and command of oral Irish.[161] It would seem that the Protestant churches were totally unsuccessful with the Fianna Fáil governments of the forties and when the Fine Gael-dominated coalition came to power in 1948 they approached Richard Mulcahy on the question with some confidence.[162] In November 1948, Dr E. C. Hodges, Bishop of Limerick, met the minister on behalf of the Board of Education, 'to submit to him some difficulties concerning Church of Ireland schools in connection with teaching through Irish'; these were outlined in a memorandum submitted to the minister based upon replies by teachers to a circular from the Board of Education.[163] This memorandum assured the minister 'that virtually no hostility to Irish was noted' but dissatisfaction with methods was expressed; it also asserted that 'teachers loyally administered the policy of the department though they admit to feelings of frustration and unhappiness about its effects upon the true education of children'.[164] The memorandum especially criticised the policy of using Irish as the medium of instruction in the infant classes and its extension to higher classes, and also drew attention to the problems in one-teacher schools; it made specific recommendations centred on reducing the role of Irish in the curriculum. In his interview with the minister, Dr Hodges said that when they had made a similar representation before, there had been a considerable mitigation of the position for them and they expected another mitigation from the new government.[165]

The reaction to Dr Hodge's memorandum within the Department of Education amounted to a total rejection of the claims made in it concerning the *bona fides* of the Board and the loyalty of Protestant teachers towards Department policy; the tone of some of the official reactions was acerbic, critical and dismissive.[166] The question was taken up again unsuccessfully in 1949 when a further submission from the Dublin School Managers of the Church of Ireland repeated the same arguments with some additional blandishments directed towards 'the new educational regime under the minister's capable supervision'.[167] When the Synod report of 1950 raised again both the language issue and 'the flood of undiluted nationalism which filled their textbooks', it reminded those who referred to the police state of Northern Ireland, 'that there was a good deal of the autocratic in the compulsory Irish of their own state'.[168] The department's reaction, on receiving this report, was again to reject emphatically the claims and assertion and to initiate a general internal examination of the attitude towards Irish in Protestant national and secondary schools. This exercise revealed a very negative attitude among the department's senior administrative and professional officials towards the demands of the Protestant schools; the general opinion was that while Protestant primary teachers were generally competent in Irish, a negative policy and reaction was created in the schools by hostile managers and parents. The demand for a lower official standard in Protestant schools was rejected out of hand, though the Chief Inspector did admit that 'in practice we may exact less from them'.[169] As to the position in Protestant secondary schools, the Department reported a wide variety of attitudes ranging from frank hostility to a positive realistic approach with the middle ground characterised by a neutral detachment. Specific schools were identified in each category and one hostile headmistress is quoted as being of the opinion that 'Irish spoiled the good accent of her girls' and that 'most teachers of Irish were socially very much inferior to the pupils'. The performance of the pupils in the public examinations was due, according to the department, to the weak provision for the subject in many of the schools.

It is of interest that the Presbyterian church was also in contact with the minister concerning Irish at this time though with a slightly different approach and with less central church support. Through Dr Irwin, the moderator, some managers of Presbyterian schools in border areas had requested an interview with the minister 'on the question of Irish in the schools'. In writing to the minister, the moderator stressed that he had no sympathy with the ideas being put forward and that he would allow the delegation to speak for themselves.[170]

There were other educational issues of a wider dimension which were of concern to the Protestant churches, in the period after 1922. The Commission on Youth Unemployment, established under the chairmanship of Archbishop McQuaid of Dublin in 1943, was examining some fundamental issues relating to school leaving age.[171] The Church of Ireland was not represented on the commission and when it applied for membership, it was informed that the body was not constituted in that way; a subsequent request that a Church of Ireland representative experienced in youth work, be included, was also refused.[172] The following year the Synod established its own Youth Council to cater for all Protestant youth, north and south.

When in the fifties Protestant schools found it difficult to secure sufficient teachers especially in rural schools, they approached the minister seeking to have the ban on married women teachers removed.[173] The minister, Richard Mulcahy, pointing out that where no other solution was possible it was permitted to appoint a married teacher in a temporary capacity, replied that he was not prepared to reopen the general question of married women teachers.[174]

Following the publication of the Council of Education report on secondary education in 1962, the Board of Education endorsed the report's rejection of the policy of 'secondary education for all'.[175] Within a few years such conservative policies on educational opportunity had been abandoned entirely in favour of a positive and enthusiastic response to the expansionist and restructuring policies of the state. The new Church of Ireland policy was expressed in the *Annual Report* of 1966; while it regarded the system as 'one of the most denominational systems surviving in Western Europe', it saw no easy way of determining the relative merits of state and church control in Ireland.[176] While maintaining that education has its own intrinsic values, they also recognised that it was a necessary element in economic planning. Its policy on educational opportunity was 'to place postprimary education at the disposal of all and to make higher education available to those who would benefit from it'. If at the creation of the state there was some ambivalence in the Church of Ireland towards the education policies of the new state, by 1966 there is a complete identification with the cultural ethos of the education system and an expression of satisfaction with the status of the Protestant churches in the education system of the Republic; according to the 1966 Report 'it is easier perhaps for the Church in the Republic to be active on behalf of all kinds and aspects of education'.[177]

Developments in Irish education in this century show the Protestant churches and their schools experiencing initial difficulties in protecting their school network for a dispersed population by a determined policy on school transport supported by state aid. On curricular issues dissatisfaction with sanctioned textbooks and with state policy on the Irish language gradually decreased until by the mid-sixties the Church of Ireland was urging the importance of the study of Irish history in Irish education.[178]

Perhaps the most striking development was the extent to which the Protestant schools, national and secondary, achieved a cohesion and a structured corporate identity. Through the agency of church bodies at national and diocesan levels its widely dispersed small national schools have been organised and formed to become an efficient network with common organisational and curricular policies. Prior to the sixties Protestant secondary schools had been governed by a variety of autonomous groups with no centralised structure; by the creation of the Secondary Education Committee in 1965 and the subsequent establishment of a Council of School Governors a new cohesion was conferred on the Protestant secondary network and a mechanism created for the rational elaboration of policy.[179]

The churches, Catholic and Protestant, have been a major element of the education system through this century. They represent the single most extensive presence in the provision of primary and secondary education; they are the proprietors of the major share of education institutions and facilities at these two levels and they constitute the largest component of the local and national management structure. All the churches manifest similar features of continuity with the last century and in this century a growing centralisation of the policy making process. They have seldom been in direct conflict on educational questions though differing fundamentally on some issues; they have effectively functioned as complementary partners in defence of the denominational system and of the managerial structures which had evolved by the end of the last century. Their presence and power have been increased significantly in the course of this century and have been further consolidated by the expansion of education provision in the last two decades.

Their contributions to policy formation have been fundamental, extensive and consistent in their main themes; while primarily defensive of the *status quo* they have touched on most aspects of policy and provision.

TABLE 8.1

The number of National Schools of of different sizes under Church of Ireland management for the years 1909 and 1927.

YEAR	TOTAL	>70	50-70	35-49	20-34	10-19	<10
1909	1152	172	162	209	350	256	3
%	100	15	14	18	30	22	0.26
1927	516	33	31	62	152	196	42
%	100	7	6	12	29	38	8

Source: relevant *Annual Reports*.

TABLE 8.2

The number and percentage distribution by size of Church of Ireland National Schools for specified years between 1927 and 1959.

YEAR	>50		20-50		<20		TOTAL
1927	64	12.4%	214	41.5%	238	46%	516
1934	51	10%	227	45%	229	45%	507
1941	26	5.6%	156	33.4%	285	61%	467
1950	26	6.2%	120	28.4%	276	65.4%	422
1959	38	9.6%	148	37.4%	210	53%	396

Source: Compiled from data in *Annual Reports*.

CHAPTER NINE

The Minister for Education
and
The Department of Education

The Minister for Education is responsible at government level for the formulation, implementation and funding of education policy. In the exercise of these functions the Minister operates through the agency of the Department of Education and in association with some other government departments, principally the Departments of Finance and Health and the Office of Public Works.

Prior to independence and the establishment of the Provisional Government in 1922, political responsibility for education policy lay with the Chief Secretary and the Lord Lieutenant, to whom the various Boards of Commissioners and the Department of Technical Instruction reported; under their respective boards, primary, inter-mediate and technical schools operated in isolation, sharing few common policy objectives, each operating within the education context specified by its own board. If in the opening decades of this century, the system lacked the impetus and cohesion of a unified department of state, their absence was compensated for by the vision and energy of men such as W.J.M. Starkie and Horace Plunkett and by the political commitment to reform in education shown by Augustine Birrell as Chief Secretary.[1]

Ministers Secretaries and the Department

The impact of a minister's contribution to education policy will vary with length of term of office, political perspective on education, party policy and the minister's status within the party; the minister's famil-iarity with the education system need not necessarily be a crucial factor but political expertise in negotiating sensitive issues may very well be. The twenty two ministers who have held the Education portfolio since 1922 have had a wide variety of vocational backgrounds including the universities, teaching, law, medicine and engineering;

the only female occupants of the post were Mrs Gemma Hussey and the present minister, Mrs Mary O'Rourke. Most of them have served short terms of office and among the four with more than five years service, Tomás Deirg's sixteen years of almost continuous tenure stands out as exceptional. Table 9.1. presents a classification of the various ministers by length of tenure and by professional familiarity or involvement with the education system. Over three quarters have served under five years, and some have served less than a year; in 1939 Seán T. Ó Ceallaigh occupied the position for less than a month during a cabinet shuffle arising from the outbreak of war. Over the thirty five years to 1957, only seven ministers occupied the position whereas in one recent year, 1982 , three different ministers served.

A majority of the ministers had some direct involvement with the system either as teachers at one level or another or through being involved in the administration. Among those who had been teachers, primary and secondary teachers predominate while two had been teaching in the vocational system. Such direct involvement with the system could give the minister a clearer perspective and perhaps a useful familiarity with the professional terminology; however close identity with one particular sector of the system could expose the minister to undue pressure and make it all the more difficult to adopt an impartial ministerial stance.

The Department of Education, established in 1924 under the Ministers and Secretaries Act, had the difficult task of coordinating the work of three entities or branches which had formerly enjoyed complete autonomy under the various boards. Forging a department identity among senior staff and overcoming the inevitable sectoral friction, not least that between professional and administrative staff, presented a major challenge to the minister and the department secretary from the beginning. The early work of the department was facilitated and significantly enhanced by the continuity and stability conferred by the long tenure of office of the early secretaries; as Table 9.2 shows, of the four who occupied the position to 1968 the first two served thirty years between them and another served twelve years. Of the four all had been intermediate inspectors, three had earlier been primary inspectors and the other had lectured in a training college. In many ways the secondary (or intermediate) branch dominated the early decades of the department; up to 1939 the office of the minister and that of the secretary were located in the secondary branch headquaters at 1 Hume St. This dominance was further emphasised by the appointment in 1923 of three secondary inspectors as general inspectors and by the practice which prevailed throughout the twenties of recruiting secondary inspectors from the ranks of the primary inspectorate.[2] This practice continued until 1930 when the first secondary inspector to be recruited externally, was appointed by the department.[3]

Despite official policy and ministerial commitment to unifying the system, the department showed few signs in its early decades of operating as a coherent unit. While MacNeill as minister was claiming in 1924 that he had unified the system and the inspectorates and created his 'clear highway' from elementary school to university, the Department of Finance in 1946 was still urging the Department of Education to unify the three inspectorates as official policy had intended twenty years earlier.[4] Each of the three branches operated according to different traditions and norms, had different relationships with the schools and contrasting internal authority patterns; the Starkie legacy of administrative hegemony over the professionals survived unchallenged in the primary branch; in the secondary branch as late as 1940 the highest administrative officer was at assistant principal level while in the technical instruction branch the chief inspector was both professional and administrative head.[5] When Joseph O'Neill was appointed secretary of the department in April 1923, the main function of the position was specified as 'to coordinate the three education services and be responsible to the minister for the whole education system'.[6] Such coordination was seldom achieved in the period prior to the mid sixties and the minister's direct responsibility for the whole system was often in question.

It is proposed to survey the policy perspectives and contributions of the various ministers from the twenties to the eighties and the policy contributions which the department made under their leadership. Since many of the twenty-two ministers served short periods in the department and it is estimated that it takes a minister two years 'to master the whole of a department', it would be unfair to subject the short terms of some office holders to detailed analysis.[7] Consequently, it is proposed to survey the ministerial contributions not on a strictly individual basis but over three distinct periods 1922-32, 1932-57 and 1957-86 and to evaluate the role of the department within the same structure on the evidence from the available official records.

Ministers, even when members of the same party, bring to office different political perspectives and policy commitments; their abilities as managers of men and public opinion will vary as will their capacity to market their policies among interest groups, in the party and in cabinet. These variations among ministers is clearly illustrated among the six ministers who held office from 1957 to 1973; in this period the economic and political climates were strikingly favourable to major policy developments in education yet no two of these ministers espoused or expressed the same policy stances with identical depth of convictions, rhetoric or ministerial political style. Personal characteristics as well as political/economic factors will influence ministerial performance. Some recent attempts have been made to categorise ministerial roles and role conceptions and to construct typologies based upon the degree of policy initiative shown by ministers.[8] Bruce Headey identifies a number of different ministerial roles, as department head, as cabinet member, as parliamentary party member and as publicist on behalf of the department; under each heading various functions and activities are listed by which it is possible to evaluate the contribution of a minister. Headey also attempts to define ministerial performance in terms of level of policy activity; thus he differentiates between minimalists, policy selectors, policy initiators, executive ministers and ambassador ministers according to their dominant characteristic ministerial style.[9] It is of course also possible to develop other typologies based on parameters surrounding the process of policy formulation such as willingness to avail of external professional advice, relationship to permanent officials and the response to dominant interest group pressure. In the course of the ministerial survey it is proposed to utilise such formal and informal typologies to characterise ministerial performance.

1922-32 Laying the Foundations
Eoin MacNeill and John Marcus O'Sullivan

Eoin MacNeill (1922-25) and John Marcus O'Sullivan (1926-32) are linked in historical sequence not only as the founding ministers who established the early policies and procedures of the Department but also because they shared similar social values and some political perspectives. Both held chairs in the National University and shared a common academic background, though O'Sullivan's early academic sojourn in Germany had exposed him to a wider, more stimulating intellectual environment than that experienced by MacNeill in Belfast and Dublin.[10]

The choice of MacNeill as the Free State's first Minister for Education was automatic and caused no surprise; he had written extensively on the subject, had been deeply involved in the educational work of the Gaelic League and most importantly, from his party's point of view, he was most acceptable to the bishops and senior clergy of the Catholic Church.[11] His short tenure of office from September 1922 to November 1925 was rendered effectively much shorter by his membership of the Boundary Commission from July 1923 to November 1925; nevertheless under his political guidance the department was established and significant changes introduced at all three levels of the system.[12]

His early extensive writings reveal a keen appreciation of the importance of education, a strong aversion to involvement of the public authority in educational provision and very little awareness or appreciation of the role of practical education; they also show a heightened regard for the pedagogic virtues which his own training had conditioned him to identify solely with the academic secondary school and the university.[13] While the early writings are substantially in agreement with his later policies they deal with topics in an open critical fashion which is notably absent from his later policy statements; that is especially so in relation to the question of popular control of education and the exclusion of lay Catholics from educational management.[14] On the whole MacNeill retained his strong conservative views on the role of the state in education and his distrust of democratic structures. In a letter to the press in 1907, he advocated an alternative local educational structure based on parental rights and inseparably united with the well-defined rights of the church; this he claimed was preferable to the existing ecclesiastical control or local government control, both of which merely strengthen the claims of the modern democratic state.[15] This latter entity, 'the modern democratic state, sovereign and independent', he regarded as hostile to the interests of Catholics and leading eventually to 'the socialist regime'. On curricular and process aspects of education policy, MacNeill held views which were consistently proclaimed from his early Gaelic League days. In matters of language revival he never shared the heady optimism generated by the enthusiasts nor the policy objectives of some of his ministerial colleagues in the Free State governments. The fate of the Irish language, according to MacNeill in 1904, depended on its use as an instrument of culture; he was convinced that 'neither government nor schools can assure the future of the language'.[16] He was convinced also of the need to embody the principle of nationality in education and later as minister, he saw his policy as seeking the conservation and development of Irish nationality.[17]

There is a clear continuity in MacNeill's opinions on education issues, although by 1922 when he became minister whatever early liberalism coloured his thinking had finally evaporated. The young questioning Gaelic Leaguer had been replaced by the cautious, unquestioning minister, member of conservative governments beset by economic problems and political instability and whose social philosophy centred on a strong commitment to the *status quo*. Moreover MacNeill, widely recognised as the politician closest to the Catholic bishops, was likely to have been the recipient of their formal and informal observations on education policy in the new state; from September 1922 he was in a position to implement a policy which was in line with these observations. In a similar fashion his friends in the Gaelic League were major influences also, especially in language policy and curricular content, though MacNeill differed fundamentally from some of his League friends as regards compulsion in language policy. Thus in two major policy areas, structure and process, MacNeill's policy options were already defined by his commitment to and aquiescence in the education policies of the Catholic Church and the Gaelic League respectively. His ministerial policy statements during his three years of office confirm this.

Within a few months of his appointment MacNeill had clearly expressed his policies and his strong views on the minimal role which he ascribed to the state, to legislators and even to himself as Minister for Education. When efforts were made to strengthen the article on education in the 1922 Constitution, MacNeill opposed the amendment on the ground, among others, that 'none of us is wise enough to define what is sufficient education for children', totally confusing minimum with uniform maximum provision.[18] He defined equality of educational opportunity in terms of capacity, not as right of access and he was utterly opposed to compulsory school attendance which he said 'he would object to in any form'.[19]

One of the policies to which MacNeill referred frequently concerned the structural articulation of the system, the divisions in the system between primary and secondary which he regarded as totally artificial.[20] 'A clear educational highway', from the most elementary to the most advanced stages of education was his aim in restructuring the system, as he outlined to the Dáil in 1925.[21]

There is no doubt that MacNeill's absence in connection with the Boundary Commission from July 1923 to November 1925 diminished his direct involvement with education policy so that he appeared to some deputies, when speaking of education in the Dáil, to be out of touch with reality, indefinite, 'wholly detached from practical affairs' and 'living in the air'.[22] In his defence, MacNeill claimed that in his absence, the officials of the department had been working progressively in forwarding his policy, a claim which was well founded.

MacNeill's education policies are characterised by some disturbing paradoxes. He was not convinced of the efficacy of the schools in language policy, yet under his leadership the schools were made the main agent of language revival. He was implacably opposed to 'statism' in education, yet presided over the first Department of Education exercising a national state function in education. He claimed that the Department of Education by 1925 was functioning as 'a united whole' and that the unification of the inspectorate was the root of such unity; twenty years later the Department of Finance was still urging the adoption of the same unification as official policy.[23] While he sought to create 'a clear educational highway by which every pupil might proceed from the most elementary to the most advanced stages', he defined equality of opportunity and the right of the child to education as 'equal opportunity in proportion to capacity'.[24] He made frequent appeals for contact between the schools and the economic and agricultural development of the local community; a circular from his department urged that education should turn the bulk of pupils towards the land.[25] Yet surprisingly he was opposed to practical education; he refers as follows to manual instruction; 'a few years ago there was a great craze in regard to this which after a brief experiment was wisely enough discontinued'. In an earlier article he had described practical education as 'simply slave education', 'an insult to human nature' and 'a menace to society'.[26]

Despite such anomalies however, much was achieved by the department during MacNeill's tenure of office. The central administrative machinery was established and the various component parts of the system drawn into formal relationship with the minister. Conferences and curricular commissions were held from which new curricula were introduced into primary and secondary schools. In the secondary system a new examination structure was introduced and a school funding mechanism based on a capitation principle was substituted for the existing payment-by-results system. Though MacNeill was very reluctant to interpose himself as minister between lay secondary teachers and the church authorities, he did secure some minimal advances for the teachers in the *Salaries and Grants Rules* of 1925.[27]

The achievement which influenced the system most fundamentally however was the launching and the gradual acceptance of the government's Irish language policy. MacNeill supplied the philosophy for such a policy but was as opposed to compulsion in language policy as he was in school attendance. The language policy in the primary school had already been launched in February 1922 before MacNeill came to office; he agreed with the general objectives of this policy, but his opposition to compulsion may have impelled him to heed teacher criticisms and to convene the Second Programme Conference of 1925.

MacNeill saw the reform of teacher training and higher education as crucial elements in the language policy; one of the general inspectors appointed by him in 1923 was given special responsibility for the training colleges and a special commission on unversity education through Irish was established which made important proposals concerning University College, Galway.[28] By the end of the twenties, the training colleges had been transformed both in their curriculum and medium of instruction. The six preparatory colleges announced in 1925 were established and by the late twenties were providing some postprimary education for Gaeltacht pupils and fluent Irish-speaking entrants to the training colleges.[29]

In relation to the language policy MacNeill followed closely the lines indicated in the document 'The Gaelicising of Ireland' prepared within the Department of Education in 1924 which advocated a gradual approach from a unilingualism based on English via bilingualism to a unilingualism based on Irish.[30] Within the constraints of his absences, he achieved a considerable amount in establishing the formative procedures of the department and in launching the various aspects of the Free State's language policy. Hence it is rather surprising to find that a recent biography by his son-in-law, Michael Tierney, based upon Mac Neill's papers, excludes from consideration his years as Minister for Education.[31] From 1923, when he became Minister for Finance, Ernest Blythe exercised a major influence on language policy and was directly responsible for many of the strategic moves which were made in the twenties.

In other areas of policy, MacNeill's influence on the system was significant; many of the developments which occurred after his resignation in 1925, the School Attendance Act, the 1930 vocational system and the primary certificate were envisaged by him. In implementing these, his successor, John Marcus O'Sullivan, owed much to the foundations laid by Eoin MacNeill.

John Marcus O'Sullivan (1881-1948), when appointed Minister in January 1926 was not as well known in political life as his predecessor, though his family had active connections with the Irish Party, for which his brother, Timothy, had been an M.P. for Kerry 1911-18. As Minister for Education he showed greater aptitude for action than for educational discourse; unlike MacNeill, he has left few, if any, written records of his educational ideas. By January 1926 when he entered office many of the procedural practices of the Department had been established and many of the new policy measures had already been aired and debated or at least identified. In his political acceptability as Minister for Education, he was remarkably similar to Eoin MacNeill. His uncle, Dr. Charles O'Sullivan, Bishop of Kerry (1917-27), who urged him into politics in 1923, would have ensured that he was well aware of episcopal opinion; one of his closest academic colleagues was of the opinion that 'with Professor O'Sullivan in control of the Department there would be no breach of European traditions as there was never any question in Catholic principles'.[32] When Cosgrave sought a minister to replace Eoin MacNeill in 1926, his choice of John Marcus O'Sullivan was goverened by the same criteria as led him initially to select MacNeill; under both Ministers he was assured of personal political loyalty, accceptability by the Catholic Church, and a prudence which would avoid any political embarrassment arising from the policies pursued.

Many of the major policy landmarks in O'Sullivan's term of office represent the carrying to fruition or into legislation of proposals or ideas first mooted in MacNeill's years; these included the Second Programme Conference for Primary Schools, the School Attendance Act 1926, the Commission on Technical Education 1926/27, the Vocational Education Act of 1930, the establishment of the preparatory colleges between 1927 and 1930 and the introduction of the primary certificate in 1929. Though these measures had been earlier referred to, it is not at all self-evident that MacNeill would have introduced them; it required O'Sullivan's tenacity and systematic approach to capitalise upon the growing expertise and efficiency of his department to implement such reforms.

However it would be incorrect to regard John Marcus O'Sullivan as a radical reformer; admittedly he did not share MacNeill's obsessional fear of the state but on questions of the relative roles of church and state in education he was equally cautious and was extremely reluctant to entertain any structural changes. He believed firmly in the 'harmfulness' of state-controlled systems of education and was apprehensive lest his ministerial power of the purse should lead gradually to an approach to a state system.[33] He saw the Irish system as 'a mixture of cooperation of voluntary effort and state support'.[34] He showed no enthusiasm for MacNeill's elusive 'clear educational highway' for the simple reason that in O'Sullivan's view, the primary system was state-aided, the secondary was private and unification between them impossible.[35]

John Marcus O'Sullivan however did manage to introduce some enlightened measures and in regard to Irish language policy he achieved significant consolidation mainly due to the supervisory attention of Ernest Blythe. In 1928 he modified the scholarship scheme based on the intermediate certificate so as to extend opportunity for girls and he secured special grants for children living on remote islands without educational facilities so that they could attend mainland primary schools.[36] He was sympathetic to the case of small rural schools and secured sanction for the continued recognition of those where daily attendance had fallen below ten.[37] This was especially beneficial to the schools under Church of Ireland management whose Board of Education petitioned the Minister unsuccessfully in 1930 and 1931 to provide a transport scheme to enable their scattered pupils to attend the nearest Protestant school. In higher education, the late twenties saw some significant developments in redefining areas of specialisation and in the allocation of institutions which formerly functioned under the Department of Agriculture and Technical Instruction. In the academic year 1929-30 state research grants were awarded for the first time to postgraduate students.[38] In curricular and process aspects, O'Sullivan's major contribution was undoubtedly in the realm of Irish language policy, while in structural aspects his Vocational Act of 1930 represents the major structural reform in Irish education between independence and the sixties. He responded to growing criticism of the primary curricular policy introduced in 1922, which Cosgrave had described as constituting 'a revolution in Irish education', by convening the Second Programme Conference to review it in 1925.[39] This conference proposed a reduction in the number of subjects, accepted that the 1922 programme was an ideal to be aimed at and proposed an interim or transitional language policy under which lower and higher courses in English and Irish could be combined according to the competence of teachers and students and instruction through Irish in the Infant classes was restricted somewhat.[40] This new programme was launched in 1926 and remained in force until the reforms of 1934.

In secondary education O'Sullivan's policy advanced the measures introduced in 1924 to extend the teaching of Irish; whereas initially a secondary school to merit recognition was required to provide either Irish or English, from 1928 onwards Irish was required among the essential subjects. Students were required to present Irish as an essential subject in the Intermediate Certificate from 1928 onwards and in the Leaving Certificate from 1934. By the end of the decade Irish was being taught in and presented as an examination subject by most secondary schools; in the examinations of June 1929, 99% of Intermediate students and 92% of Leaving Certificate students presented Irish as a subject.[41] The great vigour displayed by the minister and the department in relation to policy on the Irish language is all the more remarkable for the fact that O'Sullivan though a renowned linguist, did not himself know the language. However, much of the vigour and the official energy which propelled the policy measures came not from O'Sullivan but from Ernest Blythe, Minister for Finance from 1923 and vice-president from 1927, working closely with Joseph O'Neill, secretary of the department. It was Blythe who devised much of the language policy of the twenties and who initiated the practical measures to implement it including the Gaeltacht Commission, the preparatory colleges, An Gúm, the special role of University College Galway and various scholarship schemes for the Gaeltacht.[42] It was he who prompted the founding of Coláiste Mhuire in Dublin and facilitated the establishment of two all- Irish primary schools, Scoil Bhríde in Dublin and Scoil Fhursa in Galway.[43]

Bearing in mind the economic realities of the twenties and the Gladstonian approach to public finances adopted by the Cosgrave governments in their search for frugality and efficiency in administration, what was achieved in education policy was impressive. However when Cosgrave, speaking on behalf of the absent MacNeill in the debate on the education estimate in June 1925, promised that 'second level education for all' would have to be considered, he must surely be seen as throwing a political bone to the cooperative Labour Party which was about to publish its expansionist, reformist policy on education.[44] The magnitude of such a proposition can be clearly seen from the fact that by 1929 the average daily attendance in national schools had reached only 82% and that over 60% of the pupils aged 14-16 were not attending any school.[45]

The minister's proposed solution was to provide continuation of formal instruction for those 'by gradually bringing into operation the weapon of compulsion'. However such grandiose schemes were not to come to pass in the twenties, nor indeed in the forties or fifties; the passage of the 1930 Vocational Act was attended by sufficient problems without adding to them. These arose from the Department of Finance's major reservations on the long-term financial implications, from the Department of Local Government's concern with the financial pressure on local authorities and from the Executive Council which diluted the element of compulsory attendance in the draft bill and altered the provision for attendance officers functioning under the 1926 Act.[46] As a result of the stand taken by the Department of Finance, to the effect that unless the bill were amended 'the state would face an enormous burden of new expenditure', a tacit agreement emerged that 'did not envisage the full operation of the schemes for at least twenty years'.[47] Nevertheless, though the Department of

Finance was happy 'that the Department of Education is not beginning by opening its mouth too wide', the moratorium merely ensured that the erection of a network of permanent vocational schools would be approached in the economically more favourable climate of the postwar years.[48] There were very few areas of the educational landscape which the Department of Education did not examine in the six years during which John Marcus O'Sullivan was minister; in 1927 he appointed a Committee on Art Education which included three French experts and he also attempted a radical solution to a perennial problem, the unsatisfactory physical condition of national schools. Here however he suffered defeat and frustration; widespread criticism had been voiced in the Dáil in November 1925 and June 1926 'on the inadequacy of the measures taken to remedy the generally unsatisfactory condition of national school houses throughout the country', which O'Sullivan regarded as 'one of the principal grounds of criticism of the ministry from all parties'.[49] His proposals to replace school accommodation for one hundred and forty five thousand students over four or five years at a cost of £1.16 million, also involved a departure from the established scheme whereby local managers paid one-third of capital costs. Opposition by the Department of Finance and the Office of Public Works centred on the central issues of clerical managerial neglect, the need to protect public expenditures and whether the principle of local contribution were to be abandoned.[50] If these sensitive issues did not diminish the minister's appetite for reform and reconstruction, the laconic detachment of the Department of Finance did and the scheme was abandoned in the face of the government's general economy drive.

By 1932 when Fianna Fáil came to power, the system could be said to be operating with a purpose, many of its policy areas had been examined systematically, and the three branches were functioning through the central agency of the Minister and the Department. It had taken most of the decade from the establishment of the Provisional Government to achieve that and much of what was achieved had been achieved in the years of John Marcus O'Sullivan. Nevertheless the machinery and the network was far from perfect and some of the policies were marked by a degree of naiveté. The excellent statistical information system developed by the former commissioners had been neglected; in 1927 the Minister was unable to supply data on class size in answer to a Dáil question, because 'he was not in possession of data nor did the department have time to collect it'.[51] At the end of the twenties the department was not in possession of precise information as to whether schools and pupils were insured by managers or not eventhough the question had been a live issue as early as 1911.[52] The naiveté was most noticeable in language policy, in questions of access and participation and in the notion of coordination. It was hardly surprising that initial education expectations in the new state were so high nor that some inital successes should raise those expectations further. When Deirg succeeded O'Sullivan in March 1932, he inherited a system which though not showing extensive participation in the non-compulsory area, was functioning under settled conditions in all three levels and whose policies, if basically conservative, had been formulated as a result of informed analysis and expert opinion.

MacNeill, unlike O'Sullivan, was in a position to bring with him to the portfolio a range of policies garnered from his deep convictions and his earlier study of education. However, his long absences from the department allied to his negative self-immolating view of the ministerial role caused him to leave the initiative to his senior officials for whose policies however he was prepared to provide the necessary political Cabinet and Dáil support. In this sense using Heady's terminology, MacNeill can be classified as a minimalist minister.

O'Sullivan on the other hand, enjoyed a lengthier period of six years in office, during which his ministerial desk was littered with an embarrassment of policy initiatives from which to choose. Lacking the special expertise in the education field of his predecessor, he was naturally amenable to direction and guidance from department officials and external advisors with whose assistance he selected and implemented new policies and measures. O'Sullivan, who seemed to have no personal policy objectives, is more accurately described as a policy selector who was presented with a wide range of policy measures by enthusiastic department officials.

1932-57 SLOW EXPANSION AND LANGUAGE POLICY CLIMAX
Deirg, Ó Ceallaigh, de Valera, Mulcahy and Moylan

Of the five ministers in this period, Deirg is undoubtedly the most significant not only in the length of his term of office but also in the wide range of policy measures which he examined, introduced or attempted to have accepted. He is sometimes presented and commonly perceived as being preoccupied with language policy and has also been described as 'never completely at home in directing educational policy'.[53] However the records of departmental activity covering the years under his political leadership suggest otherwise; they portray a minister who throughout his sixteen years in office, especially in the early years, was active in promoting measures of reform in all three dimensions of policy, access, process and structure, who was subject to close scrutiny by de Valera and who was confronted by enormous resource-related issues in the physical condition of schools and the salary demands of teachers.

Throughout their sixteen years in office from 1932, but especially in the early years, Deirg and Fianna Fáil were more radical in some respects than Cumann na nGael had been. Deirg selected a number of issues bearing on educational opportunity and developed them as measures to diminish geographical and social obstacles to participation. These included maintenance grants for island children, an expanded secondary scholarship scheme, a university scholarship scheme for Gaeltacht students and a commission to examine the education of the physically and mentally handicapped and children in custodial care.[54] On the commission on special education, however, Deirg was stymied by the Department of Finance on the technical grounds that the various commissions established by Fianna Fáil had absorbed all the available senior personnel.[55]

The most spectacular early policy promoted by Deirg however was that which sought to provide second level education in the Gaeltacht where, as the report of the 1926 commission had shown, there was little or no such provision. Drawing upon the recommendations of the commission and the specific direction of the cabinet Gaeltacht committee in 1933, 'to submit proposals to increase the facilities for secondary and vocational education in the Gaeltacht', Deirg prepared a comprehensive scheme which would impose no local financial burden and would effectively provide free postprimary education in the Gaeltacht.[56] This ambitious scheme, involving free school transport by means of free bicycles and waterproof clothing, was abandoned by the Cabinet following its rejection by the Catholic bishops in 1934.[57] It would have provided higher primary schools at twenty centres throughout the Gaeltacht, offering a practical postprimary curriculum to communities which had no educational provision beyond national schools. It would appear that Deirg, in his early radicalism, sought also to create such senior schools throughout the whole system; his desire 'to reorganise the primary system throughout the country as a whole' was quickly abandoned when the Gaeltacht plan was rejected by the bishops.[58] However the commitment of de Valera and Deirg to extending educational provisions in the Gaeltacht was expressed again some years later in 1938 when they utilised Section 103 of the 1930 Vocational Education Act to establish vocational schools in Dingle, Cnoc na hAille and Inis Mór Árann.[59] Various local and national factors delayed the building of these schools and in Dingle, opposition from local secondary schools postponed the establishment until 1952 when it was confined to offering evening classes and adult education.[60]

Deirg's general policy on educational opportunity was expressed in 1937 as commitment 'to the fullest possible development of postprimary education and to some extent to a policy of postprimary education for all young persons up to the age of 16 years'.[61] This ambitious and ambiguously expressed policy was never seriously implemented though Deirg did introduce some measures which extended opportunity. The opposition of the 1935 inter-departmental committee to a general raising of the school leaving age and its espousal of limited experiments were shared by Deirg and implemented by him in the pilot projects in Cork, Limerick and

Waterford under Part V of the 1930 Act.[62] Arising from the work of the departmental committee of 1945/47 and the Commission on Youth Unemployment, the government decided in principle in October 1947, 'to raise the school leaving age to 15 as a first step to raising it ultimately to 16 years'.[63] The sensitive structural issues contingent on the implementation of such a policy and the sustained opposition of the Department of Finance, which regarded the Department of Education's estimates as hopelessly inadequate, delayed until 1972 the raising of the school leaving age to 15.[64]

On the crucial question of the physical environment of the education process both in vocational and national schools, Deirg showed unusual ministerial determination and commitment. He took a decidedly strong line with the other departments involved, Finance and Local Government, in asserting his commitment to the vocational system; in 1938 he condemned the notion that vocational education be regarded as the least of the local services, to be attended to when all other local needs had been satisfied.[65] He criticised 'the intolerable conditions' under which the vocational system had been forced to operate in practically every centre and cited the example of Killarney and Galway where in 1938 the only vocational schools were housed in old private dwelling houses.

The chronic question of the physical condition of national schools and Deirg's search for a fundamental solution have already been discussed. This question must be seen as one of the central elements in his policy, a question which according to some political colleagues, required frank and firm discussions with the Catholic bishops. There is no detailed evidence as to these discussions but he certainly returned to the question frequently, included it as a priority in his postwar plans, and raised it at cabinet where it was discussed in 1943 by the committee on economic planning.[66] The political urgency of this question is reflected in the cabinet decision that, where the state grant for the erection of a national school exceeded the normal two-thirds, consideration be given to the management of the school being vested in a commitee.[67]

Deirg's plan of 1942, contained in a special memo to de Valera, outlined a ten year scheme which required for its success the creation of a diocesan structure which would coordinate diocesan plans and arrange the central provision of the local financial contribution.[68] Such structures however were not forthcoming and his plan was frustrated. The consequences can be seen in the data presented in *Investment in Education* (1965); of the 4,821 national schools in operation in 1964, over a thousand or 22% of them had been declared obsolete by the Office of Public Works.[69] Had Deirg's comprehensive plan been accepted and implemented and had he obtained the diocesan response which he sought it is possible that the problems of the unsatisfactory national school buildings would have been solved by the mid-fifties.

When it came to postwar planning Deirg and his department showed neither imagination nor political courage. De Valera's special interest in and enthusiasm for postwar planning as part of a comprehensive government programme, found little response in the Department of Education.[70] After repeated requests from the Taoiseach's office the modest planning proposals of the Department of Education did not extend beyond a crash programme in school building and the extension of vocational education in urban areas.[71] The government's response to this plan was less than enthusiastic and in December 1944 de Valera wrote to Deirg urging him to undertake a systematic examination of the system to identify 'what should be and could be done to raise the standard of education among the mass of the people and to provide improved educational facilities'.[72] De Valera suggested that Deirg should consult the postwar plans and white papers published in Great Britain and Northern Ireland, 'to ascertain if we could derive any benefit from them'. Deirg's initial effort, based upon internal memoranda from the department's branches, proved totally inadequate and was abandoned in favour of a formal department committee to which he gave the following wide terms of reference in 1945:

> To examine the existing educational system, primary, secondary, technical, vocational and the provision available for university education and to make recommendations to the Minister as to what changes and reforms, if any, are necessary in order to raise the standard of education generally and to provide greater educational facilities for our people.[73]

In 1945 when the Cabinet proposed to publish a series of white papers on different policy sectors, Deirg was of the opinion that the white paper on education should await the report of the committee he had established.[74] However no such white paper appeared and the two years' work of senior officials on the department committee resulted in an ineffectual memorandum to the minister, the unpublished contents of which hardly deserved a wider circulation than they received. The recommendations were marked by a deep conservatism and in view of its terms of reference, by a strange reluctance to openly engage the structural implications of the committee's remit.[75] The committee proposed the establishment of new senior schools to cater for the 12-16 age group, of whom in 1943, there were 106,000 still in national schools, 30,000 in secondary schools, 7,000 in vocational schools and a further 70,000 who were not in any school.[76] These new single-sex schools, offering a comprehensive curriculum, would each serve a catchment area of five miles radius and were intended to replace the vocational system. On the question of the ownership and management of these new schools, the committee recommended as follows:

Before any definite scheme of education for pupils from 12 plus to 16 can be formulated, it will be necessary, we assume, to consult the ecclesiastical authorities in regard to the provision, maintenance and government or management of the proposed special schools under such a scheme.[77] In its final report, the committee expressed a stronger opinion on the managership of these new schools when it stated 'The general education process is essentially religious and the new system, however organised, should be subject to ecclesiastical sanction'.[78]

That this scheme constituted a grave threat to the vocational system is plainly evident from the fact that one of the committee members, a representative of the technical instruction branch, J. P. Hackett, found it necessary to include in the memorandum a personal statement on the vocational system. He asserted that vocational schools had been functioning as senior schools since the 1930 Act and asked: 'Why lavish money on school buildings and then try to empty them? Why start Education Committees and stop them when they are doing well?'[79]

However the committee and its memorandum had little effect except to delay reform further. Its report lacked any awareness of the social dimensions of education policy; nowhere in its pages are there references to 'equality of opportunity', 'secondary education for all' or even token appeals to 'cherishing all the children of the nation equally'. Instead its analysis is based upon a static vision of Irish society, in which though 'the education proposed for the new Senior Schools would be suitable for all children from the age of twelve plus', a group is identified, which includes those who will later fill the professions, for whom the type of education given in the secondary schools would be more suitable.[80] The committee and its proposals made little contribution to policy but reflected a view of the system which was dominated by ultra conservative social values; the question of extending educational opportunity was not seriously considered again until the early sixties. When in April 1948 Deirg's successor, Richard Mulcahy, sent this 1947 report to the Catholic hierarchy, he stressed that he was in no way committed to its proposals and that the document should be regarded solely as setting out the nature of the problem.[81]

In the process aspects of policy, Deirg and the department were much more active and successful, especially in relation to Irish language policy, to which Deirg devoted considerable political energy. He and de Valera accorded a high priority to language policy in accordance with Fianna Fáil's fundamental aims, but Deirg's policies sought much more in the process dimension than the revival of the language through the education system.

Sharing with de Valera a strong commitment to the principle of accountability within the system, he introduced the Primary Certificate as a compulsory examination in 1943 and the Group Certificate in the vocational system in 1947.[82] He was successful in reforming the conduct of the Primary Certificate examination, eliminated irregularities and extended the examination throughout the system despite the sustained opposition of the INTO.[83] Even when resources were scarce he secured funding for inservice courses for primary and secondary teachers and introduced specialist courses for kindergarten teachers.[84] He showed a strong commitment to improving the physical condition of schools, resisted efforts by the Local Government Department to restrain Vocational Education Committees in their building plans and criticised the inadequate provision for workshops, laboratories and physical education.[85] His commitment to better school facilities however could not accommodate the enterprising progressive national school manager in Co.Laois who in 1938 sought a grant to build a swimming pool on the school site; the Office of Public Works counselled 'a shower of cold water' for the project and this official response prevailed.[86]

In the thirties Deirg initiated efforts to improve the provision for physical education in the schools; with the assistance of the army, courses were organised for teachers and under army influence the department attempted unsuccessfully to change from the Swedish Ling system, then in use, to the Sokol system of Czechoslovakian origin, favoured by the army.[87]

Deirg's main contribution to process aspects of policy relate to language where the policy inherited from Cumann na nGael proved politically difficult to modify except in the direction of intensification. The 1934 'Revised programme for the primary school' indicated clearly the direction of department thinking under Deirg; in effect it reverted to the policy of 1922, making Irish the sole language of instruction in the infant school.[88] (A detailed study of language policy is presented in a later chapter.[89])

In the structural aspects of policy, while Deirg expressed complete satisfaction with 'church and state working hand in hand', he did encounter issues which in their resolution only emphasised the sensitivity of that 'hand-in-hand' relationship.[90] The practice of having major policy issues examined by public commissions, so frequently availed of in the first few decades of the century, was abandoned in the thirties in favour of department or inter-department committees. Few of these internal exercises yielded any significant policy contributions or shifts; the central sensitivity of issues like raising the school leaving age is clearly evident in relation to the creation of An Comhairle le Leas Óige (a Youth Council), established in 1942 as a sub-committee of Dublin V.E.C.. According to a senior official of the department, An Comhairle le Leas Óige was established 'as an alternative to the far more difficult and costly course of raising the school leaving age'.[91]

If structural change proved too challenging for the department, implementation of regulations and the application of sanctions for violations and irregularities were grist to its mill. Despite the authoritarian departmental regime of the period, the Department of Finance was not satisfied that cases of falsification of school records by teachers had been dealt with expeditiously or severely enough. Between 1935 and 1937 there were fifteen such cases which caused sharp differences of opinion between the departments and the ministers; the issue was resolved in 1938 with the publication of stricter rules as directed by the Department of Finance.[92]

The department and the minister were not permanently wed to a rigid regulatory line; in relation to the schools of the Protestant churches Deirg and de Valera exercised a flexibilty which was motivated by extra-educational considerations. In 1937 a significant concession was sanctioned to enable their national schools to employ as junior assistant mistresses those with qualifications lower than specified in the rules; it was further directed that this concession was not to appear in the published rules.[93]

The Council of Education constituted a very difficult structural issue for Deirg and de Valera, not least because in terms of its functions and powers it meant different things to its proponents and opponents. Its close association with the corporatist movement and its inclusion among the recommendations of the Commission on Vocational Organisation did nothing to endear such a Council to Fianna Fáil, nor to Deirg even though de Valera had supported such a Council as early as 1931.[94] In a memo to the cabinet in February 1945, Deirg and the department rejected the commission's argument in favour of a Council of Education as 'misleading'; in rejecting the commission's contention that the education system was state-controlled and that the state might go beyond its legitimate sphere and usurp the rights of parents, Deirg offered a direct rebuff to those who saw in the council a bulwark against state totalitarianism in education:

> The rights of the state and of parents are mentioned but there is no mention of the rights of the church. In addition the last sentence suggests that our education is state controlled and it makes no reference to the control exercised by the church in both primary and secondary education. Surely it cannot be maintained that education in this country is controlled by the state to the extent that would make possible the introduction of totalitarian regimentation and surely the control exercised by the church provides more effective safeguards against any danger of this kind than that proposed in the report.[95]

The pressures for such a council, however, forced Deirg and Fianna Fáil to face the inevitable and the minister outlined to the cabinet a possible membership of such a Council totalling 39 members, the chairman of which was to be a Roman Catholic bishop, nominated by the bishops' standing committee.[96] Despite this exercise however, Deirg never accepted the need for a council; he saw it as a body intended 'to dominate the Minister and his staff and to give authoritative outlet for all kinds of criticism and faultfinding'.[97]

In his later criticisms of the proposed council, Deirg reveals explicitly his complete satisfaction with the existing structures and his determination to avoid changing the system despite the various reform movements in postwar Europe.[98] His 1947 estimate speech rejects the INTO's *Plan of Education* and by implication the report of the department committee which he himself had established in 1945:

> The Government was not contemplating complete reorientation of the school system such as that undertaken in a neighbouring country. I do not think it was necessary. Our system had been praised as specially suitable to our conditions. It has, indeed, been described as almost ideal.[99]

After sixteen years as minister, Deirg saw education reform, especially structural reform, as 'interference' which causes 'confusion' in the system. He was thankful that 'it was a simple and practical system which conforms in its fundamental principles to the religious faith that we hold so dear'.[100]

Deirg's term of sixteen years, which has been examined in detail, was marked in its closing years by an intransigent attitude to teachers and their claims; it contrasts sharply in length but not in significance with that of de Valera's. From September 1939 to June 1940, besides occupying the offices of Taoiseach and External Affairs, de Valera discharged the role of Minister for Education and in that short time exercised a major influence on policy in addition to the general supervisory role which he exercised, as Taoiseach, on all policy.

On the question of increasing access to education de Valera achieved very little of significance once his earlier Gaeltacht attempts in 1934 were opposed. Indeed his social philosophy and his perception of educational opportunity were grounded in the total acceptance of the *status quo*, whereby 'for nine out of ten of our people, the primary school is their only educational experience', as he stated in the estimate speech of June 1940.[101] This speech reveals the innate social conservatism which de Valera brought to bear on education policy; the secondary schools he considered to be satisfactory in laying the foundations of learning and culture and in training the future leaders of the nation, though they catered for less than 15% of those aged 14-16.[102] As regards the vocational system, de Valera was not convinced in 1940 that the schools operating under the technical instruction branch of the department gave the same general satisfaction as the secondary schools. The technical schools operating from the beginning of the century had very specific aims and to a point were successful in achieving these aims; the vocational and continuation schools however did not have such specific functions assigned to them and accordingly de Valera could not say whether they were or were not worth the public money spent on them.[103]

This Dáil statement by de Valera is no casual comment delivered in the heat of parliamentary debate; it is a central item in the circulated ministerial speech, of which an English translation was also supplied. These observations may have represented de Valera's own personal convictions, derived from his personal experience and preference or his social philosophy; but it is more likely that they represent his political response to sustained pressure from the Catholic church. A decade of growth and reasonable success for the vocational system may have convinced the bishops that a major mistake had been made by them in 1930 in accepting the ministerial assurances on the act; if they could not contrive to have the act rescinded and the system abolished, they should at least have its functions redefined and secure a formal provision for religious instruction by means of a ministerial order. This is consonant with developments within the department and with the established belief that at this stage de Valera offered the vocational system to an Irish male religious order which refused the offer.[104] Furthermore expenditure on the provision of new vocational schools was drastically reduced from 1940 and reached its lowest point of £12,000 in 1946/47.[105] A department committee was established in 1942 to review the work of continuation education and to make recommendations on its organisation under urban and rural conditions. The outcome of this committee was a major document, *Memorandum V 40*, which redefined continuation education and in particular was designed to assuage any church concerns on the question. This specific aspect is clearly evident in the rhetoric employed and in the emphasis placed on religious instruction, on social and rural education and on the Irish language as an instrument of the spiritual stability of the people; 'in all schools it is essential that religious instruction be continued and that interest in the Irish language and other distinctive features of the national life be carefully fostered'.[106] *Memorandum V 40* served de Valera's political purposes admirably in deflecting church criticism at least for a few years and in harnessing the vocational schools to the cause of the language at a point when he may have feared that the primary and secondary schools were tiring of the effort.[107]

In curricular and process questions de Valera was a devotee of the twin Victorian orthodoxies of detailed specified syllabuses and regular formal evaluation. He urged the introduction of the Primary Certificate as the only mechanism to evaluate pupil progress and he weighed in heavily in support of Deirg's efforts to make it compulsory in 1942. In terms of secondary curricular policy he was apparently satisfied by the provision for language learning as expressed in the percentages studying the Classics and French; over 80% of secondary school boys studied Latin and 25% studied Greek while 85% of secondary girls studied French which was also studied by the 25% of boys who studied a modern language.[108] He favoured especially in language and literature, a detailed syllabus with specified texts, which had been absent in the secondary system since the 'open' courses were introduced in 1924. He responded to teacher criticisms and managerial demands by introducing specified texts in 1940, which reform he believed would enable the secondary schools to function more efficiently. From 1924 Science and practical subjects had been organised and inspected in secondary schools by the technical instruction branch; following the appointment of two secondary inspectors of science in 1939, this function was restored by de Valera to the secondary branch in 1940.[109]

As minister and as taoiseach, de Valera showed a special interest in higher education, which was manifested in the establishment in 1940, despite the sustained resistance of the Royal Irish Academy and the Department of Finance, of the Dublin Institute for Advanced Studies, which he modelled on the *College de France*. [110]

Fianna Fail's policy on the Irish language in the thirties derived mainly from de Valera's perception of the central role of the language in characterising Irish nationality; in this he relied heavily on the thoughts of Davis with whom he believed:

> To part with it would be to abandon a great part of ourselves, to lose the key to our past, to cut away the roots from the tree. With the language gone we could never aspire again to being more than half a nation.[111]

By 1940 de Valera was entertaining and expressing doubts about the language policy pursued in the schools, doubts which were not shared by Deirg and some other ministers. By the mid-forties however the high point of the language effort in the schools had been passed, though the rhetoric of government policy remained unchanged.

In general de Valera regarded education as an area of policy, similar to External Affairs, where it was necessary for him to keep a watchful eye. He did this not only by normal ministerial and department interaction but by directly intervening at times in senior appointments.[112] His early attachment to the egalitarian principles of the 1916 Proclamation and the First Dáil was not extended beyond the thirties and was hardly ever intended to apply to education policy where political considerations of a higher order obtained. The absolute political desire of a party with Fianna Fail's past to avoid church-state conflict on education policy reinforced the need for de Valera to eschew radicalism in social aspects of education especially in the view of those of the bishops who never did accept his basic political vision. Furthermore in education de Valera was never short of close ecclesiastical advisors whose basic interests coincided with those of the secondary schools; his ready acceptance of their counsel left de Valera with little room for manoeuvre in policy. Had he espoused a radical social vision in extending educational opportunity, it is ironically probable that his Irish language policy would have borne greater long-term fruit in the larger cohorts who would have acquired and retained a knowledge of the language.

By the early fifties however, de Valera may have suffered a subtle change in attitude towards church pressures possibly following on the 'mother and child' controversy. In 1952 when Dr McQuaid sought increased state grants for secondary schools, de Valera argued that social justice would demand that such grants be operated on a means test and not on a 'free-for-all' basis, echoing the arguments and the rhetoric so recently used by the hierarchy against Dr Noel Browne's 'mother-and-child' scheme. It has been suggested that this incident sundered the close personal friendship which previously existed between them.[113]

The period from 1948 to 1957, which produced the postwar surge of reform and reconstruction in war-torn Europe, witnessed no corresponding dramatic movement in Irish education; there is however clear evidence in this period of some critical moves and countermoves, designed to forestall or influence any emerging reforms especially those involving structural changes. Commenting on the 'integralism' which characterised Irish life in this period, Whyte says:

> All sorts of forces were at work to make Ireland a more totally Catholic state than it had yet become; more totally committed to Catholic social teaching as then understood, more totally committed to Catholic concepts of the moral law and more explicit in its recognition of the special position of the Catholic church.[114]

This process, which had been proceeding since independence, reached its climax in the postwar period; given the centrality of education in Catholic official thinking it is not surprising that education policy figured prominently. It will be recalled that the Catholic managerial bodies were especially critical in this period of official policy, especially of what they described as 'the growing tendency of the government to assume control of education', the growth of lay schools and the progressive secularisation of education.[115] Such sentiments indicated a growing resistance by Church agencies to any state initiative in the realm of education; this resistance was particularly directed against the vocational system which came under sustained attack. 'The only satisfactory answer', according to the Catholic secondary managerial bodies, 'was to scrap the vocational system as at present administered . . . and start the system over again on new and thoroughly Catholic lines'.[116] These demands are echoed in the press and in Catholic journals, some of which linked the secular nature of the vocational system with the communist regimes of Eastern Europe.[117]

It is of special interest that the structural change sought by the secondary authorities in 1947, i.e. the abolition of the vocational system, was the main structural change recommended by the department committee which sat from 1945 to 1947. This pressure on the vocational system which lasted through the fifties stemmed from demands from the hierarchy for amendments to the Vocational Act of 1930 which would make the vocational system formally denominational. This is abundantly clear from a note to the minister from the assistant secretary who had written a draft ministerial speech to be delivered to the annual congress of the vocational authorities in Limerick 1956.[118] The speech itself is bland, fulsome and nebulous and contains some observations on the vocational system reminiscent of de Valera's questioning in 1940; the note accompanying the speech however reveals its clear political purpose and reminds the minister that he and the department are attempting to placate simultaneously the Catholic hierarchy and the vocational committees. This evidence is valuable in revealing the nature of the tensions which surrounded education policy in the period during which Richard Mulcahy and Seán Moylan were ministers; the choice of these two senior experienced politicians indicates that both the Inter-Party and Fianna Fáil leaderships identified the potential tensions which could arise in education policy.

When Mulcahy came to ministerial office in 1948, he was already over sixty, was experienced in political life and had played a leading part in education debate in the preceding decades. Such involvement found him supporting the national teachers in their salary claims, agreeing with those who favoured an examination of language policy and firmly committed to the establishment of a Council of Education. He very quickly caused disillusionment among the teachers who expected from Mulcahy all they had found wanting in Deirg in relation to their professional and financial problems; where Deirg had awarded a bonus to those teachers who had not gone on strike in 1946, Mulcahy guaranteed incremental and pension rights, in respect of the strike period, to those who had. He abolished the differential rating system of teachers and changed the basis for calculating staff from attendance to enrolment numbers.[119] However in the basic issue of salary, Mulcahy diminished his early support among teachers by his selective implementation of the findings of the Roe Committee in 1949.[120]

On language policy, Mulcahy in opposition had spoken very trenchantly and had asserted that 'compulsion must be abandoned and enthusiasm kindled anew'; in office however his response was not as fundamental as he had promised.[121] He announced that he was establishing an investigation of the question and proceeded to ask a

committee of primary inspectors to examine the issue.[122] This limited
inquiry produced changes which were equally limited and did little
to mollify teachers. He considered that no other change was either
desirable or necessary other than to sanction some limited teaching of
English daily in the Infant classes where previously there had been
none.[123] In the early years of the Inter-Party government the Department of Education was under constant pressure from the Department
of Finance, whose economy drive in education expenditure included
'the general reduction of expenditure connected with policy re Irish'
and the abolition or reduction of the special bonus for Irish-speaking
Gaeltacht families.[124]

Mulcahy's main achievement was in relation to the Council of
Education, the inaugural meeting of which he addressed on 5 May
1950; his delay in establishing the council was occasioned by residual
friction as to its role and composition. When he assured the Conference of Convent Secondary Schools in June 1948 that 'what is wanted
is a Council which will recognise and proclaim the Catholic
philosophy upon which our Irish system is based, the right of
parents, the church, the state', he was also in a position to inform
them that the Catholic hierarchy had already sanctioned the Council
and had particularly approved of its advisory, non-representative
nature and of its having no function in relation to the allocation of
public funds.[125] In his inaugural speech to the Council, Mulcahy
seems to have envisaged a wider scope for the council's activities
than eventually fell to its lot; it would undertake 'a general review of
education at present provided in the three main branches up to the
age of 18 years of age' and in relation to the implications of the report
of the department committee of 1945-47, special attention should be
given as to whether the type of education considered suitable for
those over 12 could be given in primary school and if so what steps
should be taken for the provision and training of teachers.[126] The
Council in its reports did not match Mulcahy's expectations; whereas
he initially intended to seek 'the advice of the Council in defining the
functions of primary, secondary and vocational education respectively', when in 1954 he asked the council to examine secondary
education, he confined its brief to curricular issues and specifically
excluded structural questions.[127]

The cautious and conservative reports of the council faithfully
reflected the minister's own conservatism and the inertial character of
the system in the fifties. Education figured infrequently as a topic or
reference in the addresses which Mulcahy, as president, delivered to
the Fine Gael Ard Fheiseanna. In 1950, recalling the ideals and objectives inscribed in the Democratic Programme of the First Dáil and his
own role on the occasion when he formally proposed its acceptance in
1919, Mulcahy committed his party to the same ideals and to a
comprehensive social security scheme.[128] Such conference rhetoric
however, was strangely incompatible with Mulcahy's conservative

perspective and political value system. He perceived his own role as Minister to be a minimal one, 'a kind of dungarees man', who 'will take the knock out of the pipes and will link up everything'.[129] On the relative powers of state and church in education he held views which were as firm and as conservative as those of MacNeill and O'Sullivan; speaking of the function of the Council of Education he said:

> One of the foremost functions, I think that that Council would perform would be to emphasise the rights and responsibilities of parents in the matter of education, to make clear the field of authority that belonged to the church, to make clear that, whatever the functions of the state was, it had no power to inter- fere either with the rights of parents or with the authority of the church.[130]

His satisfaction with the *status quo* in the secondary realm was confirmed for him by 'a representative of the secondary schools who is in a position to speak with the highest authority' who stated that the relations of the school managers with the state approached the ideal.[131]

In the postwar period when international organisations were promoting European contacts, the Department of Education displayed a remarkable reluctance to expose the system to any exter- nal influences. In 1950 the Council of Europe in a project 'to promote closer cultural and education cooperation between European countries', proposed a comparative study of curricula and program- mes 'so that the best features of each may be available to all'. The Department's oficial response, transmitted through the Department of External Affairs, indicated that in so far as this country was concerned, schemes for reform and their subsequent implementation should not in any way, be in conflict with Catholic educational principles.[132] As regards exchange schemes, while the Department could initiate arrangements for the exchange of inspectors, no such initiative would rest with the state regarding exchange of teachers since 'all the primary and secondary schools are under private control and management'.[133]

On his return to office in 1954 Mulcahy brought little with him from his earlier experience as minister; it would appear that he possessed few personal policy objectives and relied mainly on his department officials to define his ministerial remit. His priorities, as perceived by the department, included the following: consultation with the hierar- chy on teacher training proposals, economies demanded by the Department of Finance, Dingle Vocational School, plans for the build- ing of vocational and national schools, a proposal from Ceathru Rua to establish a secondary school, a dramatic plea from Aherlow N.S., Co. Tipperary to have the building renovated and finally the strange item of two Breton Celtic scholars who had attended a congress in

Dublin in 1948, on whom the intelligence service compiled dossiers for Mulcahy.[134] These constitute a typical list of the policy items, major and minor, which might confront any minister; Mulcahy's policy response to them was determined as much by the economic recession of the fifties as by his deference to Department opinion.

Throughout his second term in office, he devoted much time to defending his department estimates from the pruning policies of the Department of Finance, in which school building and staffing, schemes for promoting Irish language policies, teacher salaries and the various cultural institutions of the state were identified for curtailment.[135] Mulcahy and the department succeeded in preserving most of the existing expenditure levels and also managed, while reducing the capital expenditure on vocational schools, to maintain the impetus of the school building programme initiated by Moylan.[136]

Richard Mulcahy served as Minister for Education in a period when the political climate was extremely reactionary, when church-state interaction in education was agitated by ultra-sensitive issues and dominated by an aggressive church approach.[137] Mulcahy's conservative political perspective and his ready response to church pressures may have diminished the long-term potential of his main creation, the Council of Education. However he may in one real sense have influenced the system, education policy and the Department of Education to a far greater extent than most other ministers. In 1951 shortly before the collapse of the Inter-Party government, Mulcahy arranged with the Minister for Finance that the department secretary, Micheál Breathnach, due to retire in 1951, be retained for two further years, that he be succeeded by L. Ó Muirithe and that T. Ó Raifeartaigh should succeed Ó Muirithe, which is precisely what transpired.[138] By so arranging the succession, Mulcahy directly influenced education policy and the Department up to 1968, long after he ceased to be minister.

In the Fianna Fáil government 1951-54, de Valera's choice of Seán Moylan as Minister for Education was very significant. Moylan, a seasoned politician and renowned leader in the War of Independence, was an especially trusted friend of de Valera's. His efforts during the teachers' strike of 1946 earned him the confidence and respect of the INTO. Moreover his institutional allegiance to the vocational system and his early radicalism provided ideal political cover for de Valera in respect of any move he might wish to make in response to church pressures to modify the vocational system. Besides, the economic situation imposed an over-riding restriction on all policies and especially on those aspects of education involving additional expenditure. Within that broad context, involving political and economic constraints, Moylan forged a policy perspective which while adhering rigorously to the *status quo* did succeed at times in revealing an imaginative and innovative approach. These constraints, however, also forced Moylan at times into upholding and expressing simultaneously what appear to be conflicting opinions.

Early in his term of office Moylan issued a clear statement of his general policy:

I feel I should make it clear, however, that it is not my intention to make any drastic changes with regard either to departmental policy or administration.[139]

Such a declaration however may have been the Pavlovian response of politicans in the aftermath of the church-state conflict on the mother-and-child scheme which brought down the previous government.[140] It could also be part of a much more deliberate plan by de Valera to reassure the bishops on education issues while he was seeking a final solution to the problems in health legislation. While the statement is literally correct in describing Moylan's ministerial performance, he did succeed in making his mark in some areas of policy.

The provision of proper and adequate school buildings was a matter of deep concern to him and he reiterated what had been said frequently by other ministers 'that the problem needed to be seriously attacked'.[141] While emphasising the importance of the local financial contribution to the cost of national schools, he also asserted that the state is also a party to the shared responsibility for education.[142] He raised substantially the expenditure on the building of vocational and national schools, so that the INTO commmented on his 'extraordinary zeal' in favour of the vocational system (Table 9.3).[143]

While he expanded the physical capacity of the system, Moylan was remarkably ambiguous on equality of educational opportunity. He criticised the restricted access to postprimary education and the educational fate of those who left school at fourteen, yet in the Dáil he rejected the concept of equality of opportunity in a passage which suggests the confusion of equality of access with equality of outcomes.[144]

If he favoured the vocational system, his attitude to secondary education, unlike de Valera's, was questioning and rather negative; he was of the opinion that secondary education did not meet the economic and social needs of the country and that vocational education filled the lacunae very effectively.[145]

The question of building a new training college for Catholic women which was under cabinet discussion between 1952 and 1954 and the associated policy issues which it raised reveal a number of paradoxes in Moylan's responses.[146] When it was proposed to remove the marriage ban on women national teachers, as a solution to the shortage of teachers, Moylan and the department were resolutely opposed on grounds which included the following: 'the woman cannot with full efficiency serve both home and school', 'two salaries coming into one house causes unfavourable comment' and 'the later months of pregnancy will occasion unhealthy curiosity'.[147] On the same issue, Moylan and the department were surprisingly very willing to dismantle the only boys' preparatory college serving the Galway and Donegal Gaeltacht, Colaiste Éinde, in order to accommodate a temporary demand for extra teachers.[148] As a compromise solution the cabinet decided that university graduates be recognised as national teachers.[149]

In the primary sector, if Moylan did not register any success on teacher salaries, he achieved considerable success in process issues in national schools. He favoured a 'narrow' curricular approach, emphasising 'the importance of imparting the basic skills efficiently', at a time when others were advocating the inclusion of technical subjects.[150] Moylan accorded a high priority to reading as a basic skill, which if encouraged and promoted would become a life-long habit. With a view to fostering such developments, he promoted school libraries and exphaised their value, 'so that books, instead of being a school duty - unavoidable- would provide the key that would open doors into a wonderland'.[151]

Moylan's most significant reform in primary education was the 'free' half-day which enabled teachers to devote time to subjects or activities outside the formal curriculum.[152] This scheme liberated teachers from the rigidity of the existing curriculum, broadened their perspectives and was a significant harbinger of the major curricular reforms of 1971.

On policy generally, Moylan favoured 'continuity and stability irrespective of political changes', a precept which he followed faithfully. On structural questions his policies were similar to those pursued by Deirg and Mulcahy, except for his positive ministerial support for the vocational system. On all other structural and access questions he satisfied deValera's higher dictat that education policy be conducted so as to avoid church-state conflict. This may have effectively stifled some of Moylan's political sentiments and restrained his reputed radicalism or perhaps he had, like most of his Fianna Fáil colleagues, already shed his earlier radicalism; the question is far from answered in the teasing ambiguity of Moylan's own Dáil observation:

> Is é mo thuairim go bhfuil an córas seo againne, agus níl a leithéid eile ar domhan, an-oiriunach don tír seo.[153] (It is my opinion that this system of ours, of which there is no comparable system on earth, is very appropriate to this country.)

The quarter century from 1932 to 1957, encompassing the economically lean years of World War Two and the potentially expansionist years of the postwar period, witnessed no dramatic policy changes in the system. The declining social radicalism of Fianna Fáil and the aggressive education policy pursued by the Catholic church in the period resulted in a common cautious response from all the parties and the four ministers. Deirg, de Valera and Moylan, no less than Mulcahy, all accepted the church-dominated *status quo* and if Mulcahy's rhetoric was inherently more fulsome than theirs, the Fianna Fáil finisters were equally committed to avoiding church-state conflict on education. Within this uniform basic approach however one can discern some differences in the dominant roles of ministers; Mulcahy and Moylan both displayed a tendency to emphasise the public relations and brokerage roles, understandably necessary in a period of teacher unrest and deep controversy.[154] His position as leader of Fine Gael enabled Mulcahy to successfully defend his department budgets in Cabinet and to resist the pruning policies of the Department of Finance. This position of political strength however could equally have been used by Mulcahy to promote progressive policies, if he had wished to do so or his department officials had presented him with them. On these grounds one could describe Mulcahy's policy leadership as minimalist.

The Fianna Fáil ministers display some evidence of policy initiation; de Valera in regard to vocational education, the secondary curriculum and higher education, Deirg perhaps most of all in relation to extending educational opportunity in the early thirties or his efforts to improve school buildings and Moylan in relation to the primary curiculum. However Deirg's reluctance or inability to respond adequately to de Valera's postwar policy quest raises the central question of the relationship between ministers and the department. Of the ministers under discussion here, Mulcahy was regarded by department officials as the most amenable to official advice; they believed that Moylan listened to external as well as to department advice.[155] That the internal advice available to ministers over this period was deeply conservative is clearly evident from the official records but perhaps especially from the report of the postwar department committee whose terms of reference offered a golden opportunity to design and promote fundamental reforms.[156]

In esence there is little basic difference between the four ministers who served between 1932 and 1957; their cautious political stance in response to the 'integralist' nature of Irish society of the period was reinforced by the innate conservatism which dominated the thinking of the Department of Education.

1957-86 EDUCATIONAL PLANNING
and
EXTENDING OPPORTUNITY
Lynch, Hillery, Colley, O'Malley, Lenihan, Faulkner, Burke, Barry, Wilson, Boland, O'Donoghue, Brady, Hussey, Cooney.

During the years covered by the terms of these fourteen ministers education gained a higher political profile and the system experienced a dramatic quantitative expansion under policies which sought to extend opportunity, to increase operational efficiency and to maximise the rate of return on the high level of public expenditure on education. The rate of progress and achievement has not been uniform over the period nor has the principal focus of policy remained constant; the rapid expansion of postprimary participation in the sixties led inevitably to the structural questions of the early seventies while the last decade has been characterised by a policy emphasis on higher education.

Policy throughout this period has been more evenly balanced as between access, process and structural dimensions, though as in other periods, structural issues were more resolutely tackled in the higher education sector than in the primary or postprimary sectors. A major feature of this period is the introduction of the planning process, following the recommendation of *Investment in Education* to establish a Planning and Development Branch in the Department. The adoption of a planning role by the department inevitably raised the level of ministerial and departmental initiative considerably,in sharp contrast with the earlier periods when both played more inertial and reactive roles.

Mr de Valera's last administration which entered office in 1957 faced a formidable set of economic and social problems on which the electorate expected policies to yield rapid solutions. Mr Lynch as Minister for Education, had not available to him the resources to initiate any major changes. However he was among the first to link the functioning of the education system with the social reality of Irish society; in his estimate speech for 1957/58 he drew attention to the educational fate of those who emigrated and commented on the haphazard manner in which pupils enrolled in one type of postprimary school rather than another. In an effort to increase the supply of teachers and reduce class size he rescinded the ban on married women teachers in 1958. In doing so, he appears to have been resolved thereby to terminate the employment of untrained teachers. He also appears to have disagreed with the moral, social and educational grounds advocated by the department as late as 1953; according to him:

> It (the ban) represented a serious loss to the state of so much teaching capacity at an age when women are best able to teach.[157]

He initiated a related change when he reformed the mechanism governing access to the training colleges; by opening up entrance and by including an interview in the assessment he hoped to improve the quality. He was also concerned with the staffing of rural one-teacher schools where unqualified teachers were frequently employed. Corporal punishment was an issue much discussed in the fifties and

Lynch in 1957 amended the rule so that 'improper or unreasonable punishment will be regarded as conduct unbefitting a teacher and will be visited with very severe sanctions'.[158]

In postprimary education he refrained from any concerted action on secondary education due to the current work of the Council of Education; he did however introduce the concept of the oral test in Irish. He succeeded in restoring the percentage cuts in grants to vocational and secondary schools as the economic climate improved. His preferential funding of the vocational and technological sectors was related to the growing public awareness of the central role of technology and science in economic development; this is also evident in the energy which Lynch devoted to the preparation of a comprehensive scheme introduced under the Apprenticeship Act, 1959.

In higher education he extended the colleges of technology in Dublin and established a commission in 1958 to examine the accommodation needs of the National University. Lynch's term of office did not witness any major changes in the system yet his two years are significant in that they ushered in the beginning of some of the policies which dominated the succeeding decades. In the mid-seventies, as taoiseach, he made a significant contribution to thinking on multi-denominational education, pluralism, community schools, the role of religious in education and the role of parents in the management of national schools.[159]

The three ministers who served from 1959-68, Hillery, Colley, and O'Malley played a special role in the evolution of the policies which characterised the sixties and yielded the 'free' education scheme of 1967. The three contributed in different ways however for their personalities, political perspectives and styles differed in a fundamental fashion; Hillery was cautious and hesitant in his moves and tentative in his rhetoric, Colley was more direct while being diplomatic, and O'Malley was characterised by a flamboyance which was allied to unusual energy and political insight.

Hillery's term of office, 1959-65, coincided with a growing demand for change and with an improving economic climate which could provide the necessary resources to finance reform. The growing party competition on education policy exercised a distinct pressure on Hillery to formulate his plans; the government's statement in October 1959, committed it to expanding the physical school facilities so as to accommodate gradually all pupils up to fifteen years of age.[160] It expected to achieve that objective without raising the school leaving age or introducing any statutory measures. By adopting such a pragmatic approach, Seán Lemass, taoiseach from June 1959, increased postprimary participation without encountering any structural controversies and bought time which allowed him to engage the churches in discussions.

The tentative nature of the policies pursued by Hillery is clearly evident in his major speech of May 1963 on postprimary education. The precise details on many aspects of the changes he announced were not yet finalised; the new comprehensive schools would operate only to age 15 after which their more academic pupils would transfer to secondary schools. The regional technical colleges which he envisaged would concentrate on providing senior cycle technical courses and the comprehensive schools would be funded jointly by the state and the Vocational Education Committees.[161] He claimed these changes to be part of a plan which was designed to promote coordination and equality of opportunity; the incomplete nature of the plan was due, most probably, to the difficulties which the minister and the department experienced in reassuring the secondary managerial bodies that the plan contained no threat to their schools and to the running battle between the department, the bishops and the managerial bodies on the definition of the 'private status' of secondary schools.[162]

Despite his inability to formulate his policy with greater clarity, Hillery achieved considerable progress in some practical measures. In the primary sphere, he introduced state subsidies for the unkeep and decoration of national schools, created posts of responsibilty for national teachers, reduced the incidence of large classes and increased the physical capacity of St. Patrick's Training College.[163] In postprimary education he promoted Science and Mathematics by means of curricular reform, attractive grant schemes, inservice courses and differential salary elements to teachers; he also encouraged modern languages and introduced oral proficiency tests in Irish. His general policy in second level sought coordination of provision and extension of educational opportunity. In higher education he initiated a modified scholarship scheme, provided the resources to relocate University College Dublin, and appointed the Commission on Higher Education. Some of his reforms constitute major steps in the structural evolution of the system; the 1965 edition of the *Rules for national schools* under Hillery's signature, gave an explicit assurance for the first time on the denominational nature of the system; in 1960 he decided to close the Catholic preparatory colleges and replace them by an extended scholarship scheme; his announcement of the regional technical colleges marked the dawn of a new era in technological education and a significant extension of rural opportunity. His provision of capital building grants to private secondary schools in 1964 marked a major structural development. Perhaps the ministerial decision which held the greatest potential was the initiation of the *Investment in Education* study in 1962, which offered a detailed blueprint to the ministers who succeeded Hillery.

His immediate successor, George Colley (1965-66) responded with alacrity to the message of *Investment in Education* and its advocacy of educational planning; in his estimate speech of June 1965 he announced the establishment of the development branch in the department and also appealed for cooperation and harmony on education issues.[164] Since many of the issues arising from Hillery's 1963 speech had generated sharp exchanges between the department and the secondary schools, Colley's primary objective was to restore harmonious relationships while advancing a policy of increased opportunity and educational planning. Futhermore secondary teachers had been deeply alienated by the recent policy developments about which teachers were not consulted. To remedy this, Colley proposed in October 1965 to establish a Consultative Committee on which teachers and managerial bodies would be represented. He also established in 1966 an Advisory Council for the Dublin Area, charged with planning educational provision in the expanding suburbs. His efforts to broaden participation in the policy process included parents, whose rights he had frequently advocated: 'I have felt and I have said this in public that deliberate efforts were made to exclude parents from education'.[165]

By December 1965, Colley had immersed himself in the process of policy clarification and was in a position to issue a document outlining the major ministerial statements and summarising policy on second level as follows:

(i)   raising the school leaving age to 15 by 1970;

(ii) provision of up to 3 years second level education for all i.e. getting pupils out of primary school by twelve plus;

(iii) provision of equality of educational opportunity to all. This does not mean that all pupils must get the same education but that each pupil must get the education suited to his needs and talents.[166]

In his 1965 estimate speech he identified those issues to which he would give priority attention; these included an integrated consultative body, the amalgamation of small national schools, the promotion of cooperation between secondary and vocational schools at centre level, the development of the comprehensive schools 'which are not and never were intended to replace, either at once or gradually, our secondary and vocational system'.[167] His perspective on educational reform was set in a wider socio-economic matrix; he committed his political energy to 'the provision of a higher level of postprimary education for the greatest possible number of our children'. In such provision he was a keen advocate of comprehensive education, for the basic reason 'that equality of educational opportunity is inherent in such a system'.[168]

On the role of the minister and the department Colley suffered from none of the desire for self-immolation which marked most of his predecessors. He stressed the need for the economic use of resources and the absolute need to plan and coordinate education provision:

> If therefore changes are to come about in our education system
> . . . there must be some point of initiative and some central
> administrative authority to translate that initiative into the
> leaven that leaveneth the whole lump. Now the only central
> point of administrative authority, in fact the only coordinating
> authority in postprimary education, is the Minister for Educa-
> tion and his Department.[169]

The minister explained that, in a situation where the state was
providing a very high percentage of the capital costs, the uncoordinated building of secondary and vocational schools could not
continue indefinitely. Common sense and the interests of the
taxpayers called for a survey of existing secondary and vocational
facilities and the coherent planning of required needs. Accordingly
Colley commissioned the Development Branch to conduct a detailed
survey of provision and needs in each county, which produced
pioneering planning studies which were discussed at local open
meetings.

George Colley was a keen advocate of the Irish language and lost no
opportunity in government to put forward policies in support of his
convictions. These convictions shared some of the fundamentalism of
de Valera, rejected arguments based on utility and spurned the policy
which seeks to place Irish on an equal footing with French or German:

> There must therefore be some other reason why Irish finds a
> place in our programmes. In fact its right to a place in an Irish
> school is the intrinsic one that it is not French, German, Italian,
> or Spanish but Irish.[170]

The structural policy with which Colley was most closely associated
was the closure and amalgamation of small national schools. He
believed passionately that the conditions obtaining in one-teacher
and two-teacher schools were a grave injustice; he initiated a policy
of amalgamation so as to create central parish schools to which free
transport was provided.[171] This policy which halved the number of
one-teacher schools and reduced considerably the number of two-
teacher schools by 1972, faced some bitter criticism and opposition
which Colley attributed to lack of information and vested interest; in
February 1966 the personal attack on him at a public meeting by Dr
Browne, Bishop of Galway, who accused him of seeking the ruin of
rural Ireland, was responded to by Colley in a manner which attracted
support for his policies.[172]

Colley's most dramatic measure was contained in his letter to
secondary and vocational school authorities in January 1966, which
appealed for cooperation and collaboration between them in provid-

ing a comprehensive curriculum at local level. In 1962, 73% of vocational schools and 63% of secondary schools had less than 150 pupils and in many centres small secondary and vocational schools competed for a limited cohort.[173] His joint approach to the postprimary schools evoked a positive response in some centres; the resulting meetings generated a new spirit between the schools which led eventually in the seventies to the development of community schools in many centres.[174]

In his very short term of office George Colley had clarifed policy significantly and had informed and developed public opinion on the nature of the reforms needed; the initial survey work of the Development Branch which he established had generated local expectations which only 'free education for all' could satisfy.

Following the publication of *Investment in Education* and the public debate which it generated, it became obvious that the gradualism inherent in Fianna Fáil's policy since 1957 was no longer an adequate response to the demands of the sixties. It fell to Donagh O'Malley to introduce the policy quantum jump to 'free' education, a transition which few other politicians of the day could have accomplished with such assurance, personal courage and political style. His major achievement was undoubtedly the 'free' education scheme of 1967 and the associated school transport system but it would be mistaken to see these as his only significant achievements. He abolished the primary certificate examination in 1967 and expressed his basic commitment to improving the physical condition of national schools by the grants scheme for upgrading heating and sanitary schemes.[175] During 1966/67 the county reports were discussed at county meetings to which, on O'Malley's instructions, parents were invited. In higher education his attempted 'merger' of Trinity College and University College Dublin was doomed to failure but his contribution to the development of the regional technical colleges was significant. He received the report of the Commission on Higher Education in 1967 and choose to ignore most of its recommendations; he established a Steering Committee on Technical Education which made a major input.[176] On language policy he surprised those who expected him to be indifferent on the question by asserting that he had no intention of presiding over the obsequies of the national language and introduced new schemes for teachers and students of the language. On the minister's specific direction, the department began the preparation of a white paper on education in 1967; this may have been in response to the various demands for legislation and a comprehensive policy statement from school authorities.

O'Malley's 'free' education and transport schemes were formed from some very deep convictions on the social role of education, the innate injustice of inequality and the long-term national benefit to be derived from expanding educational opportunity. He also revealed in his various speeches a keen awareness of social history and a comparative knowledge of the education systems of western Europe. He was keenly aware of the fate of those, 17,000 in number, who never transferred from primary to postprimary, whose formal education ended at 14 and committed himself to removing that 'dark stain on the national conscience'.[177]

His free education scheme announced in September 1966 and elaborated on in the Dáil in December, attracted some vigorous opposition and required a resolute stand by the minister against school authorities who feared the role of the state and the erosion of the private status of the secondary schools. This opposition is clearly the main theme of a remarkable ministerial address, 'Free Education and After?', delivered in February 1967 at a critical point in the negotiations between the department and the school authorities. Prefacing his comments with a claim that he was not speaking especially of Ireland, he described secondary education as 'complacent', providing an education 'which was not for every Tom, Dick and Harry' and serving a clientele which was ever increasing.[178] It had been realised in many education systems that voluntary effort was not enough, if *all* the children of the nation were to enjoy equality of educational opportunity. He described the private nature of the secondary grammar schools as having among its advantages 'that heretofore the State, that is the community in general, has largely escaped the burden of providing school accommodation'.[179] However he recognised a corresponding disadvantage:

> If we were entirely dependent on private schools, the essence of which is the right to accept or reject any particular pupil, the state could not guarantee to all children the right of access to postprimary education. A system for all but from which even one child could be arbitrarily locked out, could not be accepted by me, for with such a system we would not be cherishing all the children of the nation, not to mention cherishing them equally.[180]

Striking such a direct and fundamental political position enabled O'Malley to save his scheme against a number of alternative schemes put forward by the managerial bodies. His courage and commitment weathered the storm and 1967 witnessed the single most significant advance in Irish education in this century. His early death in 1968 cut short a political career which in a short period had transformed the system.

Brian Lenihan in his short period of office 1968/69 suffered by comparison with his predecessor and from the conflict among teachers arising from the implementation of the Ryan Tribunal on salaries. Nevertheless he succeeded in maintaining the momentum in extending opportunity; furthermore he began the shift in policy from second level to higher education. In 1968 he introduced an expanded scholarship scheme which quickly facilitated wider access not only to universities but also to the technological sector.[181] In July 1968 government policy on higher education was announced as involving the establishment of a permanent authority, a Council of Irish Universities, the de-federalisation of the National University and the amalgamation of Trinity College and University College as two colleges within a restructured University of Dublin.[182]

The four years spent by Pádraig Faulkner as minister, 1969-73, were dominated by the structural problems which arose from the rapid quantitative expansion of participation at second level. It became quite obvious that the 1967 'free' education scheme, the comprehensive schools and the policy of cooperation had not resolved the structural tensions surrounding postprimary education. Faulkner's approach tended to be extremely cautious expecially in areas which involved any element of structural change such as management committees in national schools, corporal punishment and the comprehensive schools.[183] In the three years to 1970, 50,000 new places were provided in 100 existing secondary schools, in a total of 2,000 rooms including specialist facilities. When it came to providing postprimary facilities *ab initio* in the growing suburbs, or where existing secondary and vocational schools merged, the inevitable questions of control and management arose; these led in 1970 to the emergence of a new model of postprimary provision, the community school.

In higher education, Faulkner was the first to draw attention to the heavy imbalance in favour of the arts and humanities and the relationship of this to economic and industrial development and the 'overall needs of the nation'.[184] This analysis of the output of the higher education system led eventually to a policy of quotas, limited access and positive discrimination in favour of the technological sector.

On language policy, Faulkner was closer to Colley and Deirg than to his immediate predecessors; while denying that the government's policy was to replace English by Irish he asserted that his aim was that all would acquire as a natural right a fluent knowledge of Irish, which could not be achieved except in the schools.[185]

In postprimary policy he advanced the concept of joint management of schools by Vocational Committees and private agencies; to this end he introduced in 1970 an amendment to the 1930 Act which enabled Vocational Committees to contribute financially to and share the management of such schools.[186] In curricular matters he began to examine the question of quality and turned a critical eye on the role of the public examination system. In the technological sector he established in 1972 the National Council for Educational Awards with responsibility for the promotion and validation of courses and the related awards in the non-university institutions.

The controveries which arose in the seventies on the control and management of the community schools revealed the friction and the barely concealed continuing contest between public and private ownership which the heady expansion policies of the sixties had papered over. The proposals issued by the department in 1971 and already agreed with the Catholic bishops, provided for a board of management of six, of whom four would be nominated by the secondary schools and two by the vocational authorities; it also provided that school site and buildings be vested in three trustees nominated by the bishop, one of whom would be from a list supplied by the Vocational Committee.[187] The critical comments which greeted these proposals from a variety of sources forced the minister to change the trustee arrangements. However he refused to shift his ground on the management proposals and rejected all charges of sectarianism as being based on misrepresentation and ignorance of the facts.[188] This issue dominated postprimary policy throughout the seventies and constituted a major irritant for four ministers; the first community schools operated on *ad hoc* arrangements until the deeds of trust were agreed and signed in 1981. The postprimary teacher unions were opposed to some basic clauses in the deeds, reserved places for religious teachers, a faith and morals clause on teacher appointment and the structure of teacher appointment committees; they were successful in securing formal teacher representation on the management boards of the community schools and on those of comprehensive schools from which they had also been excluded.[189] Before the community school controversy was resolved, the combined education authorities of the Protestant churches issued a major policy statement in which they criticised the reserved posts for religious teachers, the proposed Catholic catechetical inspectorate, the denominational nature of the schools and asked instead for community schools which would be 'Christian in the widest sense, open to all the children of the community'.[190]

The decade from the end of the Fianna Fáil administration in 1973 has been characterised by severe tension between demand and supply of education services. For the ministers in question funding an ever-expanding system became a major problem; total enrolments of one million students had been projected for the mid-eighties.[191] The economic recession has further restricted the scope of policy to little more than coping with the rising costs of the system; by the end of the seventies state expenditure on education was among the highest of the public services and by 1985 the education budget had reached £1 billion.

Mr Richard Burke's term of office 1973-77, was mainly characterised by developments in higher education, by changes in language policy and by initiatives in changing management structures, some of which were successful. His proposals on higher education of 1974 constituted a reversal of the policy being pursued by Fianna Fáil ministers on the relationship of the university and technological sectors.[192] Burke favoured a comprehensive structure in which the National Institutes of Higher Education would be recognised colleges of a university, all degrees would be awarded by universities and sub-degree awards would be awarded by a new Council for Technological Education. His specific proposals included two universities in Dublin, a reduced N.U.I., comprising Cork and Galway, Maynooth having the option of becoming a recognised college of one of the three universities, a conjoint Board to coordinate the two Dublin Universities and a Council of Irish Universities; he also specified the distribution of faculties as between Trinity College and University College Dublin.[193]

In 1973 shortly after taking office he announced that, as and from 1974, Irish would not be required as an essential subject in the public certificate examinations. While doing so, he echoed Donagh O'Malley's assertion, declaring that he had not become Minister to preside at the obsequies of the language; rather he hoped to rehabilitate and revitalise it.[194]

In his approach to specifying his policy of educational opportunity he was fulsomely vague, if not ambivalent:

> Everything we hold about the nature and destiny of man and especially our belief in the infinite intrinsic worth of every human being, must impel us to wage an unrelenting war, both within the educational system and outside it, against anything that prevents any child from realising his God-given potential.[195]

Richard Burke lacked the strong commitment to planning which had characterised the ministers of the sixties; it was during his term that the planning function of the department was diminished and the work of the Development Branch effectively terminated. His efforts to create a decentralised regional structure in the system did not survive the discussion and consultation stages. He did however succeed in modifying the national school managerial bodies, whereby, where committees of management were established the department would provide a substantial *per capita* grant to cover 80% of the running costs of schools[196]. This scheme effectively increased the annual expenditure on school maintenance by a factor of three and in return the churches were willing to consent to committees composed in larger schools of six church nominees, two teachers and two parents and in smaller schools of four church nominees one teacher and one parent. This structure was unacceptable to the INTO who sought tripartite equal representation; in 1980 it was modified so as to give the churches 50% and the teachers and elected parents 25% each.[197]

The return of Fianna Fáil to power in 1977, brought John Wilson to the post of Minister for Education, with a commitment in his party's election manifesto 'to set out in a White Paper the lines for future education development in Ireland'. The publication of the white paper in 1980 was a major feature of his term of office; besides envisaging various process developments it projected increased enrolments in all three levels and a pronounced emphasis on the technological sector in the development of higher education.[198]

The rising enrolments and the associated escalation in costs led in 1981 to John Boland as Minister proposing to raise the minimum age of entry to national schools, a measure which was opposed vigorously by the INTO; the issue has been raised again in 1985 by the publication of a department policy document, *The Ages of Learning*.

Mrs Gemma Hussey (1982-1986), managed to live within the constraints of the deep economic recession by cutting back on some services while at the same time taking some bold initiatives; these included a *Programme for Action in Education 1984-87*, setting out the Government's priorities, and the establishment in 1984 of a Curriculum and Examinations Board. Arising from the action programme, measures were introduced to aid the educationally disadvantaged, to delimit sexism and stereotyping in education, to extend the role of parents by the creation of a National Parents' Council and the introduction of E.E.C. funded pre-employment courses to secondary schools.[199] The minister has also made a strong commitment to adult education as an important sector in its own right along the lines of the report published in 1983.[200] In higher education she has espoused and consolidated the binary system and invested heavily in the technological sector. In late 1985 teacher salary demands caused a major confrontation with the government, reminiscent of the 1946 INTO strike, sharpened by concerted industrial action by the three teacher unions. The most spectacular initiative taken by the minister is contained in a green paper on decentralised education administration, which could in its potential significance rank with McPherson's Irish Education Bill of 1919.[201] Patrick Cooney succeeded Mrs Hussey in 1986.

Of the fourteen ministers who have held office since 1957, a number such as Peter Barry, Martin O'Donoghue, Gerard Brady and Patrick Cooney have been less than a year in office and consequently did not have sufficient time to impress their character on policy. Nevertheless even these short-term ministers shared in the general expansion of the system in the past quarter century. This significant expansion was catalysed by a strong public demand, which even in economic recession never flagged, to which the politicians responded by redefining the state's role in education in terms of a more active Department of Education. Among the younger aspiring ministers of the sixties, especially for Colley and O'Malley, the older received dogma and the associated rhetoric on the state's role were no longer acceptable; they perceived and asserted that the centre of initiative in formulating and implementing policy must be the government and the Minister. In a period when most ministers have been policy initiators and by necessity have perfected their public relations and brokerage roles, as well as developing an aggressive cabinet stance in pursuit of adequate resources, Colley and O'Malley must be seen as policy initiators and policy selectors *par excellence*.

Hillery's main role was precursorial, preparing public and political opinion for the policy changes which were still in preparation. For all of the other ministers, there was never a shortage of policies from which to choose; the problem lay in balancing the resource needs of the first and second levels with the growing demand for higher education in a society characterised by a very high dependency ratio. If all the ministers since 1957 have been policy initiators in varying degrees, they have operated in a political milieu wherein the changed role of the state in education is an accepted reality.

TABLE 9.1

The Ministers for Education since 1922 by length of office and professional familiarity with the system.

Professional Relationship	Over 5 Years	Under 5 Years
Professionally Familiar	O'Sullivan, Deirg	MacNeill, de Valera, Moylan, Faulkner, Wilson, O'Donoghue, Boland, Burke, Hussey, O'Rourke
Not Professionally Familiar	Mulcahy, Hillery,	Lynch, Colley, O'Malley, Lenihan, Brady, Barry Ó Ceallaigh, Cooney

TABLE 9.2

The Departmental Secretaries who served between 1923 and 1968, their tenure of office and previous careers.

Secretary	Tenure	Previous Career
Joseph O'Neill M.A.	1923-1944	University Lecturer at Manchester, Fribourg and Albert College; Primary Inspector 1907, Intermediate Inspector 1909-23
Micheál Breathnach M.A.	1944-1953	Secondary Teacher 1909-23, Primary Inspector 1923 Secondary Inspector 1924 General Inspector of Irish 1931, Assistant Chief Inspector 1932
Labhrás Ó Muirí, B. A.	1953-1956	Secondary Teacher (Pres. ASTI 1920), Primary Inspector 1923, Secondary Inspector 1924, Civil Service Commissioner 1926.
Tarlach Ó Raifeartaigh, M.A.	1956-1968	Lecturer St. Patrick's Drumcondra 1926-31, Secondary Inspector 1932, Assistant Chief Inspector 1944, Chief Inspector 1946, Assistant Secretary 1948.

TABLE 9.3

State expenditure on the erection of new and the enlargement of existing National Schools and on the provision and equipping of Vocational Schools by year for the period 1932-56.

Financial Year	National Schools Erection & Enlargement	Vocational Schools Erection & Enlargement
	£	£
1932/33	65,774	11,118
1933/34	100,838	56,931
1934/35	128,538	57,408
1935/36	126,967	115,691
1936/37	132,122	133,483
1937/38	159,285	95,448
1938/39	197,372	118,047
1939/40	229,222	135,286
1940/41	221,248	71,987
1941/42	212,139	41,338
1942/43	241,090	44,019
1943/44	256,511	50,805
1944/45	227,684	23,710
1945/46	176,087	16,928
1946/47	173,856	11,899
1947/48	134,942	33,395
1948/49	308,208	26,983
1949/50	513,960	91,035
1950/51	530,313	133,773
1951/52	552,151	164,668
1952/53	684,356	295,113
1953/54	1,071,053	258,862
1954/55	1,050,750	245,564
1955/56	1,042,029	328,295

Source: *Dáil Debates*, 160, 783.

CHAPTER TEN

The Department of Finance

Among those contributors to the formulation of policy not directly involved in the education process itself, the Department of Finance is undoubtedly the most significant; in most systems it is usually the department of government, other than Education which can make a major consistent input in the formulation and implementation of policy.

In the constitutions of 1922 and 1937, the functions of the Department of Finance are specified along the general lines and the fundamental principles embodied in the British financial system.[1] These fundamental principles concern the necessity for Oireachtas approval of the purpose of all monies collected or spent by the state, the establishment of a single fund into which and out of which all such monies are paid and disbursed and the definition of the unit of financial administration as the calendar year.[2] The audit of all such transactions is provided for constitutionally in the office of the comptroller and auditor-general who reports to the Oireachtas.[3] The control, regulation and management of the Civil Service was established as another major function of the Department of Finance in the early days of the state, when, according to the department secretary, the primacy of the Department of Finance emanated from 'the general conception of government embodied in our Constitution'.[4]

The supervision and control of all public expenditure by the Department of Finance places it in a special relationship with each department of government concerning the development of policies. Although its role is limited in theory to the fiscal dimension, in practice there are few aspects of policy which do not involve expenditure or the utilisation of public resources. Each department of state in the annual process of preparing and submitting its budget estimates to the Department of Finance, undergoes a thorough scrutiny of its policies and practices; this exercise affords the Department of Finance an annual opportunity to influence department policy significantly. Apart from this annual survey, all new policy proposals or departures from sanctioned procedures require the prior sanction of the Department of Finance; all proposed legislation, ministerial orders and proposals to cabinet are subject to the same process of examination. Up to the mid-seventies the personnel function in the

Civil Service was under the control of the Department of Finance, which allowed it to exercise decisive influence on the general staffing and on the appointments at senior level in all government departments.

The interaction between the Department of Finance and the Department of Education since 1922 has been methodical and meticulous, coloured at times by offical reprimand or sharp differences but on the whole, allowing for the supervisory role of the Department of Finance, it has been constructive and rational. The mechanism may appear tedious, constricting and at times unnecessarily concerned with trivial matters; yet the overall effect is to introduce a rationality into procedures, to promote consistency in the administrative process and to facilitate clarification and examination of policies. However the major objective of the Department of Finance must always be to restrain and contain Department expenditure estimates and to insist that once estimates are sanctioned, they be strictly adhered to. Consequently we frequently find rejection of proposals with which sympathy is expressed, numerous expressions of concern for the 'enormous expenditure on education' and repeated admonitions to avoid commitments to additional expenditure.[5]

This interactive process between the two departments can sometimes be drawn out and tedious but can frequently move with expedition when there is strong political support to hand or when the particular issue stems from a ministerial initiative; the various measures taken by Ernest Blythe in connection with the Irish language policy provide clear examples of the impact of ministerial support. When outright rejection was not justified or was considered inappropriate, the Department of Finance officials frequently utilised cunctatory tactics which sought to delay the introduction of desirable measures. When other means failed, the application of gentle administrative force sometimes proved very successful; when in 1938 the Department of Education was reluctant to supply a copy of its internal report on the preparatory colleges to the Department of Finance, the matter was resolved by the latter's insistence that without it the education estimates could not be considered.[6]

The official records of the inter-department transactions are dominated by the formalised language of bureaucracy; occasionally this is relieved by some colourful passages and by touches of comedy and irony in the memoranda of officials in Finance. When in 1933 the marriage ban on women national school teachers was under discussion, a press cutting was circulated in the Department of Finance reporting from Sofia that the Bulgarian Ministry of Education had dismissed all its female teachers.[7] When the Department of Education granted a concession to Protestant schools which was not to appear in the published rules, the minuted observation in the Department of Finance was: 'The considerations involved are of course, purely educational'.[8]

When occasionally issues remained unresolved between the two departments, the usual procedure was to have the questions tabled at the Cabinet or in the instances where the taoiseach intervened, one side yielded or a compromise was reached. However such unresolved conflicts were rare, due mainly to the successful strategies employed by the Department of Finance which once led an assistant secretary to minute as follows:

> Our time and labour spent on contentious issues with this department (Education) have gone for so little on occasions that I am not disposed to contest anything in which we have not a practically overwhelming case.[9]

The transactions between the departments fall into a number of identifiable categories; many concern the control of expenditure, some involve procedural infringements or official reprimands, while others concern fundamental differences of opinion. These latter occasions are outnumbered by the positive policy inputs made by the Department of Finance. Utilising the official archives, it is proposed to examine and to illustrate this interaction in greater detail by means of a few policy studies. In restraining expenditure the Department of Finance was ever conscious of the direction contained in its own annual *Estimates Circular*:

> Sanction will not be given for additional charges in respect of new or existing services unless the Minister is satisfied that the increased expenditure is essential to Government policy or compensating reductions are effected in other directions.[10]

The search for economy often involved seeking reductions in the primary subhead if the secondary subhead were exceeded as happened in the estimates for 1924/25.[11] The intensity of this economy drive in the twenties can be seen in the severe reductions imposed in 1925/27 when science laboratory grants were reduced.[12] The Department of Finance was particularly wary of commissions and their reports lest the establishment of the former or the publication of the latter would generate implicit commitment to additional expenditure. When the department opposed the establishment of a Children's Commission in 1932 on technical grounds, its real reason is revealed in an internal memo which asserts:

> The net effect of all these committees and commissions is, frankly stated, to take out of the hands of the Minister for Finance the power of controlling expenditure on the services to which the inquiries relate.[13]

In 1927 when sanctioning the publication of the 'Report on Inspection in primary schools', the Minister for Finance warned that 'no statement should be made which would fetter the discretion of this department in considering proposals involving expenditure made in this report'.[14]

The thrust of the government's language policy and especially the commitment of the Minister for Finance in the late twenties and early thirties, are evident in the question of providing school meals for Gaeltacht children; this issue provides a good example of how ministers, if and when they wish, prevail over the bureaucrats. Department officials, in true Treasury tradition, maintained that 'due to the expenditure being already incurred in pursuance of government language policy, the question of providing school meals in the Gaeltacht should be deferred'.[15] The Minister did not agree and the scheme was sanctioned by the Executive Council in November 1929.[16] Nevertheless, it is clearly not easy to defeat strong and dedicated Finance officials.

When opposition to a proposal was neither feasible nor successful, postponement was a favoured tactic; such appeals for delaying implementation were usually accompanied by soothing phrases such as 'without contesting the educational aspects of the matter'. A Department of Education request in the early fifties, for sanction to plan a seven year series of inservice courses for teachers of Geography, Mathematics and Languages was refused by asking for postponement. When the request was renewed some years later the same line was advocated with the confident assertion in an internal minute that 'we stemmed a similar tide in 1951'.[17] Upper Merrion Street was evidently still peopled by some ageing Canutes who did not share the new-found official enthusiasm for planning.

From the establishment of the preparatory colleges in the twenties the Department of Finance was critical of the level of expenditure associated with them; this attitude was no doubt reinforced by the bungling of the Department of Education on the question of a new women's training college in Galway. When this issue was before the Government in November 1932, the Department of Finance and its minister took a very strong line on 'the enormous amount of money being spent on education' and asserted that the need for a new training college would be diminished if the course were reduced to one year's duration.[18] When in 1931 the Department of Education proposed that the grant for male religious trainee teachers be greater than that for female religious trainee teachers, the Department of Finance opposed it not on egalitarian but on financial grounds.[19] Even when sympathetic to a proposal, Finance officials seldom, if ever, found themselves able to waive a rule or abandon a precedent; when a school manager was unable to defray the cost of preparing the site for his urgently needed school, it was recommended that the possibility of voluntary direct labour be investigated in preference to the state defraying the cost.[20] In 1937 it agreed with a proposal to increase the number of secondary scholarships but emphasised that such a measure could only be funded by a corresponding reduction in the Secondary Education Estimate, since in that year six new proposals would involve a substantial increase in the annual expenditure on education.[21]

In the thirties, possibly associated with the implementation of the 1930 Vocational Education Act, the Department of Finance intensified its drive for economy and restraint in educational expenditure. They were, from the outset, critical of the financial implications of the measure and were also sceptical of the reliability of the estimates prepared by the Department of Education. On examining the draft bill in May 1929, the general reaction of the Department of Finance is summarised as follows in an official minute:

> From an examination of the draft bill, it appears likely that unless the financial provisions are drastically amended the state will ultimately have to bear an enormous burden of new expenditure.[22]

The Department of Finance succeeded eventually in moderating the implications of the 1930 act but not before the Department of Education had ignored some agreed changes and circulated the bill in the Dáil without final clearance, a situation lamented as follows in a Department of Finance minute: 'So far as our control of finance is concerned, the reins seem to be on the horse's back at the moment'.[23] On a number of smaller issues, we notice again the impact of political pressures, this time by de Valera; the stated position of the Department of Finance was reversed on the Primary Certificate being made compulsory in 1942, on the provision of radios for some national schools in 1937 and on the provision of a separate national school in the newly-created Gaeltacht of Rath Chairn in Co. Meath in 1935, all with the barely concealed support of the taoiseach.[24] On other occasions, even when the issue was predominantly educational or curricular, the Department of Finance carried the day, as in 1936 when the Department of Education wished to change from the Swedish Ling system of physical education to the Sokol system from Czechoslovakia.[25]

The restraining hand is especially evident when proposals with long-term cost implications are under discussion, such as the raising of the school leaving age. This arose in 1937 when it was proposed, as an alternative to a uniform national scheme, to apply part V of the 1930 Act as an experiment to Cork City. The Department of Finance was particularly insistent that the scheme should be funded on the same principle as the vocational system, with an equal sharing of costs between the state and the local authority. The issue was settled at ministerial level by a compromise arrangement in which the state would cover the costs of those attending compulsorily and the

Vocational Committee the costs of those who attended voluntarily.[26] However the Minister for Finance was not willing to see schemes proliferate; having placed a time limit of five years on the Cork scheme, he appealed to his ministerial colleague in education to resist any suggestions for extending its scope.[27] When some Vocational Education Committees sought to build permanent schools in 1938, the local authorities were reluctant to finance them and provoked the Department of Finance into advising that the projects be postponed for a few years, observing that 'the increase in the cost of technical education has been at too rapid a rate'.[28]

These examples illustrate how in many policy areas the Department of Finance acted as an effective brake on the Department of Education; however it was realised in both departments that 'one of the certainties of education is the upward trend of expenditure' as expressed in a minute of 1929. For the Department of Finance it became a matter of priorities and of preserving a sense of proportion in policy. This balanced perspective is expressed incisively by a senior Finance official in the same minute of 1929:

> If the desirability of an improvement in the standard of education in this country, or for that matter in any other country, could be examined without regard to other considerations, there would scarcely be two opinions about the conclusions.[29]

Arising from its supervisory role and its wider perspective on policy issues than that obtaining in other departments, the Department of Finance is ideally situated to detect and if necessary to refer to the Cabinet, questions which involve departures from government policy, legal problems or possible constitutional issues. Such questions have arisen on a few occasions in regard to policy proposals in education.

In 1926, with the active support of a few other government ministers, it was proposed by the Department of Education that Louise Gavan Duffy's secondary school for girls, Scoil Bhríde, be recognised as a national school and as a Research and Practising School attached to the Faculty of Education of University College Dublin. The Department of Finance was of the opinion that the matter 'was one for decision in principle by the executive council, since it involved transforming a secondary school, which through no fault of its own had not succeeded financially into a primary school with a special relationship to University College Dublin'.[30] However Ernest Blythe, as Minister for Finance, saw no such difficulty; he convened a conference with John Marcus O'Sullivan and senior officials of the Department of Education, at which a new rule was drafted which gave recognition as a national school to Scoil Bhríde. The reconstituted school was operating within six months in government premises and the teachers were recognised as national teachers.[31]

In opposing the provision of school meals in the Gaeltacht in 1932, the Department of Finance appealed to a legal taxation principle; since the Gaeltacht in no county was coterminous with the county itself, it was not permissible to tax a county for a service which was available to only a section of itself.[32]

When grants were sought in 1928 for children on small islands without educational facilities, to board them adjacent to mainland primary schools, the Department of Finance reacted in a strange manner on a proposal whose funding might never exceed £100 p.a. Senior officials within the Department were of the opinion that the constitutional guarantee on education did not go beyond 'providing reasonable facilities for primary education'; it (the constitution) does not relieve the citizen of the obligation to cooperate with the state in having every child educated.[33] This proposal, to provide primary education for those who were receiving none, according to the same officials, opened a door for additional expenditure from public funds and 'whilst possibly achieving good in a few isolated cases, might be educationally and morally harmful'. After two years of urgent appeals from the Department of Education and frequent letters from concerned school managers, the Department of Finance relented and 'only with much difficulty' provided £100 as a maximum allocation in any one year. In doing so, it appears that they were convinced that with the passing of time 'the population now living on these islands will not increase and may indeed disappear; any scheme to board them on the mainland would ensure to that same end'.[34]

When in November 1931 the Mayo Vocational Education Committee was suspended by the Minister, two officials of the department were appointed as commissioners in its place.[35] The Department of Education wished to forego charging Mayo for their salaries, maintaining that the commissioners did their Mayo work in their spare time and during official leave. The Department of Finance and the minister, Seán McEntee, rejected this line and pursued the question with Deirg until a token £20 sum was ultimately paid.

It is difficult to differentiate in the conservative arguments put forward at times by the Department of Finance between those deriving from genuine conservative values and those which are linked tactically to expenditure cutting or constraint. When in 1951 the Council of Education sought submissions on the question of raising the school leaving age, a major debate took place in the Department of Finance.[36] The question was raised as to whether it was permissible under Article 42 of the Constitution to enforce compulsory attendance at postprimary education or to provide such education free of cost.[37] In its official reply to the Council of Education the Department of Finance repeated the constitutional limitation, stating that:

It is possible that Article 42 would not cover a general extension without exception of the present period of compulsory school attendance i.e. 8 yrs from 6 to 14.[38]

The relationship of the Department of Finance to the Department of Education and to other departments is strongly coloured by the magisterial or supervisory role and its related power to criticise and reprimand. Phrases such as 'most irregular', 'highly undesirable', 'financal loss to the state', 'official bungling', 'a serious matter', 'a very bad business for the taxpayer', 'a cause of major disquiet' and similar expressions occur in the official correspondence to indicate criticism or the displeasure of the Department of Finance. The policies or incidents which occasioned such criticism ranged from the circulation of the 1930 bill before final sanction, the irregular payment of £8,418 after 1922 to St Mary's Training College Belfast, without reference to the Department of Finance, and the state covering the total cost of teacher residences, to spending £16,000 on the steel work for a training college which was not proceeded with and sending memoranda to cabinet without prior consultation with Finance; on a number of occasions the Department of Finance derides the subservience of the Department of Education to pressure from the hierarchy, the euphemisms used in describing such pressure and the reluctance to insist on the strict observance of published statutory regulations.[39] The most frequent subject of criticism is the quality of the cost estimates presented by the Department of Education; in many policy proposals the Department of Finance tended to regard the estimates as inaccurate and inevitably to err on the low side. Their frustration is expressed clearly in the following 1936 minute: 'It would be too much to expect the department to present a complete picture of the financial implications of the proposal'.[40]

Despite much of the intervention of the Department of Finance being negative or regulatory in nature, it did make some significant contributions to the evolution of policy and this sometimes occured even when acting in its regulatory mode. In 1925 when the secondary teachers' salary rules were being drafted the Department of Education wished to amalgamate the 1914 teacher salary grant with the capitation grant and thereby abolish the legal ratio between lay teachers and religious inherent in the Birrell scheme which lay teachers regarded as their *magna carta*. The secretary of the Department of Finance (Joseph Brennan) thought it essential that the 1914 rules be observed by schools, proposed that a percentage of the capitation grant be identified as the salary grant and suggested that the atorney general examine the rules in reference to Article 8 of the 1922 Constitution.[41]

In opposing the provision of maintenance grants to island children the Department of Finance asked why preference should be given to island children and thereby raised the question of providing such grants to children in remote mainland areas.[42]

The question of the size of the local contribution to the erection of national schools was a constant issue between the departments; the Department of Education favoured the lowering of the minimum to one-quarter and later to one-sixth but the Department of Finance response was inevitable and swift, expressed in this trenchant internal direction:

> Any show of weakness in the official attitude in this matter can have but one result, grants of full cost in the end. I should favour its rejection out of hand.[43]

When the church authorities in Dublin sought a reduction in the local contribution for the national schools of the new suburbs in the late thirties, the Department of Finance reacted by proposing that the local contribution, where the burden on new parishes was too heavy, should be a diocesan responsibility.[44] When the Department of Finance observed that religious orders were usually in a position to provide a higher local contribution than the parishes, the Department of Education 'explained that there was a limit to the extent to which the archbishop would sanction the management of schools being handed over to religious orders'.[45]

The Minister for Finance played a direct role in this question when he proposed that the local authorities, specifically Dublin Corporation, should contribute to the cost of erection of national schools in new housing schemes; McEntee urged the proposal on Deirg who replied that the Archbishop of Dublin 'would not countenance any contribution towards cost of erection of national schools being provided by Dublin Corporation'. In this regard the archbishop was bound by the joint resolution adopted by the hierarchy in October 1934 which had already been communicated to the minister.[46]

This question arose again in relation to the schools of the Dublin suburbs built after the war. In 1952 the Department of Education supported a proposal that six schools in a particular suburb be managed by a church-nominated order whose proposed local contribution amounted to less than 3% of the total cost.[47] This evoked a vehement response from the Department of Finance involving projections of the profitability of the schools under various staffing arrangements of lay and religious teachers. These calculations led the Department of Finance to the conclusions that 'the earning capacity of these schools is substantial' and 'potentially at least these schools are money spinners for the order'.[48] However this detailed exercise was in vain and eventually the initial proposal of the Department of Education was sanctioned.

The central importance of this particular question is borne out by its frequency as an issue between the two Departments from the twenties onwards; the problem for the Department of Finance lay in reconciling a theoretical norm for local contributions of one third with a reality which varied from zero to the norm. The Department of Education found great difficulty in subscribing to the policy implications of the agreed local contribution and withstanding the heavy political and ecclesiastical pressure seeking to reduce the size of the contribution.

On questions of education policy, thinking in the Department of Finance was sometimes ahead of that in the Department of Education. In 1929 the Department of Finance proposed that the provision of a training college for teachers of woodwork, metalwork and engineering be examined, forty years before effective action was taken on the question.[49] In the revision of the rules in 1929, the Department of Finance questioned the appropriateness of defining suitability for managership of national schools in terms of social standing and proposed substituting the phrase 'approved by the Department'.[50] In 1939 the Department of Education proposed a scheme for the making of gramophone records as instructional aids for the national schools; in recognising the proposal as good in principle and sanctioning the scheme, the Department of Finance observed that the gramophone was giving way to radio.[51]

Though it opposed the proposal whereby in areas of the Gaeltacht where no suitable accommodation was available, housing for teachers be provided with the state assuming total cost, the Department of Finance supported the scheme on a rental basis as a necessary means of attracting good school principals to remote areas. The scheme was sanctioned and served areas in most of the Atlantic coastal counties.[52] When in 1937 the Department of Education complained of unreasonable delay in the office of the Board of Works in relation to the provision of national schools the Minister for Finance responded by sanctioning the establishment of a special school section in the office.[53]

Where legal actions arose from the exercise of the managerial function in national schools or the preparatory colleges, the Department of Finance was adamant that the state had no obligation to pay the legal costs of the manager. In one such case the manager, who was sued by a dismissed teacher, claimed that he was acting as the agent of the Department of Education and consequently sought expenses and costs.[54] The Department of Finance and the Minister for Finance rejected the claim strenuously but political pressure on the Minister for Education and the attorney general extracted a promise from John Marcus O'Sullivan to pay the costs. When it fell to the Fianna Fáil administration in 1933 to pay half the costs, the Department of Finance countered with an express directive from deValera that 'in no circumstances will any payment be made from state funds towards the legal costs of a school manager arising from actions concerning the managerial function'. However this directive was soon breached in a legal action brought by a preparatory college teacher against the Archbishop of Tuam for dismissal on her marriage.[55] In this case the high court judge directed that the Minister for Education pay the archbishop's costs.[56] The negative attitude of the Department of Finance towards commissions and their reports has already been mentioned. The most energetic reaction of all however was reserved for the report of the Commission on Youth Unemployment which sat from 1943 to 1951 under the chairmanship of Archbishop J. C. McQuaid. Strong reaction must have been anticipated by the Department of Education for it delayed presenting the outcome of the report to Government until 1958.[57] The Department of Finance was scathing in its observations and doubted, having regard to its recommendations, if the commission's time was well spent; the report was of doubtful value as a guide to the formulation of policy for the relief or abolition of unemployment among young people.[58]

There were some occasions when the two departments differed fundamentally on issues, such as the proposal to establish An Comhairle Le Leas Óige in 1941 and on making the Primary Certificate compulsory in 1942, in relation to which the Department of Finance observed as follows:

> We have been fighting a losing battle on the question of the Primary Certificate, (the Department of) Education arrived with Government authority.[59].

Possibly the most sensitive question which arose between the two departments and which also involved the Department of an Taoiseach, did not bear on education policy directly. It concerned Fr Michael O'Flanagan, a brother-in-law of Mr de Valera's, who was employed from 1932 by the Department of Education in writing a series of county histories for schools.[60] He had, it was alleged, absented himself without leave, publicly defended communism, attacked the pope and been politically active in the U.S.A. and Canada. When the secretary of Finance complained of his conduct to Education, the secretary of Education replied that national school teachers had freedom of speech; the Department of Finance was of the opinion that the Department of Education was 'suffering from cold feet'. When in January 1939 Fr O'Flanagan spoke at a London meeting in support of the Republican cause in the Spanish Civil War, the secretary of the Department of Finance complained to the Department of An Taoiseach that the Department of Education was unwilling to take any action; Mr McEntee had asked that the matter be brought to the attention of An Taoiseach. The Department of An Taoiseach replied that Mr de Valera suggested that the Minister for Finance, McEntee, might speak personally to Fr O'Flanagan.[61] This episode is of interest in illustrating the prime importance of political and ministerial direction in determining department action and initiative; when ministers are in conflict or stand back from a situation, the departments are reduced to helpless inactivity or harmless rhetoric.

To illustrate the pattern of interaction of the two departments in some greater detail a few issues of more central importance in the evolution of policy will be examined at greater length; these are the 1930 Vocational Education Act and its implementation and the raising of the school leaving age.

When the draft bill on vocational education, based upon the report of the 1927 Commission on Technical Education, came up for examination in the Department of Finance in August 1929, it caused major disquiet and met with severe opposition. The disquiet was occasioned by the inadequacy of the financial provision planned and the opposition arose from the fear that the measure would be implemented with enthusiasm and thereby cause a rapid rise in public educational expenditure.[62] The Department of Finance therefore approached the bill with questioning caution and with a determination to limit its implementation geographically and postpone its full application.

In the scheme put forward by the Department of Education in 1929, some attempt was made to quantify the demand for continuation education in the 14-16 age group; there were 74,000 of that age group who were not attending any school of whom 55,000 were expected to avail of vocational day courses.[63] This scheme also speaks of attendance at continuation schools being made compulsory. The Department of Finance sought the views of the Department of Local Government and of Industry and Commerce both of which agreed with the caution already expressed.

In its response, the Department of Finance counselled caution and a slow steady advance, recalling that the mistake made in the 1900 Technical Education scheme was its adoption over the whole country at once.[64] It proposed the following delaying measures:

(i)   for 5 years the scheme be applied only to county boroughs and larger urban areas;

(ii)   in these areas it should not begin for 2 years;

(iii)   technical education aspects to be postponed for 4 or 5 years.

An inter-department conference to examine the heads of the bill agreed to accept the principle of providing continuation education and to make it compulsory by ministerial order as, when and where it was practicable and desirable. This conference decided against providing a school transport scheme and the Minister for Education agreed that the development of vocational education should proceed only by gradual steps, indicating that he was seeking means of providing a brake on rapid development.

When the heads of the bill were before the Executive Council in August 1929 powers were granted to the Minister for Education to make special provision for continuation and technical education in the Gaeltacht and to make special grants available for that purpose.

Lest the various limits and constraints already imposed on the measure be overlooked or diluted, the Department of Finance summarised the position in a very trenchant official minute:

(i)   The minister feels bound to stipulate that every practical measure consistent with the general intention of the bill must be taken to ensure that the rate at which additional expenditure is to proceed shall be graduated and that the limit to which it may ultimately run,shall be kept in check.

(ii) The minister understands that it is not the intention to propose the establishment and maintenance of any training college for the training of teachers for the purposes of the bill.[65]

At this point the Department of Finance supplied a very effective brake by insisting that any scheme proposed would have to make provision for practical hand training for both sexes.

When the draft Bill was under discussion in March 1930, the section on compulsory attendance was amended and the Gaeltacht provision was rendered dependent on the specific sanction of the Minister for Finance; the Department of Finance was still uneasy about the lack of effective limits on incremental expenditure. It detailed its remaining criticisms as follows: the measure imposed a limited financial burden on local authorities and an unlimited one on the state, it involved differential rating proposals for different areas, it would intensify the demand for derating; and the estimate of total costs was incomplete. These features were totally unacceptable to the department and to the Minister for Finance alike and this was conveyed formally to the Department of Education.[66] In opposing unlimited expansion of provision, the Department of Finance was fortified by comparative data which it assembled showing that in education expenditure per capita of total population and as percentage of supply services, the Free State was ahead of Great Britain, Denmark, Sweden, France and Canada.[67] By June 1930 when the Bill was before the Dáil the Department of Finance was in consternation, realising that they had indeed been out-manoeuvred by the Department of Education, who had ignored the modifications advocated by the Department of Finance and had sent the bill for printing and circulation without referring back. The Department of Education had not only failed to answer requests for information on the financial effects of the measure 'but a long list of amendments notified on 24 May had not been examined from the Finance point of view'.[68] Certainly it did seem that, as the Bill was receiving the assent of the Dáil, 'the reins were on the horse's back'. But the supremacy of the Department of Finance could not be rejected so easily. By the autumn of 1930 the Department of Finance had taken a very firm grip on the reins and had imposed a tight set of restraints on the scheme. In determining state grants to committees for 1931-32 no general scheme was sanctioned but the needs of each area were taken on their merits.[69] A special formula was devised which took account of county variations in population density and ratable potential; the special provision for the Gaeltacht, it was agreed, would not be utilised in the near future and 'there was no intention in 1931 of spending money under that heading'.[70] It was agreed between the two departments that the rate of progress after 1931-32 would be much slower than that contemplated under the Act and the Department of Education itself did not envisage the operation of the scheme at full development for at least 20 years.[71] Under the imposed scheme, 15 out of the 27 county committees could introduce the scheme without any increase in state grants; in the other 12 counties and the towns and cities a grant related to population would be made. By the end of 1930 the supremacy of the Department of Finance had been reasserted; it was of the opinion that the Department of Education was behaving fairly and was confident of securing equal moderation in future years. The assistant secretary of Finance was also very impressed by the indications 'that the Department (of Education) is not beginning by opening its mouth too wide'.[72] It did not open its mouth again in relation to vocational education until the fifties.

The raising of the school leaving age, on the various occasions when it arose as a policy proposal, caused major discussion not only because of its obvious direct and indirect cost implications but also because its implementation would require some politically sensitive structural alterations in the postprimary system. The sensitivity of the question is also indicated by the delays in the implementation even when partially applied in the thirties or the longer delay between government decision in 1947 to promote legislation and the statutory raising of the school leaving age to 15 in 1972.[73] The interdepartment committee of 1933-35 recommended that experiments be conducted in selected areas utilising the vocational schools, requiring unemployed juveniles to attend full-time continuation classes, and employed juveniles to attend part-time classes. This scheme was introduced under part V of the 1930 act in Cork and later in Limerick and Waterford.

The Commission on Youth Unemployment of 1943-51, while recommending that the school leaving age be raised to 15, as a first step to raising it ultimately to 16, considered:

> That the policy most likely to yield the best results and at the same time cause the minimum of inconvenience would be to raise the school leaving age area by area according as local conditions became favourable.[74]

While the government accepted the principle, it did not propose to carry it into effect immediately nor did it expect it to be feasible for a considerable time to raise the school-leaving age on a compulsory basis.[75] In 1958 the Minister for Education proposed to the government that consideration of the question be deferred.

The Department of Finance's contribution to the debate on these various measures was realistic but mainly unenthusiastic. In response to the 1935 committee's recommendations, the Department seemed to believe that the expected educational advantage of raising the school-leaving age could not be secured 'because of the difficulty of providing a suitable reorganisation of schools', an implicit reference to the political sensitivity of the managerial and structural changes involved.[76] The department was convinced of the inevitability of a growing demand for extending educational opportunity and thought that 'in the distinctive conditions of this country, some kind of compromise is desirable'. However such desirable developments never arose from debate on the raising of the school-leaving age; by 1972 when it was raised by statute its effect had already been overtaken by the expanded participation rates consequent on 'free' education.

The more conservative side of the Department of Finance's attitude to raising the school leaving age is represented in its 1951 submission following the request by the Council of Education. Initially the internal department reaction was a distinct reluctance to offer any advice, expressed in a minute as follows:

> As a Department we have no concern with matters educational, nor can we give any advice to the Council on the question of raising the school leaving age, which is a topic to be studied by the Council soon.[77]

However, after a major internal debate this neutral stance was quickly altered to a decidedly conservative attitude and a willingness to emphasise to the council the vast costs involved, the need for a gradual approach and the possibility of compulsory postprimary education being unconstitutional. An internal memo outlining the statistical position concerning attendance at various school types among the 14-16 age group (41% of the 107,000 in 1945 were attending national, secondary or vocational schools), examined the various financial and constitutional implications of raising the school leaving age without once adverting to the principles of equity which might support such a policy.[78] The cost of providing school facilities for all to age 16 is envisaged as being very expensive and the possibility is anticipated of secondary schools seeking total current and capital costs from the state. Quoting articles 42.4 and articles 42.3.2 of the constitution, the memo questions whether compulsory postprimary education or the free provision of same by the state are constitutionally permissible. The alternative proposal, which is strongly supported, rests on a gradual approach expressed as follows:

It would seem to be the better policy to develop postprimary education for those children who wish to avail themselves of it before making it compulsory for all. The number of secondary schools and vocational schools is increasing steadily.[79]

This gradualist approach, actively canvassed by the Department of Finance, was also advocated in the *Report of the Committee on Youth Unemployment*; the department's final verdict regarded it as 'a more realistic approach as well as being less costly on the state'.[80] This was the policy pursued throughout the fifties and adopted formally by Seán Lemass in his Dáil statement in 1959. The influence of the Department of Finance on the question of the school leaving age was certainly conservative in nature but it may not have been very decisive. It is much more likely that the Department of Education's reluctance derived more from a fear of tackling the related structural questions and the anticipated church reaction than from the negative attitude of the Department of Finance.

In general the Department of Finance exerised direct influence on the education policy pursued over most of the years since the foundation of the state; this direct influence was exercised more by keeping the Department of Education on the rails of controlled expenditure than by thwarting policy initiatives. On expenditure it was usually reactionary, controlling and cautious, on expanding educational opportunity it was less than enthusiastic and, as we shall see later, on Irish language policy it was mildly hostile especially in the early decades. Even in the late fifties when the Department of Finance was advocating expansion of state initiative and central planning it saw fit to discourage the Department of Education from raising the school leaving age.

Over the decades examined here the Department of Finance never exercised the same tight control over Irish education policy which the Treasury had in the decades around the turn of the century. Nevertheless the early bureaucracy in Merrion Street had effectively learned and applied the wide range of administrative tactics and cunctatory practices developed in the Treasury. The Department of Finance role was primarily gubernatorial, directly influencing the general direction or fiscal limits of policy but never depriving or relieving the Department of Education of its basic role in formulating and implementing policy. If that policy over most of this century was timid, incoherent and conservative, this was due more to the set of values governing the policy process in the Department of Education than to the undue influence of the Department of Finance.

SECTION III

POLICY FORMULATION
AND
IMPLEMENTATION

INTRODUCTION

In the preceding section, the contributions of various groups to the policy process have been presented and examined in the context of their expressed demands upon the system. In the formulation and implementation of policy over the past eight decades these various contributions or inputs have not enjoyed equal weight nor have their relativities remained constant over time. It is intended in this section to examine the mechanism and models which have governed the formulation and implementation of policy in the context of current theory; it is proposed to examine these models and theories in relation to two major policies, language and educational opportunity in Chapter 12 and to compare the policy process in two periods in Chapter 13. Finally brief consideration is given to possible or probable developments in the system in the immediate future and associated policy implications in Chapter 14.

CHAPTER ELEVEN

The Policy Process – Models and Mechanisms

In the chapters of Section II, the contributions of the major contributors to policy are outlined. These various contributions have included the demands of the teacher associations, the published policy documents of the political parties, the formal stances of the managerial bodies, the interactive influence of the Department of Finance, the published policy statements of the churches and the actual policy outcomes as exemplified by the Ministers for Education and their department. These various inputs in the policy process have not enjoyed nor exercised equality of influence nor have their relative influences remained constant over time during this century. This particular question will be examined in this chapter with a view to discerning and describing the mechanism whereby the policy process operates including the implementation stages.

There are a number of approaches to the definition of the term 'policy' and to describing systematically what is involved in the policy process. The earlier total emphasis on decision-making, emanating from Easton's 1953 systems model, has largely been replaced by a more comprehensive approach; nevertheless the decision-making element persists as a central element of what Rose sees as 'a long series of more-or-less related activities and their consequences'.[1] Though Etzioni sees policy mainly in terms of decision-making, he places the emphasis on networks and sets of decisions and on reviewing their contexts. For Braybrooke and Lindblom, policy includes the conscious decisions and the evolutionary changes that occur in policies during their implementation.[2]

Policy, besides being more comprehensive than decision-making, is concerned with purposeful or goal-oriented rather than random or chance activity. In Harman's view policy can be both 'a position or stance developed in response to a problem or issue and directed towards a particular objective'.[3] Heclo expresses it as 'a course of action intended to accomplish some end'. However unintended policy consequences can sometimes outweigh the intended consequences; what is intended and what actually occurs as a result of the intention must be included in our definition. Based upon this viewpoint Heclo defines a policy as 'a course of action or inaction rather than specified decisions'.[4] For Jenkins, however the question is one of goals and decisions; he sees policy as 'a set of interrelated decisions concerning the selection of goals and the means of achieving them within a specified situation'.[5] This definition, though decision-based, rightfully emphasises the essential importance of implementation in the process. Policy then is concerned with a course of action, with identified goals and involves a systematic approach. The following definition by Harman would seem to accommodate these characteristics adequately:

> Policy refers to the implicit or explicit specification of courses of purposeful action being followed or to be followed in dealing with a recognised problem or matter of concern and directed towards the accomplishment of some intended or desired set of goals.[6]

Policies may differ in their scope or comprehensivity; they may as most policies do, refer to specific single issues, such as school attendance, or they may have a bearing on a wide range of related topics. Policies in the latter class, 'which involve determination of the postures, assumptions and main guidelines to be followed in developing specific policies', have been termed master policies or 'megapolicies' by Dror and may be similar to Etzioni's 'fundamental decisions'.[7] In education, 'equality of opportunity', 'efficiency in resource utilisation' or 'curricular reform' constitute common megapolicies.

The issue of rationality is central to the policy process in that the extent to which the process is or should be governed by rationality divides the field in two main groups, the rationalists and the incrementalists. Those who support rational models, derived essentially from the assumed 'rational man' of the economic and social sciences, subscribe to the view that 'rational decision-making involves selection of the alternatives which will maximise the decision-maker's values'.[8] Empirical evidence, which seemed to suggest that people neither did nor could behave as the rational model required, led Simon to question the validity of the model and offer an alternative approach in *Administrative behaviour* (1945). The 'rational comprehensive model' or the 'synoptic ideal' involves the analysis of goals, values and objectives, the examination of the alternatives and their consequences and the matching of aims to these consequences. The test of a good policy in this model 'is that it can be shown to be the more appropriate means to the desired ends'.[9]

Responding to basic criticisms on the impracticality of the rational comprehensive model, Simon has put forward his concept of 'alternative behaviour possibilities' and a further model termed 'bounded rationality' in which a restricted range of alternatives is examined in a 'satisficing' approach.[10] While the rationality models have had very little effect on how policies are actually made, the concept has played a major role in the generation of various systematic attempts to improve the policy process; Simon's original work and its systematic derivatives have sought to enhance organisational rationality.

The incremental approach has generated a number of models which have their common origin in Lindblom's creative reaction to Simon's original rational comprehensive model and his development of a simpler alternative termed 'successive limited comparison'. This simplification is achieved by limiting consideration to alternatives which differ in small degrees from existing policies and by ignoring the consequences of some possible policies.[11] For Lindblom 'the test of a good policy is not whether it maximises values but whether it secures the agreement of the interests involved'.[12] He argues that incrementalism provides a good description of how policies are actually made and a model of how they should be made; he further argues that by using it serious mistakes are avoided because, of its nature, it promotes short-step changes in policy.

In a later developement of the model, Lindblom has enunciated a strategy of 'disjointed incrementalism' (1963) as a refinement, in which 'policy-making proceeds through a series of approximations'.[13] Furthermore to promote coordination in decision-making, he has developed a concept of 'partisan mutual adjustment', which with 'disjointed incrementalism' and 'sucessive limited comparison' form the core of the incrementalist model. Two models which fit between the extremes of rationality and incrementalism have been proposed by Dror and Etzioni; Dror's 'normative operative model' seeks to combat conservatism, to combine idealism and realism and cater for the extra-rational elements and stresses the role of megapolicies.[14] Etzioni in the 'mixed scanning model' advocates a broad review of the policy field in which fundamental policies are differentiated from incremental policies.[15]

The other major theoretical divide on policy concerns the exercise of power, as to whether the political process is governed by a widespread participation or by an elite. Pluralist theory as enunciated by Dahl holds that in western democracies power is widely distributed among different groups. Elitist theory, on the other hand, rejects this view and holds that political power is concentrated in the hands of a minority, or in elites which may be based on office, wealth, technical expertise, culture, or other characteristics not widely distributed in a society.

In line with pluralist theory, interest or pressure groups play an important part in the policy process; they form 'issue communities' by aggregation of those groups with an interest in a particular issue. In many cases policy is formed within these 'communities' and thus the policy process is 'segmented'. Kogan, writing of the education system in Britain, offers a clear example of segmentation, where there exists 'a particularly strong and long-lived professional constituency which might be called the old educational establishment'. Such establishments are important elements within the policy process and usually have a longer effective 'policy life' than most politicans or officials involved in the process.[16]

According to Rose, 'public policy is best conceived of in terms of a process rather than in terms of policy making'. This policy process involves 'a lengthy, complex and often recursive series of political interactions between those within and those without government'.[17] These political interactions span a wider range than the issue of decision-making itself and include not only the content and implementation of the policy and its impact but also its resource implications, the provenance of the policy issue and the group dynamics surrounding its inclusion on the agenda of political debate. Rose has proposed a model of the policy process which reflects this wider specification; it identifies the discrete steps in the process as follows:[18]

1 Initial State	I. Issue Emerging on Agenda
2 Putting Issue on Agenda	
3 Advancement of Demands	
4 Resources and Constraints	II. Policy Formulation and
5 From No Decision to Decision	Authorisation
6 Content of Choice	
7 Implementation	III. Implementation
8 Producing Outputs	
9 Impact upon Society	IV. Policy Termination or Change
10 Routinization of Feedback	
11 Deroutinization of Stable State	

Rose's model may be reduced to a more coherent format by grouping the related steps into four main components of the policy process. This modified schema will be used to examine the policy process in Irish education.

I. Issue Emerging on Agenda

According to Schattschneider and others, getting an issue on the agenda of political debate constitutes an indicator of political power; by extension, keeping an issue off the agenda or preventing its removal from the agenda also constitute an exercise of power.[19] These complementary exercises have been termed 'the two faces of power' by Bachrach and Baratz in their analysis of the median theoretical path between elitists and pluralists. They express their conclusion as follows:

To the extent that a person or group consciously or uncon-
sciously creates or reinforces barriers to the public airing of
policy conflicts, that person or group has power.[20]

Schattschneider has expressed the same conclusion thus:

All forms of political organisation have a bias in favour of the exploitation of some kinds of conflict and the suppression of others
because organisation is the mobilisation of bias. Some issues are
organised into politics while others are organised out.[21]

Among those involved in agenda-setting in Irish education, the most
prominent are the main interest groups - teachers, managers, politicians, churches and government bodies; however significant inputs
can also be made by other agencies such as commissions of inquiry,
published research reports and single issue non-legitimised interest
groups. Contact with international movements or organisations has
also helped to place some issues on the agenda; the Washington
OECD Conference of 1961 initiated a major policy movement.
However, the major portion of the education debate takes place with
little public exposure, between the main interest groups, who also set
the agenda. Education debate at a national level in which issues
become major questions of public discourse is rare and has occurred
only on a few occasions in this century; the 1907 devolution bill, the
1919 McPherson bill, the 1946 INTO strike, the 'free' education
scheme of 1967 and some recent developments in 1985-86 represent
the totality. Parents, as a source of policy issues, have not figured as
prominently as one would expect from the primary nature of their
constitutional rights; however, lacking a recognised organised voice
until 1985, they have been unable to exercise their rights.

The commissions of inquiry which were so frequent and fruitful in
the early decades of the century were not utilised to the same extent
after 1922 when internal department committees replaced them, a
development which was favoured by the Department of Finance.[22]
The Ingram Commission on Technical Education of 1926-27 is a
classic example of a rational approach to policy; its meticulous report,
enriched by Swedish and Swiss participation, launched a major
national debate on technical education which culminated in the 1930
Act. The department committees of the thirties and forties were not so
efficacious, especially that of 1935 on raising the school leaving age
and that of 1945-47 on reforming the education system. In the sixties
the impact of *Investment in Education* was a central influence in
launching a unique national debate on education policy. In addition
to raising the level of debate and identifying issues for political
action, *Investment* also widened considerably the debate's participant
list by the manner in which it illustrated the connection between
education and socio-economic development and thus urged the

social partners to become involved.[23] Recent international studies show that policy-oriented research has little or no direct impact on policy making in education.[24] Some recent research reports and findings, especially in the later decades, have by means of a 'percolation model', raised issues of prime policy importance in Irish education and in some cases have significantly influenced the course of policy development. Research studies in the Economic and Social Research Institute, especially those of Tussing on expenditure, Hannan on schooling and sex roles, Geary and Ó Muircheartaigh on equalization of opportunity and Walsh on demography have made significant imputs to the policy process.[25] Single-issue interest groups have played an unexpected role in that while they have been few in number, they have been very successful in generating wide debate and in focussing interest on specific issues. In general these groups are non-legitimised and operate outside the ambit of the main education issue communities. They have been highly successful in attracting media support which has usually widened their geographical appeal beyond their Dublin bases. The most prominent and successful of these groups were Reform, (anti corporal punishment) the Language Freedom Movement, (anti compulsory Irish) and the Dalkey School Project, (which sought to establish and promote interdenominational national schools). Occasionally contact with other education systems through study visits or international conferences has proved a valuable mechanism by which policy issues have been placed on the agenda. Visits by inspectors and other staff to European centres were commonplace in the period prior to 1922 and introduced new curricular ideas from international centres such as the Silkeborg Seminarium in Denmark.[26] Ideas on 'free' school books and on the role of practice schools attached to training colleges emerged from similar visits to Belfast and London in the thirties. When these international contacts were resumed in the late fifties they proved to be very fruitful sources of policy initiatives especially the contacts with OECD in the sixties. The agenda of education debate however is not set by these marginal groups but by the five or six main interest groups representing the teachers, managers, churches, politicians and the government agencies. Mechanisms and procedures differ amongst them as do the specific range of policy issues which are of interest to the individual groups. While constituting the inner circle of the education debate, these interest groups do not all share equal power even in constructing the agenda; within this small group there are groupings or 'issue communities' which deal with specific issues or sets of issues. Furthermore the relative power of the various groups in drawing up the agenda has changed dramatically over this century. In the first two decades the politicians were more active, the government agencies and their officials more boldly enterprising and the teachers almost excluded or forced on the defensive. The policy agenda of this early period owed more to Augustine

Birrell and W. J. M. Starkie and less to the managerial bodies and the churches; if the major thrust of the reforms initiated by Birrell and Starkie was frustrated, the issues of structure and control were debated in a fashion that was not repeated for more than four decades. Teachers, both primary and postprimary, spent most of their organised energies up to the early sixties in pursuit of improved working conditions and in maintaining inter-union relativities. They form with the managerial bodies and the Department of Education a triangular 'issue community' in which the agenda is predominantly concerned with working conditions, school resource allocation and curricular issues. Within this 'issue community' all three participants play equivalent roles in agenda construction depending on the nature of the particular issue.

When the teachers are seeking a salary increase or improvements in working conditions, they usually introduce the question by means of conference resolutions, presidential address or by a formal submission; having submitted their case, the issue then proceeds to the conciliation stage. In a similar fashion when school managers seek extra resources from the state in relation to capitation or maintenance grants they will raise the issue and negotiate collectively with the state unless the interests of teachers are involved, when the teachers join the process. When, however, the Department of Education is seeking in time of recession to curtail expenditure, as it was in the twenties and thirties, the fifties and the eighties, it will take the initiative and propose measures involving salary reductions, reduced levels of capitation grants, lower staffing levels or higher pupil teacher ratios, the withdrawal of grants to fee-paying schools or reduced funding of school transport.[27] All of these issues, which have a strong administrative element, relate to the maintenance and funding of the system *as it is*; since the availability of resources is as variable as the strength of the economy these issues are seldom far from the centre of the debate of which they constitute the major portion. When, however, one moves outside these routine areas of policy one is dealing with a different issue community and a different set of topics. Issues, such as raising the school leaving age, the establishment of new institutions or the extension of opportunity, which involve, or are assumed to involve, a departure from the structural *status quo* or routine lower level issues which have some implications for higher issues, constitute a special category. This special issue community governs the interaction between church and state in education and exercises a major bearing on the development of policy. The setting of this agenda is shared by the state and the churches, although in the cases which we know of, it has been the state which has more usually raised the issues. The common pattern in these cases is for the Department of Education, following internal departmental examination of an issue to consult the church authorities formally, usually by correspondence with the bishops.

This occurred in relation to the establishment of the preparatory colleges (1925), the marriage ban on women national teachers (1931-33), the scheme for the improvement of the physical condition of national schools (1943), the extension of educational opportunity (1961-63) and the establishment of community schools (1970).[28] The Cabinet, in the case of de Valera's scheme for senior schools in the Gaeltacht (1934) and the 1954 proposal to recognise university graduates as national teachers, having discussed the issues, deferred a decision until discussions had been held with the Catholic bishops.[29] The churches have sometimes taken the initiative in raising issues. The Catholic bishops raised the following issues; a training college for nuns (1928), the conversion of the model schools to clerical management (1927-30) and the vocational education legislation (1930); furthermore in the period 1945-56 the bishops raised on several occasions the issue of the continuance of the vocational system.[30]

The authorities of the Protestant churches were consulted by the Department of Education at various times and they in turn took the initiative on a number of issues. These issues revolved around school transport schemes for their scattered pupils (1930) and curricular issues concerning textbook content and the Irish language (1922-1960).[31] Thus each of the main churches has exercised a special role in structuring the agenda of educational debate. This process was facilitated by the existence at the lower or routine level of participants, such as the managerial bodies, which are organically and structurally linked to the churches. Organisationally, the consultation at the lower routine level is conducted separately for primary and postprimary education but the higher level participants are the same for both, usually the representatives of the church hierarchies or other leadership and the minister and senior officers of the Department. The process is illustrated schematically in Fig. 11.1. The emphasis on defence and consolidation of the structural status quo which has characterised church policy on education in this century has been reflected both in the composition of the agenda and in the exclusion of certain topics. Prior to 1922, the reforming zeal of Birrell and Starkie and the various public commissions of inquiry maintained a flow of structural issues on the agenda; following the establishment of the Free State however questions of structure were seldom discussed, with the sole exception of the debate surrounding the 1930 Vocational Education Act. When issues bearing upon structure were raised, such as extension of opportunity, the establishment of new school types or local cooperation between secondary and vocational schools, they have seldom been addressed publicly as such; questions of structure have usually been reserved for private discussion between politicians and the churches. Issues raised by the state, upon which the church expressed a negative opinion have usually been dropped from the agenda and not raised again. Deirg's scheme for diocesan planning and supervision of national school buildings (1943), de Valera's scheme for senior schools in the Gaeltacht (1934) and the Cabinet's decision to recognise university graduates as national teachers were abandoned, all questions bearing on management and power. The only occasion on which the church was unsuccessful in a major education issue concerned the question of the Irish language in the National University of Ireland in 1910, a question on which church leadership was divided.[32] The issues raised by the churches, especially those raised by the Catholic church in relation to the model schools and the vocational system, reflect the emphasis placed on conserving the structural *status quo* . An abortive discussion of structural reform was initiated in 1974 and the topic of structure was not formally raised again until the publication in 1985 of the green paper, *Partners in education*. The avoidance of debate on issues of structure has been reinforced in its effects by the exclusion of structural issues from the terms of reference of many relevant commissions of inquiry.[33] The frequently expressed satisfaction of most ministers with the existing structures was never likely to promote structural reform as an agenda item. Even the specific direction of deValera to Deirg to conduct a fundamental postwar review of the system produced nothing more from within the Department than a proposal to abolish the vocational system in a document which is otherwise permeated with a reverence for the *status quo*.

Agenda setting at the lower level of routine issues, involves a restricted issue community, confined to the Department of Education, teachers and managers. At the higher level of policy, the participants include only the churches and the state in a process in which the churches have exercised an effective veto on the inclusion of certain issues. Lindblom's statement that 'policy is made through the complex process by which persons exert power or influence over each other' is an echo of the earlier assertion by one of the founders of group theory, A. F. Bentley:

> All phenomena of government are phenomena of groups pressing one another, forming one another and pushing out new groups and group representatives to mediate the adjustments.[34]

On this view the policy process involves 'an equilibrium between competing groups' or 'a compromise between the conflicting interests of competing groups'.[35] Public policies can thus be viewed as reflecting the dominant values of the society or 'as statements of the balance of power between societal groups'. Changing policy stances result from changes in the power structure or in the value allocation which operates in the society. Throughout the course of this century, the power structure in Irish education has not changed substantially; while the number of participant groups has increased, the relativities introduced by the new groups have not altered the established power relationships. The primary teachers, whose organisation was under interdict early in the century and the secondary teachers, whose association did not regain trade union affiliation until the sixties, spent much of the intervening decades campaigning for satisfactory working conditions. Parents, to whom churches and state accord primary rights in education, were effectively barred from taking any part in the policy process until very recently; in 1934 the bishops of the Catholic church had decided that 'no lay committee of any kind is to be associated with the manager in school management'[36] In answer to a written query from a New York educationalist in 1953, as 'to what extent parents participated in school activities', de Valera replied:

> There are few parent associations as such and parent participation in school activities is therefore usually in accordance with the desires of individual parents in this respect. The Constitution of Ireland however, lays down that the primary rights and responsibilities in education are those of the parents and our system of education is based throughout on this principle.[37]

Interests outside the formal education system, especially representatives of industry, commerce and the trade unions, did not participate in any way nor was there any mechanism by which they could do so until the sixties. By the early seventies these groups were accorded a role in various managerial, structural and advisory bodies especially in third level; by the mid-seventies all teachers had begun to occupy a more prominent place in the policy process. The expansion of second level participation in the sixties and seventies and the consequent rapid growth in the teaching force had introduced into the ASTI and the TUI a younger more radical membership and had given to both organisations the resources necessary to play a more active role in the policy process.[38] The creation by Ministerial regulation of a National Parents' Council in 1985 finally provided parents with an organised voice and a national mechanism by which their views could be expressed. The extension of the power structure to embrace these extra participants did not allow them equal voice with the existing groups but their participation made it impossible that the formulation of education policy would be conducted as it had been. These recent modifications especially the inclusion of parents will take some time to manifest their influence on the policy process but it is not self-evident at this stage that they will alter significantly the dominance exercised by the churches and the state.

We need to examine in some detail the relationship of church and state in their dominance of the policy process in education. In doing so, we find some very relevant constructs in the comparative studies of Archer on the type of formal education which existed in some

European countries prior to the development in them of state systems.[39] In the countries examined, France, England, Denmark and Russia, those who controlled education also owned it, providing its physical facilities and supplying its teaching personnel. In each society, control and ownership were concentrated in the hands of a single group, the Catholic church and its religious orders in France, the Anglican church in England, the Lutheran church in Denmark and the Orthodox church and its brotherhoods in Russia. The control of education by a dominant ownership group meant that in turn the process of education was linked to only one part of the total social structure, the social institution with which the dominant group was associated. Thus a relationship of interdependence was developed between education and one other social institution, indicated by a flow of resources and services between them. Interdependence, in the systems examined by Archer, involved a flow of human and financial resources from the dominant ownership sphere to education and a counter flow of those kinds of education outputs useful to the other institution.[40] Where churches constituted the ownership groups, the interdependence conferred substantial benefits on them; students emerged with a certain level of religious knowledge and at least a formal commitment to religious values, while some were prepared for direct recruitment into the religious organisation. Where education is related to one other social institution in a monopolistic manner, the term 'mono-integration' is used by Archer to describe the structural relationship between the institutions.[41] Where education is a mono-integrated institution, the structural relationship has certain consequences; the imbalance in the relationship leads to a subordinate role and a loss of autonomy for education and furthermore promotes a situation where educational change cannot be initiated endogenously, for, according to Archer, subordination never involves lower autonomy than when it occurs in a relationship of mono-integration'.[42] The dominant group defines education according to its own goals and controls it so closely that there are weak boundaries and little differentiation between the institutions. Typically the subordinate role means the absence of an autonomous professional body and of distinctively educational processes since the curricular content, the definition and management of knowledge and methodology are frequently confused with the values and norms of the dominant group. The subordinate and mono-integrated nature of the relationship between education and a dominant group has, according to Archer, consequences for other social institutions and for reform; these fall into three categories:

(i)   institutions which are neither helped nor hindered by the type of education provided and which are neutral *vis-a-vis* the system;

(ii) those institutions which derive adventitious benefits, whose own operation is facilitated by the outputs of the education system, and who are generally supportive of it;

(iii) those institutions whose operations are clearly obstructed by the outputs of the education system which are incompatible with their own aims or values. These social institutions tend to be agents of change and opponents of the system.[43]

The prolonged stability usually associated with education being subordinate and mono-integrated may endure either because the dominant group remains unchallenged or because it successfully resists efforts to weaken its control. The fact that a dominant group secured the mobilisation and supply of the indispensable resources for education at some earlier point in time, because no other group was interested or by virtue of mounting an effective challenge to an earlier dominant group, does not guarantee dominance in perpetuity.[44] Another group or other groups may arise which can provide schools and teachers and other resources and thus offer an alternative to the system of the dominant group. To retain its position of exclusive control, the dominant group must preserve its monopoly on charismatic, rational or traditional grounds or by a series of constraints. Other groups can be discouraged from entering the education domain by convincing them that they lack the right, the suitability, the skills, or the experience, to do so, or that the dominant group alone possesses these. The constraints can be used to obstruct or prevent other groups from supplying educational services or equipping themselves with the resources to do so. To ensure maintenance of domination, all three factors, monopoly ownership of educational facilities, protective constraints and legitimating ideology should be mutually reinforcing and the dominant group should devote adequate resources to the development of the constraints and the elaboration and universalisation of the ideology.[45] By applying the Archer model to education in Ireland, we may gain a deeper understanding of the relationships which exist or existed between the various interest groups, though it may not be feasible to apply the model in its entirety. At the establishment of the national school system in 1831, the English state and its colonial machinery in Ireland formed the dominant group which controlled education though such control was not complete. By the end of the nineteenth century, the Catholic church had become an equal partner with the state and according to Cardinal Logue, was quite happy with the structural changes achieved, though not fully satisfied. The repeated unsuccessful efforts made by the state in the early years of the century to modify the structure on a democratic, decentralised, local model, in their failure merely consolidated the church position. From 1922 to the early sixties, the church was undoubtedly the dominant group with a monopoly of ownership in the first level and most of the second level, an operational control of teacher training and employment in national elementary schools and an effective majority presence in secondary education. Throughout this century, it has elaborated and propagated in its teaching, doctrines which proclaimed the church's rights in education to be independent of any earthly power and the family's rights to be prior to those of the state, whose principal duty is to promote and protect the work of the church and the family.[46]

As acknowledged frequently by most of the Ministers for Education this definition of roles was accepted by the state at least until the early sixties. The church's dominance, legitimated by its own doctrines, has been protected from challenge by the widespread acceptance, especially by politicians and perhaps also by senior state officials involved in policy formulation, that the state or the public did not possess the rights and competences to provide education. The church position was also protected by various sanctions designed to limit any emerging challenges; secondary schools were not recognised by the Department of Education unless their founders produced a sanctioning letter from the local bishop, the concessions secured by the Catholic bishops from the minister in 1930 ensured that the vocational schools never constituted a viable challenge to the monopoly of the secondary schools. In some dioceses male religious teaching orders were not allowed to establish secondary schools lest they constitute competition for diocesan colleges.[47] The episcopal ban on any lay involvement in the management of national schools excluded the emergence of any local democratic structure in education. Despite the chronically bad condition of many national schools the church rejected all measures proposed by the INTO and the state, to change the mechanism for the provision and maintenance of national school buildings, lest such measures weaken the clerical managerial system. Church regulations forbidding attendance by Catholics at 'mixed' or secular schools guaranteed a virtual monopoly to its own. The overall effects of the church dominance and its protective strategy for the defence of that dominance was an endemic reluctance by the state to take any initiative, a disinterest among lay public and politicians, a low level of professional autonomy within the system, and an overall complacency which was oblivious of the social and geographical inequalities characterising it. There were however some important discontinuities within this structure. The ideology which protected the church's monopoly was in important respects at variance with some of the constraints used by the church. In particular church teaching on the primacy of parental rights in education was directly flouted by the 1934 episcopal ban on their involvement. The central importance of 'Catholic education in Catholic schools for all Catholic children' would logically demand that a policy of equality of educational opportunity be espoused and actively promoted by the church. However, no such development occurred; proposals for 'free education for all' were rejected as 'bordering on liberalism and socialism', deValera's Gaeltacht scheme was rejected as representing state intervention and unnecessary. The vocational system was prevented from reaching its full potential by sustained church opposition on the grounds of its suitability to impart general education; it was still church policy to denominationalise, if not dismantle, the vocational system long after it had been rendered acceptable to the church. It seems quite clear that the behaviour of the church in the education sphere was that of a dominant group and equally clear that the other groups, parents, teachers, politicians, and the Department of Education, not only accepted that reality but also accepted the consequent subordinate nature of their own roles. Few politicians adverted publicly to the church's dominant role in education, though many of them, especially Ministers for Education, from MacNeill to Moylan, affirmed their satisfaction with the existing structures and many of them denied to the state any initiating role in education. This depressed level of initiative by the state arising from church dominance has been discussed in detail by one critic in the late fifties. In outlining a programme of general reform, Professor John O'Meara of UCD identified the major weaknesses of the system as the predominance of the church, the spinelessness of the Department of Education, and the exclusion of the people from any direct influence on the system.[48] According to him, 'the church's influence on education would not only be paramount but decisive' as long as it held a very special viewpoint and retained the loyalty of the vast majority. This had created problems mainly because the state had reacted in a spineless manner to the dominant role of the church with the result that no general responsibility was exercised in relation to education. This 'unreasonable timidity' of the state *vis-a-vis* the church merely reinforced the tendency, found in may civil services, to pass the buck, except that in this case the Department of Education 'hardly handled the buck at all'. O'Meara saw the exclusion of popular control as 'the original sin of Irish education' and advocated the inclusion of professional advice at the policy making level within the department and the creation of local democratic education committees.[49]

O'Meara's castigation of the Department of Education and its officers may have been misplaced; the Department and its 'point of view' are determined more by its political leadership than by the personal proclivities of its senior officials or the influence of its policy implementors who may operationalise policy according to their own values. Given the general orientation of the main parties vis-a-vis the church, it is hardly surprising that the Ministers have been in general subservient to most, if not all, aspects of church policy. Additionally, some senior officials in their personal loyalties or due to their membership of church organisations, or their political viewpoint, may consider themselves bound to accede to church demands rather than consider alternative policy lines. It would seem that ministers and government differentiated between the churches on some issues. When the Church of Ireland sought to be formally represented on the Commission on Youth Unemployment in 1943, the chairman, Archbishop McQuaid, refused and efforts by de Valera to change the decision were fruitless.[50] What can be described as a department 'point of view' embraces at least two component parts, the current minister's policy priorities which will form the main policy emphasis and the core or residual elements of Department policy. The minister's priorities may arise from personal commitment or from party policies; in the absence of such ministerial priorities, the department will inevitably bring forward from its own stock of policy issues those which are acceptable to the minister. Thus curricular change in the twenties, planning education expansion in the sixties, higher education in the seventies and rationalisation and efficiency in the eighties can be identified among the core elements of Department policy. MacNeill's 'educational highway', Deirg's commitment to language policy or his efforts to extend opportunity and improve school buildings, Mulchay's commitment to the Council of Education, Colley's assertion of the state's role in education and O'Malley's egalitarianism are good examples of the ministerial components. The department inspectorate, acting both as policy advisors and policy implementors, may add a further dimension to the department viewpoint by modifying policies in their implementation. The sixties witnessed the emergence of a more elaborate structure among the interest groups in education which facilitated a more extensive consultation process; this in turn reflected a more sophisticated approach to policy within the Department of Education. Since then the Department has emerged as a major interest group in its own right, its demands reflecting its revised perception of its own role in the system; rationalisation and planning, efficient use of resources, extension of opportunity and curricular relevance have been prominent recent department demands on a system in which its role is now more active and central.

II Policy Formulation and Authorisation

Education, even when it is 'free' is never cheap. In most developed countries, expenditure on education constitutes a major portion of public expenditure and of that expenditure over 80% is already committed in salaries. Consequently the margin for expansion is limited even in the strongest economy. Education's labour intensity and the scarcity of resources exercise an effective control on the range of policy measures which may be considered. In Gamson's view, these conditions make for a brake on reform since to defend the *status quo* requires less resources than to promote change.[51] As we have seen, over the past six decades, one of the major concerns of the

Department of Finance has been to keep the Department of Education on the rails of sanctioned expenditure. Its enthusiasm in this exercise was significantly increased by a frequent suspicion that cost estimates accompanying Department of Education proposals were seldom realistic.[52] The opposition of the Department of Finance to increased expenditure on education and the frequent recessionary economic conditions have been very potent constraints on the real policy choices open to the Department of Education. However, 'inertia commitments' operate in education as in other sectors and while most policy measures have high costs attached, all net expenditure increases need not necessarily predicate real policy advances. There are other constraints emerging from interest group reaction, which can also effectively delimit the policy choices open to the Department of Education. These constraints may arise from opposition, either stated or anticipated, from other groups in the policy process, parents, churches, managers or teachers; they may even arise from within the Department of Education itself as happened in the twenties when the inspectors of the primary branch were opposed to reorganisation plans and to the preparatory Colleges and inspectors of all three branches were opposed to unification of the inspectorate.[53] In most cases, as issues develop within the department, informal contacts between department officials and representatives of relevant groups will provide a reliable guide as to the reaction to be expected to the policy proposal. The occasional absence of this advance intelligence has led the department at times to propose measures or make decisions which had later to be rescinded or modified; this arose in the closure of small village schools in the sixties and more significantly in 1942 when the Attendance Act was declared unconstitutional. As the process of external consultation and internal discussion proceeds within the Department of Education the finer details of possible policy options begin to emerge with greater clarity; continuing consultations with the Department of Finance narrow the policy options further to the stage at which ministerial political pronouncements are made. These political statements may sometimes run ahead of the clarifying policy process, resulting in statements which differ substantially from the eventual policy, as occurred in May 1963 in Dr Hillery's statements on the comprehensive schools.[54] Completion of the clarifying stage brings the process close to a decision and also moves the process exclusively into the ambit of the senior officials of the department. As has been observed by Rose, debate on a particular policy issue can continue for a very long time before either decision or deferral arise, though inactivity may also indicate a decision. The point of decision does not mark the endpoint but the midpoint of the policy process yet it constitutes the crucial step in the procession from arrival on the agenda to implementation or review.[55]

Policy in some areas has been characterised by inordinately long 'lead time'; some major issues have been under semi-active consideration for considerable periods before finding expression in policy measures. Thus while the raising of the school leaving age and the creation of an Advisory Council on Education were under discussion in the early decades of the century, decisions on them were not arrived at until the late forties; in relation to the leaving age, while the cabinet took a decision in principle in 1947, the legislative measure was not passed by the Dail until 1972. Similarly the proposal to link the professional training of national teachers to the universities was raised as early as 1909, yet the final decision was taken as late as 1976.[56] To illustrate this inertial process operating in a negative direction we may observe the fate of the Irish-medium preparatory colleges, which, almost from their establishment in 1927 were never short of critics including the Department of Finance, the INTO and even the Department of Education. Some of these colleges were temporarily closed, converted into war-time hospitals, or sought by health authorities as sanitoria, yet they were not closed until 1961 when Dr Hillery yielded to pressure from an assortment of groups.

Arriving at a decision in the policy process can be accelerated considerably when ministers are directly involved, though as Kogan has pointed out, ministers while involved in all major decisions will not be able to cover all aspects of policy.[57] Normally within the Department of Education the crucial decision in major policy issues would normally be taken within a small senior group based upon earlier consultations and internal discussion; this small group includes the four assistant secretaries and the secretary. The direct involvement of the Ministers for Education and Finance usually carries an issue unquestionably forward to the final decisive stage as in 1937 on the application of part V of the 1930 Act to the city of Cork. The positive involvement of the Minister for Finance constitutes a major impetus towards decision point as the various interventions of Ernest Blythe in Irish language policy demonstrate clearly.[58] Undoubtedly the intervention of the Taoiseach, when it occurred, has been decisive as in the postwar planning issue, in relation to the primary certificate (1942), the prescribed courses (1940) and senior promotions (1946).[59] These extra-Departmental inputs however are exceptional and Taoisigh and Ministers for Finance seldom participate directly.

Within the department structure, much of the routine administrative decision making occurs at branch or section level, is based upon precedent and would not normally be referred upwards. For example the decision to sanction a building grant for a national school at the normal level would be taken at assistant principal level; where above-normal grants are sought, the decision would be taken at a higher level. New policy departures, however, or major exercises such as the preparation of green or white papers will originate in and will be formulated by the senior ranks of the department's officers in close collaboration with the minister and after consultation with the

Department of Finance. These major issues will always be taken to Cabinet for final clearance or sanction as will all proposals for legislation and issues bearing on salary claims. Occasionally the Department of Finance has insisted on having unusual issues or issues of principle referred to the cabinet for decision as in the case of a secondary school being reclassified as a national school by ministerial order; on that occasion as on some other occasions, the Department of Finance was overruled by its minister, Ernest Blythe.[60] There have been a few occasions on which the normal procedures have not been followed or have not been formally adhered to. It is widely believed that the flamboyant announcement of 'free' postprimary education by Donagh O'Malley in 1966 was made without the sanction of the Department of Finance and the cabinet, though Lemass may have sanctioned or at least connived at it. Similar sidestepping of Merrion St. was attempted by the Department of Education in 1941 and in 1930 when the cabinet sanctioned proposals opposed by Finance.[61]

These exceptions however merely emphasise the routine procedure by which a large volume of department policy is made in a framework presided over by the Minister for Education. Though not immediately involved in much of the routine decisions the Minister carries ultimate political responsibility for all the policy decisions of the department .[62] A policy is guaranteed adoption if the minister favours it; however it is not abandoned if he/she does not, but joins the considerable body of long-running department policy lines, awaiting another time, or, more likely one of his or her successors. Education policies, 'purposeful action pursued by governments in pursuit of desired ends' usually include both substantive policy content and administrative procedural content. The latter will lay down operational criteria and guidelines for those charged with administering the policy e.g. specific criteria for the administration of school grants or scholarship entitlements. The substantive content forms the heart of the matter, detailing the practical measures proposed and can be categorised in a number of acceptable ways. The typology of policy content as already put forward in this work, identifies education policy content as specified in three domains or categories:

(i)   process;

(ii) access and;

(iii) structure domains.

This schema, as in Fig. 11.2, will be used to examine the historical pattern of policy content.

A consistent characteristic of policy content during this century has been the predominance of the process domain; the only exceptions have been the first two decades when policy covered all domains and the last two when structural changes at third level were a major feature of policy. The concentration on process aspects of policy by the Department of Education arose from a desire to further specific curricular objectives, from the political imperative to avoid structural or access conflicts with the church and from the nature of the instructional and curricular legacy inherited from the nineteenth century.[63] The legacy of 'payment-by-results' at primary and secondary levels, the tyranny of the examinations, a harsh inspectorial regime at primary level and uniform centrally sanctioned texts, constituted an educational formula which the infant Department of Education found easier to retain than discard. The emphasis upon process issues was enhanced for the department by its own control of the content of teacher training in the primary sector and the nature of the curricular guidance issued in its *Notes for teachers*.[64] This emphasis upon process issues did not touch higher education except in the technological sector controlled by the department itself, mainly because higher education did not feature as a serious element of policy until the late sixties. When it did and policy objectives sought to favour the technological sector, this was done more by measures in the structure domain and by the differential investment of capital and current expenditure than by process measures.[65] The central sensitivity of structure in the policy process is directly related to the low level of access issues in content and the pronounced political and department reluctance to confront issues which implied a change in or reconsideration of the structural *status quo*. The question of raising the school leaving age addressed by an inter-department committee in 1935, was again taken up in 1943 by the Commission on Youth Unemployment and once more by the department committee of 1945-47. While all agreed on the need to take action, no effective measure was taken until 1972 except decisions to avoid action. Indeed it would appear, according to Richard Mulcahy when minister, that the chairman of the Commission on Youth Unemployment, in the knowledge of the government, withheld the report of the commission 'because that report is regarded by him as one which will inevitably create serious problems for the government'.[66] Despite the egalitarian values espoused in the formal policy documents of the First Dáil and repeated assertions of commitment by parties and leaders to extending educational opportunity, little or no effort was made to develop access policies which would seek to promote effective equality of opportunity or even to define such a policy measure with accuracy. As late as 1960 an official representative body, rejected 'secondary education for all' as a valid policy objective; when throughout the sixties equality of educational opportunity became an inescapable element of access policy, it was never formulated with any degree of coherent precision. The central significance of this relationship between access and structure issues in the policy process was identified by the inter-department committee and confirmed by senior officials of the Department of Finance as early as 1935. According to the latter, the educational benefit of raising the school leaving age could not be secured 'because of the difficulty of providing a suitable reorganisation of schools'.[67] This issue has continued to be a central question, has dominated the policy process in the sixties and seventies, generating a series of structural compromises at second level, culminating in the creation of the community schools. The importance of the question and its inherent political sensitivity is indicated quite clearly in the obvious anomalies contained in the 1985 green paper, designed to promote structural reform, which excluded the national school system from its localised structure; this anomalous document may be linked to subsequent cabinet changes.[68] While process issues have constituted the major policy content in this century, structure issues have dominated the process and thereby, have depressed the frequency with which access issues are brought forward. Indeed even process issues have not been totally immune to the influence of the structural question. In establishing the vocational education system by legislation in 1930, the Department of Education, at an early stage, positively excluded the establishment of a training college for the pedagogical training of vocational teachers; rather than confront the structural questions involved, the department opted for neglecting the proper training of teachers.[69] The dominance of structural considerations has impacted on such a central element of process policy as the Irish language; when in 1967 'free' postprimary education and school transport were being organised no precautions were adopted to structurally protect the few remaining Irish-medium secondary schools.[70]

Policy content in this century reveals a pattern, on which the structural controversies of the last century and the attempted reforms of the early century have cast a long shadow. The structural legacy, inherited in 1922 has proved a resilient constant in policy and its defence and preservation have dominated the other policy domains. Apart from its direct influence on policy content, the structural legacy has also exercised a major influence on the modality of policy making. The imbalance as between process, access and structure dimensions has prevented the emergence of a consistent approach to policy based upon rationality. For perhaps a decade after the publication of *Investment in Education* (1965), during the existence of the development branch, a rational approach to policy at second level operated, based upon comprehensive statistical information and coherent planning; a similar approach to higher education was adopted in the mid-seventies and has continued to date. This rational approach to policy formulation and implementation prompted the temporary introduction of planned programme budgeting in the late sixties. In most other policy areas, especially in curricular provision, in language policy and in educational opportunity, rationality has seldom been admitted as a presiding presence in a policy process dominated by 'incrementalism'.

III Implementation and Outputs

The implementation stage as a component of the policy process cannot be assumed to follow automatically and successfully from the stages that precede it unless it is planned in detail. It concerns 'the interpretation of policy, its application to particular cases and the development of a programme or programmes'.[72] While the formulation and authorisation of new policies may be difficult tasks, their effective implementation is frequently more difficult still, a dilemma whose significance is clearly highlighted in the title of the volume, *How great expectations in Washington are dashed in Oakland or Why it's amazing that federal programmes work at all*.[73] According to Pressman and Wildavsky, one of the major obstacles to the implementation of policies as formulated and authorised in Washington was the need to use agencies at local level which Washington did not control. These local agencies had their own priorities and values and so the policy implemented was different from what national legislators intended. A similar difficulty obtains in Irish education wherein the state does not own nor control the vast majority of the local institutions providing education services according to state policy. However, the nature of the implementing agencies, is only one of the many inter-related variables characerising the implementation stage. According to the model devised by Van Meter and Van Horn, these variables include the standards and objectives, the resources applied, the implementing agencies and their activities, the prevailing economic, social and political conditions and the disposition of the implementors.[74] (Fig.11.3) Harman identifies four conditions governing the implementation of policy; these are policy design, implementation strategy, the commitment and capacity of the bureaurcratic system and environment factors.[75] According to Hood, there are limits which effectively influence the implementation of policy; he identifies 'political limits' as especially significant in the extent to which dominant groups 'distort' policy programmes in the implementation stage.[76] Pressman and Wildavsky tend to a broad pessimism concerning the likelihood of new policy programmes being implemented; evidence from some recent United States education and welfare projects provide strong support for their view.[77] They focus on 'decision-points' or clearances, at which inter-group agreement is essential for the progress of the policy; agreement is needed at so many points and the probability of such agreement so low that 'the remarkable thing is that new programmes work at all'.[78] Consequently for successful implementation, policies need to be relatively simple, implementation-oriented in design, and involve few decision points. Few policies in Irish education have met all these specified criteria during this century. Confining our attention to the megapolicies of language revival, equality of opportunity and improving the physical condition of schools, a very varied pattern emerges if we apply the criteria of Harman, Hood and Wildavsky and examine the Van Meter and Van Horn model (Fig. 11.3). Of these major policy areas, in only one, the physical condition of schools, do we see a policy design which specified clear unambiguous goals; Starkie's early programme and Deirg's sustained efforts were frustrated by Hood's 'limits' as represented by the restraining hand of the Treasury and the inertia or resistance of school managers as a dominant group, whose stance was supported by the reluctance of the bishops to contemplate any measures involving modification of the structural *status quo*. Despite the clarity of the policy goals of the department and the availability of adequate resources and appropriate standards, its failure in implementing the policy was governed by its lack of authority over the school managers, or in Van Meter and Van Horn terms, 'the negative disposition of implementors'. Over the period of this study there is only one recorded instance where an unsatisfactory manager was dismissed at the instance of the department and that did not concern the physical condition of schools.[9] In the other major policy issues, equality of opportunity and Irish language policy, the latter has been marked by a gradual descent into imprecise definition from an earlier period of strong precise policy design while the former was never defined in any but the vaguest terms. The language policy has in the last three decades experienced a number of evolutionary modifications not least the dramatic changes in the disposition of the implementors i.e. teachers, managers and inspectors, which effectively constitute a gradual erosion of the earlier policy. The imprecision on equality policy was motivated by a strong political reality; any effective policy in this field would of necessity be required to address the question of an individual student's rights in a secondary system dominated by private institutions.

Policy has been marked until the sixties and in some specific areas to the present, by a failure to plan implementation adequately at the design stage. Success in implementation has been significantly high in the routine areas where the regulation of operational codes has been conducted in a centralised disciplined fashion; in the process dimensions, the department's policies have been implemented with equal success due to a rigid examination system and an inspectorate imbued with a strong sense of discipline and duty. However a major weakness, even in the process dimensions of policy has been the failure to take account of size of school and the associated 'environment factors'; the 'new' primary curriculum of 1971 was introduced with a pedagogical model which took little if any account of reality in the small rural national schools. Two-teacher schools were never likely to be in a position to implement the new curriculum due to a combination of 'environment and social factors' which were not included in the policy design. In recent decades, especially in higher education, the policy process has been characterised by significant success in implementation; the absence of politically sensitive structural issues, the unquestioned authority which investment decisions gives to the state and the clarity of the policy goals have been crucial factors.[80]

Ineffectiveness in policy implementation is clearly evident in the question of pupil/teacher ratio and class size; this issue is fundamentally a matter of resource allocation and the matching of teacher supply and cohort size. Policy objectives on class size which were officially identified thirty years ago are now being sought by resolution at teacher conferences in 1986.[81] Many of the constraints operating negatively on the implementation of education policy can be traced directly to structural and behavioural characteristics of the system. The limited power of the minister and the department in the first and second level *vis-a-vis* managers, patrons and trustees, of whose activities the state is the major funding source, constitutes a basic weakness. The near absence of legal and statutory instruments governing the operation of the system leaves the policy process very open to the vagaries of political advantage and the interests of dominant groups. The absence of a legal framework for the system is clearly evident in the case of the Community Schools operating since 1972 whose deeds of trust though legally in operation, have not yet been made available to the public or published. The absence of a local political and administrative machinery in education in all but the vocational system removes a very effective potential local agency in implementation, simultaneously reinforces the power of the centre and of individual institutions and frustrates the emergence of a local democratic supra-institutional viewpoint on policy. This very strong centralism in the system tolerates if it does not cause a 'fingertip phenomenon', whereby standards of provision are frequently inadequate in the extremities of the system, especially in sparsely populated areas. Policy implementation can sometimes be impeded by lack of unanimity among the senior department officials, a situation which though rare, is most likely to arise in periods of unusual and dramatic policy developments, as it did in the mid-sixties between the minister and an assistant secretary.[82] The weakness of the policy process at the design stage, the constraints operating within the system concerning political feasibility and some permanent structural characteristics create a constant tendency towards an incremental style of policy which avoids any major policy shifts in direction, according to the model described by Lindblom.[83]

IV Policy Termination or Change
Policy outputs and their impact on society can be reckoned in terms of the quantitative and qualitative characteristics or dimensions of the system. Education systems, like public bureaucracies, are not inclined to regular self-examination and while there is an abundance

of empirical data on the quantitative side, major studies on educational quality do not abound.[84] It is possible however to use some indicators of quality derived from accommodation, expenditure, enrolment and retention statistics and relevant data on the instructional process which offer a basis for judgement. However, it is very difficult, as American and Swedish studies have borne out, to evaluate the impact of policies which are not accompanied by specification of the outcomes intended.[85] Many of the policies pursued in this century did not have detailed outcomes identified or outcomes which were identified were frequently expressed in vague terms; this is especially so in relation to policies in the process and access domains where outcomes were expressed in terms which render evaluation difficult. If however, one assumes that the development and expansion of the system constitute a valid policy objective it is possible to show to what extent such expansion and development occurred by examining expenditure, enrolment, staffing and pupil retention patterns; Tables 11.1 to 11.4 present data on these dimensions. In the past sixty years, current public expenditure on education has expanded significantly, has never been below 11% of total public expenditure, has been over 20% in the late twenties and early thirties and in the mid-eighties has dropped to 16% from a high of 18% in the late seventies (Fig.11.5). This pattern of expenditure has been reflected in the growth of the school network, of pupil enrolment and teacher numbers; teacher numbers have doubled and student numbers have risen by a third in the past six decades. In view of the drop-out patterns reported in *Investment in Education* for 1962, special significance attaches to Table 11.3 and Fig. 11.6 which show a sustained increase in Retention Rates for the upper primary standards and a 100% rate reached in the early seventies.[86]

While issues emerge from other sources, it is mainly from the action of the principal interest groups, teachers, managers, politicians, churches and state, that policy issues are placed on the agenda. There are two main concentrations of issues, lower level issues dealing with resource allocation, curricular issues and working conditions, topics which concern the system as it is; the higher level issues include all issues whose direct or implied consequence is a modification of the structural *status quo*. These issue concentrations provide the basis for two separate consultative processes; teachers, managers and the state confront the lower level issues whereas consultation on the higher level is usually confined to the churches and the state (Fig. 11.1). It sometimes happens that items from the lower level are transposed to the higher list by virtue of the emerging implications of the issue; the dismissal in 1984 of a secondary teacher from a convent school on grounds relating to her lifestyle and the resolution of the case in the courts, offers a clear example. The policy formulation process in Irish education is influenced significantly by the church-state relationship and by the dominant role exercised by the churches in education. The

TABLE 11.1

The number of pupils in different first and second level school types
for selected years, 1928/29 to 1974/75. x 10³

School Type	1928/29	1932/33	1961/62	1974/75
Primary	507.8	504.5	484.6	550.1
Secondary	24.6	30.0	80.4	173.2
Vocational	69.6	62.8	96.9	66.8
Industrial	6.6	6.8	3.0	0.7
Comp. & Comm.	—	—	—	13.2
TOTAL	608.6	604.1	664.9	804.00

Sources: *Tuarascáil na Roinne Oideachais.*

Note: The figures for Vocational 1928/29 to 1961/62 do not distinguish between
part-time and full-time.

TABLE 11.2

The number of full-time teachers employed in different school types at first and
second level for selected years, 1928/29 to 1974/75. x 10³

School Type	1928/29	1932/33	1961/62	1974/75
National	13.6	14.3	14.1	16.7
Secondary	2.4	2.7	5.6	9.4
Vocational	1.09	1.27	1.75	4.6
Industrial	0.42	0.47	—	—
Comp. & Comm.	—	—	—	0.92
TOTAL	17.51	18.74	21.45	31.62

Sources: *Tuarascáil na Roinne Oideachais.*

relationship between the churches and education is characterised, in Archer's terms, as mono-integrated and subordinate, defining a situation where church dominance and the protective strategy used to defend it produce a stability and inertia characterised by a state reluctance to take initiative, a low level of professional autonomy, a disinterest among public and politicians and a complacency concerning the social and geographical inequalities of the system. This central reality of Irish political and educational life has deeply influenced and constrained the content of education policy; economic necessity and the supervisory role of the Department of Finance have also been important factors. Consequently in describing the policy process, the churches must be included in Lindblom's category of 'proximate policy-makers',i.e. 'those who share immediate legal authority to decide on specific policies, together with other immediate participants in policy decisions'; the relationships among such policy makers are illustrated in Fig. 11.4.[87] Implementation of policy has been marked by reasonable success in the routine areas, especially in process aspects where the disciplinary dominance of a centralised bureaucracy and a strong inspectorate brooked few expressions of opposition; however in other policy areas, as in the physical condition of national schools, the department was singularly unsuccessful in implementing policy because of the reaction of school managers. In the megapolicies of Irish language promotion and equality of educational opportunity, implementation has been hampered by inattention at the design stage to implementation strategies, by unreal policy aims and by a reluctance to define and hold precise policy objectives.

The policy process, though faulty, has been fruitful; the education network has been physically expanded and geographically extended, educational opportunity has been dramatically increased, especially in senior-cycle second level and higher education and the subject range and course modality have been significantly modified. The policies currently in operation differ fundamentally from those of the early and the middle decades of the century; their long-term impact may include among their consequences a fundamental change in the desire and ability of the general electorate to contribute to the policy process itself.

TABLE 11.3
Retention Rates at 5th and 6th Standards National Schools 1929-79

	29/30	34/35	39/40	44/45	49/50	54/55	59/60	64/65	69/70	73/74	74/75	79/80
5th	71%	81%	84%	86%	86.2%	92 %	90.5%	96.7%	75.2%	100%	100%	100%
6th	43%	57%	61%	58.6%	56.1%	64.4%	68.3%	80.3%	90.3%	98.4%	100%	100%

Source: Compiled from *Tuarascáil na Roinne Oideachais.*

TABLE 11.4

Current public expenditure on education and percentage which such expenditure
constituted of total public current expenditure for selected years 1924 to 1984. (£ Millions)

	Total Expediture on Education (i)	Expenditure on all Services (ii)	(i) as % of (ii)
1924/25	4.0068	24.672	16.24%
1934/35	4.4711	26.531	16.85%
1944/45	5.2825	43.44	12.17%
1954/55	11.7475	104.975	11.18%
1964/65	31.7909	207.405	15.32%
1974/75	108.2519	692.703	15.62%
1979/80	485.0233	2,653.139	18.28%
1984	868.063	5,221.674	16.62%

Source: *Appropriation Accounts.*

FIGURE 11.1

The high and low-level process of consultation between the churches
and the state on education policy.

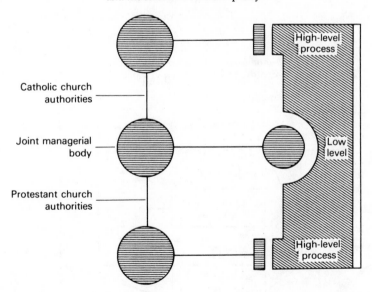

Source: *European Journal of Education,* 20, 4, (1985), 358.

FIGURE 11.2
Policy content classified by dimensions.

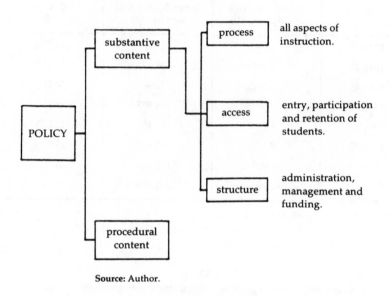

Source: Author.

FIGURE 11.3
A model of the implementation process
according to Van Meter and Van Horn.

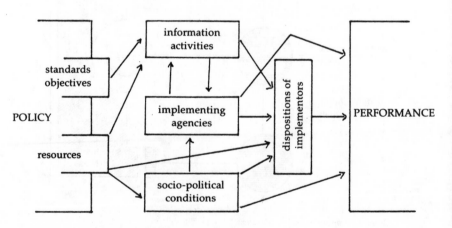

Source: *Administration and Society*, 6, (1975), 445.

FIGURE 11.4
The policy process in Irish education.

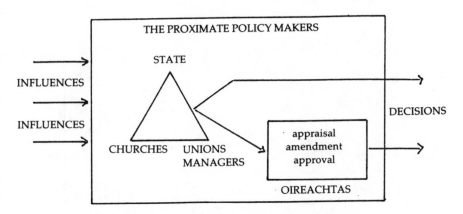

THE PROXIMATE POLICY MAKERS

STATE

INFLUENCES

INFLUENCES

CHURCHES   UNIONS
         MANAGERS

appraisal
amendment
approval

OIREACHTAS

DECISIONS

Source: Based upon B. Chubb, *Cabinet Government in Ireland*, 63.

FIGURE 11.5
State expenditure on education 1922-84, (shown in broken line) and such expenditure
expressed as a percentage of all service expenditure.

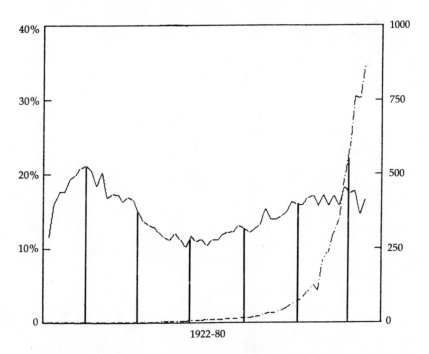

Source: Compiled from Appropriation Accounts.

FIGURE 11.6

Retention rates at standards V and VI of national schools 1930-80;
that for standard V is shown in continuous line.

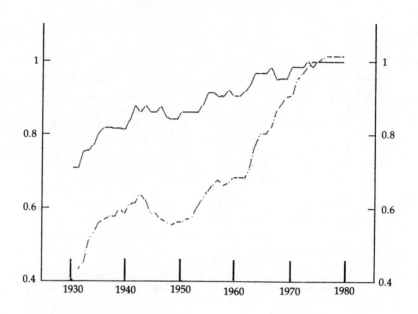

Source: author.

CHAPTER TWELVE

— TWO CASE STUDIES —

The Irish Language
and
Educational Opportunity

The Irish language and educational opportunity have been signific-ant elements of Irish education policy in this century, the former as a major policy area throughout the period and the latter as a dominant component during the last two decades. Although they differ in their timespan, they are similar as issue areas since in both, megapolicies or master policies evolved which impinged on many parts of the system, carried implications for other aspects of policy or determined in Dror's terms 'the postures, assumptions and main guidelines to be followed in developing specific policies'.[1] These two issue areas differ too is some fundamental aspects, in the manner in which they arrived on the agenda, in the nature of the decision process, in the clarity and specificity of their aims, in the nature of the related policy measures and in their implementation. It is proposed to examine each policy area in turn, to investigate these differences in detail and thereby to seek a clearer understanding of the general policy process.

The Irish Language
The formal education system during most of the last century ignored the existence of the Irish language, rejected requests to cater properly for the education of the Irish-speaking areas (Gaeltacht) and in general sought 'to encourage the cultivation of the English language and to make English the language of the schools'.[2] The 8,600 national schools and the 490 secondary schools catering for three quarters of a million pupils by the century's end, made no provision whatsoever for that segment of the population, numbering 319,602 in 1851, for whom the Irish language was a vernacular and only language, nor for the much larger group, totalling 1.5 million in 1851, who were biling-ual.[3] To argue that the national schools merely facilitated the language shift from Irish to English and 'that there were no rules

against its use', is to ignore the reality of inspectorial reports, the minutes of National Board meetings and the various submissions of the Society for the Preservation of the Irish Language, of the Gaelic Union and the very defiant policy outlined by the commissioners to the Chief Secretary in 1884.[4]

From its foundation in 1893 the Gaelic League accorded a priority to education reform; its aim, according to one of its founders, Douglas Hyde, was 'to reform all education in Ireland from the national schools to the university upon native and autochtonous lines'.[5] It sought to secure 'the intellectual independence of Ireland', an independence in which Irish history, cultural traditions and the Irish language would, in the words of Davis, 'be cherished, taught and esteemed'; it was guided by the conviction enunciated by Pearse in the editorial columns of *An Claidheamh Soluis*:

> Had the education of the country been sane and national for the last hundred years there would never have been a necessity for the language movement; when it is thoroughly sane and national again in all its branches, the necessity for the language movement will have ceased.[6]

Despite some marginal concessions gained by the League, the education authorities, both elementary and intermediate, remained substantially hostile to the language; the weak position of the language in the schools was threatened further by a motion by Judge Shaw in 1901 to delete Irish as an extra subject, which found the National Commissioners evenly divided. The ideological nature of these moves and the depth of cultural hostility they symbolised are clearly manifest in the letter of 1904 written by the eminent Trinity physicist, George Fitzgerald, a Commissioner of National Education, in which he stated; 'I will use all my influence as in the past, to ensure that Irish as a spoken language shall die out as quickly as possible'.[7]

It was inevitable that as the movement towards independence developed, the language question and its resolution would become an issue of priority. When the Gaelic League in 1915 abandoned its non-political stance, the fusion of the cultural and the separatist wings of the independence movement was assured. With the establishment of Dáil Éireann in 1919 the language in the education system had emerged as a central political issue and the prominence of Gaelic League policy in the emerging independent state was guaranteed by the appointment of its president, Seán Ó Ceallaigh, first as Minister for Irish in the Dáil cabinet and later as Minister for Education.

Despite the achievements of the League, the Irish language was not in a healthy state in the education system at the change of administration in 1922. According to the reports of inspectors, extra subjects were not taken up in many schools, and in secondary schools many of the teachers of Irish were scarcely ahead of their pupils. Of the national teachers in Gaeltacht and partly Irish-speaking areas in 1926, 13.7% and 42% respectively were unqualified in Irish.[8] In the population at large the ability to speak Irish varied considerably; while 13% of the total population were returned in 1911 as Irish speakers, in four Leinster counties the figure was under 1% while in Munster and Connacht it stood at 22% and 35% respectively.[9]

If the Irish language had declined during the previous century, had been excluded from the education system, had been associated with economic depression and had been, in the words of W. T. Cosgrave, 'subjected to neglect and contempt, ignominy and abuse', the Gaelic League was determined that an independent Irish state would redress that situation and make language revival a major political priority.[10] Such a development was guaranteed by the presence among the emerging political leaders of men such as Eoin MacNeill, Richard Mulcahy, Michael Hayes, Cathal Brugha, Ernest Blythe, Éamon de Valera, Seán Ó Ceallaigh and Seán T. Ó Ceallaigh, all of whom had been active and prominent in the Gaelic League. By the time the Treaty had been signed and the Irish Free State established in 1922, the question of language revival was firmly inscribed upon the political agenda as an issue demanding immediate attention. In the interlude between the war of independence and the Treaty, the Dáil intensified the climate of political opinion in support of language revival by the various schemes initiated by Seán Ó Ceallaigh as Minister for Irish.[11]

The aims of the language policy had been stated and formulated prior to 1922 and have been restated, modified and reformulated by various political and interest groups since. The aims of the League from its foundation in 1893 centred on 'the preservation of Irish as the national language of Ireland and the extension of its use as a spoken tongue'; among the means to this end it listed 'the national language shall be the medium of instruction in the national schools where it is the home language of the people and that greater facilities than at present be afforded for its teaching in the national and intermediate schools in all parts of the country'.[12] These two demands were the basis of the various expressions of policy by the League, those of 1913, of 1918 and of the programme which it issued in 1919.[13] This latter plan distinguished between the Gaeltacht, where Irish was the vernacular, those areas which were bilingual and those areas where English was the vernacular; for each of these areas the programme specified a different linguistic/education policy. In the Gaeltacht the language of instruction would be Irish, in bilingual areas a bilingual programme would obtain and Irish would be the language of school administration; in English-speaking areas, Irish would be taught for one hour each day in schools with a competent teacher and in those which could benefit from a travelling teacher and Irish was to be the language of school administration.[14]

When the Dáil, in early 1922, established a joint committee with the

Gaelic League, 'to investigate the position of the language and recommend a scheme for its preservation', it turned its early attention to education and not surprisingly adopted the League's education programme.[15] The Dáil Ministry of Irish initiated a number of scholarship schemes, took overall charge, with the cooperation of the Gaelic League, of the direction of the language revival in ten counties and appointed two commissions to draw up new curricular programmes for national and secondary schools.[16] Already the official reports are tinged with undue optimism; the 1922 report claims that 'there is evidence that the teachers will make every effort to put it into operation'. This report also presages with precision a feature of later policy, the provision of preparatory colleges. There is thus a clear continuity between the work and policy of the pre-Treaty Gaelic League and the political process after 1922; the bridge between them was provided by Dáil Éireann and its Ministers of Irish and Education in the years from 1919 to 1922.

The formal political responsibility after 1922 for carrying forward the policy aims and demands of the language revival fell to Eoin MacNeill, one of the founders of the Gaelic League, who however, unlike most of his colleagues, was adamantly opposed to compulsion. He was not convinced that the education system could bring about revival unaided and located his language demands within a wider framework of 'building up the character of the nation'; early in his ministerial career he assured the Dáil of his commitment, while admitting that the education policy introduced early in 1922 was the work of others:

Ba dhaoine eile a dhein an méid a dineadh. Maidir liomsa déanfaidh mé mo dhícheall chun an Ghaeilge a thabhairt ar ais.[17]
(What was achieved was done by other people. As for me I will do my utmost to revive Irish.)

Among the emerging political leaders and MacNeill's 'other people', it was Ernest Blythe who made the most comprehensive and coherent demands on the language issue. Besides being the effective driving force in formulating and implementing language policy in education, his vision encompassed a much wider penetration by the language in the administrative machinery of the state, in commerce, vocational training, publishing, the legal system and the creative arts, especially the theatre; he also saw the basic and central importance of the social and economic development of the Gaeltacht and was the initiator of the Gaeltacht Commission of 1925.[18] He summarised his general aim as follows:

In dealing with the preservation and revival of the language we have to remember that there are two problems involved and neither can be solved alone. Irish cannot be revived in the

Galltacht (English-speaking area) if the Gaeltacht disappears. In my view it is equally certain that the language cannot be preserved in the Gaeltacht if we fail to revive it in the Galltacht. The inhabitants of the present Irish-speaking districts will not consent to be made a sort of 'peculiar people' in their own land. In all our policy therefore we have to consider the Gaeltacht and the Galltacht.[19]

Pádraig Ó Brolcháin, a member of the Gaelic League and chief executive officer for National Education, was a major figure in the formulation and implementation of language policy; it was he who in February 1922 conveyed the government's policy to the Commissioners of National Education, declaring:

It is the intention of the new government to work with all its might for the strengthening of the national fibre by giving the language, history, music and traditions of Ireland their national place in the life of Irish schools.[20]

Professor T. J. Corcoran, S.J., of University College Dublin, who played an influential role in shaping language and education policy, was explicitly more specific, especially in relation to the infant classes where he would have all the work conducted through the Irish language. In his opinion:

The language should be the sole aim of that school; if, that is, the habit of using the language can be given by one teacher to a hundred children in one year it can become a permanent possession, a second nature within three years. What about English in such a school? It has no place whatsoever.[21]

The Provisional Government and later the Free State Governments entrusted the Ministry and later the Department of Education with the main responsibility in forwarding what was termed 'The Gaelicising of Ireland', this being the title of an official cabinet document circulated in 1924 outlining the aims and means of policy. In education it sought 'the substitution of Irish for English as the language of teaching, recreation and life generally in the primary and secondary schools'; in other sectors it sought to make Irish 'the normal official language in both the Gaeltacht and the English-speaking districts'.[22] The constitution of 1922 described Irish as 'the national language' and English as 'equally recognised as an official language'.[23]

This heavy political support for language policy was neither uniform nor was it accepted uncritically in some quarters. Early in the twenties there were already expressions of dissent in relation to language policy; even during the First Programme Conference of

1921-22, the national teacher representatives were opposed to the proposals that Irish be the medium of instruction for infants and for other subjects as being impracticable and premature.[24] This stance was again adopted by the INTO in the Second Programme Conference of 1925 and their argument was echoed by the Minister for Fisheries, Fionán Lynch, who expressed himself as 'entirely opposed to attempting to teach subjects through Irish where Irish is not the known language'.[25] Similar expressions of opposition emerged in the Dáil during the course of 1925.[26]

De Valera and Fianna Fáil gave a high priority to the language in the founding documents of the party and in the 1932 election manifesto, which included the following:

> To endeavour by systematic effort to preserve the Irish language and to make it again the spoken language of the people; to save the native speaker from the emigrant ship and to provide employment for him in the Gaeltacht and to make it possible for the language to spread out nationally from the Gaeltacht to the surrounding areas.[27]

Fianna Fáil's policy demands were a close echo of those of Cumann na nGael and their education dimension is clearly expressed in the words of the Minister for Education, Tomás Deirg, speaking to the national teachers in 1932:

> The heart and core of all our work in the creation of a national state must be the revival of the national language of the people; now more than ever it is the teachers of Ireland we must rely on to rebuild our nation.[28]

Even though all the political parties were united in their commitment to language revival there were various constraints operating from the beginning which impinged upon the formulation and implementation of a policy on Irish; these included the power position within the Department of Education, the attitudes of the Inspectorate and the stance of the senior officers of the Department of Finance. Within the newly created Department of Education, relations between the senior officials were never very cordial, since some, like Pádraig Ó Brolcháin, had come recently to education while others like the first secretary, Joseph O'Neill, had previously served in the intermediate and primary inspectorates.[29] Ó Brolcháin, a former official of the National Insurance Board, was Chief Executive Officer for National Education from February 1922 to his death in 1934. His official position as administrative head of primary education placed him in a position where he could promote Gaelic League policies, given the support or the allegiance of the inspectors. O'Neill, a native speaker of Irish and a scholar of some distinction, was appointed by the Cabinet in April 1923, 'as permanent secretary to coordinate the three education services'; his appointment to the most senior department rank later than Ó Brolcháin's appointment tended to create friction between them.[30] This was no doubt further aggravated by some internal doubt on O'Neill's commitment to the more extreme objectives of language policy; the O'Neill/Ó'Brolcháin tension found an echo among other Department officials, especially among the inspectors.[31]

The Treaty and the Irish language policy adopted by the incoming Provisional government caused some inspectors to opt for transfer to Northern Ireland or for resignation; the reorganisation of the primary inspectorate as planned by Ó Brolcháin caused eight senior inspectors out of fourteen to opt for the North and unsettled the rest of the inspectorate.[32] When the established order of seniority among the surviving inspectors and their individual status were threatened by the reorganisation policy, tempers flared and protesting memoranda were dispatched to the executive council.[33] However Ó Brolcháin was not that easily shaken in his purpose especially when he had the active support of the Minister for Finance. Existing inspectors with no knowledge of Irish were offered deep immersion courses or lengthy spells in the Gaeltacht; those with a command of the language were promoted and new inspectors were recruited who had a good working knowledge of the language, some of whom were active or former members of the Gaelic League.[34]

The Department of Finance and its senior officials, did not always share the policy enthusiasm of the Department of Education and were it not for the strong support of Ernest Blythe while Minister for Finance, some of the language proposals of Education would undoubtedly have perished in Merrion Street, where already by 1928 some officials were complaining of the enormous amounts of money which the state had spent on language policy and the preparatory colleges.[35] Responding to an appeal from Education for additional inspectors in 1927, Finance was of the official opinion that the burden on the inspectorate was due to the inexperience of the newly recruited or 'the intensive campaign in favour of Irish which will not have to be faced again and will certainly not be a permanent feature'.[36] The Department of Finance maintained its opposition to some of the early policy measures, including the preparatory colleges; it recommended the closure of some colleges even the college described as 'a model', Coláiste Chaoimhín, and opposed the organisation of inservice courses for teachers in colleges temporarily closed.[37] In the thirties it made efforts to modify the language requirement for entry to the professional grades of the civil service; when in the sixties, the Department of Finance adopted a more rational and supportive attitude to language policy proposals, the language was already in decline in the education system.

Despite the department tensions at senior administrative and inspectorial levels and despite the opposition of senior officials in the Department of Finance and the questioning of some politicians, the policy of the government was implemented with considerable success in the decade following independence. Measures were introduced in a number of spheres by the committed few in Education, influenced on some issues by the messianic views of Professor T. J. Corcoran, S.J. and stoutly aided by Ernest Blythe with an enthusiasm which more than compensated for the detached attitude of Eoin MacNeill and John Marcus O'Sullivan, a detachment which may have been shared by Joseph O'Neill as secretary of the department.

The basic core of the school-based aspects of language policy was contained in a regulation promulgated on 1 February 1922, in the primary programmes drawn up by the Programme Conference and in the new programme for secondary schools of 1924 produced by the Dáil Commission on Secondary Education.[38] Irish was to be taught or used as a medium of instruction in all national schools which had a competent teacher; the new curriculum in which Irish was given a new status both as a subject and a medium of instruction and in which Irish history and geography were allotted an appropriate role was to be implemented where possible.[39] The work of the infant school was to be entirely through Irish; where a local majority of parents objected to either Irish or English as an obligatory subject, their wishes were to be complied with. In secondary schools the inclusion of Irish or English in the curriculum was made a condition for recognition and the payment of grants from 1924 to 1927; from 1927 Irish and English were made mandatory. Irish was a required subject for Intermediate examination candidates from 1928 and for Leaving Certificate candidates from 1934.[40] Beyond these core measures, a wide range of policy measures was introduced in the twenties, many at the direct behest of Ernest Blythe, which collectively constituted a coherent policy strategy.

These measures were directed at the Gaeltacht and the English-speaking populations, reflecting Blythe's perception of the language question. In 1929, in defending the location of a new training college in Galway, as opposed to the Department of Finance's preference for Dublin's Phoenix Park, he wrote:

In our struggle to preserve the Irish language Galway city is the Verdun which we must strengthen and save.[41]

He involved himself directly in carrying out that policy; he established an Irish-medium national school in Galway, and by legislation and funding enabled University College Galway to develop higher education in Irish; in conjunction with Galway Vocational Education Committee and the Department of Fisheries, he initiated vocational training and apprenticeship schemes in Galway for young people from Connemara.[42] He was no less concerned for the Gaeltacht generally and those proposals which he favoured were destined to spend very short time in the bureaucratic network of his own department.[43] He introduced a school meal scheme, grants to island children, free places for Gaeltacht girls in colleges of Home Economics and a university scholarship scheme for Gaeltacht students. His major measure was the establishment of seven preparatory colleges which were intended to remedy the educational deprivation of the Gaeltacht as revealed in the Report of the Gaeltacht Commission.[44] In order to attract qualified teachers to the remote Gaeltacht schools he introduced a scheme to provide subsidised teacher residences and bonus payments to qualified teachers.[45]

In relation to the non-Gaeltacht areas, he displayed a similar personal commitment to a wide range of schemes; it seems obvious that in the Cosgrave administrations, he was the senior politician with responsibility for the language issue. Special all-Irish national schools and a special Irish-medium secondary school were established in Dublin through the direct involvement of Blythe, who provided special funding and accommodation for them.[46] The scheme introduced in 1924 to encourage secondary schools to use Irish as a medium of instruction, whereby they were classified and grant-aided according to language usage, was modified by Blythe in 1931 to attract 'big institutions like diocesan seminaries or Clongowes or Castleknock to join the work of Gaelicising education'.[47] In higher education, he linked University College Dublin with the Irish-medium primary schools and provided funds to University College Cork in 1928 to Gaelicise some of its activities.[48]

Blythe was equally involved in the wider extra-educational aspects of policy, in promoting the writing and publication of works in Irish, and in funding the preparation of dictionaries; his major creation in this field was the establishment of the state publishing body, An Gúm, and the various literary and translation schemes he promoted under its aegis.[49] By 1932 when Fianna Fáil came to power many of these language policy measures had been in operation for some years and progress was evident in some aspects. Courses had been organised for serving teachers, all but one of the training colleges had begun to use Irish as a medium of instruction and the preparatory colleges were providing native speakers of Irish as candidates for the teaching profession.[50] Three quarters of all serving national teachers were qualified in Irish and of the 5,401 national schools in operation, Irish was taught in all but 32 schools which 'were mainly schools under Protestant management situated along the border'.[51] The number of teachers qualified in Irish had been trebled in the decade and in the school year 1930-31 only 90 of the 322 teachers appointed in the Gaeltacht did not have the Bilingual Certificate.[52]

In secondary schools while the Department was not anxious to pressurise the schools, the number of schools using Irish as a medium of instruction increased steadily from 5 in 1925-26 to 24 in 1930-31 and those teaching some subjects through Irish had risen from 10 to 68.[53] In 1931 a general inspector of Irish was appointed with responsibility for promoting language policy in the Department.[54]

Throughout the thirties the language policy in the education system was implemented with renewed vigour by the minister, Tomás Deirg, and his senior officials, aided by inspectors whose promotion prospects were determined largely by their enthusiasm for and identification with the official policy. The number of Irish-medium primary and secondary schools rose to a maximum in the first decade of de Valera's long tenure of office. However as the policy began to produce results in the education system, it was associated more in the popular mind solely with the schools and its use was not extended in the adult world. Deirg was unhappy with the rate of progress and urged the national teachers to a greater effort with the reformed school programme of 1934 which effectively reverted to the 1922 position, wherein the aim of instruction in the infant classes is stated as being 'to train the children to understand Irish and to speak it as their natural language'[55] This policy change marked a turning point in the attitude of the teachers; from the mid-thirties they demanded policy modifications and in 1937 organised a national survey to provide empirical support for their demands.

While the policy launched by Cumann na nGael differed from that pursued by Fianna Fáil more in manner of execution than in content, the two parties and their language policies differed significantly in their attitudes to policy modification. Fine Gael and Ernest Blythe, despite his commitment and his unjust criticism of the INTO, were more rational in their approach and were willing to examine and assess the efficacy of the policies being implemented.[56] Fianna Fáil, despite a basic shift in policy by de Valera, were unswerving in their attachment to the original orthodoxy and were adamant in refusing an independent commission of inquiry. Perhaps the fact that language policy figured so centrally in party objectives, made it difficult for Fianna Fáil to contemplate policy modification. Through the thirties and forties the demands for policy modification grew and included those of the INTO and politicians such as Dillon, Thrift and Cogan; demands ranged from rejection of the policy objective through criticism of the means, to the need to establish a commission of inquiry.[57] The national teachers, who had from 1922 queried the wisdom of instruction through Irish where English was the home language, produced in the report of their 1937 survey, evidence that the majority of respondents disagreed with the policy.[58] In its later comprehensive policy document, the INTO produced an alternative approach based upon reality and oral competence; it pleaded for 'a fresh, keen and original' approach from the Department of Education allied to 'vision and leadership' instead of the rigid adherence to administrative routine.[59]

Deirg's public reaction to the INTO and to the other critics of his policy was mainly dismissive, holding that the reports of inspectors were indicating that the policy was successful and that there was no need for an inquiry.[60] Obviously this view was not shared by all his colleagues, even by deValera, who had slowly come to modify his own earlier viewpoints on the language in the schools; he had already come to recognise that the early policy aims were set far too high, that rigidity and intransigence merely generated hostility and apathy. He also accepted that to ask the schools to revive a language which was not spoken by a majority of the population was imposing an impossible task on pupils and teachers. By June 1940 de Valera had come to a modified conviction on the methodology of revival while still adhering to the aim of restoring Irish as a vernacular; he expressed doubts about teaching through Irish and said that the emphasis in school should be on teaching the language itself and using the vernacular as the language of instruction.[61] Despite such a shift in personal conviction no apparent policy change occurred,though deValera had promised the Dáil that if, having examined the question further,he thought the policy should be changed, he would do so.[62] In 1941 he offered to set up a commission of Dáil deputies to examine the question.[63]

Though Fianna Fáil and Deirg dismissed the evidence from the INTO survey and other demands for a policy change, it is clear that the question was of concern to the government by 1943 and may by then have become a divisive issue within the Cabinet.[64] A memorandum of March 1943 from Deirg on 'The position of the Irish language' was before the cabinet and having been deferred at a number of meetings, was finally withdrawn from the agenda.[65] It is probable that some of his colleagues, including deValera, disagreed with Deirg's document in which he admitted the widespread criticism of the policy, admitted that the out-of-school environment nullified the work of the school but rejected the view that a commission of inquiry could offer any help on school policy.[66] He proposed instead that a full-time permanent commission or board be established 'with powers not merely of investigation and formulation of schemes but with the duty and the administrative machinery to put these schemes into operation'; such a board, according to Deirg, would operate outside the educational administration. Some time later deValera was toying with the idea of establishing a special department or branch to deal with the language question. In 1952 he outlined in a message to the party Ard-Fheis his current thinking on the issue. The objective was 'the general use of the language which in the present conditions can only come from the schools'; 'the time had come to take stock . . . to examine our standards and our methods anew and dispassionately'.[67] He admitted that he had been so convinced for some years but had hesitated to advocate it in public lest it be interpreted 'as a defeat for the language cause and the occasion for a massed attack by its enemies'.

The various pressures for policy modification brought a response in 1948 under the first coalition government; Mulcahy as minister relaxed the rule on Irish in the infant classes, removed the rating system for teachers which was associated closely with language policy, and established the Council of Education in 1950 which was to review curricular policy in the national school. Under pressure from the Department of Finance the government decided on economies in expenditure on the Irish language policy and Mulcahy was directed to examine expenditure on Irish 'with a view to securing substantial reductions'.[68] This fiscal pressure on the policy was accompanied by professional doubt among some of the secondary inspectors on the wisdom of teaching the classics in secondary schools through Irish. When this doubt was expressed by two of them at a conference with the minister in January 1949, the department secretary wrote to Mulcahy disabusing him of the the idea and disproving their allegation with examination statistics.[69] Throughout the fifties the movement towards modification of policy accelerated and this is clearly evident in parliamentary exchanges such as that between de Valera and Mulcahy in 1955 during which both are anxious to avoid arriving at any specification of current policy content, opting instead to recite the history of the policy.[70] By this time, while many would not agree with the editorial view of *The Irish Times* that the language was of interest only to 'elder statesmen, rabid doctrinaires and the entrenched obscurantists of the Department of Education', it was patently obvious that a change of policy was being sought and was in fact being implemented by inaction, if not by positive decision.[71] This move towards a policy change is evident in the annual conferences of the teachers and in resolutions adopted at Fine Gael Ard Fheiseanna in 1958 and 1959.[72] These policy changes are formulated in a more general framework in Garret FitzGerald's *Towards a New Ireland* .[73]

Language policy has entered a new phase since the early fifties, a period which has witnessed a pronounced shift in state policy, a proliferation of official commissions of inquiry, a decline of usage within the public service, a widespread policy confusion and a deterioration of standards within the education system. This change in policy and its reflection within the education system are evident in all three levels of the system. Fig. 12.1. illustrates the growth and decline of Irish medium primary and secondary school from 1930 to date; it is worth observing that at no time did more than 12% of national schools teach all subjects through Irish. What is most remarkable is the very rapid early increase in Irish-medium secondary schools in the first decade after the introduction in 1925 of the classification/incentive scheme and the decline which has occurred in the last three decades. The rapid increase coincided with the pristine enthusiasms of department officials such as Pádraig Ó Brolcháin and Mícheál Breathnach and the arrival of Fianna Fáil in office in

1932; the decline is associated with the quantitative expansion of the postprimary system, with a slow erosion of department commitment and a related profound attitudinal change in training colleges and with overt political support for policy modification provided by the governments led by Fine Gael. There is also the collapse of the previous cohesion within the system; as primary and secondary schools discontinued using Irish as a medium and following the closure of the preparatory colleges in 1961, the flow of students to third level institutions who could take courses through Irish diminished rapidly, thus removing the demand for such provision. Research studies in the sixties, especially that of MacNamara, provided further impetus for official policy examination and significantly modified the attitude to the language in some training colleges.[74]

The Fine Gael policy which initiated the policy redefinition was published in connection with the *Just Society* series in 1966; its aim was 'the preservation of the language by means of realistic policies designed to secure the support of the people'.[75] Throughout the sixties language policy was the main discriminant as between Fine Gael and Fianna Fáil and between their education policies, as shown in a 1969 poll.[76] Fine Gael promised to change the compulsion attaching to the language in the education system and employment in the public service; rejecting language replacement as an unrealistic objective, it claimed that a majority did not favour substituting Irish for English.[77] It promised a policy of encouragement and freedom of choice and measures to ensure the economic and social development of the Gaeltacht. These policies, implemented from 1973, whereby Irish is no longer required as an essential subject in state examinations and as an entry requirement to the Civil Service, have had a pronounced negative impact.[78]

The commissions and councils established in the sixties and seventies identified a range of policy measures which would, it was expected, consolidate language usage, ability and status and proposed various steps which should be taken in the education system, steps which the Department of Education might reasonably be expected to have taken as part of normal policy implementation, had the approach to education policy been more rational. However most of the measures proposed in these official reports have had lukewarm response from politicians and the state; the exception has been the creation of a state body, Bord na Gaeilge, in the early seventies, a body whose creation has effectively relieved the state of direct responsibility for language policy.

From 1922 to date in the formulation and implementation of Irish language policy there have been some surprising policy outcomes which call into question the degree of rationality which characterised the policy, especially after the first decade of the state's existence. The major surprise relates to the rejection of the Gaelic League principle, a principle central to Pearse's philosophy, 'the language of the home as the language of instruction', in favour of Corcoran's proposals; given the previous successes of the League's policies and Corcoran's relative inexperience it is remarkable that he dominated language policy to the extent he did.[79]

The reluctance of the Department of Education to review its policy in the face of factual information available to it is equally surprising; through the inspectorial system it became aware, at various times, of the reality surrounding Irish in the schools, of the competence levels of teachers, of the methodologies employed and of the dominance of written skills promoted by the state examinations administered by itself, yet policy and official rhetoric remained practically unchanged. In 1941, an inspectorial report on Co Cork, which criticises 'apathy on the part of teachers and students, failure to avail of modern methods for language teaching and total neglect of the structure of the language and its essential vocabulary', describes what it calls 'a general *laissez faire* attitude'.[80] That the inertia had not been eliminated by 1974 is evident from the lack of cohesion in the introduction in 1965 of the new pedagogic approach in *Buntús Gaeilge*; up to 1974 over 60% of national teachers had received no training in the new methodology.[81] The inertia and policy confusion of the Department of Education is clear from the manner in which changing attitudes to Irish and falling standards were tolerated in the Training Colleges since the sixties and in the refusal to protect the intake of the existing Irish-medium secondary schools in 1967 when planning the 'free' education system; this occurred at a time when a government body, Comhlucht Comhairleach na Gaeilge, had criticised the Department of Education for 'failing to undertake any comprehensive planning in relation to many aspects of language policy'.[82]

The department may not have been allowed too much discretion by its political heads in the realm of language policy. On an issue in which party rivalry was so keen and on which high levels of personal commitment characterised many political leaders, it is hardly too surprising that ministers kept tight control on language policy and that senior department officials displayed little tendency to propose policy modifications.

Perhaps the most surprising feature of language policy in the six decades since 1922 has been the early 'naive optimism' which characterised the official view and which persisted despite the available evidence. According to MacNeill, 'the restoration of our language is possible, practicable and even easy', sentiments replicated by Corcoran, and by Deirg in 1934 when he asserted:

It is only a matter of years and more training in the schools until Gaelic again becomes the national language of the Irish Free State.[83]

The central surprise in language policy concerns the treatment of the

Gaeltacht despite its recognised importance in policy strategies, as acknowledged by most interested parties. On egalitarian grounds alone, leaving aside all cultural arguments, the educational neglect of the Gaeltacht constitutes a major social injustice; de Valera's 1934 plan to provide secondary education would have made a significant difference if implemented. However, higher political considerations decided the issue, similar to the political reaction evident in 1954 when the local priest and people of Ceathrú Rua in Connemara sought unsuccessfully to establish a secondary school.[84] In the eighties while a network of provision exists at first and second levels in the Gaeltacht, the major inadequacies concern curricular range and the quality of facilities at second level, consistency as to language of instruction and the teaching of English at first level. In 1986 at third level there is no institution offering all its courses in Irish or otherwise catering comprehensively for the higher education needs of the Gaeltacht, despite such provision figuring prominently in a plan prepared by Bord na Gaeilge.[85]

The issue of the preparatory colleges, established in 1926 as a central strategy in the language policy is equally baffling; no sooner were they opened than the Departments of Education and Finance were sniping at them, the INTO was fundamentally opposed to them and internal Department inquiries were held on them. One of the colleges, Coláiste Chaoimhín, described in official reports 'as a model for the development of policy . . . and in demonstrating the practicality of using the language as the sole medium of instruction', was closed in 1939; the others were closed in 1961.[86]

These various developments reveal some serious weaknesses in the policy process; undue optimism, unrealistic goals and incoherent implementation strategies have been frequently in evidence and policies have been based on a misunderstanding of the potentialities of the education system.[87] However, the policy aim, the revival of the language and its central place in the education system do still command widespread popular support. Recent studies report that in 1973, 'the average person appeared to place a high value on Irish as a symbol of national identity and wished to see its transmission to the next generation secured'.[88] These attitudes were accompanied by a marked feeling of pessimism about the future and 'a feeling that the language was irrelevant to modern life'. More recent studies suggest that supportive attitudes have remained constant in the eighties and that the language may be declining as an issue attracting strong public reaction; while less than 5% favoured discontinuing Irish as a subject in schools, 25% would favour the introduction of a bilingual programme whereby some subjects are taught through Irish.[89]

Despite such popular support the ultimate fate of the language is a matter of conjecture at this stage, given the policy weaknesses and the threatened status of the language in the Gaeltacht, after sixty years during which, for the first time in centuries, the state supported the

Irish language. The ultimate situation may approach the position described by Davis in relation to countries with two languages,

> which use one language as a medium of commerce and another as a vehicle of history, as the wings of song, as the soil of their genius and a mask and guard of their nationality'.[90]

Educational Opportunity

While educational opportunity, its extension and equalisation, have been prominent policy issues only during the last two decades, they have been present as issues in political debate to different degrees over most of this century. Some of the early references represent nothing more than individual opinion, passing parliamentary comment or the demands of small groups; one of the earliest significant calls came from the Cork Trades Council when it condemned the education system 'which ignored the fate of many'.[91] By the foundation of the Free State, political leaders and parties were well supplied with policy headlines in the 1916 Proclamation which advocated 'cherishing all the children of the nation equally' and in the Democratic Programme of the First Dáil, which gave high priority to egalitarian principles in education.[92] These founding documents may have influenced the infant Departament of Education in 1924 when its major policy document on language policy was accompanied by a shorter document defining the other elements of policy; these included 'the extension of education to a larger proportion of the population'.[93] This was to be achieved through compulsory school attendance for all between 6 and 14, special facilities for physically or mentally disabled and the provision of continuation schools for those over 14 who were not attending secondary schools.

Eoin MacNeill's promise of 'an educational highway' and a plan 'by which opportunity would be created for every pupil to proceed through the entire scale of education' must be seen in the same light as Cosgrave's earlier Dáil promise 'that secondary education for all would have to be considered', as ideological gestures to the cooperative deputies of the Labour party.[94] In that context, Labour's education policy of 1925, which advocated 'free' education for all and maintenance grants to parents was a radical document.[95] The report of Coimisiún na Gaeltachta of 1926 illustrated the extent of inequality in the Gaeltacht and drew attention to the total absence of any postprimary education in Irish, the poor physical conditions of national schools and the long distances travelled by children.[96] The report recommended that a number of free, day secondary schools be established, that adequate national schools and school equipmrnt be provided and that a school meal scheme be introduced.[97] With a view to implementing these and other proposals, de Valera established a Gaeltacht Cabinet Committee which at its first meeting instructed Deirg 'to submit proposals to increase the facilities for secondary and vocational education in the Gaeltacht'.[98] The Department of Education proposed, instead of secondary schools, 'a number of higher primary schools or senior schools which will not tend to direct the pupils towards black coat occupations but will rather train them for the life to which ordinarily the most of them will be called'.[99]

The inter-department committee on the school leaving age 1935, prompted by the Department of Industry and Commerce on grounds other than educational, came to the conclusion that 'if the school leaving age is to be raised, it must be raised only in selected areas in which the conditions are favourable and in which there is no likelihood of serious economic results'.[100] The committee was of the opinion that the existing school organisation was quite unfitted to meet the strain of raising the school leaving age to 15 or 16 and recommended instead a series of urban experiments based upon continuation education under the 1930 act. In the postwar years, despite a widespread European debate on educational opportunity, the 1945-47 department committee showed no evidence of having encountered any of the current social arguments in favour of extending participation in full-time education or of the comprehensive principle in school organisation.[101] The report, a most conservative document, reveals a timid, conditioned approach to education provision and structures despite the existing reality that only 41% of 14- 16 year olds and 12% of 16-18 year olds were in full-time education.[102]

In the late fifties and early sixties the concept of equality of opportunity had been introduced into the political debate on policy; Dáil questions on pupil-teacher ratios, drop-out from the system and the raising of the school leaving age were countered by a gradualist argument by the minister, that as demand for postprimary education increased, the relevant facilities would be provided[103]. A more interventionist note is discernible in 1962 when the planning role of the state and the provision of school facilities are seen as necessary preludes to 'postprimary education free to all'.[104] The growing debate on education policy generated by *Investment in Education* very quickly assimilated the principle of equality of opportunity without attempting to define the policy objective in any detail. However guaranteeing 'some postprimary education to all', promising free education to 15 as the Fine Gael *Just Society* document did, were very significant advances on the 1960 stance of the Council of Education which rejected the policy of 'secondary education for all'. The plan announced in 1963 by Dr Hillery to provide postprimary schools in areas lacking facilities, was described by him as 'a move in the direction, not only of a better coordination of our entire educational system, but of equality of educational opportunity'.[105] Throughout the sixties equality of opportunity became a central policy element whose force is best seen in the speech of Donagh O'Malley in 1966 announcing his 'free' education scheme; however the residual inertia in the system can also be detected in O'Malley's initial scheme, promising opportunity for free postprimary education only to the end of the Intermediate course and some assistance to support students going further. His later Dáil statement extended 'free' education to Leaving Certificate.[106]

Thus at the point when 'free' postprimary education was being promised no attempt had been made to define the degree of equality of opportunity being advocated; though it has been used as a frequent basis for policy since the mid-sixties it has usually been used without defining it in operational terms. It was difficult for the state in a system where the supply of secondary education has been governed by the operation of market forces for almost a century to guarantee equality of opportunity in a formula which would cover all possible contexts. Hence the reluctance of the state, a reluctance made more politically meaningful since the main interest groups involved were the churches.

Throughout the four decades following independence the education system operated as an elitist system in which compulsory education was available in a wide variety of educational and physical environments, in which only a fraction of the cohort experienced postprimary education and in which higher education was the preserve of a minority. The immutability of the education system over those decades is evident in the political impotence of deValera's assertion of 1940: 'for ninety per cent of the people the primary school is the only education'.[107] The conservative political sentiments which dominated the Dáil debate in 1922 on education in the Free State constitution, were powerfully present in the postwar years and were still politically represented in the years when O'Malley was moulding his scheme.[108] In addition to the inertia of the political process, the Department of Finance in its gubernatorial role exercised a major restraining force on expansion of educational opportunity.

While the system in its post-compulsory sector expanded its provision over the decades, the individual's right to sharing in that provision was mediated by circumstances of geographical location and social class. Some progress and expansion did occur; by 1929 the total number of students in the secondary schools of the Free State was greater than the total enrolled in the whole island prior to 1922.[109] While the numbers transferring to second level increased by the late forties, the system was still characterised by high drop-out rates between and within levels; only 23% of those enrolled in secondary schools in 1948-49 were in the senior cycle. The slow incremental nature of the extension of opportunity is evident from the data in Table 12.2 in relation to completion rates in secondary schools and the relative position of girls, who did not constitute 50% of Leaving Certificate candidates until 1964.

During the years from 1930 to 1966 the state examinations (Intermediate and Leaving certificate) were not available to students in vocational schools, a factor which placed them at great disadvantage.

Furthermore, the schools were located usually 'in smaller centres where it might not have been economically feasible to establish secondary schools'. In 1964 half of the total vocational schools had less than 100 students; such schools constituted 63% of the schools in Connacht. Total enrolment in vocational schools constituted on average 10.37% of the total enrolment in full-time education in the 13-17 age group in 1962/63.[110]

The degree of opportunity existing within the system and the relative retention rates as between secondary and vocational schoools is illustrated in the fate of the cohort which left the primary school in 1958. Of the 52,000, a third did not proceed to any postprimary education and the remainder suffered severe attrition as it proceeded as shown in Table 12.3. It should not be assumed that the expansion of second level facilities eliminated drop-out among Primary leavers; in 1968/69, 6,000 did not transfer to any postprimary school.[111]

Of the ten thousand who completed senior cycle in 1963, two thousand proceeded to higher education, a pattern which had characterised access to higher education for the previous four decades. The numbers attending university from 1929 to 1965 as shown in Table 12.4 , represent a very low access rate to higher education which did not alter until the seventies. In general in the four decades following the foundation of the state, education beyond the compulsory age of fourteen was not widely available, participation in second level was determined by location and social group and access to higher education was determined by the type of school attended and by socio-economic factors.

Given the absence of a coherent policy on educational opportunity and education provision, the degree of inequality revealed in *Investment in Education* is not surprising. The report drew attention to the number who left school before reaching Primary Certificate level, to the low rate of participation in postprimary and higher education by children of lower social groups and in some counties, to the high rates of early leaving from vocational schools and to a lesser extent from secondary schools.[112] It also emphasised the small proportion of vocational students who reached higher education and the low rate of participation in higher education by many social groups. Variation in participation rates by county was not found to be related to social group composition, income per head or degree of urbanisation; the mechanisms and procedures by which secondary schools are established were found to be the main factors related to Donegal, Cavan, Monaghan, Laois and Kildare having the lowest rates of 13-17 participation.[113]

In the structural and access domains of policy in many systems, equality of opportunity is the megapolicy *par excellence*, to which high political priority is attached. The various policies on promoting equality of opportunity in the past two decades were seldom part of a coherent policy strategy which sought precise objectives in the various sectors of the megapolicy. Such a strategy would seek to identify standards or criteria in equality of access to education, equal-ity of participation and equality of benefit derived. A scheme such as this would seek to eliminate social barriers and geographical constraints which limit access to education, identify economic factors which concentrate participation in postcompulsory and higher education in the upper social groups and those structural and funding factors which determine that some pupils experience ideal educational conditions while others experience unsatisfactory physi-cal conditions and inadequate pedagogical environments.

The measures of the past two decades have removed many of the factors limiting access to education especially those relating to location and opportunity cost, by the physical extension of the school network, the provision of a school transport system and the elimina-tion of school fees in the majority of schools. As has been shown in an earlier chapter (Table 3.4), the reform measures of the sixties produced a significant expansion of participation in the post-compulsory age groups; while one third of those aged 16 were in full-time education in 1964, more than two thirds of a larger cohort were doing so ten years later.

However this expansion though removing much of the inequality of access, has not eliminated some particular kinds of inequality of access. Those living on islands in the Gaeltacht find it difficult to gain access to second level education in their vernacular which does not require early migration to the mainland.[114] School type and school size are powerful determinants of access to higher education; of the cohort which entered postprimary schools in 1975/76, 60% continued to completion of the five year course; 75% of the secondary school students completed while 25% of the vocational students did so.[115] In that cohort the percentage of secondary students who entered higher education was ten times higher than the percentage of vocational students.[116] Further, for students from the Gaeltacht there is no third level institution which offers a range of courses in Irish.

Equality of access does not obtain for students in vocational schools, for those geographically remote or for those whose vernacu-lar or chosen language of instruction in higher education is Irish. Equality of participation as a policy objective requires that, where open access in higher education does not operate, participation by various groups be determined by the social composition of the population. Among the new entrants to higher education in 1980, the students from the higher socio-economic groups predominate, those from the lower groups are predictably under-represented and those from the farmers' group are approximately represented according to their demographic position as illustrated in Table 12.5.[117]

Any effective policy seeking to promote equality of participation involves measures in a number of different policy fields which require a coherent approach to implementation; depending on one's choice of time scale there are two main policy strategies available. In the shorter time scale one could introduce quotas in the admission policy to higher education with competition operating within social groups; if a longer time span is favoured then issues such as access at second level, completion rates and subject availability in different school types and sizes need to be systematically addressed. In effect this entails eliminating the undesirable effects of the existing parallel or binary system at second level by creating a single network of schools where the needs and rights of the individual take precedence over institutional structures. What is most remarkable about the geographical dimensions of educational opportunity is the historical continuity of the inequality. *Investment in education* identified a number of counties as having the lowest participation rates in second level education in 1962. By and large these were the same counties which had the lowest rates of admission to higher education in 1980. The position is illustrated in Fig. 12.2.

Equality of benefit derived, if pursued as a policy objective involves taking measures in a number of policy fields bearing upon the physical and pedagogic environment experienced by students and the benefit they derive from the experience. In effect such a policy is concerned with the quality of the system and the equity in provision obtaining within it. Such a policy requires a structure which is super-institutional and localised, and is concerned with all aspects and levels of the system; the physical conditions of schools, the quality and range of facilities, the curricular range provided and the professional development of staff would fall within the scope of such a policy of equality. This dimension of policy has been virtually absent from the policy process to date; had it been present even in an ineffective form, the inadequate physical conditions in rural schools, tolerated for so long, would not have obtained, the causative link between size of school, annual funding and range of subjects available would have been addressed and the quality of facilities in primary and postprimary schools would have been systematically upgraded.

Equality of opportunity as a megapolicy in the past two decades has not been approached in the manner just outlined but has functioned more as an ill-defined, but politically unassailable, policy slogan, which effectively continued the incrementalism enunciated by Lemass in 1958 at a faster pace. What distinguished the policy of the mid-sixties from the earlier variety was that the rate of expansion was increased dramatically by O'Malley's scheme and by the economic resources available. Open access to second level and free school transport enabled larger percentages of the cohort to continue in full-time education; however they were attending schools which varied substantially in the range of subjects available and in the quality of the facilities.[118] This aspect of inequality is doubly inequitable because the variability is linked to size and type of school and thus penalises children from sparsely populated areas or inner city areas where other infrastructural inequalities already obtain; studies in the seventies and eighties have highlighted the strong positive relationships between the quality and quantity of education received and individual prospects on a rapidly changing labour market.[119]

The two megapolicies examined in this chapter differ fundamentally in some basic ways. While one can pinpoint exactly the route by which the language policy emerged and was placed on the agenda, the policy of equality of opportunity slipped on to the agenda almost unnoticed, by a process of slow diffusion aided by the media and willing politicians who were anxious to be associated with a policy slogan which could not be contraverted. Its precise specification however was avoided lest such would raise consequential measures which were not politically opportune. The language policy however was specified as to its aims and contents at an early stage, had been worked over by many groups and was well formulated by the time it was formally adopted in 1922. It is difficult to establish when, or if, a formal policy decision was taken on equality of educational opportunity; what is quite obvious is that the government decision of 1966 to make investment in educational expansion a major priority, generated a rapid extension of opportunity.[120] This priority became the effective policy which subsumed equality of opportunity as a secondary objective.

The two megapolicies differ also in the extent to which they impinged on other parts of the system and on other policy aspects. In Dror's terms, the language policy did 'determine the postures, assumptions and main guidelines to be followed in developing specific policies'. It so dominated many dimensions of general education policy that, to some politicians and other observers, language policy was synonymous with education policy in the early decades. The equality of opportunity policy on the other hand did not enjoy this wide influence on other policy aspects mainly because its ramifications had not been worked out systematically and because most of its direct implications raised those structural questions which policy generally since 1922 had sought assiduously to avoid. Furthermore, any more radical version of equality of opportunity might not be acceptable in a society governed by a value system which was decidedly conservative.

Finally the megapolicies differ also in their implementation and in their impact. Using the schema devised by Van Meter and Van Horn, the crucial factors influencing implementation of the megapolicies are summarised in Table 12.6. It seems clear that while there may not have been total political unanimity on the language policy, a coherent set of measures was implemented with commitment for a number of decades which would have been significantly improved by rational analysis and effective evaluation. The policy on equality of opportunity however never did enjoy a systematic rational structure or a formal set of measures except for a brief period during which the official commitment was to 'real equality of opportunity'. Ironically there was more relevant research information available in the mid-sixties on inequality of opportunity than there was on the language question; the political imperative however directed that the emerging policy should avoid all 'hard' definitions of equality and that a 'soft focus' policy be adopted.

In relating the policy outcomes to the main 'actors' in the policy process, there is a distinct difference between the two areas of the Irish language and equality of opportunity. Though Fine Gael and Fianna Fáil were effectively *ad idem* on the basic objectives of language policy, Fine Gael as its original begetter and Fianna Fáil having language revival as a major party aim, the parties differed in their willingness to review the policy. Since there were voices within Fine Gael criticising the policy as early as the late twenties, it is highly likely, despite the presence of Ernest Blythe, that the policy would have been reviewed much earlier had not deValera, Fianna Fáil and Deirg come to power in 1932 and continued in office until 1948. The centrality of the language in Fianna Fáil's formal party philosophy and Deirg's strong personal commitment to language revival, ruled out any possibility of de Valera or any of his ministers departing fundamentally from the policy launched by their political opponents in 1922; they were more likely to implement the policy with greater determination. In the last thirty years the stance of the main parties has undergone a fundamental evolution on the language issue; there are now no Ernest Blythes, no Richard Mulcahys or even Eoin MacNeills within the Fine Gael party of the eighties. In the current Fianna Fáil party there may be some whose commitment to the language is beyond question but the party lacks the broad and deep dedication which characterised deValera, Deirg, Aiken and Colley. It seems that the empirical evidence of continuing popular support for the language and its place in the education system will exert pressure on the parties to retain the issue on the agenda but it is highly unlikely that the political will which inspired Ernest Blythe and Tomás Deirg will be replicated among their political successors in the coming decades.

Though the Labour Party was committed to a well-defined policy on equality of opportunity in the twenties, the two main parties did not formally espouse the issue until the sixties. When they did so, much of their rhetoric arose from a competitive pragmatism rather than from any fundamental egalitarianism or republicanism. Even within Fianna Fáil during the sixties the definitions and formulations of the party's policy on equality of opportunity varied significantly among ministers. The pronounced reluctance to specify policy content more precisely possibly arose from that same reality recognised by the Department of Finance in 1935, 'because of the difficulty of providing a suitable reorganisation of schools'. The two megapolicies examined here illustrate in their formulation and implementation some of the general characteristics of the policy process in Irish education. Where the issue lies in the process domain and when the party input is dominant, the policy is implemented with commitment; when the commitment is of the variety which refuses to examine and review policy then the result is a gradual erosion of the policy, sometimes still beneath the umbrella of the original rhetoric. Even when the empirical evidence and data are to hand indicating the appropriate policy measures, as in the case of geographical and social inequalities, the policy process does not respond with alacrity. This is especially so when the issue lies in the structure domain where a distinct inertia is observable in the process, proceeding from the central sensitivity attaching to structural questions in Irish education.

TABLE 12.1

The number of pupils enrolled in secondary schools and the number of such schools 1924/25 and 1948/49.

Year	Secondary Schools	Pupils Enrolled x 10³		
		Boys	Girls	Total
1924/25	278	14.2	8.7	22.9
1948/49	409	24.6	20.7	45.3

Source: *Commission on Youth Unemployment* 1951, 27.

TABLE 12.2

The number of candidates entered for the Intermediate and Leaving Certificate examinations, the ratio of Leaving
Certificate candidates to Intermediate and the percentage
of girls as candidates in each examination for selected years 1925-81.

YEAR	INTERMEDIATE	LEAVING	RATIO %	Inter Girls %	Leaving Girls %
1925	2,903	995	34.2	36.6	25.1
1935	5,803	2,165	37.3	43.7	38.8
1944	8,561	3,591	43.2	43.9	46.8
1954	12,311	6,098	49.5	53.8	48.2
1962	17,390	9,033	51.9	55.0	47.9
1964	19,988	11,651	58.2	54.6	50.1
1969	30,967	18,975	52.8	53.9	52.0
1974	42,220	26,892	63.7	53.0	53.4
1981	52,597	38,366	72.9	52.2	56.0

Source: Compiled from *Tuarascáil na Roinne.*

TABLE 12.3

The fate of the 1958 cohort of primary school leavers as it passed
through second level .   x 10^3

YEAR	SECONDARY	VOCATIONAL	DROP-OUT	TOTAL
Year 1 1958/59	22	12	18	52
Year 2 1956/60	20	14		34
Year 3 1960/61	16			16
Year 4 1961/62	10			10
Year 5 1962/63	10			10

Source: *Investment in Education*, 1, 175.

TABLE 12.4

Full-time and total enrolments in higher education by institution
for selected years 1928-1965.

College	1928/29 FT.	1928/29 TOT.	1938/39 FT.	1938/39 TOT.	1948/49 FT.	1948/49 TOT.	1958/59 FT.	1958/59 TOT.	1965/66 FT.	1965/66 TOT.
U.C.D			2,161	2,271	2,962	3,225	4,218	4,629	6,909	9,227
U.C.C.			853	942	936	1,115	1,275	1,605	2,281	2,957
U.C.G.		3,532	584	669	762	798	915	1,012	1,958	2,044
T.C.D.			1,543	1,594	2,236	2,539	2,268	2,567	2,999	3,295
R.C.S.I.		N.A.	N.A.	N.A.	N.A.	N.A.	601	601	611	611
TOTAL		3,532	5,141	5,476	6,896	7,677	9,277	10,414	14,758	18,134

Source: *Dáil Debates*, 239, 1554.

TABLE 12.5

The social composition of the new student intake to higher education in
1980 and the composition of the national population under 14 years in 1971.

	SOCIAL GROUP		
	Higher	Lower	Farmers
Higher Education intake in 1980	57.4 %	21.5 %	21.1 %
Population under 14 in 1971	25.9 %	53.8 %	20.3 %
Participation ratio	2.21%	0.40%	1.4 %

Source: Clancy, P. *Participation in Higher education*, compiled from Table 6, 19.

TABLE 12.6

The Van Meter and Van Horn factors operating in relation to language policy and equal opportunity in their implementation stages and the relative strengths or absences of these factors.

VARIABLES/FACTORS	LANGUAGE POLICY	POLICY ON EQUAL OPPORTUNITY
1. Standards and Objectives	Partially specified some unrealisitic	Not specified
2. Resources	Adequate in some aspects	Scarce, requires basic policy decisions
3. Disposition of Implementors	Initially favourable later opposed	Official personnel positive but helpless
4. Characteristics of important Agencies	Mistakenly confined to education sector	Lacked official commitment to basic concept
5. Communication and enforcement Activities	Compulsion as an element of policy resisted	Large segment of education system effectively opposed
6. Economic, social and political conditions	Social and political support available for most of period	Political and social support not genuinely in evidence

Source: Compiled by author.

FIGURE 12.1(b)

The number of Secondary School students (x10³) and the numbers in Secondary Schools where the medium of instruction was Irish 1927-73.

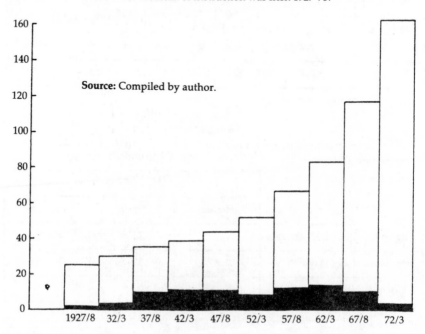

Source: Compiled by author.

FIGURE 12.1(a)

The numbers of National Schools and Secondary Schools whose medium of instruction was Irish 1922-80; National Schools in solid line.

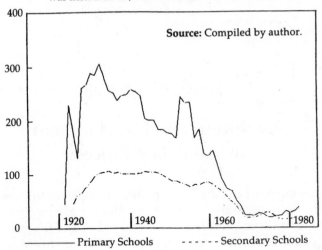

Source: Compiled by author.

——— Primary Schools   - - - - - - Secondary Schools

FIGURE 12.2(a)

Participation rates in full-time education by county in 1962. Age group 13-17.

⬭ : 30%–40%

≡ : 40%–48%

|||| : 49%–52%

National Average: 43.8%

FIGURE 12.2(b)

Admission rates to higher education by county in 1980.

⬭ : 14.5%–17.6%

≡ : 19.0%–21.4%%

|||| : 22.2%–29.0%

National Average: 19.7%

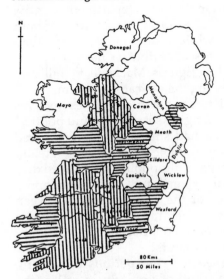

Source: *Investment in Education.*

Source: Patrick Clancy,
Participation in Higher Education, 31.

CHAPTER THIRTEEN

Evolution and Development
in the Policy Process

In the development of education policy throughout this century but especially from the foundation of the state, progress has not been sustained or uniform; the years of World War II and the postwar years up to the late fifties are especially sterile and constitute an effective watershed between the decades following 1922 and the period since the early sixties. It is proposed in this chapter to compare and contrast policy making in the first two decades of independent Ireland and the last two decades. In selecting the limits of the early period, the first two decades of the century beckon attractively as a period of remarkable innovation and lively debate; however the year 1922 offers a more rational baseline and the two decades following constitute a more coherent unit. Moreover these two decades cover the establishment of the Department of Education, the formulation and implementation of the new state's policies and the period of office of Joseph O'Neill, under whose direction the early Department identity was forged. This period too, from 1922 to 1944, offers a view of both main parties in government and while issues more urgent than education occupied those governments' attention, we have an opportunity to observe some of their leading figures, MacNeill, O'Sullivan, Blythe, de Valera and Deirg influencing the education system.

The later period from the early sixties to the mid-eighties involves a different set of political leaders, a changing set of social and political values, a teaching profession which had shaken off its depressed status and an economy which was capable of supplying greater resources to the education of an expanding population. The sixties and seventies witnessed a dramatic expansion of the system and a growing awareness and acceptance of the complex links between education and socio-economic development; during these decades also education began to enjoy an enhanced political role and to figure more prominently in formal political discourse.

It would however be mistaken to see these two periods as standing in stark contrast for they have some points of similarity as well as the obvious major differences. They both involved initiative and the breaking of new ground in policy and administration; furthermore in the formulation of policy, expert committees and other rational approaches were employed. The twenties and thirties witnessed the second attempt in the century to introduce technical education into the system, a policy initiative which was renewed with vigour and success in the sixties and seventies. There are other unexpected lines of similarity in those little-known features of the earlier period which we have come perhaps to associate solely with the later decades.

Evening classes were systematically provided in national schools until 1928 and throughout the twenties continuation and elementary classes were provided for 'juvenile street traders' in urban areas.[1] As early as 1925 school transport was provided in remote areas especially where such a measure obviated the building of new schools.[2] The development of instructional aids was begun in the thirties using radio, films and gramophone records; by 1930 the provision of a bilingual paper for students and teachers similar to the *Journal* of Hugo's Language Institute was under consideration but not proceeded with.[3] The Department of Education in the early decades was not the insular enclave sometimes suggested; it established some international contacts in Europe and the political differences between Belfast and Dublin did not prevent education contacts and occasional cross-border Department visits.[4] Long-term planning was not unknown to the Department staff in the early decades; if the Programmed Budgets of the seventies generated five-year plans, the infant Department was already submitting three-year financial plans to the Department of Finance as early as 1924.[5] Whereas the Department of Finance was frequently criticising the Department of Education for yielding unnecessarily to church pressures, there is also evidence to the contrary within the Department; some questioning occurred of the practice of allocating large national schools to orders on the proposal of Church authorities especially where such orders did not have adequate numbers of qualified teachers.[6] The Department's Irish language policy involved such interesting aspects as corporate Department membership of *The Times* Library in London which provided material for translation and publication; in 1945 its publication record attracted some Welsh publishers who sought permission to translate Irish books into Welsh.[7] The early decades are characterised by a rather more open approach to official information, possibly a legacy from the era of the Commissioners and their meticulous reports. The early annual reports of the Department are remarkably full and candid on policies and institutions and critical of school maintenance to a degree which does not appear in later years; they also included summaries of inspectors' reports, details of all public monies received by individual schools and clear expressions of Department policy, all of which have long since ceased to be features of the annual reports.[8] This openness however did not apparently extend to teachers for it would appear that it was not Department practice to answer letters from individual teachers regarding salary.[9] These early reports, however, are also given to hyperbolic accounts of the success of policies, especially so in regard to language policy.[10] These however are minor features, differences which merely emphasise the pronounced continuity in the major systemic characteristics between the earlier and later periods. That continuity is composed of a few strands, the persistence of some issues, the obvious contrast in structural complexity and policy process and the remarkable stability in the power structure. The absence of comprehensive legislation, size of school, school amalgamations, the physical condition of schools, occur and recur as themes and provide a remarkable link between the periods. The present education system functions on a minimum of legislation and is directed more by ministerial order and Departmental decision than by statutory provision of the Oireachtas. Speaking in the debate on the 1922 Constitution, T. J. O'Connell of the INTO sought to have established in basic law, the right of children to free education up to an age and stage of instruction to be prescribed by law; this was opposed by MacNeill and O'Higgins. When the latter drew attention to the possibility of some people claiming secondary education, Johnson retorted 'Succeeding parliaments will do that'.[11]

If in the seventies and eighties, second level education is available to most children, it is not available by way of individual right established by law of the Oireachtas but by Ministerial and Departmental administrative instrument. Legislation in education though frequently sought and discussed in the later decades was not universally welcome among some of the interest groups mainly because it inevitably raises the structural questions so assiduously and continuously avoided.

Size of school at both primary and secondary level, has been a major issue for almost a century. Reflecting both demographic reality and the denominational school policies pursued in the last century, the large number of small schools has been a persistent feature and has attracted amalgamation policies on a number of occasions. In the twenties, up to 250 small national schools were amalgamated before the policy was abandoned by John Marcus O'Sullivan due to episcopal and managerial resistance to the coeducation which amalgamation sometimes produced.[12] In the sixties following the publication of *Investment in education*, the problem was again highlighted and a policy of amalgamation carried through, despite some opposition from 1965 to 1973 when it was terminated.[13] Despite these various amalgamation measures, in 1980 almost 50% of all national schools were under 100 in enrolment and 22% under 50.[14] The same problem has faced and still faces postprimary schools; in 1932 of the 306 secondary schools only 48 had more than 150 pupils. Data on ten representative secondary schools in the late thirties showed sizes ranging from 48 to 250; all but three showed an annual financial loss.[15] Despite the dramatic increase in postprimary enrolment since 1965 and the official policy on school size, over 20% are under 200 in enrolment.[16] The question of coeducation is no longer seen as a barrier to amalgamation at primary level and at second level, while half of all schools are coeducational, only a quarter of secondary schools are.[17]

The question of the physical conditions of schools has rarely been absent from education debate in the course of this century, figuring in official reports in 1904, 1926 and 1965 and in the policy demands of teachers and politicians.[18] The deep intractability of this problem is possibly linked to the fiscal mechanism by which national schools are funded, the shared responsibility involved between state and local parish and the high significance accorded by the churches to the clerical managership of national schools as a key element of the denominational character of Irish education. Some of the earliest annual reports of the Department comment on falling standards and laxity and 'a general pattern of inadequate maintenance and upkeep'.[19] These early reports draw attention to the wastage of public investment involved and call for serious consideration of the question, a call which is echoed dramatically almost twenty years later by Patrick Smith, Parliamentary Secretary, in a detailed analysis of the question submitted to de Valera, in an effort to promote frank and realistic discussions with the hierarchy.[20] The problem lingered on without a solution being found, prompting the INTO to take industrial action in Co Kerry, where as late as 1969 there were national schools without electricity or running water.[21]

There are some other issues which link the two periods in a continuum, among which educational opportunity and the working conditions of teachers loom large. Admittedly some early measures were taken to overcome geographical inequalities in the twenties, although as late as 1951 children on a Co Cork island had to walk five miles to school because their numbers justified neither reopening their own school nor the provision of transport to the mainland.[22] This issue of extending opportunity and the issue of improving the working conditions of teachers belong more to the later period and constitute part of the major contrast between the periods.

However the policy links which can be identified between the early and later periods, are insignificant compared to the basic and fundamental differences. In a sense one is describing two contrasting periods, with only a few comparable characteristics; the essence of the contrast lies in the greater complexity of the education structure and the quality of the policy process which characterised the periods. In the earlier period the system was relatively undeveloped in the levels beyond primary, had a very basic administrative system and very few organised interest groups except those which had arisen in the last century. Four decades later a very much expanded Department of Education exercises a coordinating role on a much larger institutional network, manned by over forty thousand teachers and attended by almost a million students. The policy process has changed also in a number of fundamental ways; the roles of the state and the Department are enlarged and widely accepted, the number of participant groups has increased and the policy process itself has been systematised if not totally rationalised. Perhaps the extent of the changes would be most apparent to the administrative personnel in the Department of the twenties whose authoritarian relationship to the teacher associations of the period would be totally unacceptable to the unionised and consolidated teacher groups of the eighties who negotiate with the modern Department in a systematic structured fashion and have recourse also to superior national arbitration fora.

A More Complex Structure

The organisational complexity of the Department of Education marks the first major difference. For the first two decades after 1922 the Department of Education was being built up, its personnel drawn from three separate sources; by the sixties the Department had the benefit of four decades of experience, its procedures were well established and its senior officers well versed in civil service protocol.

Though the establishment of the Ministry in 1922 and of the Department in 1924 marked a sharp formal break with the previous regime, in some significant ways there was considerable continuity in the system. The school network and the *ex officio* roles of clergymen and the churches in primary and secondary schools continued unchanged; if after 1924 the major funding came from a central government department on a capitation basis, the new arrangement did not diminish by one iota the autonomy of the schools or modify their system of management. The teaching force in national and secondary schools was not substantially changed either nor indeed, with a few senior exceptions, was the inspectorate of the Department. Independence however did bring some significant modifications especially in the curriculum and in the extent to which a government department with a political head required that the education system and policy be subject to more open political debate. After 1924 a minister was responsible to the Dáil for a voted annual expenditure and his department published a formal report on the working of the system.

The transition from Boards and Commissioners to Minister and Department was however neither smooth nor sharp. In January 1922 on the installation of the Provisional Government, the Commissioners of Intermediate Education were informed by letter from the Chief Secretary that, pending the necessary steps for the transfer of power, existing Departments should continue their work 'without prejudice to the *status quo*'. Some days later, Fionán Lynch, Minister for Education of the Provisional Government, attended a meeting of the

Commissioners to inform them of the policy of the government and to clarify the exact relationship between the Provisional Government and the Board.[23] On the primary side there were however contentious issues on which departing Commissioners and incoming Department officials did not agree; when the established order of seniority among surviving primary inspectors was threatened by the reorganising policy of the government, tempers flared and protesting memoranda were dispatched to the Department of Finance and to the President of the Executive Council.[24] As late as December 1924, separate sets of estimates were presented to the Department of Finance, one from the Commissioners of Intermediate Education and the other from the Deputy Secretary of the Department of Education.[25] In 1923 before the establishment of the Department, the Commissioners issued rules for the annual examinations as usual and sought the consent of the Department of Finance. When the Board of Commisioners passed a resolution to the effect that, as the law stood, they had the exclusive right to prepare examination programmes, the matter was raised in the Dáil where Eoin Mac Neill stoutly denied that the Board had any such power.[26]

The Civil War and its associated political unrest impinged in some places on the education system and delayed the establishment of normality in the schools. In the autumn of 1922 some secondary schools were occupied by government forces and in March 1923 the Minister for Defence ordered that salary be refused to secondary teachers who were suspected of anti-government activity.[27] Teachers suspected of political activity on the Republican side were dismissed from a number of secondary schools in Dundalk and Limerick and as a consequence the schools were threatened with retaliatory action.[28] Apart however from the exigencies of the Civil War, there was considerable confusion between the old structures and the emerging system; there was no common point in time at which the transition from Boards to Department was executed for the different sectors of the system. In 1923 the powers of the former Boards of National Education and Intermediate Education were transferred by order of the Executive Council to Commissioners nominated by the Minister.[29] In each case the two new Commissioners were the incoming Secretary of the Department, Joseph O'Neill and the appropriate most senior official of the Department for Primary and Secondary education, Pádraig Ó Brolcháin and Proinsias Ó Dubhthaigh respectively.[30] The powers of the Commissioners of Education in Ireland, who dealt with Endowed Schools, were transferred to the Minister directly in 1924.[31] Responsibility for technical education was retained by the Department of Agriculture and Technical Instruction until 1927 when an order was made transferring all its functions relating to technical instruction to the Minister.[32] In 1925 the interim Intermediate Education Commissioners were abolished by order of the Executive Council and all their powers and assets transferred to the Minister for

Education.[33]

In relation to primary education the transfer of legal functions was not completed until 1935 when the National Education Commissioners were dissolved and their functions tranferred to the Minister.[34] Despite the establishment of the Department of Education in 1924 it required more than a decade before it had formally acquired all the powers and functions of all the former Boards of Education. There were other structural factors also which impeded the smooth emergence of the Department as a coherent unit; the coexistence and overlap of Dáil Éireann's Aireacht (Ministry) with that of the Provisional Government from early 1922 made it inevitable that when the Free State was established political responsibility for education was shared by a number of groups whose representatives eventually came together in the Department of Education. Thus Seán Ó Ceallaigh ('Sceilg') who was Minister for Education of Dáil Éireann until December 1921, was succeeded by Michael Hayes who remained in office until August 1922; from January to August 1922 Fionán Lynch was Minister in the Provisional Government. Any possible conflict between Dáil Éireann and the Provisional Government was avoided by a pragmatic division of responsibility whereby Michael Hayes covered intermediate and higher education while Lynch was resposible for primary education. Coincidental with the ministerial overlap, there was also the incipient struggles between the residual administrative and professional staffs on the boards and the incoming staff of the Department, introduced at the behest of various Ministers. When in September 1922, Eoin MacNeill was appointed as the Free State's first Minister for Education, some of these difficulties had been resolved and those which survived were quickly settled by the establishment structure imposed on the new Department by Cornelius Gregg and his associates in the Department of Finance.[35]

In contrast with those hectic early days of the Department the situation in the sixties presents a picture of smooth, if perhaps complacent efficiency. Its administrative machinery, grown three-fold from the twenties and spread over a number of centre-city offices, was competent in discharging all the predestined duties of the year from one set of autumnal estimates to another. Its professional personnel, divided into three inspectorates for primary, secondary and vocational education had grown considerably in number especially at postprimary level from the small group who inherited the mantle of the Intermediate and Technical inspectors in 1922. In the early sixties the expansion of the Department role, meant in turn a rapid growth in the inspectorate, the creation of a psychological service, a wider involvement in promoting curricular reform in mathematics, science and modern languages and the introduction of educational television in 1964.[36] The launch of the *Investment in education* survey in 1962, the ministerial policy document of 1963 and the publication of *Investment in education* in 1965 signalled the dawn of a new era for the Department. The Department's role in Irish education had been re-specified as a result of the ministerial and governmental acceptance of a greater state responsibility in education. The state role which Eoin MacNeill was so reluctant to admit or to discharge in 1922 fell to the ministers of the sixties with an urgency which four decades of state indifference had merely emphasised. This urgency and enhanced commitment was expressed in the creation in 1965 of the development and planning branch of the Department, in the detailed county surveys of facilities, in the establishment of comprehensive schools, in the creation of Regional Technical Colleges and National Institutes for Higher Education and the establishment of an administrative structure to promote and develop higher education.[37] The department became involved in promoting research, in various central planning exercises, in organising a school transport system, in creating a national linguistics institute and in promoting a wide array of curricular and innovative projects. The core of this programme of expansion centred on the 'free' education scheme of 1967 and the major drive to promote higher education in the seventies.

The metamorphosis of the system in the sixties is evident not only in the expanded structure and enhanced functions of the Department but also in the status and power of teachers and in the increasing sophistication of the teacher unions and the other interest groups, especially the managerial bodies. The geographical and quantitative expansion of the school network from the twenties to the seventies is clearly evident in Fig. 13.1 and in Table 13.1 which show the growth in secondary and vocational enrolment by province and the growth in the number of secondary schools by county respectively. The number of schools has increased dramatically, more so in Leinster and Munster than in Ulster and Connacht; the number of secondary schools doubled nationally in the half century but that increase was neither uniform between nor within the provinces. The inequality of provision is best illustrated in the case of Co Cavan, which figured among the counties with the lowest rates of participation in second level in 1963 and the lowest rates of entry to higher education in 1980. Throughout all of our earlier period, Co Cavan had only two or three secondary schools, all situated in the town of Cavan, The Royal School (1626), St. Patrick's Diocesan College (1874) and Loreto College (1931), all mainly boarding establishments.[38] By the sixties in County Cavan the provision of secondary schools had risen to seven and the existence also of five vocational schools extended opportunity further. However, we can observe the clear contrast between the early and later periods and also perceive the extent of the stark geographical inequality involved in the provision policies pursued in the past, by examining the degree of provision made for the postprimary population of Co Cavan in the decades since independence. This is done in Table 13.2 which compares the provision of postprimary places as a percentage of the population aged 12-18 for County Cavan and the state for various years between 1926 and 1971. County Cavan as late as 1961 provided places for less than 20% of its postprimary population while the state percentage was 30%; in the seventies the figure had risen to 38% whereas the state provision had risen to 54%. The inadequacy of the postprimary provision in County Cavan has its historical roots in the last century; similar inadequate provision is also found in counties Donegal, Monaghan and Meath.[39]

In the transformation of the education system during the past two decades, the expansion in higher education has been most significant. This has involved quantitative expansion combined with diversification and major structural modifications; the creation of a new technological sector which in 1980 enrolled half of all new entrants constitutes the major contrast with the earlier period.[40] The contrast with the earlier period is further marked by the increased localisation of participation in higher education; this is evident from Table 13.3. which shows the percentage of students at various institutions whose homes were within 30 miles of the institution.

The expansion of the school network in the last two decades has greatly increased the numbers, the status and the negotiating power of teachers within the system. It will be seen from Table 13.4 that in the last fifty years the total number of teachers in the system has more than doubled, secondary teacher numbers have increased by a factor of five almost, and primary teacher numbers have increased by fifty per cent. A most striking feature has been the rapid change in the ratio of lay to religious secondary teachers and the security of tenure which the lay teacher has won within the past three decades. In 1942 lay secondary teachers constituted 40% of the total of secondary teachers; in 1980 they constituted 82% of a teaching force which was four times larger than that of 1942.[41]

Whereas in the earlier period, teachers in general and secondary teachers in particular had little security within the system, spent much of their organisational energy in securing improved working conditions and a right to have their professional voices heard within the system, by the early seventies the teachers had secured by means of their unionised strength a position within the system which they had not enjoyed forty years earlier. The changes can be observed if one compares the INTO strike of 1946 which ended in capitulation by the teachers, to the campaign of 1985/86 in which the united teacher organisations have extracted substantial gains under a government policy change. The enhanced status and professional position of the teacher is also evident in the opening up of administrative positions within religious secondary schools to lay teachers and their membership of management boards; this is certainly a different professional world from that of 1920 when it was not the practice of the Commissioners for National Education to answer letters regarding salary from individual teachers.[42]

The expansion and transformation of the system and its growing complexity is also evident in the development of the various interest groups, especially the groups representing management. Of the twenty managerial bodies which now represent school management at first and second levels, only seven were in existence in 1945; most were created in the sixties.[43] In their response to the policy initiatives of the government in the sixties, the various managerial bodies at second level formed a number of denominational umbrella groups and then created a Joint Managerial Body as the apex of a negotiating structure which is strikingly symmetrical. Many of these umbrella groups established bureaux and professional secretariats to service their member organisations. This structure was not established however without some friction which at times diminished the cohesion especially among and within the denominational bodies. On the Catholic side, the exact role of the managerial bodies *vis-a-vis* the minister and the department was an issue upon which the bishops and some clerical leaders of the leading managerial bodies did not share a common viewpoint. By the end of the sixties however it had been established beyond doubt that the bishops and the minister constituted the primary forum for consultation after which the managerial bodies and the department would take up the consultative process within the limits established by the earlier senior consultations. In that sense there was little change in the protocol of church-state consultation on education over the sixty years from 1922, in respect of which there was little to distinguish Eoin MacNeill from P. J. Hillery on the question of ecclesiastical consultation and episcopal sanction for policy initiatives. The difference between them was that while MacNeill admitted that he yielded without question to clerical opinion on education policy issues, Dr Hillery, when asked in the Dáil why he did not consult the teacher organisations prior to announcing his 1963 plan, replied as follows:

> Matters of fundamental policy must be formulated on the sole responsibility of the minister concerned and with, where necessary, government approval. There could be no question of submitting such matters to outside bodies prior to their promulgation.[44]

This seems an admirable statement of the theory of ministerial primacy in policy formulation, except that in his press statement of 20 May 1963, the minister had said in relation to the proposed comprehensive schools:

> In the areas concerned the vast majority or perhaps all of the pupils will be Catholics and having regard to the rights of parents, who, in relation to the fundamental principles of education, are represented by the Church, and in view of the Church's teaching authority, I have had consultation, which is proceed-

ing, with the Catholic hierarchy on the management of these schools.[45]

Most, if not all ministers in all governments have observed this established protocol and have moulded policy according to the reactions received; John Marcus O'Sullivan on vocational education, Deirg and de Valera on Gaeltacht schools, Mulcahy on the Council of Education and Faulkner on community schools have observed the same procedure as MacNeill and Hillery. The developments and expansion of the sixties have not modified the order of precedence within the interest groups.

Despite such continuity there was some surprising friction and controversy involved at times in the education debate of the later period. The policy document of October 1970 on community schools, discussed prior to publication with the Catholic hierarchy, aroused considerable controversy both for the policy's contents and for the manner of its promulgation.[46] In December 1971 a group of clergymen from all denominations formally petitioned President deValera to have the proposals modified.[47] Public meetings organised in five towns in which community schools were planned, in June 1971, were used by some groups to whip up local animosity towards the Department, whose officials were pilloried by hysterical spokesmen.[48] The World Bank, source of the capital finance for the community schools, was castigated as an agency whose philosophy was foreign to traditional values and such rational measures as the amalgamation of small schools were criticised as being influenced by foreign education systems.[49] The campaign against structural reorganisation reached distasteful levels occasionally when anonymous pamphleteering poured forth venomous criticism of the department and those who supported reform.[50] These manifestations however should not be taken as representative of the system as a whole, where within a few years, following the turbulent sixties, the expanded system had settled down to its new-found equilibrium, finding no difficulty in welcoming the community schools.

The education system in the last two decades bears little relationship in terms of scale, structural complexity or geographical coverage to the system in the earlier period. In the policy process however, while some changes have occurred, the contrast between the earlier and later periods has not been so marked. It is true that some of 'the idealism and utopianism' for which there was little use and scope in the twenties emerged at times in the sixties and entered the policy debate. It is also true that under a variety of influences the larger political parties gave a higher political priority to education from the early sixties, a priority which historically echoes the urgency with which education questions were addressed in the twenties. Eoin MacNeill's 'clear educational highway' of 1925 is quite similar to the ideal structure presented in Brian Lenihan's *All Our Children* of 1969 except that neither structure conferred any basic education rights beyond those contained in the statute governing compulsory school attendance.[51]

As between the policy process in the two periods there is very little to choose on the score of rationality. The use of planned programme budgeting in the Department of Education in the late sixties may suggest that policy formulation and the related analysis were conducted as a result on a new level of rationality; however, the implementation of the programme budget was constrained by a number of resource and internal attitudinal factors which may have prevented the exercise from promoting 'a more questioning approach, an increased questioning of objectives, a consideration of alternatives and an effort to gauge the success of policies'.[52] There are significant differences in the policy process between the earlier and the later periods in relation to the range and intensity of the policy debate and especially as to the content of policy. The public debate on education as represented in articles, news reports, editorials and letters to the editor in the first two decades of the century was quite extensive in newspapers, the journals of the teacher organisations and the professional journals; in the thirties and forties the debate was confined mainly to the teacher journals with the newspapers rarely covering education topics except at conference time or in relation to major political speeches or the Irish language. In the later period however, from the late fifties onwards, popular interest in education grew rapidly as a result of increased coverage in the newspapers of various aspects of the education system and repeated calls for reform and innovation. This extensive coverage continued in the three main Dublin dailies throughout the sixties although not to the same extent in all three; the *Irish Independent* gave the least coverage, *The Irish Times* gave the greatest, while the *Irish Press* tended to carry most coverage of topics on language policy.[53] Table 13.5 shows the pattern of the articles and letters published by the *Irish Times* over the period; those reflect a growing public interest in a wide variety of topics but in their general pattern reflect also the main current policy issues in second and third level as they arose.[54] There was little concern with primary education but a major coverage of issues on secondary, vocational, comprehensive and community schools and of questions on higher education bearing upon university mergers and new institutions.[55]

This intensive coverage of education issues in the daily press indicated and perhaps helped to generate a growing interest in education policy, an interest which is reflected also in the growing high place accorded to it in political debate, as reflected in the parliamentary questions tabled in the Dáil. Table 13.6 shows the number of education issues covered in the Dail questions asked in three different periods since 1922, during which time the total number of questions has risen dramatically and the dominant categories have changed also.[56] In the period 1922/32, the topics which figured most prominently were the physical condition of national schools, the employment conditions of teachers and the Irish language. It will be seen that the range of topics covered by the questions is much wider in the sixties than in the earlier period; this changing emphasis corresponds with the quantitative expansion of the system in the later period and the rather narrow policy perspectives which prevailed in the twenties and the thirties. This is borne out by the specific question categories which did not figure earlier but are present in the sixties, equality of opportunity, funding levels, school transport, the new policies on second level, higher education, adult education and the educational needs of the handicapped. The strong presence in the later period of questions on school buildings reflects both a decline in concern with national schools and a growing local political interest in the large number of new postprimary schools built under the policy adopted from 1964 onwards. The dramatic decline in certain categories, Irish language and school attendance especially, relfects the shift in political attitudes towards the language policy and the improvement in attendance and participation throughout the period.

The press coverage of education in the sixties and the emphasis accorded to education issues in the Dáil questions both testify to the higher level of public debate which surrounded the policy process in the later period. In the decades after 1922 a very limited number of interested politicians participated in policy discussions, whereas in the sixties the participants involved not just a wider political circle but a larger segment of a more concerned and informed electorate.

The content of policy in the sixties shows a wider range of topics addressed than in the twenties and thirties. Despite the general conservatism of the period after 1922, within the education system itself there was a high degree of enthusiasm and dedication especially within the Department of Education.[57] This enthusiasm generated an urge to reform the entire system, at least administratively, an urge which was reflected in the various commissions and committees established in the first decade to examine different aspects of the system. However, apart from the curricular aspects of first and second level, the establishment of the vocational system and the question of school attendance, little political attention was paid to other questions which were widely discussed. Among these issues the role of parents in controlling the system, equality of opportunity, a Council of Education and linking teacher training to university qualifications are good examples. Eoin MacNeill appealed to deputies to bring home to the people 'that the sovereign power over their own education was at last come to the people of Ireland', when he, as minister was not sure if he could ask schools for information and some deputies were uncertain whether secondary education fell within the minister's brief and whether Dáil Éireann could discuss policy on secondary education.[58] Nothing was attempted on many of the issues discussed and their incorporation in policy did not occur until the later period except for the Council of Education which was established in 1950.

The questions of higher and adult education present further examples of issues which were effectively absent from the policy perspective of the early period, though much discussed at the time. Adult education enjoyed a new popularity in Europe in the twenties, prompted mainly by the revived Grundtvig movement in Scandinavia. Some inspectorial contacts were established in Denmark, appeals were made in the Dail for university extension courses but there was little policy response; indeed some of the adult and evening provision existing from the older system were terminated in the late twenties.[59] Policy in higher education in the twenties was limited in its scope, concentrating on aspects of agriculture and Irish language policy in the National University. Trinity College, already suffering a double isolation, political and denominational, seldom figured in policy except in official attempts to discontinue a special funding which had originated in 1918; efforts to agree on some permanent funding basis were not concluded until after 1940, when that special funding was discontinued.[60] Since the government had no policy on higher education throughout the early period, a situation which continued to the sixties, the development of the universities was effectively a matter for the individual institutions. Thus when in 1926 the library of the Commissioners of National Education, containing the valuable Starkie collection, was given to University College Dublin, rather than to Trinity College, the gesture indicated the power exercised by University College in the Free State administration as well as the political decline of the college with which Starkie was connected.[61] The official nonexistence of Trinity College in the early period is further confirmed by the efforts made in 1949 to prevent it from providing courses in the social sciences funded by the government; the President of University College Cork, sought to extract Department of Education support for his own college to supply such courses in the Dublin area if University College Dublin were not interested.[62]

Such incidents, however, testify more to the absence of policy on higher education rather than to the character of such a policy; throughout all of the early period there was little concern with higher education as the reality of educational opoportunity placed the immediate policy priority at a much lower level on MacNeill's 'clear educational highway'. Apart from any other considerations, cost considerations alone would have excluded higher education from any realistic policy agenda; similar constraints effectively ruled out any systematic provision for adult education except in so far as the vocational system had from the outset provided a network of courses under its normal schemes. Adult education and higher education had to await the seventies and eighties to be given a policy role in which they were taken seriously, funded accordingly and provided with appropriate structures.[63]

Besides encompassing a wider content range, the policy process in the later period also involved a wider network of interest groups and followed a more structured procedure. This is evident as early as 1965 in the wider range of groups which responded to *Investment in education* than normally were involved in the policy process; it is also present in the large number of interest groups who have responded to the recent discussion documents of the Curriculum and Examinations Board. Perhaps the contrast between the policy process of the earlier period and that of the present is most vividly illustrated if we compare the process from which the Vocational Education Act of 1930 emerged and the policy procedures followed in 1986 in connection with the Government's green paper on local education structures and autonomy for Regional Colleges.[64]

The Commission on Technical Instruction of 1926, examined the existing system aided by foreign experts and made a comprehensive set of proposals concerning the establishment of an alternative second level provision funded jointly by the state and the local authorities. The report of the commission attracted some public debate, confined mainly to those already involved in the education system. The process by which the proposals of the 1926 report became the provisions of the 1930 Act was the rather simple triangular one involving the Department of Education, the Department of Finance and the Cabinet; in personal terms the Act was the creation of John Ingram of the technical instruction branch of Education and Walter Doolin of Finance who between them forged a measure which met the objections and overcame the reservations of those in the Departments of Finance and Local Government who were opposed to the act.[65] Following the passing of the act, various limitations were placed upon the system by the Department of Finance and by the Minister for Education at the behest of the Catholic bishops.[66] The fate of the system since 1930 has been determined by those constraints and by the ambivalent differential social attitudes generated towards the secondary and vocational systems.

When the Minister for Education in 1985 issued a green paper on local structures in the system, she was courageously breaking new ground in two respects, firstly in the use of the paper to promote public policy discussion and secondly in addressing a topic which had been avoided in Irish education since McPherson's Bill of 1919. Publication was followed by oral and written submissions from a wide variety of bodies, interest groups and individuals. These interactions of late 1985 were followed by a second series of consultations in 1986 and it was proposed to have draft legislation prepared during the year.[67] Should this policy measure succeed and result in legislation establishing regional or Local Education Councils, it will mark a distinct difference between the earlier and the later periods.

TABLE 13.1

The growth in the number of secondary schools by county and province
between 1926 and 1971.

	1926	1931	1936	1941	1946	1951	1956	1961	1966	1971
COUNTRY	288	306	330	360	393	434	481	542	588	590
ULSTER	15	18	17	16	16	22	22	28	34	27
Cavan	2	3	3	3	3	4	3	5	7	7
Donegal	5	7	6	5	5	8	10	13	17	12
Monaghan	8	8	8	8	8	10	9	10	10	8
MUNSTER	96	97	114	138	146	161	177	199	206	197
Cork	36	36	38	47	52	62	65	75	81	79
Waterford	12	12	16	18	16	16	16	17	18	19
Kerry	9	9	9	12	17	19	25	29	28	26
Clare	6	7	8	10	11	11	12	13	15	13
Limerick	16	16	22	28	28	31	33	36	34	31
Tipperary	17	17	21	23	22	22	26	29	30	29
LEINSTER	142	154	158	159	174	189	212	234	257	278
Louth	7	7	8	9	11	11	12	13	14	14
Meath	5	8	9	8	8	10	11	11	11	9
Dublin	63	73	71	73	81	87	101	111	131	151
Wicklow	6	6	6	7	8	8	11	12	12	11
Wexford	14	14	14	13	13	12	12	12	12	14
Kildare	8	7	9	9	9	10	11	14	14	18
Carlow	7	7	7	7	7	7	7	7	7	8
Kilkenny	7	6	7	7	8	9	9	9	9	10
Laois	7	7	7	7	7	7	10	10	10	10
Offaly	7	6	7	7	8	9	7	11	11	10
Westmeath	9	10	10	9	10	14	13	14	17	16
Longford	3	3	3	3	4	5	8	10	9	7
CONNACHT	35	37	41	47	57	62	70	81	91	88
Galway	14	14	15	17	21	25	27	35	39	37
Mayo	13	13	15	17	20	21	23	26	27	26
Sligo	5	5	5	5	7	7	8	8	10	9
Leitrim	1	1	1	1	3	3	5	5	7	5
Roscommon	2	4	5	7	6	6	7	7	8	11

Moreover such a measure would constitute a critical watershed in policy development in this century, during which after 1922 questions of structure were studiously avoided lest they provoke politically undesirable church opposition. Such a development when and if it comes may offer a solution to what the Minister described in 1930 as 'the peculiar nature of our particular problems'.[68]

The policy process has undergone some fundamental changes in the course of this century, mainly in the characteristics of the process itself and also arising from the greater complexity of the system. The number of participant groups or interest groups has increased dramatically; while all those groups do not enjoy equality of involvement in the policy process, that process is no longer the simple binary model which obtained at the beginning of the century. During the last two decades the interest groups have developed more complex organisations and more active mechanisms for mutual support, including mechanisms which span the denominational divide. This recent expansion of the policy process, which included for the first time parent representatives and elements of the socio-economic system, has not altered the central reality that the policy process in Irish education is dominated by an alliance of the churches and the state. Such an alliance makes it extremely difficult for the process to address those structural problems which have characterised the system for most of the century.

TABLE 13.2

The population aged 12-18 years, the number of places in secondary and vocational schools expressed as a percentage of that population for the state and for Co. Cavan for selected years 1926-1971.

			1926	1936	1946	1961	1966	1971
	Population 12-18		407,204	385,776	359,670	365,841	381,381	396,398
STATE	School Places	Sec.	21,258	35,875	42,927	80,400	103,558	156,869
		Voc.	7,925	13,138	14,170	27,406	38,467	56,592
		TOTAL	29,183	49,013	57,097	107,806	142,025	213,421
	% Provision		7.1%	12.7%	15.9%	29.5%	37.2%	53.8%
	Population 12-18		10,892	9,936	8,236	6,985	6,875	6,853
County CAVAN	School Places	Sec.	112	366	453	732	6,875	1,517
		Voc.	—	440	348	487	662	1,089
		TOTAL	112	806	801	1,219	1,681	2,606
	% Provision		1.0%	8.1%	9.7%	17.4%	24.4%	38.0%

Source: Compiled from Departmental and Census Data.

TABLE 13.3

The percentage of students attending various university institutions whose homes were within thirty miles of the institution for various years 1938-1965.

Year	U.C.D.	U.C.C.	U.C.G.	T.C.D.
1938/39	33%	54%	58%	—
1948/49	31%	33%	49%	—
1958/59	52%	54%	43%	28%
1965/66	54%	64%	41%	27%

Source: *Dáil Debates,* 239, 1554.

TABLE 13.4

The numbers of teachers employed full-time in different school types for 1928-29 and 1980-81:   x 10³.

School Type	National School	Secondary School	Vocational School	Community and Comprehensive	TOTAL
1928-29	13.6	2.4	—	—	16
1980-81	19.4	11.7	5.7	1.2	38

Source: *Tuarascáil na Roinne Oideachais.*

TABLE 13.5

The number of articles and letters on education published in *The Irish Times* for the years 1963, 1969 and 1971 by level of education.

LEVEL	1963	1969	1971
Primary	28	9	10
Post-Primary	187	146	372
Higher	318	431	423
TOTAL	533	586	805

Source: Unpublished Survey Data.

TABLE 13.6

The questions tabled in the Dáil on education, classified by issues
for the periods 1922-32, 1932-48 and 1960-69.

CATEGORIES	1922-32		1932-48		1960-69	
	N	%	N	%	N	%
Access and School Attendance	17	7.8	62	16.1	—	—
Irish Language	38	17.4	102	26.5	20	2.3
Teacher Working Conditions	54	25.0	105	27.2	59	7.0
Curriculum and Examinations	13	6.0	28	7.2	100	11.9
Teacher Training and Preparatory Colleges	20	9.25	22	5.7	19	2.2
Vocational Education	20	9.2	28	7.2	—	—
School Buildings	56	25.7	38	9.9	453	54.0
Funding	—	—	—	—	27	3.2
Special Education	—	—	—	—	28	3.3
Higher Education	—	—	—	—	101	12.1
Educational Opportunity	—	—	—	—	84	10.0
New Policies	—	—	—	—	110	12.3
TOTALS	218	100	385	100	838	100

Source: *Dáil Debates* for years involved.

FIGURE 13.1

Enrolments in secondary and vocational schools by province in the period 1931-71
expressed in units of one hundred pupil places.
The secondary data are represented by the hatched columns.

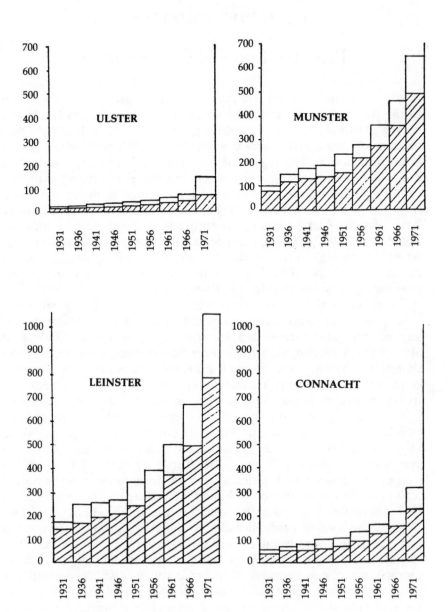

CHAPTER FOURTEEN

Possible Lines of Development

Having examined the contributions of interest groups, the evolution of the policy process, and the impact of the policies pursued in the course of this century, it is possible to make some concluding observations and to identify some possible lines of future development in education policy. The legacy of the nineteenth century has been a major factor in forming and influencing the policy process in this century; the patterns of power and patronage and the structural formulae which emerged from the controversies of the last century have played central roles in determining the agenda of education debate since 1900. It is also most probable that the major policy issues which are emerging within the system in the closing decades of the twentieth century will colour the development of policy and provision for much of the next four or five decades.

The nature of the controversies of the last century and the particular solutions which were applied not only yielded a particular power structure but also determined that these structures especially at first and second levels would acquire a central symbolic significance. The dominance by the churches and the state of the system for most of this century meant that while education was not a high profile policy area in the orthodox sense, nevertheless education, its control and its inherited structures constituted a complex central element of Irish political life. Examples abound throughout the century, from 1907 to very recent times, which illustrate the extreme sensitivity of the symbiotic relationship between the churches and the state in education policy. The subordination and mono-integration which characterise the church-education link may, according to Archer, diminish the involvement of other entitled groups in the policy process, depress the level of professional autonomy and promote an inertial complacency. Throughout most of this century especially since 1922, the system operated within a political milieu which showed no enthusiasm for empirical examination of policy effectiveness and was generally unaware of the functional weaknesses of the system. The issue of educational opportunity offers a clear example; egalitarian principles seldom if ever governed the formulation of policy and this may have been due equally to the conservative social value system, to the inefficiency of the policy process and to the political reluctance to entertain policy proposals which raised questions of structural change.

The manner in which separate school systems developed in the last century at first and second levels, reinforced the fragmentation of the system which had arisen from the rejection of local popular control. The institutional and administrative focus of the system emphasised the link between central authority and the individual local institution and depressed the concept of a localised education network of schools which discharge a collective responsibility towards a community. This phenomenon arising as early as the post-Powis decades, encouraged the proliferation of small school units and merely aggravated the effects of the demographic reality in many rural areas. Size of school has been a central policy issue in this century but has seldom attracted measures other than those designed to centralise and amalgamate.

The other major legacy from the last century concerns the emphasis upon the process aspects of policy and the associated central role ascribed to the external examinations. The centre of gravity of policy throughout most of the period under study, especially during the middle decades, lay firmly within the process dimension concerned with curriculum, syllabus, prescribed courses and the conduct of examinations. The tight centralised control, the instructional legacy of 'payment-by-results' and the political avoidance of structural and access policies produced an education ethos which viewed the process mainly, if not totally, in terms of examination success.

These various influences and systemic characteristics, derived from the last century, still manifest themselves in the policy process; some indeed exercise a dominant role in determining the quality of the education provided. The policy process is unbalanced in the range of inputs involved and in the mechanism for agenda construction; political parties, professional educators, parents and representatives of social and economic life should have a structured opportunity to participate in the policy process in a central meaningful manner. The education system of a society is of such importance, nationally and individually, that, democratic considerations aside, the quality of the policy process can only be improved by a balanced range of inputs.

The quality of the policy process needs to be improved in some major aspects. Unlike many other public policy areas, education needs a long lead-time to manifest desired outcomes; consequently policies need to be worked out and implemented consistently over periods of decades rather than years. This requires a degree of rationality in the process which has too seldom been present in the system in this century. The availability of adequate empirical research information and the existence of a systematic local and national planning mechanism, strengthen the rational complexion of the policy process.

The policy process to be effective must adopt a global perspective which sees the various elements of the system as operating in a coherent manner, somewhat in terms of the 'clear highway' advocated in 1925. The present fragmented nature of the system which functions more like a number of autonomous sub-systems, is reflected faithfully in the fragmentation of policy. This structural segmentation is reinforced by the absence at local and regional levels of a structure which would give organisational reality to the unity and continuity of the education process.

The most rationally coherent policy can be reduced to inefficiency by the quality of the attention given to the measures planned in the implementation stage. The policy process as it operated during this century offers some very vivid examples of admirable policy measures being launched without any detailed analysis being conducted of the factors influencing implementation. New curricular developments in primary and postprimary schools, admirable in their conception and philospohy, run the risk of reaching only part of the system because their implementation has not been related to the reality of small school units. In a system where the staffing and annual resource income of a school are determined on a capitation principle, the quality of the education provided is normally a linear function of school size and hence of geographical location. This particular problem illustrates the need for cohesion in the general policy; despite generous funding, curricular reform may frequently fail dismally because aspects of school organisation, funding mechanism, or staffing policies are not included in the implementation strategy. A realistic policy on equality of opportunity would not only promote equal access to and participation in the system but would ensure that a capitation funding mechanism did not differentiate between the curricular range and the quality of facility available to the students in schools of different sizes. In a centralised system such as ours, the inequality suffered by sparsely populated areas deriving from capitation funding can be aggravated by the absence of an intermediate administrative mechanism between the national centre and the individual school. In general our highly centralised system permits the policy process to operate on an inverse rule basis so that the application of a policy diminishes according to distance from the capital.

Throughout most of this century participation in the education policy process has been unbalanced and limited; contributions to the process have never been equally shared among the various groups with entitlement to participate. Given the central importance of establishing viable organic links between the education system and other sectors of the social fabric, it would seem eminently desirable to create a body with responsibility for the policy process in education which would seek to accomodate a wider range of policy inputs. Such a body would provide a forum for those interest groups whose present policy role is diminished or absent, especially parents whose constitutional rights in education have been historically ignored. Creating such a policy body will not detract in any way from the ultimate political responsibility of the relevant minister or diminish the central role of the churches as a major interest group. A statutory policy body would seek to promote a balance in the policy process, to generate a global perspective and to develop a rational cohesion in the system. In doing so, a national policy council or commission would help to diminish the complexity, increase the efficiency and enrich the public dimension of a process which is of vital concern to all.

Teachers have devoted most of their organised professional energies during this century to securing satisfactory working conditions; consequently much of their involvement in the process has been devoted to issues which could have been settled much earlier had the process and the system been rationally organised. Having, within the past two decades, achieved a satisfactory professional status within the system, teachers have begun to exert a major influence on the policy process. They have enlarged the range of policy issues of interest to them and have thereby established themselves as a major force in the policy process.

The managerial bodies have played a major role in the process throughout this century; this role has frequently been diminished by the ambiguity attaching to the role identity of these bodies. Though essentially they are the organisations which own, manage or administer the schools, they are in addition usually subservient bodies of the churches to which they are linked in various ways. This dual identity can at times diminish their potential as policy contributors and may sometimes reduce their autonomy; the controversies of the sixties served to highlight the relative status of the managerial bodies and their superior church bodies in a manner which helped to clarify the process. Despite any ambiguity surrounding their status in recent times, the managerial bodies have been major influences on policy throughout the century.

Parents, political parties and representatives of the socio- economic system have not figured as active participants in the policy process; the low level of involvement by the major parties is self-imposed and governed by the universal rule of party interest and strategy. The inclusion of the voices of industry, the economy and the trade unions seems compellingly logical in a society whose education system has been divorced from the world of work for most of this century.

The creation of a National Parents' Council in 1985 offers parents a mechanism whereby they can contribute to the formulation and implementation of education policy. The absence of a local education structure renders such a national forum centrally important in representing those whose rights in education, though guaranteed by the state and the churches, have been effectively ignored.

Given the unbalanced nature of the policy process in education throughout most of this century, both in its emphasis on some policy sectors and the exclusion of some legitimate interest groups, there is an urgent need to establish a mechanism and identify a strategy which would raise the quality of the process while also extending the list of participants.

A National Policy Council would be broadly representative of all the interests involved in education, would not exercise any administrative or executive functions within the system and could exist administratively either within the Department, attached to the Minister's office or enjoy an autonomous existence but working in close liaison with the Department. It should be sufficiently resourced to commission policy studies from which it could offer a range of policy options to the minister. Similar councils operate with great success in a number of European countries and have significantly enriched the policy process.

The creation of such a Council could be very cost effective in increasing productivity in a policy sector which is among our higher areas of public expenditure. Its existence would not imply any diminution of the role of the Department of Education; on the contrary the Department's decision-making role would thereby operate on a more rational and coherent range of options. In a period when economic reality renders it unlikely that the public resources for education will be maintained at the levels of the past decades, it is imperative that the participant groups within the system reach a working consensus on the ordered application of the available resources. A National Policy Council offers one mechanism for developing such a constructive consensus.

APPENDIX 1

Letter from Seoirse Ó Colla, T.D., Minister for Education, to the Authorities of Secondary and Vocational Schools, January 1966.

A Cháirde,

In the course of discussions which I have had recently with the various educational bodies, proposals for the improvement of our postprimary system were examined and a very considerable degree of unanimity arrived at. It seems to me that we are now at the stage when the future policy of my department should be outlined to all concerned in the provision of postprimary education. I write accordingly to you because I look to you to accord me your full cooperation in the effort to provide for every pupil, to the greatest extent which our resources will allow, an education suited to his needs and aptitudes.

It is a truism that education is a unity. Its focus is on the student as an individual and its aim from the beginning is to direct, to guide, to lead out the pupil's resources, moral and mental, so that he may develop the proper use of all his talents. Emphasis on the mode or means may change as the pupil passes from childhood into manhood but the aim and purpose are constant.

Such an aim and purpose call for equality of educational opportunity for all. My concern in writing to you here is the achieving of such equality in the postprimary phase.

Before proceeding with this theme, however, I wish to record my appreciation and admiration of the initiative and enterprise displayed by the school authorities, secondary and vocational. As a result of their efforts there are at present in this country some 600 Secondary schools and some 300 Vocational schools, so that it is now possible to envisage as a practical proposition in the near future the provision of postprimary education for all the children of the country; more than that, to envisage the provision of an education suited to the many different aptitudes and abilities of these children.

The government has already signified its intention to raise the school-leaving age by the end of the decade. This step will create problems of accommodation and teaching power as well as of curriculum content. The solutions to the problems must be found

393

before the raising of the school-leaving age becomes effective and it is my intention to seek them without delay. But the first step must be to consider how the facilities now available can be used to best advantage.

Hitherto, for reasons which it is not necessary to examine here, secondary schools and vocational schools pursued their educational endeavours along widely separated paths; indeed they formed two separate systems, each with its own schools, its own curricula and courses of study, its own examinations and its own cadre of teachers. The secondary system offered courses of an academic nature almost entirely, while those offered by the vocational system were mainly of a practical nature, the student opting for either system of his choice, regardless of where his abilities lay. Those suited to the system received an excellent educational service, those not suited, in number not inconsiderable, made the best they could of it.

There are two good reasons, at least, for urging that the barriers between the systems be broken down: first, the denial of a suitable education tends towards frustration in the pupil; second, our national survival demands the full use of all the talents of our citizens.

The first steps in this direction have already been taken. It has been decided that from 1969 the Intermediate Certificate examination will be open to candidates from the secondary and vocational schools in common. New courses have been added and the subject syllabuses are being revised. The courses and syllabuses thus revised will be issued during the current school year and will be effective for both secondary and vocational schools in September 1966. Since the courses will require a minimum of three years' study - on which the pupils will generally enter between the ages of twelve and thirteen - the present day continuation course in vocational schools is being extended from two to three years.

I should say here that it is not intended that the Day Group Certificate Examination, now available to pupils in Vocational schools, will be discontinued. That examination, within its present subject limits, will remain and will as heretofore be available to pupils of the Vocational schools. The common syllabus for the Group Certificate Examination and the Intermediate Certificate examination enables me to allow pupils from Secondary schools who propose to take up apprenticeship-training before completing the Intermediate Certificate course to present for the Day Group Certificate Examination on the completion of the second year of their course.

Furthermore, pupils who take the Intermediate Certificate Examination but who do not pass in sufficient subjects to earn the award of the Intermediate Certificate may be awarded the Group Certificate on the results of that examination if they are successful in the subjects appropriate to the Group Certificate course. These steps will establish a common standard for all postprimary schools. Moreover, they are necessary preliminaries to our main task which, as I have said earlier, is providing, to the best of our ability, an education suited to his needs and talents for every student.

As you are aware, my department is at present engaged in a survey of the facilities available in all postprimary schools in this country. This survey, when completed, together with the information already available in regard to school population, will enable us to answer in regard to any area in the country such questions as (1) What is the number of pupils for whom postprimary provision is needed? (2) What facilities are needed to provide for these pupils? (3) What facilities are already available in the area? (4) What additional facilities are needed? The processing of the information so collected will take some considerable time, I feel we cannot afford to wait.

While the time has come when the operation of two rigidly separated postprimary systems can no longer be maintained, this is not to say that the secondary or the vocational school need lose its distinctive character. What I have in mind is that there should be a pooling of forces so that the shortcomings of one will be met from the resources of the other, thus making available to the student in either school the postprimary education best suited to him. For example, the vocational school could offer facilities for the teaching of woodwork to pupils of the secondary school while that school would give facilities for the teaching of Science to the pupils of the vocational school. The provision of any necessary additions to the existent facilities would be by arrangement with the authorities of both schools.

As you are aware, comprehensive schools are in the course of erection in three localities - Cootehill, Carraroe and Shannon. These schools will provide postprimary education for all pupils in their areas. They will offer a very broad curriculum, comprising both academic and vocational disciplines. The services of psychological as well as teaching personnel will be available to guide the pupils in regard to the courses of study best suited to their abilities. Apart from their local importance these schools are of general significance because they will signpost the way to an integrated postprimary system of education. Let me add that I do not anticipate that the number of public comprehensive schools will be very great. My aim is that secondary and vocational schools, by the exchange of facilities and by other forms of collaboration, should make available a curriculum broad enough to serve the individual needs of all their students, and thereby to provide the basis of a comprehensive system in each locality.

The extent and nature of the cooperation between schools will be governed largely by local circumstances but it is suggested that an approach might be made on the following lines:

(1) In each locality the authorities of the secondary schools (including secondary tops) and the vocational schools should confer and formu-

late proposals on the utilisation of existing accommodation or facilities and, where necessary, the provision of additional facilities.

(2) That the Department of Education be represented at such conference by a member of the department's inspectorate (primary, vocational or secondary). The functions of the department's representative would be to help the school authorities in their consideration of the problem and to transmit to the department for approval any arrangement proposed for the interchange of facilities.

(3) That the following points be considered at the conference:

(a) Are there any general classrooms or special subject rooms not being fully utilised at present in any of the schools and, if so, to what extent would it be possible for pupils from other schools to use these rooms?

(b) Would it be feasible to make ad hoc arrangements of a temporary or improvised nature to provide additional accommodation and other facilities where such are not at present adequate?

(c) Taking the needs of the schools collectively, are additional facilities necessary and how and where could they most effectively be provided?

(d) Is the teaching potential in the area being utilised to best advantage? The possibilities of a greater degree of specialisation through interchange of teachers might be explored in this regard.

(e) Would it be feasible to introduce the teaching of such subjects as Art, Music, Woodwork etc., where they are not already taught, if a teacher, or teachers, were employed to serve all the schools in the area.

(f) Could the interchange of pupils between one school and another - one secondary school and another, or a secondary school and a vocational school - for particular subjects be arranged, if such were desirable?

(g) If there are obstacles in the way of an interchange which would be desirable in the interest of the pupils concerned and of the better utilisation of resources, how might such obstacles be overcome?

(h) Would it be feasible to form a class, composed of both secondary and vocational school pupils, for a particular subject, where the provision of that subject would not be justified in terms of the numbers seeking it in either school taken separately?

Problems will arise. Indeed, I am already aware of some of the difficulties in the way of effective cooperation and collaboration. Insofar as these problems concern my Department I do assure you that I will use all the resources available to me to find satisfactory solutions. The welfare of the pupil is our common purpose and I am confident that with mutual goodwill and cooperation we cannot fail to improve our educational system and offer better opportunities to all the pupils in our schools.

Mise, le meas
Seoirse Ó Colla, Aire Oideachais.

APPENDIX 2

A Formal Petition by a group of Clergymen to President de Valera in 1970 on the Community School issue.

A Uachtaráin, A Shoillse,

We, the undersigned, who are active in the ministries of the following religious bodies, the Roman Catholic Church, the Church of Ireland, the Presbyterian Church, the Methodist Church and the Society of Friends, wish to present a formal petition to Your Excellency.

We are gravely disturbed by the long-term consequences for our country arising from the proposals presently being implemented with regard to the community schools. At a time when education should be a unifying factor in our community, we see these proposals as being exceptionally divisive. Such proposals cannot be regarded as being in the national interest.

We regret that these proposals, in effect, constitute a repeal of the 1930 Vocational Education Act, under which our vocational schools have functioned so efficiently for forty years on a basis of multi-denominational cooperation and harmony.

Since the democratically expressed opposition and alternative proposals of the people of Tallaght and the views of other representative bodies have been ignored, we appeal to You, to seek to have the present policy on community schools altered.

Rev. Paul S. Cardew, Church of Ireland, Rathfarnham. Rev. Phillip M. Day, Church of Ireland, St. Mary's, Crumlin. Rev. Ernest W. Gallagher, Methodist, Rathmines and Terenure. Rev. Alistair Graham, Church of Ireland, Clontarf. Rev. Denys F. Horgan O. P. Roman Catholic, Tallaght. Rev. Dennis Cooke, Methodist Centenary, St. Stephen's Green. Rev. Derek Pringle, Church of Ireland, Raheny. Rev. Éamonn Gaynor, C. C., Quin, Co Clare. Rev. Conor O'Donovan S.J., Roman Catholic, Milltown Pk., Dublin. Rev. E. E. O'Donnell S.J., Roman Catholic, Milltown Pk., Dublin. Rev. Philip Fogarty S.J., Roman Catholic, Milltown Pk., Dublin. Canon F. R. Alexander, Church of Ireland, Clondalkin / Rathcoole. Rev. John W. Morrow, Presbyterian Dean of Residence, TCD. Rev. Robert J. Black, Church of Ireland, St. Ann's, Dawson St. Rev. Stephen Doyle O.P., Roman Catholic, Tallaght. Victor L. H. Bewley, Religious Society of Friends, Brittas. Brian H. Murdock, Religious Society of Friends, Rathgar. Rev. James Good, Roman Catholic, Limerick. Rev. Terence P. McCaughey, Presbyterian, TCD.

APPENDIX 3

Letter from J. M. O'Sullivan T.D., Minister for Education, to Dr Keane, Bishop of Limerick on the 1930 Vocational Education Act, 31 October 1930.

My Lord,
On Thursday 16th instant, His Grace the Archbishop of Tuam, His Lordship the Bishop of Clogher and Your Lordship, representing the Irish Hierarchy, discussed with me certain aspects of the Vocational Education Act in which the church was particularly interested. I gathered that it was the sections dealing with the continuation education for young persons between the ages of fourteen and sixteen that especially claimed attention. On that occasion I indicated that I should take an opportunity of communicating formally with Your Lordship, for the information of the bishops, my own view and the views of my department on these matters.

First I should like to deal with the general scope and purpose of the act especially in reference to the provision of continuation education, for it is here particularly that misconceptions have arisen in some quarters.

I may say at once that the title of the act, viz., 'Vocational Education Act', is not intended merely for reference purposes - to provide the act with a name as it were - but is meant to indicate its purpose and to delimit its scope. On many occasions before the introduction of the bill as well as subsequently, I have made it clear that vocational - not general- education was the subject matter of the act. It is not and was never intended to be in any degree a general education act.

For the purpose of better organisation and to prevent much of the confusion that had prevailed under our technical system, I have found it advisable to divide vocational education into continuation education and technical education; but both these branches as legislated for by this act remain essentially vocational. By their very nature and purpose the schools to be provided under this act are distinctly not schools for general education. General education, after the age of 14 years, as well as before the age of 14 years, will continue to be given in primary and in secondary schools. When we can afford to make more universal a system of general education for postprimary pupils it cannot be through the medium of these continuation schools.

I have repeatedly expressed - and quite definitely in my speech on the Second Reading of the Bill in the Dáil - my dislike of the term 'continuation education', as it was liable to be misunderstood. What

I had in mind might in some ways be more clearly expressed by the terms 'technical education of a more specialised character'. The use of these terms would, however, have meant very clumsy drafting. The work of the continuation schools is intended to be a re-organised system of introductory technical classes for students between the ages of fourteen and sixteen years, such as exists widely at present. Anybody, however, acquainted with the history of technical education in this country will understand why I shrank from the use of the word 'Introductory'.

The instruction is to be continuation instruction in the sense that the instruction of young people will be continued after the age of fourteen. It is not, however, and was never intended to be, continuation education in the sense that it continues the type of education given in primary schools or continues the atmosphere that prevails in them. I consider that a distinct break with that type of education and that atmosphere is essential for the success of the continuation courses if they are to fulfil the purpose for which we intend them. On the occasion of the second reading of the bill in the Dáil, I clearly pointed out that it was an essential note of these courses that the future occupation should be kept continually before the students. Apart from the compulsory powers that it provides and its financial provisions, the Act aims at the re-organisation and reform of the existing 'technical' system and I trust that the type of education in the continuation courses provided by committees will steadily become more definitely vocational than the similar education which is at present being given in technical schools, and that where subjects, other than handwork, etc., are taught, they will be taught with a definite reference to employment and as 'practical' subjects.

The fundamental distinction between these vocational schools and primary schools I emphasised in several passages in my speech when moving the second reading of the bill in the Dáil and also in my speech in the Seanad. Summing up my attitude in reply to the various speeches on the second reading of the bill I said:

> I could not accept the view that this bill is simply an extension of primary education. I do not intend it to be such. It is rather a reform so far as that can be legislatively managed of the existing system of technical education which, as I explained, whatever may have been the intention of the legislators, does, in practice, embrace a large amount of continuation education.

The strictly vocational character was so marked that the main opposition that I had to face during the passage of the bill into law, (apart from some criticism of the financial clauses), both inside and outside the Oireachtas, came from those who wished to widen its scope and to make larger provision for general and cultural education. This was the attitude specially taken up by the Gaelic League and by some of those interested in the spread of the Irish language. However, I resisted any amendments put forward on these lines precisely because they went beyond the scope of the bill by tending to remove the purely vocational character. To deputations who expressed fear that the distinctly vocational character of the bill would prejudice the work at present being done for Irish under the technical system, I indicated that whereas for full grown adults attendance at the course in Irish alone might still be possible, for young people, on the other hand, attendance would normally be at a course of subjects of which Irish might indeed be one, but one of a group with others which would be 'practical' as distinct from cultural. All through I was most careful to secure that no new principle of control in education should be introduced by this act. I stated this very distinctly at the close of my introductory speech already referred to above. I do not pretend that the system established in this country meets all ideals, but I believe that when all practical difficulties are taken into account there is no need to be uneasy about the present act.

I strove to secure, with success, as I believe, that the act should not run counter to established Catholic practice in this country, or to the spirit of the Maynooth decrees governing these matters. This was one of the reasons why I insisted so strongly on the vocational character of the instruction to be provided under the act. The second reason was that I felt there was a great deal in the criticism so often heard that our education system has hitherto been too one-sidedly theoretical and that however excellent the education given in the primary and secondary schools may be, it was not sufficiently balanced by a system of a more 'practical' type. This is sometimes adduced as one of the reasons why our young people so readily turn their backs on agriculture and industrial pursuits. With more justice it might be urged that for these latter not nearly enough in the way of adequate provision of instruction was being done. That, I confess, is one of the reasons why I am keen that both as to matter and method and aims there should - right through - in the vocational course be a definite break with the primary system. For the great bulk of our young people the education at present provided for instance in secondary schools, is neither available nor suitable. Our existing technical system was in many respects somewhat out of date, it no longer met our needs; but it required reform and reorganisation, rather than abolition and the substitution of something entirely new. In addition to the better articulation of 'continuation' and 'technical' education and the substitution of a smaller, and, I hope, more efficient type of committee, there were two other important changes introduced.

The committees were sadly in need of adequate finances to enable them to carry on their work and to provide more effective vocational training than at present. The act makes possible the provision of such adequate finances to the committees.

In addition the act confers certain compulsory powers on the Minister for Education. Such powers, however, do not come automatically into force at any fixed date. They can be applied to any particular district only when the minister thinks fit - that is, presumably, when he is satisfied that the conditions in any such district warrant and require it. Thus, so far as this act is concerned, the extension of compulsory attendance between the ages of fourteen and sixteen over the whole country will probably be a gradual process. Further, the powers conferred on the minister by this act are restricted in various ways. The number of hours for which he can compel the attendance of students between fourteen and sixteen years of age is limited to one hundred and eighty per annum. Care has also been taken that this power cannot be used to compel the students, to which the compulsory clauses have been made applicable, to attend any particular type of school. The obligations can be satisfied not only by attendance at the courses provided by the committees but in a variety of other ways - for instance by continued attendance at the National School. As, in that part of the act that deals with the enforcement of continuation education, we are still dealing with a general problem where compulsion may become universal, not with the conditions of admission to a definite trade or profession, I believed that a wide liberty of choice should be left to the parent.

Another matter which Your Lordships raised was the question of coeducation and night schools especially in the country districts. I think that the committees ought so to fix the hours of their continuation classes in these districts that boys and girls would not attend the schools on the same evening and that, as far as possible, night classes should be avoided.

The only matter that now remains on which to make my position clear is the very important one of religious instruction. I may point out that, with the exception of a special reference to the Schools of Music in Cork and in Dublin, no subject of instruction is mentioned in the act. The act does not profess to set out a curriculum. I think, however, that facilities for the giving of religious instruction should be provided by the vocational committees. I cannot believe that any committee will fail in this respect. If, however, in any individual case the committee should fail I see no reason why we should not use our general powers of approval of courses to bring pressure to bear on them to make the necessary provisions. The facilities should be real facilities, that is, rooms should be set apart in the schools for this purpose and the time for religious instruction should be incorporated with the general class plan. The amount of religious instruction should bear a relation to the length of the course of which it should thus form a part. I cannot, as their Lordships will understand, compel any student to avail himself of the facilities provided. I may point out, however, that we exercise no such compulsory powers in the case of either the primary or secondary schools. In the conditions at present prevailing in this country it may indeed be doubtful whether the exercise of any such power by the state, were it constitutionally permissible , would be either necessary or, in the long run, healthy. I gathered from your Lordships that so far as Catholic instruction is concerned, the Bishops would undertake the responsibility of providing the actual teaching when facilities are given.

I may add that to facilitate the coming into force of the new act my department is at present sending out general instructions to the committees. We will avail of the opportunity to bring to their notice this and the other matters mentioned. It only remains for me to thank the bishops for their readiness in giving me an opportunity of putting my views before them.

Yours sincerely,
J. M. O'Sullivan, Minister for Education.

Select Bibliography

SCHEMA
Primary sources
1. Public and private archives and manuscripts.
2. Official publications i) pre-1922, ii) post-1922.
3. Newspapers and journals.
4. Published contemporary memoirs and documents.
5. Works of reference.

Secondary sources
6. Specialist studies on education and policy.
7. Relevant general historical works.

Primary sources
1. Public and private archives and manuscripts
State Paper Office: Dáil Éireann files 1919-22; Cabinet Files and Documents, 1922-54.
Department of the Public Service, files in the E series, 1920-40.
Department of Education, some files relevant to period 1924-54.
Department of Finance, files in the S and F series, 1922-55.
University College, Dublin, Archives Department: MacNeill papers, Blythe papers, Mulcahy papers.
National Library, Manuscript Division: MacNeill papers, Thomas Johnson papers, Gaelic League papers.
Trinity College Library, Manuscript Library: John Dillon papers.
Public Record Office, Newspaper cuttings on education.
Documents and papers in private ownership relating to various issues in education in the periods 1910-34 and 1956-76.

2. Official publications
i) Pre- 1922.
Copy of the letter from the Chief Secretary of Ireland to the Duke of Leinster, on the formation of a Board of Commissioners for Education in Ireland, H.C. 1831-2, XXIX.
Report of the Commissioners Appointed to Inquire into the Nature and Extent of the Instruction afforded by the Several Institutions in Ireland for the Purpose of Elementary or Primary Education; also into the practical working of the system of National Education, Vol. I, Part 1, H.C. 1870, XXVIII, Pts. II-V.
Royal Commission on Manual and Practical Instruction in Primary Schools Under the Board of National Education in Ireland, Final Report. H.C. 1898, XLIV. Further reports, evidence and appendix in H.C. 1897, XLIII and H.C. 1898, XLIV.
Report of the Commissioners of Intermediate Education (Ireland), Final Report. H.C., 1899, XXII. First report, appendices and evidence in H.C., 1899, XXII, XXIII, XXIV.
Report of the Commissioners on University Education (Ireland), Final Report, H.C. 1903, XXXII. First, Second and Third Reports in H.C. 1902, XXX1, XXX11.
Report of Mr F. H. Dale, His Majesty's Inspector of Schools, Board of Education, on Primary Education in Ireland. H.C. 1904, XX.
Report of Messrs F. H. Dale and T. A. Stephens, His Majesty's Inspectors, Board of Education, on Intermediate Education in Ireland. H.C. 1905, XXVIII.
Report of the Royal Commission on Trinity College, Dublin and the University of Dublin, Final Report. H.C. 1906, LVL.
Report of Vice-Regal Committee of Inquiry into Primary Education (Ireland) 1913, Final Report. H.C. 1914, XXVIII.
Report of Vice-Regal Committee of Inquiry into Primary Education (Ireland) 1918, Final Report. H.C. 1919, XXI.

Report of Vice-Regal Committee on the Condition of Service and Remuneration of Teachers in Intermediate Schools and on the Distribution of Grants from Public Funds for Intermediate Education in Ireland. H.C. 1919, XXI.
Annual Reports of the Commissioners of National Education (Ireland), 1834 to 1921.
Annual Reports of the Commissioners of Intermediate Education (Ireland), 1879-1920.
Annual Reports of the Department of Agriculture and Technical Instruction, 1901-20.
ii) Post-1922.
Department of Education, *Programme for Students in Training 1924-25,* (1924).
Department of Education, *Rules and Programmes for Secondary Schools,* (1924).
National Programme Conference, *Report and Programme,* (1926).
Committee on Inspection of Primary Schools, *Report,* (1927).
Commission on Technical Education, *Report,* (1928).
Department of Education, *Notes for Teachers,* (1933-34).
Department of Education, *Revised Programme of Primary Instruction,* (1934).
Inter-Departmental Committee on the Raising of the School Leaving Age, *Report,* (1936).
Department of Education, *Organisation of Whole-Time Continuation Courses, Memorandum V 40/1942.*
Department of Education, *Terms of Reference to the Council of Education and Inaugural Addresses,* (1950).
The Council of Education, *(1) the Function of the Primary School, (2) the Curriculum to be Pursued in the Primary School,* (1954).
The Council of Education, *The Curriculum of the Secondary School,* (1962).
Commission on the Restoration of the Irish Language, *Summary of the Final Report,* (1963).
Department of Education, *Rules for National Schools,* (1965).
White Paper on the Restoration of the Irish language, (1965).
O.E.C.D. Survey Team, *Investment in Education,* (1965).
Commission on Higher Education 1960-67, *Presentation and Summary of Report,* (1967).
Steering Committee on Technical Education, *Report to the Minister for Education on Regional Technical Colleges,* (1967).
Tribunal on Teacher Salaries, *Report presented to the Minister for Education,* (1969).
Comhairle na Gaeilge, *Irish in Education,* (1974).
Advisory Committee, *Adult Education in Ireland,* (1973).
Department of Education, *Educational Development,* (1980).
Department of Education, *Annual Report,* 1924-25 to 1963-64.
Department of Education, *Statistical Report,* 1964-65 to 1980-81.
Department of Education, *Partners in Education,* (1985).

3. **Newspapers and journals**
American Political Science Review, An Claidheamh Soluis, British Journal of Political Science, Catholic Herald, The Clongownian, Dublin Review, European Journal of Education, European Journal of Political Research, Comhar, Feasta, Freeman's Journal, Gairm, Irish Catholic Directory, Irish Education Review, Irish Independent, Irish Journal of Education, Irish Monthly, Irish News, Irish People, Irish Press, Irish Review, Irish School Weekly, Irish Teachers' Journal, Irish Times, The Leader, Oideas, Public Administration Review, Roscommon Herald, School & College Yearbook, Studies, Sunday Press, Times Educational Supplement, Weekly Freeman.

4. **Published contemporary memoirs and documents**
Acta et decreta synodi plenariae episcoporum Hiberniae habitae apud Thurles, (Dublin, 1851).
Acta et decreta synodi plenariae episcoporum Hiberniae habitae apud Maynutiam, (Dublin, 1900, 1927, 1956).
A. Birrell, *Things past redress,* (London, 1936).
E. Cahill, S.J., *The framework of a Christian state,* (Dublin, 1932).
J. Connolly, *Labour in Irish history,* (Dublin, 1973).
Séamas Fenton, *It all happened,* (Dublin, 1949).
J. W. Kavanagh, *Mixed education: The Catholic case stated,* (Dublin, 1859).
W. McDonald, *Reminiscences of a Maynooth professor,* (London, 1925).
M. McInerney, *Peadar O'Donnell, Irish social rebel,* (Dublin, 1974).
W. J. O'Neill-Daunt, *Journal,* (Cork, 1875).
Horace Plunkett, *Ireland in the new century,* (London, 1904).
John O'Leary, *Recollections of Fenians and Fenianism,* (Dublin, 1896).
W. J. M. Starkie, *Recent reforms in Irish education,* (Dublin, 1911).
Thomas Wyse, *Education reform,* (London, 1836).

5. Works of reference

C. E. Beck, *Perspectives on world education*, (Wisconsin, 1973).

B. F. Chubb, *The government and politics of Ireland*, (London, 1982).

R. J. Hayes, *Sources for the history of Irish civilisation*, (Boston, 1970).

James MacCaffrey, *A history of the church in the nineteenth century*, (Dublin, 1910).

R. B. McDowell, *The Irish administration 1801-1914*, (London, Toronto, 1964).

James Meenan, *The Irish economy since 1922*, (Liverpool, 1970).

T. W. Moody & F. X. Martin, *The course of Irish history*, (Cork, 1966).

M. Moynihan, (ed.), *Speeches and statements by Éamon de Valera 1917-1973*, (Dublin, 1980).

T. Nealon, *Guide to the Dáil and Senate*, (Dublin, 1982).

Secondary Sources
6. Specialist studies in education and policy

Donald H. Akenson, *The Irish education experiment*, (London, 1970);*Education and enmity: The control of schooling in Northern Ireland 1922-1950*, (London, 1973); *A mirror to Kathleen's face*, (Toronto, 1973).

Margaret S. Archer, *Social origins of educational systems*, (London, 1979).

J. J. Auchmuty, *Irish education, a historical survey*, (Dublin, 1937).

Graham Balfour, *The educational systems of Great Britain and Ireland*, (Oxford, 1903).

A. F. Bentley, *The process of government*, (Harvard, 1967).

Raymond Boudon, *Education, opportunity and social inequality: changing prospects in western society*, (New York, 1974).

David Braybrooke & Charles Lindblom, *A strategy for decision*, (New York, 1963).

R. K. Carty, *Party and parish pump: electoral politics in Ireland*, (Wilfrid Laurier University Press, 1981).

B. F. Chubb, *Cabinet government in Ireland*, (Dublin, 1974).

P. Clancy & C. Benson, *Higher education in Dublin: a study of some emerging needs*, (Dublin, 1979).

P. Clancy, *Participation in higher education*, (Dublin, 1984).

J. A. Coolahan, *The ASTI and post- primary education in Ireland 1909-1984*, (Dublin, 1984); *Irish education- history and structure*, (Dublin, 1981).

P. J. Corish, (ed.), *The church since emancipation: Catholic education*, (Dublin, 1971).

D. Easton, *The political system*, (New York, 1953); *A framework for political analysis: a systems analysis of political life*, (New Jersey, 1965).

Ronan Fanning, *The Irish Department of Finance 1922-58*, (Dublin, 1976).

Brian Farrell, *The founding of Dáil Éireann: parliament and nation building*, (Dublin, 1971).

I. G. Fenwick, & P. McBride, *The government of education in Britain*, (London, 1978).

T. Garvin, *The evolution of Irish nationalist politics*, (Dublin, 1983).

C. Ham & M. Hill, *The policy process in the modern capitalist state*, (London, 1984).

D. Hannan, & R. Breen, *Schooling and sex roles*, (Dublin, 1983).

S. Henig, *Political parties in the European Community*, (London, 1980).

C. C. Hood, *The limits of administration*, (London, 1976).

J. R. Hough, *Educational policy - an international survey*, (London, 1984).

T. Husén & M. Kogan, (eds.), *Educational research & policy*, (Oxford, 1984).

M. Kogan, *The politics of education*, (Harmondsworth, 1971);*Educational policy-making, a study of interest groups and parliament*, (London, 1975).

C. E. Lindblom, *The policy-making process*, (New Jersey, 1968).

T. J. McElligott, *Education in Ireland*, (Dublin, 1966); *Secondary education in Ireland 1870-1922*, (Dublin, 1981); *A teaching life*, (Dublin, 1986).

Milbrey W. McLaughlin, *Evaluation and reform*, (Mass., 1975).

John C. McQuaid, *Catholic education, its function and scope*, (Dublin, 1942); *Higher education for Catholics*, (Dublin, 1961).

P. Mair, *Issue dimensions and party strategies in the Irish Republic 1948-1981*, (Florence, 1982).

M. Manning, *Irish political parties*, (Dublin, 1972).

Arnold J. Meltsner, *Policy analysts in the bureaucracy*, (Univ. of California, 1976).

D. W. Miller, *Church, state and nation in Ireland 1898-1921*, (Dublin, 1973).

A. Mitchell, *Labour in Irish politics 1890-1930*, (Dublin, 1974).

T. W. Moody & J. C. Beckett, *Queen's College Belfast 1845-1945, the history of a university*, (London, 1959).

Kingsmill H. Moore, *An unwritten chapter in the history of education*, (London, 1904).

T. J. Morrissey, *Towards a national university*, (Dublin, 1983).

T. J. O'Connell, *A history of the INTO 1868-1968*, (Dublin, 1969).

J. J. O'Meara, *Reform in education*, (Dublin, 1958).

S. M. Parkes, *Kildare Place - A history of the Church of Ireland Training College 1811-1969*, (Dublin, 1983).

P. H. Pearse, *The Murder Machine*, in Ó Buachalla (ed.) *A significant Irish educationalist*, (Cork, Dublin, 1980).

C. Pollitt *et al.*, *Public policy in theory and practice*, (Milton Keynes, 1979).

Jeffrey L. Pressman & Aaron Wildavsky, *Implementation*, (Univ. of California, 1973).

E. Randles, *Post-Primary education in Ireland 1957-70*, (Dublin, 1975).

J. J. Richardson, & A. G. Jordan, *Governing under pressure*, (Oxford, 1979).

R. Rose, (ed.), *Policy-Making in Britain*, (London, 1974).

E. Rumpf, & A. C. Hepburn, *Nationalism and socialism in twentieth century Ireland*, (Liverpool, 1977).

E. E. Schattschneider, *The semi-sovereign people*, (New York, 1960).

A. M. Schroder, *Das religiusproblem in der Irisch-Englischen schulpolitik*, (Charlottenburg, 1935).

Brian E. Titley, *Church, state and the control of schooling in Ireland 1900-1944*, (Dublin, 1983).

A. Dale Tussing, *Irish educational expenditure - past, present and future*, (Dublin, 1978).

P. J. Walsh, *William J. Walsh*, (Dublin, 1928).

T. J. Walsh, *Nano Nagle and the Presentation Sisters*, (Dublin, 1959).

J. H. Whyte, *Church & state in modern Ireland 1923-1970*, (Dublin, 1971); *Catholics in western democracies*, (Dublin, 1981).

Aaron Wildavsky, *The art & craft of policy analysis*, (London, 1980).

7. Relevant general historical works

J. C. Beckett, *The Making of Modern Ireland*, (London, 1966).

D. A. Kerr, *Peel, priests and politics*, (Cambridge, 1982).

J. J. Lee, *The modernisation of Irish society 1848-1918*, (Dublin, 1973).

J. J. Lee, (ed.), *Ireland 1945-'70*, (Dublin, 1979).

F. S. L. Lyons, *Ireland since the famine*, (London, 1973).

J. A. Murphy, *Ireland in the twentieth century*, (Dublin, 1975).

K. B. Nowlan & T. D. Williams, (eds.), *Ireland in the war years and after 1939-'51*, (Dublin, 1969).

E. A. Norman, *The Catholic Church and Ireland in the age of rebellion 1859-'73*, (London, 1965).

Leon Ó Broin, *The chief secretary Augustine Birrell in Ireland*, (London, 1969).

P. S. O'Hegarty, *Ireland under the union*, (Dublin, 1922).

T. P. O'Neill & P. Ó Fiannachta, *De Valera*, (Dublin, 1968).

T. D. Williams, (ed.), *The Irish struggle*, (Dublin, 1966).

NOTES TO THE TEXT

Where the Departments of Finance, of Education and the Public Service, and the National Library, the State Paper Office and the Public Record Office are cited as archival locations in these notes they are indicated thus: D.F., N.L.I., S.P.O., P.R.O.

CHAPTER 1

1. Akenson, D. H., *The Irish education experiment*, (London, 1970).
2. *Census of Ireland 1901.*
3. Ó Tuama, S., (ed.), *The Gaelic League Idea*, (Dublin, 1972); Akenson, *The Irish education experiment*, ch. 9; *Census 1851*; Ó Buachalla, S., 'Educational policy and the role of the Irish language, 1831-1981' in *European Journal of Education*, xix, no. 1 (1984), 75-92.
4. *Hansard, 3*, vol. 4, 1249-1305, H.C., (1831-2).
5. Cousin, Victor, 'Rapport sur l'etat de l'instruction publique en Prusse' in Knight, E. W. (ed.), *Reports on European education*, (London, 1930); Wyse, Thomas, *Education reform*, (London, 1836); Auchmuty, J. J., *Irish education, an historical survey*, (London & Dublin, 1937).
6. Kingsmill Moore, H., *An unwritten chapter in the history of education*, (London, 1904); Brenan, M., *Schools of Kildare and Leighlin*, (Dublin, 1935); Parkes, Susan M., *Kildare Place, A history of the Church of Ireland training college, 1811-1969*, (Dublin, 1983).
7. McCaffrey, James, *History of the Church in the 19th century*, (Dublin, 1910).
8. Walsh, T. J., *Nano Nagle and the Presentation Sisters*, (Dublin, 1959).
9. *Investment in education*, (1965), l, 167.
10. O'Sullivan, James J., 'The education of Irish Catholics, 1778-1831'. (unpublished Ph. D. thesis, Queen's University, Belfast, 1958).
11. Akenson, *The Irish education experiment*, 392.
12. Data compiled from the report of the Powis Commission, H.C., 1870, XXVIII.
13. Akenson, *The Irish education experiment*, 214-24.
14. *Decreta Synodi Plenariae Episcoporum Hiberniae Apud Thurles 1850*, (Dublin, 1853).
15. Balfour, Graham, *The educational systems of Great Britain and Ireland*, (Oxford, 1903), 95.
16. Minutes of the commissioners of national education, Ireland, for 21 Nov 1863 and 26 June 1886, (P.R.O.).
17. *Report of the commissioners of national education in Ireland, 1883*, 15-18.
18. *Report of the department of education, 1924-25*, 33-4.
19. *Report of royal commission of inquiry into primary education (Ireland)*, [C6], H.C. 1870, XXVIII; Murphy, James, *Church, state and schools in Britain 1800-1970*, (London, 1971).
20. Akenson, *The Irish education experiment*, 315.
21. Balfour, *The Irish education experiment*, 97.
22. Akenson, *The Irish education experiment*, 311.
23. Schroder, A. M., *Das religiusproblem in der Irisch-Englishen schulpolitik*, (Charlottenburg, 1935).
24. *Report of royal commission of inquiry into primary education (Ireland) 1870*, 1, pt. 1, 522-534.
25. *Thirty second report of the commissioners of national education in Ireland, 1865*, 13, [3713], H.C. 1866, XXIX.
26. Balfour, *Educational systems*, 101.
27. *Report of the commissioners to inquire into the state of popular education in England, 1861.*
28. Akenson, *The Irish education experiment*, 315.
29. *Report of Mr F. H. Dale, H.M.I., on primary education in Ireland*, (Cd. 1891), 984, H.C. 1904, XX.
30. *Investment in education*, 1, Tables 9. 3 & 9. 4, 227-8.
31. Murphy, *Church, state and schools*, ch. 3.
32. *A Bill to improve national education in Ireland*, H.C. 1892, (420), iv.
33. *Sixty seventh report of the commissioners of national education in Ireland, 1900*, 12-13.
34. *Appendix to sixtieth report of the commissioners of national education in Ireland 1893*, 3-10.
35. 'Resolutions of the assembled archbishops and bishops of Ireland on the education bill', in *I.E.R.*, xiii (1892), 472.
36. 'The right to educate, to whom does it belong?' in *I.E.R.*, iii, (1867), 281, 410, 541.
37. *I.E.R.*, ii, (1881), 627.

38. *I.E.R.* , xvii, (1896), 643.
39. *Sixty sixth report of the commissioners of national education in Ireland, 1899*, 13.
40. *National programme of primary instruction Dublin 1922*, 24; School Attendance Act 1926; McKenna, L., 'State rights in Irish education' in *Studies*, xvi, (1927), 215; O'Connell, T. J., *A History of the INTO, 1868-1968*, (Dublin, 1969), 386-92.
41. Akenson, *The Irish education experiment*, 324-329.
42. *Sixty seventh report of the commissioners of national education in Ireland 1900*, 28, [Cd. 704], H.C. 1901, xxi.
43. *Minutes commissioners of national education in Ireland*, of 16 April 1876, of 12 March 1872 and of 14 Dec 1875; McDowell, R. B., *The Irish administration 1801-1914*, (Dublin, 1964), 101; *Minutes Commissioners of National Education in Ireland*, of 22 Jan 1878.
44. Akenson, *The Irish education experiment*, 318.
45. *Minutes commissioners of national education in Ireland*, of 3 Oct 1876; Balfour, *Educational systems*, 101.
46. Lyons, F. S. L., *The Irish Parliamentary Party 1890-1910*, (Westport, Conn., U.S.A., 1951), 69.
47. National Board circular, Nov 1848; *Freeman's Journal*, 5 Feb 1859.
48. O'Connell, *History of INTO*, 9.
49. Ibid., 38-39.
50. Ibid., 45.
51. *The Irish Independent*, 24 Apr 1899.
52. O'Connell, *History of INTO*, 58.
52. Ibid., 37.
53. Balfour, *Educational systems*, 193.
54. *Report from the select committee on foundation schools and education in Ireland*, H.C. 1837-38, VII, 76.
55. *Report of the royal commission into the endowments, funds and purpose of education in Ireland*, H.C. 1857-58, XXII.
56. Archer, R. L., *Secondary education in the nineteenth century*, (Cambridge, 1921), 175; Beck, C. E., *Perspectives on world education*, (Wisconsin, 1973), 22.
57. Norman, E. A., *The Catholic Church and Ireland in the age of rebellion*, (London, 1965), 59.
58. Quoted by O'Rahilly, A., in *Studies*, (1962), 147-155.
59. *Census of Ireland 1902*, Table 156.
60. Ibid., Table 186.
61. *Dublin Review*, Jan -April, (1876).
62. McElligott, T. J., *Secondary education in Ireland 1870-1922*, (Dublin, 1966), ch. 4.
63. 'The right to educate, to whom does it belong?', *I.E.R.* , iii, (1867), 281, 410, 541; 'Educational dangers', *I.E.R.* , iv, (1868); 'Resolutions of the bishops of Ireland, 18 Aug 1869', *I.E.R.* , v, (1869), 582.
64. Lyons, F. S. L., *Ireland since the famine*, (London, 1973), 90- 103.
65. Coolahan, J. A., 'The payment-by-results policy in the national and intermediate

schools of Ireland', (unpublished M. Ed. thesis, Trinity College, Dublin 1975).
66. *Report of Mr F. H. Dale and Mr. T. A. Stephens on Intermediate education in Ireland*, H.C. (1905), XXVIII, 709.
67. *Report of the Commissioners of Intermediate Education 1907*.
68. Dale and Stephens, *Intermediate education*, 756. Note: Unlike the system in the National Schools the payment-by-results scheme did not necessarily benefit the individual secondary teacher.
69. *Report of the commissioners on intermediate education (Ireland), 1899*, H.C. 1899, XXII, 502.
70. *Journal of the Statistical and Social Inquiry Society of Ireland*, for the years 1876, 1878, 1880, 1882.
71. *I.E.R.* , 1881, 1885, 1886, 1887, 1896, 1897; *The Irish Monthly*, 1875, 1877, 1891, 1895.
72. For an extensive bibliography see Hayes, R. J., *Sources for the history of Irish civilisation*, (Boston, 1970), 6, 712-14.

CHAPTER 2

1. Akenson, *The Irish education experiment*, Chapter IX.
2. For a detailed analysis of this topic see Norman, *The Catholic Church and Ireland*.
3. Ibid., 33; Bowen, D., *Paul Cardinal Cullen*, (Dublin, 1983); Kerr, D. A., *Peel, priests and politics*, (Cambridge, 1982).
4. *Royal commission of inquiry into primary education (Ireland)*, 1, i, 70.
5. Norman, *The Catholic Church and Ireland*, 17.
6. *Decreta Synodi Plenariae Episcoporum Hiberniae*, MDCCCL, 52-59.
7. Healy, J., *Maynooth College, its centenary history*, (Dublin, 1895).
8. Dalton, E., *History of the archdiocese of Tuam*, (Dublin, 1928).
9. O'Neill-Daunt, W. J., *Journal*, 27 May 1870.
10. Norman, *The Catholic Church and Ireland*, 96; Parliamentary Papers, 1870, xxviii, 1226.
11. O'Leary, John, *Recollections of Fenians and Fenianism*, 11 (Dublin, 1896), 36.
12. *The Irish People*, 7 Jan 1865.
13. Norman, *The Catholic Church and Ireland*, 10.
14. Bowen, *Paul Cardinal Cullen*, Chs. 2, 3.
15. Butler, C., *The Vatican Council 1869-70*, (London, 1962), 176.
16. Letter from Cullen to Manning, 13 Oct 1871.
17. Norman, *The Catholic Church and Ireland* 432; *Select committee on the Callan schools*, P. P. (1873), ix, 1, 320.
18. Kavanagh, J. W., *Mixed education, the Catholic case stated* (Dublin, 1859); *Freeman's Journal*, 25 Aug 1859; *I.E.R.*, iv, (1868): v, (1869).
19. 'Resolutions of the Irish bishops', *I.E.R.*, ii, (1881), 627- 631.
20. Walsh, P. J., *William J. Walsh* (Dublin,

1928), 12.
21. Miller, D. W., *Church, state and nation in Ireland, 1898-1921* (Dublin, 1973); Morrissey, T. J., *Towards a national university* (Dublin, 1983), 288.
22. Rev. W. Walsh, President of Maynooth, Rev. W. Delaney S.J. and Rev. Reffé C.S.Sp., Blackrock College.
23. Letter from Moran to Walsh, 4 Sept 1878, in Walsh, P. J., *William J. Walsh*, 75.
24. Circular of Commissioners of National Education, 1849.
25. Circular of Commissioners of National Education, 1850.
26. Miller, *Church, state and nation*, 32-34.
27. O'Connell, T. J., *History of INTO*, 42-93.
28. *Freeman's Journal*, 9 March 1885.
29. Uncatalogued documents in INTO Archives.
30. *Irish Teachers' Journal*, 23 Dec 1893.
31. *Irish Teachers' Journal*, 14 July 1894.
32. *I.E.R.*, xvii, (1896), 762.
33. Miller, *Church, state and nation*, 33-34; O'Connell, *History of INTO*, 45.
34. A school manager quoted in the *Irish Teachers' Journal*, 8 Sept 1894, 4; *Irish Independent* 10 June 1898.
35. 'Pastoral address of the Irish bishops on the management of catholic schools', *I.E.R.*, xix, (1898), 75-78; *Irish Independent*, 24 June 1898.
36. O'Connell, *History of INTO*, 55.
37. Letter from Dr Walsh to Gort INTO, *Irish Independent*, 30 July 1898.
38. O'Connell, *History of INTO*, 58.
39. *Irish Independent*, 24 April 1899.
40. *Irish News*, 2 June 1904; O'Connell, *History of INTO*, 59; *Weekly Freeman*, 15 April 1899.
41. O'Connell, *History of INTO*, 60; *Freeman's Journal*, 18 April 1900; *Irish Times*, 19 April 1900.
42. *I.E.R.*, xxi, 1901.
43. INTO Circular, Oct. 1900.
44. 'The right to educate, to whom does it belong?' in *I.E.R.*, iii, (1867), 280.
45. 'Resolutions of the assembled archbishops and bishops of Ireland on the education bill', in *I.E.R.*, xiii, (1892), 472; *I.E.R.*, xvii, (1896), 643.
46. *I.E.R.*, xix, (1900), 466.
47. *I.E.R.*, xx, (1900); 'Pastoral Address 1927', *Acta et Decreta*, 1927, 157.
48. Morrissey, *National University*, 89-112.
49. Beckett, J. C.., *The making of modern Ireland 1603-1923* (London, 1966), 332.
50. *Sixty sixth report of the commissioners of national education in Ireland 1899-1900*, xiv, 9.

CHAPTER 3.
1. *Commission on manual and practical instruction in primary schools*, Final report, [C. 8923], H.C. 1898, xliv; *Commission of inquiry into Intermediate education in Ireland*, Final report, [C9511] H.C. 1899, xxii.
2. *Revised programme of primary instruction for national schools*, Sept 1900; Minutes of the Commissioners of National Education, (N.L.I., Ms. 05574, 240.)
3. *The Irish Teachers' Journal*, xxxiv, issues of 15, 22 and 29 Sept 1900.
4. Intermediate education in Ireland act, (63, 64 Vict.).
5. *Report of Mr. Dale on primary education in Ireland*, H.C. I904, xx; *Report of Dale and Stephens on Intermediate education in Ireland*, [C. 2546], H.C. 1905, xxviii, 709.
6. Ó Tuama, S., (ed), *The Gaelic League idea*. (Cork, 1972).
7. *An Claidheamh Soluis*. 1903-1909; Ó Buachalla, S., 'An Piarsach mar oideachasóir', i *Feasta*, xxxix, nos. 5, 7, (1976).
8. *Bill to provide for the establishment and function of an administrative council in Ireland and for other purposes connected therewith*, H.C. 19O7, (182), ii, 481; *Hansard*, H.C. 1907, 174, 93; *An Claidheamh Soluis*, 27 April 19O7; *The Irish Independent*, 17 May 1907; *Vice-Regal Committee of Inquiry into primary education (Ireland)* 1918, (Cd. 60), H.C. 1919. XXI; *Vice-Regal Committee on the conditions of service and remuneration of teachers in Intermediate schools and on the distribution of grants from public funds for Intermediate education in Ireland*, (Cd. 66) H.C. 1919, xxi, 645; *A Bill to make further provision with respect to education in Ireland*, 1919, (214), 1, 407.
9. *An Claidheamh Soluis*, issues of May 1907.
10. *Report of Vice-Regal Committee on conditions etc.* 1919. *op. cit.*, 765-769.
11. Ibid., 666-675.
12. *A Bill to make further provision with respect to education in Ireland*, HC. 1919, (214); ibid., HC. 1920, (35).
13. 'Statement of the standing committee of Irish bishops on the proposed education bill for Ireland', *I.E.R.*, xiv, (1919), 504.
14. Statement by the General Council of County Councils on McPherson's Bill in *The Irish Independent*, 12 Dec 1919.
15. Carson, E., quoted in *The Irish Independent*, 19 Dec 1919.
16. *The Irish Independent*, 13 Mar 1920; *The Freeman's Journal*, 17 Mar 1920; *The Irish Independent*, 5 Mar 1920; *The Irish Independent*, 2 Dec 1919.
17. O'Connell, T. J., *History of the INTO*, 307-331; *The Leader*, 5 Mar 1920.
18. *Hansard*, 136, 13 Dec 1920, 213.
19. Chubb, B., *Cabinet government in Ireland*, (Dublin, 1974) Chapter 3; Farrell, B., *The founding of Dáil Éireann* (Dublin, 1971).
20. *Dáil Éireann Minutes* from 19 Sept 1919 to 31 May 1920.
21. *Dáil Éireann Minutes of Aireacht* for 4 Mar 1920, S.P.O.
22. O'Connell, *History of the INTO*, 306.
23. *The Irish Independent*, 14 Jan 1920.
24. Letter of Rev W. Dwane, Limerick to *The Irish Independent*, 10 Jan 1920.
25. *Proceedings of Dáil Éireann*, Session of 27

October 1919.

26. *Dáil Éireann file*, (S.P.O. DE 2/54).
27. *Report of the commissioners on university education (Ireland)*, (Cd. 1483-4), H.C. 1903, xxxii, i; *Report of royal commission on Trinity College and the University of Dublin*, (Cd. 3311-2), H.C. 1907, xli.
28. Bailey, K. C., *A history of TCD 1892-1942* (Dublin, 1947).
29. *The Irish Times*, 4 Jan. 1904.
30. 'Statement of the standing committee of the Catholic archbishops and bishops of Ireland, 25 July 1906' in *Irish Catholic Directory and Almanac*.
31. Moody, T. W., and Beckett, J. C., *Queen's College Belfast 1845- 1945, The history of a university*, (London, 1959), 381.
32. Chillingworth, H. R., 'TCD at the beginning of the century', *Hermathena*, (1943), 42; *The Irish Universities Act*, H.C. 1908, (358), 11, 1097. 33 *Hansard*, 1911, XXVI, 23 May 1911, 210-212.
34. Ibid., 12 June 1914, 704.
35. *The Irish Educational Review*, Oct 1909, July 1913; *The Irish Journal of Education*, Apr 1910 and Jan 1911.
36. *Parliamentary Papers*, 1913, L. 772.
37. *The Irish Educational Review*. 11 Aug 1913, 690; Correspondence between the Chief Secretary and the CHA, *Parliamentary Papers* 1913.
38. *Parliamentary Papers*, 1914, ixiv, (Cd. 7368).
39. UCD Archives, Mulcahy Papers, P7/C/l/70, item XV.
40. *Coimisiún na Gaeltachta*, 1926, 20.
41. Ó Tailliúr, P., 'Annotated list of Gaelic League pamphlets', *Comhar*, Feabhra-Lúnasa 1964.
42. 'Irish education', 358-368; 'The educational problem in the Home Rule Parliament', 356-358; 'An ideal in education', 369-370, in Ó Buachalla, Séamas, (ed.), *A significant Irish educationalist*, (Cork, 1980)
43. 'Ministerial Career of S. Ó Ceallaigh', (S.P.O., DE 2/54).
44. 'Reports of Aireacht na Gaeilge June 1920 and Aug 1921, (S.P.O. DE 2/54).
45. Ibid., Report 1921, (S.P.O. DE 2/54), 7; *National programme for primary instruction 1922*; (S.P.O., Cabinet Minutes for 20 Feb 1920, DE 1/2).
46. Tuairisc Aireacht na Gaeilge, 1921, (S.P.O. DE 2/54).
47. Ibid., 8.
48. MacNeill, Eoin. 'A view of the state in relation to education' in *The Irish Review*, (1 Oct 1922), 3; MacNeill Eoin, 'Education, the idea of the state', *The Irish Review*, (11 Nov 1922), 28.
49. *The Times Educational Supplement*, 29 Oct 1921, 323.
50. *The I.L.P. and T.U.C. report for 1922*, 59-63; *Labour's policy on education; I.L.P. and T.U.C. report 1925; The Irish Independent*, 6 Aug 1925.
51. Meenan, James, *The Irish economy since 1922*, 92; see also Governor General's address to Dáil, 3 Oct 1923.
52. O'Connell, *History of the INTO*, 198-202.
53. *Dáil Debates*, 1, 696; *Dáil Debates*, 11, 547.
54. *Dáil Debates*, 8, 407; S.P.O., Cabinet Files, S3891.
55. S. P. 0., DE 2/396.
56. Mitchell, A., *Labour in Irish politics*, (Dublin, 1974), 188.
57. Lynch, Patrick. 'The social revolution that never was' in T.D. Williams (ed.), *The Irish struggle 1916-1926*, (Dublin, 1966), 53.
58. UCD Archives, MacNeill papers, LAI/E/78 and LAI/E/82; Department of Finance (hereafter D.F.) S82/13/29, S20/8/35; *Report Department of Education 1924-25*, 6-8.
59. *National programme of primary instruction*; 'Concerning the teaching of the Irish language in the National Schools', Ministry of Education, *Public notice no. 4*, 1 Feb. 1922.
60. *Report and programme presented by the national programme conference to the Minister of Education 1926; Revised programme of primary instruction 1934*.
61. *Dáil Commission on secondary education*, (Dublin, Dec. 1922) *Dáil Debates*, 17 Aug 1921.
62. *Report of the Department of Education 1924/25*, 51; *Report of the Department of Education for the school years 1925, 26, 27*.
63. Derived from figures in *Report of Department of Education 1927-28*.
64. *Report of the Department of Education 1925-27*, 6.
65. *Report of the Department of Education 1927-28*, 11.
66. Ibid., 22; D.F., S18/7/26.
67. O'Connell, *History of the INTO*, 413.
68. *Teachers' superannuation bill 1928*, *Dáil Debates*, 18 July 1928, 848.
69. *Dáil Debates* 32, 24 Oct 1929; Ibid, 30, 28 June 1929, 2013; UCD Archives, MacNeill papers, LAI/E/37.
70. *Report of commission on technical education 1926*, iv.
71. *Dáil Debates*, 34, 14 May 1930, 1733.
72. Whyte, J. H., *Church and state in modern Ireland*, (Dublin 1971), 37-38.
73. Ibid., 21.
74. *Fianna Fáil election manifesto to the electors 1932*, quoted in Moss, W., *Political Parties in the Irish Free State*, 208.
75. Whyte, *Church and state*, 45-51.
76. O'Connell, *History of the I.N.T.O.* , 208, 209.
77. Ibid, 265.
78. Ibid., 267-268; D.F., S18/14/33.
79. D.F., S19/2/33.
80. Comhairle na Gaeilge, *An Ghaeilge sa chóras oideachais*, 16-17; O'Connell, *History of the INTO*, 365.
81. *Seanad Debates*, 34, 1397; D.F., S18/10/38.
82. *Dáil Debates*, 78, 6 June 1940, 1565; Address to INTO Congress at Killarney, 1940.
83. D.F., S24/2/38.
84. D.F., S24/2/38; S.P.O., Cabinet Files,

S2512.

85. S.P.O., Cabinet Files, S12891 'B'.

86. Whyte, *Church and state*, 122.

87. He was a member of the 1925 programme conference, the Gaeltacht commission 1926 and the university committee 1925.

88. Texts of speeches and notes relating to 1948 general election, (UCD Archives, Mulcahy Papers, P 7/C/11, 122).

89. *Dáil Debates*, 115, 296; O'Connell, *History of the INTO*, 242.

90. *The Irish Independent*, 25 Nov 1949 and 1 Dec 1949; *The Irish Times*, 10 Dec 1949; D.F., S18/2/45.

91. *Dáil Debates* 110, 1101-1102; Clann na Poblachta manifesto, *The Irish Independent*, 24 Jan. 1948.

92. *The Irish Times*, 5 Apr 1950; *The Sunday Press*, 9 Apr 1950.

93. *The Irish Independent*, 5 Apr 1950; *Irish Trade Union Congress annual report 1949/50*, 37, 38.

94. *Dail Debates*, 110, 1093.

95. *Report of the council of education, the primary school; Report of the council of education the curriculum of the secondary school*; Ibid., par. 428.

96. *Dáil Debates*, 110, 1089.

97. *Irish School Weekly*, 51, (Apr. 1949).

98. McInerney, M., *Peadar O'Donnell, Irish social rebel*, (Dublin 1974), 102.

99. *The Irish School Weekly*, 55, (5 Dec and 12 Dec 1953).

100. The occasion was the opening of a new vocational school at Banagher, Oct 1953; *The Irish School Weekly*, 55, (20 Oct 1953); *Dáil Debates*, 126, 1743.

101. *Tuarascáil na Roinne Oideachais*, 1951 and 1954.

102. Sheehan, John, 'Education and society in Ireland 1945-70' in Lee, J. J. (ed.), *Ireland 1945-70*, (Dublin, 1979), 61-72.

103. *Fine Gael policy for a just society*, 3 *Education*.

104. Irish Labour Party, *Challenge and change in education*, (1963); *Labour party outline policy* (1969), 65-82.

105. *Investment in education; Report to the minister on regional technical colleges*.

106. *Policy conference on economic growth and investment in education*, 1962.

107. *Investment in education*, 1, Ch. xiii, 350-355.

108. Ibid., 1, 176, Chs. vi and ix.

109. Chart 6.7, Ibid., 1, 172, Note: these percentages do not refer to the same cohorts.

110. Table 6.32, Ibid., 1, 154-163.

111. Table 9.4, Ibid., 1, 228.

112. *Dáil Debates*, 177, 188.

113. Ibid., 177, 470

114. Ibid., 180, 930-946; Ibid., 191, 15.

115. Press conference by minister, 20 May 1963.

116. Ibid., par. 20.

117. *Tuarascáil na Roinne Oideachais 1980/81*, 42.

118. Ó Buachalla, S., 'Policy and Structural Developments in Irish Higher Education', in *European Journal of Education*, 19, 2, (1984), 165-171.

119. Dáil Éireann, *Appropriation accounts*, 1963, 1973; Tussing, Dale A., *Irish educational expenditures past, present and future*, (Dublin, 1978).

120. *Book of Estimates and public capital programme for 1985*.

121. Clancy, P. and Benson, C., *Higher education in Dublin*, (Dublin, 1979).

122. Clancy, P., *Participation in higher education*.

123. Curriculum and Examinations Board, *Issues and structures in education*.

124. Geary, R. C. and Ó Muircheartaigh, F. S., *Equalization of opportunity in Ireland*, (Dublin, 1974); Geary, R. C. and Henry, E. W., 'Education and Socio-Economic Class' in *The Irish Journal of Education*, 13, (1979), 5-24.

125. Chubb, *Cabinet government in Ireland*.

126. *Tuarascáil na Roinne Oideachais 1964/65 and 1980/81*.

127. Ibid., 1924/25 and 1980/81.

128. Ibid., 1925-62 incl.

129. Clancy, P., *Higher education*; Hannan, D. and Breen, R. et al., *Schooling and sex roles*, (Dublin, 1983).

130. McCarthy, C., *A Decade of upheaval*, (Dublin, 1973); McCarthy, C., *Trade Unions in Ireland 1894-1960*, (Dublin, 1977); O'Connell, *History of the INTO*; Coolahan, J. A., *The ASTI and post-primary education in Ireland. 1909-1984*, (Dublin, 1984).

CHAPTER 4

1. Lindblom, Charles E., *The Policy making process*, (New Jersey, 1968), 29; Chubb, *Cabinet governemnt in Ireland*, Ch. 7.

2. Akenson, *The Irish education experiment*, Ch. IX.

3. Chubb, *Cabinet government in Ireland*, 65.

4. As of January 1985, the INTO had 24,000 embers. The original title of the organisation was The Irish National Teachers' Association.

5. O'Connell, *A History of the INTO*, Ch. 1.

6. Henley was later on the staff of the Church of Ireland Training College, Kildare Street, from its establishment in 1884.

7. The 1927 address, which concerned postprimary education and the 1941 address which discussed broad education policy are good examples.

8. O'Connell, *History of the INTO*, 467.

9. Presidential address 1914: *The Irish School Weekly*, 18 April 1914.

10. Presidential address, 1913, *The Irish School Weekly*, 29 March 1913.

11. *The Irish School Weekly*, lvii, (1911), 103.

12. *Final Report: Vice-Regal inquiry into primary education (Ireland), 1913*, (Cd. 7235), H.C.

1914.

13. *The Irish School Weekly*, 29 March 1913, 55.
14. O'Connell, *History of INTO*, 415.
15. *The Irish School Weekly*, 29 March 1913, 55.
16. Ibid.
17. Starkie, W. J. M., *The History of Irish Primary and Secondary Education during the Last Decade*, (Dublin 1902) 9-11.
18. George Goschen as Chancellor of the Exchequer in 1895, introduced an 'equivalent grant' to Scotland and Ireland, based upon the capitation grant awarded to English schools.
19. O'Connell, *History of INTO*, 188-196.
20. Ibid., 197.
21. *The Irish School Weekly*, 16, (1923), 510.
22. *Public service temporary economies Act* 1933, (37), 1043.
23. *The Irish School Weekly*, 14, (1933), 318.
24. O'Connell, *History of INTO*, 261.
25. *INTO Annual report 1942*, 35.
26. O'Connell, *History of INTO*, 211.
27. *The Irish Times*, 20 May 1946.
28. Recently at the Wexford 1980 Congress: *The Irish Times*. 10 Apr 1980.
29. Private communication from a participant; O'Connell, *History of INTO*, 253.
30. The Mangan Award: *The Annual report of INTO 1963-64*.
31. *The Annual report of INTO 1964-65*, 6.
32. Coolahan, *The ASTI and post-primary education*, 273-308.
33. O'Connell, *History of INTO*, 42-56.
34. Ibid., 52.
35. *The Irish School Weekly*, issues of April 1916; O'Connell, *History of INTO*, 62-68.
36. *Acta et Decreta*, 1927, 387.
37. O'Connell, *History of INTO*, 70-93.
38. Ibid., 93.
39. The Frank Edwards case in Waterford 1937 and the Máirtín Ó Cadháin case in Galway 1938.
40. D.F., S22/4/37.
41. *Sixty seventh and eighty sixth Reports of the commissioners of national education in Ireland, 1900 and 1920; An Roinn Oideachais, Turasgabháil*, 1922-1980.
42. O'Connell, *History of INTO*, 97.
43. The list included the national schools in Cavan, Newbridge, Loughrea and Lanesboro.
44. O'Connell, *History of INTO*, 112.
45. Letter from Cardinal D'Alton to Dr Hillery, Feb. 1962 and letter from D. J. Kelleher to Dr Hillery, Feb. 1962: in O'Connell, *History of INTO*, 119.
46. *Report of tribunal on teachers' salaries*, 1968.
47. Table 4.1.
48. D.F., S22/4/37.
49. Table 8.2., *Investment in education*, 2, 257.
50. Presidential address, *The Irish School Weekly*, 25 April 1908.
51. *Confidential report on inspectorial returns, Feb 1907*.
52. O'Connell, *History of INTO*, 434-436.
53. *Dáil Debates*, 23, 2054, 24 May 1928.

54. *Tuarasgabháil na Roinne Oideachais*, 1932-47.
55. *Dáil Debates*, 80, 1638, 6 June 1940.
56. O'Connell, *History of INTO*, 436.
57. *Tuarasgabhail na Roinne Oideachais*.
58. *Investment in education*, 1, 259.
59. INTO, *School buildings and their maintenance, upkeep and repair*, (1926).
60. O'Connell, *History of INTO*, 439.
61. Presidential address, *The Irish School Weekly*, 2 Apr 1932.
62. *The Irish Independent*, 30 March 1932.
63. *Dáil Debates*, 13, 470-473; 13, 477-478; 23, 2502; 70, 1006; 83, 1191; *Seanad Debates*, 27, 388.
64. INTO, *A Plan for Education*, (Dublin, 1947), 84-98.
65. *Seanad Debates*, , 32, 1902; *Dáil Debates*, 106, 342; *Irish Catholic Directory*, 1946, 681; Mescal, J., *Religion in the Irish System of Education*, (Dublin, 1957), 77-109.
66. Memo by P. Smith, T.D., to the Minister for Education, 31 July 1945 and letter, enclosing this memo, to the Taoiseach: S.P.O., S12891.
67. O'Connell, *History of INTO*, 440.
68. Ibid., 449.
69. Letter from deValera to Deirg, 16 December 1944 and Deirg's reply 24 February 1945: S.P.O. S12891 'B'.
70. The following are examples: *The educational needs of disadvantaged children* (1979), *Inservice education and the training of teachers* (1980), *Education for the physically handicapped* (1981), *A proposal for growth-the administration of national schools* (1980), *An examination of the educational implications of school size* (1982), *Early childhood education* (1983) and *Educational disadvantage* (1984).

CHAPTER 5
1. In 1984 ASTI membership totalled 10,860. In 1981/82 there were 11,864 teachers employed in secondary schools of whom 9,845 were lay teachers and 2,019 were nuns, priests and brothers, of whom 1,309 were nuns.
2. The six lay teachers included P. J. Kennedy, the first president of ASTI, Thomas MacDonagh the 1916 leader and poet, E. Fitzgerald, Cormac Ó Cadhlaigh, later Professor of Irish in UCD and Michael J. O'Shea, who in January 1909 circularised colleagues convening the first meeting.
3. O'Connor, Joseph, 'Old, unhappy far off things, A personal reminiscence' in *The School and College Yearbook*, (1956), 17.
4. *Report of the commission on Intermediate education (Ireland)* [C. 9512], H.C. 1899, xxii, 502; ASTI, *An outline history*, 6; The Association of Intermediate and University Teachers, Ireland. *Secondary education in Ireland, a plea for reform*, 7.

5. Its first president was P. J. Kennedy and its first secretary was P. F. Condon, who had been secretary of the older organisation.
6. The ASTI, *An outline history*, 5.
7. *Irish Journal of Education*, 1, no. 3, (Mar 1910), 46, (hereafter cited as *Journal*).
8. The ASTI, *An outline history*, 6.
9. *Journal*, 1, 10, (Dec 1910), 172-181.
10. The statutory percentage ratio introduced in 1896 by George Goschen, Chancellor of the Exchequer, whereby England, Scotland and Ireland received funds from excise duties for the funding of education.
11. *Journal*, 11, no. 6, (June 1911), 93.
12. *Journal*, 1, no. 10, (Dec 1910), 186.
13. *Journal*, III, no. 11, (Mar 1912), 2.
14. Following the demise of the *Irish Journal of Education* in 1917, the ASTI did not publish a journal for twenty years. From February 1920 to August 1937 the INTO provided space for a weekly column in *The Irish School Weekly* which was contributed by the ASTI General secretary, T. J. Burke.
15. From Annual Reports of CEC published for each Convention.
16. *Report of the Commissioners of Intermediate Education (Ireland)*, 1882, (Cd. 3580), xxiv.
17. Report of Dale and Stephens.
18. Intermediate Education Board for Ireland, *Selections from the report of the temporary inspectors 1901-1902*, 3.
19. *Irish Education Review*, iii, no. 1, (1909), 55.
20. *Journal*, 1, no. 7, (1910), 120.
21. O'Nolan, F. P., 'The state of Irish secondary teachers', in *Journal*, 1, no. 10, (1910), 182.
22. *The Irish Education Review*, iii, no. 10, (1910), 625.
23. Fr. P. Cullen, C. M., of Castleknock College, speaking at the Mansion House meeting on Nov 5th 1910.
24. *Journal*, 11, no. 7, (1911), 97.
25. *Parliamentary Debates*, 1911, xxvi, 210-211.
26. *Irish Education Review*, v, no. 12, (1912), 753.
27. *Irish Education Review*, vi, no. 12, (1913), 106.
28. *Parliamentary Papers*, (Cd. 6294), lxxi, 1913; *Irish Education Review*, vi, no. 10, (1913), 615-640.
29. *Journal*, II, no. 7, (1911), 98.
30. *Journal*, II, no. 10, (1911), 159.
31. *Journal*, III, no. 6, (1912), 97.
32. *Journal*, IV, no. 5, (1913), 77.
33. *Intermediate Education (Ireland) Act*, 1914, 425 Geo. V.
34. The Schedule to the Act specified the following salaries; men: £140 or £110 with board; women: £90 or £70 with board.
35. *Commissioners of Intermediate Education, annual report*, 1917/18.
36. ASTI, *Security of tenure*, 14.
37. *Irish School Weekly*, lxviii, no. 34, 826.
38. *Irish School Weekly*, lxviii, no. 30, 729; no. 40, 958; no. 43, 1006; no. 43, 1030; *The Cork Examiner*, 3 May, 6 May, 8 May 1920.
39. ASTI *An outline history*, 16.

40. *Dáil Debates*, 1 Dec 1922, 2599-2601.
41. Communication from minister to ASTI as quoted in *Official convention programme, ASTI, 1926*, 14; 'Intermediate Education Amendment Act 1924', (S.P.O., S3891); *Iris Oifigiúil*, 67, (8 Aug. 1924).
42. *Consilii Plenarii Manutiani, Acta et Decreta*, 1927.
43. ASTI, *Minutes of Standing Committee*, 12 December 1925.
44. ASTI, *Official programme*, 1926, 12.
45. ASTI, *Official programme*, 1932, 15.
46. ASTI, *Official programme*, 1933, ll.
47. ASTI, *Official programme*, 1934, 15.
48. ASTI, *Security of tenure*, 14 and 34.
49. *The Irish Monthly*, cii, no. 608, (1924), 68.
50. Letter from CHA to ASTI, 20 October 1925, in *Security of tenure*, 30.
51. Letter from Dr O'Doherty, hon. sec. to the Episcopal standing committee, July 1926, Ibid., 36.
52. *Consilii Plenarii Manutiani*, MCMXXVII, Appendix, 284.
53. ASTI, *Security of tenure*, 32.
54. This special report was *Security of tenure*.
55. ASTI, *Official convention programme*, 1936, 12.
56. Coolahan, John. *The ASTI*, 135-138.
57. ASTI file on dismissals; Coolahan, *The ASTI*, 142-48.
58. Ibid., 147.
59. *Dáil Debates*, l, 1 December 1922, 2579-2599; *Seanad Debates*, l, 21 Feb 1923, 402-410.
60. ASTI, *An outline history*, 20.
61. *Dáil Debates*, iii, 3 Oct 1923, Appendix 7.
62. ASTI, *Official programme 1924*, 12; D.F., S19/1/24.
63. Internal memo to minister n. d. ; internal evidence suggests it was compiled in spring 1924; (Mulcahy papers, UCD Archives, P 7/C/70).
64. Ibid.
65. In the interval between the establishment of the Free State and the foundation of the Department of Education (1924), the authority of the Board of Commissioners was vested in two commissioners, Seosamh Ó Neill and Proinsias Ó Dubhthaigh according to an order made on 31 March 1923; D.F., S19/17/24.
66. Fanning, Ronan, *The Irish Department of Finance 1922-58*, (Dublin 1976), Ch 3, 105.
67. There is an echo of this proposal in correspondence to T. M. Healy, Governor General, in Nov 1923 from the Ursuline Convent Waterford, which complains of a tendency in recent years 'to promote the interests of lay teachers to the detriment of religious teachers in secondary schools re grants. (U.C.D. Archives, MacNeill papers, LAI/E/75.)
68. Internal departmental memorandum to minister, 1924(UCD Archives, Mulcahy papers, P 7/C/70); Statement on Intermediate Education made to minister 20 May 1924, signed by J. Thompson, Rev. J.

C. Troy, Rev. J. J. Crehan, J. H. Kane, and T. J. Burke (UCD Archives, Mulcahy papers, P 7/C/l/70.)

69. ASTI memorandum, 'On the position of lay secondary teachers' signed by Tomás de Búrca, 20 May 1924(UCD Archives, Mulcahy papers, P 7/C/l/70.)
70. Ibid.
71. *Dáil Debates*, 8, 712.
72. An Roinn Oideachais, *Rules for the payment of increments of salary of secondary teachers*, (March 1925).
73. The 1946 scales gave incremental maxima of £410 (married men), £290 (single men) and £260 (women).
74. ASTI, *Official Programme 1952*.
75. *The school and college yearbook 1965*, 101.
76. *Report of teachers' salaries committee 1960*, 97.
77. Ibid., 122; Coolahan, *The ASTI*, 193.
78. *Report of tribunal on teachers' salaries 1968*, 5.
79. Ibid., 9-15.
80. ASTI, *Official Programme 1969*, 51; Coolahan, *The ASTI*, 267-316.
81. Coolahan, *The ASTI*, 295-305.
82. These two organisations existed simultaneously in the early fifties and their amicable merger was negotiated in 1955 by Professor Liam Ó Buachalla of UCG.
83. Aontas Múinteoiri Éireann, *Rule Book*, 2.
84. *Gairm*, (April 1956); *Gairm*, (January 1956).
85. Circular from Department of Education, 7 March 1967.
86. *Gairm*, 6 Oct 1967.
87. *Gairm*, 20 Oct 1972.
88. *Gairm*, June 1958, July 1960, July 1961 and July 1964.
89. *Gairm*, 31 Oct 1969.
90. *Gairm*, 2 Dec 1966; HEA, *Report on teacher education*.
91. *Gairm*, June 1959, 'Resolutions'.
92. *Gairm*, July 1960, Presidential address and issues for 1961, 1962 and 1963.
93. *Gairm*, Oct 1965 and May 1966.
94. C. McCarthy, 'A fresh look at vocational education' in TUI, *News and Views*, 18 Dec 1965.
95. VTA, *General secretary's report to congress 1972*.
96. TUI, *Policy document on community schools*, (Oct 1973).
97. TUI, *Observations on ANCO apprenticeship document and union recommendations*, (1973).

CHAPTER 6

1. From its foundation to Oct 1963 the ISA was known as 'The Schoolmasters' Association'.
2. Prior to 1965, some of these orders were affiliated to the CHA though the major order, the Irish Christian Brothers was not.
3. Maurice C. Hime was later headmaster of Foyle College, Derry and an active apologist for Irish intermediate education

in his books, *Home education*, (London, 1887), *The Efficiency of Irish schools*, (London, 1889).
4. *Rules of the Schoolmasters' Association*, (Dublin, 1877).
5. McElligott, *Secondary Education*, Chs 2 and 3.
6. Letter of Dr Walsh to each Catholic bishop dated 21 Sep 1878, in Walsh, *William J. Walsh*, 78.
7. Minutes of ISA, 1 Oct 1910.
8. McElligott, *Secondary education*, Ch. 10.
9. Document incorporated in ISA Minutes dated May 1917.
10. McElligott, *Secondary education*, Ch. 13. ll. *Irish Times*, 27 Oct 1930.
12. *Irish Times*, 11 Nov 1929.
13. *Irish Times*, 27 Oct 1930.
14. *Irish Times*, 8 Nov 1926.
15. Internal department memo., (U.C.D. Archives, Mulcahy Papers, P 7/11/152).
16. Letter of Dr W. J. Walsh, 21 Sept 1878, referred to above.
17. Ibid.
18. Among the early prominent members of the CHA were Fr. Reffe (Blackrock College), Fr. W. Delaney, S.J., Fr. Bodkin (Castleknock), Fr. Henry (St. Malachy's College, Belfast), Dr. Egan (Catholic University School), Fr. O'Leary (Killarney), Fr. Boyle (Armagh), Dr. Molloney (Balinasloe), and Dr. Hassan (Derry).
19. Letter in *The Freeman's Journal*, 2 Oct 1881.
20. *The Freeman's Journal*, 23 August 1883.
21. See Ch. 5 of this work and Ch. 10 of McElligott, *Secondary education*.
22. *The Irish Educational Review*, vi, no. 1, 1913, 48.
23. Coolahan, *The ASTI*, 58-63.
24. (U.C.D. Archives, Mulcahy Papers, P 7/C1/70).
25. *Dáil Debates*, 16, 405.
26. Ch. 10 of this work.
27. Coolahan, *The ASTI*, 198-205.
28. In 1934 the CHA was represented by its chairman, Dr J. C. McQuaid and its secretary Dr J. Staunton of St Kieran's College, Kilkenny, who was later bishop of Ferns.
29. CHA meeting, May 1947.
30. CHA meeting, Oct 1947.
31. ASTI letters to CHA, Dec 1965 and CCSS Reports, 1963-65.
32. CHA meetings of 1951, 1952 and 1955 and *Report on Salary 1960-64*.
33. Pearse, P. H., *The Murder Machine*, (Dublin, 1915).
34. *Dáil Debates*, 78, 1565; Estimate Speech, 6 June 1940.
35 Perhaps the best example is that of Mr. deValera and Cardinal D'Alton, Dr J. C. McQuaid and Dr E. Leen, C. S. Sp.
36. Coolahan, *The ASTI*, 204.
37. In the resolution forwarded to the commissioners by the ISA on 6 April 1902 there is reference to 'the convent schools' committee.

38. Letter from Department of Education, 26 March 1929, to various education bodies in *Report of the Department of Education 1928-29*, 75.
39. Dr W. F. Butler had been assistant commissioner of Intermediate education from 1910 and after 1924 was principal officer in the secondary branch of the Department of Education at 1 Hume St.
40. These rules were incorporated in a new constitution which was adopted in 1973.
41. *Annual report CCSS 1966*, 77; Ibid, 1976, 1.
42. *Annual report CCSS 1949*, 75.
43. *Annual report CCSS 1950*, 32.
44. *Annual report CCSS 1946*, 1949.
45. *Annual report CCSS 1931*, 10.
46. *Annual report CCSS 1946*, 16.
47. *Annual report CCSS 1941*, 20, 60.
48. *Annual report CCSS 1952*, 42.
49. *Annual report CCSS 1945*, 30.
50. Ibid., 31.
51. Ibid., 36.
52. Ibid., 40.
53. Ibid., 39.
54. Ibid., 29.
55. Ibid., 30.
56. *Annual report CCSS 1947*, 35, 36.
57. *Annual report CCSS 1946*, 61.
58. *Annual report CCSS 1947*, 49.
59. Ibid., 16.
60. Ibid., 55.
61. Ibid., 56.
62. Ibid., 57.
63. *Annual report CCSS 1948*, 13.
64. Ibid., 35.
65. Ibid., 37.
66. *Annual report CCSS 1949*, 52.
67. *Dáil Debates*, 195, 1441, 13 Dec 1962.
68. While the JMB contained representatives of the CHA, the CCSS, the Christian Brothers, the IHA and of the AIH, the impetus towards its formation came from Fr John Hughes (CHA) with the active assistance of Mother Jordana (CCSS) and Br P. J. Walsh (Christian Brothers).
69. *Constitution of the Federation*, 1958, 1.
70. Cannon, P. G., 'Investment in education', paper read to the Statistical and Social Inquiry Society, 25 Mar 1966.
71. Memorandum of Federation, dated 30 June 1960. (Private papers)
72. Published by the Federation in May 1962 under the names of its officers Eunan O'Donnell, Joseph O'Dwyer, Seán Hamilton, Vincent Russell and Patrick G. Cannon. A supplementary volume was published in 1963.
73. *Dáil Debates*, 195, 1445, 13 Dec 1962.
74. *Dáil Debates*, 196, 23 Jan 1963.
75. *Dáil Debates*, 195, 1442-1450, 13 Dec 1962.
76. *Dáil Debates*, 196, 23 Jan 1963.
77. The FLCSS joined the JMB in 1967.
78. *Journal of Proceedings of the General Synod 1964: Report of the Board of Education*, 94.
79. In 1959 there were 45 Protestant secondary schools catering for 6,295 pupils of whom 4,368 were Church of Ireland members. The schools varied in size from 479 (Wesley College, Dublin) to 25 (Bishop Hodson's School at Elphin).
80. *Journal of Proceedings of the General Synod, 1962: Report of Board of Education*, 118.
81 General Synod, *Report on Secondary Education*, (1965), 6.
82. Ibid.
83. Ibid., 24.
84. SEC Report in *Proceedings of the General Synod 1967*.
85. SEC Report in *Proceedings of the General Synod 1969*. The earlier council was known as the Protestant Secondary Schools' Council.
86. Much of the factual and anecdotal information in this section, while obtained from authoritative sources, cannot be attributed.
87. *To the authorities of secondary and vocational schools*, 1 Jan 1966: Appendix 1 of this work.
88. This special committee consisted of Rev M. Canon Mooney, Tuam, Rev J. Hughes, S. J., Rev E. D. Creed, Provincial, Christian Brothers, Rev B. Browne, Presentation College, Bray, Mother M. Jordana, O. P., Mother M. Fidelma, Convent of Mercy, Galway, Mr. Seán Hamilton, Principal, High School, Bandon.
89. *Council of Managers of Catholic Secondary Schools: Constitution 1967*, article 6.
90. Ibid., article 7 (a).
91. The Council consists of eight members, two representatives each from the CHA and the TBA, three from the CCSS and one from the FLCSS.
92. Press statement of Dr P. Hillery, 20 May 1963.
93. Ibid., 12, 15.
94. Department of Education, Circular 39/64, 29 Apr 1965.
95. Mr. O'Malley met the Catholic bishops on 4 Oct, the Protestant church leaders on 13 Oct and the Joint Managerial Body on 16 Dec. For one account of what transpired see Randles, E., *Post-Primary education in Ireland 1957-70*, (Dublin, 1975), 248-253.
96. It is understood that this alternative scheme emerged from meetings held in the Dublin archdiocese.
97. See for example *Have the Snakes Come Back?*, Vera Verba Publications, (Dublin, 1975).
98. Figure 6. 2.
99. Employer-Labour Conference, *Adjudication report No. 6.*, (24 February 1975).

CHAPTER 7
1. Fenwick, I. G. and McBride, P., *The Government of education in Britain*, (London, 1978), 212.
2. For a detailed analysis of the political system see Chubb, *The government and politics of Ireland*.

3. The Irish Labour Party and Trade Union Congress, (ILP and TUC), *Annual Report 1918*, 12.

4. Chubb, *The government and politics of Ireland*, Ch. 3, 70; Garvin, T., *The evolution of Irish national politics*, (Dublin, 1983).

5. Chubb, *The government and politics of Ireland*, 95.

6. Table 3. 5, Ibid., 96.

7. Carty, R. K., *Party and parish pump: electoral politics in Ireland*, (Ontario, 1981), Table 4.4, 96.

8. 1932-1948 and 1957-1973.

9. Mair, P., *Issue dimensions and party strategies in the Irish Republic 1948-1981*, (Florence, 1982), 27.

10. Ibid, 31.

11. Kogan, Maurice, *The Politics of educational change*, (London, 1971), 147.

12. Mitchell, A., *Labour in Irish politics*; Chubb, *The government and politics of Ireland*, Ch. 3, 70; Manning, M., *Irish political parties*.

13. Mitchell, *Labour in Irish politics*, 65-67.

14. Chubb, *The government and politics of Ireland*, 334; Table 3.2 in Carty, *Electoral politics in Ireland*, 36.

15. Chubb, *The politics and government of Ireland*, 83.

16. Carty, *Electoral politics in Ireland*, 72-75.

17. Elements of education policy are also to be found in *The Nation Organised*, (Dublin, 1936).

18. Mitchell, *Labour in Irish politics*, 16. The 'free' education referred to here probably meant the abolition of the fees charged in national schools until abolished in 1892 following the Irish Education Act which made school attendance to 14 compulsory and consequently free.

19. Ryan, D., (ed.), *James Connolly, Socialism and Nationalism*, (Dublin, 1924), Appendix 1, 185.

20. Connolly, J., *Labour in Ireland*, 304.

21. McDonald, W., *Reminiscences of a Maynooth Professor*, (London, 1925), 185.

22. *Annual report of ILP and TUC 1916*, 53.

23. *Annual report of ILP and TUC 1917*, 8.

24. Ibid., 66.

25. *Annual report of ILP and TUC 1918*, 45, 60, 63.

26. Dublin United Trades Council and Labour League, *Let labour lead*, (Dublin, 1918), 10.

27. *Annual report of ILP and TUC 1918*, 29.

28. Lynch, P., 'The social revolution', 45.

29. Dáil Éireann, *Miontuairisci an Chéad Dála 1919-1921*. Opening Session, 21 Jan 1919, 23.

30. Lynch, 'The social revolution', 46.

31. *Annual Report of the ILP and TUC 1920*, 31; Ó Buachalla, S., 'Education as an Issue in the First and Second Dáil' in *Administration*, 25, no. 1, 57-75.

32. Mitchell, *Labour in Irish politics*, 122-129.

33. Dáil Éireann, cabinet minutes, 4 Mar 1920, (SPO DE 1/2).

34. *Annual report of ILP and TUC 1920*, 12-13.

35. Dáil Éireann, cabinet minutes, 20 Feb. 1920, (SPO DE 1/2). Cabinet Minutes: DE I/2, meeting of 20 February 1920.

36. Manning, *Irish political parties*, 10.

37. Rumpf, E. and Hepburn, A. C., *Nationalism and Socialism in twentieth century Ireland*, (Liverpool, 1977), 62-63.

38. Communications from Professor Basil Chubb, who interviewed Thomas Johnson on the question.

39. *Annual report of the ILP and TUC 1924*, 81.

40. The members of the committee were T. Johnson, (chairman), T. J. O'Connell, (vice-chairman), Tomás de Búrca (ASTI), Thomas Farren, Seán C. MacGuaighin, Frances A. H. Heagen, Cormac Breathnach (INTO) and Dr R. MacDonald (Technical).

41. Dr R. MacDonald of the Municipal Technical Institute, Dún Laoghaire, would not agree to allow the adverse comments on the Department's Inspectorate to be applied to the Inspectors of the Technical Instruction Branch. He also wished to see the Urban District Committees of Technical Instruction retained.

42. *Labour's policy on education*, 21, quoting from section IX, 'When we are Free', of *The Murder Machine*.

43. Ibid., 21.

44. Ibid., 10-13. Note: The concept of an 'Extern Minister' was based upon all-party agreement on policy and a funding mechanism which was not dependent on cabinet procedures. Such a minister and the advisory committee would have a role similar to that of the present Swedish National Board of Education; in such a structure the Department of Education would have a diminished policy role.

45. Ibid., 14.

46. Ibid., 19.

47. Ibid., 20.

48. Ibid., 18-19.

49. Lynch, 'The social revolution', 53.

50. 'Postwar planning', (SPO S12891 'A').

51. The Irish Labour Party. *Challenge and change*, 1.

52. Ibid., 10, 11.

53. Ibid., 13.

54. Ibid., 56.

55. Rumpf, E., *Nationalism and socialism in Ireland*, 156, 157; Busteed, M. A. and Mason, H., 'Irish Labour in the 1969 Election', in *Political Studies*, xviii, 3, (1970).

56. *Labour party outline policy (education) 1969*, 65-82.

57. Ibid., 68-69.

58. Ibid., 112-118.

59. Manning, *Irish Political Parties*, 9-19.

60. Chubb, *The government and politics of Ireland*, 81-82.

61. Manning, *Irish political parties*, 15-17; Garvin, *The evolution of Irish nationalist politics*, 168.

62. Nealon, T., *Guide to the Dáil and Senate*, (Dublin, 1982).

63. Chubb, B., 'Ireland' in S. Henig (ed.), Political parties in the European Community, (London, 1980).
64. Ibid., 125.
65. Table 7. 2
66. Rumpf, Nationalism and socialism in Ireland, 220.
67. Chubb, The government and politics of Ireland, 58.
68. Garvin, Evolution of Irish nationalist politics, 158.
69. Chubb, 'Ireland', 119-124.
70. Garvin, Evolution of Irish nationalist politics, 158.
71 Chubb, The government and politics of Ireland, 81.
72. Rumpf, Nationalism and socialism in Ireland, 132.
73. Manning, Irish political parties, 31.
74. Gallup poll, Apr. 1969: in Appendix A, Table l, Manning, Irish political parties, 14.
75. Irish Marketing Surveys, (1977).
76. Chubb, Government and Politics, 82.
77. Debate on the Constitution, 18 Oct 1922, Dáil Debates, 1695.
78. Ibid., 1699.
79. Ibid., 1700.
80. Ibid., 1702.
81. The national programme conference, National programme of primary instruction, (1922), 24; Retention rate is calculated on enrolment at standard six or standard five over enrolment in standard two, four or three years previously.
82. Dáil Debates, 18 Oct 1922, 1702.
83. Ibid., 1710.
84. Dáil Debates, 4 Jan. 1923, 548.
85. Dáil Debates, 16, 406, 1926.
86. Dáil Debates, 13, 190, 1925.
87. (Mulcahy Papers, P 7/C/132, UCD Archives).
88. Fine Gael policy for a just society - education, 67-69.
89. Ibid., 4.
90. Ibid., 32.
91. Ibid., 1.
92. Ibid., 4.
93. Ibid., 19.
94. Ó Buachalla, S., 'Irish demographic issues and educational planning', European Journal of Education, 17, no. 1, 1984.
95. Department of Education, Action programme for education in the 80's, 31, 76, (1984).
96. Ibid., 29.
97. Ibid., 38.
98. Fianna Fáil. A national policy, 18.
99. A national policy, 13; see also M. Moynihan (ed.), Speeches and statements by Éamon de Valera 1917-1973, (Dublin, 1980), 133.
100. A national policy, 17.
101. Garvin, Evolution of Irish nationalist politics, 154.
102. Ibid., 157.
103. Ibid., 156.
104. Ibid., 155.
105. Rumpf, Nationalism and socialism in Ireland, 103-107, 125-128.
106. Chubb, Government and politics of Ireland, 81.
107. Rumpf, Nationalism and socialism in Ireland, 103.
108. Irish Labour Party, Annual report 1932, 7.
109. Rumpf, Nationalism and socialism in Ireland, 126.
110. Garvin, Evolution of Irish nationalist politics, 154.
111. Murphy, John A., 'The Irish party system' in Nowlan, Kevin B. and Williams, T.D. (eds.), Ireland in the war years and after, 151.
112. 'The republican goals' in Moynihan, Speeches and statements, 52-53.
113. 'Taking stock' in Moynihan, Speeches and statements, 522.
114. Rumpf, Nationalism and socialism in Ireland, 220.
115. Ibid., 223.
116. O'Hegarty, P. S., Ireland under the union, (Dublin, 1922), 781.
117. Murphy, The Irish party system, 150.
118. Dudley Edwards, R., 'Church and State in Modern Ireland', in Nowlan, Kevin B. and Williams, T.D. (eds.), Ireland in the war years and after, 109-119; this would apply especially to prominent members such as Frank Aiken and Tommy Mullins.
119. Ibid., 111-113.
120. Garvin, Evolution of Irish nationalist politics, 179.
121. See for instance Whyte, Church and State, 130.
122. See Department of Education, Ár nDáltai Uile, (Dublin, 1969) and White Paper on Education, (Dublin, 1980).
123. Moynihan, Speeches and statements, 131.
124. Ibid., 188.
125. Ibid., 342.
126. Ibid., 467.
127. Dáil Debates, lxxviii, 6 June 1940, 1569.
128. Fianna Fáil manifesto 1977, 40.
129. Ibid.
130. Ó Buachalla, S., 'Education as an issue in the first and second Dáil'.

CHAPTER 8.

1. Table 6. 2 of this work.
2. Administration Yearbook & Diary 1982-83, 99-103.
3. Akenson, The Irish education experiment, 395.
4. The bishops' pastoral in I.E.R, xx, (1900).
5. Miller, Nation, church and state, 437-442.
6. Ch. 6, Figs. 6.1 and 6.2.
7. Whyte, Church and State, 19.
8. I.E.R. , xviii, (1898), 83.
9. I.E.R. , xx, (1900), 553.
10. Ibid.
11. I.E.R. , xxii, (1902), 459.
12. I.E.R. , xxiv, (1904), 171.
13. Ibid.
14. Strauss, E., Irish nationalism and British

democracy, (London, 1951), 214-215; *An Claidheamh Soluis*, editorials in issues of May 1907.

15. Miller, *Nation, church ans state*, 439.
16. *The Irish Independent*, 16 Feb 1920.
17. *I.E.R.*, xiv, (1919), 504-507.
18. 'Official Statements in 1919' in *Irish Catholic Directory*, 1920, 499.
19. Ibid., 517.
20. Ibid., 498.
21. Ibid., 517.
22. *I.E.R.*, xiv, (1919), 504.
23. *Dáil Éireann*: cabinet minutes, 4 Mar 1920, (S.P.O., DE 1/2).
24. *I.E.R.*, xv, (1920), 150.
25. *Dáil Éireann*, minutes, 27 Oct 1919, 162.
26. Akenson, *Education and enmity*, 39-71.
27. Statement of northern bishops, 27 Mar 1923, in *Irish Catholic Directory*, (1924), 602.
28. *Irish Catholic Directory*, (1925), 563.
29. *The Times Educational Supplement*, 29 Oct 1921, 323.
30. *Irish Catholic Directory*, (1928), 558.
31. Pastoral address issued by the archbishops and bishops of Ireland to their flocks on the occasion of the Plenary Synod held in Maynooth 1927, *Acta et Decreta*, 1927, 157.
32. *The Christian Education of Youth*, 10, 11, 14.
33. Ibid., 20, 22.
34. Ibid., 28-38.
35. Ó Néill, Tomás agus Ó Fiannachta, Pádraig, *De Valera*, (Dublin, 1968), ii, 328.
36. Cahill, E., S.J., *Framework of a Christian State*, (Dublin, 1932), 350.
37. Ibid., 361.
38. Ibid., 371, 372.
39. Ibid., 376.
40. McKenna, L., 'State rights in education', in *Studies*, xiv, 1927, 220.
41. Department committee on school inspection; E 47/1/27.
42. O'Neill, Joseph, 'The educationalist', in *Studies*, xxxii, (1943), 158.
43. His major works: *State policy in Irish education*, (Dublin, 1916); *The Catholic schools of Ireland*, (Louvain, 1931); *The National University of Ireland 1908-32*, (ed.), (Dublin, 1932); various articles in *Studies*, *The Irish Monthly* of which he was editor and in *The Catholic Bulletin*, of which he was joint editor.
44. *Vice-regal committee on Intermediate education, 1918: Note on appeal against notice of dismissal, report*, (Cd. 8724), H.C., xi.
45. Corcoran, T. J., 'The Catholic philosophy of education', in *Studies*, xix, (1930), 206.
46. D.F., S18/3/41.
47. Devane, R., 'Adolescence and the vocational education bill' in *I.E.R.*, xxxvi, (1930), 20-24.
48. Brenan, M., 'The Catholic school system of Ireland', in *I.E.R.*, iii, (1938), 257-271. See also his 'The vocational schools' in *I.E.R.*, lvii, (1941), 13-27.
49. Lucey, Cornelius, 'Making the school system of Ireland Catholic', in *I.E.R.*, lii,

(1938), 405-417.
50. Ibid., 411-412.
51. Ibid., 412-417.
52. *The Irish Times*, 6 May 1950.
53. D.F., S25/1/33.
54. McQuaid, J. C., *Higher education for catholics*, (Dublin, 1961).
55. McGrath, F., 'The university question', in P. J. Corish (ed.), *The Church since emancipation: Catholic education*, (Dublin, 1971), 142.
56. William Cardinal Conway, *Catholic schools*, (Dublin, 1971), 6.
57. 'Lenten pastoral of Cardinal Logue 1907' in *Irish Catholic Directory*, (1908), 456.
58. Akenson, *The Irish education experiment*; Norman, *The Catholic Church and Ireland*; Bowen, Paul, *Cardinal Cullen*; Kerr, D. A., *Peel, priests and politics*, (Cambridge, 1982).
59. McDonald, *Reminiscences of a Maynooth professor*, 163-194.
60. Ibid., 185.
61. *This Week*, 4 June 1971, 12; 'The priests in education', in *Christus Rex*, 24 Apr 1970, 79.
62. Press statement of Dr P. J. Hillery, 20 May 1963.
63. Memo to Executive Council, Nov 1932, (D.F., S20/7/32).
64. D.F., 2/30/28.
65. *Acta et Decreta Concilii Plenarii Episcoporum Hiberniae 1927*.
66. Memo of 19 June 1930, (D.F., S20/11/30).
67. D.F., S22/4/31.
68. Evidence by department in the High Court, (D.F., S18/1/38).
69. Memo by J. O'Neill dated 15 July 1926, (D.F., S18/7/26).
70. Letter from the secretary to the hierarchy to the Department, dated 25 June 1925.
71. Letter from Department of Education to hierarchy dated 10 April 1926.
72. D.F., S20/18/28.
73. D.F., S18/1/38.
74. *The Irish Times*, 5 July 1939; *The Irish Independent*, 20 Feb 1940.
75. Appendix 3: Letter from minister for education, John Marcus O'Sullivan to Dr Keane, Bishop of Limerick, 31 Oct 1930.
76. It is strongly implied that the minister envisaged continuation classes being held in the evening.
77. *Acta et Decreta*, 1927, 120, 402.1.
78. D.F., S84/4/30.
79. Letter from the registrar of UCG, Mons S. Hynes, to the minister for finance, dated 1 July 1926, (D.F., S18/2/26).
80. D.F., S20/4/28; D.F., S22/2/33.
81. Internal department memo to the minister for finance, dated 21 Nov 1932, (D.F., S20/4/28).
82. Memo dated 1 Mar 1939, (D.F., S25/2/39).
83. UCD Archives, Mulcahy Papers, P 7/C/154.
84. 'Reply from Dr Fergus, secretary to the hierarchy, 24 June 1954', (Ibid.).
85. D.F., S20/28/26.

86. O'Connell, *History of INTO*, 434-449.
87. Ibid., 441.
88. D.F., S22/4/37.
89. Letter from S. McEntee to T. Deirg, 18 June 1937, (D.F., S22/4/37).
90. Letter from T. Deirg to S. McEntee, 18 June 1937, (Ibid.).
91. Cabinet meeting 11 Jan 1935, (D.F., S22/2/35).
92. Facefield N. S., Co Mayo from 2 Feb to 6 Mar 1942.
93. Letter from minister for education, T. Deirg to Dr Staunton, bishop of Ferns, 31 May 1943, (S.P.O., S12891).
94. Letter from Dr Staunton to Mr. Deirg 26 Oct 1943, (Ibid.).
95. Department memo to Minister for Finance dated 22 Dec 1949, (D.F., A 22/2/35).
96. Letter from minister to Dr Staunton, 10 Jan 1945.
97. D.F., S22/2/35.
98. Letter and memo from Patrick Smith, T.D., to Taoiseach and Minister for Education 31 July 1945, (S.P.O., Cabinet Papers, S12891).
99. O'Connell, T. J., History of INTO, 448.
100. The Inter-departmental committee of 1935, The commission on youth unemployment 1943-51, department committee on reform of the education system 1945-47.
101. *Report of Coimisiún na Gaeltachta 1926*, 11.
102. Meeting of Gaeltacht Committee of Cabinet on 29 June 1932, (S.P.O. Cabinet minutes, S6506 and S9409).
103. Memo from Department of Education to Department of Finance 30 Dec 1933, (D.F., S20/1/34).
104. Letter from Department of Education to Department of Finance, 22 Jan 1934, (S.P.O., S2512).
105. D.F., S20/1/34.
106. Note from secretary to Government to Department of Education, 3 Feb 1934, (S.P.O., S2512).
107. Memo from Department of Education to cabinet, Oct 1947.
108. S.P.O., S12891 'B'. The committee met in Feb 1945 and reported to the minister on 27 June 1947.
109. Letter from Department of Education to Dr Staunton, Apr 1948 (S.P.O., S12891 'B').
110. See Chapter 6.
111. Whyte, Church and State, 21.
112. Ibid., 370.
113. *Acta et Decreta, 1900*, *432.
114. *Acta et Decreta, 1927*, *385; *Acta et Decreta, 1956*, *259.
115. *Acta et Decreta, 1900*, *435. 5.
116. Ibid., *440.
117. *Acta et Decreta, 1927*, *387.
118. Ibid., *388.
119. *Acta et Decreta, 1956*, *260. 1.
120. Ibid., *260. 2.
121. Ibid., *263.
122. *Acta et Decreta, 1900*, *471; *Acta et Decreta, 1927*, *402.1.
123. *Acta et Decreta, 1900*, *486, *490; *Acta et Decreta, 1927*, *404. *Acta et Decreta, 1956*, * 287.
124. *Journal of Proceedings General Synod of Church of Ireland 1908* containing Annual report of the Board of Education: (hereafter cited as *Annual report*.
125. *Annual report, 1917*.
126. *Annual report, 1914*.
127. *Annual report, 1906*.
128. *Annual report, 1918*.
129. *Annual reports, 1915, 1915*.
130. *Annual report, 1907*.
131. *Annual report, 1910*; Ó Buachalla, S., 'Educational policy and the role of the Irish language 1931 to 1981', *European Journal of Education*, xlx, no. 1, (1984), 83.
132. *Annual report, 1918*.
133. *Annual report, 1904*.
134. *Annual report, 1919*.
135. *Annual report, 1920*.
136. *Annual report, 1921*.
137. *Annual report, 1923*.
138. *Report and Programme*, The National Programme Conference 1925, 4.
139. *Church of Ireland Gazette*, 9 May 1930.
140. *Annual report, 1929*, 227.
141. *Annual report, 1928*, 256.
142. *Annual report, 1931*, 236.
143. *Annual report, 1939*, 227.
144. *Annual report, 1943*, 203.
145. *Annual report, 1954*, 109.
146. *Annual report, 1957*, 103.
147. *Annual report, 1963*, 101.
148. *Annual report, 1923*, 202.
149. *Annual report, 1923*, 203.
150. This was the author of *Séadna*, an tAthair Peadar Ó Laoghaire.
151. This series was published by The Educational Company of Ireland, Dublin.
152. *Annual report, 1935*, 224.
153. *Annual report, 1938*, 217; The winner was Miss D. Casserly of Diocesan Girls' School whose volume was published by Talbot Press.
154. *Annual reports, 1950, 1951*.
155. Canon J. R. Ross at the 1960 synod.
156. Moody, T. W. & Martin, F. X., *The course of Irish history*, Cork, 1966); *Annual report, 1967*.
157. *Annual reports, 1925, 1928*.
158. *Annual report, 1935*.
159. *Annual reports, 1936, 1937*.
160. *Annual report, 1939*.
161. *Annual report, 1942*.
162. *Annual report, 1949*.
163. Memo., 18 Nov 1948, (UCD Archives, Mulcahy Papers, P 7/C/153).
164. Ibid., 1.
165. UCD Archives, Mulcahy Papers, P 7/C/ 152.
166. Internal memo. by an assistant secretary, (P 7/C/11, 152).
167. UCD Archives, Mulcahy Papers, P 7/C/ 11, 153.

168. *The Irish Times,* 11 May 1950.
169. Memo. by chief inspector primary branch, 6 June 1950.
170. Letter 26 Feb 1951, (P 7/C/152).
171. D.F., S106/6/51.
172. *Annual report, 1944.*
173. *Annual report, 1957.*
174. *Annual report, 1955.*
175. *Annual report, 1963; The Secondary Curriculum,* 1962, pars. 428, 429.
176. *Annual report, 1966.*
177. Introduction, *Annual report, 1983.*
178. *Annual report, 1967.*
179. See Chapter 6 on The managerial bodies.

CHAPTER 9.
1. Starkie, W. J. M., *Recent reforms in Irish education: history of primary and secondary education during the last decade,* (Dublin, 1902); Plunkett, Horace, *Ireland in the new century,* (London, 1904); Birrell, A., *Things past redress,* (London 1936); Ó Broin, Leon, *The chief secretary, Augustine Birrel in Ireland,* (London, 1969).
2. D. P. S., E 57/6.
3. This was Thomas Fitzgerald.
4. D. P. S., E 48/1/46.
5. D. P. S., E 48/1/40.
6. D. P. S., E 57/3.
7. Kogan, Maurice, *The politics of education,* (London, 1971), 43.
8. Headey, Bruce, *British cabinet ministers,* 54.
9. Ibid., 76-77.
10. Martin, F. X. and Byrne, F. J., *The scholar revolutionary: Eoin MacNeill 1887-1945,* (Dublin 1973).
11. Brennan, Robert, *Allegiance,* (Dublin, 1950), 153.
12. *Dáil Debates,* 4, 1224; 13, 796.
13. UCD Archives, MacNeill Papers. LAI/F/30, 93.
14. Ibid., (LAI/E/76, LAI/F/166).
15. Ibid., (LAI/F/76).
16. Ibid., (LAI/E/75).
17. Ibid., (LAI/F/166).
18. *Dáil Debates,* 1, 1699.
19. Ibid., 1, 1700.
20. *Dáil Debates,* 13, 190.
21. Ibid., 13, 192.
22. Ibid., 13, 194.
23. D. P. S., E 48/1/31; E 51/2/33; E 48/1/46.
24. *Dail Debates,* Debate on Constitution, 1, 1695, 1699.
25. Ibid., 13, 189; 13, 353.
26. Ibid., 2, 2574; 'Practicalism in education', UCD Archives, MacNeill Papers, LAI/E/88.
27. UCD Archives, Mulcahy Papers, P 7/C/I/70; S.P.O., Cabinet Papers, S4650/9. *Note:* In 1926 the Attorney General was of the opinion that Rule 4 was contrary to article 8 of the 1922 Constitution.
28. UCD Archives, MacNeill Papers. LAI/E/37.
29. 'Scheme for preparatory colleges' UCD Archives, Mulcahy Papers. P 7/C/I/70, *Tuarascáil na Roinne Oideachais,* 1931/32,

15.
30. 'The gaelicising of Ireland', UCD Archives, Mulcahy Papers, 7/C/1/71.
31. Tierney, M., *Eoin MacNeill,* (Oxford, 1982).
32. Gwynn, Aubrey, 'John Marcus O'Sullivan' *The Clongownian* (1948), 27-29.
33. *Dáil Debates,* 38, 1900.
34. *Dáil Debates,* 30, 2052.
35. *Dáil Debates,* 14, 1010.
36. D.F., S19/4/30; D.F., S20/8/28.
37. D.F., S20/29/31. See Chapter 8 and *Annual report of Church of Ireland Board of Education, 1931.*
38. D.F., S21/1/29; Among the recipients were Tadhg Twomey, UCC and Vincent Barry, UCG
39. *Dáil Debates,* 12, 812.
40. *Report and programme of the national programme conference,* 1925/26.
41. *Tuarasgbháil na Roinne Oideachais 1928/* 29, 166.
42. UCD Archives, Blythe papers, P 24/302B, P 24/303. P 24/304, P 24/342, P 24/345.
43. D.F., S20/39/41; S19/8/31; S20/9/29.
44. *Dáil Debates,* 12, 820.
45. *Tuarasgbháil na Roinne Oideachais 1928-* 29, 8; D.F., S84/13/29.
46. D.F., S84/13/29.
47. D.F., S24/4/30.
48. Internal Department of Finance memo. by H. P. Boland 21 Nov 1930, (D.F. S24/4/30).
49. D.F., S20/28/26.
50. D.F., S20/26/26.
51. *Dáil Debates,* Question by Deputy J. Good, 27 Oct 1927, 21, 6.
52. D.F., S20/9/29.
53. O'Connell, T. J., *History of INTO,* 209; Titley, E. Brian, *Church, State and the control of schooling in Ireland 1900-44,* (Dublin, 1983), 128.
54. D.F., S20/8/28; D.F., S19/4/30.
55. D.F., S101/11/32.
56. Minutes of the cabinet committee on the Gaeltacht, (S.P.O., S59409).
57. D.F., S20/1/34; see above ch. 8, ref. 114.
58. 'Higher primary schools in the Gaeltacht', memo to Department of Finance, 30 Dec 1933, (S.P.O., Cabinet papers, S2512).
59. D.F., A 24/2/38.
60. Interview of CBS superior, Dingle with Minister for Education, 24 June 1954, (UCD Archives, Mulcahy papers P7/C/54).
61. D.F., S18/47/33.
62. Internal memo. of Department of Finance, (D.F., S18/47/33).
63. Letter from Roinn an Taoisigh to Department of Finance, 1 Nov 1947, (D.F., S18/47/33).
64. Letter from the Department of Education to the Department of Finance, 5 Apr 1937, (D.F., S24/3/37).
65. Letter, 26 Jan 1938, from the Department of Education to the Department of Local Government and Public Health, (D.F., S24/3/37).
66. Minutes of cabinet committee on

economic planning, 14 Apr 1943, (S.P.O., S12891'A').

67. Minutes of cabinet committee on economic planning, 12 May 1943, (S.P.O., S12891'A').

68. Letter from Deirg to de Valera, 12 Jan 1945, (S.P.O., S12891).

69. *Investment in Education*, 1, 259.

70. Letters from de Valera to Deirg and from Taoiseach's Department to Department of Education between 8 July 1942 and 2 Oct 1942, (S.P.O., S12891'A').

71. Submission by Department of Education 7 Dec 1944, (S.P.O., S12891'B', S13529).

72. Letter from de Valera to Deirg 16 Dec 1944, (S.P.O., S12891'B').

73. Letter from Deirg to de Valera 24 Feb 1945, (S.P.O., S12891'B'). *Note*: The members of this Department committee were, Labhrás Ó Muirithe, (chairman), Pádraig Ó Dubhthaigh, P. S. Ó Tighearnaigh, S. Mac Cionnaith, P. E. Ó Suilleabháin, J. P. Hackett, T. Ó Raifeartaigh, L. Mac Giolla Osa, E. Ó Cuirc, D. Ó Laoghaire (rúnaí).

74. Letter from Minister for Education to Department of an Taoiseach, 29 Aug 1945, (S.P.O., S12891'B').

75. Report and interim report of the department committee to examine the education system, 1947, (S.P.O., S12891 'A', 'B').

76. S.P.O., S12891'B', Table 2.

77. Interim report, par. 11, (S.P.O., S12891'A').

78. Memorandum (Final Report), par 25, (S.P.O., S12891'B').

79. Note on continuation schools with reference to par. 31, signed by J. P. Hackett, 18 July 1947, (S.P.O., S12891'B').

80. Memo., par. 32, (S.P.O., S12891

81. Letter from Minister for Education, to Dr Staunton, secretary to the hierarchy, 10 Apr 1948, (S.P.O., S12891'B').

82. D.F., S20/9/36.

83. Internal memo 11 Mar 1942, Ibid.; Estimate speech by Minister for Education, 3 June 1942; Letter from McEntee to Deirg 3 June 1942, (D.F., S20/9/36). *Note*: In its first compulsory year, 1943, of 56 X 10³ eligible candidates, 44 X 10³ were presented and of the 2,656 centre superintendents, 1,620 were national teachers.

84. D.F., S20/20/41; Department of Education Circular 14/44; D.F., S20/38/40.

85. Memo. from Minister for Education to Department of Finance, 5 Apr 1937, (D.F., S24/3/37).

86. D.F., S20/31/38.

87. D.F., S25/1/33; Internal memo and official reply 10 Oct 1936. (D.F., S18/18/36).

88. *Revised programme of primary instruction*, 1934.

89. Chapter 12.

90. *Dáil Debates*, 94, 394.

91. Note by T. Ó Raifeartaigh, 27 May 1953, (D.F., S18/3/41).

92. D.F., S20/10/35.

93. D.F., S20/18/37.

94. *Dáil Debates*, 38, 1746.

95. Cabinet memo 17 Nov 1944, (S.P.O., S12753 'A').

96. Addendum to memo 19 Feb 1945, (S.P.O., S12753 'A').

97. Minister's reply to the Dáil motion on the council of education, March 1945, (S.P.O., S12753 'A').

98. Minister's estimate speech, 22 May 1947, *Dáil Debates*.

99. Ibid.

100. Ibid.

101. *Dáil Debates*, 77, 1565.

102. Department of Finance internal memo, 23 Aug 1951, (D.F., S18/2/45).

103. Translated from: 'agus ní féidir liom a radh i láthair na huaire cé aca is fiú nó nach fiú an costas iad', *Dáil Debates*, 77, 1565.

104. Based upon confidential information.

105. *Dáil Debates*, 160. 783.

106. Department of Education, *Memorandum V 40*, Introduction, 2.

107. *Dáil Debates*, 77, 1569.

108. Ibid., 1570.

109. D. P. S., E 48/1/31, E 48/1/46, E 57/19.

110. D.F., S18/10/38.

111. Éamon de Valera, 'The Ireland that we dream of' in Moynihan, *Speeches and statements*, 446.

112. Appointment of chief inspector and two assistant chief inspectors, July 1946, (D. P. S., E 57/19).

113. Personal communication from Prof. T. P. O'Néill.

114. Whyte, *Church and state*, 158.

115. Chapter 6, refs. 55-66 incl.

116. *Annual report, CCSS, 1949*, 52.

117. *The Irish Monthly*, lxxvi, 903, (1948); *The Roscommon Herald*, editions of 16 Oct 1948 and 30 Oct 1948.

118. Note from T. Ó Raifeartaigh to the Minister, R. Mulcahy, 5 June 1956 and typescript of 'Address by the Minister at the IVEA Congress', Limerick 12 June 1956, (UCD Archives, Mulcahy Papers, P7/C/161).

119. *Dáil Debates*, 115, 296; Letter from Department of Finance to Department of Education, 23 Oct 1950.

120. *Dail Debates*, 120, 824.

121. 'Fine Gael election address' in *Irish Independent* 26 Jan 1948.

122. *Dáil Debates*, 110, 1099.

123. *Dáil Debates*, 115, 303.

124. Department of Finance memo to cabinet, 21 Apr 1948, (S.P.O., S16240).

125. *Annual report, CCCS, 1948*, 35.

126. The Council of Education, 'Terms of reference and general regulations', (1950), 14-15, (S.P.O., S12753'B').

127. *Dáil Debates*, 152, 467.

128. UCD Archives, Mulcahy P /C/123.

129. *Dáil Debates*, 159, 1494.

130. *Dáil Debates*, 110, 1093.

131. *Dáil Debates*, 115, 331.

132. Memo 28 Oct 1950, (UCD Archives, Mulcahy Papers, P 7/C/9/44).

133. (UCD Archives, Mulcahy Papers, P 7/C/9/44).

134. (UCD Archives, Mulcahy Papers, P 7/C/154).

135. Letters and memoranda between Ministers for Education and Finance during Aug and Sept 1954, (UCD Archives, Mulcahy Papers, P 7/C/154).

136. Letter from Department of Education to Department of Finance, 6 Oct 1954, (UCD Archives, Mulcahy Papers, P 7/C/154).

137. Memoirs of Dr A. J. McConnell, former Provost of Trinity College, Dublin in *The Irish Press*, 12, 13 and 14 Aug 1985.

138. Letter from R. Mulcahy, Minister for Education to P. McGilligan, Minister for Finance, 11 Apr 1951, (UCD Archives, Mulcahy Papers, P 7/C/152).

139. *Dáil Debates*, 126, 1697.

140. Whyte, *Church and state*, Chs VII-IX incl.

141. *Dáil Debates*, 127, 238; 126, 1698.

142. Ibid.

143. *Dáil Debates*, 160, 783.

144. *The Irish School Weekly*, lv, 20, (Oct 1953); *Dail Debates* 126, 1743, 1744.

145. *The Irish School Weekly*, lv, 20, (Oct 1953); *Dáil Debates*, 132, 1088. *Translation*: 'The work and activity characteristic of secondary schools undergo very little change over time. Not everyone is happy with the eternal preoccupation with secondary education'.

146. Memoranda to the Government 11 Oct 1952 and 13 Oct 1952, 14 Feb 1953 and 19 Feb 1953, 27 Nov 1953 and 3 Dec 1953, from the Departments of Finance and Education respectively, (D.F., S20/7/32).

147. *Dáil Debates*, 126, 1741, 1742; Memo. 14 Feb 1953, (D. E., F 32/113).

148. Memo. for the Government from the Department of Education, 11 Oct 1952, (D.F., S20/7/32).

149. Memo. 19 Feb 1953, (D.F., S20/7/32); Letter from L. Ó Muirithe, secretary of the Department of Education to Dr Fergus, secretary to the hierarchy, (UCD Archives, Mulcahy Papers, P 7/C/154).

150. *Dáil Debates*, 139, 243.

151. *Dáil Debates*, 126, 1746.

152. (UCD Archives, Mulcahy Papers, P 7/C/154); Department of Education circulars 10/54 and 8/54.

153. *Dáil Debates*, 131, 1084.

154. Headey, *British cabinet ministers*, 54.

155. Information gained from interview with Dr T. Ó Raifeartaigh, Feb 1979.

156. Report and interim report of the departmental committee to examine the educational system 1945-47, (S.P.O., S12891 'A' and 'B').

157. *Dáil Debates*, 168, 1501.

158. *Dáil Debates*, 162, 308.

159. Press release, Fianna Fáil, Dublin 11 Apr 1975; *The Sunday Press*, 17 Jan 1975.

160. *Dáil Debates*, 177, 470.

161. Department of Education, *Statement by Dr P. J. Hillery, T.D., Minister for Education in regard to postprimary education*, (20 May 1963), pars. 21, 23, 24, 25.

162. Meetings sought by the Catholic managerial bodies in June 1963 with the minister.

163. *Dáil Debates*, 182, 79; 189, 842.

164. *Dáil Debates*, 216, 967, 179, 182.

165. *Dáil Debates*, 220, 1797.

166. Department of Education, *Policy in relation to postprimary education*, 1965.

167. *Dáil Debates*, 216, 968, Estimate Speech.

168. 'The Comprehensive school', *The Sunday Press*, 9 Jan 1966.

169. 'Changes in Irish education', address by George Colley, T.D., Minister for Education, to the Cork branch of Tuairim, 15 Nov 1965.

170. Ibid., 11.

171. Author's interview with G. Colley, Mar 1974.

172. Interview and author's personal recollection of Galway meeting, 5 Feb 1966.

173. *Investment in Education*, 1, 284, 266.

174. Cooperative ventures developed in Ballinamore, Co. Leitrim and in Boyle, Co. Roscommon.

175. Department of Education, *Estimate Speech, 1967/68*.

176. *Report to the Minister for Education on regional technical colleges*. (Prl. 371), (Dublin), 1967.

177. Statement by D. O'Malley, Minister for Education, Dún Laoghaire 10 Sept 1966.

178. 'Free Education and After?', address by D. O'Malley at Clontarf, 16 Feb 1967, 3.

179. Ibid., 5.

180. Ibid., 6.

181. *Local authorities (Higher education grants) act*, 1968.

182. Department of Education, press release 6 July 1968; address by the Minister for Education, Brian Lenihan, T.D. to the Higher Education Authority at its first meeting, 12 Sept 1968.

183. Estimate closing speech, 1969/70 by Minister for Education.

184. Ibid., 40.

185. Ibid., 1.

186. Statement by Minister for Education on introducing the *Vocational Education (Amendment) Bill*, 1970.

187. Press statement from Government information bureau, 13 May 1971; *Dail Debates*, 253, 1963.

188. *Dail Debates*, 254, 494, 1082, 1921; 258, 852; 253, 1971.

189. ASTI, Report of special convention, Apr 1979; TUI, Annual Congress, Apr 1980; *The Irish Times*, 11 Apr 1980.

190. *The Irish Times*, 10 Oct 1979.

191. NESC (1976), *Population projections 1971-86, the implications for education*; Tussing, A. Dale (1978), *Irish educational expenditure, past, present and future*, (Dublin 1978)

Department of Education, *White paper on educational development*, (1980); Ó Buachalla, S., 'Irish demographic issues and educational planning', *European Journal of Education*, 17, no. 1, (1982).

192. Statement by R. Burke, T.D., Minister for Education, 16 Dec 1974.

195. Ibid., 6-10.

196. Department of Education, *Scheme of capitation grants*, (1974).

197. *The Irish Times*, 8 October 1980.

198. *White paper on educational development*, (1980), Chapter 1.

199. *Progress report on the first year of the programme for action in education (1984-87)*, (Dublin, 1985); Press release, Department of Education, 21 Jan 1985.

200. *Lifelong Learning*, Report of the Commission on Adult Education, (1983), (Pl. 2292).

201. An Roinn Oideachais, *Partners in education*, (1985).

CHAPTER 10.

1. Fanning, Ronan, *The Irish Department of Finance 1922-58*, (Dublin, 1976), 51, 265, 520; *Constitution of the Irish Free State*, articles 36, 37, 54, 61; *Bunreacht na hÉireann 1937*, articles 28, 33.

2. Hogan, G. P. S., 'The Constitutional Basis of Financial Control, *Administration*, vii, 2, 158.

3. *Bunreacht na hÉireann*, Article 33.

4. Brennan, Joseph, 1923, quoted in Fanning, *Department of Finance*, 68.

5. D.F., S20/11/30; D.F., S20/4/28.

6. D.F., S84/23/36.

7. D.F., S20/7/32; *The Irish Times*, 2 September 1933.

8. D.F., S20/18/37.

9. Note by H. P. Boland, (D.F., S23/4/31).

10. Circular re department estimates, (D.F., S19/4/30).

11. D.F., S19/l/24.

12. Estimates 1925-26, 1926-27, (D.F., F 152/45/25).

13. D.F., S101/11/32.

14. D.F., S46//17/27.

15. D.F., S84/62/32.

16. Executive council meeting 9 Nov 1929, (D.F., S84/62/32).

17. D.F., S20/25/49; D.F., S19/2/57.

18. D.F., S20/4/28.

19. D.F., S20/3/30.

20. D.F., S22/9/39.

21. D.F., S19/4/30.

22. D.F., S84/13/29.

23. Memo. to secretary, 3 June 1930, (D.F., S84/13/29).

24. D.F., S20/9/36; D.F., S20/16/36; D.F., S22/6/35.

25. D.F., S18/18/36.

26. D.F., S24/2/37.

27. Letter, dated 28 January 1938, (D.F., S24/2/37).

28. D.F., S24/3/37.

29. D.F., S84/13/29.

30. D.F., S18/5/26.

31. Conference and memo., 28 May 1926, (D.F., S18/5/26).

32. D.F., A 84/62/32.

33. D.F., S20/8/28.

34. Internal memo. 11 Nov 1929, (D.F., S20/8/28).

35. D.F., S18/32/32: the commissioners were J. Ingram and R. O'Connor.

36. D.F., S18/2/45.

37. Memo. dated 23 Aug 1951, (D.F., S18/2/45).

38. Ibid.

39. D.F., S19/17/24; *Report of Committee of Public Accounts 1925*; D.F., S20/4/28; D.F., S22/2/33; D.F., S20/11/30; D.F., S20/28/31; D.F., S20/10/35.

40. D.F., S18/18/36.

41. D.F., S19/1/24.

42. D.F. /, S20/8/28.

43. Memo. from H. P. Boland to W. Doolin, 20 Mar 1928, (D.F., S22/1/28).

44. Internal memo., 7 Apr 1937, (D.F., S22/4/37).

45. Conference held on 7 April 1937, (D.F., S22/4/37).

46. Memo. by W. Doolin, 11 May 1937, (D.F., S22/4/37).

47. Ibid.

48. Internal memo., 3 Dec 1952, (D.F., S22/4/37).

49. D.F., S20/30/28.

50. D.F., S20/9/29.

51. D.F., S18/8/39.

52. D.F., S22/1/31.

53. D.F., S22/15/37.

54. D.F., S20/18/28.

55. D.F., S18/1/38. Case of Mrs M. McDonnell (M. Ní Giolláin) v. Archbishop Gilmartin of Tuam.

56. *The Irish Independent*, 20 Feb 1940, 4 June 1940.

57. D.F., S106/6/51.

58. Memo. to cabinet, Nov 1958, (D.F., S106/6/51).

59. Minute of 23 Sept 1942, (D.F., S20/9/36).

60. D.F., S18/22/32.

61. *The Irish Times*, 9 Jan 1939; *The Catholic Herald*, 6 Jan 1939.

62. D.F., S84/13/29.

63. Memo. from the Department of Education, July 1929, (D.F., S84/13/29).

64. Official minute, 26 July 1929, (D.F., S84/13/29).

65. Letter of 23 August 1929, (D.F., S84/13/29).

66. Letter of 10 Apr 1930, (D.F., S84/13/29).

67. Internal Department of Finance memo., (D.F., S84/13/29). *Note*: The validity of these data may not be high; some of the systems cited had significant local as well as central public funding.

68. Memo. to secretary, Department of Finance from H. P. Boland, 3 June 1930, (D.F., S84/13/29).

69. Internal memo., 13 Nov 1930, (D.F., S84/13/29).

70. Ibid.
71. Internal memo. by W. Doolin, 12 Nov 1930, (D.F., S84/13/29).
72. Marginal comment in memo by H. P. Boland, (D.F., S84/13/29).
73. Letter from Department of An Taoiseach to the Department of Education, 1 Nov 1947, (D.F., S18/47/33).
74. *Report of the commission on youth unemployment 1951*, pars. 63-64 incl.
75. Memorandum to the Government dated 10 November 1958.
76. Memo. on report, 23 Oct 1935, (D.F., S18/47/33).
77. D.F., S18/2/45.
78. Memo initialled M. B., 23 Aug 1951, (D.F., S18/2/45).
79. Ibid.
80. 'Nóta breise' or addendum to the memo. initialled M. B., of 23 Aug 1951, (D.F., S18/2/45).

CHAPTER 11.
1. Easton, D., *The political system*, (New York, 1953); *A framework for political analysis*, (New Jersey, 1965); *A systems analysis of political life*, (New York, 1965); Rose, R. (ed.), *Policy making in Britain*, (London, 1974).
2. Braybrooke, David and Lindblom, Charles, *A strategy for decision*, (New York, 1963), 249.
3. Harman, Grant, 'Conceptual and theoretical issues', in Hough, J. R., (ed.), *Educational policy*, (London, 1984), 13.
4. Heclo, H. Hugh, 'Policy analysis' in *British Journal of Political Science*, 2, (1978), 83-108.
5. Jenkins, W. I., *Policy Analysis*, 15.
6. Harman, 'Conceptual and theoretical issues', 13.
7. Dror, Y., 'From management sciences to policy sciences' in C. Pollit et al (eds.), *Public policy in theory and practice*, (London, 1979); Etzioni, A., 'Mixed scanning: a third approach to decision making' in *Public Administration Review*, 27, (1967), quoted in Ham, C. and Hill, M., *The policy process in the modern capitalist state*, 84-88.
8. Ham & Hill, *Policy process*, 77.
9. Lindblom, C., 'The science of muddling through', quoted in Richardson, J. J. and Jordan, A. G., *Governing under pressure*, 21.
10. Richardson and Jordan, *Governing under pressure*, 20-21.
11. Ibid., 21-23.
12. Ham & Hill, *Policy process*, 82.
13. Ibid.
14. Ibid., 84-87, 91.
15. Ibid., 84-88.
16. Kogan, *The Politics of Education*, 44; Richardson and Jordan, *Governing under pressure*, 54.
17. Rose, R., (ed.), 'Models of change' in *The dynamics of public policy*, 10.
18. Rose, R., 'Comparing public policy', *European Journal of Political Research*, 1, (1973), 1.
19. Schattschneider, E. E., quoted in Richardson and Jordan, *Governing under pressure*, 79.
20. Bachrach, Peter and Baratz, Morton S., 'Two faces of power', in *American Political Science Review*, 56, (1962), 947-52.
21. Schattschneider, E. E., *The semi-sovereign people*, (New York, 1960), 71.
22. For specific references to these commissions and committees consult ch. 3 in this work; D.F., S101/11/32.
23. *Investment in Education*, Vol. 1, Ch. 15.
24. Husen, T. & Kogan, M., *Educational research and policy*, (Oxford, 1984), 6-31.
25. Tussing, *Irish educational expenditure*; Hannan, D., *Schooling and sex roles*, (Dublin, 1983); Geary, R. C. & Ó Muircheartaigh, F. S., *Equalization of opportunity in Ireland: statistical aspects*, (Dublin, 1974); Walsh, Brendan, M., *Population and employment projection 1971-86*, NESC, No. 5. 1975.
26. D.F., S20/2/32; D.F., S105/26/38.
27. Budget speech, Dáil Éireann, 29 Jan 1986; *The Irish Times*, 30 Jan 1986.
28. D.F., S18/1/38; S18/7/26; S22/4/37; S20/7/32; letters 31 May 1943, 26 Oct 1943, 10 Jan 1945, (S.P.O., S12891).
29. D.F., S20/1/37; S.P.O., S25129; (UCD Archives, Mulcahy Papers, P 7/C/154).
30. D.F., S20/4/28; S20/11/30; S84/13/29; (UCD Archives, Mulcahy Papers, P 7/C/152).
31. *Annual Report 1931*, 236. *Annual Reports 1939, 1942, 1929; Annual Reports 1923, 1935, 1938, 1950, 1951 and 1960*.
32. Morrissey, Thomas J., *Towards a national university*, (Dublin, 1983), 321; Ó Buachalla, *A Significant Irish Educationalist*, 215-221.
33. 1950 Council of Education, (D.F., S18/2/45).
34. Bentley, A. F., *The process of government*, (Harvard, 1967).
35. Richardson and Jordon, *Governing under pressure*, 4.
36. D.F., S22/4/37.
37. Letter from Mr. deValera, to Mrs. Chapey of New York, 15 Dec 1953, (S.P.O., S12891 'B').
38. Coolahan, *The ASTI*.
39. Archer, Margaret Scotford, *Social origins of educational systems*, Ch. 2.
40. Ibid., 59-61.
41. Ibid., 60.
42. Ibid., 63.
44. Ibid., Ch. 3, 89-93.
45. Ibid., 92.
46. See chapter 8 above.
47. *Investment in education*, Vol. 1, 167; Perhaps the most celebrated case concerned the establishment of the national and secondary schools of the Irish Christian Brothers in Roscommon on foot of the specific terms of the Conmee bequest of 1860. Before the schools were opened in 1937 the case had been through the High Court in Dublin

and the Roman rota.

48. O'Meara, J. J., *Reform in education*, (Dublin, 1958).

49. Ibid., 15-17.

50. D.F., S106/6/51; Personal communication from Professor T. P. O'Néill.

51. Gamson, William A., *Power and Discontent*, (Illinois, 1968), 63.

52. D.F., S18/18/36.

53. D.P.S., E 48/1/27; D.P.S., E 47/1/26; Fenton, S., *It all Happened*, (Dublin, 1949), 205.

54. Press Statement by Dr P. J. Hillery, 20 May 1963.

55. Rose, 'The dynamics of public policy', 12.

56. 'The university and the schools', *An Claidheamh Soluis*, 23 Jan 1909.

57. Kogan, *Politics of education*, 156-60.

58. D.F., S20/4/28; F 87/4/26; S18/7/26; S22/1/31; S20/49/31; S22/4/31; S19/8/31; S19/5/31; S25/4/29; S20/9/29; S18/8; S18/9/29; S18/6/28.

59. S.P.O., S12891'A', S12891'B'; D.F., S20/9/36; Estimate Speech, 3 June 1942; D.P.S., E 48/1/31, E 48/1/46; D.P.S., E 57/19, Appointment of Chief Inspector and two Assistant Chief Inspectors, July 1946.

60. D.F., S18/5/26. The school in question was Miss Louise Gavan Duffy's Scoil Bhríde in Pembroke Road which was moved to Government premises in Earlsfort Terrace.

61. Comhairle le leas óige, (D.F., S18/3/41); D.F., S84/13/29.

62. Chubb, *Cabinet government in Ireland*, 77.

63. Coolahan, 'origins of the payment-by-results policy in education'; Akenson, *The Irish educational experiment*, Ch. VI, 'The politics of the curriculum'.

64. The series, *Notes for Teachers*, written by senior members of the inspectorate on specific subject areas of the curriculum, constituted the official guide to curricular content; their contents were reviewed on a regular basis.

65. *White paper on educational development*, 1980, ch. x.

66. Letter from R. Mulcahy to P. McGilligan, 11 April 1951, (UCD Archives, Mulcahy Papers, P 7/C/152).

67. Internal memo., 23 Oct 1935, (D.F., S18/47/33).

68. Department of Education, *Partners in education*, 9-16.

69. Memo., 23 Aug 1929, (D.F., S84/13/29).

70. An Roinn Oideachais, *Liosta na Meán Scoileanna*, (1960-75).

71. O'Mahony, Seán, 'The working of the first programme budget in education', in *Administration*, Vol. 20, 3, (1972), 16-26; see also, *Administration*, Vol. 19, (1971), 222-231.

72. Harman, 'Conceptual and theoretical issues', 17.

73. Pressman, Jeffrey L. & Wildavsky, Aaron, *Implementation*, (Univ. of California, 1973), 143.

74. Van Meter, D. S. & Van Horn, C. E., 'The policy implementation process: a conceptual framework' in *Administration and Society*, 6, (1975), 445-88.

75. Harman, 'Conceptual and theoretical issues', 24-25.

76. Hood, C. C., *The limits of administration*, (London, 1976), 6-9.

77. McLaughlin, Milbrey Wallin, *Evaluation and Reform*, (Mass., 1975); Boudon, Raymond, *Education, opportunity and social inequality: changing prospects in western society*, (New York, 1974).

78. Pressman & Wildavsky, *Implementation*, ch. xvi, 109.

79. D.F., S20/24/44; this occurred in the parish of Ballintemple, Co Cavan in 1944, when the manager moved teachers around arbitrarily and employed extra teachers independent of the Department of Education.

80. Ó Buachalla, S., 'Policy and structural development in Irish higher eduation', 165-71.

81. INTO Conference, *Irish Times*, 20 Mar 1986.

82. Based upon confidential communication.

83. Lindblom, 'The science of muddling through'; *The policy making process*, (New Jersey, 1968).

84. I.I.E.P., *Qualitative aspects of educational planning*, (Paris, 1969); *Evaluation in education*, 2, 3, (Oxford, 1978).

85. Husen, T., 'Issues and their background' in Husen and Kogan, *Educational research and policy*; Wildavsky, Aaron, 'Learning from education', in Wildavsky, Aaron, *The art and craft of policy analysis*, (London, 1980).

86. These *Retention Rates*, RR 5 and RR 6, are calculated on the basis of the enrolment in standard X and the enrolment in standards X-3 and X-4, three and four years earlier; the earlier values may be depressed somewhat by the practice of grade repetition, much in vogue in the early period.

87. Chubb, *Cabinet government*, 63.

CHAPTER 12.

1. Dror, Y., 'From management systems to policy sciences', in Pollit et al, *Public policy in theory and practice*, 25.

2. Ó Buachalla, 'Educational Policy and the Role of the Irish Language'.

3. *Census of Ireland for 1851*, pt. vi.

4. Akenson, *The Irish education experiment*, 378-384; National Education, (Ireland), *Teaching of Irish*, H.C., 1884, LXI, 1, 2.

5. Ryan, W. J., *The pope's green island*; Ryan, Desmond, *Remembering Sion*; Ó Cuiv, B., *Aspects of the Irish language*; Gaelic League Series, *Irish in university education*, (Dublin 1902).

6. 'The Education Question' in *An Claidheamh Soluis*, 13 Aug 1904.

7. Quoted by the recipient, Dr Douglas Hyde at the Mansion house meeting of 13 July 1904.

8. Inspectorial Reports, Appendix to the *Sixty*

Ninth report of the Commissioners of National Education in Ireland for year 1902, (Cd. 1890), 1903; Intermediate Education Board for Ireland, *Selections from the reports of the temporary inspectors,* 1901-1902, 34.

9. *The Irish Catholic Directory and Almanac,* (1908 and 1911).

10. *Report, Coimisiun na Gaeltachta,* (1926), Appendix iii, 108.

11. *Dáil Éireann proceedings,* First and Second Dáil: reports of Aireacht na Gaeilge 1920, 1921.

12. 'National conference on the teaching of Irish 1913', (N.L.I., MacNeill Papers, MS 10, 895) *The Irish Education Review,* 7, 119-24; (S.P.O., DE 2/54), The Gaelic League Educational Programme; Coiste an Oideachais, 30 Oct 1918, (N.L.I., MacNeill Papers, Ms 9798).

13. Those involved in drafting this programme were Máire Ní Chinnéide, Sean Ó Ceallaigh and Micheál Ó hAodha, with assistance from Professor T. J. Corcoran, S.J.

14. Report of Aireacht na Gaeilge June 1920, (S.P.O., DE 2/54); The Dáil members included Ernest Blythe, Cathal Brugha and Piaras Béaslaí.

15. Dáil Éireann, *Report of ministry of the national language,* Aug 1921, (S.P.O., DE 2/54).

16. Dáil Éireann, Department of Education, *Report from 11 Jan to 21 Apr 1922,* (S.P.O., DE 2/474); These conferences were the First programme conference (1920) and the Dáil commission on secondary education (1921).

17. *Dáil Debates,* 1 Dec 1922, 2557. *Translation:* 'What was done was done by others. As for me I shall do my utmost to revive Irish'.

18. Various items in Blythe Papers especially P 24/231 and items P 24/301 to P 24/339, (UCD Archives).

19. Letter 16 Oct 1931 to Professor Liam Ó Briain of University College Galway, (UCD Archives, Blythe Papers, P 24/304).

20. D.P.S., E 58/33/24; *The School Weekly,* 11 Feb 1922.

21. 'How the Irish language can be revived', *The Irish Monthly,* 51, (1923), 26-30. (It is generally believed that Professor Corcoran did not have any knowledge of the Irish language nor take steps to learn it).

22. 'The Gaelicising of Ireland', (UCD Archives, Mulcahy Papers, P 7/C/71).

23. *Constitution of the Free State of Ireland,* Article 4.

24. O'Connell, *History of INTO,* 347.

25. *Dáil Debates,* 5, 430; *Dáil Debates,* 13, 195, 209.

26 *Dáil Debates,* 8, 273, 282.

27. *Election manifesto of Fianna Fáil,* 1932.

28. Ministerial speech at INTO congress 1932.

29. D.P.S., E 47/1/26.

30. D.P.S., E 57/3.

31. O'Neill was a prolific writer: his historical novels include *Wind from the north* (1934), *Land under England,* (1935), *Day of wrath* (1936), *Philip,* (1940) and *Chosen by the queen* (1947). He also wrote an unpublished autobiographical novel.

32. D.P.S., E 47/1/26.

33. Letters, 6 July 1922 and 10 Aug 1922, (D. P. S., E 47/1/26).

34. The following were assimilated as class II Inspectors on 1 December 1922: J. Fenton, M. Franklin, H. Morris, M. F. Hollins, F. J. O'Tierney, P. MacSweeney; Fenton was promoted to deputy chief inspector on 12 April 1923, the other five together with R. J. Little were promoted to the rank of Divisional Inspector on 16 May 1923. Twelve inspectors, who were known collectively as the 'Twelve Apostles', were appointed in 1923; they were Miss A. Walsh, Miss B. Murphy, Mr. M. Hughes, Mr. M. Walsh, Mr. L. Murray, Mr. M. Kinsella, Mr. J. J. O'Connor, Mr. J. B. Dolan, Mr. J. Hayes, Mr. T. C. Twomey, who were appointed in July and Mr. C. J. Watters and Miss M. F. Geehin who were appointed in September. Later in 1923 and early in 1924 five further inspectors were appointed, Mr. L. Close, Mr. T. Sullivan, Mr. M. Dundon, Mr. J. McMahon and Mr. Wm. Falconer.

35. Memo. by H. P. Boland to Minister for Finance, (D.F., S20/4/28). .

36. Official reply from H. P. Boland to J. O'Neill, 17 Nov 1927, (D. P. S., E 47/2/31).

37. D.F., S20/26/37; D.F., S22/2/23; D.F., S20/23/43.

38. Public Notice No. 4, *Concerning the teaching of the Irish language in the national schools; National programme of primary instruction,* issued by the National Programme Conference 1922; Dail commission on secondary education 1921-22.

39. *National programme primary instruction,* 3-5, 15.

40. Department of Education, *Rules and programme for secondary schools,* (1924); D.F., S19/1/24.

41. Note, 31 Dec 1929, (D.F., S20/4/28). .

42. (UCD Archives, Blythe Papers, P 24/348, 24/370); D.F., F 87/4/26.

43. Perhaps the shortest was the proposal to establish Scoil Fhursa in Galway, which cleared all stages in two days, 12-13 August 1931: D.F., S20/49/31.

44. D.F., S84/64/32; S20/8/28; S18/7/26; S2/30/28; S19/2/33; *Report Coimisiún na Gaeltachta,* 11-27; (UCD Archives, Mulcahy Papers, P 7/C/1/70).

45. D.F., S22/1/31; S20/9/29.

46. D.F., S18/5/26; S19/8/31. These schools were Scoil Mhuire (Marlborough St.), Scoil Bhríde (Earlsfort Terrace) and Coláiste Mhuire (initially Harcourt St., later Parnell Square) all of which were housed in government premises.

47. D.F., S19/1/24; Letter from Blythe to J. M. O'Sullivan, 19 Dec 1930, (D.F., S19/5/31).
48. (UCD Archives, Blythe papers, P 24/352).
49. D.F., S18/21/31; D.F., S18/9/29; D.F., S1/8/30.
50. Tuarascáil na Roinne Oideachais, 1930/31, 42.
51. (UCD Archives, Blythe Papers, P 24/304); of the 14,000 teachers 10,000 had a qualification in Irish.
52. Dáil Debates, 9 Dec 1931, 2595.
53. Tuarascáil na Roinne Oideachais, 1931/32, 37.
54. This was Micheál Breathnach, appointed as a Primary Inspector in 1923, transferred to the Secondary Inspectorate in July 1924, who was promoted as assistant Chief Inspector in Nov 1932. He died in April 1987 aged 101.
55. Department of Education, Revised programme of primary instruction, 1934, 5.
56. The Leader, 13 June 1942; D.F., S9/5/31.
57. O'Connell, History of the INTO, 369; Dáil Debates, 44, 741; 55, 115; 66, 155; 44, 840; 106, 357.
58. INTO Report on committee of inquiry, 1942, 15-25.
59. INTO A plan for education, (1947), 41-42; 104-123.
60. Dáil Debates, 74, 2420; 70, 923; 66, 245; 83, 1229.
61. Dáil Debates, 78, 1568.
62. Dáil Debates, 78, 1570.
63. Education estimate 1941, Dáil Debates.
64. S.P.0., S13180; S15562; S15744.
65. Mmemo to cabinet, 30 Mar 1943, (S.P.O., S13180).
66. Ibid., par. 2.
67. (S.P.0., S15744); Message from Utrecht to Fianna Fáil Árd Fheis, 30 Oct 1952, (S.P.O., S13180).
68. D.F., S18/13/48.
69. (UCD Archives, Mulcahy Papers P 7/C/160).
70. Dáil Debates, 17 May 1955: see also Irish Times, and Irish Press for 18 May 1955.
71. The Irish Times, editorial 18 May 1955.
72. Tables 4.1 and 5.1 in this work; (UCD Archives, Mulcahy Papers P 7/C/123).
73. FitzGerald, G., Toward a new Ireland, 154, 155.
74. MacNamara, J., Bilingualism and Irish education.
75. Fine Gael, Irish language policy, (1966), 1.
76. Whyte, J. H., 'Ireland: politics without social bases', in Rose, R., (ed.), Electoral behaviour: A comparative handbook.
77. Fine Gael, Irish Language Policy, (1966), 2, 9.
78. Ó Riagáin, P., Public and teacher attitudes towards Irish in the schools, (Dublin, 1985), 6.
79. Titley, E. Brian, Church, state and the control of schooling in Ireland, 1900-44, (Dublin, 1983), 94-100.
80. Inspectorial report by P. E Ó Suilleabháin on Co Cork, 1941, (Papers in private ownership).
81. Oideas, 14, 37.
82. Comhlucht Comhairleach na Gaeilge, Tuarascáil 1966-68, 33; Andrews, Liam, A Black Paper on Education, (Dublin, 1981).
83. Tierney, Eoin MacNeill, 78; Tomás Deirg in an interview with The Boston Traveller, 26 Oct 1934; Ó Cuiv, B., A View of the Irish language, 130.
84. Correspondence between Fr A. Ó Mórain, the Taoiseach and the Department of Education and report by Micheál Ó Siochfradha, dated 1954, (UCD Archives, Mulcahy Papers P 7/C/154).
85. Bord na Gaeilge, Plean gniomhaíochta don ghaeilge, 30.
86. D.F., S20/4/28; D.F., S22/2/33; D.F., S25/4/37; D.F., S25/2/39; (UCD Archives, Blythe Papers, P 24/302B). Coláiste Móibhí, attached to the Church of Ireland College of Education continues to function as a preparatory college.
87. Report committee on Irish language attitude research, (1975), 356.
88. Ó Riagáin, Public and teacher attitudes, 5.
89. Ibid., 6.
90. Ó Fiaich, Tomás, 'The language and political thought', in Ó Cuiv, A view of the Irish language, 110.
91. Sligo Conference 1916, Annual report I.L.P. and T.U.C., 53.
92. Dáil Éireann, Miontuairiscí an Chéad Dála 1919-21, Session, 21 Jan 1919, 23.
93. 'Further educational needs', (UCD Archives, Mulcahy Papers, P 7/C/71).
94. Dáil Debates, 13, 356; Dáil Debates, Debate on constitution, 18 Oct 1922, 1702.
95. Labour's policy on education, 14.
96. Report Coimisiún na Gaeltachta, 18, 19, 20; the only secondary school serving the Gaeltacht was C.B.S. Dingle which operated through English in 1926.
97. Ibid., 59, 60.
98. Minutes of cabinet Gaeltacht committee, first meeting 29 June 1933, (S.P.O., S9409); Memo. from Minister for Education to cabinet on education in the Gaeltacht, (D.F., S20/1/34).
99. Memorandum to Department of Finance, 30 Dec 1933, (D.F., S20/1/34).
100. Report of inter-departmental committee on raising of the school leaving age, 17, 18.
101. Interim report of departmental committee, (S.P.O., S12891'B').
102. (S.P.O., S12891 'B', 2, 3).
103. Dáil Debates, Questions by Dr Noel Browne, May 1957 and February 1958: 16, 479; 165, 372: 165, 948.
104. Dáil Debates, 195, 2061.
105. Press release by Minister for Education, 20 May 1963.
106. Dáil Debates, 225, 1872.
107. Dáil Debates, 78, 1565.
108. Dáil Debates, 18 October 1922, 1695-1710.
109. Internal memo, 15 Dec 1931, (D.F., S18/36/31).

110. *Investment in education*, 1, ch. x, 283-285; Table 6.32, 158.
111. Rudd, Joy, *National school terminal leavers*.
112. *Investment in education*, 1, 176.
113. Ibid., 154-168.
114. In 1985 a small second level school was sanctioned for Inis Oirr in the Aran Islands with a view to solving this problem.
115. Table 9.24 in Clancy, *Participation in higher education*.
116. Table 10. 26, Ibid.
117. The social group categories are calculated by aggregating groups 3, 4, 5, 6 and 7 as higher and the others, except farmers, as lower.
118. Ó Buachalla, 'Irish demographic issues and educational planning'.
119. Geary, R. C., *Relations between lack of education, unemployment and age amongst males*, (Dublin, 1978).
120. *Dáil Debates*, 223, 2194.
121. Van Meter, D. S. & Van Horn, C. E., 'The policy implementation process: a conceptual framework', in *Administration and society*, 6, (1975), 445-88; Mazmanian, Daniel A. and Sabatier, Paul A., *Effective policy implementation*.

CHAPTER 13.

1. D.F., S18/3/26.
2. D.F., S20/8/25.
3. (UCD Archives, Blythe Papers, P 24/343); D.F., S18/18/36, S18/9/35, S18/18/39.
4. D. P. S., E 104/48/28, E 104/19/27, E 103/22/33; D.F., S20/2/32. The 1926 commission had Swiss and Swedish members and Rev. L. McKenna, S.J., chairman of the 1927 Inquiry on Inspection, toured Scotland, Belgium, Holland, Germany and France on behalf of the department.
5. D.F., S19/1/24.
6. D.F., S22/4/37; In 1952 concern was expressed in the department because the order of nuns to which six Dublin national schools had been allocated by Church decision had only 24 qualified members for the 59 posts in the schools it already had.
7. D.F., S18/3/45.
8. *Tuarascáil na Roinne Oideachais 1925-26-27*, 21, 35.
9. D.F., S20/1/24. This was the case of Mr. Martin Leydon, who took legal action on a salary cut.
10. *Tuarascáil na Roinne Oideachais, 1931-32*.
11. *Dáil Debates*, 18 Oct 1922, 1695-1707.
12. A special meeting of the Catholic bishops of 26 May 1926 declared: 'Mixed education in public schools is very undesirable especially among older children'; *Dail Debates*, 16, 409; The minister on 7 June 1926 confirmed to the Dail that there was a very strong objection 'to having boys and girls taught in the same school'.
13. *Dail Debates*, 241, 1782. Up to June 1969, 141 national schools had been closed or amalgamated; *Dáil Debates* 242, 1878, a question was asked on the foreign influences prompting the amalgamation policy.
14. *Tuarascáil staitistiúil na Roinne Oideachais, 1980-81*, 18.
15. D.F., S19/1/38.
16. *Tuarascáil staitistiúil na Roinne Oideachais, 1980-81*, 18.
17. Ibid., 59.
18. Dale Report 1904; *Report coimisiún na Gaeltachta 1926. Investment in education*, 1965.
19. *Tuarascail na Roinne Oideachais, 1925-26-27*, 27, 35.
20. (S.P.O., S12891); D.F., S22/2/35.
21. *Dáil Debates*, 241, 949: of 4,343 national schools in 1968/69 1,200 schools were not equipped with electric current; *Dail Debates*, 238, 2455; Two national schools in Kerry, at Glenbeigh and Curaheen, were without heating and lighting in March 1969; D.F., S23/1/39. As early as 1923 a boat service was provided in Connemara to bring 8 children from Illaunaerach (Oileán Aerach) to Innisbarra to attend school. See also D.F., S20/8/28, case of Island Eddy near Kilcolgan, Co. Galway where in 1928 there were 7 children of school going age but where there had been no education facilities for twenty five years.
22. *Dáil Debates*, 127, 1219. The Island in question was Reengaroga near Baltimore, Co. Cork.
23. *Minutes of the Commissioners of Intermediate Education*, 19 Jan 1922.
24. Letter from the committee of divisional and senior inspectors to the secretary of the Department of Finance, 6 July 1922, (D.P.S., E 47/1/26); Appeal by Enrí Ó Muirgheasa on behalf of the junior inspectors to President Cosgrave, 30 Sept 1922.
25. Estimates 1925/26, (D.F., F 152/48/24).
26. *Dáil Debates*, 2, 248, 23 Mar 1923.
27. Killorglin Secondary School was occupied from Aug to Dec 1922 and Cork Model School was also involved.
28. Question by Cathal O'Shannon, T.D., on St. Mary's College, Dundalk, *Dail Debates*, 21 Sept 1922.
29. Orders 7 and 10 of 1923, *Iris Oifigiúil*, 21 Aug 1923.
30. D.F., S19/17/24; S20/9/29.
31. D.F., S18/11/24.
32. D.F., S18/11/27.
33. *Intermediate Education Commissioners (transfer of functions) order*, 1925; D.F., S19/17/24.
34. Order 264 of 1935, 2 Aug 1935; D.F., S20/18/35.
35. D.P.S., E 47/2/31; Fanning, *The Department of Finance* 98, 43.
36. The Secondary Branch recruited seven inspectors in 1962.
37. Ó Buachalla, 'Policy and structural development in higher education', 165-71.
38. There had been a Christian Brothers'

school (primary and secondary) in Cavan town up to 1886 when it was forced to close because its growing secondary enrolment was considered a threat to the Diocesan College, St. Patrick's.

39. Table 6.32 in *Investment in education*, 1, 158.

40. Clancy, *Participation in higher education*, 12.

41. *Tuarascáil na Roinne Oideachais 1942*, and *Tuarascáil staitistiúil na Roinne Oideachais 1980-81*.

42. D.F., S20/1/24.

43. See Table 6.1. of this work.

44. *Dáil Debates*, 203, 598.

45. Minister for Education's press statement 20 May 1963, par 20.

46. *The Irish Times*, 12 Nov 1970.

47. Press Release, 10 Dec 1971; Appendix 2 of this work.

48. *The Irish Independent*, 18 June 1971.

49. Question by Deputy Liam Burke of Fine Gael, *Dáil Debates* 242, 1878.

50. *Have the snakes come back?*, (Dublin, 1975), a pamphlet published anonymously is a typical example.

51. *Dáil Debates*, 13, 190; Department of Education, *All our children*.

52. O'Mahony, S., 'Programme budgeting in the Department of Education' in *Administration*, 19, 3, (1971), 220-30.

53. In a typical month in 1971, the number of articles and letters published was as follows: *Irish Times*, 89, *Irish Independent*, 48 and *Irish Press*, 54.

54. Data from an unpublished survey directed by author and conducted by Ernest Hipwell in 1971.

55. This extensive coverage of education led the *Irish Times* in 1972 to establish a specialist weekly *The Education Times* under the editorship of John Horgan.

56. The data on Dáil questions for 1960/69 is based upon the years 1960, 1963, 1966 and 1969.

57. MacGearailt, Tomás, 'The great power sharers of Marlborough Street, a memory of early days in the inspectorate', in *The Education Times*, Vol. 3, (22 , 29 May 1975), 8-9.

58. *Dáil Debates*, 4 Jan 1923, 548; *Dáil Debates*, 21 Sept 1922; *Dáil Debates*, 12 Nov 1925, 247.

59. *Dáil Debates*, 13, 275.

60. D.F., F 68/9/33; D.F., S24/5/25.

61. D.F., S18/2/26.

62. Minute of meeting 5 Dec 1949, in the Department of Education between Dr Alfie O'Rahilly of UCC and T. Ó Raifeartaigh, assistant secretary, (UCD Archives, Mulcahy Papers, P 7/C/153).

63. *Lifelong learning in Ireland*, (1983); *White paper on educational development*, (1980); *Priority areas in adult education*, Aontas, (1986); *Education in Ireland*, (Brussels, 1982).

64. An Roinn Oideachais, *Partners in education*, (1985).

65. D.F., S84/13/29; S24/4/30.

66. D.F., S24/4/30; see Appendix 3.

67. In the Cabinet changes of February 1986, Mrs. Hussey was replaced as Minister for Education by Mr. Cooney and the fate of the green paper is uncertain.

68. Debate on second stage of bill in Dáil, 14 May 1930, 1734. (D.F., S84/13/29).

INDEX